Non-Governmental Organisations in International Law

Non-governmental organisations (NGOs) are playing an increasing political role on the international scene, and their position in relation to international law is generally regarded as important but informal. Their actual legal status has not been the subject of much investigation. This book examines the legal status of NGOs in different fields of international law, with emphasis on human rights law. By means of a thorough examination and systematisation of international legal rules and practices, Anna-Karin Lindblom explores the rights, obligations, *locus standi* and consultative status of NGOs. This investigation is placed within a wider discussion on the representation of groups in the international legal system. Lindblom argues, on the basis of a discourse model of international decision-making, that non-governmental organisation is an important form of public participation that can strengthen the flawed legitimacy of the state-centric system of international law.

ANNA-KARIN LINDBLOM, LL.D., is Special Adviser in human rights issues in the Ministry of Justice (Division for Democratic Issues), Sweden. She was previously a lecturer in public international law at Uppsala University, Sweden.

CAMBRIDGE STUDIES IN INTERNATIONAL AND COMPARATIVE LAW

Established in 1946, this series produces high quality scholarship in the fields of public and private international law and comparative law. Although these are distinct legal sub-disciplines, developments since 1946 confirm their interrelation.

Comparative law is increasingly used as a tool in the making of law at national, regional and international levels. Private international law is now often affected by international conventions, and the issues faced by classical conflicts rules are frequently dealt with by substantive harmonisation of law under international auspices. Mixed international arbitrations, especially those involving state economic activity, raise mixed questions of public and private international law, while in many fields (such as the protection of human rights and democratic standards, investment guarantees and international criminal law) international and national systems interact. National constitutional arrangements relating to 'foreign affairs', and to the implementation of international norms, are a focus of attention.

The Board welcomes works of a theoretical or interdisciplinary character, and those focusing on the new approaches to international or comparative law or conflicts of law. Studies of particular institutions or problems are equally welcome, as are translations of the best work published in other languages.

General Editors	James Crawford SC FBA *Whewell Professor of International Law, Faculty of Law, and Director, Lauterpacht Research Centre for International Law, University of Cambridge* John S. Bell FBA *Professor of Law, Faculty of Law, University of Cambridge*
Editorial Board	Professor Hilary Charlesworth *Australian National University* Professor Lori Damrosch *Columbia University Law School* Professor John Dugard *Universiteit Leiden* Professor Mary-Ann Glendon *Harvard Law School* Professor Christopher Greenwood *London School of Economics* Professor David Johnston *University of Edinburgh* Professor Hein Kötz *Max-Planck-Institut, Hamburg* Professor Donald McRae *University of Ottawa* Professor Onuma Yasuaki *University of Tokyo* Professor Reinhard Zimmermann *Universität Regensburg*
Advisory Committee	Professor D. W. Bowett QC Judge Rosalyn Higgins QC Professor J. A. Jolowicz QC Professor Sir Elihu Lauterpacht CBE QC Professor Kurt Lipstein Judge Stephen Schwebel

A list of books in the series can be found at the end of this volume.

Non-Governmental Organisations in International Law

Anna-Karin Lindblom

CAMBRIDGE
UNIVERSITY PRESS

CAMBRIDGE UNIVERSITY PRESS
Cambridge, New York, Melbourne, Madrid, Cape Town, Singapore,
São Paulo, Delhi, Dubai, Tokyo

Cambridge University Press
The Edinburgh Building, Cambridge CB2 8RU, UK

Published in the United States of America by Cambridge University Press, New York

www.cambridge.org
Information on this title: www.cambridge.org/9780521850889

© Anna-Karin Lindblom 2005

This publication is in copyright. Subject to statutory exception
and to the provisions of relevant collective licensing agreements,
no reproduction of any part may take place without the written
permission of Cambridge University Press.

First published 2005
Reprinted 2008

A catalogue record for this publication is available from the British Library

ISBN 978-0-521-85088-9 Hardback

Transferred to digital printing 2009

Cambridge University Press has no responsibility for the persistence or
accuracy of URLs for external or third-party Internet websites referred to in
this publication, and does not guarantee that any content on such websites is,
or will remain, accurate or appropriate. Information regarding prices, travel
timetables and other factual information given in this work are correct at
the time of first printing but Cambridge University Press does not guarantee
the accuracy of such information thereafter.

Contents

Acknowledgements	*page*	xv
List of abbreviations		xvii

Part I   Theoretical framework   1

1   The main issues and their context   3

    1.1   Introduction   3

    1.2   The legitimacy of international law   6

      Introduction   6

      Democracy and representation
in international law   6

      A changing international scene: globalisation
and the diffusion of state power   12

      The transnationalisation of civil society and
the increasing role of NGOs   15

      Legitimacy and international law   22

      Conclusion: the role of NGOs in a discourse
model of international law   28

    1.3   The diversity of NGOs: definitions and
delimitations   36

      Definitions of 'NGO' in international
instruments and doctrine   36

      Defining 'NGO' for the purpose of the study   46

2   Historical and conceptual background   53

    2.1   Introduction   53

    2.2   The historical view of the subjects
of international law   54

    2.3   Intergovernmental organisations as subjects
of international law   58

vii

viii CONTENTS

2.4	The *'sui generis'* subjects of international law	63
	Introduction	63
	The Order of Malta	64
	The International Committee of the Red Cross	68
2.5	The classical concepts relating to international legal personality in modern doctrine	74
2.6	The relationship between personality and the making of international customary law	77

3 International legal theory and non-state actors 79

3.1	Introduction	79
3.2	The actors of international law in international legal theory	82
	Introduction	82
	The rule approach	84
	Who are the actors of international law?	84
	How can it be determined that a new actor has become part of the legal system?	87
	The process approach	91
	Who are the actors of international law?	91
	How can it be determined that a new actor has become part of the legal system?	96
	International law and international relations	100
	Who are the actors of international law?	103
	How can it be determined that a new actor has become part of the legal system?	107
3.3	Conclusions	109
	Introduction	109
	States as the dominant actors of international law	111
	The increasing role of non-state actors	111
	States and the conferral of international legal status	112
	Generally accepted sources	113
	An inductive method	115

Part II Legal and empirical survey 119

4 Rights and obligations 121

4.1	Theoretical background	121
	The concept of 'rights'	121

	Non-state rights-holders on the international plane	123
	Introduction	123
	The intention of the parties	127
	The terms of the treaty	128
	Rights and legal remedies	130
	Conclusion	133
4.2	Organisation rights	134
	Human rights, group rights and organisation rights	134
	Organisation rights in international law	139
	Introduction	139
	The International Covenant on Civil and Political Rights	140
	The International Covenant on Economic, Social and Cultural Rights	147
	The UN Declaration on Human Rights Defenders	152
	The ILO Conventions	154
	The Aarhus Convention	160
	The European Convention on the Recognition of the Legal Personality of International Non-Governmental Organisations	164
	Council of Europe Fundamental Principles on the Status of Non-Governmental Organisations in Europe	166
	The European Convention on Human Rights	168
	The rights to freedom of assembly and association	169
	The right to freedom of expression	172
	The right to a fair trial	173
	The right to freedom of religion	174
	The right to respect for private life	176
	The right to peaceful enjoyment of one's possessions	176
	The legal nature of rights under the European Convention	177
	The European Social Charter	177

The American Convention on Human Rights	181
The African Charter on Human and Peoples' Rights	183
4.3 International obligations	187
Introduction	187
Limitations of organisation rights	190
The ILO Conventions	192
The UN Declaration on Human Rights Defenders	192
The obligations of NGOs in their co-operation with IGOs	193
Formal IGO–NGO co-operation	193
Operational IGO–NGO co-operation	198
Codes of conduct	198
4.4 International humanitarian law and non-state actors	201
Introduction	201
International humanitarian law and humanitarian organisations	205
4.5 Conclusions	215
5 Standing before international judicial and quasi-judicial bodies	218
5.1 Introduction	218
5.2 International bodies	219
The International Court of Justice	219
International criminal courts	224
The UN Treaty Bodies	224
The Human Rights Committee	224
The Draft Optional Protocol to the ICESCR	230
The Committee on the Elimination of Racial Discrimination	231
The Committee Against Torture	234
The Committee on the Elimination of Discrimination Against Women	235
The 1503 Procedure	236
The ILO freedom of association procedures	237
The UNESCO procedure for individual communications	239
The World Bank Inspection Panel	241

5.3	Regional bodies	246
	The European Convention on Human Rights and its monitoring bodies	246
	The procedure	246
	The concept of 'non-governmental organisation' and the victim requirement	247
	NGOs as parties before the Commission and the Court	253
	Issues raised in cases brought by NGOs	255
	The European Social Charter collective complaints procedure	257
	The European Court of Justice	264
	The Inter-American System for Human Rights	271
	The procedure	271
	The Inter-American Commission	274
	The Inter-American Court	277
	The African Commission and Court for Human and Peoples' Rights	279
	The African Commission	279
	The African Court	285
	The Aarhus Convention procedure for individual communications	285
	The citizen submission procedure under the North American Agreement on Environmental Cooperation	288
5.4	Conclusions	298
6	Non-party participation before judicial and quasi-judicial bodies	300
6.1	Introduction	300
6.2	The World Court	303
6.3	International criminal courts	310
	The International Criminal Court	310
	The International Criminal Tribunal for the former Yugoslavia	310
	The International Criminal Tribunal for Rwanda	314
6.4	The WTO dispute settlement procedure	317
6.5	The European Commission and Court of Human Rights	328
	The Commission	328

xii CONTENTS

	The Court	328
6.6	The European Court of Justice	345
6.7	The Inter-American Commission and Court of Human Rights	350
	The Inter-American Commission	350
	The Inter-American Court of Human Rights	354
	Contentious cases	355
	Advisory opinions	358
6.8	The African Commission and Court of Human and Peoples' Rights	361
6.9	Conclusions	363
7	Co-operation with intergovernmental organisations	366
7.1	Introduction	366
7.2	The United Nations	367
	Introduction	367
	The General Assembly and the Security Council	369
	ECOSOC consultative arrangements	374
	General	374
	ECOSOC Standing Committee on Non-Governmental Organizations	382
	ECOSOC subsidiary bodies and extra-conventional mechanisms	387
	The UN treaty bodies	395
	Introduction	395
	The Human Rights Committee	396
	The Committee on Economic, Social and Cultural Rights	397
	The Committee Against Torture	399
	The Committee on the Elimination of Discrimination against Women	401
	The Committee on the Elimination of Racial Discrimination	402
	The Committee on the Rights of the Child	404
	Committee on the Protection of the Rights of All Migrant Workers and Members of Their Families	406
	Discussions on reform of UN–civil society relationships	406

7.3	The International Labour Organization	410
	The tripartite structure	410
	Consultative status	415
7.4	The Council of Europe	416
7.5	The European Union	425
7.6	The Organization of American States	431
	General	431
	The General Assembly and the General Secretariat	435
	The OAS Councils	436
	The Inter-American Commission on Human Rights	437
7.7	The African Union	438
	General	438
	The African Commission on Human and Peoples' Rights	440
7.8	Conclusions	444
8	Participation in international conferences	446
8.1	Introduction	446
8.2	Rules for NGO participation in UN conferences	448
8.3	The United Nations Conference on Environment and Development	450
8.4	The World Conference on Human Rights	455
8.5	Third Session of the Conference of the Parties to the Framework Convention on Climate Change	460
8.6	The Rome Conference for an International Criminal Court	463
	Introduction	463
	Qualitative research interviewing	465
	The legal framework for NGO participation	467
	Influence on the negotiations	470
	General	470
	The modalities for NGO participation	471
	Strategies and working methods of NGOs	472
	The internal strategy of the CICC	477
	The role of different organisations	478
	In what respect were the negotiations influenced?	478
8.7	Conclusions	479

xiv CONTENTS

9 Agreements with states and intergovernmental
organisations 487
9.1 International agreements and non-state
actors 487
9.2 Agreements between states and NGOs 494
9.3 Agreements between IGOs and NGOs 496
Introduction 496
Memoranda of understanding and framework
agreements 498
Project agreements 503
9.4 Conclusions 506

Part III   Conclusion 511
10 Summary and concluding remarks 513
10.1 The legal status of NGOs in international law 513
10.2 Possible developments of the legal status
of NGOs through standard-setting 521
10.3 NGOs and the legitimacy of international law 523

Bibliography 527
Interviews 545
Index 547

Acknowledgements

This book would never have been written without the help of various persons and institutions. My sincere gratitude goes first and foremost to Professor Iain Cameron of the Faculty of Law at Uppsala University, who has put much time and energy into reading and discussing the manuscript and given very constructive comments. This book draws on a doctoral thesis presented in 2001 at Uppsala University, and Iain was a much-appreciated supervisor for that project. I am also indebted to Professor Ove Bring, who offered helpful viewpoints during the first period of the research project. Professors Philippe Sands, Scott Davidson, G. J. H. van Hoof, and Inger Österdahl all gave valuable comments during the public examination of the thesis in 2001.

I am very grateful for the financial assistance of the Faculty of Law of Uppsala University during the period when I worked on the doctoral thesis. Colleagues at the Faculty created a friendly and stimulating atmosphere. I would especially like to thank the members of the public law seminar group, who read and gave useful input on parts of the thesis manuscript. A special thanks goes to Dr Christina Johnsson, with whom I discussed theoretical issues of common concern, as well as many other matters. Thanks also to the librarians at the Law Library and the Dag Hammarskjöld Library at Uppsala University, as well as the library of the Ministry of Foreign Affairs, for much help during the work on both the thesis and the book.

I am very grateful to those who gave me time and important information during interviews, as well as to everyone at intergovernmental and non-governmental organisations who provided me with material.

The Swedish Foundation for International Cooperation in Research and Higher Education financed a much-appreciated stay at the Lauterpacht Research Centre for International Law of Cambridge

University. It was a privilege to experience the stimulating environment at the Centre, and I would like to thank everyone there for their friendliness and hospitality. I am also grateful to the Foundation Staten och Rätten (the State and the Law), which provided me with a scholarship so that I could update and revise my thesis.

My present colleagues at the Ministry of Justice have extended valuable encouragement. Finally, a special thanks goes to my family for much emotional and practical support.

Abbreviations

ACHPR	African Commission for Human and Peoples' Rights
ACISMOM	Association of Italian Knights of the Order of Malta
ADB	Asian Development Bank
AFN	Assembly of First Nations (Canada)
AIRE	Advice on Individual Rights in Europe (Centre, UK)
AJIL	American Journal of International Law
AP	Additional Protocol (Geneva Convention)
APRODEH	Asociación Pro Derechos Humanos (Colombia)
APW	Agreements for the Performance of Work (WHO)
ARIS	Anti Racism Information Service (CERD)
ASIL	American Society of International Law
ASOPAZCO	Association for Peace in the Continents (Cuba)
AU	African Union
BYIL	British Yearbook of International Law
CAPECE	Petroleum Environment Capacity Enhancement (Cameroon)
CAT	Convention against Torture
CBO	Community-based organisation
CEDAW	Convention on the Elimination of all Forms of Discrimination
CEDHU	Comisión Ecuménica de Derechos Humanos (Chile)
CEJIL	Center for Justice and International Law
CERD	Convention on the Elimination of All Forms of Racial Discrimination
CFI	Court of First Instance
CICC	NGO Coalition for an International Criminal Court
CIDI	Inter-American Council for Integral Development

xvii

LIST OF ABBREVIATIONS

CIEL	Center for International Environmental Law
CLO	Civil Liberties Organisation
CMC	Center for Marine Conservation
CMPDH	Comisión Mexicana para la Defensa y Promoción de Derechos Humanos
CODESRIA	Council for the Development of Economic and Social Research in Africa
CoE	Council of Europe
CONECCS	Consultation, the European Commission and Civil Society
CONGO	Conference of NGOs in Consultative Relationship with the United Nations
COP	Conference of the Parties
CoR	Committee of the Regions (EU)
CRC	Convention on the Rights of the Child
CSD	Commission on Sustainable Development (ECOSOC)
CSO	Civil society organisation
D&R	Decisions and Reports of the European Commission of Human Rights
DRC	Documentation and Advisory Centre on Racial Discrimination (Denmark)
DSB	Dispute Settlement Body
DSU	Agreement Establishing the World Trade Organization (1994), Annex 2, Understanding on Rules and Procedures Governing the Settlement of Disputes (Dispute Settlement Understanding)
EC	European Community
ECHO	Humanitarian Office of the European Commission
ECHR	European Convention for the Protection of Human Rights and Fundamental Freedoms
ECJ	European Court of Justice
ECOSOC	Economic and Social Council
ECCOSOC	Economic, Social and Cultural Council (AU)
EEC	European Economic Community
EFL	Environmental Foundation Ltd
EJIL	European Journal of International Law
EP	European Parliament
EPIL	Encyclopedia of Public International Law
ESC	Economic and Social Committee (EC)

LIST OF ABBREVIATIONS   xix

ETS	European Treaty Series
EU	European Union
Europol	European Police Office
FAO	Food and Agriculture Organization
FASM	Association of Muslim Students (Denmark)
FCCC	Framework Convention on Climate Change
FEDEPAZ	Fundación Ecuménica para el Desarollo y la Paz (Peru)
FIDH	International Federation of Human Rights
FIELD	Foundation for International Environmental Law and Development
GA	General Assembly (UN)
GATT	General Agreement on Tariffs and Trade
GC	Geneva Convention
GDP	Gross domestic product
GONGO	Government-organised non-governmental organisation
HRC	Human Rights Committee
HRIC	Human Rights in China
HRLJ	Human Rights Law Journal
HRQ	Human Rights Quarterly
HUDOC	Database of the case-law of the supervisory organs of the European Convention on Human Rights
IADB	Inter-American Development Bank
IBRD	International Bank for Reconstruction and Development (World Bank)
ICBL	International Campaign to Ban Landmines
ICC	International Chamber of Commerce
ICC	International Criminal Court
ICCPR	International Covenant on Civil and Political Rights
ICESCR	International Covenant on Economic, Social and Cultural Rights
ICJ	International Court of Justice
ICLQ	International and Comparative Law Quarterly
ICPD	International Conference of Population and Development
ICRC	International Committee for the Red Cross
ICRC	International Convention on the Rights of the Child
ICTR	International Criminal Tribunal for Rwanda
ICTY	International Criminal Tribunal for the Former Yugoslavia
IDA	International Development Association

LIST OF ABBREVIATIONS

IFI	International financial institution
IFTU	International Federation of Trade Unions
IGO	Intergovernmental organisation
IL–IR	International law–international relations
ILO	International Labor Organization
ILP	International legal process
ILR	International Law Reports
IMF	International Monetary Fund
INGO	International non-governmental organisation
INTGLIM	International Task Group on Legal and Institutional Matters (UN)
IPR	Intellectual property rights
IRA	Irish Republican Army
ISO	International Organization for Standardization
IUCN	International Union for the Conservation of Nature
JCIDP	Jamuna Char Integrated Development Project
JCWI	Joint Council for the Welfare of Immigrants (UK)
JPAC	Joint Public Advisory Committee (NAAEC)
LOA	Letter of Agreement (FAO)
MAP	Mangrove Action Project
MIND	The National Association for Mental Health (UK)
MNE	Multinational organisation
MOU	Memorandum(a) of Understanding
NAAEC	North American Agreement on Environmental Cooperation
NAFTA	North American Free Trade Agreement
NCAI	National Congress of American Indians
NGO	Non-governmental organisation
OAS	Organization of American States
OAU	Organization of African Unity
ODA	Official development assistance
OECD	Organization for Economic Co-operation and Development
OHCHR	Office of the United Nations High Commissioner for Human Rights
OMCT	World Organisation against Torture
OP	Optional Protocol
OSCE	Organization for Security and Co-operation in Europe

OSICAN	Organization of Indigenous Syndics of the Nicaraguan Caribbean
PCIJ	Permanent Court of International Justice
PEN	Philippine Ecological Network
PLO	Palestine Liberation Organization
POEM	Umbrella Organization for the Ethnic Minorities (Denmark)
PrepCom	Preparatory Committee
QCEA	Quaker Council for European Affairs
QUANGO	Quasi-non-governmental organisation
RECIEL	Review of European Community and International Environmental Law
RENACE	Red Nacional de Acción Ecológica
SWANUF	South-West Africa National United Front
SWAPO	South-West Africa People's Organization
TIAS	US Treaties and Other International Agreements
TNC	Transnational corporation
TRP	Transnational Radical Party (Chechnya)
TUC	Trades Union Congress (UK)
UDHR	Universal Declaration of Human Rights
UEAPME	Union Européene de l'Artisinat et de Petites et Moyennes Entreprises
UN	United Nations
UNAMIR	United Nations Assistance Mission for Rwanda
UNCED	United Nations Conference on Environment and Development (Rio Conference)
UNCITRAL	United Nations Commission on International Trade Law
UNCLOS	United Nations Convention on the Law of the Sea
UNDEP	United Nations Development Program
UNEP	United Nations Environment Programme
UNESCO	United Nations Educational, Scientific and Cultural Organization
UNHCR	United Nations High Commissioner for Refugees
UNICEF	United Nations Children's Fund
VCLT 1969	Vienna Convention on the Law of Treaties (1969)
VCLT 1986	Vienna Convention on the Law of Treaties between States and International Organizations or between International Organizations
WFP	World Food Programme

WHO	World Health Organization
WTO	World Trade Organization
WWF	World Wide Fund for Nature
YILC	Yearbook of the International Law Commission

PART I • THEORETICAL FRAMEWORK

1 The main issues and their context

1.1 Introduction

My aim in this study is to investigate the present legal status of non-governmental organisations (NGOs) in international law, and to discuss this status in relation to the functioning and legitimacy of the international legal system. The seemingly technical issue of international legal status is closely related to broader questions about participation and representation of different groups on the international plane and the legitimacy of international law. The overall perspective chosen here is therefore a systemic one, which sees questions about the role of NGOs as legal actors as issues of how international law functions, and ought to function, as a system. It should nevertheless be clarified at the outset that it is not asserted that NGOs are 'good'. In fact, NGOs are neither good nor bad. This study concentrates on non-governmental organisation (without an 's') as a form of association, rather than on particular organisations, and on the role of NGOs generally within the international legal context.

Part I contains the theoretical framework of the study. This first, introductory, chapter outlines the political and legal setting in which the study is placed. It deals with a number of basic characteristics of international law as well as international political developments and discusses issues of the legitimacy of international law and the role of NGOs in that context. The chapter also examines different definitions of 'non-governmental organisation' and specifies the term for the purpose of the investigation, along with the delimitations which have been necessary. Chapter 2 includes a historical and conceptual background to the issue of the actors of international law, while chapter 3 provides a theoretical and methodological platform for the investigation. Part II

4   THEORETICAL FRAMEWORK

(chapters 4–9) is the study 'itself', i.e. a survey of international legal rules and practices which relate to NGOs. Part III (chapter 10) contains the conclusions of the study.

The topic of NGOs is vast. It should thus be observed that a study on the rather narrow and somewhat dry topic of the international legal status of NGOs can only contribute a detail to the overall picture of the role and work of these organisations. I believe, however, that it is both possible and justified to concentrate on this detail thanks to the impressive and multi-faceted research on NGOs which has already been carried out, and which is growing steadily. The majority of investigations have been conducted within the fields of political science and sociology. There are several studies that focus on the role of NGOs in international relations, on their interaction with intergovernmental organisations (IGOs), on their working methods or on particular NGOs.[1] There is also a considerable number of international legal works, mainly articles, on NGOs but they generally do not discuss the general issue of legal status.[2] An increasing number of books and

---

[1] To mention a few books of a more general character (the articles are too numerous to be listed here): John Boli and George M. Thomas (eds.), *Constructing World Culture: International Nongovernmental Organizations since 1875*, Stanford University Press, 1999; Henry F. Carey and Oliver P. Richmond (eds.), *Mitigating Conflict: The Role of NGOs*, Frank Cass, 2003; Ann C. Hudock, *NGOs and Civil Society: Democracy by Proxy?*, Cambridge: Polity Press, 1999; Margaret E. Keck and Kathryn Sikkink, *Activists Beyond Borders: Advocacy Networks in International Politics*, Cornell University Press, 1998; William Korey, *NGOs and the Universal Declaration of Human Rights: A Curious Grapevine*, London: Palgrave, 2001; Craig Warkentin, *Reshaping World Politics: NGOs, the Internet and Global Civil Society*, Oxford: Rowman & Littlefield, 2001; Thomas G. Weiss and Leon Gordenker (eds.), *NGOs, the UN, and Global Governance*, Boulder, CO: Lynne Rienner, 1996; Claude E. Welch, Jr. (ed.), *NGOs and Human Rights: Promise and Performance*, Philadelphia: University of Pennsylvania Press, 2001 and *Protecting Human Rights in Africa: Strategies and Roles of Non-Governmental Organizations*, Philadelphia: University of Pennsylvania Press, 1995; and Peter Willetts (ed.), *'The Conscience of the World': The Influence of Non-Governmental Organisations in the UN System*, Oxford: Hurst & Co., 1996.

[2] One exception is Rainer Hofmann, *Non-State Actors as New Subjects of International Law: International Law – From the Traditional State Order Towards the Law of the Global Community*, Proceedings of an International Symposium, Berlin: Duncker and Humblot, 1999. See also Yves Beigbeder, *Le rôle international des organisations non-gouvernamentales*, Brussels: Bruylant, 1992 and *The Role and Status of International Humanitarian Volunteers and Organizations: The Right and Duty to Humanitarian Assistance*, Dordrecht: Martinus Nijhoff, 1991; Mario Bettati and Pierre-Marie Dupuy (eds.), *Les ONG et le Droit International*, Paris: Economica, 1986; Theo C. van Boven *et al.* (eds.), *The Legitimacy of the United Nations: Towards an Enhanced Legal Status of Non-State Actors*, Netherlands Institute of Human Rights, SIM Special, 19, Utrecht, 1997; Sara Guillet, *'Nous, peuples des nations unies . . .': l'action des organisations non-gouvernamentales dans le système international de protection des droits de l'homme*, Centre de Droit International de Paris I, Perspectives internationales,

THE MAIN ISSUES AND THEIR CONTEXT 5

articles examine the influence of NGOs on international law-making.[3] The major international legal textbooks, for their part, still seem to regard international legal rules which deal with private actors as anomalies that do not alter the general principle that international law is about relations between states and IGOs. NGOs are in consequence only briefly mentioned in most such textbooks.[4]

10, Montchrestien, 1995; Morita Hiroshi, *International Human Rights and in Particular Reference to the Role of Non-Governmental Organizations*, Dissertation University of Alberta, Faculty of Law, 1993; J. J. Lador-Lederer, *International Non-Governmental Organizations and Economic Entities: A Study in Autonomous Organization and Ius Gentium*, Leyden: A. W. Sijthoff-Leyden, 1963; Chiang Pei-heng, *Non-Governmental Organizations at the United Nations: Identity, Role and Function*, New York: Praeger, 1981; Howard B. Tolley, Jr., *The International Commission of Jurists: Global Advocates for Human Rights*, Philadelphia: University of Pennsylvania Press, 1994; Lyman Cromwell White, *International Non-Governmental Organizations: Their Purposes, Methods and Accomplishments*, New Brunswick: Rutgers University Press, 1951. The relevant articles are too many to list here, but are cited throughout the study.

[3] Bas Arts, *The Political Influence of Global NGOs: Case Studies on the Biodiversity Conventions*, Utrecht: International Books, 1998; Claire Breen, 'The Role of NGOs in the Formulation of and Compliance with the Optional Protocol to the Convention on the Rights of the Child on Involvement of Children in Armed Conflict', 25 HRQ (2003), pp. 453–481; Maxwell A. Cameron *et al.* (eds.), *To Walk Without Fear: The Global Movement to Ban Landmines*, Oxford University Press, 1998; Cynthia Price Cohen, 'The United Nations Convention on the Rights of the Child: Involvement of NGOs', in Theo Van Boven *et al.* (eds.), *The Legitimacy of the United Nations: Towards an Enhanced Legal Status of Non-State Actors*, Netherlands Institute of Human Rights, SIM Special, 19, Utrecht, 1997, pp. 169–184; Virginia Leary, 'A New Role for Non-Governmental Organizations in Human Rights: A Case Study of NGO Participation in the Development of International Norms on Torture', in Antonio Cassese (ed.), *UN Law/Fundamental Rights*, Alpen aan den Rijn: Sijthoff & Nordhoff, 1979, pp. 197–209; Niall MacDermot, 'The Role of NGOs in Human Rights Standard-Setting', *UN Bulletin of Human Rights*, 90/1, pp. 42–49; Louis Maresca and Stuart Maslen (eds.), *The Banning of Anti-Personnel Landmines: The Legal Contribution of the International Committee of the Red Cross 1955–1999*, Cambridge University Press, 2000. See also Kenneth Anderson, 'The Ottawa Convention Banning Landmines, the Role of International Non-governmental Organizations and the Idea of International Civil Society', 11 EJIL (2000), pp. 91–120, which is mostly a discussion on the (non-)democratic aspects of NGO influence.

[4] See, e.g., I. A. Shearer, *Starke's International Law*, 11th edn., London: Butterworths, 1994 – no mention, apart from the Order of Malta as a non-state entity, p. 103; Sir Robert Jennings and Sir Arthur Watts (eds.), *Oppenheim's International Law*, I, 9th edn., London: Longman, 1996, pp. 21–22; Malcolm N. Shaw, *International Law*, 4th edn., Cambridge University Press, 1997, pp. 138, 192 – very briefly and p. 171 (the Order of Malta); Iain Brownlie, *Principles of Public International Law*, 5th edn., Oxford University Press, 1998 – no mention at all (as far as I can see), with the exception of the Sovereign Order of Jerusalem and Malta, p. 65; D. J. Harris, *Cases and Materials on International Law*, 5th edn., London: Sweet & Maxwell, 1998, pp. 15, 142–143 (the latter on the Order of Malta); Henry G. Schermers and Niels M. Blokker, *International Institutional Law: Unity within Diversity*, 3rd rev. edn., Dordrecht: Martinus Nijhoff, 1999, pp. 32–33, 128–129, 132–133. Peter Malanczuk, *Akehurst's Modern Introduction to International Law*, 7th edn., London: Routledge 1997, pp. 96–100, is more elaborate.

6   THEORETICAL FRAMEWORK

1.2 The legitimacy of international law

Introduction

Below, I will explore how the issue of the legal status of NGOs is linked to the question of the legitimacy of international law. This is done through placing the issue in a wider context of today's international legal and societal system. The focus will be on three factors, which I believe are of particular relevance to the international legal role of NGOs. These factors are: first, that the rules on recognition of states and government do not, in practice, require democratic government, which means that large sections of the world's population are not represented on the international plane; secondly, the diffusion of state power which is due to a number of factors that can be summarised as globalisation; and, thirdly, a transformation in the way that identities and loyalties are shaped in the globalised society as evidenced by, *inter alia*, the increasing numbers and political influence of NGOs. Bearing these three phenomena in mind, I shall examine different conceptualisations of legal legitimacy and their relation to the individual and to civil society. In the concluding section, I shall suggest that the deliberative model of democracy can help explain the role and function of civil society and NGOs in international law.

Democracy and representation in international law

According to traditional international law, a government in effective control of the territory is generally accepted as the representative of the population within that territory even if it has assumed power through violent or otherwise undemocratic methods. Moreover, the government will continue to be regarded as the people's representative even if it commits serious violations of international rules on human rights. The dominant theory on the recognition of governments and of states rests on the criterion of *de facto* effective control of the government.[5] As the international representative of the population, a government enjoys an

---

[5] There are signs that this is changing, see section 1.2. Moreover, even today one can say that when judging whether the degree of effective control is sufficient for statehood, some consideration can be taken of the manner in which the government came to power – e.g. if there has been a breach of the right to self-determination. James Crawford, *The Creation of States in International Law*, Oxford: Clarendon Press, 1979, pp. 84–118; Sean D. Murphy, 'Democratic Legitimacy and the Recognition of States and Governments', in Gregory Fox and Brad R. Roth (eds.), *Democratic Governance and International Law*, Cambridge University Press, 2000, pp. 125 ff.

THE MAIN ISSUES AND THEIR CONTEXT   7

exclusive right from the international legal perspective to perform a number of important acts which will bind the population as a whole, such as to become a member of international organisations, to negotiate and cast the vote of that state in such organisations, to adhere to international agreements and to declare war or peace.[6]

It has, however, been suggested in international legal doctrine that international law does not, or should not, remain unconcerned with the way a people is governed. The major debate was initiated in 1992 by Thomas Franck and his article 'The Emerging Right to Democratic Governance'.[7] In his article, Franck suggested that democratic governance was gradually becoming a global entitlement in international law. More precisely, Franck described the development of international legal rules defining the minimal requisites of a democratic process capable of validating the exercise of power and measuring the legitimacy of each government.[8] He suggested that the building blocks of an emerging norm of 'democratic entitlement' were three: self-determination (understood as the right of a people to determine its collective political destiny), the human right of free political expression, and a participatory electoral process.[9] Franck based these three components mainly on the UN Charter and on the International Bill of Human Rights, but also on certain elements of state practice. He suggested that the *right to self-determination* applied not only in a colonial context, but to peoples everywhere, whether in a dependent territory or an independent state. While the rights of minorities are generally regarded as individual rights, not including any right to secession, Franck proposed that there may be an exception to this rule where a people, which is geographically separate and has its own ethnic and/or cultural characteristics, has been placed in a position or status of subordination.[10] The right to *free*

---

[6] According to Article 46 of the Vienna Convention on the Law of Treaties (VCLT) (1969), a treaty is binding upon a state even if the government has acted in breach of national law regarding the competence to conclude treaties.

[7] Thomas Franck, 'The Emerging Right to Democratic Governance', 86 AJIL (1992), pp. 46–91. See also Thomas Franck, *The Principle of Fairness in International Law and Institutions*, Oxford University Press, 1995, pp. 25–46.

[8] Franck, 'The Emerging Right to Democratic Governance', pp. 49–50.   [9] *Ibid.*, pp. 52 ff.

[10] *Ibid.*, pp. 58–59. The character of minority rights is the subject of much debate; *see*, e.g., Badinter Arbitration Commission, Opinion No. 2, 11 January 1992; Antonio Cassese, *Self-Determination of Peoples: A Legal Reappraisal*, Cambridge University Press, 1995; Thomas D. Musgrave, *Self Determination and National Minorities*, Oxford University Press, 1997; Harris, *Cases and Materials*, pp. 113 ff; Rosalyn Higgins, *Problems and Process: International Law and How We Use It*, Oxford: Clarendon Press, 1994, p. 124.

8   THEORETICAL FRAMEWORK

political expression was understood as inclusive of the rights to freedom of thought, freedom of association and freedom of expression as specified in the International Covenant on Civil and Political Rights (ICCPR).[11]

The third building block of the democratic entitlement, the requirement of a *participatory electoral process*, was according to Franck supported by Article 21 of the Universal Declaration of Human Rights, Article 25 of ICCPR and a UN General Assembly resolution declaring that periodic and genuine elections are a necessary and indispensable element in the effective enjoyment in a wide range of human rights and developments within the regional human rights mechanisms.[12] Franck concluded that:

> The democratic entitlement, despite its newness, already enjoys a high degree of legitimacy, derived both from various texts and from the practice of global and regional organizations, supplemented by that of a significant number of non-governmental organizations.[13]

Franck has also later observed that there is a clear development towards a democratic entitlement in the sense that governments are increasingly making legal provisions for determining their governments by multi-party secret ballot elections.[14]

Sean D. Murphy has investigated the relationship between national political situations and the recognition of states and governments.[15] On the basis of a detailed review of events in the international arena which need not be repeated here, Murphy concludes, *inter alia*, that (a) while

---

[11] Franck, 'The Emerging Right to Democratic Governance', p. 61. Article 19(2) reads: 'Everyone shall have the right to freedom of expression; this right shall include freedom to seek, receive and impart information and ideas of all kinds, regardless of frontiers, either orally, in writing or in print, in the form of art, or through any other media of his choice.'

[12] A/RES/46/137, *Enhancing the Effectiveness of the Principle of Periodic and Genuine Elections*, 17 December 1991, and Franck, 'The Emerging Right to Democratic Governance', pp. 63 ff.

[13] Franck, 'The Emerging Right to Democratic Governance', p. 90. It is interesting that Franck here takes account not only of the practice of states and IGOs, but also the practice of NGOs. Franck is of the opinion that, while the United Nations and the regional human rights organisations are regarded as the main actor in validating governments, NGOs have a supplementary role to play, pp. 76, 90. Franck has later specified the relevant practice of NGOs as their 'activities', see *The Principle of Fairness in International Law and Institutions*, p. 138.

[14] According to the Article (which refers to reports in the *New York Times* and from the US State Department, 130 governments were legally committed to such elections in 1997, and most of them had joined the trend during the 1990s. Franck, 'Legitimacy and the Democratic Entitlement', in Gregory Fox and Brad R. Roth (eds.), *Democratic Governance and International Law*, Cambridge University Press, 2000, p. 27.

[15] Murphy, 'Democratic Legitimacy and the Recognition', pp. 123 ff.

THE MAIN ISSUES AND THEIR CONTEXT 9

democratic legitimacy is increasingly becoming a factor in recognition practice, there is no international norm obligating the international community not to recognise an emerging state simply because its political system is undemocratic, and (b) if there is an emphasis on democratic legitimacy as regards the recognition of governments, it arises primarily where a democratic government is internally overthrown by non-democratic forces.[16]

Like Murphy, Crawford is sceptical about the relevance of democracy to recognition practice. He points to the inconsistent state practice in relation to undemocratic regimes:

from wholesale regional intervention in Sierra Leone and Liberia, to limited measures of disapproval and economic sanctions in Myanmar and Nigeria, to toleration and acceptance (as with the Kabila government in Congo/Zaïre and or that of Buyoya in Burundi), and even to complicity (as with the 'preventive' coup in Algeria).[17]

Crawford also refers to the discussion and voting in 1999 in the UN Commission on Human Rights regarding a resolution on the right to democracy.[18] In the resolution, the Commission on Human Rights recalled 'the large body of international law and instruments, including its resolutions and those of the General Assembly, which confirm the right to full participation and the other fundamental democratic rights and freedoms inherent in any democratic society', and affirmed that 'the rights of democratic governance' include a number of human rights, such as the rights to freedom of opinion and expression, of thought, conscience and religion, and of peaceful association and assembly.[19] The resolution was adopted by fifty-one votes to none with two abstentions, but the debate on the resolution was lengthy, and a couple of proposals by Cuba on changing the title and the operative paragraph of the resolution were supported by a number of states.[20] It can be

---

[16] *Ibid.*, pp. 146, 153.
[17] Crawford, 'Democracy in International Law – A Reprise', in Gregory Fox and Brad R. Roth (eds.), *Democratic Governance and International Law*, p. 117.
[18] Crawford, 'Democracy in International Law', Cambridge University Press, 2000, p. 116.
[19] E/CN.4/RES/1999/57, *Promotion of the Right to Democracy*, 28 April 1999, para. 6 of the Preamble and para. 2.
[20] A proposal to delete the expression 'right to democracy' from the title was rejected by a vote of 12 in favour and 28 opposed with 13 abstentions, while the proposal to replace operative para. 3 of the resolution was defeated by 9 votes in favour and 27 opposed, with 17 abstentions, UN Press Release, HR/CN/99/61, *Resolution on Promotion of Democracy Adopted by Commission on Human Rights*, 27.04.1999.

10   THEORETICAL FRAMEWORK

observed that in subsequent resolutions the General Assembly has given some support to the right to take part in elections and in government.[21]

The democratic norm theory has met criticism with regard to its understanding of democracy. Susan Marks asserts that the focus on procedures means that

the extent to which social and material conditions affect the opportunities for political participation is made to appear irrelevant. The real inequality among citizens is masked by the formal equality of participation among voters.[22]

Marks contends that the right to democratic governance as proposed in international legal theory has the character of 'low intensity democracy', as it identifies democracy with the holding of multi-party elections, the protection of civil rights and the establishment of the rule of law. It tends therefore to stabilise existing power relations.[23] There are also problems with the international dimension of the democratic norm thesis, as elaborated mainly by Anne-Marie Slaughter, because it is limited in the sense that it is pan-national rather than an attempt to democratise global governance, and aims at a multi-layered process of democratisation rather than promoting the universalisation of national democracy.[24] In sum, 'A move to promote democracy through international law becomes a step in securing systematic inequalities among states, within states, and in global governance generally'.[25] Instead, Marks proposes a 'principle of democratic inclusion'. She does this to signal a very different conception from that which informs the proposed norm of democratic governance. According to the principle of democratic inclusion, everyone should have the right to a say in decision-making that affects them. The principle includes not only those

---

[21] In a 2001 resolution, the Assembly calls upon 'States to promote and consolidate democracy, inter alia, by ... Guaranteeing that everyone can exercise his or her right to take part in the government of his or her country, directly or through freely chosen representatives.' A/RES/55/96, *Promoting and Consolidating Democracy*, 28 February 2001, para. 1d(i). The resolution was adopted by 157 votes to none, with 16 abstentions, A/55/PV.81, 81st Plenary Meeting, 4 December 2000, p. 16. See also A/RES/54/173, 15 February 2000, and A/RES/58/180, 17 March 2004 and, on the other hand, A/RES/58/189, 22 March 2004.

[22] Susan Marks, *The Riddle of All Constitutions: International Law, Democracy, and the Critique of Ideology*, Oxford University Press, 2000, p. 61.

[23] Marks is here referring to arguments presented by Gills, from whom the expression 'low intensity democracy' originates, but in her conclusions she basically endorses this reasoning. Marks, *The Riddle of All Constitutions*, pp. 52, n. 8, and 74–75.

[24] *Ibid.*, pp. 86 ff.   [25] *Ibid.*, p. 101.

operating within nation-states, but also those that operate among nation-states and in transnational arenas.[26] Marks thereby endorses David Held's view that democracy requires 'a model of political organization in which citizens, wherever located in the world, have voice, input and political representation in international affairs, in parallel with and independently of their own governments'. Democracy is thus to be seen as an ideal of popular self-rule and political equality, an ideal that has relevance not only in national, but in also in international political settings.[27]

It is clear that the right to political participation, to democratic elections and several related rights have a firm basis in international treaty law. The question whether all these human rights together and in combination with state practice provide evidence for an emerging right to democratic governance is however uncertain, for several reasons. There is considerable disparity between, on the one hand, the substantial support in international and regional treaty law for human rights related to democratic governance and, on the other, state practice. While there is indeed a trend towards more democratic systems of government among states on paper, democratic rights are, as we all know, often violated in reality. Also, there is still rather weak support in state practice for the hypothesis that non-democratic states are treated differently in international recognition practice as compared to democratic states and governments.

It can thus be concluded that, in spite of Franck's democratic norm theory, international law excludes large groups from international representation based on popular consent. This also means that international law has internal contradictions. While it guarantees democratic rights in treaty law, the law on recognition of states and governments only incidentally takes a respect for democratic rights on the national plane into account. As is illustrated by Marks' critique, this lack of representation is not really a problem for the democratic norm theory, which is more concerned with the validation of national governments

---

[26] *Ibid.*, pp. 109, 119.

[27] *Ibid.*, pp. 109–110, citing Daniele Archibugi and David Held in their introduction to *Cosmopolitan Democracy: An Agenda for a New World Order*, Cambridge: Polity Press, 1995, p. 13. See also, regarding 'the emerging participatory notion of international environmental law', Jonas Ebbesson, 'The Notion of Public Participation in International Environmental Law', 8 *Yearbook of International Environmental Law* (1997), p. 60, and about public participation in international environmental law generally, Daniel Bodansky, 'The Legitimacy of International Governance: A Coming Challenge for International Environmental Law', 93 AJIL (1999), pp. 617 ff.

12 THEORETICAL FRAMEWORK

than with how international law should redress the *de facto* situation of lacking political representation and political equality. Nevertheless, it is interesting that the democratic norm theory – as well as Marks' critique – evidences a growing interest and recognition in international law for democratic principles which used to be left aside as an issue of primarily, if not solely, national concern.

In addition to the problem of international representation of people(s) living under authoritarian rule, the democratic links between international fora and individuals in states where the government has been democratically elected are sometimes weak. One explanation for this is the phenomenon of globalisation, which will be discussed below, while another is the position of minorities in national democratic systems. Indigenous peoples and minorities which are distinct from the rest of the population with regard to culture, religion or language often find themselves in the position of a constant political minority – for example, due to the fact that state frontiers have divided them into several smaller groups. If there are no constitutional mechanisms that can compensate for this situation, the consequence may be democratic exclusion on both the national and international level.[28] Although the existence of minority rights in international human rights law demonstrates that it is considered legitimate for the international community to take an interest in the protection of indigenous peoples and cultural, religious and linguistic minorities, the rights pronounced for their protection are mainly of an individual character or constructed to be exercised within the state, and do not address the question of international representation of the groups.[29]

A changing international scene: globalisation and the diffusion of state power

The relationship between state and society seems to be transforming through a number of intersecting phenomena that are occurring within and between the arenas of the state, IGOs and private actors.

---

[28] On the problem of democratic exclusion of minorities in national democracy, see Christina Johnsson, *Nation States and Minority Rights: A Constitutional Law Analysis*, Uppsala University, 2002, pp. 59 ff. and Charles Taylor, 'The Dynamics of Democratic Exclusion', 9.4 *Journal of Democracy* (1998), pp. 143 ff.

[29] On the character of minority rights, see section 4.21, the Human Rights Committee's General Comment No. 12, *The Right to Self-Determination of Peoples* (in particular, para. 4), 13 March 1984, and No. 23, *The Rights of Minorities*, 8 August 1994 and Johnsson, *Nation States and Minority Rights*, pp. 35–40, 118 ff.

THE MAIN ISSUES AND THEIR CONTEXT 13

These phenomena are often summarised as 'globalisation' without much further specification. It seems that the majority of academics recognise globalisation as a fact, and that these political and social changes are relevant to issues of democracy, to international law and in particular to the question of its actors. Not myself belonging to the field of political science, I shall rely on other scholars in considering the political developments in this field in order to sketch a background to the study.

In his trilogy *The Information Age*, the sociology professor Manuel Castells has given a thorough account of globalisation and the particular phenomena that affect the role and influence of the state and of private actors in society. More precisely, Castells describes globalisation as a diffusion of state power which is due to several factors.[30] First, the interdependence of financial markets and the co-ordination of currencies decrease the state's possibilities of controlling its monetary – and, ultimately, budgetary – policies. Secondly, there is increasing transnationalisation and relocation of production, which cause employment as well as fiscal problems for the state. The third factor is interrelated with the second: the welfare state experiences problems when commercial bodies operate in global markets where there are differences in costs for social benefits. Castells claims that the downward spiral of social benefits which is or may be the effect of these differences results in a situation where 'a fundamental component of the legitimacy and stability of the nation-state fades away'. Fourthly, the media, which used to be a tool for information and opinions in the hands of the state, are becoming privatised and globalised. And, finally, growing multilateralism in several areas, such as foreign policy and defence, constrains state power internationally, as evidenced by the increasing role of the UN Security Council and regional defence alliances, international economic institutions and the European Union, for example.[31] Castells describes the relation

---

[30] Manuel Castells, *The Information Age: Economy, Society and Culture*, II, *The Power of Identity*, Oxford: Blackwell, 1997, pp. 243 ff., and III, *End of Millennium*, 2nd edn., Oxford: Blackwell, 2000, pp. 377 ff. The same factors are identified by Ulrich Beck, in *What is Globalization?*, Cambridge: Polity Press, 2000, pp. 1–18. See also Hans-Peter Martin and Harald Schumann, *The Global Trap: The Assault on Prosperity and Democracy*, London: Zed, 1997; Jürgen Habermas, *The Postnational Constellation: Political Essays*, Cambridge: Polity Press 2001, pp. 65 ff.; and David Held and Mathias Koenig-Archibugi (eds.), *Taming Globalization: Frontiers of Governance*, Cambridge: Polity Press, 2003.

[31] Castells also describes other factors, such as the globalisation of crime, Castells, *The Power of Identity*, pp. 259 ff. As regards the largest states, it can be questioned whether their power has really been constrained by multilateralism.

14 THEORETICAL FRAMEWORK

between these different developments and the functioning of representative democracy in the national setting in the following words:

> The main transformation concerns the *crisis of the nation-state as a sovereign entity and the related crisis of political democracy*, as constructed in the past two centuries. Since commands from the state cannot be fully enforced, and since some of its fundamental promises, embodied in the welfare state, cannot be kept, both its authority and its legitimacy are called into question. Because representative democracy is predicated on the notion of a sovereign body, the blurring of boundaries of sovereignty leads to uncertainty in the process of delegation of people's will.[32]

If globalisation means that governments are not in full control of the national political scene, the link between national democracy and the decisions taken in international bodies appears even weaker. The problem of 'democratic deficit' has been much discussed in relation to the European Union, but its application is extending outside the regional arena.[33] The socio-political changes of globalisation also correspond to a perforation of state sovereignty in different fields of international law and, again, the strengthened role of intergovernmental and regional organisations.[34]

Reflecting on this situation, Robert Dahl poses the question whether the national democratic process cannot simply move up to the international level. In his view, such a suggestion is excessively optimistic, as 'Crucial decisions mainly come about through bargaining', and 'Limits are set not by democratic processes but mainly by what negotiators can get others to agree to.'[35] If Dahl is right, the problem of democratic deficit in multilateral decision-making bodies is intrinsic and will grow with increasing internationalisation.[36] In the report of the Panel of Eminent Persons on Civil Society and UN Relationships, the weak influence of traditional democracy in matters of global governance is noted as one reason why citizens in different parts of

---

[32] Castells, *End of Millennium*, p. 377 (emphasis in original).

[33] Dahl states that 'virtually all observers agree that a gigantic "democratic deficit" remains' within the European Union, in spite of nominally democratic structures, such as the parliament. Robert A. Dahl, *On Democracy*, New Haven: Yale University Press, 1998, p. 115.

[34] See further Christoph Schreuer, 'The Waning of the Sovereign State: Towards A New Paradigm for International Law?', 4 EJIL (1993), pp. 447–471.

[35] Dahl, *On Democracy*, pp. 114–115.

[36] See section 1.2 for a brief description of suggestions on how these problems can be (partly) remedied.

THE MAIN ISSUES AND THEIR CONTEXT   15

the world are urging greater democratic accountability for international organisations.[37]

The transnationalisation of civil society and the increasing role of NGOs

Civil society and its role in democracy is an issue which has been much discussed in the social sciences, particularly after the transitions in Eastern Europe and Latin America.[38] A very basic explanation of 'civil society' is 'the space of uncoerced human association and also the set of relational networks ... that fill this space'.[39] The more specific understanding of the concept is debated, one central problem being whether the concept should include the market, notably corporations. The majority of writers support the view that civil society is best analysed within the framework of a three-part setting, which distinguishes between the state, the economy and civil society, and which allows the discussion to differentiate questions concerning the autonomy of the market and the promotion of commercial interests from questions about the role of (non-commercial) civil society.[40] That is also how the concept should be understood here.

It is generally held that democracy presupposes, or at least benefits from, a strong civil society.[41] With his empirical study of the regions of

---

[37] A/58/817, 11 June 2004, pp. 8, 24. See also section 7.2.

[38] The concept of civil society itself has a longer history, however. For a collection of articles describing the background of the concept and the present debate, see Robert Fine and Shirin Rai (eds.), *Civil Society: Democratic Perspectives*, London: Frank Cass, 1997.

[39] Michael Walzer, 'The Concept of Civil Society', in Michael Walzer (ed.), *Toward a Global Civil Society*, Providence and Oxford: Berghahn Books, 1995, p. 7.

[40] See, e.g., Jean Cohen, 'Interpreting the Notion of Civil Society', in Walzer, *Toward a Global Civil Society*, p. 36 and, in the same volume, Kai Nielsen, 'Reconceptualizing Civil Society for Now', pp. 43 ff. and Young, 'Inclusion and Democracy', pp. 157 ff. All three writers build on an understanding of civil society that was elaborated by, among others, Antonio Gramsci and Jürgen Habermas, see Jürgen Habermas, for example, *Between Facts and Norms: Contributions to a Discourse Theory of Law and Democracy*, Cambridge: Polity Press, 1996, pp. 44–45, 75, 329 ff; *The Inclusion of the Other: Studies in Political Theory*, Cambridge: Polity Press, 1998, pp. 108–109, 249; Jean Grugel (ed.), *Democracy without Borders: Transnationalization and Conditionality in New Democracies*, London: Routledge, 1999, p. 12. For a thorough examination of different understandings and usages of 'civil society', as well as critique of the civil society–market distinction, see John Keane, *Global Civil Society?*, Cambridge University Press, 2003, pp. 2 ff., 75–88.

[41] Michael Walzer states that: 'The subject is of great interest just now because of the argument that democracy requires a strong and lively civil society – if not for the sake of its initial formation then for the sake of its coherence and stability over time.' Walzer, *Toward a Global Civil Society*, p. 1. See also, e.g., Morten Kjaerum, *The Contributions of Voluntary Organisations to the Development of Democratic Governance*, in Ann McKinstry Micou and Birgit Lindsnaes (eds.), *The Role of Voluntary Organisations in Emerging*

16   THEORETICAL FRAMEWORK

Italy, Robert Putnam investigated 'the conditions for creating strong, responsive, effective representative institutions', the overarching question being why some democratic governments succeed and others fail. One of the results of the study was that 'Democratic engagement is strengthened, not weakened, when it faces a vigorous civil society.'[42]

The World Bank, often criticised by NGOs and non-governmental networks, makes the connection between a strong voluntary sector and sustainable development, and advises governments to welcome a wider role for NGOs and to allow and foster a strong civil society participating in public affairs.[43] In 1995, the World Bank commissioned an NGO – the International Center for Not-for-Profit Law – to give best practice advice on national legislation that could provide a healthy climate for NGOs.[44]

The concept of 'civil society' is itself undergoing a transformation in parallel with globalisation. In former days, when state and society was conceived, organised and experienced as coextensive, civil society had

> *Democracies: Experiences and Strategies in Eastern and Central Europe and South Africa*: The Danish Centre for Human Rights and the Institute of International Education, 1993, p. 13; Grugel, *Democracy without Borders*, pp. 12, 159; Marks, *The Riddle of All Constitutions*, p. 59, (without using the expression 'civil society'); and UN documents A/RES/55/96, *Promoting and Consolidating Democracy*, 28 February 2001, Preamble, para. 11, A/RES/54/173, *Strengthening the Role of the United Nations*, 15 February 2000, Preamble, paras. 7 and 10 and E/CN.4/RES/2000/47, *Promoting and Consolidating Democracy*, 24 April 2000, Preamble, para. 10, paras. 1e (viii–x).

[42] Putnam thereby concluded that Tocqueville, who in the 1830s had found that civil associations contributed to the effectiveness and stability of democracy in America, was right. Robert D. Putnam, *Making Democracy Work: Civic Traditions in Modern Italy*, Princeton University Press, 1993, pp. 89, 182, referring to Alexis de Tocqueville, *Democracy in America* (eds. J. P. Mayer and M. Lerner.), New York: Anchor Books, 1969. More concretely, Putnam studied, *inter alia*, associational life as demonstrated by numbers of and membership in private associations, see Putnam, *Making Democracy Work*, pp. 83–120.

[43] John D. Clark of the World Bank NGO Unit, in the Introduction to *Draft World Bank Handbook on Good Practices for Laws Relating to Non-Governmental Organizations*, Prepared for the World Bank by the International Center for Not-for-Profit Law, 1997, pp. 3–4.

[44] *Draft World Bank Handbook on Good Practices for Laws Relating to Non-Governmental Organizations*, p. 3. Among the recommendations made in the Handbook are, *inter alia*, that laws governing NGOs should be written and administered so that it is relatively quick, easy and inexpensive to establish an NGO as a legal person; that NGOs should have the same rights, privileges, powers and immunities as are generally applicable to legal persons; and that the laws governing NGOs should require certain minimum provisions in the NGO's governing documents. Such minimum provisions should include, e.g., that the highest governing body (assembly of members or board of directors) must meet with a given frequency, that the governing body is the sole body with power to amend the basic documents of the organisation or decide upon merger, split up, or termination and that it must approve the financial statements of the organisation. *Ibid.* pp. 31, 34, 49. See also Leon E. Irish, Robert Kushen and Karla W. Simon, *Guidelines for Laws Affecting Civic Organizations*, New York: Open Society Institute, 2004.

the 'same boundaries as the political community'.[45] As identities and solidarity are globalised, 'transnational civil society' is becoming an increasingly frequent term in academic literature.[46] This expression emphasises the fragmentation and internal struggle of international social movements, while other writers prefer the term 'global civil society' in order to express optimism and a belief in globally shared values.[47] Within the international legal discipline, Thomas Franck visualises an era of 'new communitarianism', where:

> The sense of community once fostered by town meetings and chats across white picket fences increasingly [is] being facilitated by discourse on the Internet or in co-operative efforts on behalf of Amnesty International, Human Rights Watch committees, or the World Wildlife Fund.[48]

In spite of the differences between these conceptualisations of civil society, they share the view that modern civil society and NGOs create *new social spaces*, transnationally and independently of states.[49]

Thus, while state relations, the power structures of financial actors and the mass media are becoming globalised, NGOs and other groups in civil society seem to be undergoing a corresponding development.[50]

---

[45] Walzer, *Toward a Global Civil Society*, p. 3; Beck, *What is Globalization?*, p. 64.

[46] See, e.g., Beck, *What is Globalization?*, pp. 64 ff; Richard Falk, *Law in an Emerging Global Village: A Post-Westphalian Perspective*, New York: Transnational Publishers, 1998, p. 37; Keck and Sikkink, *Activists Beyond Borders*, pp. 1 ff., 33; Anthony Clark Arend, *Legal Rules and International Society*, Oxford University Press, 1999, p. 175 (on 'transnational organisations'); and Anne-Marie Slaughter, 'Building Global Democracy', 1 *Chicago Journal of International Law* (2000), p. 225. Keck and Sikkink recognise that networks are organised around shared values and discourses, but lack convincing studies on something resembling a global civil society, *Activists Beyond Borders*, p. 33.

[47] See e.g. Falk, *Law in an Emerging Global Village*, pp. 38–39 and Habermas, *The Inclusion of the Other*, p. 127. Gordenker and Weiss write about a 'world civil society', in Weiss, *Beyond UN Subcontracting*, p. 42. John Keane uses the concept of global civil society while at the same time stressing its complexity, see *Global Civil Society?*, pp. 17–20. For a critical approach to the concept, see Boli and Thomas (eds.), *Constructing World Culture*, p. 17.

[48] Thomas M. Franck, *The Empowered Self*, Oxford University Press, 1999, p. 90.

[49] Beck, *What is Globalization?*, p. 65. Globalisation of identities and the growth of a 'global' or 'transnational' civil society may seem to be a process of inclusion and increasing contacts between individuals. However, it also excludes large groups and geographical areas. It is a striking fact that 90 per cent of the world's population still has no access to computers, Brian Urquhart, 'Between Sovereignty and Globalisation: Where Does the United Nations Fit In?', The Second Dag Hammarskjöld Lecture, Dag Hammarskjöld Foundation, Uppsala, 2000, p. 15. According to OECD calculations of the 'digital divide', there were eighty-two Internet hosts per 1,000 inhabitants in OECD countries in October 2000, but only 0.85 in non-OECD countries, OECD, *Understanding the Digital Divide*, Paris: OECD Publications, 2001, p. 8.

[50] The concept of civil society is further discussed and defined in section 1.2.

18   THEORETICAL FRAMEWORK

The traditional interest groups – national political parties – are in the decline, at least in Western Europe.[51] This trend is possibly related to the weakening role of the state, at which political parties direct their efforts, and a more general development towards a society where groups and identities are more complex and issue-oriented. Different campaigns illustrate this development, such as the International Campaign to Ban Landmines (ICBL) which was formed by six NGOs in 1991 as a flexible network for the co-ordination of initiatives and calls for a ban on antipersonnel landmines.[52] In September 1997, 121 states negotiated and adopted the Convention on the Prohibition of the Use, Stockpiling, Production and Transfer of Anti-Personnel Mines and on Their Destruction. One month later, the ICBL and its co-ordinator Jody Williams received the Nobel Peace Prize. By then, over 1,000 organisations and groups were affiliated to the ICBL, but the campaign had so little organisational structure that it was unable to receive the prize cheque.[53] Today, the ICBL represents over 1,100 international, regional, national and local NGOs and groups in over sixty countries. Several other NGOs have received the Nobel Peace Prize, one example being Médecins Sans Frontières which was awarded the Prize in 'recognition of the organization's pioneering humanitarian work on several continents'.[54]

There are several similar examples of NGOs and networks that have received attention for their work. Other, more controversial, examples include the widespread consumer boycotts and anti-globalisation protests which have exerted increasing pressure on governments on the national plane, as well as in connection with intergovernmental meetings.[55] This was evident in the chaotic events taking place in relation to the meetings of the WTO in Seattle in November 1999 and of the IMF

---

[51] Peter Mair, *Party System Change: Approaches and Interpretations*, Oxford: Clarendon Press, 1997, p. 78. At the same time, the large and well-known NGOs, such as Amnesty International, the ICRC and Greenpeace, have lost members in Sweden, Jussi Svensson, 'Ras för organisationer', *Dagens Nyheter*, 25 July 2001.

[52] Information obtained at the ICBL website, www.icbl.org, 13 February 2001.

[53] The Norwegian Nobel Committee, Press Release 10 October 1997, and the American Society of International Law, *Proceedings of the 92nd Annual Meeting: The Challenge of Non-State Actors*, 1–4 April, 1998, p. 35.

[54] The Norwegian Nobel Committee, Press Release 15 October 1999. Other examples include Amnesty International in 1977 and the ICRC in 1994 and 1963.

[55] Castells has identified 'social movements against the new global order' as a key trend in shaping modern identity: 'Along with the technological revolution, the transformation of capitalism, and the demise of statism, we have experienced, in the last quarter of the century, the widespread surge of powerful expressions of collective identity that

THE MAIN ISSUES AND THEIR CONTEXT 19

and the World Bank in Prague in September 2000, for example. Such loosely organised mass movements are another face of globalisation, and they use its infrastructure for their own purposes. Anti-globalisation campaigns have set up websites on the meetings of international financial institutions (IFIs) with information on the organisation of protests, transportation, safety, accommodation, etc., for example. Similar mass protests regarding a wide range of issues seem to be being carried out more and more frequently on a national as well as an international plane.[56] It is evident that these protest campaigns involve and are supported by diverse groups with different objectives, allied only for the purpose of protesting against the globalisation of economies, and that they would not be able to have such a strong impact on intergovernmental bodies without the use of modern information technology.

The growth of the international NGO sector illustrates increasing private contacts across national borders. According to the *Yearbook of International Organizations*, there were 3,733 international NGOs in 1972; in 2003, this number had grown to 49,471.[57] This increase is reflected in the number of NGOs in consultative status with the UN ECOSOC: forty-one NGOs were granted consultative status in 1948, 377 in 1968; in August 2004 the number had risen to 2,534.[58] Some NGOs have

challenge globalization and cosmopolitanism on behalf of cultural singularity and people's control over their lives and environment. These expressions are multiple, highly diversified, following the contours of each culture, and of historical sources of formation of each identity. They include proactive movements, aiming at transforming human relationships at their most fundamental level, such as feminism and environmentalism. But they also include a whole array of reactive movements that build trenches of resistance on behalf of God, nation, ethnicity, family, locality, that is, the fundamental categories of millenial existence now threatened under the combined, contradictory assault of techno-economic forces and transformative social movements.' Castells, *The Power of Identity*, p. 2.

[56] One example of protests that transcended national frontiers were the protests over fuel prices carried out in Britain and on the European continent during the autumn of 2000, see 'Borders Are No Barriers to Public Discontent Over Fuel Prices', *International Herald Tribune*, September 23–24, 2000, p. 8. Another famous example of a successful consumer boycott is the 1995 campaign organised by Greenpeace against Shell to prevent the sinking of an oil platform in the North Atlantic.

[57] *Yearbook of International Organizations*, ed. 40, vol. 1B, 1999/2000, appendix 3, p. 2738. The total number of international NGOs includes, however, 390 recently reported and not yet confirmed NGOs, and 4,191 non-active or dissolved organisations. That an NGO is 'international' is determined in the *Yearbook* by seven criteria, such as its aim, membership and structure, appendix 2, p. 2735.

[58] A/53/170, *Arrangements and Practices for the Interaction of Non-Governmental Organizations in All Activities of the United Nations System*, 10 July 1998, para. 2, and *List of NGOs in Consultative*

20 THEORETICAL FRAMEWORK

considerable resources at their disposal. One striking example is the International Committee of the Red Cross (ICRC), which in 2003 had a headquarters budget of close to 95 million Euro and a field budget amounting to 606 million Euro.[59] States exist whose gross domestic product (GDP) is smaller than this.

The ICRC's budget, although impressive, is almost totally dependent on financial support from governments.[60] In that regard, the finances of Amnesty International are more interesting. The international budget adopted by Amnesty for the financial year April 2003–March 2004 reached almost 36 million Euro.[61] The organisation's work is financed through donations from its members and the public – no funds are sought or accepted from governments, with the exception of support for certain projects on human rights education.[62] The budget represents approximately one-quarter of the estimated income likely to be raised during the year by the movement's national sections to finance their campaigning and other activities.[63] The World Wide Fund for Nature (WWF, formerly World Wildlife Fund) also belongs to the group of large and powerful international NGOs. WWF International's operating income for the year 2002 amounted to over 65 million Euro, of which around 17 per cent was derived from governments and aid agencies.[64]

The membership of large NGOs is another interesting factor. Amnesty has 1.8 million members and subscribers in over 150 countries and

---

Status with ECOSOC, 4 August 2004, published online at www.un.org/esa/coordination/ngo/pdf/INF_List.pdf.

[59] The budgets amounted to 149.9 and 959.8 million Swiss Francs respectively, exchange rate as of 18 October 2004. ICRC, *ICRC Annual Report 2003*, Geneva, 2004, p. 33.

[60] In the year 2003, 79.9 per cent of the contributions came from governments, 8.8 per cent from the European Commission and 6 per cent from the National Societies. *ICRC Annual Report 2003*, p. 33.

[61] The budget amounted to £25,375,000, exchange rate as of 18 October 2004. *Amnesty International Report 2004* (section 'What is AI? – Finances'), accessible online at http://web.amnesty.org/report2004/aboutai-eng, as of 17 October 2004.

[62] Amnesty International accepts governmental grants solely for projects concerning human rights education which have been approved of in advance by the International Executive Committee. For instance, the Irish section has carried out human rights education in Albania with financial support from the Irish government. Explanation given in a letter from the Swedish section of Amnesty International, 1 March 2001, on file with the author.

[63] *Amnesty International Report 2004* (section 'What is AI? – Finances').

[64] Its operating expenditure was slightly higher. *WWF Annual Report 2002*, World Wide Fund for Nature, December 2002, Insert: Financial Report 2002, p. 2.

territories.[65] The ICRC and Red Crescent Movement comprises 181 national societies and 97 million members and volunteers.[66]

Globalisation also has an impact on solidarity and on the state as distributor of support and foreign aid. As states encounter increasing fiscal problems in the transnational financial system, a situation is developing where 'rich and poor no longer sit at the same [distributive] table of the national state'.[67] NGOs, on the other hand, can act independently of territorial boundaries. According to a report issued by the UN Secretary-General in 1998, NGOs collectively constitute the second largest source of development assistance in terms of net transfers.[68] The World Food Programme (WFP) reports that NGOs deliver more official development assistance (ODA) than the entire UN system, excluding the World Bank and the International Monetary Fund (IMF).[69] In 1995–6, 30 per cent of official development assistance in Sweden, 29 per cent in Switzerland and 25 per cent in Norway was channelled through NGOs.[70] Although the considerable sums of money that are distributed by international NGOs in different regions of the world are usually derived from governmental sources, the question can be asked whether such organisations are adequately represented on the international plane by national governments alone.

---

[65] *Amnesty International International Report 2004* ('What is AI? – Finances'), accessible online at http://web.amnesty.org/report2004/aboutai-eng, as of 17 October 2004. The expression 'members and subscribers' is used due to the fact that the procedure for obtaining membership is different for different national sections of Amnesty. Some sections regard all persons who support the organisation financially as members, while other sections require an explicit declaration of will in order for a person to become a member. 'Members and subscribers' thus means all persons who are members or support the organisation financially. Explanation given in a letter from the Swedish section of Amnesty International, 1 March 2001, on file with the author.

[66] Red Cross and Red Crescent website, accessible online at http://www.ifrc.org/who/society.asp, as of 17 October 2004.

[67] Beck, *What is Globalization?*, p. 67.

[68] A/53/170, *Arrangements and Practices for the Interaction of Non-Governmental Organizations in All Activities of the United Nations System*, 10 July 1998, para. 2.

[69] WFP/EB.1/2000/5/2, *Evaluation Reports, Agenda item 5, Thematic Evaluation of WFP–NGO Partnerships*, 20 December 1999, para. 11.

[70] Ian Smillie, 'NGOs and Development Assistance: A Change in Mind-Set?', in Thomas G. Weiss (ed.), *Beyond UN Subcontracting: Task-Sharing with Regional Security Arrangements and Service Providing NGOs*, New York: St Martin's Press, 1998, p. 185. The Organization for Economic Co-operation and Development (OECD) has reported that the proportion of total aid from member countries channelled through NGOs rose from 0.7 per cent in 1975 to 3.6 per cent in 1985, and at least 5 per cent in 1993–94, Hudock, *NGOs and Civil Society*, p. 3.

22   THEORETICAL FRAMEWORK

An interesting reflection of the increasingly transnational role of non-state actors can be seen in the field of international standardisation and regulation. New quasi-legal areas of regulation, developed by IGOs, expert bodies and other non-state actors, are spreading under labels such as *lex mercatoria, codex alimentarius* and ISO standardisation.[71] Large transnational corporations (TNCs) and groups of international NGOs adhere to self-regulating instruments in the form of codes of conduct. Such normative 'grey zones' break the necessary connection between law and state, both by suggesting that non-state actors can produce 'law', and by creating regulation on a transnational scale, i.e. irrespective of national borders.[72]

Legitimacy and international law

It has already been described how the international legal system excludes large groups from international representation. It has also been discussed how globalisation affects the traditional democratic processes of the state in a way that weakens or disrupts the links between decisions affecting the individual and national democratic processes. The increase and trans-nationalisation of civil society has been illustrated by the size, numbers and strength of NGOs and social movements formed around common interests rather than around national identity.

---

[71] By '*lex mercatoria*' is usually meant a body of norms developed by international commercial arbitrators on the basis of customary transnational business practice. However, there are divergent views on the terminology as well as the legal quality of such norms, which is well illustrated by the fact that one of the major books on the subject includes two 'concurrent introductions', one written by a scholar who is of the opinion that *lex mercatoria* is law and the other written by a scholar of the opposite view, see Thomas E. Carbonneau (ed.), *Lex Mercatoria and Arbitration: A Discussion of the New Law Merchant*, revised edn., The Hague: Kluwer Law International, 1998, pp. xix–xxv. For a thorough review of the nature and terminology of *lex mercatoria*, see Klaus Peter Berger, *The Creeping Codification of Lex Mercatoria*, The Hague: Kluwer Law International, 1999, pp. 37 ff. '*Codex alimentarius*' refers to setting of standards for food safety, notably by the Codex Alimentarius Commission, which is a body of experts jointly brought together by the World Health Organization (WHO) and the Food and Agriculture Organization (FAO). 'ISO standardisation' refers to the international standards set in many different fields by the non-governmental International Organization for Standardization (ISO). Although states are free to accept or reject such standards, they have significant influence on domestic regulations, as the General Agreement on Tariffs and Trade (GATT) Uruguay Round Agreements give them a privileged position, Bodansky, 'The Legitimacy of International Governance', p. 619. Bodansky also discusses the legitimacy and nature of expert standards in more general terms.

[72] Gunther Teubner (ed.), *Global Law Without a State*, Aldershot: Dartmouth, 1997, pp. 10–11.

THE MAIN ISSUES AND THEIR CONTEXT   23

The question now to be discussed is whether the fact that the democratic links between international law and the individual are weak or sometimes non-existent is a problem. It can be asserted that international law should, as it does now, focus primarily on effectiveness, which means that control of territory is the important criterion for international representation. However, it will be argued here that weak and missing democratic links have serious implications for the legitimacy of international law as a system, and that this is a problem which needs to be addressed, for several reasons.[73]

First, it needs to be considered how 'legal legitimacy' should be understood. One well-known conceptualisation of the term has been elaborated by Thomas Franck, who perhaps sparked the discussion on the legitimacy of international law and its relation to concepts such as democracy and fairness.[74] According to Franck, 'Legitimacy is a property of a rule or rule-making institution which itself exerts a pull towards compliance on those addressed normatively because those addressed believe that the rule or institution has come into being and operates in accordance with generally accepted principles of right process.'[75] There are four paradigms of right process that legitimate the international system of rules and rule-making (i.e. the secondary rules of international law), namely (i) that states are sovereign and equal, (ii) that their sovereignty can be restricted only by consent, (iii) that consent binds and (iv) that states, in joining the international community, are bound by the ground rules of that community.[76] On this basis, Franck elaborates indicators of the legitimacy of the primary rules of international law. These indicators are pedigree (or symbolic validation), determinacy, coherence and adherence.[77]

---

[73] It can be held that the difference between rule and system legitimacy may be somewhat misleading in international law. As Buchanan points out, the 'system' is extremely decentralised and seldom gives rise to either/or choices or decisions to reject or accept international law *in toto*. Allen Buchanan, *Justice, Legitimacy, and Self-Determination: Moral Foundations for International Law*, Oxford University Press, 2004, p. 301.

[74] Thomas Franck, *The Power of Legitimacy Among Nations*, Oxford University Press, 1990; 'The Emerging Right to Democratic Governance', pp. 46–91; *The Principle of Fairness in International Law and Institutions*.

[75] Franck, *The Power of Legitimacy Among Nations*, p. 25, and *The Principle of Fairness in International Law and Institutions*, p. 26.

[76] Franck, *The Principle of Fairness in International Law and Institutions*, p. 29.

[77] Franck, 'The Emerging Right to Democratic Governance', p. 51, and *The Principle of Fairness in International Law and Institutions*, pp. 30 ff.

24 THEORETICAL FRAMEWORK

Franck's notion of legitimacy as applied to international law is thus kept within the framework of the state-centric community. Still, it would be misleading to say that Franck regards the internal conditions of a state as irrelevant to international law. He approaches this question from another angle. He constructs a concept of 'fairness' which is understood as the composite of two independent and potentially adversary variables: legitimacy and distributive justice. Law's primary objective is to achieve a negotiated balance between the need for order and the need for change. *Fairness discourse* is the process by which the law, and those who make the law, seek to integrate these two variables. Franck contends that 'The issue is not a society's definition of fairness in any particular instance, but rather the openness of the process by which those definitions are reached. This process is applied by the judiciary and by legislative bodies. However, the most important instrument for fairness discourse is democratic electoral politics ... Attention must therefore be paid to democracy as a right protected by international law and institutions.'[78] Further, he argues that:

fairness discourse requires fairness in the selection of participants. At present the term 'global discourse' suggests a conversation between nations. That limited view, however, is wrong. Not only is it inaccurate, overlooking the many actors – multinational corporations, churches, service organizations, gender- and ethno-culturally specific groups, scientific networks, and a myriad others – who are already part of this discourse. In addition, and centrally, the mental model's wrongness lies in its unfairness.[79]

Franck thus attaches importance to the *democratic process* as a part of the global fairness discourse, on the national as well as the international plane. His view is normative in the sense that he suggests that international law should rest on a more inclusive national fairness discourse. However, the fact that the global fairness discourse of today *de facto* excludes large groups does not lead Franck to question the legitimacy (or the validity) of international law. Nor does he discuss the 'compliance pull' of primary rules of international legal rules in relation to individual persons in undemocratic states.[80] In other words, states are regarded as entities, not as aggregates of persons, when the legitimacy of international rules is to be assessed.

---

[78] Franck, *The Principle of Fairness in International Law and Institutions*, p. 83. [79] *Ibid.*, p. 484.
[80] On 'compliance pull', see Franck, 'The Emerging Right to Democratic Governance', p. 51, and *The Principle of Fairness in International Law and Institutions*, pp. 25 ff.

In a later work, Franck has connected the legitimacy of global and regional institutions to the issue of unrepresentative regimes. The initiatives of such institutions cannot, in Franck's view, be perceived as legitimate and fair if any significant number of the participants in the decision-making process are unresponsive to the views and values of their own people: 'In the legitimacy of national regimes resides the legitimacy of the international regime.'[81]

In a recent book by Allen Buchanan, a moral construct of legitimacy is developed.[82] Buchanan first claims that 'An entity has political legitimacy if and only if it is morally justified in exercising political power', and that 'an entity that exercises political power is morally justified in doing so only if it meets a minimal standard of justice, understood as the protection of basic human rights'.[83] This notion of legitimacy serves as the point of departure for an examination of the legitimacy of the international legal system. Buchanan carries out this examination by criticising the view that state consent is the basis for legitimacy in international law, which he describes as 'moral minimalist'. Three examples are given in order to reveal the weakness of this view: (i) consent given by a state signing a peace treaty at gunpoint can count as state consent, (ii) it is false to characterise the current system as one in which the state consent super-norm is satisfied, particularly bearing in mind international customary law and (iii) to assume that state consent to norms confers legitimacy within a system in which many states do not represent the interests of their citizens is committing the error of treating states as if they were moral persons in their own right, rather than being institutional resources for human beings.[84] In consequence of the latter example, state consent to international legal norms cannot show that their enforcement on other collectivities and individuals is morally justified.[85] Buchanan's own model of system legitimacy is justice-based and includes several factors, the most important of which is the protection of basic human rights. He also suggests that while it is difficult to imagine that much can be done to achieve 'genuine [i.e. individual] democratic global governance' at present, making international institutions more representative of individuals and more

---

[81] Franck, 'Legitimacy and the Democratic Entitlement', in Gregory H. Fox and Brad R. Roth (eds.), Democratic Governance and International Law, Cambridge University Press, 2000, p. 31.

[82] Allen Buchanan, Justice, Legitimacy, and Self-Determination: Moral Foundations for International Law, Oxford University Press, 2004.

[83] Ibid., pp. 233–234.   [84] Ibid., pp. 303–305.   [85] Ibid., p. 309.

26   THEORETICAL FRAMEWORK

accountable to individuals, as both individuals and as members of non-state groups, would contribute to democratising the international legal system, thereby increasing its system legitimacy.[86]

It is interesting that Buchanan's criticism of the state consent view on the legitimacy of international law breaks through the state-centric paradigm while partly kept inside it. The moral basis of Buchanan's theory can be criticised for subjectivity and for a problem pointed out by Habermas, i.e. that morality cannot serve as the basis for legitimacy in a diverse and pluralistic society. On the other hand, the 'morality' which is used as a parameter for legitimacy is to a great extent already incorporated into international law in the form of human rights law, however vague its rules might be. Buchanan's proposal that, while there is little hope for a genuine democratisation of international law within a reasonable time, making international institutions more representative of individuals and more accountable to individuals, as both individuals and as members of non-state groups, draws attention to the role of NGOs and of civil society in general.

In declaring that individual democratic global governance is presently out of reach, Buchanan takes a more cautious view than David Held, who is known for advocating cosmopolitan democracy. In Held's view, it is the *individual* who is the holder of the ultimate right to choose. He states that 'The idea of democracy derives its power and significance ... from the idea of self-determination; that is, from the notion that members of a political community – citizens – should be able to choose freely the conditions of their own association, and that their choices constitute the ultimate legitimation of the form and direction of their polity.'[87] Held elaborates a 'principle of autonomy', which insists on 'the people', in contrast to state sovereignty, determining the conditions of their own association.[88] He claims that consent through elections based on territory or state is problematic because of national, regional and global interconnectedness. Held asks: which is the relevant community, what is the relevant constituency and to whom do decision-makers have to justify their decisions? Instead, he builds a model of cosmopolitan democracy, which 'transcends the particular claims of nations and states and extends to all in the "universal

---

[86] Ibid., pp. 323, 315.
[87] David Held, *Democracy and the Global Order: From the Modern State to Cosmopolitan Governance*, Cambridge: Polity Press, 1995, p. 145.
[88] Ibid., p. 147.

community"'.[89] States would 'wither away' in this system and would no longer be the sole centres of legitimate power within their own borders, while people would enjoy multiple citizenships – political membership in the diverse political communities which significantly affected them.[90] As has been mentioned above, in line with Held's ideas, Susan Marks proposes a 'principle of democratic inclusion', according to which everyone should have the right to a say in decision-making that affects them.[91]

While David Held's theory is primarily a vision for the future, his view on legitimacy and the role of non-state actors in cosmopolitan democracy provides interesting points of reference for today's international legal system. His 'principle of autonomy', which insists on 'the people' determining the conditions of their own association, perforates the walls of state sovereignty and emphasises political membership in the diverse political communities which significantly affect individuals.

An important point of reference for discussions on legitimacy and law in the democratic state is, of course, Jürgen Habermas. According to Habermas, law can claim legitimacy only if it can meet with the assent of all possibly affected persons in a discursive process of legislation that in turn has been legally constituted.[92] The discourse principle by which the legitimacy of a rule is determined thus lies at a level which is conceptually prior to the distinction between law and morality. In Habermas' view, moral or ethical reflections can never by themselves account for the legitimacy of law in complex, pluralistic societies.[93]

Like Held, Habermas finds the ultimate basis for legal legitimacy in the consent of the individual. By requiring that consent should be given in a situation of rational discourse, he also adds a *procedural* dimension which is interesting for analysing international law. The discourse theory also places much importance on a 'vibrant civil society' in

---

[89] *Ibid.*, pp. 18, 228.
[90] Held, *Democracy and the Global Order*, p. 233. See also 'From Executive to Metropolitan Multilateralism', in David Held and Mathias Koenig-Archibugi (eds.), *Taming Globalization: Frontiers of Governance*, Cambridge: Polity Press 2003, pp. 160–186.
[91] Marks, *The Riddle of All Constitutions*, pp. 109, 119.
[92] Habermas, *Between Facts and Norms*, pp. 107–110.
[93] With the discourse principle, Habermas also overcomes the tension between popular sovereignty and human rights. Habermas, *Between Facts and Norms*, pp. 104–107, 118 ff.

28   THEORETICAL FRAMEWORK

general and on civil society organisations in particular, as will be elaborated below.[94]

Conclusion: the role of NGOs in a discourse model of international law

Common to several of the conceptualisations of legitimacy described above is the fact that the ultimate source of legal legitimacy is placed in the individual. While Franck's model of legitimacy is an exception in this regard, his theory reaches the individual through the proposed democratic entitlement and fairness discourse. In other words, all four conceptualisations adhere to the principle that law, national as well as international, should be based on the assent of the people, i.e. individuals.

For the purpose of the present study, Habermas' concept of legitimacy will be used. According to this, as we have seen, law can claim legitimacy only if it can meet with the assent of all possibly affected persons in a discursive process of legislation that in turn has been legally constituted. This construction of legitimacy has several advantages. First, the concept itself avoids the choice between law and morality and can therefore, at least potentially, be accepted by the proponents of different 'schools' of law, as well as by different regions and cultures. Secondly, it embraces both primary and secondary rules. Thirdly, it insists on a discursive process which includes all possibly affected persons, thus adding qualitative elements to the way in which decisions are taken. And, fourthly, it links the issue of legitimacy with the individual which is, in my view, the most reasonable understanding of the concept.

The acceptance of a concept of legal legitimacy that is ultimately linked to the individual implies, of course, a standpoint that international law is not legitimate. This is, however, not the same thing as arguing that international law *should* be legitimate. It can, as has been stated above, very well be argued that international law should, as it does today, rest primarily on *effectiveness* – or, in other words, on state consent. Nevertheless it is argued here that the flawed legitimacy of international law is a problem which needs to be addressed, for several reasons. First and foremost, the view that the international community should aim at a legitimate legal system is a moral standpoint. However, there are also more functional arguments which support such a view.

---

[94] Habermas, 'Postscript to Faktizität und Geltung', 20 *Philosophy and Social Criticism* (1994), p. 147, *The Inclusion of the Other*, p. 251 and *Between Facts and Norms*, pp. 355 ff.

THE MAIN ISSUES AND THEIR CONTEXT   29

One such argument is 'compliance pull', as explained by Thomas Franck. Although the primary addressees of international law are states, it is ultimately up to individuals to comply with international rules. States are, after all, only aggregates of individuals.[95] As the international legal system expands into new and wider fields, the group of people who are expected to comply with international law grows. For example, international environmental law is applied not only by government officials, but also (at least indirectly) by private entities and persons, such as shipping companies and industries.

More generally speaking, the weak legitimacy of international law may affect the more general sense within the community that international legal rules created by states are acceptable because they are based on the assent of the population in many countries. The knowledge that decisions in international law on important and far-reaching issues are taken by governments in international fora without any participation from a large part of the world's population might add to a feeling of frustration among people in democratic as well as undemocratic countries. There is a risk that the democracy deficit in international law is or becomes one component in an erosion of people's faith and engagement in traditional political processes. This type of frustration may have been a contributing factor to the mass protests held in connection with many high-level intergovernmental meetings. Franck points out that legitimation serves to reinforce the perception of *communitas* on the part of community members. This should be made true also for international law.[96]

Yet another argument for strengthening the legitimacy of international law through political participation of unrepresented groups has been touched upon earlier. Any system of law should be coherent in the sense that one field of law should not contradict another. According to Franck's theory of legitimacy, coherence is one element of legal legitimacy, thus also affecting the compliance pull of a given norm. Bearing in mind the strong support for human and discursive rights in

---

[95] Kelsen contends that: 'The statement that states as juristic persons are subjects of international law does not mean that individuals are not the subject of the obligations, responsibilities, and rights established by this law. It only means that individual human beings are indirectly and collectively, in their capacity as organs or members of the state, subjects of the obligations, responsibilities, and rights presented as obligations, responsibilities, and rights of the state.' Hans Kelsen, *Principles of International Law*, 2nd edn., New York: Holt, Rinehart & Winston, 1966, pp. 194–195.

[96] Franck, *The Principle of Fairness in International Law and Institutions*, p. 26.

30   THEORETICAL FRAMEWORK

international treaty law, the problem of people(s) and groups that are unrepresented in international fora should not be neglected.

Finally, it is reasonable to assume that decisions taken on the basis of an inclusive discursive process are of a better quality than decisions taken by a more limited and partly unrepresentative group of people without any process of external consultation. Information is lost in undemocratic decision processes and many points can be left unconsidered. This is not rational within a legal system which embraces a whole world, with everything that this implies in terms of plurality, differences and inequalities.

The question that follows is what such a position means for the international decision-making process. My platform for that discussion is, in spite of what has been stated above, a conviction that the international system is not ready for direct representation of people(s) and groups in actual decision-making, at least not outside specified areas of law. In my view, the model built by Held and others of a cosmopolitan democracy has great advantages and can serve as a useful point of reference for important reforms. At the same time, I do not think that a transformation to a whole new system of international governance will be possible for a long time. This means that the views and proposals presented in this study are based on an acceptance of a state-centric international legal system as a fact.

That being said, it should be considered what a discourse perspective on international law implies in practical terms. In order to do this, Habermas' theories need to be recalled. Although his work focuses on the national arena, I find that his proceduralist paradigm is helpful in putting intergovernmental decision-making in a wider perspective.[97] In the national context, Habermas claims that the success of deliberative politics depends on the institutionalisation of the corresponding procedures and conditions of communication, as well as on the interplay of institutionalised deliberative processes with informally developed public opinions.[98] Although discourse theory is primarily modelled on a nation-state which grants political rights for its citizens, it is significant for the international arena as it 'corresponds to the image of a decentred society, albeit a society in which the political public sphere has been

---

[97] As regards the domain of international law, Habermas expresses some hope for a more peaceful and just political and economic world order, but points out that it is unthinkable 'without the kind of policies that could only be carried out under pressure from a mobilized global civil society'. Habermas, *The Inclusion of the Other*, p. 127.

[98] Habermas, *Between Facts and Norms*, p. 298.

THE MAIN ISSUES AND THEIR CONTEXT 31

differentiated as an arena for perception, identification, and treatment of problems affecting the whole of society'.[99]

Habermas emphasises the importance of a 'robust' civil society and that formal, institutionalised deliberation should be open for input from informal public spheres. There must be channels of communication between the public sphere and a strong civil society, where mobilised publics find a basis in associations distinct from both state and economy. At the same time, Habermas makes it clear that, within the boundaries of the public sphere, civil society actors can acquire only influence, not political power. In the national context, public influence is transformed into communicative power only after it has passed through the filters of the institutionalised procedures of democratic opinion and will formation into legitimate law-making: 'Not influence per se, but influence transformed into communicative power legitimates political decisions.'[100]

The main arena of Habermas' discourse theory is the nation-state.[101] The question still lingers to what extent his model of deliberative politics can be applied to the international level. Habermas has himself answered this question in a book on the conditions for democracy in a globalised context.[102] The overriding question put by Habermas is: 'How can we envision the democratic legitimation of decisions beyond the schema of the nation-state?'[103] The vision of cosmopolitan democracy suggested by Held is rejected by Habermas, who argues that rather than a 'world state', a less demanding basis of legitimacy in the organisational form of an international negotiating system, which already exists, needs to be found.[104] Although conventional procedures for decision-making and political representation can never be entirely replaced, Habermas contends that a discourse-theoretical understanding of democracy changes the theoretical demands placed on the legitimacy conditions for democratic politics. Factors such as a functioning public sphere, the quality of discussion, accessibility and the discursive character of opinion and will formation can contribute to meeting the procedural demands of communicative and decision-making processes. Habermas continues:

Supposedly weak forms of legitimation then appear in another light. For example, the institutionalised participation of non-governmental organizations

---

[99] *Ibid.*, p. 301.   [100] *Ibid.* and p. 371.
[101] For Habermas' view on the concept of nation-state, see, e.g., *Between Facts and Norms*, pp. 492 ff. and *The Postnational Constellation*, pp. 63–65.
[102] Habermas, *The Postnational Constellation*, pp. 58–112.   [103] *Ibid.*, p. 110.
[104] *Ibid.*, pp. 107–109.

32   THEORETICAL FRAMEWORK

in the deliberations of international negotiating systems would strengthen the legitimacy of the procedures insofar as mid-level transnational decision-making processes could then be rendered transparent for national public spheres, and thus be reconnected with decision-making procedures at the grass-roots level.[105]

Thus, although a conceptualisation of legitimacy which is based on the will of the individual can never find a substitute for conventional democratic procedures for decision-making and political representation, discourse theory can be instrumental in identifying ways to strengthen the legitimacy of the international (legal) system.[106]

On the basis of what has been said above, it seems clear that the legitimacy of international law can be strengthened if international fora are made more transparent and open for participation from a wide range of groupings and interests from different sectors and segments of society, such as indigenous peoples, minorities with cultural, linguistic or religious characteristics, academia, trade unions, religious associations, other NGOs, etc.[107] In accordance with the discourse principle, decisions should be based on rational discourse which is inclusive of all possibly affected persons. Andrew Linklater has specifically engaged in the question of the dialogical community of international relations in the context of globalisation and ethnic fragmentation. He argues that, as globalisation erodes traditional concepts of community, the critical project needs to be reconstructed: it 'requires normative and sociological accounts of more inclusive communication communities which introduce unprecedented forms of dialogue between the radically different'.[108] Systematically excluded groups and victims of transnational harm should enjoy rights of participation. According to Linklater: 'Wider universalities of discourse which increase the range of permissible disagreements would represent a significant shift beyond the Westphalian era of classical sovereign states and their

---

[105] Ibid., pp. 110–111.

[106] Considering that a 'global democracy' is not possible, Van Rooy proposes the 'compromise solution' of a 'Supplementary Democracy', which can be summarised as an amplification of existing mechanisms that promote broader civic participation and greater accountability, Alison Van Rooy, The Global Legitimacy Game: Civil Society, Globalization and Protest, New York: Palgrave Macmillan, 2004, pp. 137–140.

[107] On the recognition of minority interests through a deliberative understanding of democracy, see Steven Wheatly, 'Deliberative Democracy and Minorities', 14 EJIL (2003), pp. 507–527.

[108] Andrew Linklater, The Transformation of Political Community, Cambridge: Polity Press, 1998, p. 5.

THE MAIN ISSUES AND THEIR CONTEXT   33

totalising projects.'[109] As has been mentioned above, Susan Marks also endorses the importance of wide participation with the principle of democratic inclusion.[110]

The precise role that should be played by different non-state entities in different contexts depends on their special characteristics and interests, and on what issues are to be discussed. A variety of solutions and mechanisms are possible, and many are already in place. For example, the International Labour Organization (ILO) provides an interesting example of direct decision-making power for non-governmental groups which are representative of certain sectors of society and which have special competence. Other possibilities are advisory, consultative or participatory status, special committees composed of representatives of different interests, observers and working groups. Several proposals for reform of the United Nations have been presented in the report of the Panel of Eminent Persons on Civil Society and UN Relationships, as will be described in chapter 7.[111] I shall not discuss which solution is most appropriate for different actors, fora and issues, but shall focus exclusively on the role of NGOs. The legal survey in part II of the book will show that there are many different forms of contact in place between NGOs and IGOs.

Before we embark on the main topic of the study, some clarifications need to be made about the view of NGOs which is adopted here. Discussions about NGOs often focus on whether these organisations are 'good' or 'bad'. Naturally, these questions need to be asked. As has been touched upon above, NGOs are self-appointed, often oriented towards a single issue, mostly based in the North, often have their basis in the middle class and are often not accountable to the people on whose behalf they claim to speak.[112] Keohane states that NGOs are often not very transparent, but, 'perhaps more seriously, their legitimacy and their accountability are disconnected'. The claims of NGOs to a legitimate voice over policy are based on the disadvantaged people on whose

---

[109] *Ibid.*, pp. 107–108.   [110] Marks, *The Riddle of All Constitutions*, pp. 109–110.
[111] See section 7.2 and A/58/817, 11 June 2004.
[112] For example, Kenneth Anderson, formerly a Director of the Human Rights Watch Arms Division, 'sharply questions whether the Ottawa Convention and the process leading up to it represents any real "democratization" of international law', see Kenneth Anderson, 'The Ottawa Convention Banning Landmines', the Role of International Non-governmental Organizations and the Idea of International Civil Society', 11 EJIL (2000), p. 91. Alison van Rooy has included a whole list (as a reflection of 'a growing chorus of complaint') of critical statements on NGOs, see *The Global Legitimacy Game*, pp. 2–3.

34   THEORETICAL FRAMEWORK

behalf they claim to speak, but they are internally accountable to wealthy people in rich countries, who do not experience the result of their actions. However, Keohane considers that NGOs on the whole wield influence only through persuasion and lobbying. Apart from moral claims and media presence they are relatively weak, and they are highly vulnerable to threats to their reputations. His conclusion is therefore that 'we should not demand strong internal accountability of relatively weak NGOs'.[113] Another point relating to the critique of the NGO community is made by Van Rooy, who observes that one need not be legitimate in order to voice an opinion. It is in relation to issues such as negotiation of treaties that legitimacy through representation becomes relevant.[114]

While these problems are important they are, in my view, not the primary issue in a discussion on the role of NGOs in international law. Because of the democratic deficit in international law, resulting from both the rules on the representation of populations and from globalisation, diverse and conflicting information, opinions and concerns of different groups are needed in the fora where international law is made and applied. The criticism often heard about NGOs thus loses some of its relevance. With a view of the international system that is based on Habermas' theories of democratic discourse, the focus is placed on the procedure of *communicative action*, rather than on specific actors. As Habermas states, a discourse-theoretical understanding make supposedly weak forms of legitimation appear in another light.[115]

It should also be observed that the focus of this study is more on non-governmental organisation as a form or a method than on the character or role of particular NGOs. Although this distinction may seem artificial, I think it needs to be upheld for the purpose of the discussion on legitimacy. In other words, the question whether international law should provide and protect a form of political participation through non-governmental organisation is on another and more fundamental level than the issue of which particular organisations should be entitled to participate in which particular situations. There is no guarantee that there are sufficient links between unrepresented groups and NGOs to

---

[113] Robert A. Keohane, 'Global Governance and Democratic Accountability', in David Held and Mathias Koenig-Archibugi, *Taming Globalization: Frontiers of Governance*, Cambridge: Polity Press, 2003, p. 148.

[114] Van Rooy, *The Global Legitimacy Game*, p. 138.

[115] Habermas, *The Postnational Constellation*, p. 111.

provide these groups with a say. Nevertheless, an international system which protects the right to non-governmental organisation and which allows NGOs to participate provides a form and a possibility for anyone who seeks to take part in international (legal) discourse.[116]

What is the more precise shape of the associational form of 'non-governmental organisation' will be discussed in the next section on the definition of the concept. However, such criteria can specify only the basics. The autonomy of the NGO community means that its diverse and unco-ordinated character is intrinsic. I believe that Iris Marion Young has a point when she reflects that:

> Particular attributes of civil society make possible its self-determining, opposi-tional, communicative, and creative aspects. The value of civil society lies precisely in the fact that its activities are voluntary, diverse, plural, often locally based, and relatively uncoordinated among one another.[117]

It should be stressed that I do not suggest that NGOs should have a general right to vote or negotiate alongside governments in inter-national bodies.[118] The role of NGOs which is in focus of this study is rather one of 'public participation'. It is an underlying assumption of this study that the regulated participation of NGOs as informants and partners of dialogue in intergovernmental fora is a phenomenon that is healthy for the overall functioning of international law.[119] The partici-pation of NGOs in international law cannot make it 'democratic', but it

[116] The Panel of Eminent Persons on Civil Society and UN Relationships suggests in its final report that the United Nations can make an important contribution to strengthening democracy and widening its reach by helping to connect national democratic processes with international issues and by expanding roles for civil society in deliberative processes, A/58/817, 11 June 2004, p. 24.

[117] Young, *Inclusion and Democracy*, pp. 52, 189. She expresses the same ideal regarding communicative democracy: 'A strong communicative democracy, I conclude, needs to draw on social group differentiation, especially the experience derived from structural differentiation, as a resource. A democratic process is inclusive not simply by formally including all potentially affected individuals in the same way, but by attending to the social relations that differentially position people and condition their experiences, opportunities, and knowledge of society. A democratic public arrives at objective political judgement from discussion not by bracketing these differences, but by communicating the experiences and perspectives conditioned by them to one another.' *Ibid.*, p. 83.

[118] This has, however, proved to be a solution in some areas, such as the making of international labour law within the ILO.

[119] Marks endorses this view. She asserts that the processes of international law should be made more inclusory, and that NGOs should 'take up a central role in the framing of international legal norms'. Marks, *The Riddle of All Constitutions*, p. 113.

36   THEORETICAL FRAMEWORK

can to some extent contribute to strengthening its legitimacy.[120] From a more pragmatic point of view, co-operation with NGOs also helps to bring information and expertise into intergovernmental fora and inform the public of the decisions taken there.[121] This needs to be kept in mind at times when new forms of threats from non-state actors may make the state community close the doors to its meeting rooms. The questions of what type of participation and which NGOs or actors should be entitled to participate should be regulated by international law – ideally by rules and practices which are themselves based on an open and transparent decision-making procedure which allows for participation by those affected.

1.3 The diversity of NGOs: definitions and delimitations

Definitions of 'NGO' in international instruments and doctrine

There is no generally accepted definition of the term 'non-governmental organisation' in international law. As will be demonstrated throughout this book, each area of law that relates to NGOs establishes its own definition, as a reflection of the fact that the status and legal framework for NGOs varies from one part of international law to another.

This study will take the same approach, i.e. outline a definition only for the purpose of the study. In order to define the concept of 'non-governmental organisation', it needs first to be considered for what purpose a definition is needed. Part II of this book consists of a legal survey of existing international rules and practices which relate to NGOs. Parts I and III, which include the theoretical framework and the concluding chapter 10, have the purpose of placing the legal survey in a wider context of more principled issues and drawing some conclusions on the basis of the legal survey as regards the role of NGOs in international law. The study is thus to a great extent a reflection of

---

[120] As mentioned above, Kenneth Anderson is highly critical of the idea that the participation of NGOs in international law-making means a 'democratisation' of international law, and even suggests that such processes 'should be seen as a step in the development of global transnational elites at the expense of genuinely democratic, but hence local, processes', Anderson, 'The Ottawa Convention Banning Landmines', pp. 91–120. See, on the other hand, Asher Alkoby, 'Non-State Actors and the Legitimacy of International Environmental Law', 3 *Non-State Actors and International Law* (2003), p. 97.

[121] See also the final report of the Panel of Eminent Persons on Civil Society and UN Relationships, A/58/817, 11 June 2004, p. 26.

existing law. I shall therefore elaborate a definition which builds on those that are already used in different parts of international law. The definition used is thus not normative and meant as a suggestion for international law as it ought to be, but merely a reflection of international law as it is.

The definition thus elaborated is also used as a delimitation of the study, which does not cover other non-state actors such as indigenous peoples, minorities, corporations, liberation movements or terrorist groupings.[122] It is possibly the case that the more general status and role of NGOs in international law is best discussed in relation to other non-state actors. The focus in this study will, however, be almost exclusively on NGOs. In other words, suggestions and viewpoints on NGOs presented here – such as the above considerations on the role of NGOs in relation to the legitimacy of international law – should not be interpreted as excluding the possibility that the same considerations may also be valid for other actors. The concentration on NGOs is made for practical reasons – the topic of NGOs is vast, and in spite of the fact that this study is fairly extensive, it does not cover all aspects of NGOs.

In order to elaborate a definition of NGO which builds on existing international legal rules, the definitions used in different areas of international law need to be examined. A natural starting point is Article 71 of the UN Charter. This is a comparatively old provision contained in an authoritative instrument of universal application, and the way it has been interpreted can be considered typical for how NGOs are usually regarded. Moreover, it was with the drafting of the UN Charter that the term 'non-governmental organisation' became the commonly used term in international law.[123] However, Article 71 of the UN Charter does not contain any definition itself, but simply provides that:

The Economic and Social Council may make suitable arrangements for consultation with non-governmental organizations which are concerned with matters within its competence. Such arrangements may be made with international organizations and, where appropriate, with national organizations after consultation with the Member of the United Nations concerned.

When the arrangements for consultation with NGOs were revised in 1950, the following definition of 'NGO' was established:

---

[122] It is recognised that the distinctions are not clear in all cases, such as when terrorist groups establish and fund NGOs. In practice, the question of what should be regarded as an NGO needs to be examined on a case-by-case basis.
[123] White, *International Non-Governmental Organizations*, p. 3.

38   THEORETICAL FRAMEWORK

Any international organization which is not created by intergovernmental agreement shall be considered as a non-governmental organization for the purposes of these arrangements.[124]

Apart from making 'international' a criterion, the resolution described NGOs only by what they were *not*, i.e. not created by an intergovernmental agreement.[125] The present provisions on the ECOSOC consultative arrangements include a more elaborate definition:

Any such organization that is not established by a governmental entity or intergovernmental agreement shall be considered a non-governmental organization for the purpose of these arrangements, including organizations that accept members designated by governmental authorities, provided that such membership does not interfere with the free expression of views of the organization.[126]

The word 'such' refers to the conditions for the establishment of consultative relations with an NGO that are enumerated in this and previous paragraphs of the resolution. These conditions include:

1. the aims and purposes of the organization shall be in conformity with the spirit, purposes and principles of the UN Charter,
2. the organization shall be of recognized standing within the particular field of its competence or of a representative character,
3. the organization shall have established headquarters with an executive officer
4. the organization shall have a democratically adopted constitution, and that
5. the organization shall have a representative structure with appropriate mechanisms of accountability to the members.[127]

The above criteria should be seen in relation to the provisions concerning suspension and withdrawal of consultative status. Such a measure can be taken, for example, 'If an organization clearly abuses its status by engaging in a pattern of acts contrary to the purposes and principles of the Charter of the United Nations including unsubstantiated or

---

[124] E/RES/288(X), *Review of Consultative Arrangements with Non-Governmental Organizations*, 27 February 1950, para. 8. Just as the 1950 resolution, the first arrangements set up conditions for consultative status, but did not include any definition of 'NGO', E/43/ Rev. 2, *Arrangements for Consultation with Non-Governmental Organizations*, 21 June 1946.

[125] It is not surprising that the term 'NGO' has been criticised for the same reason, see, e.g., Kjærum, 'The Contributions of Voluntary Organisations', p. 13.

[126] E/RES/1996/31, *Consultative Relationship between the United Nations and Non-Governmental Organizations*, 25 July 1996, para. 12.

[127] *Ibid.*, paras. 2, 9–12.

THE MAIN ISSUES AND THEIR CONTEXT   39

politically motivated acts against Member States of the United Nations incompatible with those purposes and principles.'[128] This means that political parties and liberation movements cannot achieve consultative status under the resolution. The resolution's definition of 'NGO' in para. 12 does not at first seem to exclude such entities. However, if the provisions on suspension and withdrawal are read in conjunction with the definition and the first criterion for consultative status, i.e. that the 'aims and purposes of the organisation shall be in conformity with the spirit, purposes and principles of the UN Charter', political parties and liberation movements do indeed fall outside the scope of the definition: at least that is how the resolution is interpreted.[129] The same line of reasoning seems to be applicable to violent and criminal groups. It can be observed that, although political parties cannot obtain consultative status, international organisations of national political parties or groupings, such as the Liberal International and the Socialist International, are accepted.[130]

It is rather striking that there is no explicit requirement for a non-profit-making aim. Such a requirement is however implicit in para. 2, which states that the aims and purposes of the organisation shall be in conformity with the spirit, purposes and principles of the UN Charter. That a non-profit-making aim is indeed a condition for the granting of consultative status is also supported by para. 13 of the resolution, which provides that the basic resources of the organisation shall be provided 'in the main part' from contributions of the national affiliates or other components or from individual members, as well as by the practice of the Council Committee of NGOs as regards the granting of consultative status.[131] It can be noted that this latter provision is placed after the definition of 'non-governmental organisation', which is given in para. 12 and refers to previous provisions. It does not seem, in other words,

---

[128] *Ibid.*, para. 57(a).
[129] The term 'organisation' is defined in the resolution as 'non-governmental organizations at the national, subregional, regional or international levels', *ibid.*, para. 4 (emphasis added). A few liberation movements have obtained observer status with the UN, see chapter 7 in this volume.
[130] Both have general consultative status, see list of NGOs in consultative status with ECOSOC, accessible online at www.un.org/esa/coordination/ngo/pdf/INF_List.pdf, as of 19 October 2004. See also Willetts, 'The Conscience of the World', p. 4.
[131] Financial contributions or other support that comes directly or indirectly from a government shall be 'openly declared'. E/RES/1996/31, *Consultative Relationship between the United Nations and Non-Governmental Organizations*, 25 July 1996, para. 13. See also section 7.2.

40   THEORETICAL FRAMEWORK

that a non-profit-making aim is formally part of the definition itself. Nothing is said in the resolution about national juridical personality. All in all, it can be seen that the UN ECOSOC's definition of 'NGO' can be understood only by following a rather winding interpretative path through the different provisions of the resolution.

The Council of Europe (CoE) first decided to establish arrangements for consultative relationship with NGOs in 1951.[132] The present arrangements are divided into two categories – participatory status for international NGOs and partnership for national NGOs.[133] Quite surprisingly, the resolutions do not contain any definition of the term 'NGO', and only a few conditions for the establishment of participatory or partnership status are set out. That the scope of the resolution on participatory status excludes commercial bodies is, however, clear from the Preamble, which refers to 'co-operation between the Council of Europe and the voluntary sector'. The Preamble of the resolution on partnership status makes no explicit reference to a non-profit-making aim, but puts the role of NGOs into a context of public opinion and democracy. The lack of an explicit requirement of a non-profit-making aim in the two resolutions is particularly surprising considering the fact that the term 'non-governmental organisation' in the European Convention on Human Rights has long since been interpreted in the practice of the monitoring bodies as being inclusive of commercial actors.[134]

Another important instrument for NGOs adopted within the CoE is the Convention on the Recognition of the Legal Personality of International Non-Governmental Organisations (1986).[135] Article 1 states that:

This Convention shall apply to associations, foundations and other private institutions (hereinafter referred to as 'NGOs') which satisfy the following conditions:

    a. have a non-profit-making aim of international utility;
    b. have been established by an instrument governed by the internal law of a Party;

---

[132] Council of Europe Resolution (51) 30 F, *Relations with International Organisations, both Intergovernmental and Non-governmental*, 3 May 1951.

[133] Council of Europe, Committee of Ministers, Resolution Res(2003)8, *Participatory Status for International Non-Governmental Organisations with the Council of Europe*, and Resolution Res(2003)9, *Status of Partnership between the Council of Europe and National Non-Governmental Organisations with the Council of Europe*, both adopted on 19 November 2003.

[134] See section 5.3 for further information on the requirements for consultative status and on the arrangements within the CoE generally, see section 7.4.

[135] ETS no. 124. See also section 4.2.

THE MAIN ISSUES AND THEIR CONTEXT　41

   c. carry on their activities with effect in at least two States; and
   d. have their statutory office in the territory of a Party and the central
      management and control in the territory of that Party or of another
      Party.

The Explanatory Report to the Convention makes it clear that the term 'private' in this context means that the NGO does not 'exercise prerogatives of a public authority'. The condition of a 'non-profit aim of international utility' is commented on in the Explanatory Report in a manner that refers to NGOs in general:

> An NGO must not have a profit-making aim. This condition distinguishes NGOs from commercial companies or other bodies which exist to distribute financial benefits among their members.[136]

The Explanatory Report indicates that a trade union is an NGO, although it may promote an increased income of its members, while a commercial company is not. This is also in accordance with other legal instruments of the CoE, such as the European Social Charter Additional Protocol providing for a System of Collective Complaints.[137] An NGO may make a profit, the Report explains further, in connection with a given operation, if that operation is to serve its non-profit-making aim. The expression 'of international utility' means that the NGO must not be simply of national or local utility, but of benefit to the international community. Political parties and other political organisations whose aims and activities are centred on the domestic situation of a given country are thereby excluded.[138]

    In 2002, the CoE adopted the Fundamental Principles on the Status of Non-Governmental Organisations in Europe.[139] Although this is not a

---

[136] *Explanatory Report on the European Convention on the Recognition of the Legal Personality of International Non-Governmental Organisations*, Strasbourg, 1986, p. 7.

[137] Article 1 of the Protocol refers to international organisations of employers and trade unions and 'other international non-governmental organisations'. The monitoring bodies have interpreted 'non-governmental organisation' in Article 34 of the European Convention on Human Rights, as well as its predecessor Article 25, to include trade unions and commercial companies.

[138] *Explanatory Report on the European Convention on the Recognition of the Legal Personality of International Non-Governmental Organisations*, Strasbourg, 1986, pp. 7–8. The requirement of 'International utility' is further specified in the Report by reference to the UN Charter and the Statute of the Council of Europe, p. 8.

[139] *Fundamental Principles on the Status of Non-Governmental Organisations in Europe and Explanatory Memorandum*, Council of Europe, May 2003 (adopted at multilateral meetings held in Strasbourg from 19 to 20 November 2001, 20 to 22 March 2002 and 5 July 2002). See also section 4.2.

42   THEORETICAL FRAMEWORK

binding document of international law, the Principles are interesting as an expression of the member states' view on NGOs, as well as for being rather elaborate in their description of the characteristics of non-governmental organisations. In specifying the meaning of the term 'NGO', the Principles declare that:

1. NGOs are essentially voluntary self-governing bodies and are not therefore subject to direction by public authorities. The terms used to describe them in national law may vary, but they include associations, charities, foundations, funds, non-profit corporations, societies and trusts. They do not include bodies which act as political parties.
2. NGOs encompass bodies established by individual persons (natural and legal) and groups of such persons. They may be national or international in their composition and sphere of operation.
3. NGOs are usually organisations which have a membership, but this is not necessarily the case.
4. NGOs do not have the primary aim of making a profit. They do not distribute profits arising from their activities to their members or founders, but use them for the pursuit of their objectives.
5. NGOs can be either informal bodies, or organisations which have legal personality. They may enjoy different statuses under national law in order to reflect differences in the financial or other benefits which they are accorded in addition to legal personality.

The most specific point in para. 1 is the exclusion of political parties from the definition. This exclusion is in line with how the ECOSOC resolution on consultative status is interpreted. On the other hand, political parties fall under the term 'non-governmental organisation' in Article 34 of the European Convention on Human Rights.[140] In the Explanatory Memorandum, it is stated that the political parties are excluded from the scope of the Fundamental Principles because they are the subject of separate provisions from those applicable to NGOs in general under most national laws.[141] The exception is thus made more for practical reasons than as a matter of principle. The Memorandum also makes it clear in relation to para. 1 that trade unions and religious congregations are within the scope of the Fundamental Principles, although this is not stated explicitly. Paragraph 4 includes an important explanation in relation to bodies that have the primary aim of making profit, which are not within the ambit of the Principles. This is in

[140] See section 5.3.
[141] *Fundamental Principles on the Status of Non-Governmental Organisations in Europe and Explanatory Memorandum*, p. 18.

THE MAIN ISSUES AND THEIR CONTEXT 43

accordance with most other international documents relating to NGOs. The point made in para. 5 as regards informal bodies is, however, more unusual. The Explanatory Memorandum makes it clear that 'the text acknowledges the principle that an NGO may wish to pursue its activities without having legal personality to that end, and it is important that national law should do likewise. Furthermore, in some countries, the distinction between NGOs with legal personality and those without does not exist.'[142]

The Organization of American States (OAS) adopted Guidelines for Participation by Civil Society Organizations in OAS Activities in 1999. The Guidelines build on and specify the 1971 Standards on Cooperative Relations.[143] Interestingly enough, neither the new Guidelines nor the background material explain the introduction of the term 'civil society organisation' (CSO), although the 1971 Standards use the expression 'non-governmental organisation'. If the two definitions are compared it can, however, be noted that 'CSO' is a wider term, as the Standards define 'NGO' as 'any national or international organization made up of natural or juridical persons of a private nature', while the 1999 Guidelines speak of 'any national or international *institution, organization, or entity'*.[144] The 1999 Guidelines set up conditions for civil society organisations to obtain status with the OAS, but these conditions are not connected to the definition as such.

Attempts to define NGOs and examine the issue of their international legal status were made early within the non-governmental sector itself. In 1910, a first initiative was taken within the *Institut de Droit International*. The project was discussed on different occasions over the years, and in 1950 a concrete proposal was formulated for a convention with the purpose of determining *'les conditions d'attribution d'un statut international à des associations d'initiative privée'*.[145] The final text did not really answer the question about international legal status, but was a suggestion for states to recognise certain rights for NGOs within their

---

[142] *Ibid.*, p. 19.

[143] AG/RES. 57 (I-0/71, *Standards on Cooperative Relations Between the Organization of American States and the United Nations, its Specialized Agencies, and Other National and International Organizations*, 23 April 1971.

[144] *Ibid.*, para. 2(c), and CP/RES. 759 (1217/99), *Guidelines for Participation by Civil Society Organizations in OAS Activities*, 15 December 1999, para. 2 (emphasis added).

[145] *Annuaire de l'Institut de Droit International*, 1950, Tome I, pp. 547–548.

44 THEORETICAL FRAMEWORK

respective jurisdictions, and the text never resulted in the adoption by states of an international convention.[146]

The organisations in focus of the project were labelled '*associations d'initiative privée*', defined in Article 2 in the following way:[147]

Les associations internationales visées à l'article 1er sont des groupements de personnes ou de collectivités, librement créés par l'initiative privée, qui exercent, sans esprit de lucre, une activité internationale d'intérêt général, en dehors de toute préoccupation d'ordre exclusivement national.[148]

In other words, the members of the Institute and its rapporteur Suzanne Bastid identified a set of criteria for the identification of a private international organisation worthy of international legal protection, namely (1) that it should be freely created by private initiative, (2) that it should have a non-profit-making aim and (3) that it should perform international activity in a sphere of general, and not purely national, interest.

It is apparent that definitions of the term 'non-governmental organisations' vary according to the circumstances. Each institution has its own definition elaborated for its own purposes. It is natural that the approach within the doctrine is likewise functional. There is a wide spectrum of definitions and explanations of 'NGO'.[149] One publication that discusses the definition of 'NGO' at great length is the

---

[146] Article 1 defining the scope of the proposed Convention, reads: 'Chacune des Parties contractantes s'engage à reconnaître aux associations internationales et aux fondations d'interêt international les droits définis dans la présente Convention …' The proposed rights include 'le bénéfice du traitment de droit commun le plus favorable, accordé aux associations nationales à but non lucratif, notamment en ce qui concerne l'exercise de leur activité, la perception des cotisations, l'acquisition et la possession des biens meubles et immeubles', *Annuaire de l'Institut de Droit International*, 1950, Tome II, pp. 384–386. One of the members of the Commission working on the project doubted its utility because of the limited rights that could be set out in an international instrument, *Annuaire de l'Institut de Droit International* 1950, Tome I, pp. 623–624. On the European level, there has been an instrument of a comparable character since 1986, namely the above-mentioned European Convention on the Recognition of the Legal Personality of International Non-Governmental Organisations, which entered into force in 1991.

[147] The English-speaking member called them 'non-governmental organisations brought into being by private initiative', *Annuaire de l'Institut de Droit International*, 1950, Tome I, p. 584.

[148] *Annuaire de l'Institut de Droit International*, 1950, Tome II, p. 353.

[149] See, e.g., Boli and Thomas (eds.), *Constructing World Culture* (adopting the definition of international NGO used in the *Yearbook of International Organizations*), p. 20; Schermers and Blokker, *International Institutional Law*, p. 32; Willetts, '*The Conscience of the World*', pp. 3–5; White, *International Non-Governmental Organizations*, pp. 7 ff.; Hermann H.-K. Rechenberg, *Non-Governmental Organizations, EPIL*, 3, Amsterdam: North-Holland, 1997, p. 612, and Lador-Lederer, *International Non-Governmental Organizations*, p. 60.

THE MAIN ISSUES AND THEIR CONTEXT   45

above-mentioned *Draft World Bank Handbook on Good Practices for Laws Relating to Non-Governmental Organizations*, which states:

> As used in this Handbook, 'nongovernmental organization' (NGO) refers to an association, society, foundation, charitable trust, nonprofit corporation, or other juridical person that is not regarded under the particular legal system as part of the governmental sector and that is not operated for profit – viz., if any profits are earned, they are not and cannot be distributed as such. It does not include trade unions, political parties, profit-distributing cooperatives, or churches.[150]

This definition is narrower than those described earlier as, apart from requiring a non-profit-making aim and autonomy from the governmental sector, it excludes several groups of entities which are otherwise often included, i.e. trade unions and churches. Political parties are excluded by some other definitions as well, as has been described above. It should be observed, however, that the reason for excluding these groups from the scope of the handbook was purely practical: most legal systems have special rules for such entities, and the objective of the Handbook was to discuss national legislation, not international law.[151]

The variety of definitions of 'NGO' is a reflection of the *ad hoc* approach to NGOs of IGOs and the international legal system in general. As will be shown later in the study, different bodies and rules take distinct approaches to NGOs and other entities, and very little about legal status can be assumed simply on the basis of the fact that an entity is labelled 'NGO'. The variety of definitions may be regarded as a problem. For instance, some members of the NGO sector itself may wish to be clearly distinguishable from other groups. To the extent that government-organised non-governmental organisations ('GONGOs'), other entities with hidden agendas or even organised criminal groups hide behind an NGO façade, it is obvious that transparent and public interest NGOs need to distinguish themselves from those entities.[152] Moreover, it may be a problem that the term 'NGO' says so little about what an organisation really is while the common usage of the term may give the impression that there is a general understanding of the concept.

There are, however, also positive aspects to this *ad hoc* approach. Most importantly, it is a considerable advantage that there is no external

---

[150] *Draft World Bank Handbook on Good Practices Relating to Non-Governmental Organizations*, p. 19.
[151] *Ibid*, p. 21.
[152] The term 'GONGO', as well as others, such as 'QUANGO' (quasi-non-governmental organisation), are used in, e.g., the *Draft World Bank Handbook on Good Practices Relating to Non-Governmental Organizations*.

46 THEORETICAL FRAMEWORK

regulation (except in national law) of a sector whose existence and strength depends on private initiatives and diversity. This also entails flexibility for IGOs and other bodies to find the partners and forms of co-operation that suit a particular context best. The latter aspect means, on the other hand, that the control is to a large extent held by the various bodies with which NGOs seek to co-operate or influence. If in the future NGOs, as a category, become actors with a recognised and defined legal standing in international law, a definition with specified criteria will have to be formulated, just as for states today.

Defining 'NGO' for the purpose of the study

It has been explained above that, as a large part of this book is a description of existing law, a definition which builds on those that are already used in different parts of international law is most suitable for our purpose. This means that the definition which will be elaborated is not intended to have a normative dimension, but is merely a reflection of international law as it stands.

In order to construct a definition on the basis of present international law, the common elements of existing definitions and practices need to be identified. The first, and most obvious, element which is part of all definitions above, and which is also accepted here, is the requirement of autonomy from the state, i.e. the '*non-governmental*' requirement. This factor can be divided into three components. First, there is general agreement that an NGO is not established by intergovernmental agreement, or otherwise by governments. Secondly, it is free from governmental influence, at least in a formal sense. In practice, many NGOs depend on governmental or intergovernmental funding, which of course has a negative impact on their independence. However, if organisations that accept governmental funding were excluded from the category of 'NGOs', not many would remain. It can also be observed that IGOs generally accept that NGOs which uphold formal relations (such as consultative status) with them receive funding from governments, provided that such funding is openly declared. To be free from governmental influence also means that an NGO as a principle, cannot have members who represent the government.[153] A third aspect of the

---

[153] In practice, many officials within government agencies are also members of NGOs. However, if they are not members as representatives of the government this should, in my view, normally not be regarded as altering the non-governmental character of the organisation. On the other hand, 'hybrid NGOs', which officially comprise NGOs, governments and/or IGOs, cannot be regarded as non-governmental. One example of

'non-governmental' element is that NGOs do not perform public functions or wield governmental powers, as has been clarified in the case-law of the monitoring bodies of the European Convention on Human Rights.[154]

A second element of the concept of NGO concerns the *aim* of such organisations. Most international instruments on NGOs cover a wide range of entities and do not require NGOs to have any specific type of objectives. The ECOSOC arrangements for consultative status can be used as an illustration of this. Under the ECOSOC resolution, it is required that 'the aims and purposes of the organisation shall be in conformity with the spirit, purposes and principles of the UN Charter'.[155] It is also stated in the resolution that the consultative status of an organisation can be suspended or withdrawn if it clearly abuses its status by engaging in a pattern of acts contrary to the purposes and principles of the Charter, including unsubstantiated or politically motivated acts against UN member states incompatible with those purposes and principles. Further, consultative status can be suspended or withdrawn in cases where there exists substantiated evidence of influence derived from proceeds resulting from internationally recognised criminal activities such as the illicit drugs trade, money laundering or the illegal arms trade.[156] Rather than positively formulating specific conditions regarding the aim of an NGO, the resolution thus seems to aim at excluding (i) entities that have profit as their primary objective, (ii) political parties and subversive groups, and (iii) entities which promote or use violence, or have clear connections with criminality. I shall deal with each of these groups separately and then discuss whether international law in general requires that NGOs should have specific types of objectives.

The requirement that an NGO be *not-for-profit* is shared by most definitions in international legal instruments, such as the ECOSOC consultative arrangements, the European Convention on the Recognition of

---

such an organisation is the International Union for the Conservation of Nature (IUCN), which includes seventy-seven states, 114 government agencies and more than 800 NGOs.

[154] In *16 Austrian Communes and Some of their Councillors* v. *Austria*, Admissibility decision of 31 May 1974, the European Commission for Human Rights found that local government organisations such as communes, which exercise public functions on behalf of the state, are clearly 'governmental organisations' as opposed to 'non-governmental organisations' entitled to bring complaints under the Convention. See also *Holy Monasteries* v. *Greece*, Admissibility decision of 5 June 1990, *Finska Församlingen i Stockholm and Hautaniemi* v. *Sweden*, Admissibility decision of 11 April 1996, and section 5.3.

[155] E/RES/1996/31, *Consultative Relationship between the United Nations and Non-Governmental Organizations*, 25 July 1996, para. 2.

[156] *Ibid.*, para. 57a–b.

the Legal Personality of International Non-Governmental Organisations, the Council of Europe (CoE) Fundamental Principles on the Status of NGOs and the CoE arrangements for participatory status of international NGOs. One exception is the European Convention on Human Rights, which also grants *locus standi* before the Court to commercial bodies. In fact, all private entities are entitled to bring a case to the Court as long as the victim requirement is satisfied. Considering that the rationale of the Convention is human rights protection, it is not surprising that the definition is wider than in other instruments.

I shall adhere to the common understanding that an NGO is not-for-profit. What this means more concretely is clarified in the CoE Fundamental Principles on the Status of NGOs, which state that 'NGOs do not have the primary aim of making a profit. They do not distribute profits arising from their activities to their members or founders, but use them for the pursuit of their objectives.'[157] It can be observed that a definition of 'NGO' that excludes commercial bodies adheres to the dominating understanding of civil society as distinct from both the economy and the state.[158]

Most international instruments exclude *political parties* from the definition of 'NGO'. This is the case with, for instance, the European Convention on the Recognition of the Legal Personality of International Non-Governmental Organisations, the ECOSOC consultative arrangements and the CoE Fundamental Principles on the Status of NGOs. Political parties are, on the other hand, not excluded by the definition used in Article 34 of the European Convention on Human Rights concerning *locus standi*, which entitles political parties to bring cases to the European Court of Human Rights in the capacity of victims of violations of the Convention. In the light of what has been stated above about the rationale of the Convention, this is not surprising. As I have chosen to use a definition that adheres to the most common concept of NGO in international law, the definition used here will also exclude political parties. From a more normative point of view, however, it can be considered that the need for international representation of oppositional political groups may be strong when a state is under authoritarian rule. Political parties are also particularly central to the

---

[157] *Fundamental Principles on the Status of Non-Governmental Organisations in Europe and Explanatory Memorandum*, para. 4. See also *Draft World Bank Handbook on Good Practices Relating to Non-Governmental Organizations*, p. 19, where it is explained that 'if any profits are earned, they are not and cannot be distributed as such'.
[158] See section 1.2.

functioning of democracy; thus, even if political parties are not included in the understanding of 'NGO' used here, this does not mean that the issue of their position on the international plane is unimportant.

It is evident that organisations that *promote or use violence or have clear connections with criminality* are excluded from the common understanding of 'NGO' in international law. This condition is, for example, included in the ECOSOC consultative arrangements resolution by the requirement mentioned above that the aims and purposes of an NGO shall be in conformity with the spirit, purposes and principles of the UN Charter. In accordance with this and other international legal instruments, the term 'NGO' used here will be exclusive of organisations that promote or use violence or have clear connections with criminality. It can be observed that with the threat of terrorism the distinction between peaceful NGOs and violent groups and organisations is becoming more important. Making a correct distinction in deciding on such issues as consultative status requires substantial knowledge and information. There is also a risk that the threat of terrorism may be used as an excuse for generally restricting non-governmental access to intergovernmental fora.

In addition to excluding commercial bodies, political parties and entities that promote or use violence or have connections with criminality, it needs to be considered whether international instruments should formulate other requirements in relation to the objective of NGOs. Such requirements are in fact unusual, and no such conditions will be formulated here. One example that has already been mentioned above is, however, the European Convention on the Recognition of the Legal Personality of International Non-Governmental Organisations, which states that NGOs should have an aim of 'international utility'. It should be observed that this condition is connected to the fact that the Convention deals only with international NGOs. It thus needs to exclude NGOs which address issues of a purely national character. Nevertheless, I think it should be stated that defining 'NGO' in relation to its objective contradicts the autonomous and diverse character of the NGO community, and is also impractical since it makes it difficult to decide which organisations are NGOs and which are not. Is, for instance, the preservation of a minority language a cause that is of international utility, or is it a matter for persons belonging to the minority only? Or is it a national question? Even if international law takes a clear position that the protection of minorities is a question of international concern,

50 THEORETICAL FRAMEWORK

the example illustrates the difficulties with requirements that NGOs should deal only with certain issues. Another type of organisation that some might wish to exclude from the definition is that of industrial or similar associations that promote profit for a particular industry, even though the organisation itself does not distribute profit. For instance, the Union of Arab Banks, which is an NGO in general consultative status with the UN ECOSOC, describes itself as 'corner stone in the process of building and developing banking cooperation for the benefit of economic, financial, and banking development in the Arab world'.[159] It could be questioned whether such organisations should be put on an equal footing with NGOs which promote interests of a clearly public or general character, such as human rights or the protection of the environment, and thereby be eligible for formal status with IGOs and have standing to file complaints and *amicus curiae* briefs with international courts and quasi-judicial bodies, etc. My view is, however, that distinctions on the basis of objective are both inappropriate and difficult. If, for example, local tea producers in a Third World country are adversely affected by a World Bank project, their interest in filing a complaint through their common association with the World Bank Inspection Panel can hardly be seen as less legitimate than the interest of a Geneva-based NGO to file a complaint with the African Commission for Human and Peoples' Rights (ACHPR) regarding an individual who has suffered a human rights violation and who has not authorised the NGO to do so. The position that international law should not formulate positive conditions in connection with the objective of NGOs does, however, not mean that IGOs should not adapt their procedures and provisions regarding co-operation with NGOs to what can be regarded as suitable for a particular context or field of law.

The element of *organisation* in the definition poses the difficult question whether an NGO has to be legally constituted under national legislation, i.e. have legal personality or some form of formal status under national law. A related question is whether it needs statutes and a democratic internal structure. For the purpose of describing and discussing the international legal status of NGOs, I propose that it is not the status under national law that is decisive, but the capacity of the organisation to act *in its own name* within the international legal context. Such an element in the NGO concept is expressed in several

---

[159] Union of Arab Banks website, accessible online at www.uabonline.org/UABWeb/profile/profile.htm, as of 20 October 2004.

THE MAIN ISSUES AND THEIR CONTEXT 51

international legal instruments through requirements concerning, for example, established headquarters, a democratically adopted constitution and a representative structure (all three conditions included in the ECOSOC resolution) or, in other cases, the practices followed in examining new applications for consultative or similar status. For instance, under the CoE arrangements for participatory status for international NGOs, there is no explicit requirement regarding formal status, while the resolution states that an NGO seeking participatory status should submit, *inter alia*, its statutes. Thus, there must be some form of formal structure in order for an NGO to act under international law. It can also be assumed on the basis of existing international legal instruments that an NGO should have a democratic, representative structure, although it is not entirely clear what this means in practice.

A formal structure does, however, not necessarily imply legal personality under national law. As was mentioned above, the CoE Fundamental Principles on the Status of NGOs take the position that such status is not necessary for an entity to be categorised as an NGO, since an organisation may wish to pursue its activities without having legal personality, and since, in some countries, the distinction between NGOs with legal personality and those without does not exist.[160] A definition requiring national legal personality would also exclude organisations or groups which seek to enjoy the right to freedom of association but are hindered by the authorities through, for example, denial of registration or dissolution. It can be observed that Article 22 of the ICCPR on the freedom of association protects not only NGOs with legal personality, but also *de facto* organisations.[161] Moreover the case-law of the monitoring bodies of the European Convention on Human Rights demonstrates that NGOs in such a position are entitled to lodge cases with the European Court of Human Rights.[162] The concept of 'NGO' as understood in this book therefore includes groups lacking legal personality under such special circumstances. At the same time, it can be stated that most NGOs in fact do enjoy legal personality under national law.

---

[160] *Fundamental Principles on the Status of Non-Governmental Organisations in Europe and Explanatory Memorandum*, p. 19.

[161] Manfred Nowak, *UN Covenant on Civil and Political Rights. CCPR Commentary*, Kehl am Rhein: N. P. Engel, 1993, p. 387.

[162] E.g., *Freedom and Democracy Party (ÖZDEP)* v. *Turkey*, 8 December 1999, paras. 1–12, and *Stankov and United Macedonian Organisation Ilinden* v. *Bulgaria*, Admissibility decision, 29 June 1998. See also section 5.3.

52 THEORETICAL FRAMEWORK

In sum, the definition of 'NGO' used in this study implies that it:

1. is 'non-governmental', meaning that it is established by private initiative, is free from governmental influence, and does not perform public functions,
2. has an aim that is not-for-profit, meaning that if any profits are earned by the organisation they are not distributed to its members but used in the pursuit of its objective,
3. does not use or promote violence or have clear connections with criminality, and
4. has a formal existence with a statute and a democratic and representative structure, and does normally, but not necessarily, enjoy legal personality under national law.

For the sake of clarity, it can be repeated that no distinction will be made here on the basis of an organisation's objective, apart from the requirements just mentioned. NGOs have diverse objectives and forms, and include such different entities as, for example, associations, charities, foundations, churches and religious congregations, non-profit corporations and trade unions, be they national or international in character.

2   Historical and conceptual background

2.1 Introduction

The issue of legal subjects is at the core of any legal system. As for international law, its very name, as well as its traditional definition as 'the body of rules which are legally binding on states in their intercourse with each other' also determines the range of its actors.[1] The circle seems to be closed for good. Even though it has long been accepted that international law is more complex than this definition suggests, the classical view lingers on and the concepts related to the issue of personality seem to be adapted to it. It is important to take a closer look at how the issue of the subjects of international law has traditionally been considered, for the argument that a new actor has acquired international legal status will inevitably be examined by reference to the traditional theory. My aim in this chapter is to describe this classical theory as well as some alternative views, how the concepts related to the issue of legal subjects have been used and which actors besides states have successively been accepted as legal subjects. This brief presentation will provide a background for chapter 3, which will deal with the modern theories of international law and outline my own methodology for the study.

---

[1] Sir Robert Jennings and Sir Arthur Watts (eds.), *Oppenheim's International Law*, I, 9th edn., London: Longman, 1996, p. 4 (hereafter *Oppenheim's International Law*). It is however recognised in *Oppenheim's International Law* that 'states are not the only subjects of international law. International organisations and, to some extent, also individuals may be subjects of rights conferred and duties imposed by international law', *ibid*.

54   THEORETICAL FRAMEWORK

2.2 The historical view of the subjects of international law

The horizontal and positivist interstate model of international law is closely connected to the nation-state system as it emerged after the Peace Treaty of Westphalia of 1648.[2] The concept of sovereignty has deep historical roots, but was mainly developed as a doctrine after Westphalia.[3] The general model of international law as a system of rules between sovereign states has basically kept its grip since then, even if alternative views have become more common as international law and politics in fact involved more and more actors.

While legal personality and the related concepts have until recently not been examined with regard to non-governmental organisations, historical theories about the relationships between states, intergovernmental organisations and individuals can provide an understanding of the classical view on non-state actors in international law. A discussion on this subject that was presented in one of the early editions of Oppenheim's *International Law* illustrates how legal personality was looked upon between the two world wars, i.e. before the development of international human rights law:

The conception of International Persons is derived from the conception of the Law of Nations. As this law is the body of rules which the civilised States consider legally binding in their intercourse, every State which belongs to the civilised States, and is therefore a member of the Family of Nations, is an International Person. And since now the Family of Nations is on the way to becoming an organised community under the name of the League of Nations with distinctive international rights and duties of its own, the League of Nations is an International Person *sui generis* besides the several States. But apart from the League of Nations, sovereign States exclusively are International Persons – i.e. subjects of International Law ... It must be specially mentioned that the character of a subject of the Law of Nations and of an International Person can be attributed neither to monarchs, diplomatic

---

[2] See, e.g., Richard Falk, *Law in an Emerging Global Village: A Post-Westphalian Perspective*, New York: Transnational Publishers, 1998, p. 4 and Christoph Schreuer, 'The Waning of the Sovereign State: Towards A New Paradigm for International Law?', 4 EJIL (1993), p. 447 (who, however, draws a more complex picture).

[3] An elaborate historical description is presented by E. N. Van Kleffens in 'Sovereignty in International Law', 82 Recueil des Cours I (1953), pp. 13–83. See also Helmut Steinberger, 'Sovereignty', EPIL, 4, Amsterdam: North-Holland, 2000, pp. 500–521; *Oppenheim's International Law*, I, pp. 124–125; and Malcolm N. Shaw, *International Law*, 4th edn., Cambridge University Press, 1997, pp. 22–23.

envoys, private individuals, nor churches, nor to chartered companies, nor to organised wandering tribes.[4]

Oppenheim thus asserted that it could be concluded logically from the nature of international law that private actors could never acquire international legal personality. It should be noted that Oppenheim regarded the concept of international legal personality as 'derived' from the concept of the 'Law of Nations'; accordingly, only nations, i.e. states, could be international persons. As regards rights pertaining to the individual, Oppenheim was equally certain:

The assertion that, although individuals cannot be subjects of International Law, they can nevertheless acquire rights and duties from International Law, is untenable as a general proposition. International law cannot grant international rights to individuals, for international rights and duties can only exist between States, or between the League of Nation and States.[5]

Although this was at the time the dominant view, there was already discussion on the subject.[6] The same year, the question of whether it was possible for individuals to hold rights under an international treaty was at issue in a case before the Permanent Court of International Justice, the *Danzig Railway Officials* Case. The Court stated:

It may readily be admitted that, according to a well established principle of international law, the *Beamtenabkommen*, being an international agreement, cannot, as such, create direct rights and obligations for private individuals. But it cannot be disputed that the very object of an international agreement, according to the intention of the contracting Parties, may be the adoption by the Parties of some definite rules creating individual rights and obligations and enforceable by the national courts ... The intention of the Parties, which is to be ascertained from the contents of the Agreement, taking into consideration the manner in which the Agreement has been applied, is decisive.[7]

The Court thereby clarified that there is no obstacle inherent in international law to prevent states from conferring international rights on

---

[4] Lassa Oppenheim, *International Law: A Treatise*, I, 4th edn., London: Longmans, Green & Co., 1928, pp. 133–134.

[5] Oppenheim, *International Law: A Treatise*, p. 520. International treaties speaking about rights for individuals represented 'nothing more than an inaccuracy of language', in Oppenheim's view, p. 519.

[6] Oppenheim, *International Law: A Treatise*, p. 134.

[7] 'Advisory Opinion on the Jurisdiction of the Courts of Danzig', (1928) PCIJ Series B No. 15, pp. 17–18. There are even older examples. The Treaty between five Central American States establishing the Central American Court of Justice included provisions for individuals to bring cases directly before the Court, Shaw, *International Law*, p. 179.

56   THEORETICAL FRAMEWORK

individuals and making them legal subjects in that respect, if this is the intention of states.[8]

The eighth edition of Oppenheim's *International Law*, published almost thirty years later, was edited by Sir Hersch Lauterpacht. In the new version of the text relating to the position of the individual in international law it was contended that states occasionally did confer international 'rights *stricto sensu*', i.e. on individuals 'rights which they acquire without the intervention of municipal legislation and which they can enforce in their own name before international tribunals' on individuals.[9] On this basis, and based on the fact that international law also imposed international duties on the individual, Lauterpacht concluded that the quality of individuals as subjects of international law was 'apparent'. In fact, Hersch Lauterpacht had advocated the position that individuals were subjects of international law at least as early as in 1947–8, in other words soon after the Second World War, when he had been associated with the preparations for the trials of German war criminals.[10] Lauterpacht held that the positivist view that only states were subjects of international law was 'unable to stand the test of actual practice'.[11] He made this argument referring to, *inter alia*, the rules of international law on the issue of piracy and to the rules on the 'fundamental rights of the individual' which, according to English doctrine, were part of the law of the land.[12] Commenting on the contemporary doctrinal discussions on the issue of subjects of international law, Lauterpacht stated 'The orthodox positivist doctrine has been explicit in the affirmation that only States are subjects of international law', and then in a footnote: 'That traditional doctrine is now rejected by the great majority of those who have devoted special study to the matter – though it continues to linger in some repetitious statements in text-books.'[13]

---

[8] The same position was held more recently in the case of *LaGrand* (*Germany* v. *USA*), 27 June 2001, accessible online at the ICJ's website, www.icj-cij.org/icjwww/idocket/igus/igusframe.htm, as of 4 November 2004. See also James Crawford, 'The ILC's Articles on Responsibility of States for Internationally Wrongful Acts: A Retrospect', 96 AJIL (2002), pp. 887–888.

[9] H. Lauterpacht (ed.), *Oppenheim's International Law*, I, 8th edn., London: Longmans, Green & Co., 1955, pp. 638–639.

[10] Elihu Lauterpacht (ed.), *International Law, Being the Collected Papers of Hersch Lauterpacht*, 2, *The Law of Peace*, Cambridge University Press, 1975, p. 487.

[11] *Ibid.*, p. 491.   [12] *Ibid.*, pp. 490–491.

[13] *Ibid.*, p. 489. See also Hans Kelsen, *Principles of International Law*, 2nd edn., New York: Holt, Rinehart & Winston, 1966 (1st edn. 1950), pp. 203 ff., where it was acknowledged that individuals were subjects of international obligations, while the existence of international rights was held to depend on the possibility of enforcement.

HISTORICAL AND CONCEPTUAL BACKGROUND 57

As will be demonstrated below, Lauterpacht's view that the status of the individual as a subject of international law was 'apparent' is far from a generally recognised view even today.[14] It is fascinating how the reasoning on this subject has kept repeating itself over such a long time, although the legal status of the individual has been successively strengthened.

One of the earlier attempts to launch the idea of an international legal order inclusive of all kinds of actors was made by the American professor Philip Jessup, who published his work 'Transnational law' in 1956.[15] Jessup asserted that the term 'international' law was misleading because it suggested that 'one is concerned only with the relations of one nation (or state) to other nations (states)'.[16] With the expression 'transnational law' Jessup wanted to conceptualise 'the law applicable to the complex interrelated world community which may be described as beginning with the individual and reaching on up to the so-called "family of nations" or "society of states"'.[17] In other words, Jessup regarded what is now understood as private international law and international law as one and the same legal system, including 'all law which regulates actions or events that transcend national frontiers'.[18] Transnational law could involve 'individuals, corporations, states, organizations of states, or other groups'. Jessup specifically referred to the '140 intergovernmental organizations and over 1,100 nongovernmental organizations commonly described as international', that made one realise 'the almost infinite variety of transnational situations that may arise'.[19] The term 'transnational law' has lived on in modern legal theory, as will be described in chapter 3.[20]

---

[14] See section 3.2.
[15] Jessup himself refers to Scelle's monistic conception of law, according to which individuals were the only subjects of law. Philip C. Jessup, *Transnational Law*, New Haven: Yale University Press, 1956, p. 3, referring to Scelle, *Précis de droit de gens*, Paris, 1932. In 1948, Jessup had published *A Modern Law of Nations*, which also took up the issues of subjects of international law and the position of the individual. He suggested that international law should be defined as 'law applicable to states in their mutual relations and to individuals in their relations with states', but still regarded as an 'inescapable fact' that the fundamental changes of law could take place only through state action. Philip C. Jessup, *A Modern Law of Nations*, New York: Macmillan, 1948, pp. 16–17.
[16] Jessup, *Transnational Law*, p. 1.   [17] *Ibid.*   [18] *Ibid.*, p. 2.   [19] *Ibid.*, p. 4.
[20] See section 3.2. See also Harald Konjung Koh, *Transnational Legal Process*, The 1994 Roscoe Pound Lecture, *Nebraska Law Review*, 1996, pp. 181–207; Anne-Marie Slaughter *et al.*, 'International Law and International Relations: A New Generation of Interdisciplinary Scholarship', 92 AJIL (1998), pp. 337–338.

2.3 Intergovernmental organisations as subjects of international law

The issue of international legal personality has been considered mainly in relation to intergovernmental organisations in international legal doctrine and case-law. This topic has been discussed thoroughly, and I shall not describe all its aspects. My intention is instead to examine how international legal personality was once extended to include IGOs in order to consider whether it is possible to make analogies with the international legal position of NGOs today.

The early IGOs did not have any legal personality on the international plane; instead, one member state acted on behalf of all the member states.[21] Although the United Nations was not the first IGO to be recognised as an international legal person, the advisory opinion delivered by the International Court of Justice (ICJ) in the case of *Reparations for Injuries Suffered in the Service of the United Nations* was an important development of the notion of international legal personality, because it partially cut IGOs loose from their constituent instruments.[22] The main question that was put to the Court was whether the United Nations, as an organisation, had 'the capacity to bring an international claim' against a government regarding injuries that the organisation alleged had been caused by that state. One of the Court's preliminary observations on the question submitted to it concerned what was meant by the formula 'capacity to bring an international claim'. The Court found that this was tantamount to asking whether the organisation had international personality.[23] After having noted that this question was not settled explicitly in the Charter, the Court deliberated on the question whether the UN members had nevertheless intended to give the organisation legal personality. It stated:

---

[21] Henry G. Schermers and Niels M. Blokker, *International Institutional Law: Unity within Diversity*, 3rd rev. edn., Dordrecht: Martinus Nijhoff, 1999, p. 977.

[22] In the 7th edition of *Oppenheim's International Law* from 1948, it was stated that 'The question of the legal nature of the League was a matter of considerable controversy. The predominant opinion was that the League, while being a juristic person *sui generis*, was a subject of International Law and an International Person side by side with the several States.' Lassa Oppenheim, *International Law: A Treatise*, I, 7th edn., London: Longmans, Green & Co., 1948, pp. 344–345. See also Hermann Mosler, *The International Society as a Legal Community*, Alphen aan den Rijn: Sijthoff & Noordhoff, 1980, p. 33, on the European Commission of the Danube.

[23] *Reparations for Injuries Suffered in the Service of the United Nations*, ICJ Reports, 1949, p. 178.

The subjects of law in any legal system are not necessarily identical in their nature or in the extent of their rights and their nature depends upon the needs of the community.[24]

The Court observed that, in order for the United Nations to achieve its ends, international legal personality was indispensable. After examining the functions given to the organisation in the Charter, as well as the practice of the United Nations as concerned, *inter alia*, the conclusion of treaties, the Court stated that:

the Organization was intended to exercise and enjoy, and is in fact exercising and enjoying functions and rights which can only be explained on the basis of the possession of a large measure of international personality and the capacity to operate upon an international plane ... Accordingly, the Court has come to the conclusion that the Organization is an international person. That is not the same thing as saying that it is a State, which it certainly is not, or that its legal personality and rights and duties are the same as those of a State ... What it does mean is that it is a subject of international law and capable of possessing international rights and duties, and that it has capacity to maintain its rights by bringing international claims.[25]

The next question was whether the international rights of the United Nations included the kind of international claim in question:

Whereas a State possesses the totality of international rights and duties recognized by international law, the rights and duties of an entity such as the Organization must depend upon its purposes and functions as specified or implied in its constituent document and developed in practice.[26]

The Court concluded that, since the functions of the United Nations were of such a character that they could not be effectively fulfilled if they involved concurrent action by all its member states, these states had indeed endowed the United Nations with the capacity to bring international claims when necessary for the discharge of its functions.[27] Another important clarification was made with respect

---

[24] *Ibid.*   [25] *Ibid.*, p. 179.   [26] *Ibid.*, p. 180.

[27] The Court explained that the competence to bring an international claim is 'the capacity to resort to the customary methods recognized by international law for the establishment, the presentation and the settlement of claims. Among these methods may be mentioned protest, request for an inquiry, negotiation and request for submission to an arbitral tribunal.' The Court continued: 'When the Organization brings a claim against one of its Members, this claim will be presented in the same manner, and regulated by the same procedure.' *Ibid.*, pp. 177–178.

60   THEORETICAL FRAMEWORK

to whether the United Nations could bring a claim for injuries against a state which was not a member of the organisation. On this point, the ICJ found that the fifty member states of that time represented 'the vast majority of the members of the international community', and so they had the power of bringing into being an entity with *objective* international legal personality, i.e. legal personality valid in relation to, or opposable to, all other subjects of international law.[28] For comparison, it can be mentioned that the legal personality of such *sui generis* entities as the Order of Malta has been regarded as *qualified*, i.e. valid only in relation to the states that consent to it.[29]

The advisory opinion in the *Reparation for Injuries* case laid down a foundation as regards what is understood by international legal personality and how it is created that is still generally accepted today. For the purpose of the present study, there are five key points of the Court's opinion: (1) The subjects of law can be different and their nature depends on the need of the community; (2) while states possess the totality of international rights and duties recognised by international law, other subjects of international law may have different combinations of rights, duties and capacities; (3) if an entity has the capacity to bring an international claim, this means that it has international legal personality; (4) capacities need not be expressly conferred on an IGO, but can be inferred from functional necessity and practice, and (5) a vast majority of states can create an IGO that possesses international objective legal personality, opposable also to states that have not consented to this through membership or otherwise.

The International Law Commission (ILC) has considered the issue of the legal personality of IGOs as part of its work on the relations between states and IGOs, which was placed on its agenda by the General Assembly in 1958. In 1992, however, the General Assembly decided

---

[28] *Ibid.*, p. 185. The expression 'objective legal personality' is sometimes also understood as something different, namely the idea that IGOs have legal personality in international law independently of the will of their member states, provided that they have at least one organ which has a will distinct from that of the member states. Schermers and Blokker, *International Institutional Law*, pp. 978-979, Finn Seyersted, 'International Personality of Intergovernmental Organizations: Do their Capacities Really Depend upon the Conventions Establishing Them?', 34 *Nordisk Tidsskrift for International Ret og Jus Gentium* (1964), pp. 1-112.

[29] Shaw, *International Law*, p. 191, James Crawford (who uses the terms 'objective' and 'special' legal personality), *The Creation of States in International Law*, Oxford: Clarendon Press, 1979, p. 26. See also section 2.4.

HISTORICAL AND CONCEPTUAL BACKGROUND   61

that the work should not be pursued.[30] The Special Rapporteur, suggesting that IGOs, individuals as well as some other bodies were indeed new subjects of international law, stated that an IGO must enjoy a 'functional independence' *vis-à-vis* the states which establish it.[31] He summarised the functional powers of IGOs in the following way:

> Although international organizations can be given only functions and powers which are related to their purposes, they must be given all the powers necessary for the realization of those purposes. This goes beyond the limits which this theory seeks to supplement.[32]

The draft articles submitted by the Special Rapporteur suggested that IGOs should 'enjoy legal personality under international law and under the internal law of their member States', that they should have the capacity to contract, to acquire and dispose of property and to institute legal proceedings. It was further suggested that the capacity of an IGO to conclude treaties should be governed by the 'relevant rules of that organization and by international law'.[33] Some comments were made within the Commission on the wording of the draft articles, but in general there was support for the Special Rapporteur's report.[34]

Schermers and Blokker assert that the theory of implied powers, as expressed in the *Reparations for Injuries* opinion, is the dominant theory on the legal personality of IGOs. The theory of attributed powers and the theory of objective legal personality are alternative views, the latter advocated mainly by Seyersted.[35] Peter Bekker adheres to a 'pragmatic school of thought' on the international personality of IGOs, in support of Seyersted's theory.[36] Bekker takes 'the *concrete exercise* of, or at least the potential ability to exercise, certain rights and the fulfilment of

---

[30] A/RES/1289 (XIII), *Relations between States and Intergovernmental Organizations*, 5 December 1958; A/RES/47/33, Report of the International Law Commission, 25 November 1992. For an extensive description of the Commission's work on the subject, see Peter H. F. Bekker, *The Legal Position of Intergovernmental Organizations*, Dordrecht: Martinus Nijhoff, 1994, pp. 9 ff.

[31] Special Rapporteur Díaz Gonzáles, YILC 1985 vol. II, Pt. One, p. 107.

[32] *Ibid.*, p. 110.   [33] *Ibid.*, p. 157.   [34] *Ibid.*, pp. 86–87.

[35] Schermers and Blokker, *International Institutional Law*, pp. 978–979. The theory of attributed powers is also called the theory of delegated powers, see YILC 1985 vol. II, Pt. One, p. 109.

[36] Bekker, *The Legal Position of Intergovernmental Organizations*, pp. 55–56. Seyersted's main theory in relation to IGOs is that its international personality is not established by the provisions of its constitution or the intention of its framers, but by the objective fact of its existence. Seyersted, *International Personality of Intergovernmental Organizations*, p. 61 (emphasis in original).

62 THEORETICAL FRAMEWORK

certain obligations as the basis for concluding that an international organization has an international personality distinct from that of its member states'.[37] Bekker summarises his approach as follows:

An international organization shall be entitled to (no more than) what is strictly necessary for the exercise of its functions in the fulfilment of its purpose.[38]

The views expressed on the issue of the international legal personality of IGOs in the *Reparations for Injuries* case, in the reports of the ILC and in the writings by Schermers and Blokker, Bekker and Seyersted are – although different in some respects – to a large extent shared. The question is to what degree any conclusions can be drawn from these theories for the purpose of the examination and discussion on the legal status of NGOs. A few points can be made in this regard. *First*, a basic observation and starting-point for analysis is that all IGOs have been established by states as opposed to NGOs, which are by definition established by private initiative. As the existence and position of all IGOs can be regarded as originally derived from state intent, there is considerably more room for a dynamic development of their legal status than in the case of NGOs, at least from the point of view of the traditional theory of international law. It is not easy to argue for a theory of implied powers in relation to NGOs, especially not if implied powers are seen as a consequence of the objective of the organisation. It could possibly be held that the conferral of certain capacities or status – for instance, in relation to co-operation with an IGO – would be meaningless without the conferral of other aspects of legal status, and that the latter could therefore be implied. It can be mentioned as an illustration that some IGOs, such as the European Union and the United Nations High Commissioner for Refugees (UNHCR) contract NGOs for operational work, as will be described in chapter 9. Some components of legal status may be necessary for the NGO to be able to carry out such work, such as the capacity to conclude agreements with other IGOs or states.

Secondly, neither the ICJ in the *Reparation for Injuries* case, nor the writers referred to above, have determined the legal position of IGOs on the basis of an *a priori* notion of international legal personality or the explicit attribution of legal personality in the constituent instrument. Rather, the status of a particular IGO has been evaluated on the basis of its actual existence and its functions, purposes and practices. Such an approach could be applied also to NGOs insofar as rights, duties and

---

[37] Bekker, *The Legal Position of Intergovernmental Organizations*, pp. 54–55.   [38] *Ibid.*, p. 5.

capacities have actually been conferred on an organisation by treaty or otherwise. If a corresponding connection to original state intent is to be maintained, however, the legal personality of an NGO could never extend outside the area of the rights, duties and capacities actually enjoyed by it.[39]

Thirdly, and finally, it is of interest to note that the ICJ stated that a majority of states could confer objective personality on an IGO, i.e. personality that is opposable also to other states. Considering the status of the ICRC and the Order of Malta, which will be described below, it seems possible that some NGOs may also acquire objective personality.

2.4 The '*sui generis*' subjects of international law

Introduction

As is generally known, there are some entities which have been recognised by states and IGOs as legal persons, although they are not states, are not created by states and are, at least currently, non-territorial. The existence of such '*sui generis*' subjects of international law illustrates the fact that if states accept a non-state entity as a new international legal person there are no obstacles inherent in international law itself to prevent such a development.[40] Furthermore, it is interesting that this personality is not derived from a direct intent on the part of states to create a new subject of international law, as in the case of IGOs. I shall briefly examine two of these private subjects of international law – the Order of Malta and the ICRC – in order to describe what acts they perform under international law and what is the general attitude of the international community towards them. The Order of Malta and the ICRC have been chosen as examples as they both, at least roughly, fall within the definition of 'non-governmental organisation' used in this study.[41] They therefore demonstrate a potential that, at least theoretically, all NGOs have.

---

[39] But see the decision of the Trial Chamber of the ICTY regarding the ICRC, described in section 2.4.

[40] The expression '*sui generis*' seems to indicate that private subjects of international law will always be exceptional. I have used notation marks in order to indicate an attitude which is more neutral to possible developments. It can be observed that Lassa Oppenheim called the League of Nations an international person *sui generis* in his statement cited above, see *International law: A Treatise*, I, 4th edn., 1928, pp. 133–134, and section 2.2.

[41] See, however, section 2.4 on the characterisation of the ICRC.

64   THEORETICAL FRAMEWORK

Other non-state entities, such as the Holy See and insurgent groups, are of some interest for the sake of comparison, in spite of their territorial connections. It is generally recognised that the Holy See, as distinct from the Vatican City, is an international legal person.[42] It is a party to international agreements and maintains diplomatic relations with over 170 states, as well as with the European Union and the Order of Malta.[43] The Holy See also concludes concordats on behalf of the catholic church, i.e. bilateral agreements between the Holy See and a state, whereby the Holy See as the head of the Catholic Church regulates the relations of the church in a given state with the government of that state.[44] The Holy See, however, distinguishes itself from NGOs as defined in this study through its position as head of the Vatican.[45] Belligerent and insurgent groups, for their part, may acquire some kind of position under international law in times of conflict by entering into agreements with states or by being bound by international humanitarian law.[46]

The Order of Malta

The Sovereign Military and Hospitaller Order of Saint John of Jerusalem, of Rhodes and of Malta, in short the Order of Malta, was founded as a monastic community in 1099 and became an independent organisation to give religious and hospital care to Christian pilgrims and crusaders in Jerusalem around 1100.[47] Although the Order of Malta as a religious

---

[42] *Oppenheim's International Law*, pp. 326–328; Shaw, *International Law*, p. 172; D. J. Harris, *Cases and Materials on International Law*, 5th edn., London: Sweet & Maxwell, 1998, p. 138; Crawford, *The Creation of States in International Law*, pp. 156–160; Hermann Mosler, 'Subjects of International Law', EPIL, 4, Amsterdam: North-Holland, 2000, pp. 719–720. See, however, Ian Brownlie, who states that the Holy See can have international legal personality only in relation to states which are prepared to enter into relations with such institutions on the international plane, *Principles of Public International Law*, 5th edn., Oxford University Press, 1998, p. 64.

[43] Official website of the Holy See accessible online at http://www.vatican.va (section 'Bilateral and Multilateral Relations of the Holy See'), as of 28 October 2004.

[44] Chris N. Okeke, *Controversial Subjects of Contemporary International Law: An Examination of the New Entities of International Law and their Treaty-Making Capacity*, Rotterdam University Press, 1974, p. 67.

[45] Italy recognised the international personality of the Holy See and its exclusive sovereignty and jurisdiction over the city of the Vatican through the Lateran Treaty of 1929, *Oppenheim's International Law*, I, pp. 326–328. Okeke, *Controversial Subjects*, p. 68.

[46] See, e.g., Shaw, *International Law*, p. 173 and Brownlie, *Principles of Public International Law*, p. 63. See also section 4.4 and chapter 8.

[47] Yves Beigbeder, *The Role and Status of International Humanitarian Volunteers and Organizations: The Right and Duty to Humanitarian Assistance*, Dordrecht: Martinus Nijhoff, 1991, p. 212. The official name of the Order is given in Article 1, para. 1, of its

HISTORICAL AND CONCEPTUAL BACKGROUND   65

order has connections with the Holy See, which approves the appointment of the Grand Master, it is independent of it as a sovereign Order of Knighthood.[48]

The Order of Malta takes its name from the island of Malta, which was given to it in 1530 by Emperor Charles V. It ruled Malta until 1798, when the island was taken by Napoleon. Before that, the Order had been sovereign on Rhodes.[49] In 1834, the Order established its headquarters as a humanitarian organisation in Rome, where it is still located today.[50] The Order has around 12,000 Knights and Dames and more than 1 million associate members, and its humanitarian work includes the operation of around 200 hospitals, dispensaries and nursery schools.[51]

It is interesting to note from an international legal point of view that the Order of Malta, although being a private entity currently without territory, is generally regarded as a subject of international law.[52] Its diplomatic relations include embassies in nearly sixty countries and legations in five, and it issues diplomatic passports.[53]

The sovereignty and independence of the Order have been discussed in several judgments from Italian national courts. In a case from 1935-7, the Italian Court of Cassation stated:

With the recognition of the Church and of the Byzantine Empire, the Order established, after the conquest of territory of its own, its independence and

---

Constitutional Charter and Code, promulgated on 27 June 1961, published in *Bolletino Ufficiale*, Rome, 12 January 1998.

[48] *Constitutional Charter and Code* of the Order of Malta, Article 4, para. 1 and Article 13, para. 13 and Beigbeder, *The Role and Status of International Humanitarian Volunteers and Organizations*, p. 212.

[49] *Constitutional Charter and Code* of the Order of Malta, Article 1, para. 1.

[50] Harris, *Cases and Materials*, pp. 142, 143.

[51] Beigbeder, *The Role and Status of International Humanitarian Volunteers and Organizations*, pp. 212, 213; Shaw, *International Law*, p. 171; and *Constitutional Charter and Code* of the Order of Malta, Article 3, para. 1.

[52] See the annex to the resolution mentioned below, A/48/957, *Request for the Inclusion of an Additional Item in the Agenda of the Forty-Eighth Session*, 29 June 1994, according to which sixty-four member states of the United Nations have recognised the Order's 'full sovereignty as an equal member of the international community', and the cases from the Italian courts mentioned below. See also *Oppenheim's International Law*, p. 329 (fn. 7, implicitly); Shaw, *International Law*, p. 171; Harris, *Cases and Materials*, pp. 142, 143; Crawford, *The Creation of States in International Law*, pp. 26, 155, 160; and Beigbeder, *The Role and Status of International Humanitarian Volunteers and Organizations*, p. 212. The latter does not explicitly mention the Order's international legal personality, but describes it as 'internationally recognized as sovereign and independent of any civil power'. Brownlie states that the international legal capacities of the Order are 'limited', *Principles of Public International Law*, p. 65.

[53] H. J. A. Sire, *The Knights of Malta*, New Haven: Yale University Press, 1994, pp. 271, 285.

66   THEORETICAL FRAMEWORK

sovereignty ... The Grand Master was recognised as Sovereign Head of Rhodes with all the attributes of such a position, which included ... the right of active and passive legation together with the right of negotiating directly with other States and of making conventions and treaties ... Such attributes of sovereignty and independence have not ceased, in the case of the Order, at the present day – at least not from the formal point of view in its relations with the Italian State. Nor has its personality in international law come to an end notwithstanding the fact that as a result of the British occupation of Malta such personality cannot be associated with the possession of territory.[54]

A case from 1974 originated in an action brought by an employee of one of the Order's hospitals against the Association of Italian Knights of the Order of Malta (ACISMOM).[55] ACISMOM, which is one of the national associations of the Order of Malta, claimed that the Court lacked jurisdiction since ACISMOM was a subject of international law recognised by Italy. The Court again confirmed that the Order of Malta was a subject of international law and granted it jurisdictional immunity, stating that the Order 'constitutes a sovereign international subject and, though deprived of territory, is equal in all respects to a foreign State with which Italy has normal diplomatic relations'. As regards the position of ACISMOM in relation to the Order of Malta, the Court observed quite interestingly that:

The term 'national' therefore means only that the individual association is intended to operate within the nation for which it was set up, and not that it becomes a corporate body under the legal system of that nation. The associations are public bodies under the legal system of the Maltese Order and they are entitled to the same legal treatment due to the Sovereign Military Order of Hospitallers of Malta.[56]

---

[54] *Nanni* v. *Pace and the Sovereign Order of Malta*, 1935–37 8 A.D.2. Italian Court of Cassation, in Harris, *Cases and Materials*, p. 143.

[55] *Association of Italian Knights of the Order of Malta* v. *Piccoli*, Italian Court of Cassation, 6 June 1974, in 65 ILR (1984), pp. 308–312.

[56] *Association of Italian Knights of the Order of Malta* v. *Piccoli*, Italian Court of Cassation, 6 June 1974, in 65 ILR (1984), p. 310. A case which is interesting as a comparison is *Bacchelli* v. *Comune di Bologna*, which concerned the Order of Santa Maria Gloriosa. In this case, the Court of Cassation discussed the indications of international legal personality and the importance of the attitude of the international community in this regard. The Court came to the conclusion that, for determining the status of the Order of Santa Maria Gloriosa, the Order of Malta could not be relied upon as a precedent since it was a unique exception which was to be explained by reference to its historical background and 'the (anomalous) survival in the case of the Order of the requisites of independence or of sovereignty'. *Bacchelli* v. *Comune di Bologna*, Italian Court of Cassation, 20 February 1978, in 77 ILR (1988), pp. 621–626. See also section 2.5.

HISTORICAL AND CONCEPTUAL BACKGROUND   67

The Court also mentioned that Italian law (in particular Law No. 23 of 1938 regarding personnel in the service of the Association operating in Italy) has expressly recognised that the latter has the nature of a public international body.[57]

Although the Order of Malta as a humanitarian organisation does not have the mandate entrusted to the ICRC in international humanitarian law by the Geneva Conventions of 1949,[58] an earlier document (the Final Act of the 1929 Diplomatic Conference in Geneva) contained the following recommendation with regard to the Order:

> In view of a request by the Sovereign and Military Order of the Hospitallers of St. John of Jerusalem, called the Order of Malta, the Conference considers that the provisions laid down by the Geneva Convention governing the position of Aid Societies with armies in the field are applicable to the national organizations of this Order.[59]

The Order is one of the few non-state entities which have been granted observer status at the UN General Assembly.[60] The documentation on the granting of observer status provides some interesting information about the Order's status and the general attitude of states towards it. In June 1994, twenty-eight states proposed the inclusion on the agenda of the UN General Assembly of an additional item regarding observer status for the Order of Malta in the Assembly.[61] A fairly thorough account of the role and status of the Order was given in an annex to the resolution, which also expressed the official position of a large group of states towards the Order. For instance, it was stated in the annex that sixty-four member states of the United Nations had recognised the Order's 'full sovereignty as an equal member of the international community'.[62] It was also said that the members of the Order were 'loyal

---

[57] *Association of Italian Knights of the Order of Malta* v. *Piccoli*, Italian Court of Cassation, 6 June 1974, in 65 ILR (1984), p. 310.

[58] However, some provisions of the Geneva Conventions of 1949 and the additional protocols extend protection to humanitarian organisations in general, see section 4.4.

[59] *Final Act of the Diplomatic Conference*, Geneva, 27 July 1929, recommendation II. The Diplomatic Conference of Geneva of 1929 was convened by the Swiss Federal Council for the purpose of revising the Geneva Convention for the Amelioration of the Condition of the Wounded and Sick in Armies in the Field of 1906 and adopting a new convention in relation to the treatment of prisoners of war.

[60] A/RES/48/265, *Observer Status for the Sovereign Military Order of Malta in the General Assembly*, 24 August 1994.

[61] A/48/957, *Request for the Inclusion of an Additional Item in the Agenda of the Forty-Eighth Session*, 29 June 1994, and A/48/957/Add. 1, 22 July 1994.

[62] *Ibid.*, annex, para 1.

68   THEORETICAL FRAMEWORK

citizens of their respective countries, a condition that is not compromised by their membership in the Order, which is a supplemental, supranational honour'.[63]

Other information provided in the annex includes the fact that, in addition to the diplomatic or official representatives present in many countries, the Grand Magistry of the Order is represented by accredited delegations to numerous international agencies, including the UN offices at Geneva and Vienna, the Commission of the European Union and the CoE.[64] The Order of Malta was granted observer status at the UN General Assembly in August 1994 in consideration of 'the long-standing dedication of the Sovereign Military Order of Malta in providing humanitarian assistance, and its special role in international humanitarian relations'.[65] The resolution was adopted without vote after the presentation of a draft by seventy-two states.[66]

In sum, the Order of Malta is an entity with a very special history of both territorial sovereignty, which the Order was for a time able to defend by force, and connections to the Holy See. The Italian Court of Cassation has underlined this *'sui generis'* character of the Order, stating that it cannot be regarded as a precedent for other non-state entities. As is clear from chapter 1, my definition of 'non-governmental organisation' embraces the Order of Malta. The Order therefore provides an interesting demonstration of the flexible character of international law, which can clearly accommodate particular NGOs as international legal subjects if this is accepted by the international community. The Order of Malta also illustrates what attributes of international legal personality can potentially be held by non-state entities.

The International Committee of the Red Cross

The ICRC is an independent part of the International Red Cross and Red Crescent Movement, which also encompasses the International Federation of Red Cross and Red Crescent Societies and the different National Societies. Each body of the movement is independent and exercises no authority over the others. According to Article 1 of its

---

[63] *Ibid.*, para. 2.   [64] *Ibid.*, para. 8.

[65] A/RES/48/265, *Observer Status for the Sovereign Military Order of Malta in the General Assembly*, 30 August 1994, Preamble, para. 2.

[66] A/48/L.62, 22 August 1994 and A/48/L.62/Add. 1, 25 August 1994. Voting information given at the UN website accessible online at http://www.un.org/Depts/dhl/res/ resa48.htm, 'Resolutions adopted by the General Assembly at its 48th session', accessed on 25 October 2004.

HISTORICAL AND CONCEPTUAL BACKGROUND 69

Statute, the ICRC is 'an independent humanitarian organization having a status of its own'.[67] It is a Swiss association created under the Swiss Civil Code and enjoys Swiss legal personality. The twenty-five members of the ICRC shall be Swiss citizens.[68]

Within the context of the present study, the most interesting feature of the ICRC is its special status under international humanitarian law.[69] This status has a long history. As a result of his experiences from the Battle of Solferino, Henry Dunant wrote *A Memory of Solferino* (1862) and made several proposals in order to alleviate the suffering of the victims of armed conflicts. One proposal was to declare army medical services neutral and to give them a distinctive emblem. Another was to form, in peacetime, voluntary relief societies to act as auxiliaries to army medical services in times of war.[70] The ICRC, which was initially called the International Committee to Aid the Military Wounded, met for the first time in 1863 to examine the proposals.[71] The same year, the first voluntary aid societies were set up.

Although the influence of the ICRC on the development of international humanitarian law has only an indirect connection to the issue of its legal status, a brief description is of interest at this point, as the Committee to a great extent participated in the making of the rules which gave it its special status. In 1864, when the International Committee to Aid the Military Wounded had existed for only a year, the

---

[67] *Statutes of the International Committee of the Red Cross*, as adopted on 24 June 1998, International Review of the Red Cross No. 324, pp. 537–543.

[68] *Statutes of the International Committee of the Red Cross*, Articles 2, 7(1).

[69] For more general information about the Red Cross and Red Crescent Movement, see, e.g., Beigbeder, *The Role and Status of International Humanitarian Volunteers and Organizations*. pp. 61–79, 139–177; Christophe Lanord, 'The Legal Status of National Red Cross and Red Crescent Societies', *International Review of the Red Cross*, No. 840 (2000), pp. 1053–1077; Peter Macalister-Smith, *International Humanitarian Assistance: Disaster Relief in International Law and Organization*, Dordrecht: Martinus Nijhoff, 1985, pp. 22–34, 75–92; Louis Maresca and Stuart Maslen (eds.), *The Banning of Anti-Personnel Landmines: The Legal Contribution of the International Committee of the Red Cross 1955–1999*, Cambridge University Press, 2000; Peter Nobel, 'The Red Cross–Red Crescent Movement: A Model for Non-State Participation?', in Theo Van Boven *et al.* (eds.), *The Legitimacy of the United Nations: Towards an Enhanced Legal Status of Non-State Actors*, Netherlands Institute of Human Rights, SIM Special, 19, Utrecht, 1997, pp. 77–86; and Yves Sandoz, *The International Committee of the Red Cross as Guardian of International Humanitarian Law*, Geneva: International Committee of the Red Cross, 1998.

[70] Sandoz, *The International Committee of the Red Cross*, p. 4.

[71] Finnemore, in John Boli and George M. Thomas (eds.), *Constructing World Culture: International Nongovernmental Organizations since 1875*, Stanford University Press 1999, p. 155.

70   THEORETICAL FRAMEWORK

Committee convened an international conference with delegates from sixteen states to discuss a draft convention it had prepared. During this Conference, the Geneva Convention for the Amelioration of the Condition of the Wounded in Armies in the Field was adopted.[72] By the end of the year, the convention had been ratified by ten states.[73] As a result of the initiatives and work of the Committee, the convention was revised and other conventions adopted over the years. Just as for these earlier conventions, the ICRC was responsible for the initiative that led to the conclusion of the four Geneva Conventions of 1949, as well as the two additional protocols of 1977.[74] Moreover, the texts of both the conventions and the additional protocols were drafted by the ICRC after a process of consultation with the state parties to the Geneva Conventions and NGOs.[75] During the break-up of the former Yugoslavia, the ICRC (because of the mixed international–internal nature of the conflict) presented an extract of the most basic norms of the Geneva Conventions to the belligerent parties, who adopted the agreement.[76] The ICRC also played a key role in the international efforts to ban antipersonnel landmines, leading to the signing of the 1997 Convention on the Prohibition of the Use, Stockpiling, Production and Transfer of Anti-Personnel Mines and on their Destruction.[77]

The ICRC has a unique mandate in international humanitarian law directly formulated in the Geneva Conventions.[78] For instance, common Article 3 to the Geneva Conventions provides that 'An impartial humanitarian body, such as the International Committee of the Red Cross, may offer its services to the Parties of the conflict.' The most remarkable provision of the Conventions in this regard is perhaps Article 10 of Geneva Conventions I–III, according to which the ICRC or another humanitarian organisation can assume the powers of a

---

[72] Finnemore, in Boli and Thomas, *Constructing World Culture*, p. 159.

[73] ICRC website at http://www.icrc.org/eng/history, 'Founding and early years of the International Committee of the Red Cross (1863–1914)', as of 10 May 2001.

[74] Claude Pilloud *et al.*, *Commentary on the Additional Protocols of 8 June 1977 to the Geneva Conventions of 12 August 1949*, International Committee of the Red Cross, Dordrecht: Martinus Nijhoff, 1987, pp. xxx ff.

[75] *Ibid.*, p. xxxi; Maresca and Maslen, *The Banning of Anti-Personnel Landmines*, p. 1.

[76] Jean-François Berger, *The Humanitarian Diplomacy of the ICRC and the Conflict in Croatia (1991–1992)*, Geneva: International Committee of the Red Cross, 1995, pp. 25–29; Ove Bring, *Folkrätt för totalförsvaret: En handbok*, Stockholm: Norstedts Juridik, 1994, p. 224.

[77] For a thorough account of this work, see Maresca and Maslen, *The Banning of Anti-Personnel Landmines*.

[78] See also section 4.4.

HISTORICAL AND CONCEPTUAL BACKGROUND 71

protecting power including, *inter alia*, the right to visit prisoners of war (Article 126 of Geneva Convention III) and to monitor compliance with the rules of Geneva Convention IV relating to the protection of civilian persons (Articles 55 and 61).[79]

The Statutes of the ICRC have, interestingly enough, been adopted by both the components of the Red Cross and Red Crescent Movement and by the state parties to the Geneva Conventions, i.e. almost all the states of the world.[80] The statutes establish, *inter alia*, the legal status, headquarters and role of the ICRC and its relations with other parts of the movement.[81] In Article 6, the ICRC's relations outside the movement are outlined: 'The ICRC shall maintain relations with government authorities and any national or international institution whose assistance it considers useful.'

Maintaining relations with governments is thus part of the organisation's tasks under the statutes. The four-yearly International Conference of the Red Cross and Red Crescent brings together delegations both from the Red Cross and Red Crescent institutions (the International Committee of the Red Cross, the International Federation of Red Cross and Red Crescent Societies and the National Societies) and from states parties to the Geneva Conventions. At the same time, it should be noted that the membership of the Committee is composed solely of individual Swiss citizens.

The ICRC is generally recognised as possessing international legal personality, a fact that is related to its special status under international humanitarian law.[82] In this context, it should be observed that the ICRC

---

[79] My point, as is stated elsewhere, is to demonstrate that the international legal system can accommodate and integrate non-state actors. It is therefore interesting to note that Beigbeder, in *The Role and Status of International Humanitarian Volunteers and Organizations* (pp. 79–80) differentiates the ICRC from what he calls 'the "real" NGOs'. Beigbeder notes that: 'We have seen that the ICRC, although legally established as a NGO, has a mandate and responsibilities in relation with governments, in particular with regard to the formulation and monitoring of international humanitarian law, which distinguishes it from the "real" (non-Red Cross) NGOs.' The consequence of Beigbeder's argument seems to be that NGOs that are endowed with a specific role directly under international law cease to be NGOs – or, in other words, that international law is by definition a system which can involve only states and IGOs.

[80] Sandoz, *The International Committee of the Red Cross*, p. 4.

[81] Articles 2–5 of the Statutes of the International Committee of the Red Cross, as adopted by the Assembly of the ICRC on 24 June 1998, *International Review of the Red Cross*, No. 324 (1998), pp. 537–543.

[82] See, e.g., Article 1 of the Agreement between the International Committee of the Red Cross and the Swiss Federal Council to determine the legal status of the Committee in

72   THEORETICAL FRAMEWORK

does not consider itself to be an NGO in the ordinary sense of the term, mainly because of its special status, but also due to the fact that the Committee – although being an independent body – is part of the International Red Cross and Red Crescent Movement, in which states participate to determine the ICRC's statutory authority to offer services or otherwise intervene in armed conflict.[83] It was also mentioned above that the Statutes of the ICRC have been adopted not only by the organisation itself, but also by the states parties to the Geneva Conventions.

An interesting aspect of the special status of the ICRC is the headquarters agreements that it has concluded with seventy-four states.[84] The purpose of these agreements, which will be more closely examined in section 9.2, is to facilitate the independent action of ICRC delegates and the ICRC itself. The Agreement concluded between the ICRC and the Swiss Federal Council to determine the legal status of the ICRC in Switzerland, explicitly says that: 'The Federal Council recognizes the international legal personality and the legal capacity in Switzerland of the International Committee of the Red Cross.' The ICRC is also granted inviolability of premises and archives as well as immunity from legal process and execution, etc.[85] ICRC delegates on mission are entitled to a Swiss diplomatic passport.[86]

In an interesting decision delivered by the International Criminal Tribunal for the Former Yugoslavia (ICTY), the Trial Chamber established that the ICRC has a position not only under the Geneva Conventions, but also under customary international law.[87] The decision followed a motion filed by the prosecution seeking a ruling from

---

Switzerland, *International Review of the Red Cross*, No. 293 (1993), pp. 152–160; International Tribunal for the Former Yugoslavia, Trial Chamber, *Prosecutor* v. *Simić et al.*, Decision on the prosecution motion under rule 73 for a ruling concerning the testimony of a witness, 27 July 1999, paras. 35 and 46 and n. 9; *ICRC Annual Report 2000*, Geneva: ICRC, 2001, p. 220; Schermers and Blokker, *International Institutional Law*, p. 33; and Shaw, *International Law*, p. 192.

[83] Letter from the ICRC legal division, 22 June 2001, on file with the author. See also Nobel, *The Red Cross–Red Crescent Movement*, pp. 77, 80–81.

[84] *ICRC Annual Report 2003*, p. 21.

[85] Articles 1, 3, 4, 5 of the Agreement between the International Committee of the Red Cross and the Swiss Federal Council to determine the legal status of the Committee in Switzerland, *International Review of the Red Cross*, No. 293 (1993), pp. 152–160.

[86] Beigbeder, *The Role and Status of International Humanitarian Volunteers and Organizations*, p. 67.

[87] International Tribunal for the Former Yugoslavia, Trial Chamber, *Prosecutor* v. *Simić et al.*, Decision on the prosecution motion under rule 73 for a ruling concerning the testimony of a witness, 27 July 1999, and JL/P.I.S./439-E, Press release, *Trial Chamber III Rules that ICRC Need not Testify before the Tribunal*, The Hague, 8 October 1999.

the Trial Chamber as to whether a former ICRC employee could be called to give evidence of facts that had come to his knowledge by virtue of his employment as an interpreter. The Chamber noted the principles derived from the mandate entrusted to the ICRC by international law under the Geneva Conventions and the additional protocols – in particular, the principles of impartiality, neutrality and independence, as well as the working principle of confidentiality.[88] It considered that the right to non-disclosure of information in the possession of employees in judicial proceedings is necessary for the effective discharge by the ICRC of its mandate. Therefore, the parties to the Geneva Conventions and the additional protocols had assumed a conventional obligation to ensure non-disclosure of information in judicial proceedings of information relating to the work of the ICRC, and the ICRC had a right to insist on such non-disclosure.[89] As regards customary international law, the ratification of the Geneva Conventions by 188 states could be considered as reflecting the *opinio juris* of these state parties, which led the Chamber to conclude that the ICRC had a right under customary international law to non-disclosure of information. The evidence of the former employee of the ICRC sought by the prosecutor should therefore not be given.[90]

According to the Rules of Procedure for the International Criminal Court (ICC), information provided by the ICRC is privileged, and consequently not subject to disclosure, unless the ICRC waives this privilege or the information is contained in public statements and documents of the Committee.[91]

---

[88] International Tribunal for the Former Yugoslavia, Trial Chamber, *Prosecutor* v. *Simić et al.*, Decision on the prosecution motion under rule 73 for a ruling concerning the testimony of a witness, 27 July 1999, paras. 51–59.

[89] It is interesting to note that this reasoning is parallel to the functional approach adhered to by the ICJ in relation to the United Nations in the *Reparation for Injuries* case, where the Court stated that: 'The functions of the Organization could not be effectively discharged if they involved the concurrent action, on the international plane, of fifty-eight or more Foreign Offices, and the Court concludes that the Members have endowed the Organization with capacity to bring international claims when necessitated by the discharge of its functions.' *Reparations for Injuries Suffered in the Services of the United Nations*, ICJ Reports, 1949, p. 180.

[90] International Tribunal for the Former Yugoslavia, Trial Chamber, *Prosecutor* v. *Simić et al.*, Decision on the prosecution motion under rule 73 for a ruling concerning the testimony of a witness, 27 July 1999, paras. 73–74.

[91] International Criminal Court, ICC-ASP/1/3, *Rules of Procedure and Evidence*, Adopted by the Assembly of State Parties, 3–10 September 2002, rule 73(4).

74   THEORETICAL FRAMEWORK

A final point worth noting about the ICRC is that it is one of the very few non-state actors which has been granted observer status at the UN General Assembly. This status was given in consideration of 'the special role carried on accordingly by the International Committee of the Red Cross in international humanitarian relations'.[92]

2.5 The classical concepts relating to international legal personality in modern doctrine

In the 1920s, Oppenheim distinguished between *subjects of international law* and *international legal persons*. Not-full sovereign states could be 'only subjects of law', thus being 'imperfect' international persons.[93] The same distinction is made in the Restatement (Third), written in 1987:

> This part deals with entities that are persons under international law, i.e. those that, to varying extents, have legal status, personality, rights, and duties under international law and whose acts and relationships are the principal concerns of international law. The literature of international law has sometimes referred to 'subjects' of international law (rather than persons). But the term 'subjects' may have more limited connotations, suggesting that such entities have only rights and obligations.[94]

This explanation is both confusing and circular, in that it suggests that 'legal status' and 'personality' are *indicia* of persons under international law. It is, however, clear that the Restatement (Third) regards legal subjects as entities that may have 'only rights and obligations'. This means that legal personality would include something more, presumably legal capacity and maybe also a capability, or an entitlement, to participate in the formation of international customary law. The Restatement supports the former element, for it states that individuals have been accorded some aspects of personality, as some international agreements give individuals remedies before international bodies. The relationship between legal personality and international law-making is not discussed.[95] In modern international legal doctrine, the

---

[92] A/RES/45/6, *Observer Status for the International Committee of the Red Cross*, 16 October 1990. In 1994, observer status was also granted to the International Federation of the Red Cross and Red Crescent Societies, A/RES/49/2, *Observer Status for the International Federation of the Red Cross*, 19 October 1994.

[93] Oppenheim, *International Law: A Treatise*, p. 134.

[94] *Restatement of the Law Third: The Foreign Relations Law of the United States*, The American Law Institute, 1987, I, p. 70 (hereafter 'Restatement (Third)').

[95] Restatement (Third), pp. 24 ff., 70–71.

connotations 'subject of international law' and 'international legal person(ality)' are generally used interchangeably.[96] I shall follow that practice here.

As regards other concepts that are related to international legal personality and the practical meaning of the term the views are slightly varied, as will be discussed in more detail in relation to the modern theories of international law.[97] It is generally held that being an international legal person means that an entity is, or is capable of being, endowed with *rights*, *duties* and *capacities* directly under international law. For instance, the Restatement explains that: 'In principle, however, individuals and private juridical entities can have any status, capacity, rights or duties given to them by international law or agreement.'[98] In Akehurst's *A Modern Introduction to International Law*, Malanczuk suggests a more precise list of requisites for legal personality, 'the central issues of which have been primarily related to the capacity to bring claims arising from the violation of international law, to conclude valid international agreements, and to enjoy privileges and immunities from national jurisdictions'.[99] The term *'legal capacity'* does not seem to suggest any predetermined combination of legal abilities but can signify all or one of several elements – for instance, ability to be a party to international treaties, to send and receive legations, or to institute international judicial proceedings.[100] 'Legal capacity' will be used in this study in this general sense, denoting all these different elements, which can be held by different actors in different combinations. As regards IGOs, capacities are sometimes referred to as *powers*, e.g. in discussions about the theories of attributed or implied powers.[101] This expression appears to emphasise the link between state intent and the

---

[96] See, e.g., Peter Malanczuk, *Akehurst's Modern Introduction to International Law*, 7th edn., London: Routledge, 1997, p. 91, which is more elaborate; *Oppenheim's International Law*, p. 16 (implicitly); Brownlie, *Principles of Public International Law*, p. 57 (implicitly); Bekker, *The Legal Position of Intergovernmental Organizations*, pp. 55–56 (implicitly). According to Jan Klabbers, however, subjectivity is a status conferred by the academic community, while personality is (in principle) a status conferred by the legal system. Jan Klabbers, *An Introduction to International Institutional Law*, Cambridge University Press, 2002, p. 43.
[97] See section 3.2. [98] Restatement (Third), p. 70.
[99] Malanczuk, *Akehurst's Modern Introduction to International Law*, p. 91.
[100] See, e.g., the Report of the International Law Commission to the General Assembly on the topic of relations between states and international organisations, YILC 1990, vol. II, pt. Two, pp. 86–87.
[101] See YILC 1990, vol. II, Pt. Two, pp. 86–87, and the discussion on IGOs on p. 61.

76 THEORETICAL FRAMEWORK

objectives of the organisation. For NGOs and other non-state actors, I shall therefore consequently use the term 'capacities'.[102]

Shaw, among others, adds the element of general *recognition* to personality, stating that 'International personality is participation plus some form of community acceptance. The latter element will be dependent upon many different factors, including the type of personality in question. It may be manifested in many forms and may in certain cases be inferred from practice.'[103] The interrelationship between recognition, in the widest sense, and international legal personality will be discussed in chapter 3 on theory.[104] It is of interest to observe in this context, however, that the element of recognition, understood as the general attitude of the international community towards an entity, has been discussed in Italian law in relation to international orders. In the case of *Bacchelli* v. *Comune di Bologna* already mentioned, the Court was confronted with the question whether the Order of Santa Maria Gloriosa enjoyed international legal personality, and whether the Grand Master could claim fiscal immunity on that ground. The Court stated:

One of the fundamental indications of the effective position of the body is the attitude of the members *par excellence* of the international community, i.e. the conduct of the States as a whole with regard to: the treatment which the body receives in respect of its claim to autonomy; entering into regular diplomatic relations with it; allowing it to participate by full right in international organizations, etc.[105]

The Court held that the debate on the constitutive or declaratory theories of recognition of states was out of place in this context, and concentrated on the 'effectiveness' of the claimed sovereignty. After having examined the evidence in this regard, the Court concluded that: 'It is not the lack of recognition by the Italian State, but the insubstantiality of the premises

---

[102] A related terminological question is whether an entity can be a subject of law or a legal person to a greater or lesser extent, or if the answer is simply 'yes' or 'no'. In the view of Schermers and Blokker, to be an international legal person 'means only *to be capable* of bearing rights and duties', *International Institutional Law*, p. 981 (emphasis in original). According to other writers, an entity can be a subject of law in some respects or have a limited legal personality. Brownlie states that 'the entity concerned may still have legal personality of a very restricted kind', *Principles of Public International Law*, p. 57. In *Oppenheim's International Law*, the expression legal subject 'to a limited extent' is used, p. 17.

[103] Shaw, *International Law*, p. 139. See section 3.2.   [104] Chapter 3.

[105] *Bacchelli* v. *Comune di Bologna*, Italian Court of Cassation, 20 February 1978, in 77 ILR (1988), p. 625.

upon which the supposed international personality of the Order of Santa Maria is based, which leads to the finding that the "Grand Master" is to be treated as equal to a common citizen.'[106]

2.6 The relationship between personality and the making of international customary law

As has been mentioned above, treaty-making capacity is generally seen as one component, as well as an *indicium*, of international legal personality. The linkage between legal personality and customary international law is not as clear. In general textbooks on international law, personality is often discussed without any reference to the development of customary law.[107] However, since states are both subjects and the creators of international law, the question might be put whether there is a relationship between international law-making and legal personality. Article 38 of the Statute of the International Court of Justice defines customary law as 'international custom, as evidence of a general practice accepted as law'. Although it is not explicit in the article who are the actors forming the custom or accepting it as law, it is generally held that states are the relevant actors in this regard. Nevertheless, it can be discussed how static that definition is and what its relation is to international legal personality.

Four alternative views can be suggested. First, it can be held that there is no relationship and that – no matter if IGOs and other entities are or become subjects of international law – states will continue to be the only law-makers. Secondly, one may take the view that some entities (not only states) have personality and some of these participate in law-making, without any connection of one to the other. Thirdly, it might be suggested that there is a relationship in the sense that participation in law-making is a consequence of unlimited international personality, and that full international legal persons are entitled to such participation. Fourthly, it can be held that participation in the creation of international customary law is an *indicium* of personality.

Although Michael Byers is a contemporary writer who borrows conceptual tools from the discipline of international relations (I shall

---

[106] *Ibid.*, pp. 625–626.

[107] *Oppenheim's International Law*, pp. 16–22; Shaw, *International Law*, pp. 137 ff.; Harris, *Cases and Materials*, pp. 101 ff. (with the exception of a couple of questions on p. 143); Malanczuk, *Akehurst's Modern Introduction to International Law*, pp. 91 ff.

78   THEORETICAL FRAMEWORK

return to this later), I believe that his theories can illustrate the classical view of the relationship between international legal personality and law-making. Byers asserts that having full legal personality means an entitlement to participate in the process of law creation.[108] In his view, the 'principle of personality' *qualifies* participation in law-making, which means that he supports the third of the views described above. That this theory is the classical one is supported by the traditional notion of state sovereignty, which contradicts the possibility that a non-state entity can have an independent influence on the legal system that is binding on states. More generally, it is also reasonable to assume that there is a link between the possibility of an entity participating in law-making and itself being bound by these rules, which is problematic in the case of non-state actors. To take into account the informal or indirect influence of non-state actors on law-making for determining their legal status – i.e. to interpret their influence as an *indicium* of legal personality – would be to take a step further away from the classical doctrine. For example, Van Hoof remarks that although private persons and organisations have come to play a more important role as both subjects of international law and as participants in the creation of law, this has not basically altered the traditional paradigm, as private participation is always 'indirect', i.e. channelled through state consent.[109]

The practice of intergovernmental organisations, as distinct from the practice of states that take place within such organisations, has been discussed as one potential candidate of customary law formation by entities other than states.[110] But even if it is accepted that IGOs themselves participate in the formation of customary law, this can be regarded as relatively uncontroversial, since IGOs are created and, to a greater or lesser extent, controlled by states. Direct non-state participation in the formation of customary law, on the other hand, would question the whole traditional paradigm. Nevertheless, supporters of modern strands of international legal theory often put emphasis on the influence of non-state actors on the formation of both treaty law and customary law. I shall describe this in more detail in chapter 3.

---

[108] Michael Byers, *Custom, Power and the Power of Rules: International Relations and Customary International Law*, Cambridge University Press, 1999, p. 75. For a more thorough description of Byers' view on international legal personality, see section 3.2.

[109] G. J. H. Van Hoof, *Rethinking the Sources of International Law*, The Hague: Kluwer, 1983, p. 63.

[110] For an overview, see Karol Wolfke, *Custom in Present International Law*, 2nd rev. edn., Dordrecht: Martinus Nijhoff, 1993, pp. 79–83.

3 International legal theory and non-state actors

3.1 Introduction

Most topics of academic legal writings have probably been chosen because there are no answers, or contradictory ones, to a particular problem in the recognised legal sources. One approach is to choose, explicitly or implicitly, one of several international legal 'methods', 'theories' or 'schools', or to attempt to create a new one. If such a choice is explicitly described before the legal problem is embarked upon, the study is provided with a scholarly appearance. The idea of the investigation and the choice of method may seem to be the result of 'some nonmethodological method, a nonpolitical academic standard that allows that method or politics to be discussed from the outside of particular methodological or political controversies'.[1] Koskenniemi argues that the initial question of what method should be chosen for the study assumes:

> the existence or accessibility of some perspective or language that would not itself be vulnerable to the objections engendered by the academic styles that carry labels such as 'positivism', 'law and economics', 'international law and international relations', 'legal process', 'feminism' and 'critical legal studies'. But there is no such neutral ground.[2]

Even if it were possible to choose a theory and method from such neutral ground, this choice would require a meta-method, which in turn would require a meta-meta method and so on. This, of course, is not how it happens, personal choices must be admitted at some point. The choice of the writer to make a 'positivist' study, an 'idealist' study or

---

[1] Martti Koskenniemi, 'Letter to the Editors of the Symposium', 93 AJIL (1999), p. 352.
[2] *Ibid.*

80 THEORETICAL FRAMEWORK

something else is often a choice of style of argument and, in some cases, of the preferred solution. It could be argued that it would be more honest simply to argue for the 'best' solution rather than to elaborate on theory. I believe, however, that an explicit decision about theoretical choices will in most cases make the argument more transparent. An active choice of theoretical approach will also require some degree of consciousness about moral and political preferences affecting the study.

As regards the topic of the actors of international law and their legal status, different theories and methods might lead to different results, as will be shown below.[3] Yet, these theories are often generally formulated and difficult to compare because they have different objectives or take different professional roles as their starting point.[4] The rule approach to international law could be described as the judge's usual, concrete working method, as seen from a position within the system itself. Although it draws a more general picture of international law as a system of rules, its main objective is not to explain what law is, but how to find a solution. By contrast, the process and policy orientations observe the processes that shape law and policy from a distance. They direct their explanation and message to the entire legal profession, and suggest that lawyers should aim at the realisation of common values. Lawyers belonging to critical theories or post-modern views locate the whole of their discussion at the meta-level, leaving the task of solving concrete legal conflicts to their unfortunate colleagues within the judiciaries and foreign ministries.

There is some dispute over the definitions of 'theories', 'methods' and 'schools'. This mixture of ontological and epistemological elements is a consequence of the lack of a general agreement on what constitutes the 'rule of recognition' in international law – or indeed if there is one.[5] The

---

[3] Section 3.2.

[4] Richard Falk has stated: 'There is a tendency to discuss which approach to international legal studies is the correct one. This produces rather sterile arguments by advocates of one approach against those of another. Such polemics overlook the important fact that the main established approaches all serve a useful function, and this usefulness normally accounts for their existence ... One way of avoiding the necessity for choice is to recognize that each particular approach has its own set of intellectual objectives.' 'International Legal Order: Alwyn V. Freeman v. Myres McDougal', 59 AJIL (1965), p. 66.

[5] According to Hart, such a rule of recognition would specify sources of law and provide general criteria for the identification of its rules. In international law, 'we must wait and see whether a rule gets accepted as a rule or not; in a system with a basic rule of recognition we can say before a rule is actually made, that it *will* be valid *if* it conforms to the requirements of the rule of recognition'. H. L. A. Hart, *The Concept of Law*, Oxford University Press, 1961, pp. 209, 229 (emphasis in original).

theoretical question about what law is and what it is not overlaps with the problem of method, of how one can find knowledge about law and a solution to a particular problem. A strictly rule-oriented lawyer would hold that existing rules provide solutions to most international legal problems, and only sources that provide evidence about these rules are relevant. If there is no rule for a particular problem, the lawyer should leave it aside. On the other hand, a theory that regards international law as vague in its nature and legal decisions as always incorporating an element of choice accepts that all answers cannot be found in the existing rules themselves, or in evidence about these rules. Such a theory would therefore adopt a more open attitude to sources. International law – international relations theory, for its part, asserts that the legal paradigm and legal concepts are no longer adequate tools for dealing with changing realities. This theory consequently accepts that new legal methods will have to be elaborated with the help of instruments from international relations.

The issue of international legal actors – or, more specifically, the legal status of NGOs – lies at the crossroads of changing political realities and traditional principles, of *lege lata* and *lege ferenda* and of different theoretical approaches. The question however, is, if or how differences in theory become apparent when applied to the same concrete problem. Below I shall examine how different theoretical approaches attack the problem of the actors of international law. More specifically, the first issue to be considered is the problem of who the actors in international law are according to different theoretical approaches, and how the question of 'actors' relates to concepts such as subjects and objects of law, legal personality and legal capacity. This is the ontological side of the problem.[6] The second issue is of an epistemological nature and raises questions about the method and sources employed by different approaches when answering the question of how it can be determined that a new actor has become part of the legal system. Because of the interconnectedness between international legal theory and method, the discussion will include some elements of method although its main objective is to describe international legal theory and different approaches to non-state actors.

---

[6] For reasons of clarity, parts of the discussion in chapter 2 on the historical view on international legal personality will be repeated here.

82   THEORETICAL FRAMEWORK

On the basis of the different theoretical approaches described, some basic assumptions on international law will be formulated together with a method, or a general approach to international law and its concepts, for the purpose of investigating the legal status of NGOs.

3.2 The actors of international law in international legal theory

Introduction

The different theories and methods will be presented in three main categories, the rule-oriented approach, the process-oriented approach and the international law–international relations approach. In reality, the number of views that scholars of international law take on theoretical and methodological issues are almost as many as the scholars themselves. Naturally, a categorisation of theories draws only a simplified picture. That is partly the point. However, it is also to some extent synthetic to place one theory beside another, as different theories have different purposes and sometimes deal with different issues. It is, for instance, not unlikely that a person who argues for a process-oriented approach for international law in scholarly writings uses a rule-oriented method when faced with the task of solving a concrete legal problem as a judge or legal adviser.[7] Most writings within the field of international law–international relations do not attempt to answer a particular legal problem. One proponent of this theoretical strand explains that it 'does not purport to be ... a true "legal method" capable of answering doctrinal questions, like the positivist approaches'.[8] Several writers can also be categorised in different ways. In particular, the process approach

---

[7] Another way of looking at the problem is to say that the theoretical/methodological discussions are performed at a different level than the legal practice, or at a certain distance from it, which just continues its work without taking much notice of the academic discourse. Koskenniemi writes: 'If international law consisted in a small number of argumentative rules through which it was possible to justify anything, what were the consequences to ... my practice in the legal department of the Foreign Ministry? Or more accurately: I posed no question but continued writing articles about valid law and memoranda to the Minister arriving at definite interpretive statements ... This was the problem of the relationship between academic theory/ doctrine ... and practice, or of the relation between my (external) description of the structure of legal argument and my (internal) participation in that argument.' Koskenniemi, 'Letter to the Editors of the Symposium', p. 356.
[8] Kenneth W. Abbot, 'International Relations Theory, International Law, and the Regime Governing Atrocities in Internal Conflicts', 93 AJIL (1999), p. 362.

INTERNATIONAL LEGAL THEORY AND NON-STATE ACTORS 83

and the international law–international relations theories are close in some respects and in their treatment by some writers.[9]

Notwithstanding these problems, and the fact that most lawyers would probably define their own position as somewhere in the middle of the range of theories, I shall use a simplified categorisation to illustrate alternative theoretical views on the actors of international law. As the rule approach and the process approach can be seen as representatives of the two ends of a scale in international legal argument they are useful for clarifying the discussion. The international law–international relations theories are interesting for another reason; they attempt to find ways to open up the legal paradigm to phenomena traditionally categorised as 'non-law' in order to reshape legal tools so that they can deal with new phenomena, such as non-state actors.

Not only are the theoretical and methodological views varied: even the descriptions and categorisations of these views are many and diverse. Some would prefer to describe rule-oriented lawyers as 'positivists'. The expression 'rule-oriented' has been chosen here in consequence of my aim to describe different views on the general structure of international law and how such views relate to its subjects and to other actors. The rule approach is thus understood as the theory that holds that there are international legal rules that are more or less 'ready' to apply, and that legal decisions ought to be taken through the application of these rules. In that sense, it is indeed the same thing as 'positivism' (and this is probably the label that the writers referred to would apply to themselves).[10] But 'positivism' is also often regarded as the opposite of naturalism and the belief in a higher law, or morality, while a 'process-oriented' approach to international law is something different. Such an approach does not necessarily have to do with morals or values outside the legal system itself (although it might have, e.g., in the theory elaborated by the New Haven school). What is meant here by a 'process approach' is the view that international law is created by a constant and complex process of

---

[9] E.g. the New Haven school and Harald Honju Koh, 'Transnational Legal Process', The 1994 Roscoe Pound Lecture, 75 *Nebraska Law Review* (1996), pp. 181–207. Some writers who use international relations theory are however more rule- than process-oriented, particularly Anthony Clark Arend, *Legal Rules and International Society*, Oxford University Press, 1999, pp. 26 ff. and (to some extent) Michael Byers, *Custom, Power and the Power of Rules: International Relations and Customary International Law*, Cambridge University Press, 1999, pp. 7, 49–50.

[10] By some called 'formalism', see Mary Ellen O'Connell, 'New International Legal Process', 93 AJIL (1999), p. 335.

84   THEORETICAL FRAMEWORK

decisions, not only in courts but also within foreign ministries, IGOs and, according to some, by non-state actors. According to this view, rules are just 'accumulated *past* decisions', and there are no, or almost no, cases or situations when a rule is just 'applied'.[11]

The rule approach

Who are the actors of international law?

The primary objective of the rule approach to international law can be considered to be to provide the judge or decision-maker with a method to deal with concrete legal problems, rather than to investigate the nature of international law or its place in society. It is thus more a method than a theory. Some more committed rule-oriented writers, however, draw a broader picture, advocating the importance of upholding a clear distinction between law and politics in order to avoid the dangers of 'pathological' phenomena such as relative normativity or social, political or moral considerations being dwelt on in court. Prosper Weil, for example, has criticised 'the lack of rigor too often shown nowadays in handling the distinction between the non-normative and the normative'.[12] In the *South West Africa* case, Judges Spencer and Fitzmaurice emphasised that various considerations of a non-juridical character – social, humanitarian and other – were matters for the political rather than the legal arena.[13] But apart from these more general considerations, the rule approach has its stronghold among lawyers who, while admitting that the line between law and politics or between *lege lata* and *lege ferenda* is not always clear, need a technique for the usage of legal sources in order to be able to do their job and provide answers to legal problems. In their contribution to a seminar on method at the American Society of International Law, Bruno Simma and Andreas Paulus noted that 'the lawyer's role is not to facilitate the decision-maker's dilemma between law and politics (and, occasionally, between law and morals), but to clarify the legal side of things'.[14] The problem-solving aim of the rule orientation does not, however, necessarily mean traditional or strictly internal legal methods. For example, Anthony Clark Arend has

---

[11] Rosalyn Higgins, *Problems and Process: International Law and How We Use It*, Oxford: Clarendon Press, 1994, p. 3 (emphasis in original).

[12] Prosper Weil, 'Towards Relative Normativity in International Law', 77 AJIL (1983), p. 415. The expression 'pathological' is also Weil's, at pp. 416, 417.

[13] *South West Africa* case, ICJ Reports, 1962, p. 466.

[14] Bruno Simma and Andreas L. Paulus, 'The Responsibility of Individuals for Human Rights Abuses in Internal Conflicts: A Positivist View', 93 AJIL (1999), p. 307.

INTERNATIONAL LEGAL THEORY AND NON-STATE ACTORS 85

outlined a method for determining when an international legal rule is at hand, but has also included discussions and conclusions from the field of international relations theory in this method.

For the rule orientation, the question about the relevant actors of international law is a question about its subjects. An actor that is not a subject of international law may have political or even legal influence but will still remain on the outside of the legal system, and is therefore irrelevant. In their elaborate book on international institutional law, Schermers and Blokker have observed that the European Union 'has no international legal personality of its own. It therefore has no status, *and does not exist*, in international law.'[15] Although the international legal personality of IGOs differs from that of NGOs, the expression used is illustrative for a rule-oriented view on personality and the legally relevant actors of international law.

As illustrated by Schermers' and Blokker's statement, a characteristic of the rule orientation is the notion of international law as structured around *dichotomies*: it is public as opposed to private, it is international as opposed to national, it is law as opposed to politics.[16] In a discussion about the position of the individual in international law, for example, Harris states that:

For the most part, however, the individual remains an object, not a subject, of international law whose most important characteristic for international law purposes is his nationality.[17]

Harris' statement seems to indicate that an entity cannot be something between a subject and an object, or almost a subject. The question is not one of degree; if you are not on the inside of the legal system, you are on the outside.[18]

---

[15] Henry Schermers and Niels M. Blokker, *International Institutional Law: Unity within Diversity*, 3rd rev. edn., Dordrecht: Martinus Nijhoff, 1999, p. 977 (emphasis added).

[16] This has been thoroughly discussed and criticised by feminist theories of national and international law, see, e.g., Hilary Charlesworth *et al.*, 'Feminist Approaches to International Law', 85 AJIL (1991), pp. 613–645 and Hilary Charlesworth, 'Feminist Methods in International Law', 93 AJIL (1999), pp. 379–394.

[17] D.J. Harris, *Cases and Materials on International Law*, 5th edn., London: Sweet & Maxwell, 1998, p. 142.

[18] However, Harris also suggests that there are exceptions to the general rule, since 'The "procedural capacity of the individual" has more recently been recognised before the European Court of Justice and in treaties on human rights.' Thus, Harris recognises that the individual – and probably also other non-state actors – are something other than 'objects' of international law to the extent that they have procedural capacity. Harris, *Cases and Materials*, p. 142.

86   THEORETICAL FRAMEWORK

The concepts of 'capacity', 'personality', 'subject' and 'object' are the classical tools of the rule-oriented approach. Usually seen in the light of their long usage within the national legal field, these concepts give the impression of clearly defined legal concepts. Within the field of international law, however, this clarity is somewhat illusory, as there are no generally accepted definitions of the concepts. While there is a common understanding that the expressions 'subject of law' and 'legal personality' have to do with rights, obligations and legal capacity, it is not possible to deduce a fixed set of powers or capacities from the fact that an entity is a legal person. For the rule-oriented approach, legal personality is like a jigsaw puzzle, from which different entities have different pieces.[19] But, in the view of the rule-oriented lawyer, a non-state actor cannot possess *all* the pieces:

The common denominator of all subjects of international law is the quality of being endowed with legal capacity. Corresponding to the different role and relevance of units participating in the relations of the international society, the range of legal capacity is not uniform. Only independent States possessing sovereign equality in their mutual relations enjoy all-round legal capacity comprising any legal position provided by the international legal order. All other subjects of international law possess only a capacity which is limited to the function they are to fulfil in that legal order.[20]

The whole traditional international legal paradigm, the notion of international law itself – its structure, how it is created and from where it derives its binding force – excludes the possibility that non-state actors have any substantial role. This would be a contradiction in terms, for: 'International law is the body of rules which are legally binding on states in their intercourse with each other.'[21]

---

[19] According to Schermers and Blokker, however, the question of personality requires an 'absolute, "black and white" answer (yes or no)', while the question of legal powers depends on which powers have been attributed to the IGO. Schermers and Blokker, *International Institutional Law*, p. 981. See also Article 4(1) of the Statute of the International Criminal Court, which provides that 'The Court shall have international legal personality. It shall also have such legal capacity as may be necessary for the exercise of its functions and the fulfilment of its purposes.'

[20] Hermann Mosler, 'Subjects of International Law', *EPIL*, 4, Amsterdam: North-Holland, 2000, p. 710.

[21] Sir Robert Jennings and Sir Arthur Watts (eds.), *Oppenheim's International Law*, I, 9th edn., London: Longman, 1996, p. 4. It is, however, recognised in *Oppenheim's International Law* that 'states are not the only subjects of international law. International organisations and, to some extent, also individuals may be subjects of rights conferred and duties imposed by international law.' *Ibid.*

We are reminded of the dualistic structure of international law. Public international law regulates the relations between states, not the relations of private actors established within national jurisdictions. NGOs and other non-state actors do, by definition, not belong within this field of law.

How can it be determined that a new actor has become part of the legal system?

As was mentioned earlier, the question of how a new actor becomes part of the legal system is the question of the existence of a new international legal person for the rule-oriented lawyer. In the *Reparations for Injuries* case, the ICJ used a teleological method for answering the question of the legal personality of the United Nations. A teleological method is about as far as the rule approach can go in terms of discretion when answering a legal question. The Court stated:

in the Opinion of the Court, the Organization was intended to exercise and enjoy, and is in fact exercising and enjoying, functions and rights which can only be explained on the basis of possession of a large measure of international personality and the capacity to operate upon an international plane ... Accordingly, the Court has come to the conclusion that the Organization is an international person ... [22]

Thus, in the case of the legal personality of IGOs, it is the intention of the member states that is central. This intention need not be manifested explicitly, but can be implied from 'functions and rights' and practices. Although the state-created IGOs have a different character than NGOs, the *Reparation* opinion may give some indication as to the Court's general approach to the concept of legal personality as induced from facts 'on the ground' rather than deduced from an *a priori* notion of international law and its 'true' subjects.

The view expressed on the more general issue of international legal personality in the most recent edition of *Oppenheim's International Law* is in line with the ICJ's approach:

To the extent that bodies other than states directly possess some rights, powers and duties in international law they can be regarded as subjects of international law, possessing international personality.[23]

---

[22] *Reparation for Injuries Suffered in the Service of the United Nations*, ICJ Reports, 1949, pp. 178–179.

[23] *Oppenheim's International Law*, I, p. 16.

88   THEORETICAL FRAMEWORK

The appropriate method for determining legal personality according to this view consists of one single step: investigating to what extent a particular entity does in fact directly possess some rights, duties and powers (or capacities). The legal personality of the particular entity investigated is equivalent to the combination of legal relations identified.

Some rule-oriented writers suggest that the recognition by states of an entity as capable of possessing international rights, duties and capacities is a separate criterion for legal personality, additional to such possession as a matter of fact. In his article on the 'Subjects of International Law' in the *Encyclopedia of Public International Law*, Mosler asserts that:

Subjects of international law are States, international organizations and institutions possessing the status of legal capacity in international relations, and organized groups or corporate entities of various kinds *whose legal capacity to take part in legal relations is recognized by States* ... The common denominator of all subjects of international law is the quality of being endowed with legal capacity.[24]

The suggestion that an entity must, first, be recognised as capable of taking part in legal relations and, second, have rights, etc. actually conferred upon it in order to be a legal person seems somewhat complicated. An interpretation that could solve this problem would be to regard the actual conferral of rights and duties as implying, or even being the same thing as, the required recognition. Mosler's continued discussion on the subjects of international law does not provide clear support for such an interpretation, however. He distinguishes between different kinds of entities, among which only states are 'primary subjects', as 'The legal capacity of all other subjects is derived from States; they are either created by States or, if they have otherwise come into being ... recognised by States. These may be called secondary subjects of international law.'[25]

---

[24] Mosler, 'Subjects of International Law', p. 710 (emphasis added). See also Shaw, who states that 'International personality is participation plus some form of community acceptance. The latter element will be dependent upon many different factors, including the type of personality in question. It may be manifested in many forms and may in certain cases be inferred from practice.' Malcolm N. Shaw, *International Law*, 4th edn., Cambridge University Press, 1997, p. 139.

[25] Mosler, 'Subjects of International Law', p. 718. It is not entirely clear if Mosler uses the term 'legal capacity in international law' as synonymous with, or something different from, legal personality.

Mosler's view on the position of the individual can illustrate his general approach to the legal status of non-state actors. He observes that international law 'takes account of the individual', and that the 'human person does not as such take part in international relations and is, consequently, not a subject of international law in the proper sense'. On the other hand, the individual is 'not solely an object of rules of international law' and has an 'important position' as regards the substantial and procedural rights contained in the European and American human rights conventions.[26] Mosler seems reluctant to say that international law 'applies' to individuals in some respects or that the individual has 'procedural capacity' under some international treaties. The whole argument is based on the distinction between states and other actors, and this distinction seems to prevent the individual from being a subject in 'the proper sense' even with regard to human rights treaties. Still, it is entirely clear to Mosler that states, as a community, are capable of creating new subjects of international law.[27]

Mosler is not the only writer who distinguishes recognition from the actual possession of rights, duties and/or capacities. According to Brownlie, 'an entity of a type recognized by customary law as *capable* of possessing rights and duties and of bringing international claims, and having these capacities conferred upon it, is a legal person'.[28] Brownlie continues:

If the first condition is not satisfied, the entity concerned may still have legal personality of a very restricted kind, dependent on agreement or acquiescence of recognised legal persons and opposable on the international plane only to those agreeing or acquiescent.[29]

Recognition in customary international law is probably what Mosler means by the expression 'whose legal capacity to take part in legal relations is recognized by States'. Brownlie's statement can be interpreted only as meaning that recognition in customary law is not the same thing as actual conferral of rights, duties and/or capacities. Such recognition seems to be of a general kind, opposable *erga omnes* and valid for all different aspects of legal personality. As Mosler, Brownlie argues from the standpoint that certain types of entities are the only

---

[26] *Ibid.*, pp. 725, 711–712, 724.   [27] *Ibid.*, p. 718.

[28] Ian Brownlie, *Principles of Public International Law*, 5th edn., Oxford University Press, 1998, p. 57.

[29] *Ibid.*

90 THEORETICAL FRAMEWORK

'real' subjects, i.e. the only subjects that are recognised as capable of having all rights, duties and capacities. Brownlie notes:

The number of entities with personality for particular purposes is considerable ... Thus, the individual is in certain contexts regarded as a legal person, and yet it is obvious that he cannot make treaties. The *context* of problems remains paramount.[30]

The point of Brownlie's argument appears to be that, because an entity has particular rights, duties or capacities one cannot assume that it has other, or the full range, of rights, duties and capacities. Such a conclusion is consistent with the views expressed by the ICJ in the *Reparation for Injuries* case and in *Oppenheim's International Law*. Thus, to the rule-oriented lawyer, legal status and personality are not 'contagious'. Different instances of legal status for non-state actors under treaty law are seen as individual phenomena that are exceptions to the general rule of 'non-personality'. One capacity does not imply another capacity, and personality opposable to one state is not necessarily opposable to another. Mosler demonstrates this view clearly when he claims that: 'Procedural rights to enforce substantive rights by the individuals themselves must be characterized as special treaty law rather than as prescribed by general international law.'[31]

According to this approach, a new legal person has thus not been created until the number or scope of treaty provisions which endow it with some form of legal status covers the major part of international law, or when states have expressed general recognition by way of customary law.

On the basis of the writings described above, the rule approach to international legal personality can be summarised in the following way:

- The possession of rights, duties and powers is relevant for the question of legal status and for legal personality, and may even be regarded as the same thing as legal personality.
- States are the only international legal persons that possess the full range of rights, duties and capacities, and are the only entities that are capable of enjoying such possession under international law as we know it today.

---

[30] *Ibid.*, p. 68 (emphasis in original).
[31] Mosler, 'Subjects of International Law', p. 726.

- States can create new, 'imperfect', subjects of international law.
- All non-state international legal persons derive their legal personality from states.[32]

The process approach
Who are the actors of international law?

The theory described here as the process approach to international law in fact comprises a rather diverse group of writers who present different lines of reasoning. Two major categories can be discerned within the group of writers with a process approach to law. The first category is the policy orientation, as represented by the New Haven school and by a couple of other scholars. Writers in this category are, *inter alia*, Chen, Lasswell, McDougal and Reisman as representatives of the New Haven school, and Judge Rosalyn Higgins with her somewhat modified interpretation of the policy orientation. The second category is the international legal process, with its successor the new international legal process (called by some 'transnational legal process'). Within this category we find Chayes, Erlich and Lowenfeld as representatives of international legal process, and Harold Koh and Mary Ellen O'Connell as spokespersons of new international legal process. I shall also briefly mention legal pluralism.

The policy orientation characterises international law as a *process*, a flow of individual decisions, rather than a system of rules. To writers of the policy orientation, the distinction between law and politics is not particularly interesting, because law is the interlocking of authority with power. Moreover, the distinction between law as it is and law as it ought to be is described as a false dichotomy.[33] 'When ... decisions are made by authorised persons or organs, in appropriate forums, within the framework of certain established practices and norms, then what

---

[32] A different view as regards IGOs was elaborated mainly by Seyersted, who argued that if an IGO had at least one organ with a will distinct from that of the member states, it was *ipso facto* an international legal person. Such personality was not derived from states, but a consequence of the international legal order itself. Finn Seyersted, 'International Personality of Intergovernmental Organizations: Do Their Capacities Really Depend upon the Conventions Establishing Them?', 34 *Norsk Tidschrift for International Ret Og Jus Gentium* (1964). As already mentioned in section 2.3, however, the theory of objective personality is not the dominant view today, but rather the theory of implied powers (as expressed by, e.g., the ICJ in the *Reparation for Injuries* case), see Schermers and Blokker, *International Institutional Law*, pp. 978–979.

[33] See Higgins, *Problems and Process*, p. 10.

92 THEORETICAL FRAMEWORK

occurs is *legal* decision-making. In other words, international law is a continuing process of authoritative decisions.'[34] Chen explains:

Authority refers to the normative expectations of relevant social actors – expectations of community members about who is to make what decisions, in what structures, by what procedures, and in accordance with what criteria.[35]

It follows from the policy orientation's lack of absolute distinctions between law and politics, or *lege lata* and *lege ferenda*, that the need for a clear definition of who are the actors of international law is not as important as for the rule approach. The starting point is an all-inclusive birds'-eye view – or indeed the observations of an 'extra-galactic observer' – over the processes that shape law and policy in the world.[36] These observations of power systems, threats to humankind and values of the global community lead to a highly abstract, yet at the same time detailed, method for the jurisprudence of the world. The policy orientation's primary objective is not to provide practical tools for determining such concrete problems as which actors possess rights directly under the international legal system, but it nevertheless presents many general observations on the actors of the 'world community process'.

The New Haven school divides the 'world community process' that produces policy and law into two interrelated categories, and identifies relevant actors for each one of them. Within the '*global process of effective power*' the nation-state stands out as the major participant, while the power of many 'functional groups' is increasing. It is further pointed out that the individual is the ultimate actor in all groups. Within the '*global process of authoritative decision*', the officials of nation-states continue to be important decision-makers, but are joined by the officials of IGOs, NGOs and other non-territorial entities.

The policy orientation is both a theory and a methodology. There is 'genuine pluralization', and 'with the appearance of many new participants, there is also a broadening of access'.[37] In order to become more relevant, jurisprudence should adopt a policy-oriented method that can assist in assessing the transnational legal system and clarify goals and

---

[34] Rosalyn Higgins, 'Policy Considerations and the International Judicial Process', 17 ICLQ (1968), pp. 58–59 (emphasis in original).

[35] Lung-chu Chen, *An Introduction to Contemporary International Law: A Policy-Oriented Perspective*, New Haven: Yale University Press, 1989, p. 17.

[36] Myres MacDougal and Michael W. Reisman, 'International Law in Policy-Oriented Perspective', in St J. MacDonald and Douglas M. Johnston, *The Structure and Process of International Law*, Dordrecht: Martinus Nijhoff Publishers, 1986, pp. 103–129.

[37] *Ibid.*, p. 107.

policy alternatives in the emerging future.[38] Such jurisprudence should recognise that the whole of humankind constitutes a community, and extend its focus of inquiry to include it. Accordingly, the policy-oriented jurisprudence offers 'a comprehensive inventory of possible modes of participation' in decision-making:

> Besides the traditional nation-state, whether independent or associated with another actor, the world social and decision processes include intergovernmental organizations, non-self governing territories, autonomous regions, and indigenous and other peoples, as well as private entities such as multinational corporations, media, nongovernmental organizations, private armies, gangs and individuals. An actor with actual or potential influence is a candidate for participation in the decision process.[39]

The most important actors from the policy-oriented lawyer's viewpoint are thus the 'authorised decision-makers', who are mainly state officials but to an increasing extent also officials of other organisations and entities. Jurisprudence at large should, however, have a much wider scope of inquiry, including all actors with influence.

In her book *Problems and Process*, Judge Rosalyn Higgins presents a less abstract, and possibly less value-focused, version of the policy orientation. She discusses the actors of international law at some length in a chapter titled 'Participants in the International Legal System'. Higgins explains:

> But I believe that there is room for another view: that it is not particularly helpful, either intellectually or operationally, to rely on the subject–object dichotomy that runs through so much of the writings. It is more helpful, and closer to perceived reality, to return to the view of international law as a particular decision-making process. Within that process (which is a dynamic and not a static one) there are a variety of participants, making claims across state lines, with the object of maximizing various values. Determinations will be made on those claims by various authoritative decision-makers – Foreign Office legal Advisers, arbitral tribunals, courts.
>
> Now, in this model, there are no 'subjects' and 'objects', but only *participants*. Individuals *are* participants, along with states, international organizations (such as the United Nations, or the International Monetary Fund (IMF) or the ILO), multinational corporations, and indeed private non-governmental groups.[40]

---

[38] *Ibid.*, p. 113.

[39] Siegfried Wiessner and Andrew R. Willard, 'Policy-Oriented Jurisprudence and Human Rights Abuses in International Conflict: Toward a World Public Order of Human Dignity', 93 AJIL (1999), p. 323. For a similar, but less provocative, statement by the 'founders' of the New Haven school, see MacDougal and Reisman, 'International Law in Policy-Oriented Perspective', p. 117.

[40] Higgins, *Problems and Process*, p. 50 (emphasis in original).

94 THEORETICAL FRAMEWORK

Still, Higgins holds on to the view that: 'International law is, for the time being, still *primarily* of application to states.'[41]

The protagonists in the early international legal process (ILP) were more interested in the questions of how international legal rules were used by the shapers of foreign policy than of the content of actual legal rules. They observed that international legal issues arose mainly in the process of making policy decisions, rather than before courts, and focused especially on the way international law was incorporated into decisions within foreign offices.[42] The ILP clearly shared the policy orientation's view of international law as mainly a constant process of decisions. New ILP, which is broader in scope and includes a normative element that is lacking in classical ILP, advocates 'dynamic' decision-making.[43] The view that New ILP has of law-making demonstrates a non-legalistic approach to the question of actors of international law, for law-making is 'a process of value-creation in which courts, agencies and the people engage in a process of democratic dialogue'.[44] Koh describes New ILP (in his terminology labelled 'transnational legal process') and its view on the actors of international law in the following way:

Transnational legal process has four distinctive features. First, it is nontraditional: it breaks down two traditional dichotomies that have historically dominated the study of international law: between domestic and international, public and private. Second, it is nonstatist: the actors in this process are not just, or even primarily, nation-states, but include nonstate actors as well. Third, transnational legal process is dynamic, not static. Transnational law transforms, mutates, and percolates up and down, from the public to the private, from the domestic to the international level and back down again. Fourth and finally, it is normative. From this process of interaction, new rules of law emerge, which are interpreted, internalized, and enforced, thus beginning the process all over again.[45]

---

[41] *Ibid.*, p. 39 (emphasis in original).

[42] O'Connell, 'New International Legal Process', pp. 334–337.

[43] O'Connell explains the difference between the two schools, *ibid.*, p. 339. According to her description, classic ILP describes what is actually occurring and explains actual events, while New ILP also deals with the question of how international law *should* deal with a particular question.

[44] Koh, 'Transnational Legal Process', p. 188. The article is also cited and discussed in O'Connell, 'New International Legal Process', p. 338.

[45] Koh, 'Transnational Legal Process', p. 184. While labelling his own theory 'transnational legal process', Koh's view is categorised as 'new international legal process' by Mary Ellen O'Connell, and as 'constructivist' international law–international relations theory by Slaughter, Tulumello and Wood. O'Connell, 'New International Legal Process', p. 335, and Anne-Marie Slaughter, Andrew S. Tulumello and Stepan Wood, 'International Law and

A related theory is legal pluralism. According to Gunther Teubner, its central thesis is that 'globalization of law creates a multitude of decentralised law-making processes in various sectors of civil society, independently of nation-states'.[46] For Teubner, technical standardisation, human rights and intra-organisational regulation in multinational enterprises (MNEs) are all forms of rule-making by private actors. At a time when sovereign states are losing their controlling potential and globalisation is highly fragmented, *Lex mercatoria* – the transnational law of economic transactions – is in Teubner's view the most successful example of global law without a state.[47] This global law can be accurately explained only by a theory of legal pluralism and should not be measured against the standards of national legal systems: 'Global law grows from the social peripheries, not from the political centres of nation-states and international institutions.' The theory shifts its attention from rules and sanctions to discourses and communicative networks, and the central elements of a legal order are legal acts, not legal rules.[48] Pluralistic theory, as the other process orientations, thus breaks down the traditional distinctions between the legal and the non-legal, between legal sources and empirical material and between legal persons and other actors.[49]

The issue of the actors of international law can be divided into the aspects of participation in decision-making processes and of the application of rules to different actors. As has been clear already, the process orientation is mainly concerned with the aspect of *participation*. Most process-oriented lawyers seem to regard state officials as the main 'authorised decision-makers' in the law-creating process. It is, however, emphasised by the approach that account is also taken of the non-state actors that are taking part in this process to an increasing extent.[50] The role of non-state actors in shaping law is illustrated by Koh when he observes that NGOs are 'helping shape the direction of governmental

International Relations: A New Generation of Interdisciplinary Scholarship', 92 AJIL (1998), p. 368.

[46] Gunther Teubner (ed.), *Global Law Without a State*, Aldershot: Dartmouth, 1997, p. xiii.
[47] For references to writers who discuss the nature and terminology of *lex mercatoria*, see section 1.2.
[48] Teubner, *Global Law Without a State*, pp. 3–13.
[49] Teubner goes as far as to claim that 'It has proved hopeless to search for a criterion delineating social norms from legal norms. The decisive transformation cannot be found in the inherent characteristics of rules, but in their insertion in the context of different discourses. Rules become legal as communicative events emerge using the [legal/illegal] binary code and produce microvariations of legal structure.' *Ibid.*, p. 13.
[50] Koh points out that 'the actors are not just, or even primarily, nation states', 'Transnational Legal Process', p. 184.

96   THEORETICAL FRAMEWORK

policies', and Teubner when he points to how law has emerged from, *inter alia*, standard-making procedures in technical areas and professional rule production.

For the determination of the question *whether international law applies to non-state actors*, the process orientation rejects the classical concepts related to this issue, such as 'legal subject' and 'legal personality'. It also rejects the traditional dichotomisation of law, and thereby the *a priori* exclusion of entire fields of society by the use of categorisations such as 'domestic', 'private', or 'object'.[51] What this more inclusive approach means for the concrete application of rules is not thoroughly discussed. Higgins observes that states are still at the heart of the international system, but she also emphasises that individuals possess international rights.[52] Policy-oriented Wiessner and Willard note that 'in some contexts, certain participants are authorised to invoke human rights prescriptions and others are not', but conclude that 'policy-oriented jurisprudence does not promise or guarantee one correct, single answer ... It does offer a detailed and self-aware approach to any problem.'[53]

How can it be determined that a new actor has become part of the legal system?

In her discussion on the position of the individual in international law, Higgins denies that the classical concepts of subject, object, etc., or the general nature of international law, can be the 'cause' of the 'procedural disability' that characterises the position of the individual in some respects.[54] In other words, she rejects deduction from the concepts themselves as a method of inquiry in this field. Higgins observes 'We have erected an intellectual prison of our own choosing and then

---

[51] *Ibid.*, p. 185, and Higgins, *Problems and Process*, p. 49. Not all writers discuss this explicitly, but their wide perspectives illustrate such a view; see for instance Wiessner and Willard in the AJIL symposium on method, who reformulated the question that was posed to them since they thought it was too narrow: 'The topic of this symposium was further clarified in a request from its editors that we cover the desirability *vel non* of holding individuals criminally or otherwise accountable for "atrocities committed during civil wars – murder, torture, rape indiscriminate attacks etc". ... We posit that it is most useful to construe the topic under consideration in terms of proper response by the world community to large-scale incidents of violence in internal contexts.' Wiessner and Willard, 'Policy-Oriented Jurisprudence', p. 318.

[52] Higgins, *Problems and Process*, pp. 39, 53.

[53] Wiessner and Willard, 'Policy-Oriented Jurisprudence', pp. 324 and 334.

[54] Higgins, *Problems and Process*, p. 53.

declared it to be an unalterable constraint', and there is no inherent reason why the individual should not be able to invoke international law.[55] Referring to the writings of Sir Hersch Lauterpacht, Higgins supports the view that 'the individual does have certain rights owed to *him* under international law (and not just to his state)'.[56] This indicates that she regards the question of rights as relevant for a discussion about the actors of international law. Then she asks herself precisely what is meant when it is said that international law applies to individuals – if it means that individuals can invoke it or that they are obliged to follow it. But at this point Higgins gives up, conceding that: 'These are difficult questions, and we need to approach the underlying issues step by step.'[57]

More clearly policy-oriented writers, as was discussed earlier, put their main emphasis on decision-making, rather than on the application of law. It is the 'global constitutive process' that establishes the framework of institutions and processes for authoritative decision-making and identifies 'authoritative decision-makers', i.e. the most powerful law-making actors.[58] According to Wiessner and Willard, 'an actor with actual or potential influence is a candidate for participation in the decision process'.[59] The policy orientation also emphasises the dynamic character of the decision-making process by suggesting that

---

[55] *Ibid.*, p. 49.   [56] *Ibid.*, p. 53 (emphasis in original).

[57] *Ibid.*, p. 54. In a couple of her dissenting opinions to the decisions of the ICJ, Higgins has applied something that reminds one of a process approach in that she seems to admit a greater freedom for the judge in decision-making, while at the same time emphasising the importance for the Court to explain its reasoning step by step. This is perhaps most clearly illustrated by her dissenting opinion in the *Legality of the Threat or Use of Nuclear Weapons* case, where she argues that the Court effectively pronounced a *non liquet* on the key issue of the case. *Legality of the Threat or Use of Nuclear Weapons*, Advisory Opinion, 8 July 1996, Dissenting Opinion of Judge Higgins, paras. 2, 6–7. See also Falk, commenting on Judge Higgins' 'value-oriented contextualism' in '*Nuclear Weapons, International Law and the World Court: A Historic Encounter*', 9 AJIL 1997, p. 66. In the description of the process approach to international law in her book *Problems and Process*, Higgins holds that the process-oriented lawyer does not recognise any *lacunae* in international law, because with this method 'there are still the tools for authoritative decision-making on the problem (by the use of analogy, by reference to the context)'. She also states that, in the case of outdated rules, law as process leaves more room for interpretation and choice in accordance with later developments and values than the rule orientation does. Higgins, *Problems and Process*, p. 10.

[58] The 'global constitutive process' is one of two categories of decisions within the 'global process of authoritative decision', the other category being decisions that control and regulate the transnational value processes. MacDougal and Reisman, 'International Law in Policy-Oriented Perspective', p. 107.

[59] Wiessner and Willard, 'Policy-Oriented Jurisprudence', p. 323.

98   THEORETICAL FRAMEWORK

it enables scholars, advisers and decision-makers to be maximally effective while 'empowering non-state entities to play greater roles in decision'.[60]

The New ILP, in Koh's version, requests the lawyer to take the full scope of *societal interaction* into consideration when analysing the process and normativity of transnational law. As with the policy orientation, Koh focuses on the influence of actors as the determining factor for deciding their relevance. He recognises the importance of both states and non-states in shaping law: 'As transnational actors interact, they create patterns of behaviour and generate norms of external conduct which they in turn internalize.'[61] Koh observes that non-state actors are also influential as regards the national implementation of international law, which in its turn shapes new policies:

Transnational legal process forces states to become more law-abiding ... When such a state violates international law, that violation creates frictions and contradictions that disrupt its ongoing participation in the transnational legal process. Transnational public law litigation brought by nongovernmental organizations is designed precisely to provoke judicial action that will create such frictions, thereby helping shape the normative direction of governmental policies. If this is so, nongovernmental organizations are not just observers of, but important players in, transnational legal process. Their actions influence the process and their inaction ratifies its outcomes.[62]

For Koh, the critical factor when determining whether an actor has been accepted into the system of transnational law is thus the influence such an actor has on the shaping of law and policy.

New ILP may, however, look different when faced with a concrete legal problem. Mary Ellen O'Connell describes New ILP as dynamic and non-statist, including both state and non-state actors on the same level.[63] Yet, when discussing the question of individual responsibility for grave breaches of law in internal conflicts, O'Connell concludes that:

---

[60] Wiessner and Willard conclude: 'Human rights activists and nongovernmental organizations, for example, have been critical to the development of prescriptions, including the formation of the international criminal court.' *Ibid.*

[61] Koh, 'Transnational Legal Process', p. 188. The article is also cited and discussed in O'Connell, 'New International Legal Process', pp. 204, 205.

[62] Koh, 'Transnational Legal Process', p. 207.

[63] O'Connell, 'New International Legal Process', p. 338, and Koh, 'Transnational Legal Process', p. 184.

Sufficient state practice and *opinio juris* exist to permit the view that, through the operation of custom, the 'grave breaches' regime can now be applied to internal armed conflict ... The evidence was certainly solid enough for a duly established decision maker to find a new rule.[64]

As demonstrated by this argument, the actors that determine the law are, first, states by way of their practice and *opinio juris* and, secondly, the 'duly established decision maker', in this case the ICTY. Moreover, the question whether the individual can be held responsible directly under international law in this particular situation is answered through the traditional method of examining customary law. The rather discrete role of non-state actors in this operation is to participate in the formation of social values which should be taken into account by the decision-maker.[65] The only way for a non-state actor to become a legally relevant actor, in the sense of having obligations under international law, is to be recognised as such by states in their formation of law.

The question of whether a new actor has been accepted into the legal system is closely related to the issue whether a general acceptance can be inferred from the fact that a certain actor is a participant in some respects. It was mentioned earlier that the rule approach, as represented by Mosler, answers this question clearly by stating that the procedural capacity of the individual under certain human rights treaties 'must be characterized as special treaty law rather than as prescribed by general international law'.[66] According to the rule approach, general recognition is thus decisive for an actor to be fully accepted into the system. Although this question is not answered directly by the process orientation – it would not be put that way – it is clear from the discussions referred to above that the process approach has a wider notion of sources, a less state-centred view on international law in general and that it permits greater independence for the lawyer (and legal jurisprudence as a whole) in the development of law. In the case of an actor that already possesses some rights, capacities and other attributes of legal status, it is therefore not unlikely that the process-oriented lawyer or decision-maker will determine that a new actor has been accepted into the legal system in a more general sense.

---

[64] O'Connell, 'New International Legal Process', p. 348. [65] *Ibid.*, p. 349.
[66] Mosler, 'Subjects of International Law', p. 726.

100   THEORETICAL FRAMEWORK

International law and international relations

'International relations is a discipline where theories of international relations compete.'[67] These theories seek to analyse causes, patterns and consequences of the behaviour of states and other actors in the international arena. Theories of international relations and of international law thus observe and analyse the same realities from the perspectives of two different paradigms.[68] It is not my intention to describe international relations, or the interdisciplinary perspectives of international law–international relations, in any detail. The focus here is on the single question of the actors of international law.

International relations theory has, like international law, traditionally concentrated on states.[69] The theory of realism, and its successor neo-realism, has dominated the field since the disillusioned era following the Second World War.[70] Realism regards states as the only or principal actors of international politics. In an anarchical international system, states engage in a power struggle to protect their interests, of which security is paramount. Moreover, realism denies all need to 'open the boxes' of states, in other words it sees states as unitary actors. For this theory, law has no place, only power. Neo-realism, as represented by authors such as Kenneth Waltz, considers that the interacting units in the international system are states. States all carry out the same functions, and they all possess sovereignty, an attribute which is

[67] Martin Hollis and Steve Smith, *Explaining and Understanding International Relations*, Oxford: Clarendon Press, 1990, p. 10.

[68] Although one discipline has not always regarded the other as particularly relevant, there are early exceptions. Cambridge Law Professor Alexander Pearce Higgins published *Studies in International Law and Relations* in 1928. Higgins advocated a balance between *Realpolitik* (which he considered had a 'truth underlying its grotesque and hideous appearance') and law: 'In considering the principles which should guide statesmen in the conduct of international relations, we shall do well to remember the wise words of Francis Bacon and thus avoiding the danger he indicates that "philosophers make imaginary laws for imaginary commonwealths, and their discourses are as the stars, which give little light because they are so high". Let us follow the advice which he gives and turn to the statesmen and diplomatists who have to deal with the hard concrete facts of state life, where they are faced with the conflicting desires and ambitions of the representatives of other states.' Alexander Pearce Higgins, *Studies in International Law and Relations*, Cambridge University Press, 1928, p. 5.

[69] For overviews of different theories of international relations with references to writers, see Hollis and Smith, *Explaining and Understanding International Relations* and Kenneth W. Abbott, 'International Relations Theory, International Law, and the Regime Governing Atrocities in Internal Conflicts', 93 AJIL (1999), pp. 361–379.

[70] *Ibid.*, p. 364.

axiomatically linked to the anarchical structure of the system. Having said this, neo-realism does not claim that states are the only actors on the international scene, only the most important ones.[71]

Among other major contemporary theories of international relations, liberalism demonstrates the most open attitude to non-state actors.[72] Liberalism regards individuals and private groups as the fundamental actors in international relations. In contrast to realism, liberalism does not regard the state as a unitary actor, but as a conglomerate, whose preferences are determined by domestic politics. One description of liberalism is that the 'black box of sovereignty becomes transparent, allowing examination of how and to what extent national governments represent individuals and groups operating in domestic and transnational society'.[73] Accordingly, the dominant group on the national plane will determine the state's international behaviour. Moreover, private groups and individuals form networks and communities and carry out activities across national borders. It should be noted, however, that according to the liberalist description, the 'box' is 'transparent', not open or perforated; the state is still regarded as the representative of non-state actors on the international plane. Transnational liberals take a step further and emphasise the breaking down of the domestic–international distinction. I shall return to this below.

Other international relations theories are also generally state-centred. Institutionalism, which focuses on the conditions for co-operation among states seen as unitary actors, is of some general interest to international lawyers as (unlike realism) it supports the view that international legal rules and institutions can have some effect on state behaviour.[74] Some scholars within regime theory do acknowledge significant roles for private actors.[75] For instance, Robert Cox emphasises the role of classes and intellectuals.[76] The theory of constructivism

---

[71] Hollis and Smith, *Explaining and Understanding International Relations*, pp. 104 ff., Kenneth N. Waltz, *Theory of International Politics*, New York: McGraw-Hill, 1979, pp. 68–69.

[72] Although strands within both institutionalism and constructivism also acknowledge roles for non-state actors, see Abbott, 'International Relations Theory', pp. 365–367.

[73] Anne-Marie Slaughter Burley, 'International Law and International Relations Theory: A Dual Agenda', 87 AJIL (1993), p. 207.

[74] Anthony Clark Arend, *Legal Rules and International Society*, Oxford University Press, 1999, pp. 5, 119.

[75] Slaughter, Tulumello and Wood, 'International Law and International Relations', p. 36 and Abbott, 'International Relations Theory', p. 365.

[76] Andreas Hasenclever, Peter Meyer and Volker Rittberger, *Theories of International Regimes*, Cambridge University Press, 1997, pp. 195 ff.

102   THEORETICAL FRAMEWORK

rejects the possibility that states and other actors have objectively determined interests and emphasises social contexts; shared understandings and norms constitute and define such basic notions as the state, state sovereignty and national interests. Constructivists argue that actors, their identities and their interests are shaped through social interaction on the basis of international norms and ideas. This theory does not deny a role to non-state actors in international relations, as it contends that foreign policy decisions are governed both by the meanings that states attribute to social objects and by their self-understandings.[77]

The theoretical developments that the twin disciplines of international law and international relations have seen within their respective fields are to a great extent parallel. For instance, realism has been one of the main theoretical approaches in international relations as well as in international law, and Hans Morgenthau is regarded as one of the main representatives of both disciplines, although 'realism' does not necessarily mean the same thing for each of them.[78] Transnationalism is a theoretical approach to international relations, to the relationship between public and private international and national law, as well as to international law on the borderland with international relations ('transnational legal process').[79]

The initial theoretical discussions on international law–international relations were mainly concerned with emphasising the importance of one discipline to the other and identifying possible common areas of research.[80] More recently, international lawyers have also begun to

---

[77] *Ibid.*, p. 188.

[78] See, e.g., Hollis and Smith, *Explaining and Understanding International Relations*, pp. 22 ff. and Martti Koskenniemi, *From Apology to Utopia: The Structure of International Legal Argument*, Helsinki: Finnish Lawyers' Publishing Co., 1989, pp. 167 ff. (although Koskenniemi labels Morgenthau's theories 'Scepticism'). Kenneth Abbott, who is one of the proponents of international law–international relations theories, points out that 'realism' in one discipline should not be confused with 'realism' in the other. Abbot, 'International Relations Theory', p. 364, n. 24.

[79] Hollis and Smith, *Explaining and Understanding International Relations*, pp. 32 ff., Philip C. Jessup, *Transnational Law*, New Haven: Yale University Press, 1956 and Koh, 'Transnational Legal Process', pp. 181-207. The term 'transnational law' is also used by Slaughter in 'International Law and International Relations Theory', p. 230, although in a different meaning than Jessup's.

[80] E. g. Kenneth W. Abbott, 'Modern International Relations Theory: A Prospectus for International Lawyers', 14 *Yale Journal of International Law* (1989), pp. 335–411, Robert J. Beck *et al.* (eds.), *International Rules: Approaches from International Law and International Relations*, Oxford University Press, 1996 and Slaughter Burley, 'International Law and International Relations', pp. 205–239.

elaborate theoretical and methodological tools that can make it possible for this discipline to incorporate international relations theory into their work on legal problems. The changes that are taking place in the international arena as well as within the international legal system itself – mainly the weakening of state sovereignty in its different aspects – have been regarded as creating a situation where the legal conceptual framework does not provide sufficient tools of analysis. It is therefore natural that attempts are being made to create new analytical tools which borrow ideas and concepts from other disciplines.

Who are the actors of international law?

One of the reasons for international lawyers to turn to international relations theory for input has been the inability of traditional views on international law to deal with non-state actors. The liberalist Anne-Marie Slaughter uses the theories of international relations to see through the 'black box' of state sovereignty:

And above all, they will want a theoretical framework that takes account of increasing evidence of the importance and impact of so many factors excluded from the reigning model: individuals, corporations, nongovernmental organizations of every stripe.[81]

The question about actors in the international system as a whole is answered in the following way:

The first Liberal assumption is that the primary actors in the international system are individuals and groups acting in domestic and transnational civil society ... Second, Liberals assume that the 'State' interacts with these actors in a complex process of both representation and regulation.[82]

Slaughter suggests that law should be seen in its context. The model of the international system that forms the basis of law should be compared with the models used by international relations theorists, because these scientists are concerned with the empirical validation of their models. If by such a comparison it is found that the primary actors in the international system are not states, international law will

---

[81] Slaughter, 'International Law and International Relations Theory', p. 227. The emergence and increasing importance of non-state actors is also given as an explanation for the need for an interdisciplinary model in Slaughter, Tulumello and Wood, 'International Law and International Relations Theory', p. 370. Slaughter describes her own approach as 'liberal theory'. Slaughter Burley, 'International Law and International Relations Theory', pp. 207, 227.

[82] Slaughter, 'International Law in a World of Liberal States', 6 EJIL (1995), p. 508.

104 THEORETICAL FRAMEWORK

become irrelevant.[83] Slaughter's view is thus mainly normative, while she does not provide any clear answers as to who the current actors of international law are.[84] In another context, however, she has stated that the challenge of non-state actors is both an empirical and a conceptual one, and that we 'need to redraw our conceptual maps' in ways that help us to solve a number of practical problems.[85]

The liberalist strand of International law–International relations theory thus finds non-state actors relevant to law, and proposes a transnational legal system that can regulate the complex web of relations between private actors and governmental actors. What it does not seem to do, however, is to assert that NGOs or other non-state actors have status under the *present* international legal system.[86] Other writers within the liberal strand of international law, such as Richard Falk and Thomas Franck, also put emphasis on the role of civil society and the waning of state sovereignty in a normative language, rather than investigating legal possibilities for civil society under the international legal system as it stands today.[87]

Nevertheless, some international lawyers have formulated interdisciplinary theories which also deal with the present status of non-state actors and the issue of personality. Michael Byers has outlined a legal theory that takes account of international relations by examining the relationship between law and power and by investigating to what extent the legal paradigm is susceptible to power, with special focus on customary law.[88] Byers seeks to explain how judges and lawyers

---

[83] *Ibid.*, p. 504.

[84] Slaughter observes that liberal international relations theories generally have been characterised as normative rather than positive. *Ibid.*, pp. 507–508.

[85] American Society of International Law, *Proceedings of the 92nd Annual Meeting: The Challenge of Non-State Actors*, April 1–4, 1998, p. 36.

[86] Spiro warns international lawyers of leaning too heavily on international relations theory as, even though the institutionalist, constructivist and liberal strains of international relations theory have recognised that international law is of some importance to international relations, these theories have 'a hard time dealing with non-state actors apart from their influence on states'. Even liberals, Spiro points out, find non-state actors relevant only insofar as they define state preferences. Peter J. Spiro, 'Globalization, International Law, and the Academy', 32 *New York University Journal of International Law and Politics* (2000), p. 582.

[87] Richard A. Falk, *Law in an Emerging Global Village: A Post-Westphalian Perspective*, New York: Transnational Publishers, p. 33 ff.; Thomas M. Franck, 'The Democratic Entitlement', 29 *University of Richmond Law Review* (1994), pp. 1–39 and 'Community Based on Autonomy', in Jonathan I. Charney *et al.*, *Politics, Values and Functions: Essays in Honour of Professor Louis Henkin*, Dordrecht: Martinus Nijhoff, 1997, pp. 43–64.

[88] Byers, *Custom, Power and the Power of Rules*.

determine the existence and content of individual legal rules, and the role of power in that process.

Byers notes that the term 'personality' refers to the capacity of an individual or entity to hold rights and be subject to obligations within a particular legal system.[89] However, personality may also be a requirement, or an entitlement. He recognises that different degrees of personality may exist – within a legal system some entities may be capable to hold more rights, obligations and capacities than others. Any entity with full legal personality, however, is capable of holding as many rights, etc. as the other entities. In other words, Byers distinguishes *full* legal personality from *partial* legal personality. As the topic of Byers' study is the relationship between power and international customary law, he focuses on discussing personality in that context. Byers observes that in a system where the subjects of law are also its creators, having full legal personality also means that the entity is formally entitled to participate in the process of law creation to the same extent as any other entity. He continues:

In the international legal system the principle of personality has the consequence that only those individuals or entities which have international legal personality are entitled to participate in the process of customary international law, and only those individuals or entities which have full international legal personality are entitled to participate fully in that process.[90]

Byers' perspective is thus not how power affects law, but rather how law affects the application of power. Accordingly, Byers views personality as a principle that qualifies power.

Byers notes that states are usually considered to be the only holders of full legal personality in international law.[91] As regards NGOs, he recognises that they have a great deal of influence on the process of customary international law. This influence has, however, been exercised within the framework of the state-centric system. Byers continues:

Non-governmental organisations do not have international legal personality and are therefore incapable of participating directly in the customary process ... States [have] allowed non-governmental organisations to participate, to a limited degree, in certain bodies of some international organisations, such as the Sub-Commission of the United Nations Human Rights Commission. However, such participation should not lead one to conclude that non-governmental organisations play any sort of direct role in the customary process, for it

---

[89] *Ibid.*, p. 75.   [90] *Ibid.*   [91] *Ibid.*

106 THEORETICAL FRAMEWORK

is the behaviour of the States they seek to persuade which then develops, maintains or changes customary international law.[92]

The same perspective is adopted in relation to individuals and TNCs. Although TNCs are legal persons under national law and have a great deal of influence on states, they have – at best – only limited legal personality on the international plane. The absence of legal personality renders TNCs 'largely incapable' of participating in an independent capacity in the formation of customary law. As for the individual, some human rights are *erga omnes* obligations to the individual *and* to other states, and some criminal responsibility entails responsibility *erga omnes*. However, Byers concludes, '*erga omnes* rules represent only a small portion of the rights and obligations which States have under international law in respect of individuals and other non-state entities'.[93]

Anthony Clark Arend also turns to international relations theory in order to explain law and its changing nature in a wider context, while seeking to retain law's special place and character. He asserts that 'there is a need to rehabilitate the status of international law within the political science community' and turns to international relations because he thinks that 'there is a need to provide a methodology of international law that returns the discipline to an examination of empirical data'. Arend suggests that 'the changing nature of the international system requires that certain fundamental principles of international law be reexamined'.[94] By emphasising the need to examine empirical data, Arend makes the point that too much scholarship in international law focuses on the value of different theoretical approaches, while what should be evaluated is 'the behaviour of ... international actors'.[95] Arend mentions that the 'new role of nonstate actors may affect the nature of international law', and asks 'what role these nonstate actors play in the constitutive process of legal rules'. Arend concludes that:

I believe that nonstate actors generally do not participate *directly* in the law-creating process. Nonstate actors, with some exceptions that will be discussed below, do not interact with states in an unmediated manner. Nonstate actors may be the origin of a proposed legal rule, but in order for the proposal to become law, it must be accepted by states.[96]

---

[92] *Ibid.*, p. 86.   [93] *Ibid.*, p. 79.   [94] Arend, *Legal Rules and International Society*, p. 4.
[95] *Ibid.*, p. 7.   [96] *Ibid.*, p. 43 (emphasis in original).

Arend thus uses international relations theory in a manner similar to Byers: he looks into international relations theory in order to 'return ... to an examination of empirical data', but regards the traditional theory of participation in the law-creating process as stable. States are still the central actors, while non-state actors can sometimes participate through states. However, Arend also admits that there might be exceptions to this general rule, and refers to peoples and IGOs. The reason that these entities are mentioned is that they are sometimes capable of concluding international agreements and, in the case of IGOs, adopting decisions that are binding on member states.

How can it be determined that a new actor has become part of the legal system?

Byers does not explain how personality is created, but sees close links between recognition and personality. He does make a rather illustrative remark about individuals, however:

Although the assimilation of rights is clearly something of a legal fiction which addresses the procedural incapacity of individuals and corporations to bring claims in international law, it has the consequence that States are considered to have legal obligations towards other States concerning the treatment of those other States' nationals.[97]

In other words, Byers regards diplomatic protection as the overriding principle, rejecting the idea that states' conferral of rights on individuals through rules of international law affects the international legal personality of the individual. Rather, such rights are 'a legal fiction'. Byers seems to be of the opinion that legal personality could be endowed on a non-state actor only by a clear rule of general international law, or possibly by rights combined with procedural capacity.

As described above, Arend asserts that the fundamental aspect of actors in the international system may be undergoing change and points to the 'increase in the role played by a host of nonstate actors', understood as including both intergovernmental and non-governmental organisations. Arend raises the question whether this development may affect the development and nature of international law:

As noted earlier, under traditional legal theory, international law was created by states. If nonstate actors are entering into the international negotiating process

---

[97] Byers, *Custom, Power and the Power of Rules*, p. 80.

108   THEORETICAL FRAMEWORK

in different ways, scholars may need to reassess their assumptions about how international law is constituted.[98]

For the purpose of considering how Arend answers the question of how a new actor of international law can be identified, it is of interest to examine his proposed method for determining the existence of a rule of international law and possible changes in international law.

Arend proposes a method for the determination of a legal rule based on a few fundamental assumptions about international law, including that states are its primary actors, that they are essentially unitary and that they are sovereign.[99] In an attempt to combine positivism and the New Haven approach, Arend proposes a test of 'authority' and 'control' for the determination of whether states have consented to a particular rule. In the case of customary law, Arend explains, asking whether a rule is authoritative and controlling is essentially the same thing as asking whether there is state practice and *opinio juris*. Tests of treaty law and general principles are also suggested to focus entirely on state behaviour and consent.[100]

Arend considers the expression 'members of the international community', which is used by the New Haven approach for the incorporation of a wider range of actors in the determination of authority, too vague. Thus, although Arend sets out with the assumption that there is an 'increase in the role played by a host of nonstate actors', and that this development may affect the development and nature of international law, he leaves these assumptions aside when he formulates his method. As was mentioned above, Arend holds that non-state actors 'do not enter into the process of creating general international law in an unmediated fashion ... Only state interaction can produce custom'.[101] In other words, it is state practice and *opinio juris* that is of relevance for the identification of a new rule of customary law, and it is therefore states that decide whether a new actor should become part of the international legal system.[102]

Arend also explains that, if peoples and IGOs have a limited ability to enter the international law-making process, their authority to do so is

---

[98] Arend, *Legal Rules and International Society*, p. 9.   [99] *Ibid.*, pp. 86–87.
[100] *Ibid.*, pp. 87–90.   [101] *Ibid.*, p. 176.
[102] Arend suggests, however, that trends point towards a different kind of international system, a system of a neo-medieval character, in which states would only be one actor among many. In such a system, the process of creating customary international law could become much more complex. *Ibid.*, pp. 177, 184–185.

derived from the consent of states, so these actors are not 'truly independent'.[103] In other words, even if a non-state actor concludes international agreements, it does not participate in the law-creating process in a true sense. As all non-state actors can be said to have derived their legal position from state consent at some point in history, the consequence of Arend's theory seems to be that no other entities than states can ever become independent participants in international law-making.

In conclusion, it can be observed that even when international lawyers borrow from international relations theory, they seem unwilling to reach outside the traditional paradigm of international law. This is perhaps especially clear concerning the theories of Michael Byers, who seems to use a deductive method for examining the concept of legal personality, and Anthony Clark Arend, who starts out with observing the need to reconceptualise international law in order to deal with new actors, yet returns to the state-centric paradigm in more concrete discussions. Slaughter's model has a similar characteristic. Her fundamental assumption is that non-state actors are the main players on the international arena, but she does not make concrete suggestions as to how international law can be adjusted in order to incorporate such a reality.

3.3 Conclusions

Introduction

An examination of the different theoretical views on the role and status of non-state actors in international law is a rather unsatisfactory experience; it appears to produce more questions than answers. The theoretical approaches do not seem to attempt to engage in any dialogue: the identity of each view is rather upheld by its opposition to other views. Moreover, these identities are sometimes emphasised by the elaboration of new conceptual worlds. It is difficult, sometimes even impossible, to make any meaningful comparison as to how the same concrete problem is or would be tackled by the different approaches.[104] Koskenniemi asserts that:

---

[103] Arend, *Legal Rules and International Society*, p. 44.

[104] This seems to be confirmed by the AJIL Symposium on Method, which put the same concrete question to a number of writers of different methods. One of the participants declined to answer the question, and the answers received were so different in scope and objective that some are difficult to compare (which is itself an interesting result). 93 AJIL (1999), pp. 291–423.

110 THEORETICAL FRAMEWORK

theoretical discourse has repeatedly ended up in a series of opposing positions without finding a way to decide between or overcome them. 'Naturalism' is constantly opposed with 'positivism', 'idealism' is opposed with 'realism', 'rules' with 'processes' and so on. Whichever 'theoretical' position one has attempted to establish, it has seemed both vulnerable to valid criticisms from a contrasting position and without determining consequence of how one should undertake one's doctrinal task.[105]

These problems have been rather evident above. However, it should be admitted that I have sought conflict by contrasting one view with the other rather than trying to find any synthesis. The texts described have been selected because of their clear support for one model or the other. The rule and process approaches represent the ends of a scale of possible views, where the majority of international lawyers would probably support a mixture of these theories and occupy a position somewhere in the middle. The international law–international relations theory, for its part, cannot really be placed on such a scale, as it consists of rather diverse views with the only common characteristic that they seek to redefine legal concepts by borrowing instruments from international relations theory.

I shall not attempt to construct a new theory with new concepts and language in opposition to the theories already described. On the contrary, I will attempt to use them all. In spite of – and because of – the contradictions that exist between different theoretical strands, I believe that it is useful to try to identify the assumptions that are shared by them. The aim is not to construct a meta-theory, but rather a minimalist model for the purpose of conducting the present study. This model identifies some very basic assumptions that are or could be shared by most theories, and conducts the investigation of the concrete problem in focus of this study – the question of the legal status of NGOs in international law – on the basis of those ideas. There seem to be four such basic assumptions that represent a smallest common denominator for the different legal theories. These are (1) that states are the dominant actors of international law, (2) that the international political role of non-state actors is increasing and that international law will somehow

---

[105] Koskenniemi, 'From Apology to Utopia', p. xv. The explanation is 'That there is no real discourse going on within legal argument at all but only a patterned exchange of arguments relates to the way the Rule of Law leads lawyers to deal with concrete social disputes in a *formal and neutral* way. Discourse points constantly away from the material choice which the problem for any non-lawyer would immediately be about.' *Ibid.*, p. 456 (emphasis in original).

need to deal with this situation, (3) that states are able to confer legal status on actors on the international plane and (4) that treaties and other generally recognised sources can provide relevant information on the existence of international legal rules, although some theories prefer a wider notion of sources.

States as the dominant actors of international law

For the rule-oriented lawyer, states are both the dominant (or only) law-makers and the primary subjects of international law. Policy-oriented jurisprudence, for its part, asserts that while the individual is the ulti-mate actor of world policy process, states are the dominant actors. This is the case within the 'global process of effective power', where the nation-state stands out as the major participant, although the power of many 'functional groups' is increasing. Moreover, the officials of states are the most influential decision-makers within the 'global process of authoritative decision' that structures law and policy. As regards the major actors for the application of law, Higgins observes that: 'International law is, for the time being, still *primarily* of application to states.'[106] New ILP focuses primarily on states, and although transna-tional legal process emphasises how non-state actors influence the creation and application of law, the point is still that such actors influ-ence the behaviour of states. The international law–international relations theories described above clearly present states as the main actors. Although liberalism breaks down sovereignty and describes private individuals and groups as the main actors, this is done more as an ideal. Even liberalism does not assert that private actors are domi-nant today.

The increasing role of non-state actors

Without going into detail about the different theoretical variations, it can be observed that all the writers referred to recognise the increasing political role of non-state actors. This is not surprising since such a development is clearly evidenced by facts such as statistical data.[107] It is perhaps more interesting to note that most writers also appear to recognise a need for the legal system somehow to relate to these changes. For the process approach, one of its rationales is the need to broaden the scope of law in order to include a wider range of actors. Such a need to adapt the scope of law is recognised by other theories

---

[106] Higgins, *Problems and Process*, p. 39 (emphasis in original). [107] See section 1.2.

112   THEORETICAL FRAMEWORK

as well. Anthony Clark Arend, who outlines a theory on the border between international law and international relations, suggests that: 'If nonstate actors are entering into the international negotiating process in different ways, scholars may need to reassess their assumptions about how international law is constituted.'[108] In their article about positivism, Bruno Simma and Andreas Paulus observe that other actors than states (IGOs, NGOs, etc.) are growing in importance, and if 'norm perception in the international sphere now focuses on the will of states less than previously, the sources of law, and the interpretative tools to understand them, will also have to change'.[109]

States and the conferral of international legal status

For rule-oriented lawyers, it is clear that states create international law and change it as they like. It follows that states can confer legal status on non-state actors and even create new international legal persons, even if such personalities may be regarded as 'secondary' in relation to states. The assumption that states can confer legal status on non-state actors is also supported by case-law from the Permanent Court of International Justice (PCIJ) and the ICJ, notably the *Danzig Railway Officials* case and the *Reparation for Injuries* case, as well as the generally recognised position of non-state entities such as the ICRC and the Order of Malta.[110] As regards the process approach, the question of whether states can confer legal status on non-state actors can be answered only hypothetically, as the issue is not phrased in such a way by this theory. It is clear, however, that Rosalyn Higgins, who is both a process-oriented scholar and a Judge of the ICJ, is of the view that there is no inherent reason why the individual should not be able to invoke international law, and she supports the view that 'the individual does have certain rights owed to him under international law (and not just to his state)'.[111] Moreover, as the New Haven school regards state officials as the most influential decision-makers, it seems logical that states can strengthen the legal status of non-state actors. The fairly traditional method used by Mary Ellen O'Connell for solving international legal problems also seems to support the view that states are free to create new legal subjects. Finally,

[108] Arend, *Legal Rules and International Society*, pp. 7–9.
[109] Simma and Paulus, 'The Responsibility for Human Rights Abuses in Internal Conflicts: A Positivist View', p. 306.
[110] See chapter 2.   [111] Higgins, *Problems and Process*, p. 53.

international law–international relations theory clearly accepts states as creators of international law.

Generally accepted sources

The 'extra-galactic' panorama of the processes of law- and policy-making that is described by the process orientation and the internal view of the rule orientation are entirely different perspectives with a distinct purpose. Therefore, they do not ask the same questions, and in part, do not use the same sources. As the objective of the process approach is to broaden the lawyer's traditional perspective, there is no point for it to discuss the validity of treaty law or recognised customary law. For the rule-oriented lawyer, who works inside the legal system with concrete problems arising from the application of its rules, one important step is to identify and clarify existing rules. The different perspectives on international law and its sources are thus to a great extent the instruments of different professional roles. It might be assumed that few process-oriented lawyers would reject existing treaty law as irrelevant if they were put in the position of a judge. Their point is rather that treaty law represents only a small part of the picture, and that it is vague in its nature. Neither does international law–international relations theory deny the legal validity or relevance of treaties. For rule-oriented lawyers, on the other hand, rules that can be identified through the use of the generally accepted sources constitute the whole picture. The existence and identification of rules of customary law represent a classical topic of dispute between different strands of international legal theories and methods. This means that provisions in treaty law that expressly relate to NGOs represent one part of a 'smallest common denominator' when it comes to determining their legal status. Likewise, case-law which interprets treaty provision should be a source which can be accepted by different 'schools' for the present type of study.

Resolutions of IGOs have often been the topic of disagreement among proponents of different theoretical models. The value of such resolutions as state practice or evidence of *opinio juris* in relation to emerging norms of customary international law is a much-discussed issue. Most resolutions examined in this study are, however, of a different kind, as they establish frameworks for the relations of IGOs with NGOs. Resolutions and decisions concerning consultative status for NGOs with different IGOs or the rules of procedure of their different organs, for example, belong to the internal law of international institutions and

114   THEORETICAL FRAMEWORK

generally bind the organ which has adopted it, the lower organs of the organisation, as well as states when they act in their capacity as members of the organisation.[112] Such resolutions can therefore hardly be disputed as relevant material for a study on the status of NGOs.

In sum, the material used in this study for examining the international legal status of NGOs includes treaties, case-law of international and regional courts and quasi-judicial bodies, resolutions and declarations of IGOs, the practices of IGOs as regards their relations with NGOs and doctrinal works. In addition, agreements concluded between states and IGOs on the one hand and NGOs on the other will be examined. Although the rule orientation would probably not regard such agreements as relevant for the issue of international legal personality, it seems likely that they would be accepted as information on the (international) legal status of NGOs.

One exception from the use of generally accepted sources of international law will, however, be made in order to discuss the issue of the influence of NGOs on the development of international law. While this issue runs through most of the examination of the legal status of NGOs, as these organisations use different rules as platforms for asserting an influence, it is often held that NGOs also influence international law by asserting pressure directly on legal decision-makers. It is clear that the influence of NGOs on international law-making at diplomatic conferences and similar events would be classified as extra-legal, and therefore irrelevant, by the classic rule approach. At most, this theory could admit that NGOs *de facto* put pressure on states, which may affect the outcome of decision-making processes. Information on that type of pressure does not fit into the 'lowest common denominator' model outlined above, and so there is no specific chapter on this issue.[113]

Nevertheless, I have found it of interest to examine whether, in the view of the 'law-makers', NGOs can in fact assert an influence within the framework of their participation in international meetings and conferences. Such an investigation can provide information as to whether provisions about NGO participation are any more than empty letters. It is also of interest for a discussion *de lege ferenda* to look at who

---

[112] Schermers and Blokker, *International Institutional Law*, pp. 741–746; Philippe Sands and Pierre Klein, *Bowett's Law of International Institutions*, 5th edn., London: Sweet & Maxwell, 2001, p. 441.

[113] Several other studies on the influence of NGOs on the development of international law have been made. For references, see section 1.1.

the actors behind international law really are. If non-state actors formally have no influence on the voting of states to an international treaty, while in reality states change their positions through pressure from NGOs, transnational corporations or other lobby groups, it might have to be considered whether such influence should be taken account of or regulated in some way.

The example of the participation and influence of NGOs in the creation of the Statute of the International Criminal Court has been chosen for the examination of the influence of NGOs on international law-making at international conferences.[114] I shall also briefly touch upon different instances of NGO pressure throughout the discussion. While it is mentioned in chapter 5 on international tribunals that NGOs have no *locus standi* before the ICJ, for instance, it is also shown how NGOs asserted strong pressure on the WHO to request an advisory opinion on the legality of the use of nuclear weapons.[115]

An inductive method

On the basis of the 'minimalist' model outlined above, a method, or approach, to international legal concepts and material should be considered. In carrying out the work of identifying rules which have to do with the legal status of NGOs, I shall not use any *a priori* notions of the 'real' nature of international law or of international legal personality. This can be described as an inductive method, or approach, to international law, in the sense that the actual provisions, relations and practices on the 'ground' is law itself and that, at least sometimes, general rules can be induced from many separate rules. Some (not all) rule-oriented scholars have a tendency to make deductions from the 'nature' of international law and from the classical concept of international legal personality in order to find out which parts of international law are relevant for international legal status. Provisions that grant consultative status for NGOs at an intergovernmental organisation, for instance, have been rejected as irrelevant for the question of legal personality.[116] Such a method seems to indicate that there is

---

[114] Section 8.6.   [115] Section 5.2.

[116] Rechenberg observes: 'if an NGO is granted consultative or observer status by an IGO, it simultaneously acquires a certain international legal status (albeit not that of a subject of international law)'. Hermann H.-K. Rechenberg, 'Non-Governmental Organizations', EPIL, 3, Amsterdam: North-Holland, 1997, p. 617. It should be observed that Rechenberg thus recognises that such resolutions provide information on the *legal status* of NGOs.

THEORETICAL FRAMEWORK

some basic rule of international law which determines the content of international legal personality. A sort of ideal picture of legal personality is used as the standard by which actors are to be measured, and if they fall short of that standard they are 'objects' – or, legally speaking, non-existent. But, as we have seen, there is no general rule which identifies the subjects of international law, and the views in doctrine are varied.

Furthermore, the traditional dichotomies which characterise international law cannot be respected as absolute boundaries within the framework of this study. The definition of international law as 'public' in contrast with 'private' international law renders any substantial legal status for private actors an anomaly. In my opinion, actual provisions and practices that explicitly relate to NGOs should be examined, irrespective of how they would be classified in terms of 'public'–'private' or 'subject'–'object'. The argument about whom or what is a subject and whom or what is an object in international law has been going on for at least a century, and there does not seem to be any way out of that debate. It is not unlikely that we shall have to accept an increasingly complex web of actors in the future with different legal status, for which the classical categories will fall short. In order to find out what the relations in such a system are, we shall need to examine them without the use of pre-defined concepts.

In line with what has been said above, I shall not use the concepts of 'international legal personality' and 'subject of international law'. The explanations of these terms are varied, and some scholars reject them altogether. For others, the terms in themselves determine what material is relevant for analysing the international legal position of a particular actor. The classical concepts are thus not helpful in describing the position of NGOs in international law. Instead, the more neutral term 'legal status' will be used. 'Legal status' is here understood as a broad concept, which embraces all kinds of provisions and practices which explicitly take account of NGOs or which can be used by these organisations for acting in the international legal context, irrespective of which field of international law the material belongs to.

At the same time, it should be admitted that the structure of the study is traditional in the sense that it is systematised into rights, obligations and different categories of legal capacities, such as procedural capacity and the capacity to conclude agreements under international law.[117] This structure may be helpful for those who would like to use the material assembled in the legal survey to measure NGOs against the concepts of 'subject of international law' and 'international legal personality'. In the present study, however, no such attempts will be made.

Finally, it should be explained that there is a vast amount of international legal or quasi-legal material relating to NGOs, and it has not been possible to cover it all within the framework of the study. My primary aim has been to concentrate on instruments which relate to NGOs explicitly and in a direct manner. As a consequence, human rights law has come to dominate the study. I have also chosen to focus on the United Nations as the most important IGO. As NGOs are important actors before several UN human rights bodies, this has also led to some concentration on human rights law.

---

[117] As a consequence, there is repetition, mainly as regards the regional human rights systems, which are discussed in chapters 4–6. This was difficult to avoid, as the topic of the study is not the regional systems as such, but the different components of legal status which NGOs have before these bodies.

PART II • LEGAL AND EMPIRICAL SURVEY

4 Rights and obligations

4.1 Theoretical background

The concept of 'rights'

'Right' and 'obligation' are not unproblematic as concepts of international law. Because of the interconnectedness of the issue of international rights and obligations pertaining to non-state actors with the issue of the subjects of international law, it is still somewhat controversial to assert that individuals – or, indeed, NGOs – can be bearers of rights or obligations directly under the international legal system. As has been touched upon earlier in this book, there is substantial debate in international legal theory as to the meaning and implications of the concept of 'right' as related to non-state actors.[1] Although there is neither room nor need within the framework of the present study for a lengthy description of the different theories and positions put forward in this discussion, a brief analysis of the concept is called for before it is examined to what extent international law does in fact confer rights on NGOs.

A useful starting-point for discussions on the legal rights concept is Professor Wesley Hohfeld's theory, which was first put forward in 1913. In his book, Hohfeld separated eight different aspects of 'right' grouped into four pairs, where each term was defined by its correlative opposite. The two pairs most relevant for the purposes of analysing the position of private entities in international law are right (claim)–duty and power–liability.[2] While admitting that legal relations are *sui generis*, Hohfeld asserted that his scheme included all possible variations of legal

---

[1] Section 3.2.

[2] The other pairs are privilege–no-right and immunity–disability, Wesley Newcomb Hohfeld, *Fundamental Legal Conceptions as Applied in Legal Reasoning*, New Haven: Yale University Press, 1919, p. 36. Hohfeld's classification is, however, more elaborate;

122   LEGAL AND EMPIRICAL SURVEY

relations. At the same time, it should be noted that Hohfeld concentrated on private law, his examples being taken from the law of contracts, torts, property, etc. It should also be observed that the model was not intended as a method of determining whether rights, powers or immunities existed or should exist; it 'solves no problem of social justice or juristic policy, but it does much to define and clarify the issue', as was stated in the Foreword to Hohfeld's book.[3]

Two observations should be made about Hohfeld's model in this context. First, he separated a wider understanding of right, which included all possible aspects of legal relations, from right 'in the strictest sense'. Secondly, the concept of right '*stricto sensu*' was separated from the power to enforce the right. Using a terminology similar to Hohfeld's, the question examined in this chapter is not 'rights' in the wide, but in the strict sense. What will be studied here is thus not whether NGOs have the 'right' to institute proceedings before international courts or the 'right' to intervene in such proceedings – i.e. have different capacities under international law – but whether states have duties under international law to treat NGOs in a specific manner on the domestic plane, corresponding to rights held by NGOs. Such international rules are mainly found within the fields of international human rights law and labour law. It is a different issue whether a right *presupposes* the capacity to enforce the right in order to be considered a right 'in the strictest sense'. That question will be discussed separately.

According to Hohfeld, duty is the 'invariable correlative' of right 'in the strictest sense', which means that a right '*stricto sensu*' cannot exist without a correlative duty. *A*'s right is thus (defined by) *B*'s duty.[4] A similar thought has been expressed by Joseph Raz in modern rights theory; he states that 'by definition rights are nothing but grounds of duties'.[5] Neil MacCormick, for his part, prefers a theory which asserts

---

he distinguishes 'jural correlatives' from 'jural opposites' and relations *in personam* from relations in rem, see pp. 65 ff.

[3] Arthur L. Corbin, in Hohfeld, *Fundamental Legal Conceptions*, p. xi.

[4] Hohfeld, *Fundamental Legal Conceptions*, pp. 38–39.

[5] Joseph Raz, *The Morality of Freedom*, Oxford University Press, 1986, p. 176. See also 'Legal Rights', 4 *Oxford Journal of Legal Studies* (1984), p. 5: 'To say that a person has a right is to say that an interest of his is sufficient ground for holding another to be subject to a duty.' Nino, however, denies an absolute relationship between rights and duties: 'Intuitively, rights serve as basis for duties because they have a wider scope. For example, they may justify acts of self-defence which violate other rights. Theoretically, there could be rights which do not provide a basis for actual or potential duties. This seems to lead to an impasse, since, apparently, there is no meaning of "right" which does not imply

RIGHTS AND OBLIGATIONS   123

the primacy of rights – rights are grounds for identifying duties – but still recognises the relationship.[6] Within the field of international law, Henkin states that: 'According to the common view, one has a legal right only against some other; to say one has a legal right against another is to say that one has a valid legal claim upon him and that the addressee has a corresponding legal obligation.'[7] In spite of their differences, all these views admit the necessary relationship between rights and duties, and I will adhere to this position for the purpose of the study.

Non-state rights-holders on the international plane
Introduction

Because of the interrelationship between national and international law, the question of international rights pertaining to NGOs and other non-state actors raises special difficulties. As has been mentioned earlier in this study, the Permanent Court of International Justice found in 1928 in the *Danzig Railway Officials* Case that individuals can hold rights under an international treaty if the intention of the contracting states is to create such rights.[8] The same position was expressed in the *LaGrand* case in 2001.[9] Yet, it is still often questioned whether human rights are 'real' rights under international law. Malanczuk, in *Akehurst's Modern Introduction to International Law*, observes that:

Very many rules of international law exist for the benefit of individuals and companies, but that does not necessarily mean that the rules create rights for the individual and companies, any more than municipal rules prohibiting cruelty to animals confer rights on animals. Even when a treaty expressly says

---

obligations.' Nino then elaborates a definition of 'rights' which, instead of duties, includes a criterion of it being 'wrong' to deprive a person of a certain situation (right), Carlos Santiago Nino, *The Ethics of Human Rights*, Oxford: Clarendon Press, 1991, pp. 30–34. It should be noted, however, that the 'right' to act in self-defence cannot be understood as a 'right *stricto sensu*' but rather as an 'immunity' according to Hohfeld's scheme. Hohfeld's notion of 'right *stricto sensu*' is rejected by Nino as being too narrow.

[6] Neil MacCormick, *Legal Right and Social Democracy*, Oxford: Clarendon Press, 1982, p. 144.
[7] Louis Henkin, *The Age of Rights*, New York: Columbia University Press, 1990, p. 34.
[8] Section 2.2, and *Advisory Opinion on the Jurisdiction of the Courts of Danzig* (1928) PCIJ Series B No. 15, pp. 17–18. For other similar examples, see Sir Robert Jennings and Sir Arthur Watts (eds.), *Oppenheim's International Law*, I, 9th edn., London: Longman, 1996, p. 847.
[9] *LaGrand* case (*Germany v. USA*), 27 June 2001, accessible online www.icj-cij.org/icjwww/idocket/igus/igusframe.htm, as of 4 November 2004. See also James Crawford, 'The ILC's Articles on Responsibility of States for Internationally Wrongful Acts: A Retrospect', 96 AJIL (2002), pp. 887–888.

124   LEGAL AND EMPIRICAL SURVEY

that individuals and companies shall enjoy certain rights, one has to read the treaty very carefully to ascertain whether the rights exist directly under international law, or whether the states party to the treaty are merely under an obligation to grant municipal law rights to the individuals or companies concerned. The international rules concerning the protection of human rights are a good example of the difficulty of deciding whether individuals derive rights from international law, or whether they merely derive benefits.[10]

In *Oppenheim's International Law*, international rights are linked to the capacity to enforce the rights:

Although treaties may speak of the rights of individuals as if they were derived from the treaties themselves, this, as a rule, is not normally the position. Such treaties, rather than creating the rights, impose the duty upon the contracting states to establish them in their national laws ... States can, however, and occasionally do, confer upon individuals, whether their own subjects or aliens, international rights *stricto sensu*, i.e. rights which they acquire without the intervention of municipal legislation and which they can enforce in their own name before international tribunals.[11]

Examples of *stricto sensu* rights referred to in this context are, *inter alia*, the rights recognised in the *Danzig Railway Officials* case and the rights monitored by the European Court of Human Rights.

According to Harris, the access to an international legal remedy is of importance for assessing whether an international legal rule creates a right for the individual. Harris observes, however, that such access is still an exception to the ordinary rule:

For the most part, however, the individual remains an object, not a subject, of international law whose most important characteristic for international law purposes is his nationality. It is this, for example that determines which state (his national state) may protect him against the extravagances of another.[12]

Thus, while Harris admits that the individual may acquire international legal rights, he refers to diplomatic protection to support the view that the individual normally lacks such rights. Diplomatic protection arises in cases of dispute between a host state and a foreign national whose rights have been denied and who has as a result suffered injuries. If the foreign national is unable to internationalise the dispute and take it out

---

[10] Peter Malanczuk, *Akehurst's Modern Introduction to International Law*, 7th edn., London: Routledge, 1997, p. 100.

[11] *Oppenheim's International Law*, I, p. 847. See also D. J. Harris, *Cases and Materials on International Law*, 5th edn., London: Sweet & Maxwell, 1998, p. 142.

[12] Harris, *Cases and Materials*, p. 142.

RIGHTS AND OBLIGATIONS 125

of the sphere of local law, the state of nationality can, at its discretion, espouse the individual's claim and invoke the responsibility of the host state.[13] As only states may invoke state responsibility, it can be argued that they are the only proper subjects of international legal rights.[14]

Although other writers hold that individuals are indeed holders of international legal rights – irrespective of whether the rights-holder has access to an international enforcement mechanism – the scepticism of writers such as Malanczuk and Harris needs consideration before possible 'NGO rights' are surveyed.[15] Should some, or all, of the body of human rights law not be regarded as rights *stricto sensu*, but merely benefits, these provisions would hardly be relevant for the question of international legal personality at all.

According to Hohfeld's logic, the existence of a legal right presupposes a corresponding legal duty directed towards the rights-holder. The problem as regards the rights of the individual is whether the obligation of contracting states to comply with the agreement entered into is directed towards the individuals whom the provisions are intended to protect or towards other states. Louis Henkin addresses the crucial point as follows:

According to a common view, one has a legal right only against some other; to say one has a legal right against another is to say that one has a valid legal claim upon him and that the addressee has a corresponding obligation in the relevant

---

[13] A/53/10, *Report of the International Law Commission on the Work of its Fiftieth Session*, 1998, para. 63.

[14] See also the *Barcelona Traction* case, in which the ICJ stated that 'a State may exercise diplomatic protection by whatever means and to whatever extent it thinks fit, for it is *its own right* that the State is asserting'. *Barcelona Traction, Light and Power Company, Limited*, ICJ Reports, 1970, p. 44 (emphasis added). The Court's statement does, however, not exclude the possibility that there may be a parallel right on the part of the individual towards the violating state. See also Crawford, who explains that Article 33 of the ILC's Draft Articles on State Responsibility takes no position on the question whether the rights bestowed in a treaty on a private entity are held by that entity directly or by the state, 'The ILC's Articles on Responsibility of States for Internationally Wrongful Acts', pp. 887–888.

[15] See, e.g., Malcolm N. Shaw, *International Law*, 4th edn., Cambridge University Press, 1997, p. 190: 'this vast array of practice with regard to the international rights and duties of the individual under customary and treaty law clearly demonstrates that individuals are subjects of international law'. Shearer states in *Starke's International Law* that: 'Irrespective of municipal legislative implementation of the rules therein contained, there is no question that, however exceptionally, many modern treaties do bestow rights or impose duties upon individuals.' Nevertheless, he calls these norms 'exceptional instances', I. A. Shearer, *Starke's International Law*, 11th edn., London: Butterworths, 1994, pp. 53, 61.

126   LEGAL AND EMPIRICAL SURVEY

legal system. The instruments are designated as dealing with the rights of individuals, and there is reference to individual rights in every article. But the state's obligation and the individual's right are not necessarily correlative, or even in the same legal order.[16]

Henkin's observation about the language of international agreements seems sympathetic. It cannot be completely ignored that the makers of international law, i.e. states, have in fact chosen the term 'right' for the legal relationship they have intended to create.[17] Still, the problem of correlation between right and duty remains unsolved if the individual right is seen as belonging solely within the national legal domain.

For the sake of clarity, four potential combinations of legal relationships involved in human rights law can be distinguished:

(a)   The individual is a holder of human rights under international law, and states' corresponding obligations under international law are addressed only towards the individual rights-holders. The individual is thus a bearer of international legal rights *stricto sensu*.

(b)   The individual is the beneficiary of international human rights law, while the state's international legal duty to comply with these rules is directed only towards other states. The state may be obliged towards the individual under national law to respect the right, but this question is outside the scope of international law.

(c)   The individual is a holder of a right *stricto sensu* (irrespective of whether she has the capacity to enforce the right), the state thus being under an international obligation towards the individual, while at the same time the state has an international duty towards other states, or towards the international community as a whole.[18]

---

[16] Henkin, *The Age of Rights*, p. 34. Hohfeld writes: 'If X has a right against Y that he shall stay off the former's land, the correlative (and equivalent) is that Y is under a duty toward X to stay off the place.' Hohfeld, *Fundamental Legal Conceptions*, p. 38.

[17] See also Cassese, who observes that: 'It would indeed be contradictory or even illogical to refer, in an international treaty, to a "right" of peoples and then actually to mean that what is granted is not a legal entitlement proper but simply an indirect benefit accruing to peoples because of the interplay of rights and obligations between Contracting States.' Antonio Cassesse, *Self-Determination of Peoples: A Legal Reappraisal*, Cambridge University Press, 1995, pp. 143–144.

[18] The ILC has discussed whether the definition of an 'injured state' in Draft Article 43 on state responsibility should be changed from a state which is entitled to invoke the responsibility of another state when the obligation is owed to 'the international community as a whole' to 'the international community of States as a whole'. The Rapporteur, James Crawford, did not agree that any change was necessary, and stated that 'the international community includes entities in addition to States; for example the European Union, the International Committee of the Red Cross, the United Nations itself'. A/CN.4/517, *Fourth Report on State Responsibility*, 31 March 2000, para. 36.

(d) International human rights law does not normally create rights *stricto sensu* on the part of individuals, as states' obligations are directed towards other states, which are the only actors that can enforce international legal rights. However, when the individual has the capacity to enforce the right, a duty on the part of the state towards the individual has been created.

The combination of legal relationships described under (a) cannot provide the full explanation, as it disregards state responsibility for breaches of human rights law. Malanczuk seems to adopt view (d), or possibly (b), while Harris adheres to (d).[19] Both thus deny the possibility that the individual may be a holder of rights *stricto sensu* even without access to an enforcement mechanism.

As with many questions relating to international legal personality, a general discussion on the subject of individual rights under international law seems to provide few answers. It is therefore necessary to examine the particular instruments and contexts in which rights or benefits have been created.

The intention of the parties

The starting point for such an investigation was given by the PCIJ in the *Danzig Railway Officials* case already mentioned. The case concerned an international agreement (the so-called *Beamtenabkommen*) which regulated the conditions of employment for the Danzig railway officials working on the Polish railway system. Poland argued that the *Beamtenabkommen*, being an international agreement, created rights and obligations between the contracting parties only, and that Poland was responsible for breaches of the agreement only in relation to the Free City of Danzig. Danzig contended, for its part, that the *Beamtenabkommen*, though an international agreement in form, was intended by the contracting parties to regulate the legal relationship between the Railway Administration and its officials, and that it was the

---

[19] Malanzcuk, however, later demonstrates that he supports view (d), not (b), see below. See also Kelsen, who made the distinction between tribunals whose jurisdiction states are obliged to recognise and those to which states adhere as contracting parties. Kelsen also added the element of enforcement action, which is the prerogative of states, not of international tribunals. He concluded that 'in the absence of any provision in the treaty conferring a procedural capacity upon individuals – endowing individuals with the "faculty of independent action to enforce these rights" – they are not the subjects of international rights'. Hans Kelsen, *Principles of International Law*, 2nd edn., New York: Holt, Rinehart & Winston, 1966, pp. 231–234.

128 LEGAL AND EMPIRICAL SURVEY

substance rather than the form which ought to determine its juridical character. The Court found that:

> it cannot be disputed that the very object of an international agreement, according to the intention of the contracting Parties, may be the adoption by the Parties of some definite rules creating individual rights and obligations and enforceable by the national courts ... The intention of the Parties ... is decisive.[20]

According to the Court, it is thus the intention of the parties which should be at the centre of attention. This argument seems to be well in line with Hohfeld's rights analysis; if the parties intended to create rights *stricto sensu* they were also willing to undertake the corresponding duty. The issue whether there are enforcement mechanisms accessible for the rights-holder is another, or related but secondary, question.

But how is the intention of the parties to be ascertained? Below it will be discussed which factors may provide evidence of an intention on the part of treaty-makers to create international legal rights. These factors will later be used for identifying rights held by NGOs under international law.

The terms of the treaty

In the *Danzig Railway Officials* case, the PCIJ examined the question of how it was to establish an intention of the parties to create international rights:

> That there is such an intention in the present case can be established by reference to the terms of the *Beamtenabkommen*. The fact that the various provisions were put in the form of an *Abkommen* is corroborative, but not conclusive evidence as to the character and legal effects of the instrument. The intention of the Parties, which is to be ascertained from the contents of the Agreement, taking into consideration the manner in which the Agreement has been applied, is decisive. This principle of interpretation should be applied by the Court in the present case.[21]

The contents of an international agreement may include several types of provisions which can provide guidance as to the nature of the legal relationship(s) created by it. First, there is often a specific provision describing the legal obligation of the contracting parties. Naturally, such provisions are of great interest as evidence of a legal obligation towards the rights-holder. One example of such a provision is Article 2 of the ICCPR:

---

[20] *Advisory Opinion on the Jurisdiction of the Courts of Danzig* (1928) PCIJ Series B No. 15, pp. 17–18.
[21] *Ibid.*

Each State Party to the present Covenant undertakes to respect and to ensure to all individuals within its territory and subject to its jurisdiction the rights recognized in the present Covenant.

The corresponding article of the International Covenant on Economic, Social and Cultural Rights (ICESCR) gives a rather different message as regards state obligation:

Each State Party to the present Covenant undertakes to take steps, individually and through international assistance and co-operation, especially economic and technical, to the maximum of its available resources, with a view to achieving progressively the full realization of the rights recognized in the present Covenant.

The specificity of the rights provision itself is also important evidence of an intention to create a legal obligation. It is reasonable to assume that a very detailed provision is intended to create a clear obligation directly, while more programmatic rules may create a more diffuse or dynamic responsibility, which might change with time and circumstances.

However, the treaty provisions on legal obligation or the specificity of rights may not always provide any clear guidance as to whether the parties have the intention to create rights. Other provisions or factors may come into play, such as whether the treaty is generally regarded as self-executing or directly applicable. While national legislation is left aside here, it can be asserted that the fact that a treaty was intended to establish rights which are directly enforceable in domestic courts provides evidence of an international legal obligation towards the rights-holders. The distinction elaborated by Thomas Buergenthal between self-executing treaties and what he calls 'directly applicable treaties' might be of some interest in this regard.[22] Buergenthal's point is that, while the question whether a given treaty is self-executing or not is a domestic law question, some treaties are *concluded for the purpose* of creating directly enforceable rights, i.e. directly applicable treaties.[23] The latter, according to Buergenthal, put a stronger obligation on states as regards implementation on the national plane and to allow individuals to invoke the treaty provisions in national courts. As a 'directly applicable' treaty, in the sense explained by Buergenthal, is intended to create directly enforceable rights, one may assume that it also creates a

---

[22] Thomas Buergenthal, 'Self-Executing and Non-Self-Executing Treaties in National and International Law', 235 *Hague Recueil* (1992), pp. 313–400.
[23] *Ibid.*, p. 322.

130   LEGAL AND EMPIRICAL SURVEY

clearer legal obligation towards the individual on the international plane. On the other hand, the fact that a treaty was not intended to be 'directly applicable' cannot constitute conclusive evidence that there is no legal obligation on the part of contracting states towards the rights-holder.

Rights and legal remedies

The existence of legal rights has often been seen as closely connected with the question whether the rights-holder has access to a legal remedy in the case of a violation of the right. As already indicated, Malanczuk puts strong emphasis on this relationship:

One way of proving that the rights of individuals or companies exist under international law is to show that the treaty conferring the rights gives the individuals or companies access to an international tribunal in order to enforce their rights.[24]

Sir Hersch Lauterpacht, on the other hand, rejected a necessary relationship between rights and procedural capacity to defend the right. As early as 1947, he stated that:

The existence of a right and the power to assert it by judicial process are not identical. In the municipal sphere there are persons, such as minors and lunatics, who though endowed with rights are unable to assert them by their own action.[25]

The assertion that rights and access to remedies are distinct – although often connected – legal phenomena corresponds to Hohfeld's theory, according to which the legal correlatives 'right' (understood as claim) and 'duty' are distinct from the conceptual pair 'power' (understood as competence or capacity) and 'liability'.[26] For this and other reasons explained above, I have chosen to regard rights as such whenever a treaty expressly proclaims 'rights'.[27] In my opinion, the lack of enforcement mechanisms does not prove that rights proclaimed in a treaty are

---

[24] *Akehurst's Modern Introduction to International Law*, p. 101.

[25] Sir Hersch Lauterpacht, 'The Subjects of the Law of Nations', 63 *The Law Quarterly Review* (1947), p. 455.

[26] Hohfeld, finding the expression 'capacity' unfortunate, suggests 'ability' as the nearest synonym, but then his discussion has a broader scope than procedural capacity. With 'power' Hohfeld means all the powers connected to a legal relation – e.g. the owner's power to extinguish his/her own legal interests over certain property through abandonment. See Hohfeld, *Fundamental Legal Conceptions*, p. 51.

[27] It was mentioned above, with reference to Louis Henkin, that it must be considered of at least some importance that states have actually chosen the term 'right' in a number of international treaties.

not 'real' or 'legal' rights. On the other hand, Hohfeld's separation of rights from powers/capacities does not necessarily imply that the rights-holder's access to an enforcement mechanism lacks importance when it comes to identifying a right. Rather than interpreting the lack of such access as evidence that there is no right *stricto sensu*, the argument seems to work the other way around. It is reasonable to assume that, if international enforcement mechanisms have been created in relation to a particular legal provision, the contracting parties *intended to create* an international legal right and to undertake the corresponding obligation. It can be observed that, if Malanczuk's, Oppenheim's and Harris' statements are understood this way, their views are not incompatible with those of Lauterpacht and Hohfeld. This line of reasoning also gains support from the ILC, which discussed the issue of diplomatic protection and its relation to the rights of the individual in 1998. The ILC Special Rapporteur on diplomatic protection recognised the developments within international law, whereby the individual has acquired 'some legal personality' independently of the state of which it is a national:

The Special Rapporteur referred to the emergence of a large number of multilateral treaties recognizing the right of individual human beings to protection independently from the intervention by states and directly by the individuals themselves through access to international forums. In this context he referred to the right of petition. He further referred to the recognition of basic human rights as creating obligations *erga omnes* and creating an interest on the part of all states. These developments, together with the proliferation of bilateral investment promotion and protection agreements and the establishment of bodies whereby a national of one state could present a claim against another state, created a legal framework outside the traditional area of diplomatic protection.[28]

In other words, treaties may bestow rights on individuals. This fact is supported by the existence of monitoring mechanisms which provide access for the individual, and which are regulated by a body of law outside the area of diplomatic protection.[29]

---

[28] A/53/10, *Report of the International Law Commission on the Work of its Fiftieth Session*, 1998, paras. 65–66.
[29] See also the Special Rapporteur's report, in which he states that: 'The State can no longer claim to enclose the individual within its exclusive sphere of national competence, since the international order bestows rights on him directly and places all States under an obligation to ensure that those rights are respected. Under certain conditions, individuals can even obtain a hearing and defend their rights before international bodies or committees established by international human rights treaties (the right of petition). The dualist approach taken by the original promoters of diplomatic

132   LEGAL AND EMPIRICAL SURVEY

International monitoring mechanisms provide different degrees of access for individuals, groups and NGOs. In some treaty monitoring systems only the rights-holders themselves have *locus standi* before a tribunal. When the *locus standi* of an individual or an organisation is based on the actor's own interest in the case – such as within the European human rights system – it can be concluded that all categories of non-state actors who have brought cases are actual rights-holders under the treaty and that the contracting states have a clear legal obligation towards all these actors. In other systems, such as the Inter-American system for human rights, there is no victim requirement, which means that cases may be brought before the commission by persons or organisations with no connection to the particular case or violation.[30] In such situations, it is reasonable to regard the enforcement mechanism as evidence of a general legal obligation towards the beneficiaries of the treaty provisions. It can, however, not be concluded solely on the basis of the complainant's access to the enforcement mechanism that the *complainant* is also holder of international rights under the treaty.

Another factor of importance is the character of the legal remedy in question. The legal remedies available to private actors in international law are often of a quasi-judicial character. For instance, violations of the rights enumerated in the ICCPR are examined by the Human Rights Committee (HRC). The Committee cannot issue legally binding decisions, only 'forward its views' to the State Party concerned and to the individual victim.[31] Nevertheless, the access to a quasi-judicial body supervising compliance with the treaty does provide some evidence that contracting states which have accepted the complaints procedure have also taken on an international legal obligation regarding the individual rights. Other forms of monitoring compliance with convention rights are state-reporting systems, which have been established under

protection is therefore no longer appropriate in such cases', A/CN.4/484, *Preliminary Report on Diplomatic Protection*, 4 February 1998, para. 35.

[30] See, e.g., section 5.3 on the Inter-American Commission on Human Rights, which provides for unrestricted access for NGOs and other actors to bring complaints, as long as at least a potential victim is identified.

[31] See section 8.2. It is possible that a practice of regarding these views as binding is developing. McGoldrick (writing in the 1980s) has stated that: 'Over a decade of practice under the OP [the optional protocol to the ICCPR] has demonstrated the feasibility of individual petition systems at the international level as the ECHR has at the regional level. In this respect the OP represents a signal contribution to the recognition of the individual as a proper subject of international law.' Dominic McGoldrick, *The Human Rights Committee: Its Role in the Development of the International Covenant on Civil and Political Rights*, Oxford: Clarendon Press, 1994, p. 198. The Optional Protocol has been in force since 1976.

several treaties, such as the ICCPR, ICESCR and the Convention on the Elimination of all Forms of Discrimination Against Women (CEDAW). Such systems underline the legal obligation of State Parties on the international plane, but provide no particular standing for non-state actors who have suffered violations. It could therefore be held that the reporting system mainly provides evidence of the legal obligation between the parties. On the other hand, it could also be argued that the reporting system has been established in order to monitor states' fulfilment of their obligations towards rights-holders.

Each system and situation will have to be studied separately, as different combinations of circumstances surrounding the rights will provide evidence of different strength as to the international legal obligation towards the rights-holders. Even though it has been concluded that rights may exist without enforcement and monitoring mechanisms, it is helpful to highlight examples of rights which are clearly held by non-state actors under international law.

Conclusion

The separation of rights from the power to enforce rights promotes conceptual clarity. Moreover, it should be borne in mind that the makers of international human rights law have chosen the term 'rights' for the legal relationships they intended to create. Legal language constitutes an important message in itself, intended to create values and to affect legal actors so that they undertake or refrain from certain conduct. For these reasons, I have chosen not to question the validity or 'legality' of rights expressly pronounced in international law.

Some writers, however, assert that the obligation of the contracting parties towards non-state actors and the corresponding rights under human rights treaties lie primarily on the national plane. Such a viewpoint does not exclude the possibility that there is also a legal obligation towards the rights-holder on the international plane. It is nevertheless important for the rights-holders themselves, as well as the legal community in general, to clarify to what extent the rights held and the corresponding obligation lie on the international level. In order to answer this question, the intention of the parties as expressed in the treaty text needs to be examined. The existence of enforcement mechanisms in relation to a right may also provide such evidence.

In this chapter, different fields of international law will be surveyed in order to identify rights which are held by NGOs directly under these rules. The question of whether NGOs also have obligations under

134 LEGAL AND EMPIRICAL SURVEY

international law will be dealt with in a separate section. Finally, international humanitarian law, which is a field with special characteristics with regard to non-state actors, will be discussed.

Before the survey of rights is carried out, however, the character of rights pronounced for non-state actors within international law needs to be analysed in order to find out whether rights can be held by organisations as such or only by their members.

4.2 Organisation rights

Human rights, group rights and organisation rights

Certain rights in modern human rights law benefit groups and peoples. Such 'collective rights' or 'group rights' are intended to protect not only the interests of an individual belonging to the group, or the aggregation of the interests of all the individuals of the group, but also the interests of the group as such.[32] Examples of rights which are usually classified as group rights are the right of peoples to existence (as distinguished from the individual right to life), the right to self-determination and the right of minorities to preservation of a separate identity.[33]

Group rights are not a new phenomenon in international law. As a consequence of the territorial changes following the First World War, a system for the protection of minorities was established under the

---

[32] See, e.g., Ian Brownlie, *Treaties and Indigenous Peoples*, Oxford: Clarendon Press, 1992, pp. 29–54 and 'The Rights of Peoples in Modern International Law', in James Crawford (ed.), *The Rights of Peoples*, Oxford: Clarendon Press, 1988, p. 2; Allan Rosas, 'So-Called Rights of the Third Generation', in Asbjörn Eide *et al.* (eds.), *Economic, Social and Cultural Rights: A Textbook*, Dordrecht: Martinus Nijhoff, 1995, pp. 243–245; Natan Lerner, *Group Rights and Discrimination in International Law*, Dordrecht: Martinus Nijhoff, 1991, pp. 34–37; Harris, *Cases and Materials*, pp. 625–626, 722–725; Athanasia Spiliopoulou Åkermark, *Justifications of Minority Protection in International Law*, The Hague: Kluwer Law International/Iustus Publishing Co., 1997, pp. 42–48. The categorisation of certain rights as 'group rights' by these and other authors does not, however, always mean that the group itself is regarded as the holder of the right, or that the protection of the group as such provides the justification for the right; see Roland Rich, 'Right to Development: A Right of Peoples?', in Crawford (ed.), *The Rights of Peoples*, pp. 43–44 and below. I will use the term 'group rights' as a neutral concept inclusive of both the understanding that the individual members of the group are the rights-holders and the understanding that the right is held by the group as such.

[33] Lerner, *Group Rights*, pp. 34–35; Patrick Thornberry, *International Law and the Rights of Minorities*, Oxford: Clarendon Press, 1991, pp. 57–58; James Crawford, 'The Rights of Peoples: "Peoples" or "Governments"?', in Crawford, *The Rights of Peoples*, pp. 56–66; Allan Rosas, 'The Right to Self-Determination', in Asbjörn Eide *et al.*, *Economic, Social and Cultural Rights*, pp. 82, 252, and Åkermark, *Justifications of Minority Protection*, p. 44.

League of Nations. This system included several treaties, individual provisions in peace treaties and declarations containing minority rights, created for the purpose of both granting equality to individuals belonging to minorities in relation to other nationals of the state and making possible the preservation of the group's characteristics.[34]

There has been substantial debate in the doctrine as to the justification and actual existence of group rights in international law. Some deny altogether that there are indeed rights held under international law by groups as such, preferring to regard them as rights held by the individuals belonging to the group, while others accept the idea but debate which rights belong to this category.[35] Bearing in mind that the notion of human rights has strong roots in a liberal-democratic tradition of thinking, focusing on protection of the individual and individual freedom, it is not surprising that the idea of group rights have by some been regarded as hard to reconcile with the notion of human rights:

> but in a liberal scheme rights belong solely to individuals, as their 'trumps' against the power of the group. Thus any theory that suggests that the group as such may itself be the holder of rights appears inherently anti-liberal and therefore incompatible with the usual 'Western' formulation of human rights.[36]

In other words, a strengthened position of the group might threaten the rights and freedoms of individuals outside, or inside, the group.[37]

---

[34] For a description of the system, see, e.g., Lerner, *Group Rights*, pp. 11 ff. and Joel E. Oestreich, 'Liberal Theory and Minority Group Rights', 21 HRQ (1999), pp. 110–114. As regards the ideas underlying the minority protection system, see the Advisory Opinion of the PCIJ in the case of *Minority Schools in Albania* of 6 April 1935, PCIJ Series A/B No. 64, p. 17.

[35] See, e.g., Yoram Dinstein, 'Collective Human Rights of Peoples and Minorities', 25 ICLQ (1976), pp. 102–120; Lerner, *Group Rights*; Thornberry, *International Law and the Rights of Minorities*; Marlies Galenkamp, 'Collective Rights: Much Ado About Nothing? A Review Essay', 9 *Netherlands Quarterly of Human Rights* (1991), No. 3, pp. 291–307; Åkermark, *Justifications of Minority Protection*. As regards the definition of 'group rights' in international law, Brownlie holds that there are at least two criteria for the notion of group rights. First, group rights are certain types of individual rights which tend to be exercised by the individual as a member of a group – e.g. the right to enjoy rights without discrimination as to race, religion, etc. Secondly, group rights involve elements of recognition of the cultural and other identity of the group, a recognition which is not ensured by the ordinary application of the provisions representing individual rights. Brownlie thus includes both an individual and a corporate conception of group rights in his view. Brownlie, *Treaties and Indigenous Peoples*, p. 29.

[36] Oestrich, 'Liberal Theory and Minority Group Rights', p. 116.

[37] It is also sometimes asserted that, to the extent that group rights exist, they cannot be 'human' rights. For a vast number of references to works discussing these issues, see Peter Jones, 'Human Rights, Group Rights, and Peoples' Rights', 21 HRQ (1999), pp. 80–81.

136 LEGAL AND EMPIRICAL SURVEY

Moreover, the recognition of group rights might be regarded as a threat to the territorial sovereignty of the state and thus to stability in the international community.

One solution to the conflict between the idea of individual human rights and group rights is to require that group rights must always be justified on the individual plane. For instance, Joseph Raz lays down the following conditions for the existence of a group right:

> First, it exists because an aspect of the interest of human beings justifies holding some person(s) to be subject to a duty. Second, the interests in question are the interests of individuals as members of a group in a public good and the right is a right to that public good because it serves their interest as members of the group. Thirdly, the interest of no single member of that group in that public good is sufficient by itself to justify holding another person to be subject to a duty.[38]

It is the second and third conditions which, according to Raz, distinguish collective rights from individual rights. At the same time, Raz emphasises that rights – even collective rights – can exist only if they serve the interests of the individuals: 'The right rests on the cumulative interests of many individuals.'[39]

The political scientist Peter Jones distinguishes between the 'collective' and the 'corporate' conception of group rights.[40] Group rights interpreted as collective rights are rights held by the individuals forming the collective, while according to the corporate conception of group rights, the rights-holder is the group as such, defined by legal personality or by other factors, such as language or culture. A collective group right is thus 'theirs', while a corporate right is 'its'. Jones observes that the corporate conception of group rights is familiar in relation to legal corporations. His article is, however, more concerned with moral than with legal rights.[41] Jones finds that, from a moral point of view, only the collective conception of group rights, as exemplified by the right to self-determination, is in sympathy with the morality of human rights, while the corporate conception of rights 'belong to a quite different and potentially conflicting morality'.[42]

'Corporate rights' as described by Jones is a useful concept for rights held by organisations. In order to avoid confusion with the common

---

[38] Raz, *The Morality of Freedom*, p. 208. [39] *Ibid.*, p. 209.
[40] Jones, 'Human Rights, Group Rights, and Peoples' Rights', pp. 83–88.
[41] *Ibid.*, p. 87. [42] *Ibid.*, p. 107.

understanding of 'corporations' as commercial bodies I will, however, call rights held by NGOs and other organisations *organisation rights*.

Jones' viewpoints raise the question whether organisation rights are problematic in relation to (other) human rights. The two main arguments against the corporate conception of group rights on the international plane seem to be, first, that they may constitute a threat towards individual rights and freedoms and, secondly, that they may constitute a threat to stability within the international community. It could therefore be argued that any candidates for the category of organisation rights should be analysed from the perspective of the individual and deconstructed into aggregates of separate, individual rights.

The problem of organisation rights as related to individual rights and freedoms was discussed during the drafting of Article 8 of the ICESCR, which protects the rights of trade unions. Some delegates held that trade union rights were contrary to the general conception of human rights, as they relate to only one category of persons and are held by collectives rather than individuals.[43] However, when one considers which kind of conflicts may arise between an organisation and its members or other individuals, it seems that such conflicts – although easy to imagine – are not a product of the international protection afforded to organisations in general. This is mainly due to the character of organisation rights, as codified in current international law. With some anticipation of the result of the survey of organisation rights in international law in this book, it can be observed that they are basic, mostly consisting in the right to exist and to function freely as an organisation without interference from the state. In other words, organisation rights are mainly of a formal, not a material, character. International labour law is an exception in the sense that it includes rights of a more material kind, such as the right to collective bargaining. This right can come into conflict with, for instance, the interests of the employer or of employees not belonging to the trade union. I suggest, however, that the organisation right to collective bargaining does as such not constitute a threat to human rights as it can be interpreted in a way which is consistent with individual rights.

Another – and, indeed, fundamental – difference between organisation rights and other group rights, notably minority rights, is that one

---

[43] Matthew C. R. Craven, *The International Covenant on Economic, Social and Cultural Rights: A Perspective on its Development*, Oxford: Clarendon Press, 1995, p. 250. See also section 4.2 on organisation rights in the ICESCR.

138   LEGAL AND EMPIRICAL SURVEY

chooses to belong to an organisation – at least as long as the negative freedom of association is respected – while people are born into minorities and peoples.[44] This means that there is another scope for individual choices in relation to organisations than in relation to cultural minorities or peoples, where the question of belonging to the group is closely connected to a person's identity and life in general. The conflicts which may arise between individual rights and the group rights of a minority, thus do not seem to be actualised in the case of organisation rights.

There is indeed one case where organisation rights may come into conflict with human rights: if racist, non-democratic or terrorist organisations use international law to protect their identity and position. Although it might be held that it is not the right to associate as such which poses a threat to human rights (but rather the ideologies and activities of the organisation), legal rights protecting the organisation create a platform for its work. The protection afforded to organisations in international law is, however, not a problem in this respect. In present-day international law, there are legal grounds for states to exempt such organisations from organisation rights, and even treaty obligations on contracting states to prohibit them.

Finally, it may be considered whether organisation rights pose a threat to the stability of the state, or even to the international community. This question has been much discussed in relation to the rights of peoples and minorities. It is a fairly obvious observation that the basic organisation rights which have been recognised so far do not as such conflict with state stability. On the contrary, they are an integral part of democracy, and it can rather be argued that they promote stability.[45]

---

[44] On the negative freedom of association, see Manfred Nowak, *UN Covenant on Civil and Political Rights: CCPR Commentary*, Kiel: N. P. Engel, 1993, pp. 387–389 and Sarah Joseph, Jenny Schultz and Melissa Castan, *The International Covenant on Civil and Political Rights: Cases, Materials, and Commentary*, Oxford University Press, 2000, pp. 439–440.

[45] The Turkish government has argued before the European Court of Human Rights in cases regarding organisations which pursue Kurdish interests that the organisations threaten national security and the territorial integrity of the country (see, e.g., *Freedom and Democracy Party (ÖZDEP)* v. *Turkey*, 8 December 1999). In such cases, it is the particular agendas or activities of the organisations in question that are regarded as a threat, rather than the fact that organisations may in general be established. Accordingly, human rights treaties (e.g. ICCPR, Article 22, para. 2 and ECHR, Article 11, para. 2) recognise that state parties may restrict the right to freedom of association for the protection of certain interests, while not allowing that the right as such is suspended.

Organisation rights in international law

Introduction

The structure of rights relating to the existence and activities of private organisations corresponds to that of other group rights: either they are designed to protect the rights of the individual members, such as the right to form and join organisations, or they offer protection for the organisation as such, or both. Our survey of organisation rights in international law will concentrate on the two latter categories. As a background to this survey it may nevertheless be useful briefly to mention some of the individual rights related to organisations.

The individual's right to participate in organisational life is protected by several international human rights instruments. According to Article 20 of the Universal Declaration of Human Rights, everyone has the right to freedom of peaceful assembly and association and also the right not to be compelled to belong to an association. Article 23(4) of the Declaration protects the right to form and to join trade unions. The same right is guaranteed by the ICESCR, Article 8(1a). The ICCPR, in Article 22, establishes the right to freedom of association with others, including the right to form and join trade unions.

In addition to the protection offered by these conventions of a general character, rights relating to organisations have been established in several specialised fields of law. For instance, the European Framework Convention for the Protection of National Minorities establishes that every person belonging to a national minority has the right to establish religious organisations and associations.[46] Similarly, Article 2(4) of the Declaration on the Rights of Persons Belonging to National or Ethnic, Religious and Linguistic Minorities states that persons belonging to minorities have the right to establish and maintain their own associations.[47] According to Article 7(c) of CEDAW, women have the right 'to participate in non-governmental organizations and associations concerned with the public and political life of the country'.

It should be observed that it is not the primary aim of this chapter to examine the material content of the rights provisions which are found to include elements of organisation rights. The content of rights will be described only to the extent that they have a particular connection to organisations. I have also limited the survey of rights to treaties, with

---

[46] Framework Convention for the Protection of National Minorities, ETS No. 157, Article 8.
[47] Adopted by General Assembly resolution A/RES/47/135, 3 February 1993.

140 LEGAL AND EMPIRICAL SURVEY

the exception of two non-binding instruments of particular relevance to NGOs: the UN Declaration on Human Rights Defenders and the Council of Europe Fundamental Principles on the Status of Non-Governmental Organisations in Europe. Resolutions which establish rights for NGOs in their co-operation with IGOs are examined later.[48] The discussion on the obligations of NGOs, on the other hand, includes both instruments of varying normative character as well as the obligations formulated for NGOs in resolutions concerning IGO–NGO co-operation. The international responsibilities or obligations of NGOs constitute an area of law which is new and possibly still under development. It is therefore interesting to examine as much as possible of the material that is there. Rights and obligations under international humanitarian law are dealt with later in the chapter.[49]

The International Covenant on Civil and Political Rights

Article 22 of the ICCPR provides that:

1. Everyone shall have the right to freedom of association with others, including the right to form and join trade unions for the protection of his interests.
2. No restrictions may be placed on the exercise of this right other than those which are prescribed by law and which are necessary in a democratic society.

According to Manfred Nowak, the right to freedom of association, as protected by Article 22 of the ICCPR, includes not only the individual right of freedom to form or join an organisation, but also 'the collective right of an existing association to perform activities in pursuit of the common interests of its members'.[50] State parties are obliged not to interfere with the founding of associations, or with their activities, and to protect the formation of associations against interference by private parties. Moreover, state parties are under a positive duty to provide the legal framework for the founding of juridical persons under domestic

---

[48] Chapter 7.   [49] Section 4.4.

[50] Nowak, *UN Covenant on Civil and Political Rights: CCPR Commentary*, p. 387. According to the decision of the majority of the Human Rights Committee regarding communication No. 118/1982 (*J.B. et al.*, represented by the *Union of Provincial Employees* v. *Canada*), the right to strike is, however, excluded from the scope of the Article. This decision was based on an analysis of the *travaux préparatoires* and an interpretation of Article 22 as compared to Article 8 of the Covenant on Economic, Social and Cultural Rights, see Manfred Nowak, 'Survey of Decisions Given up Till July 1986', 7 HRLJ (1986), p. 302, and Joseph, Schultz and Castan, *The International Covenant on Civil and Political Rights*, pp. 434–439.

law.[51] The Human Rights Committee has declared in its jurisprudence that complicated registration procedures for trade unions and other NGOs are contrary to the Covenant. It stated in its concluding observations regarding a state party report that it was 'concerned about the difficulties arising from the registration procedures to which non-governmental organizations and trade unions are subjected', and continued:

The Committee, reiterating that the free functioning of non-governmental organizations is essential for protection of human rights and dissemination of information in regard to human rights among the people, recommends that laws, regulations and administrative practices relating to their registration and activities be reviewed without delay in order that their establishment and free operation may be facilitated in accordance with article 22 of the Covenant.[52]

The Committee has also explained that prohibitions regarding the activities of NGOs must be limited.[53] For instance, a general prohibition imposed on the right of civil servants to organise a trade union and bargain collectively, as well as their right to strike, has been found to raise 'serious concerns' in relation to Article 22.[54] Furthermore, the Committee has stressed the importance of independence for human rights NGOs, and has criticised measures preventing NGO officials from taking part in its meetings.[55]

As regards the character of the organisations protected, the scope is broad. Purposes may be political, religious, ideological, economic, social, sports, etc. and the legal form of association is unrestricted. Even *de facto* organisations, lacking juridical personality, are protected. Organisations founded under public law are, however, not covered by Article 22.[56]

---

[51] Nowak, 'UN Covenant', p. 387.
[52] CCPR/C/79/Add.86, *Concluding Observations of the Human Rights Committee: Belarus*, 19 November 1997, para. 19.
[53] CCPR/C/79/Add.87, *Concluding Observations of the Human Rights Committee: Lithuania*, 19 November 1997, para. 20.
[54] CCPR/C/79/Add.104, *Concluding Observations of the Human Rights Committee: Chile*, 30 March 1999, para. 25. See also CCPR/C/79/Add.105 (Canada), 7 April 1999, para. 17.
[55] CCPR/C/79/Add.43, *Concluding Observations of the Human Rights Committee: Tunisia*, 23 November 1994, para. 12 and CCPR/C/79/Add.65 (Nigeria), 24 July 1996, para. 290. In the latter case, two officials of the Nigerian NGO Civil Liberty Organisation were prevented from taking part in the meeting of the Human Rights Committee and had their passports confiscated by the authorities.
[56] Nowak, 'UN Covenant', p. 387.

142   LEGAL AND EMPIRICAL SURVEY

For NGOs, the right to freedom of association under Article 22 is the most fundamental right in the Covenant which (at least according to Nowak) includes elements of organisation rights. It can be discussed whether Article 21 on the right to peaceful assembly also includes elements of organisation rights; Nowak states that this is one of the Articles which 'ensure rights also to groups of persons or to juridical persons'.[57] However, he is also of the opinion that assemblies held by associations are primarily protected by Article 22.[58] Unfortunately, the Human Rights Committee has not adopted any General Comments or Recommendations on the rights to freedom of association and peaceful assembly. It should also be observed that, since only individuals are entitled to submit complaints to the Human Rights Committee regarding violations of the Covenant, the Committee's jurisprudence does not include case-law concerning the extent to which the Covenant protects NGOs as such.[59]

There are other provisions in the Covenant which might include aspects of group or organisation rights, notably Article 18 on the right to freedom of religion.[60] Some support for such an interpretation of Article 18 can be found in a General Comment of the Human Rights Committee, where it states that:

> In addition, the practice and teaching of religion or belief includes acts integral to the conduct by religious groups of their basic affairs, such as the freedom to choose their religious leaders, priests and teachers, the freedom to establish seminaries or religious schools and the freedom to prepare and distribute religious texts or publications.[61]

In addition, there is no reason to exclude the possibility that rights which are neutral to the character of the rights-holder, such as the right to a fair and public hearing under Article 14(1), can possibly also be held by NGOs. It would take this discussion too far to examine all of the Convention rights in order to determine whether they include

---

[57] *Ibid.*, p. 658.   [58] *Ibid.*, p. 374.

[59] Optional Protocol to the International Covenant on Civil and Political Rights, Article 2.

[60] Article 18(1) reads: 'Everyone shall have the right to freedom of thought, conscience and religion. This right shall include freedom to have or to adopt a religion or belief of his choice, and freedom, either individually or in community with others and in public or private, to manifest his religion or belief in worship, observance, practice and teaching.'

[61] Human Rights Committee, *General Comment No. 22* (adopted in 1993), para. 4, in HRI/GEN/1/Rev.5, *Compilation of General Comments and General Recommendations Adopted by Human Rights Treaty Bodies*, 26 April 2001, p. 144. See also Nowak, 'UN Covenant', p. 658.

RIGHTS AND OBLIGATIONS 143

aspects of organisation rights or whether they are purely individual in their character. It is possible that all the rights which are not necessarily connected to a physical person, such as the right to life or the right not to be subjected to torture, may also be held by organisations, but in the absence of clear support for such an interpretation from the Human Rights Committee or from states parties, the answer is uncertain.

There is, however, an inadmissibility decision from the Human Rights Committee regarding a complaint submitted under the Optional Protocol which seems to contradict the possibility that companies, and thus possibly other juridical persons, have any rights under the Convention. The case of *Lamagna* v. *Australia* concerned the owner of a nursing care centre, who complained that she had been subjected to unfair, unreasonable and unjust treatment in relation to subsidies that she had been denied by the authorities. She did not, however, invoke any specific articles of the Covenant. The Committee stated:

> However, the author who purchased the nursing as an enterprise is essentially claiming before the Committee violations of the rights of her company, which has its own legal personality. All domestic remedies referred to in the present case were in fact brought before the Courts in the name of the company, and not of the author, furthermore the author has not substantiated that her rights under the Covenant have been violated. ... The Committee considers that the author, by claiming violations of her company's rights, *which are not protected by the Covenant* has no standing within the meaning of article 1, of the Optional Protocol, in respect of the complaint related to her company and that no claim related to the author personally has been substantiated for purposes of article 2 of the Optional Protocol.[62]

The Committee thus declared the complaint inadmissible. The decision can be interpreted in several ways. The first is simply that companies do not have rights under the Covenant, thus not excluding the possibility that other juridical persons, such as NGOs, may have such rights. Secondly, the decision could be understood as indicating that juridical persons in general cannot have such rights. Thirdly, the Committee's statement can be understood as not specifically referring to the company, but to the *rights* which might have been actualised by the complaint. This would mean that the Committee, to some extent, anticipated a decision on the merits by indicating that the complaint would not have been successful even if it had been submitted on behalf of the

---

[62] *Lamagna* v. *Australia*, Communication No. 737/1997, CCPR/C/65/D/737/1997, 30 April 1999, para. 6.2 (emphasis added).

144 LEGAL AND EMPIRICAL SURVEY

complainant herself. Such an interpretation enjoys some support from the fact that no rights in the Covenant were invoked and that the circumstances of the case did not fall clearly under any of its provisions. In my opinion, the Committee's statement is unclear, and for the purposes of this study it can be concluded only that it does not totally exclude the possibility that NGOs enjoy protection under the Covenant.

In conclusion, it is possible that several of the rights enunciated by the ICCPR can be held by NGOs. Nowak's commentary provides clear support for such an interpretation, while the position of the Human Rights Committee is uncertain. The right to freedom of association under Article 22 is the most fundamental of the rights possibly held by NGOs.

The question which remains to be answered is to what extent there is evidence that the contracting states to the ICCPR are under an international legal obligation towards NGOs as to the fulfilment of these rights. I have suggested above that such evidence can be found through an examination of the treaty text and of the supervisory mechanisms set up to monitor the implementation of the convention rights.

The general obligation of states parties to the ICCPR is expressed in Article 2:

1. Each State Party to the present Covenant undertakes to respect and to ensure to all individuals within its territory and subject to its jurisdiction the rights recognized in the present Covenant, without distinction of any kind, such as race, colour, sex, language, religion, political or other opinion, national or social origin, property, birth or other status.

2. Where not already provided for by existing legislative or other measures, each State Party to the present Covenant undertakes to take the necessary steps, in accordance with its constitutional processes and with the provisions of the present Covenant, to adopt such laws or other measures as may be necessary to give effect to the rights recognized in the present Covenant.

Paragraph (1) expresses a general undertaking of the contracting parties to respect the Convention and to apply it in a non-discriminatory way towards all individuals within its territory. It should be noted that the obligation is absolute, in the sense that it does not take account of available resources or other circumstances, as is mentioned in the corresponding article in the ICESCR.

During the drafting of the Convention, there was disagreement among states as regards Article 2.[63] Some state representatives saw

---

[63] McGoldrick, *The Human Rights Committee*, pp. 12–13.

Article 2(1) as an expression of an absolute and immediate obligation of the contracting parties. According to this view, states could become parties to the Covenant only after having taken the necessary legislative measures to secure the rights. These representatives criticised Article 2(2), because it was regarded as leaving room for states to fulfil their obligations only progressively. Other states argued that certain elasticity was required as regards the obligation posed on state parties, and there was a need to take account of the constitutional processes of different countries. A US proposal to include a provision stating that 'the provisions of the Covenant shall not themselves become effective as national law' was decisively rejected.[64]

From the national perspective, Article 2(2) has been differently interpreted by courts in different countries, some taking such implementation clauses to provide evidence of state parties' intent to refuse applicability, others seeing it as an expression of respect for the different constitutional approaches to application of international law in the domestic field.[65] The present wording of Article 2(2) represents a compromise, meaning that the direct applicability of the ICCPR is an unanswered question from the perspective of international law, leaving it open for each particular state to decide what legislative measures are necessary for the implementation of the Convention. The Human Rights Committee has stated that 'article 2 of the Covenant generally leaves it to the States parties concerned to choose their method of implementation'.[66] Nevertheless, the Committee has demonstrated a certain tendency to promote the direct applicability of the Covenant, and noted in its *Annual Report 1999* that domestic courts increasingly applied the standards contained in the ICCPR.[67]

As indicated above, the ICCPR is provided with a facultative mechanism for complaint under the Optional Protocol to the Convention. Under Article 2 of the Optional Protocol, individuals who claim that any of their rights enumerated in the Covenant have been violated and

---

[64] Mc Goldrick, *The Human Rights Committee*, p. 271.

[65] See Benedetto Conforti, 'National Courts and the International Law of Human Rights', in Benedetto Conforti and Francesco Francioni (eds.), *Enforcing International Human Rights in Domestic Courts*, The Hague: Martinus Nijhoff, 1997, p. 9.

[66] Human Rights Committee, General Comment No. 3 (adopted in 1981), para. 1, in HRI/GEN/1/Rev.5, *Compilation of General Comments and General Recommendations Adopted by Human Rights Treaty Bodies*, 26 April 2001, p. 112.

[67] A/54/40, *Report of the Human Rights Committee*, I, 21 October 1999, paras. 124, 404, and Nowak, 'UN Covenant', p. 54.

146   LEGAL AND EMPIRICAL SURVEY

who have exhausted all available domestic remedies may submit a written communication to the Human Rights Committee for consideration. After having considered communications received in the light of all information made available to it by the individual and by the state party concerned, the Committee adopts a view which is forwarded to the state party concerned and to the individual. The view is not binding on the state party, but the opinions delivered by the Committee are publicised and generally considered authoritative, although often not complied with.[68]

According to the wording of Article 2, communications may only be submitted by *individuals* claiming to be the victim of a violation of the rights enumerated in the Covenant. The fact that communications may not be submitted by organisations as alleged victims of violations has been confirmed by the Committee in several of its opinions.[69] The jurisprudence of the Human Rights Committee also excludes the possibility that communications are submitted through a representative individual alleging breaches of an organisation right or a group right, since the Optional Protocol provides a procedure for the protection of individual rights only.[70] Nowak notes in his commentary that 'a variety of Articles (e.g. 1, 18, 21, 22, 23, 25 or 27) ensures rights also to groups of persons; but under a literal reading of Arts. 1 and 2 OP, a violation of these rights cannot be remedied by the affected groups or organizations but only by individual members of such'.[71] Thus, the only possibility is for individual members to submit communications individually or jointly alleging violations of their individual rights.

There is also a reporting system established under the ICCPR. According to Article 40 of the Covenant, state parties undertake to submit reports on the measures they have adopted in order to give effect to the

[68] McGoldrick, *The Human Rights Committee*, pp. 151–152, 201, 202, and Nowak, 'UN Covenant', p. xix. Nowak's view is, however, that the views of the Committee 'are generally complied with'.

[69] See section 5.2.

[70] See Communication No. 40/1978 (*Hartikainen v. Finland*), which was submitted by the Secretary-General of the Union of Free Thinkers of Finland on behalf of the organisation as well as on his own behalf, in Joseph, Schultz and Castan, *The International Covenant on Civil and Political Rights*, p. 43, the case of *Lamagna v. Australia* mentioned above, Communication No. 737/1997, CCPR/C/65/D/737/1997, 30 April 1999, No 163/1984, and (regarding the right to self-determination) Communications No. 78/1980 (*A. D. v. Canada*; submitted on behalf of the Mikmaq tribal society), in A/39/40, *Report of the Human Rights Committee*, 1984, pp. 200–203, and No. 167/1984 (*Lubicon Lake Band v. Canada*), in 96 ILR (1994), pp. 667–707, particularly at para. 32.1.

[71] Nowak, 'UN Covenant', p. 658.

rights recognised in the Covenant and on the progress made in the enjoyment of those rights.[72] This system, as well as the facultative interstate complaint system under Article 41, underlines the legal obligation state parties have towards other contracting states to comply with the treaty.[73] It is, however, more doubtful whether the existence of these mechanisms provides evidence of the legal obligation towards the rights-holders.

It can be concluded that, although the ICCPR formulates rather precise rights relating to organisations, it cannot be ascertained that these rights protect NGOs as such, and the evidence of state obligation towards NGOs on the international plane is not particularly strong. The right to freedom of association with its different components, such as the right to found organisations and to function freely, is of course fundamental for NGOs. However, the ICCPR is not very useful as an instrument for NGOs when it comes to defending this and other rights under the Covenant, as NGOs lack standing under the Optional Protocol as victims before the Human Rights Committee. Apart from submitting general information to the Committee – for example, in the form of parallel reports – the only remedy available to NGOs for defending these rights is the 1503 procedure, which deals with the examination of situations which appear to reveal a consistent pattern of gross violations of human rights and thus cannot be used for individual cases of violations of organisation rights.[74]

The International Covenant on Economic, Social and Cultural Rights

Most rights pronounced in the ICESCR are clearly of a personal nature, such as the right to social security and the right of everyone to an adequate standard of living. Although there are rights which benefit groups, such as the right to self-determination guaranteed in Article 1, the provision that is most relevant for the question of organisation rights is Article 8:

---

[72] It can be observed, however, that many states show a lack of respect as to their obligation to submit reports. During its 54th session, the Human Rights Committee noted that eighty-three States Parties to the Covenant, or nearly two-thirds of all States Parties, were in arrears with their reports, A/54/40, *Report of the Human Rights Committee*, I, 21 October 1999, para. 49.

[73] The interstate complaints system has so far never been used.

[74] See section 5.2.

148   LEGAL AND EMPIRICAL SURVEY

1. The States Parties to the present Covenant undertake to ensure:

(a) The right of everyone to form trade unions and join the trade union of his choice, subject only to the rules of the organization concerned, for the promotion and protection of his economic and social interests. No restrictions may be placed on the exercise of this right other than those prescribed by law and which are necessary in a democratic society in the interests of national security or public order or for the protection of the rights and freedoms of others;

(b) The right of trade unions to establish national federations or confederations and the right of the latter to form or join international trade-union organizations;

(c) The right of trade unions to function freely subject to no limitations other than those prescribed by law and which are necessary in a democratic society in the interests of national security or public order or for the protection of the rights and freedoms of others;

(d) The right to strike, provided that it is exercised in conformity with the laws of the particular country.[75]

International standards relating to trade unions provide the most obvious example of organisation rights in international law. These rights can be seen as deriving from the general right to freedom of association, but were given a special status because of the important role historically played by trade unions in the realisation of other economic and social rights.[76] During the drafting of the ICESCR, criticism was raised against special protection for trade unions. It was considered contrary to the notion of human rights that rights related to only one category of persons, and that they were held by collectives rather than individuals. However, the majority found it unsuitable to guarantee the individual right to form and join trade unions but at the same time deny trade unions a right to function freely, and that in order effectively to guarantee the individual right to form and join trade unions, trade unions themselves had to be guaranteed the right to act.[77]

The text which was finally adopted as Article 8 of the ICESCR is described by Craven in his book on the Covenant as a hybrid of

---

[75] It can be discussed whether the right to the enjoyment of just and favourable conditions of work with its different components under Article 7 might include aspects of organisation rights. Considering the clear reference to trade unions in Article 8, however, it seems unlikely that other rights include an implicit organisation right.

[76] Craven, *The International Covenant on Economic, Social and Cultural Rights*, pp. 248–249.

[77] *Ibid.*, pp. 250, 255–256.

individual and collective rights. The wording of the text provides clear examples of organisation rights, including the right of trade unions to establish national federations or confederations and the right of federations and confederations to join international trade union organisations under Article 8(1b) and the right of trade unions to 'function freely subject to no limitations other than those prescribed by law and which are necessary in a democratic society', guaranteed by Article 8(c).[78]

The observations made by the Committee on Economic, Social and Cultural Rights on state party reports contain little information as to what different components are included in the organisation rights guaranteed by the Covenant.[79] As regards the right to function freely, the Committee has emphasised that the right shall be subject to no restrictions, except under the conditions mentioned in the provision.[80] One example of a restriction contrary to the Covenant mentioned by the Committee is to prevent trade unions from registration if national legislation requires registration.[81] The Committee has also criticised a government office created to monitor trade unions.[82] Furthermore, it has stated that Article 8 enshrines the right to collective bargaining.[83] According to Craven, who notes that the precise scope of the provision was left undefined by the drafters, the right to function freely also includes the right to call conferences and meetings without interference.[84] As regards the right to federate, the Committee has been critical of the need for approval from the authorities for trade unions to join an international organisation.[85]

In addition to the rights which are explicitly said to be held by organisations, the right under Article 8(a) to form trade unions and join the trade union of one's choice and the right to strike under Article 8(d) might include corporate elements. The right under Article 8(a) to form trade unions and join the trade union of one's choice, 'subject only to the rules of the organization concerned', implies the

---

[78] Craven's own comment is that it would be preferable if the collective right to federate had been inferred from the individual right, since this would mean that the individual right would prevail in case of conflict. *Ibid.*, pp. 255–256.

[79] Unfortunately, no General Comment has been adopted regarding Article 8.

[80] E/C.12/1/Add.46, *Concluding Observations*, 1 September 2000, para. 35.

[81] E/C.12/1/Add.7/Rev.1, *Concluding Observations*, 6 December 1996, para. 17.

[82] E/C.12/1990/SR.40, para. 63, cited in Craven, *The International Covenant on Economic, Social and Cultural Rights*, p. 273.

[83] *Ibid.*, para. 9 and E/C.12/1/Add.59, *Concluding Observations*, 21 May 2001, para. 39, and E/C.12/1/Add.9.

[84] Craven, *The International Covenant on Economic, Social and Cultural Rights*, p. 256.

[85] E/C.12/1987/SR.6, para. 45, cited in Craven, *The International Covenant on Economic, Social and Cultural Rights*, p. 273.

150 LEGAL AND EMPIRICAL SURVEY

organisation right of trade unions to establish internal rules and maintain control over their own membership.[86] The right to strike seems to include both an individual and an organisation right.[87]

The Covenant should also be examined in order to consider the question to what extent there is evidence that the state parties to the Covenant are under a legal obligation towards the organisations under international law. The general obligation of state parties to implement the ICESCR is articulated in Article 2(1):

Each State Party to the present Covenant undertakes to take steps, individually and through international assistance and co-operation, especially economic and technical, to the maximum of its available resources, with a view to achieving progressively the full realization of the rights recognized in the present Covenant by all appropriate means, including particularly the adoption of legislative measures.

The Committee on Economic, Social and Cultural Rights has adopted two General Comments relating to state party obligation, one on *The Domestic Application of the Covenant* (*General Comment 9*) and one on *The Nature of States Parties Obligations* (*General Comment 3*).[88] The differences between the ICCPR and the ICESCR as to the nature of party obligations have been given a clear expression in the respective treaty texts. As regards the phrase in Article 2(1) regarding steps 'with a view to achieving progressively the full realisation of the rights recognized', the Committee observes that the concept of progressive realisation constitutes a recognition of the fact that full realisation of all rights in the Covenant will generally not be able to be achieved in a short period of time, and that in this sense the obligation differs significantly from that contained in Article 2 of the ICCPR, which embodies an immediate obligation to respect and ensure all of the relevant rights. Nevertheless, the Committee observes that the phrase:

must be read in the light of the overall objective, indeed the raison d'être, of the Covenant which is to establish clear obligations for States parties in respect of the full realization of the rights in question. It thus imposes an obligation to move as expeditiously and effectively as possible towards that goal.[89]

---

[86] Craven, *The International Covenant on Economic, Social and Cultural Rights*, p. 266.
[87] *Ibid.*, p. 278.
[88] Committee on Economic, Social and Cultural Rights, *General Comment 9* and *General Comment 3*, in HRI/GEN/1/Rev.5, *Compilation of General Comments*, 26 April 2001, pp. 58–62, 18–21.
[89] Committee on Economic, Social and Cultural Rights, *General Comment 3*, 14 December 1990, para. 9, in HRI/GEN/1/Rev.5, p. 20.

Furthermore, the Committee stresses that some of the obligations undertaken by state parties are of immediate effect:

In particular, while the Covenant provides for progressive realization and acknowledges the constraints due to the limits of available resources, it also imposes various obligations which are of immediate effect.[90]

The undertaking to guarantee that relevant rights will be exercised without discrimination was mentioned as an example of an obligation of 'immediate effect', but the Committee did not specify all such obligations.[91] As for the obligation relating to the rights contained in Article 8, it should be noted that it is specifically stated in the Article that the states parties *undertake to ensure* these rights. This can be compared with the provisions guaranteeing rights which are of the type which require substantial economic resources, such as the right to an adequate standard of living, which all include the phrase 'The State parties to the present Covenant recognize the right ...' The expression 'undertake to respect and ensure' is used in the ICCPR, which pronounces an immediate obligation.[92] It can therefore be concluded that the Committee regarded all obligations phrased in the former way, and thus including Article 8, to be of 'immediate effect'.[93]

As to the domestic application of the Covenant, the Committee on Economic, Social and Cultural Rights discussed this issue in its *General Comment 9*. The Committee noted that the Covenant does not stipulate the means by which it is to be implemented in national law and that there is no provision obligating its comprehensive incorporation.[94] Nevertheless, the Committee holds the opinion that:

while the Covenant does not formally oblige States to incorporate its provisions in domestic law, such an approach is desirable. Direct incorporation avoids problems that might arise in the translation of treaty obligations into national law, and provides a basis for the direct invocation of the Covenant rights by individuals in national courts. For these reasons, the Committee strongly encourages formal adoption or incorporation of the Covenant in national law.[95]

The Committee thus advocates a development of national legal systems towards incorporating the rights provisions. It specifically mentions

---

[90] *Ibid.*, para. 1, p. 18.   [91] *Ibid.*   [92] See Article 2(1).
[93] This view is supported by Craven, *The International Covenant on Economic, Social and Cultural Rights*, p. 261. See also Nowak, 'UN Covenant', p. 372.
[94] Committee on Economic, Social and Cultural Rights, *General Comment 9*, para. 5, in HRI/GEN/1/Rev.5, *Compilation of General Comments*, 26 April 2001, p. 59.
[95] *Ibid.*, para. 8, p. 60.

152   LEGAL AND EMPIRICAL SURVEY

that 'It is especially important to avoid any a priori assumption that the norms should be considered to be non-self-executing', and points to the fact that many of the treaty provisions are specific enough to be applied directly in national courts.[96] In this context, it should be noted that Article 8 on trade union rights is one of the more specific rights in the Covenant. Furthermore, through the reference made in para. 3 to the ILO Convention 1948 on the Freedom of Association, there is a body of international rules which can complement and specify Article 8 of the ICESCR.

The only supervisory mechanism in operation under the Covenant is the submission under Article 16 of state party reports on the measures which they have adopted and the progress made in achieving the observance of the Covenant rights for consideration by the Committee on Economic, Social and Cultural rights. A draft Optional Protocol for the submission of individual communications is still under consideration in the Commission on Human Rights. According to the proposed text for Article 2, 'Any individual or group claiming to be a victim of a violation' may submit a communication to the Committee for examination.[97] The issue whether organisations as such can be considered to be victims of violations of the rights set forth in the ICESCR is not discussed in the Committee's report on the Protocol.[98] If and when the Protocol enters into force, and if organisations are given *locus standi* within the complaints system, the evidence of state party obligation towards the rights-holders on the international plane will be fairly strong. Bearing in mind the quasi-judicial character of the mechanism, however, the organisation rights under the Covenant will not be fully instrumental for trade unions which seek to defend their interests on the international level.

The UN Declaration on Human Rights Defenders

The Declaration on the Right and Responsibility of Individuals, Groups and Organs of Society to Promote and Protect Universally Recognized Human Rights and Fundamental Freedoms was adopted by consensus by the UN General Assembly in December 1998 after a negotiation

---

[96] It also pointed out that attempts during the drafting process to include a specific provision in the Covenant to the effect that it be considered 'non-self-executing' were strongly rejected. *Ibid.*, para. 11, p. 61.

[97] E/CN.4/1997/105, *Status of the International Covenants on Human Rights*, 18 December 1996, Annex, para. 31.

[98] *Ibid.*, paras. 19–20. For a more elaborate description of the Draft, see section 5.2.

RIGHTS AND OBLIGATIONS   153

process of thirteen years.[99] Although it is a legally non-binding document, it can be observed that it specifically refers to the rights of individuals in relation to NGOs. The Declaration does not explicitly pronounce rights pertaining to NGOs as such; nevertheless, organisation rights are implied in the text considering that all the rights formulated are bestowed on 'everyone, individually and in association with others'.[100]

The most important right from an NGO perspective is Article 5, which provides that:

For the purpose of promoting and protecting human rights and fundamental freedoms, everyone has the right, individually and in association with others, at the national and international levels:

    a.   To meet or assemble peacefully;
    b.   To form, join and participate in non-governmental organizations, associations or groups;
    c.   To communicate with non-governmental or intergovernmental organizations.

Other rights closely connected to the activities of NGOs include:

- The right to seek, obtain, receive and hold information about all human rights and fundamental freedoms (Article 6a)
- The right freely to publish, impart or disseminate to others views, information and knowledge on all human rights and fundamental freedoms (Article 6b)
- The right to submit to governmental bodies and agencies and organisations concerned with public affairs criticism and proposals for improving their functioning (Article 8, para. 2)
- The right to offer and provide professionally qualified legal assistance or other relevant advice and assistance in defending human rights and fundamental freedoms (Article 9, para. 3c)
- The right to unhindered access to and communication with international bodies with general or special competence to receive and consider communications on matters of human rights and fundamental freedoms (Article 9, para. 4).

---

[99] A/RES/53/144, *Declaration on the Right and Responsibility of Individuals, Groups and Organs of Society*, 8 March 1999.

[100] The delegation of the United Kingdom to the Working Group which drafted the Declaration, however, specifically stated that the rights included in a proposed Article 3 (on the right to participate in peaceful activities against violations of human rights) were 'those of individuals, exercisable individually or in association with others, rather than of groups as such'. E/CN.4/1993/64, *Drafting of a Declaration*, 1 March 1993, para. 35.

154 LEGAL AND EMPIRICAL SURVEY

Many of the activities mentioned in the Articles are usually performed within the framework of an NGO, and have certainly been created in order to protect their work.

In April 2000, the Commission on Human Rights established the mandate of a Special Representative of the Secretary-General on Human Rights Defenders.[101] The Special Representative receives communications about violations against human rights defenders from, *inter alia*, any individual, group, or NGO with reliable knowledge of such violations.[102] The overwhelming majority of communications sent by the Special Representative to governments concern cases in which human rights defenders have been targeted in their capacity as members of NGOs. Many violations of the rights contained in the Declaration are regarded by the Representative as violations against NGOs, rather than violations committed against individuals.[103]

The ILO Conventions

The ILO has adopted more than 180 conventions covering a broad range of subjects within the area of labour law. It is not possible to review all the conventions within the framework of the present study in order to identify organisation rights. I have therefore concentrated on the conventions which have been recognised by the ILO Governing Body as fundamental conventions, since they are of a general nature and should be implemented and ratified by all member states of the ILO.[104] According to the ILO Declaration on Fundamental Principles and Rights at Work (1998), all member states of the ILO have an obligation arising from their membership to respect and realise four principles concerning the rights contained in the fundamental conventions, of which the first is the right to freedom of association and the effective recognition of the

---

[101] E/CN.4/RES/2000/61, *Human Rights Defenders*, 27 April 2000, para. 3.
[102] E/CN.4/2004/94, *Promotion and Protection of Human Rights: Human Rights Defenders*, 15 January 2005, para. 25.
[103] *Ibid.*, para. 27 and Summary.
[104] This decision was taken by the ILO Governing Body in 1995. The Conventions are Nos. 29 (Forced Labour Convention), 87 (Freedom of Association and Protection of the Right to Organise Convention), 98 (Right to Organise and Collective Bargaining Convention), 100 (Equal Remuneration Convention), 105 (Abolition of Forced Labour Convention), 111 (Discrimination Convention), 138 (Minimum Age Convention) and 182 (Worst Forms of Child Labour Convention), the latter having been added after its adoption in 1999. *General Report of the Committee of Experts on the Application of Conventions and Recommendations*, 2001, 89th Session, para. 62.

right to collective bargaining.[105] The principle thus corresponds to the subject matters of the two ILO conventions of primary interest for trade unions and other NGOs, namely the Freedom of Association and Protection of the Right to Organise Convention (No. 87) of 1948 and the Right to Organise and Collective Bargaining Convention of 1949 (No. 98).

The Freedom of Association and Protection of the Right to Organise Convention has been ratified by 142 states.[106] It protects not only the rights of individual workers and employers to establish and join organisations, but also the rights of workers' and employers' organisations.[107] Article 3 reads:

Workers' and employers' organisations shall have the right to draw up their constitutions and rules, to elect their representatives in full freedom, to organise their administration and activities and to formulate their programmes.[108]

The ILO Committee of Experts on the Application of Conventions and Recommendations has stated that in order for the right to draw up a constitution and rules to be fully guaranteed, national legislation should lay down formal requirements only as regards trade union constitutions, and constitutions should not be subject to prior approval at the discretion of the public authorities.[109] The right of workers' and employers' organisations to organise their administration and activities and formulate their programmes includes, *inter alia*, the right to hold trade union meetings, the right of trade union officers to have access to places of work, the right to strike and, in general, any activity involved in the defence of members' rights.[110] In practice, the difficulties most

---

[105] ILO Declaration on Fundamental Principles and Rights at Work, 86th Session, June 1998, para. 2.

[106] As of October 2004. Information obtained at the ILO database ILOLEX at www.ilo.org/ilolex/english/newratframeE.htm.

[107] This part of the study focuses on the existence of organisation rights in international law, rather than on the material content of rights. For a thorough examination of the material content of the right of workers to freedom of association, see Petra Herzfeld Olsson, *Facklig föreningsfrihet som mänsklig rättighet* (*The Workers' Freedom of Association as a Human Right*), Uppsala: Iustus Förlag, 2003.

[108] The convention is co-ordinated with ICCPR and its Article 22 on the right to freedom of association through a provision in ICCPR Article 22(3), stating that nothing in Article 22 of ICCPR shall authorise state parties to the ILO Convention on the Freedom of Association and Protection of the Right to Organise Convention to take legislative measures which would prejudice the guarantees provided for in that Convention.

[109] Report of the Committee of Experts on the Application of Conventions and Recommendations, *Freedom of Association and Collective Bargaining*, International Labour Conference, 81st session, Geneva, 1994, para. 109.

[110] *Ibid.*, para. 128.

156   LEGAL AND EMPIRICAL SURVEY

frequently encountered in national legislation concern restrictions or prohibition of political activities and the right to strike.[111] Other organisation rights enunciated in the Freedom of Association and Protection of the Right to Organise Convention include the right of workers' and employers' organisations not to be liable to be dissolved or suspended by administrative authority (Article 4) and the right of these organisations to establish or join federations (Article 5).

The rights-holding organisations are also subjected to obligations under the Convention. According to Article 8, workers and employers and their respective organisations shall respect the law of the land in exercising the rights provided for in the Convention:

> The general obligation of the contracting parties is formulated in Article 1: Each Member of the International Labour Organisation for which this Convention is in force undertakes to give effect to the following provisions.

The general obligation in Article 1 is reflected in Article 8(2), stating that 'the law of the land shall not be such as to impair, nor shall it be so applied as to impair, the guarantees provided for in this Convention'. More specific obligations are included in Article 3(2), according to which the public authorities shall refrain from any interference which would restrict the rights to draw up constitution and rules, etc. under para. 1, and in Article 7, which provides that the acquisition of legal personality by workers' and employers' organisations shall not be subject to conditions which would restrict the application of the rights guaranteed by Articles 2, 3 and 4 of the Convention.

The Right to Organise and Collective Bargaining Convention of 1949 (No. 98) includes a mixture of, on the one hand, provisions phrased as individual or organisation rights, and, on the other, provisions containing more or less detailed instructions for contracting states to establish machinery and take other measures to promote the objectives formulated in the Convention. The direct rights formulated deal with different aspects of the right to organise. Under Article 2, 'workers' and employers' organisations shall enjoy adequate protection against any acts of interference by each other or each other's agents or members in their establishment, functioning or administration'. Paragraph 2 of the same Article provides examples of acts of interference, such as those which are designed to promote the establishment of workers' organisations under the domination of employers or employers' organisations.

---

[111] *Ibid.*, para. 57.

Article 3 provides that state parties shall establish 'machinery appropriate to national conditions', where necessary, for the purpose of ensuring respect for the right to organise. The Committee of Experts has stated that, in order to ensure that the measures are effective in practice, 'national legislation should explicitly lay down these substantive provisions, as well as appeals and sanctions in order to guarantee their application'.[112]

A convention of particular interest to organisations of workers and employers, although it is not one of the eight fundamental ILO Conventions, is the Tripartite Consultation Convention of 1976 (No. 144). States which become parties to the Convention undertake to establish procedures for consultations with workers' and employers' organisations in relation to different ILO activities, such as reporting on the implementation of ILO Conventions and proposals for the denunciation of ratified Conventions, on a yearly or more frequent basis (Article 5).[113] The Articles are not formulated as direct organisation rights, but rather as obligations undertaken by state parties. Other conventions include obligations of a similar kind, for example the Equal Remuneration Convention of 1951 (No. 100), which provides that 'Each Member shall co-operate as appropriate with the employers' and workers' organisations concerned for the purpose of giving effect to the provisions of this Convention'.

The question of evidence of a legal obligation on state parties towards the rights-holding organisations on the international plane is somewhat special in the case of ILO conventions. Although workers' and employers' organisations do not have direct access to a tribunal which can adopt legally binding decisions, but only to a complaints mechanism, it should be kept in mind that the ILO is a tripartite body, where representatives of workers' and employers' organisations participate on an equal footing with state representatives in the work of the ILO, including in the drafting of legal instruments.[114] The traditional international–national divide of international law, according to which the domain of private organisations is the domestic plane and national legislation, therefore does not seem to describe the area of international labour law appropriately. Another factor of interest to the question of

---

[112] *Ibid.*, para. 232.
[113] See also *Consultation Recommendation No. 113* of the ILO General Conference, 44th session, 1960.
[114] See section 7.3.

158   LEGAL AND EMPIRICAL SURVEY

international legal obligation towards workers' and employers' organisations is that all member states of the ILO are considered bound by at least the basic rights related to the freedom of association and collective bargaining, irrespective of whether they have ratified the conventions on these subjects.

As for the international supervision of compliance with the rights of workers' and employers' organisations, there are two categories of procedures which may be actualised.

First, the *regular system of supervision* includes the submission of government reports and their examination. According to Article 22 of the ILO Constitution, each of the members agrees to make an annual report to the ILO on the measures which it has taken to give effect to the provisions of conventions to which it is a party. The report shall be communicated to representative organisations of workers and employers (Articles 3, 23).

Secondly, the *special procedures for supervision* (i.e. those for specific allegations) include three different mechanisms, of which two are accessible for organisations of workers and employers. Article 24 permits an industrial association of employers or workers to make a so-called 'representation' to the ILO claiming that a given member state has failed to apply an ILO Convention to which it is a party. After the examination of complaints by an *ad hoc* committee, the Governing Body considers the report in private.[115] It may decide to publish the report or to initiate a complaint under Article 26 of the Constitution. After a procedure of examination involving a commission of inquiry, the complaint may eventually be referred by the government(s) concerned to the ICJ for final decision.[116] The Article 26 procedure, which is also accessible to member states, has only seldom been used, and has never resulted in a decision by the ICJ.[117]

In addition, the International Labour Conference set up two new procedures in the 1950s, since the failure of many states to ratify Conventions Nos. 87 and 98 made it impossible to supervise their application under the other mechanisms. One of these is the Fact-Finding and Conciliation Commission on Freedom of Association, which examines

---

[115] For details of this procedure, see the *Standing Orders Concerning the Procedure for the Examination of Representations under Articles 24 and 25 of the Constitution of the International Labour Organization.*

[116] See further Articles 27–34 of the ILO Constitution.

[117] One example of a complaint submitted by workers' delegates is GB.281/8, *Complaint Concerning the Non-Observance by Colombia*, June 2001.

complaints referred to it by the ILO Governing Body. The Commission is essentially an investigatory body, but may also examine the possibilities of settling problems by agreement. It may examine complaints regarding states which have or have not ratified the ILO conventions on freedom of association; in the latter case, however, only with the consent of the state concerned.[118] The Commission has only rarely been convened.[119]

More importantly, complaints of alleged breaches of trade union rights are examined by the Committee on Freedom of Association, which was established in 1951 as a tripartite body following a decision by the ILO Governing Body.[120] This procedure is more elaborately described later in this book.[121] The Committee receives complaints concerning ILO member states which may or may not have ratified the ILO's freedom of association conventions.[122] The Committee can recommend an examination by the Governing Body, which may communicate the Committee's conclusions to the government concerned.

The general question of direct applicability of the rights in the ILO Labour Conventions has been addressed by the Committee of Experts, which has stated that 'Most of the Conventions do not consist of provisions directly prescribing to a citizen that he shall do or leave undone a particular act, but are rather addressed to the country as such, and oblige it to deal with a particular question in a particular way'.[123] The organisation rights in the Freedom of Association and Protection of the Right to Organise Convention and the Right to Organise and Collective Bargaining Convention are, however, relatively specific in their character compared to provisions of a more programmatic character in

---

[118] The ILO Conventions on freedom of association include, apart from the above described Conventions Nos. 87 and 98, No. 11 (Right of Association, 1921), No. 135 (Workers' Representatives Convention, 1971), No. 141 (Rural Workers' Organisations Convention, 1975), No. 151 (Labour Relations Convention) and No. 154 (Collective Bargaining Convention, 1981).

[119] Report of the Committee of Experts on the Application of Conventions and Recommendations, *Freedom of Association and Collective Bargaining*, International Labour Conference, 81st session, Geneva, 1994, paras. 17–18. According to the ILO website (at www.ilo.org/public/english/standards/norm/enforced/foa/index.htm), it had only examined six cases as of November 2004.

[120] *ILO Law on Freedom of Association: Standards and Procedures*, Geneva: International Labour Office, 1995, p. 128.

[121] See section 5.2.

[122] The procedures for examining the complaints are, however, different depending on whether the member state which is criticised has ratified the conventions or not, see *ILO Law on Freedom of Association*, p. 129.

[123] International Labour Conference, 47th Session, *General Report of the Committee of Experts on the Application of Conventions and Recommendations*, 1963, para. 22.

160 LEGAL AND EMPIRICAL SURVEY

other conventions – for instance, the Social Policy Convention of 1947 (No. 82).[124] It is clear that the obligations of contracting states under both Conventions are absolute, as the provisions are not programmatic or progressive. Still, both conventions include provisions specifically addressed to the problem of incompatibility of national law with international law, which seems to reflect the intention of the General Conference of the ILO not to make the conventions directly applicable. In the case of the Right to Organise and Collective Bargaining Convention, this assumption is supported by the Committee of Experts' statement that national 'legislation should explicitly lay down these substantive provisions'.[125]

It can be concluded that the evidence of an international legal obligation of ILO member states towards the holders of the organisation rights guaranteed by the ILO conventions is relatively strong. The rights are specific to their character and correspond to an absolute and immediate legal obligation. The organisation rights set forth are connected with a number of different procedures for supervision. Although the procedures usually do not lead to binding decisions, complaints made by organisations of workers or employers in accordance with Article 24 of the ILO Constitution may eventually – at least hypothetically – lead to a decision by the ICJ. This fact, taken together with the ILO tripartite structure and the practice of examining of complaints concerning states which have not ratified the Conventions on Freedom of Association, underline the international obligation towards the rights-holders.[126]

The Aarhus Convention

The Convention on Access to Information, Public Participation in Decision-Making and Access to Justice in Environmental Matters was adopted in 1998 by the Fourth Ministerial Conference 'Environment for Europe' of the UN Economic Commission for Europe and entered into force in October 2001.[127] The Convention, which is also known as the

---

[124] But there are also, on the other hand, more specific conventions, e.g., the Prevention of Major Industrial Accidents Convention (No. 174, 1993).

[125] Report of the Committee of Experts on the Application of Conventions and Recommendations, *Freedom of Association and Collective Bargaining*, International Labour Conference, 81st session, Geneva, 1994, para. 232.

[126] In addition, a withdrawal by a state from the ILO does not cancel the obligations of a state arising from ratification of a convention, ILO Constitution, Article 1(5).

[127] The Convention was adopted in Aarhus, Denmark, on 25 June 1998, see ECE/CEP/43, 21 April 1998.

Aarhus Convention, links environmental rights with human rights by focusing on the interaction between public authorities and the public in a democratic context. While other environmental treaties adopted during the 1990s formulate participatory rights for NGOs and other parts of civil society as regards certain specified fields of environmental law – such as to combat desertification – the Aarhus Convention deals with public participation as such.[128] In the perspective of a study on the legal status of NGOs in international law, the Convention is therefore of particular interest:[129] Article 1 of the Convention clarifies the objective of the treaty:

> In order to contribute to the protection of the right of every person of present and future generations to live in an environment adequate to his or her health and well-being, each Party shall guarantee the rights of access to information, public participation in decision-making, and access to justice in environmental matters in accordance with the provisions of this Convention.

The two main addressees of rights under the Convention are 'the public' and 'the public concerned'. These two concepts are both defined in the Convention as inclusive of NGOs. 'The public' is specified as 'one or more natural or legal persons, and, in accordance with national legislation or practice, their associations, organizations or groups'. 'The public concerned' is defined as 'the public affected or likely to be affected by, or having interest in, the environmental decision-making; for the purposes of this definition, non-governmental organizations promoting environmental protection and meeting any requirements under national law shall be deemed to have an interest'.[130] In other words, NGOs which promote environmental interests are regarded as legitimate spokespersons of the public and holders of all rights which the Convention bestows on 'the public' and 'the public concerned', irrespective of their connection to the particular environmental matter at stake.

---

[128] See, e.g., the UN Convention to Combat Desertification (1994), Articles 3(c), 10(f), 13(b), 14(2) and 16(d), the Framework Convention on Climate Change, Articles 4(1)(i) and 7(2.1), the Convention on Biological Diversity (1992), Article 23(5), and further Alexandre Kiss and Dinah Shelton, *International Environmental Law*, 2nd edn., New York: Transnational Publishers, 2000, pp. 135–137. For a general survey of citizen's right of access to information and participation in international law on the environment and development, see Philippe Sands and Jakob Werksman, 'Procedural Aspects of International Law in the Field of Sustainable Development: Citizens' Rights', in Konrad Ginther *et al.* (eds.), *Sustainable Development and Good Governance*, Dordrecht: Martinus Nijhoff, 1998, pp. 178–204.

[129] For general information on the Aarhus Convention, see Kiss and Shelton, *International Environmental Law*, pp. 156–159.

[130] Articles 2(4) and 2(5).

162   LEGAL AND EMPIRICAL SURVEY

Article 3 contains general provisions. One example of such a provision of particular interest for NGOs is Article 3(4):

each Party shall provide for appropriate recognition of and support to associations, organizations or groups promoting environmental protection and ensure that its national legal system is consistent with this obligation.

It can be observed that this provision does not explicitly state rights for NGOs and groups, but expresses the obligations of state parties in relation to these actors. However, the focus of this provision on the obligations of state parties should be seen in the light of the explicit mention of the overarching rights of access to information, public participation in decision-making and access to justice in environmental matters as guaranteed in Article 1.[131] As was concluded in section 4.1, a duty on state parties towards an actor has a necessary correlative in the right of the actor towards state parties.[132] It is thus clear that the Aarhus Convention indeed formulates rights for NGOs, such as the right to appropriate recognition and support by state parties to the Convention under Article 3(4).[133]

The more specific rights which are bestowed on the 'public concerned' include the right to be informed at an early stage of environmental decision-making procedure of, *inter alia*, the proposed activity, the nature of possible decisions and the public authority responsible for making the decision.[134] In the context of environmental decision-making procedures, 'the public' shall be allowed to submit comments, information, analyses or opinions that it considers relevant to each activity.[135] Members of the public shall also have access to administrative or judicial procedures to challenge acts and omissions by private

---

[131] Moreover, Article 3 contains a general provision on non-discrimination which is formulated as a right: 'Within the scope of the relevant provisions of this Convention, the public shall have access to information, have the possibility to participate in decision-making and have access to justice in environmental matters without discrimination as to citizenship, nationality or domicile and, in the case of a legal person, without discrimination as to where it has its registered seat or an effective centre of its activities.'

[132] See section 4.1.

[133] See also Ebbesson, who notes that 'while formally addressed to states, these international norms are ultimately directed at individuals through the intermediary of national institutions', Jonas Ebbesson, 'The Notion of Public Participation in International Environmental Law', 8 *Yearbook of International Environmental Law* (1997), p. 55.

[134] Article 6(2 a–c).   [135] Article 6(7).

persons and public authorities which contravene provisions of the national law relating to the environment.[136]

The rights-based approach of the Convention is clearly expressed in Article 1, cited above. Article 3 specifies the obligation of state parties in an absolute manner. The state parties to the Convention 'shall', for instance, take the necessary legislative, regulatory and other measures and provide for appropriate recognition of and support to associations, organisations or groups promoting environmental protection and ensure that its national legal system is consistent with this obligation. In the implementation guide to the Aarhus Convention, it is observed that:

Whereas most multilateral environmental agreements cover obligations that Parties have to each other, the Aarhus Convention covers obligations that Parties have to the public. It goes further than any other convention in imposing clear obligations on Parties and public authorities towards the public as far as access to information, public participation and access to justice are concerned.[137]

In comparing obligations that state parties have *vis-à-vis* each other with obligations that they have to the public, the implementation guide expresses rather clearly that the obligations state parties have under the Aarhus Convention towards the public, including NGOs, are intended to lie on the international level, thus creating corresponding international rights. That the Convention creates rights for NGOs directly under international law is also supported by the establishment of a compliance mechanism accessible for NGOs. The Compliance Committee which has been established under Article 15 of the Convention receives communications regarding state parties' compliance with the Convention from, *inter alia*, NGOs.[138] If the Committee determines that the state party concerned is or has been failing to comply with the Convention, it can recommend the Meeting of State Parties to take different measures, such as provide advice, make recommendations, issue declarations of non-compliance, issue cautions, and/or suspend the special rights and privileges accorded to the party concerned under

---

[136] Article 9(3).

[137] Economic Commission for Europe, *The Aarhus Convention: An Implementation Guide*, ECE/CEP/72, United Nations Sales Publication, 2000, p. 1.

[138] ECE/MP.PP/2/Add.8, *Report of the First Meeting of the Parties, Addendum, Decision I/7, Review of Compliance*, 2 April 2004. The procedure set up according to this decision is further described in section 5.3.

164   LEGAL AND EMPIRICAL SURVEY

the Convention.[139] Although the compliance mechanism is of a quasi-judicial character, it is thus relatively strong. State parties also undertake to submit reports on their implementation of the Convention to the Meeting of State Parties, which reviews these reports.[140]

It can thus be concluded that the Aarhus Convention creates rights for NGOs directly under international law. These rights include the right to recognition of and support to NGOs promoting environmental protection, the right to access to information, the right to participation in decision-making and the right to access to justice in environmental matters. The Aarhus Convention seems to be another step towards a growing recognition of the importance of public participation in international environmental law.[141] Agenda 21 had already recognised that 'non-governmental organizations play a vital role in the shaping and implementation of participatory democracy' and stated that 'the fullest possible communication and cooperation between international organizations, national and local governments and non-governmental organizations should be promoted in institutions mandated, and programmes designed to carry out Agenda 21'.[142]

The European Convention on the Recognition of the Legal Personality of International Non-Governmental Organisations

The European Convention on the Recognition of the Legal Personality of International Non-Governmental Organisations was adopted by the Council of Europe in 1986 and entered into force on 1 January 1991.[143] It still has only ten state parties.[144] According to Article 1 of

---

[139] ECE/MP.PP/2/Add.8, *Report of the First Meeting of the Parties, Addendum, Decision I/7, Review of Compliance*, 2 April 2004, paras. 18 and 37.

[140] Articles 5(4) and 10(2).

[141] See, e.g., *Agenda 21*, A/CONF.151/26, Annex II, *Report of the United Nations Conference on Environment and Development*, 1992, para. 23.2 (on 'broad public participation in decision-making' as 'One of the fundamental prerequisites for the achievement of sustainable development'); Ebbesson, 'The Notion of Public Participation', pp. 51 ff., Daniel Bodansky, 'The Legitimacy of International Governance: A Coming Challenge for International Environmental Law?', 93 AJIL (1999), pp. 617–619; and Philippe Sands and Jakob Werksman, 'Procedural Aspects of International Law in the Field of Sustainable Development: Citizens' Rights', in Konrad Ginther *et al.* (eds.), *Sustainable Development and Good Governance*, Dordrecht: Martinus Nijhoff, 1998, pp. 178–204.

[142] *Agenda 21*, A/CONF.151/26, II, *Report of the United Nations Conference on Environment and Development*, 1992, paras. 27(1) and (4).

[143] ETS No. 124.

[144] As of 23 October 2004 (according to the Council of Europe Treaty Office at http://conventions.coe.int/Treaty/EN/CadreListeTraites.htm).

the Convention, it applies only to associations, foundations and other private institutions which (a) have a non-profit-making aim of international utility, (b) have been established by an instrument governed by the internal law of a state party, (c) carry on their activities with effect in at least two states, and (d) have their statutory office in the territory of a state party and the central management and control in the territory of that state or of another state party.[145] The requirement that the NGO carries out its activities in at least two states refers to states in general; these need not be state parties of member states of the Council of Europe.[146] The conditions must be met throughout the period of the NGO's activity in a state party.[147]

Article 2 of the Convention provides that

1. The legal personality and capacity, as acquired by an NGO in the Party in which it has its statutory office, shall be recognised as of right in the other Parties.
2. When they are required by essential public interest, restrictions, limitations or special procedures governing the exercise of the rights arising out of the legal capacity and provided for by the legislation of the Party where recognition takes place, shall be applicable to NGOs established in another Party.

According to the Explanatory Report on the Convention, no special procedure has to be followed by an NGO in order for its legal personality and capacity to be recognised in the other state parties, provided that it meets the conditions in Article 1.[148] The principle of the statutory office means that the NGO will have the same legal capacity and personality in all the contracting states as it has in the state where the statutory office is located. There were two reasons for basing the legal personality and capacity of an NGO on the law of the state where it has its statutory office. First, it was held that the NGO had manifested a wish to be subject to a given system of law in deciding on its statutory office, and that this wish should be respected. Secondly, the principle chosen made

---

[145] Concerning these conditions, see section 1.3.

[146] *Explanatory Report on the European Convention on the Recognition of the Legal Personality of International Non-Governmental Organisations*, Strasbourg, 1986, para. 11.

[147] The *Explanatory Report* states: 'Failure to satisfy any of these conditions automatically removes the right to invoke the Convention.' *Ibid.*, para. 24.

[148] *Ibid.*, para. 13.

166   LEGAL AND EMPIRICAL SURVEY

it possible to avoid any break in continuity in the legal personality of an NGO if its real seat changed.[149]

Article 3 specifies the proof of the NGO's existence to be presented to the authorities of the state in which the NGO wishes to be recognised. This evidence includes the NGO's memorandum and articles of association or other basic constitutional instruments, accompanied by documents establishing administrative authorisation, registration or any other form of publicity in the state which granted the legal personality and capacity.[150]

According to Article 4 of the Convention, the application of an NGO may be excluded only if the NGO which invokes it

(a) contravenes national security, public safety, or is detrimental to the prevention of disorder or crime, the protection of health or morals, or the protection of the rights and freedoms of others; or

(b) jeopardises relations with another State or the maintenance of international peace and security.

Article 4 operates independently of Article 1, which means that an NGO can fall under Article 4 even if the conditions in Article 1 are met.[151]

Reservations to the Convention may not be made, but it can be denounced at any time.[152]

Although it is clear that the Convention establishes legally binding obligation for the states which become parties to it, its significance is still limited because of the small number of state parties. It should also be observed that NGOs do not have access to any complaints procedure in cases of breach of the Convention. Nevertheless, the Convention is interesting as a demonstration of how the question of the legal status of NGO can apply outside the state where it is based.

Council of Europe Fundamental Principles on the Status of Non-Governmental Organisations in Europe

The Fundamental Principles on the Status of Non-Governmental Organisations in Europe were adopted by the participants in a series of multilateral meetings held in Strasbourg during 2001 and 2002. The foundation of the Principles had already been laid in an earlier document: the Guidelines to Promote the Development and Strengthening

---

[149] *Ibid.*, para. 14.   [150] See *Explanatory Report*, paras. 19–22.
[151] *Ibid.*, paras. 23–24.   [152] Articles 9, 10.

of NGOs in Europe of 1998.[153] In a decision in April 2003, the Deputies took note with appreciation of the Fundamental Principles and instructed the Secretariat to give them the widest possible circulation.[154]

The Preamble of the Fundamental Principles refers to the European Convention on the Recognition of the Legal Personality of International Non-Governmental Organisations discussed above and to the desirability of enlarging the number of its contracting parties. The Fundamental Principles can be seen as a way to promote such a development, but at the same time the Convention and the Principles have in some ways different scopes and objectives. While the Convention on the Recognition of the Legal Personality of International Non-Governmental Organisations deals with international NGOs which have legal personality under national law, the Fundamental Principles on the Status of Non-Governmental Organisations in Europe seek to promote national legislation which, *inter alia*, assists the setting up of NGOs and lays down arrangements for the acquisition of legal personality, regardless of whether the NGO is national or international in character.[155]

Apart from referring to the Convention on Legal Personality, the Preamble of the Fundamental Principles includes several statements which can put the Principles into context. For example, the Preamble mentions the importance of NGOs in the development, realisation and continued survival of democratic societies, and states that NGOs make an invaluable contribution to the achievement of the aims and principles of the UN Charter and of the Statute of the Council of Europe. The Principles also recognise that the operation of NGOs entails responsibilities as well as rights, among which the rights to freedom of association and to peaceful assembly are specifically mentioned.

The operative part of the Fundamental Principles begins by laying down four basic principles:

1. That NGOs come into being through the initiative of individuals or groups of persons. That the national legal and fiscal framework applicable to them should therefore permit and encourage this initiative.
2. That all NGOs enjoy the right to freedom of expression.

---

[153] *Fundamental Principles on the Status of Non-Governmental Organisations in Europe and Explanatory Memorandum*, Council of Europe, May 2003, *Explanatory Memorandum*, paras. 6–7.

[154] CM/Del/Dec(2003)837, *Decisions Adopted*, Item 2.3, 17 April 2003.

[155] The definition of 'NGO' formulated in the Principles has been discussed in section 1.3.

168 LEGAL AND EMPIRICAL SURVEY

3. That NGOs with legal personality should have the same capacities as are generally enjoyed by other legal persons and be subject to the same administrative, civil and criminal law obligations and sanctions generally applicable to them.
4. That any act or omission by a governmental organ affecting an NGO should be subject to administrative review and be open to challenge in an independent and impartial court with full jurisdiction.[156]

On the basis of the four main principles, rather detailed provisions are formulated on a number of subjects relating to NGOs, such as establishment, statutes, membership, legal personality, property and fund-raising and transparency and accountability.[157]

My purpose in mentioning the Fundamental Principles in the context of the international rights of NGOs is not to discuss the various principles in detail. The Principles are declared in a document which is of a non-binding character and do not in themselves establish international rights for NGOs. However, the elaboration of the document and the acceptance of the Principles expressed by the meeting of the Deputies provides support for the supposition that customary law may be developing among Council of Europe member states with the effect of recognising basic international rights for NGOs (thus not only for their members), such as the right to freedom of association and the right to freedom of expression. From such a point of view, the Principles add support to rights expressed in other European and international instruments, such as the European Convention on Human Rights, the European Convention on the Recognition of the Legal Personality of International Non-Governmental Organisations and the ICCPR.

The European Convention on Human Rights

The European Convention for the Protection of Human Rights and Fundamental Freedoms (ECHR) does not contain any explicit organisation rights.[158] The rights provisions are phrased so that rights are bestowed on 'everyone' or on 'men and women', while the fundamental freedoms include the expression 'no one'. Nevertheless, several rights and freedoms have aspects of organisation rights. This is evidenced by the fact that organisations have instituted cases before the Commission and the Court. As applications are declared admissible only if the victim requirement is met – i.e. if the applicant has been the victim of a

---

[156] *Fundamental Principles on the Status of Non-Governmental Organisations in Europe*, paras. 6–9.
[157] *Ibid.*, paras. 10–78.   [158] ETS No. 005.

violation of one of the rights set out in the Convention – it can be concluded that the Commission and the Court have regarded the applicant organisations as rights-holders in all cases which have been decided on the merits.[159]

The rights to freedom of assembly and association
Article 11(1) of the Convention provides that:

Everyone has the right to freedom of peaceful assembly and to freedom of association with others, including the right to form and to join trade unions for the protection of his interests.

The Court has heard cases regarding both the right to freedom of peaceful assembly and the right to freedom of association. One example of a case where the organisation right to peaceful assembly was at issue is *Plattform 'Ärzte für das Leben'* v. *Austria*.[160] Although the Court did not find a violation of the right to peaceful assembly under Article 11 in this case, the fact that it was decided on the merits and the reasoning of the Court demonstrates that the right to freedom of peaceful assembly can be held by organisations. The Court stated that the right implies both a duty on the part of the state not to interfere and a positive obligation to take reasonable and appropriate measures to enable individuals and associations to enjoy the right to peaceful assembly. Furthermore, the right has a horizontal dimension in that it requires positive measures to be taken in the sphere of relations between individuals and private entities.

The right to freedom of association also includes elements of organisation rights. Harris, O'Boyle and Warbrick observe that the 'association' mentioned in the Article 'is capable of enjoying fundamental rights against the state and will generally have rights and owe duties to its members'.[161] The notion of 'association' has an autonomous meaning under the Convention, meaning that Article 11 can also be called into consideration in relation to an entity which is not recognised as an

---

[159] See Article 34 of the Convention and section 5.3, which includes a survey of cases brought by NGOs before the Court.

[160] *Plattform 'Ärzte für das Leben'* v. *Austria*, 21 June 1988 (see also section 5.3). Judgements and decisions of the Convention monitoring bodies which are accessible in the Council of Europe HUDOC database (at http://hudoc.echr.coe.int/hudoc/) are referred to by title and date only. If the cases are not included in the database, reference is made to a publication.

[161] D. J. Harris, M. O'Boyle and C. Warbrick, *Law of the European Convention on Human Rights*, London: Butterworth, 1995, p. 421.

170   LEGAL AND EMPIRICAL SURVEY

association in national law.[162] The Commission has, however, formulated something like a lowest common denominator by stating that the notion of 'association' presupposes 'a voluntary grouping for a common goal'.[163] The fact that the range of organisations protected under the right to freedom of association is wide is demonstrated by the fact that organisations of many different kinds – political parties, religious congregations and organisations for the promotion of certain ideals or cultural interests, etc. – have been the subject of consideration under Article 11.[164] Professional associations which are instituted by law and which perform public functions have, however, not been considered as associations by the Convention monitoring bodies within the meaning of Article 11.[165] Trade unions are expressly mentioned in the Article, and such organisations have been at issue in several cases.[166]

As to the material content of the organisation right to freedom of association, an absolute obligation on state parties to provide a legal framework for every form of association is outside the scope of Article 11.[167] On the other hand, Van Dijk and van Hoof assert that there is an implied obligation to ensure that national law assigns at least sufficient legal status for an association for it to 'stand up effectively for the interests of their members'.[168] The right to form an association is mentioned expressly only as regards trade unions. However, since the Court has stated that trade union freedom is only 'one form or a special aspect of freedom of association', the right to form an association is implied in

---

[162] P. van Dijk and G. J. H. van Hoof, *Theory and Practice of the European Convention on Human Rights*, 3rd edn., The Hague: Kluwer Law International, 1998, p. 591, and Harris, O'Boyle and Warbrick, *Law of the European Convention*, p. 421. According to Alkema, 'association' is a notion which comprises 'in principle, all kinds of legal persons', which should be interpreted to include any corporate body irrespective of its status in domestic civil law. Evert Alkema, 'Freedom of Associations and Civil Society', 34 *A Yearbook of the European Convention on Human Rights* (1994), pp. 56 and 71.

[163] Opinion of the Commission in the case of *Young, James and Webster* v. *the United Kingdom*, 14 December 1979, para. 167, p. 36, in *Digest of Strasbourg Case-Law Relating to the European Convention on Human Rights*, 3, Cologne: Carl-Heymann-Verlag, 1984, p. 506.

[164] Court judgements which originate in applications brought by non-profit-making legal entities include: *Grande Oriente d'Italia di Palazzo Giustiniani* v. *Italy*, 2 August 2001; *Freedom and Democracy Party (ÖZDEP)* v. *Turkey*, 8 December 1999; *Socialist Party and Others* v. *Turkey*, 25 May 1998; *United Communist Party of Turkey and Others* v. *Turkey*, 30 January 1998; *National Union of Belgian Police* v. *Belgium*, 27 October 1975; and *Swedish Engine Drivers' Union* v. *Sweden*, 6 February 1976. See also section 5.3.

[165] See, e.g., the case of *Le Compte, Van Leuven and De Meyre* v. *Belgium*, 23 June 1981, paras. 64–65.

[166] See below.   [167] Harris, O'Boyle and Warbrick, *Law of the European Convention*, p. 423.

[168] Van Dijk and van Hoof, *Theory and Practice of the European Convention*, p. 600.

RIGHTS AND OBLIGATIONS 171

the right to freedom of association in general.[169] Once the association has been established, the state's obligation is mainly negative – i.e. it has the duty not to interfere with the activities of an association – and infringements of the rights to freedom of association and assembly must be justifiable under Article 11(2).[170]

A general positive obligation to provide organisations with *locus standi* in domestic courts has been rejected by the Commission.[171] The applicant association was refused *locus standi* for an administrative court action against a decision on authorisation for the construction of a nuclear power station. The association invoked grounds of environmental protection and public health. The Commission found that the claim did not involve an assertion of the association's own rights and stated that the right to freedom of association does not include or imply a general right to seize the courts in all matters falling within the ambit of the statutory activities of organisations irrespective of the existence of a legal interest of their own.[172]

As has already been mentioned, the right to form and join trade unions is explicitly included in Article 11.[173] Three examples of court judgements which originated in applications filed by trade unions are *National Union of Belgian Police* v. *Belgium, Swedish Engine Drivers' Union* v. *Sweden,* and *Wilson, National Union of Journalists and Others* v. *the United Kingdom,* which all concerned the right to freedom of association.[174] According to the Commission, the right to form trade unions under

---

[169] *National Union of Belgian Police* v. *Belgium,* 27 October 1975, para. 38. This principle was confirmed in the case of *Young, James and Webster* v. *the United Kingdom,* 13 August 1981, para. 52.

[170] Article 11(2) reads: 'No restrictions shall be placed on the exercise of these rights other than such as are prescribed by law and are necessary in a democratic society in the interests of national security or public safety, for the prevention of disorder or crime, for the protection of health or morals or for the protection of the rights and freedoms of others.'

[171] *X. Association* v. *The Federal Republic of Germany,* 26 D&R (1982), pp. 270–271.

[172] See, by contrast, the case of *Canea Catholic Church* v. *Greece,* 16 December 1997, which concerned the right to a fair trial for organisations which seek to defend their own interests.

[173] In the *Young, James and Webster* case, the Court recalled that 'the right to form and to join trade unions is a special aspect of freedom of association', referring to the *National Union of Belgian Police* judgement of 27 October 1975. *Young, James and Webster* v. *The United Kingdom,* 13 August 1981, para. 52.

[174] *National Union of Belgian Police* v. *Belgium,* 27 October 1975; *Swedish Engine Drivers' Union* v. *Sweden,* 6 February 1976; and *Wilson, National Union of Journalists and Others* v. *the United Kingdom,* 2 July 2002. See also *Young, James and Webster* v. *the United Kingdom,* 13 August 1981 and *A. Union.* v. *Federal Republic of Germany,* 34 D&R (1983), pp. 173–176.

172   LEGAL AND EMPIRICAL SURVEY

Article 11 involves 'the right of trade unions to draw up their own rules, to administer their own affairs and to establish and join trade union federations'.[175] The Court has made it clear that Article 11 also protects the right of a union to be heard during collective bargaining, while not guaranteeing the right have a collective agreement concluded.[176] In general, state parties to have a positive obligation to secure the right of trade unions to strive for the protection of its members' interests. For example, the Court has judged that a state party which permits employers to use financial incentives to induce employees to surrender important union rights fails in its positive obligation under Article 11.[177] The Court's case-law also includes cases which actualise the relationship between a trade union and its members and the state's obligation to regulate these private relationships. In this context, the so-called 'negative freedom of association' – the right of individuals not to be compelled to be a member of an association – has been recognised.[178] In general, it can be observed that the ILO conventions, such as the Freedom of Association and Protection of the Right to Organise Convention (No. 87), have been taken into account by the Convention monitoring bodies in their interpretation of Article 11.[179]

The right to freedom of expression
The right to freedom of expression is guaranteed by Article 10(1) of the Convention:

Everyone has the right to freedom of expression. This right shall include freedom to hold opinions and to receive and impart information and ideas without interference by public authority and regardless of frontiers.

The right to freedom of expression is closely connected with the rights to freedom of peaceful assembly and freedom of association. For NGOs,

---

[175] *Cheall* v. *the United Kingdom*, 42 D&R (1985), p. 185.
[176] *National Union of Belgian Police* v. *Belgium*, 27 October 1975. The Court first expressed the right to be heard as a right belonging to the members: 'In the opinion of the Court, it follows that the members of a trade union have a right, in order to protect their interests, that the trade union should be heard', but continued 'What the Convention requires is that under national law trade unions should be enabled ... to strive for the protection of the members' interests' (para. 39).
[177] *Wilson, National Union of Journalists and Others* v. *the United Kingdom*, 2 July 2002, para. 48.
[178] See, e.g., *Young, James and Webster* v. *The United Kingdom*, 13 August 1981 and *Gustafsson* v. *Sweden*, 25 April 1996.
[179] See, e.g., *Van der Mussele* v. *Belgium*, 23 November 1983, para. 32 ff. and *Sigurdur A. Sigurjónsson* v. *Iceland*, 30 June 1993, para. 35.

RIGHTS AND OBLIGATIONS   173

the activities performed as a consequence of the right to function freely as a separate body will often include the promotion and expression of certain values, ideas or opinions. This connection is demonstrated by the fact that the right to freedom of expression has frequently been at issue in cases brought by non-governmental corporate entities before the Commission and the Court. At least nine cases which actualise issues relating to the right to freedom of expression have been brought by NGOs before the Court, five of which concern publications or activities in the mass media.[180] The cases brought under Article 10 by different forms of juridical persons clearly demonstrate that the Convention monitoring organs accept corporate bodies as victims of violations, and thus holders, of the right to freedom of expression under the Convention.

The right to a fair trial
The right to a fair trial as regards civil proceedings is equally valid for organisations as for individuals. Three examples of cases brought by non-profit entities are *Canea Catholic Church* v. *Greece*, *Procola* v. *Luxembourg*, and *Ekin Association* v. *France*.[181] The case of *Apeh Üldözötteinek Szövetsége and Others* v. *Hungary* is of particular interest to NGOs, as it concerned the question whether the 'right' to register an association came within the scope of Article 6:

The case was instituted before the Commission by an unregistered organisation, APEH, and three Hungarian nationals. The organisation had been denied registration by the Supreme Court as its intended name was contrary to the Civil Code. The applicants alleged, in particular, that the proceedings concerning the registration had been unfair, in breach of Article 6(1) of the Convention.

---

[180] *Informationsverein Lentia & Others* v. *Austria*, 24 November 1993 and 28 November 2002 (friendly settlement); *Otto-Preminger Institut* v. *Austria*, 20 September 1994; *Vereinigung demokratischer Soldaten Österreichs and Gubi* v. *Austria*, 19 December 1994; *Vereniging Weekblad Bluf!* v. *the Netherlands*, 9 February 1995; *Radio ABC* v. *Austria*, 20 October 1997; *Vgt Verein Gegen Tierfabriken* v. *Switzerland*, 28 June 2001; *Ekin Association* v. *France*, 17 July 2001; and *Unabhängige Initiative Informationsvielfalt* v. *Austria*, 26 February 2002. In *Open Door and Dublin Well Woman* v. *Ireland*, 29 October 1992, the applicant was a not-for-profit company. Other cases which concern the right to freedom of expression and which originated in complaints filed by juridical persons include the cases of *The Sunday Times* v. *the United Kingdom* (several judgements); *Observer and Guardian* v. *the United Kingdom*, 26 November 1991; *Bladet Tromsø and Stensaas* v. *Norway*, 20 May 1999; and *Bergens Tidende and Others* v. *Norway*, 2 May 2000. See also section 5.3.

[181] *Canea Catholic Church* v. *Greece*, 16 December 1997; *Procola* v. *Luxembourg*, 28 September 1995; *Ekin Association* v. *France*, 17 July 2001.

174   LEGAL AND EMPIRICAL SURVEY

The Court recalled that, for Article 6(1), in its 'civil' limb, to be applicable there must be a dispute over a 'right' that could be said to be recognised under domestic law. The outcome of the proceedings must also be directly decisive for the civil right in question. In the present case, the 'right' in dispute was the right to register an association for the purposes of the Hungarian Associations Act. The Court observed that, according to that Act, associations obtained their legal existence only by virtue of their court registration. It followed from that rule that an unregistered association constituted only a group of individuals whose position in any civil-law dealings with third parties was very different from that of a legal entity. For the applicants, it was consequently the applicant association's very capacity to become a subject of civil rights and obligations under Hungarian law that was at stake in the registration proceedings. In those circumstances, the Court found that the proceedings complained of concerned the applicant association's civil rights and that Article 6 was thus applicable. The Court concluded that there had been a violation of Article 6(1) as the principle of equality of arms had not been respected in the proceedings.[182]

The right to freedom of religion
This right is protected by Article 9, which provides that:

Everyone has the right to freedom of thought, conscience and religion; this right includes freedom to change his religion or belief and freedom, either alone or in community with others and in public or private, to manifest his religion or belief, in worship, teaching, practice and observance.

Although the Commission originally took the position that the right to freedom of religion and belief was purely individual to its character,[183] this position was changed in 1979 with the case of *X. and Church of Scientology* v. *Sweden*:

When a church body lodges an application under the Convention, it does so in reality, on behalf of its members. It should therefore be accepted that a church body is capable of possessing and exercising the rights contained in Article 9(1) in its own capacity as a representative of its members.[184]

The rights to freedom of belief and religion are not restricted to churches, but can also be held by organisations. In the case of *ISKCON*

---

[182] *Apeh Üldözötteinek Szövetsége and Others* v. *Hungary*, 5 October 2000.
[183] The Commission's earlier view was expressed in the case of *Church of X* v. *the United Kingdom*, in which it stated that 'a corporation being a legal and not a natural person, is incapable of having or exercising the rights mentioned in Article 9, paragraph (1) of the Convention', 29 *Collection of Decisions of the European Commission of Human Rights* (1969), p. 75. It can be observed that the Commission also excluded the possibility that the legal entities possess the right to education under Protocol 1, Article 2.
[184] *X. and Church of Scientology* v. *Sweden*, 16 D&R (1979), p. 70.

et al. v. *the United Kingdom*, one of the applicants was a charity registered in the United Kingdom, the International Society for Krishna Consciousness Ltd (ISKCON). Although the Commission found that the interference with ISKCON's right to freedom of religion could be regarded as 'necessary in a democratic society' and declared the application inadmissible as manifestly ill-founded, it did not question that ISKCON as an organisation was capable of holding such rights.[185] In another case, *Cha'are Shalom Ve Tsedek* v. *France*, the Court found that 'an ecclesiastical or religious body may, as such, exercise on behalf of its adherents the rights guaranteed by Article 9 of the Convention', and that 'ritual slaughter must be considered to be covered by a right guaranteed by the Convention, namely the right to manifest one's religion in observance, within the meaning of Article 9'.[186]

However, according to an older case, not all rights under Article 9 can be held by organisations. In the case of *Verein 'Kontakt-Information-Therapie' (KIT) and Siegfried Hagen* v. *Austria*, the Commission stated that: 'Insofar as Article 9 (Art. 9) is concerned, the Commission considers that a distinction must be made in this respect between the freedom of conscience and the freedom of religion, which can also be exercised by a church as such.'[187] It thus seems that the rights to freedom of thought and to freedom of conscience are both of a purely individual character, which is logical considering their personal character.

---

[185] Application No. 20490/92, *ISKCON and 8 Others* v. *United Kingdom*, 8 March 1994. The organisation also claimed violation of, *inter alia*, its right to peaceful enjoyment of one's possessions under Protocol 1, Article 1 taken alone and in conjunction with Article 14 of the Convention. See also Application No. 20471/92, *Kustannus Oy Vapaa Ajattelija AB, Vapaa-Ajattelijain Liitto – Fritänkarnas Förbund RY and Kimmo Sundström* v. *Finland*, and van Dijk and van Hoof, *Theory and Practice of the European Convention*, p. 552.

[186] *Cha'are Shalom Ve Tsedek* v. *France*, 27 June 2000, paras. 72 and 74. The Court did, however, not find a violation of Article 9 alone or taken together with Article 14 on the prohibition of discrimination, as had been alleged.

[187] Application No. 11921/86, *Verein 'Kontakt-Information-Therapie' (KIT) and Siegfried Hagen* v. *Austria*, para. 1. In the case of *Grande Oriente D'italia Di Palazzo Giustiniani* v. *Italy*, the Court declared that an application brought by an association was inadmissible under Articles 8, 9 and 10, alone and in conjunction with Articles 13 or 14. The case concerned a regional law laying down the principles governing appointments to public offices. The law required candidates for those offices to produce a declaration certifying that they were not freemasons. Acting through its Grand Master, the association complained of the prejudice caused it by the law in question. This decision might seem inconsistent with the above cases on freedom of religion. However, as the alleged violation concerned candidates for public office, it is logical that only individuals could be regarded as victims. The association was accepted as applicant as concerned the right to freedom of association, see judgement of 2 August 2001.

176   LEGAL AND EMPIRICAL SURVEY

The right to respect for private life
Article 8(1) reads: 'Everyone has the right to respect for his private and family life, his home and his correspondence.' In a decision on inadmissibility, the Court has discussed whether a private association may be entitled to protection under Article 8. It stated that:

> the question nevertheless arises whether the applicant association can claim to be a victim of the alleged violation of its right to respect for its 'home' ... The Court recalls that to interpret the words 'private life' and 'home' as including certain professional or business activities or premises would be consonant with the essential object and purpose of Article 8, namely to protect the individual against arbitrary interference by the public authorities ... It may therefore be arguable that a legal person may rely on the right to respect for its 'home' where the premises, on which it carries out its business activities or – in the case of the applicant association – its activities with an idealistic goal, are subject to interference.

Thus, although Article 8 may at first sight seem to be of a purely individual character, it appears that organisations enjoy the right to respect for their premises.[188]

The right to peaceful enjoyment of one's possessions
Article 1 of the First Protocol to the European Convention protects the right to property. The first sentence of Article 1 reads: 'Every natural or legal person is entitled to the peaceful enjoyment of his possessions.' This is the only Convention right which expressly mentions juridical persons as holders. The victim requirement stated in Article 34 on the standing of non-state actors before the Court is equally upheld as regards the right to property, meaning that the property of the legal person and its individual shareholders or members are seen as separate issues.[189] Corporate bodies which have brought cases before the Convention monitoring organs have included a large number of companies, but also non-commercial entities such as trade unions and religious congregations. One example of the latter category is the case of *Holy Monasteries* v. *Greece*, which originated in applications brought by eight Greek Orthodox monasteries.[190] Accordingly, NGOs have the right

---

[188] *Verein Netzwerk* v. *Austria*, Admissibility decision, 29 June 1999.
[189] Harris, O'Boyle and Warbrick, *Law of the European Convention*, p. 517.
[190] *Holy Monasteries* v. *Greece*, 9 December 1994. See also, e.g., *Canea Catholic Church* v. *Greece*, 16 December 1997 (in which the Court, however, found it unnecessary to examine the allegations regarding the right to property), *National Federation of Self-Employed* v. *The United Kingdom*, 15 D&R (1979), pp. 198–203 and *Greek Federation of Customs Officers et al.* v. *Greece*, 81-B D&R (1995), pp. 123–129.

to peaceful enjoyment of their possessions under Protocol 1 to the Convention.

The legal nature of rights under the European Convention
In examining the legal nature of organisation rights under the Convention, the standing of NGOs under Article 34 (former Article 25) seems to provide a clear answer to the question. As already mentioned, in order for a private body to have *locus standi* under Article 34 it is a requirement that the applicant be the victim of a violation of the Convention ('the victim requirement'). Although the lack of access to an international legal remedy does not mean, in my view, that a right guaranteed in an international convention is not a right *stricto sensu*, the establishment of *locus standi* for the rights-holder does indeed provide evidence that the state parties have undertaken an international legal obligation towards them.[191] NGOs are thus rights-holders under the ECHR.

The subject matters of the cases brought by legal persons demonstrate that not only the rights directly connected with associations as such are held and protected by legal persons. It has not been considered necessary to go through the possible corporate elements of all the rights set out in the Convention. Although it is evident that some of the rights can be held only by individuals, such as the right to physical integrity under Article 3, other rights which have not been discussed above may well be held by NGOs or other corporate bodies.

The European Social Charter

The revised Social Charter entered into force in 1999. Just like the former version, the revised Charter is divided into two parts, of which Part I is a political instrument expressing that the contracting parties accept as their aim to promote the realisation of certain rights and principles. By contrast, the introduction to Part II expresses a clear legal obligation:

The Contracting Parties undertake, as provided for in Part III, to consider themselves bound by the obligations laid down in the following articles and paragraphs.

---

[191] As a consequence of their rights, NGOs also have the right to just satisfaction under the Convention. In the case of *Comingersoll SA* v. *Portugal*, the Court made it clear that juridical persons can be afforded non-pecuniary damages, see judgement of 6 April 2000.

178   LEGAL AND EMPIRICAL SURVEY

The system of supervision of the legal rights protected under Part II of the Charter includes a reporting system, under which state parties undertake to report on a regular basis to the European Committee of Social Rights, which examines the reports and gives a legal assessment of these states' fulfilment of their undertakings. The state reports and the conclusions of the Committee of Experts are submitted for examination by the Governmental Committee of the Charter, which adopts resolutions and issues recommendations requesting states to bring national law and practice in conformity with the Charter. There is also a complaints procedure established under the Additional Protocol providing for a system of collective complaints, which will be discussed below.

Most legal rights protected under Part II of the Charter are individual rights. However, the Charter also includes some provisions which bestow rights on organisations. Some of the clearest examples will be mentioned here. This does not exclude the possibility that other rights which are mostly held by individuals may under certain circumstances also be held by corporate bodies.

Article 3 concerns the right to safe and healthy working conditions. The different undertakings of the provision shall be implemented 'in consultation with employers' and workers' organisations'. Such consultation should take place at both the national level and at the level of the enterprise. According to the European Committee of Social Rights (also called the Committee of Independent Experts), national consultation can be performed, for example, within tripartite bodies responsible for the drawing up and amendment of occupational health and safety laws and for laying down regulations and guidelines. It is, however, sufficient if the responsible authority consults workers' and employers' organisations on a regular basis.[192]

Article 5 protects the right to organise. According to the provision, the contracting parties undertake: 'With a view to ensuring or promoting the freedom of workers and employers to form local, national or international organisations for the protection of their economic and social interests and to join those organisations, ... that national law shall not be such as to impair, nor shall it be so applied as to impair, this freedom.' Article 5 protects both the individual right of workers to

---

[192] See, e.g., Committee of Independent Experts, Conclusions XIV-2, the Netherlands, Sweden and the United Kingdom. The requirement of regularity was stated in, e.g., Conclusions V, p. 23, cited in *Case Law on the European Social Charter*, 1995, p. 26.

establish or join a trade union and the organisation right of the trade unions thus established to organise and function in the interest of their members.[193] The organisation right includes organisational activities, such as the election of officers, the management of funds and the conduct of meetings, as well as the right to function effectively in general.[194] Furthermore, the state is obliged to provide protection against reprisals on the ground of trade union activities.[195] Trade unions also have the right under this Article to discipline members who, for instance, refuse to take part in lawful strikes, and legislation prohibiting such action would constitute interference with trade union autonomy in breach of Article 5.[196]

Article 6 provides that, with a view to ensuring the effective exercise of the right to bargain collectively, the contracting parties undertake, *inter alia*, to promote joint consultation between workers and employers (para. 1) and to promote machinery for voluntary negotiations between employers or employers' organisations and workers' organisations, with a view to the regulation of terms and conditions of employment by means of collective agreements (para. 2). The European Court of Human Rights has stated in the case of *National Union of Belgian Police* that Article 6(1) of the Charter does not provide a material right to consultation, only an obligation for states to promote consultation.[197]

Under Article 6(4), the contracting states recognise the right of workers and employers to collective action in cases of conflicts of interest, including the right to strike, subject to obligations that might arise out of collective agreements previously entered into. As the rights are, according to the wording of the provision, bestowed on workers and employers collectively, it is reasonable to assume the provision also protects organisation rights of workers' and employers' organisations.

---

[193] Donna Gomien, David Harris and Leo Zwaak, *Law and Practice of the European Convention on Human Rights and the European Social Charter*, Strasbourg: Council of Europe Publishing, 1996, p. 390.

[194] *Ibid.* On the obligation of contracting states to protect trade unions from interference on the part of employers, see also Conclusions I, p. 31, as cited in *Case Law on the European Social Charter* 1995, p. 42.

[195] Committee of Independent Experts, Conclusions XIV-1, e.g., Austria, France and Norway.

[196] Committee of Independent Experts, Conclusions XIV-1, Austria and France.

[197] *National Union of Belgian Police* v. *Belgium*, 27 October, 1975, para. 38. The Court commented on Article 6 of the Charter for the sake of interpreting Article 11 of the Convention.

180   LEGAL AND EMPIRICAL SURVEY

The Committee of Social Rights has criticised legislation restricting the right of trade unions to take action to 'their own' employer, making it impossible for them to take action, *inter alia*, against the company which may hire the workers through an intermediary company.[198]

The position of workers' and employers' organisations, as well as other NGOs, has been considerably strengthened by the Additional Protocol Providing for a System of Collective Complaints, which entered into force in July 1998.[199] The organisations provided with this possibility are (a) certain international organisations of employers and trade unions, (b) other international NGOs with consultative status with the Council of Europe and appearing on a special list which is drawn up for this purpose by the Governmental Committee and (c) representative national organisations of employers and trade unions within the jurisdiction of the state against which the complaint has been lodged.[200]

It is clear that the rights enumerated in Part II of the Charter are not merely undertakings of contracting states to provide individuals with certain benefits. The practice of the Charter monitoring bodies supports the conclusion that the Charter also include corporate rights for workers' and employers' organisations, and the existence of the Collective Complaints Procedure further underlines a right–obligation relationship on the international plane. However, as the collective complaint procedure is open also to organisations which have not themselves suffered a violation of one of the corporate rights in the Charter, not all complainants are rights-holders. Moreover, it should be noted that the supervisory bodies of the Charter cannot issue legally binding decisions. Instead, the Committee of Independent Experts draws up a report in which it 'presents its conclusions' as to whether the Charter has been satisfactorily applied.[201] The report is passed on to the Committee of Ministers, which shall adopt a recommendation to the state party concerned if the Committee of Independent Experts has found that the Charter has not been satisfactorily applied.[202] The value of the procedure for organisations whose rights have been violated is thus not particularly strong.

---

[198] Committee of Independent Experts, Conclusions XIV-1, United Kingdom.
[199] Additional Protocol to the European Social Charter Providing for a System of Collective Complaints, ETS No. 158.
[200] See section 5.3.   [201] Collective Complaints Protocol, Article 8(1).
[202] Articles 8(2) and 9(1).

The American Convention on Human Rights

Just as its European counterpart, the American Convention on Human Rights uses the word 'everyone' as the holder of many of the rights guaranteed.[203] As has been demonstrated above, it is clear that NGOs and other legal entities may be rights-holders under the European Convention. However, juridical persons have not been recognised as rights-holders under the American Convention.

The provision on *locus standi* before the Inter-American Commission on Human Rights grants standing to 'Any person or group of persons, or any nongovernmental entity legally recognized in one or more member states of the Organization' (Article 44 of the Convention). It is thus clear that NGOs may submit petitions to the Commission. Petitions are often submitted by NGOs or by other physical or juridical persons on behalf of one or several alleged victims.[204] Legal entities may, however, not submit petitions on their own behalf. This is due to Article 1(2) which provides that: 'For the purposes of this Convention, "person" means every human being.' In the case of *MEVOPAL, SA* v. *Argentina*, which concerned, *inter alia*, the right to a fair trial, the Inter-American Commission referred to Article 1(2) and declared that:

For the purposes of this Convention, person means every human being. Under this provision and in accordance with the reiterated doctrine of this Commission and the jurisprudence of the Court, the Commission holds the term 'victim' to be every person protected by the Convention as established generically in Article 1(1) in accordance with the regulations establishing the rights and freedoms specifically recognized therein. Moreover, in accordance with the second paragraph of the transcribed regulations, the person protected by the Convention is 'every human being' – in Spanish 'todo ser humano', in French 'tout être humain'. Consequently, the Commission considers that the Convention grants its protection to physical or natural persons, excluding juridical or ideal persons from its field of application, inasmuch as the latter are legal fiction and do not enjoy real existence in the material order. This interpretation is confirmed on verifying the true significance attributed to the phrase 'person is every human being' with the text of the Preamble to the Convention which recognizes that the essential rights of man are 'based on attributes of his human personality' and reiterates the necessity of creating conditions which permit every individual to 'achieve the ideal of free human beings enjoying freedom from fear and want'.[205]

---

[203] OAS Treaty Series No. 36. See, e.g., Articles 3, 4, 11, 12.   [204] See section 5.3.

[205] Case of *MEVOPAL, SA* v. *Argentina*, Report No. 39/99, paras. 16–17, in *Annual Report of the Inter-American Commission on Human Rights 1998*, April 16, 1999.

182   LEGAL AND EMPIRICAL SURVEY

The Commission thus considered the petition 'obviously out of order' in terms of the requirements established in Article 47(c) in conformity with Article 1(2) of the American Convention, and declared it inadmissible. With this decision, the Commission confirmed an earlier practice established in the cases of *Banco del Perú* and *Tabacalera Boquerón*.[206]

It can nevertheless be observed that there are several rights pronounced by the Convention which indirectly afford protection to NGOs. For instance, Article 16 recognises the right to freedom of association, Article 15 the right to peaceful assembly and Article 13 the right to freedom of expression. Most cases lodged with the Commission concern breaches of the most fundamental rights, such as the right to life, the right to humane treatment and the right to personal liberty. However, a few cases have actualised the right to freedom of association and the right to freedom of expression and have indirectly concerned organisations.[207] The Court's case-law also provides a couple of examples which concern these rights – for instance, Advisory Opinion No. 5 on *Compulsory Membership in an Association Prescribed by Law for the Practice of Journalism*, which raised the issue of the negative aspect of the right to freedom of association.[208] There are also examples of cases which concern peoples or cultural groups.[209]

Although the practice of the Commission in relation to legal persons as victims of Convention rights is entirely clear, it can be observed that the wording of the different rights provisions varies. Article 1(2) makes it clear that, for the purposes of the Convention, 'person' means every human being. It is, however, only some of the rights provisions which

---

[206] *Banco del Perú* v. *Perú*, Report No. 10/91, in OEA/Ser.L/V/II.79.rev.1, *Annual Report of the Inter-American Commission on Human Rights, 1990–1991*, February 22, 1991 and *Tabacalera Boquerón* v. *Paraguay*, Report No. 47/97, in OEA/Ser.L/V/II.98, *Annual Report of the Inter-American Commission on Human Rights, 1997*, April 13, 1998. See also Case of *Metropolitan Nature Reserve*, Report No. 88/03 in OEA/Ser.L/V/II.118, *Annual Report of the Inter-American Commission on Human Rights, 2003*, December 29, 2003, para. 33.

[207] See, e.g., *Susana Higuchi* v. *Perú*, Report No. 119/99 (in which the petitioner alleged that the state had refused to register her as a candidate for a political group before national elections), in OEA/Ser.L/V/II.106, *Annual Report of the Inter-American Commission on Human Rights, 1999*, April 13, 1999 and *Clemente Ayala Torres et al.* v. *Mexico* (in which the petitioners were representatives of a political party), Report No. 48/99 in OEA/Ser.L/V/II.102, *Annual Report of the Inter-American Commission on Human Rights, 1998*, April 16, 1999.

[208] Inter-American Court of Human Rights, Advisory Opinion OC-5/85, *Compulsory Membership in an Association Prescribed by Law for the Practice of Journalism*, November 13, 1985. See also Series C: Decisions and Judgments, No. 72, *Baena Ricardo et al.* v. *Panama*, 3 February 2001 and No. 73, '*The Last Temptation of Christ' (Olmedo Bustos et al.)* v. *Chile*, 5 February 2001.

[209] For instance No. 79, *Mayagna (Sumo) Community of Awas Tingni* v. *Nicaragua*, 31 August 2001.

employ this term (for example, Article 3 on the right to juridical personality, Article 4 on the right to life and Article 5 on the right to humane treatment). Other provisions, including some of those most directly connected to the activities of NGOs (Article 13 on the right to freedom of expression, Article 16 on the right to freedom of assembly, Article 12 on the right to freedom of religion), state that 'Everyone has the right to'. As pointed out above, this is the same expression as is used in the European Convention, which does indeed recognise the rights of legal persons. The right to peaceful assembly under Article 15 has been given a passive form: 'The right of peaceful assembly, without arms, is recognized.' In the case of *MEVOPAL SA* v. *Argentina*, described above, which was declared inadmissible *ratione personae* by the Commission, the petitioner alleged violations of the right to a fair trial (Article 8), the right to property (Article 21) and the right to equal protection (Article 24). Of these, the first and the last are guaranteed for 'persons', while the second is guaranteed for 'everyone'.[210] The Commission's reference to and discussion of Article 1, however, does not seem to leave any room for a distinction between these two categories of rights.

The African Charter on Human and Peoples' Rights

The title of the African Charter on Human and Peoples' Rights gives an immediate impression of a different approach to rights than most international or regional human rights instruments. The Charter explicitly includes a collective notion of rights and articulates several group rights, such as the right to existence and the right to self-determination (Article 20) and the right of all peoples to freely dispose of their wealth and natural resources (Article 21).[211] Most rights are, however, bestowed on 'every individual'. This is also the case with the right to free association. Article 10 provides that:

1. Every individual shall have the right to free association provided that he abides by the law.
2. Subject to the obligation of solidarity provided for in Article 29 no one may be compelled to join an association.

---

[210] The Declaration on the Rights and Duties of Man, by contrast, consistently includes expressions such as 'person' and 'individual'. It can also be observed that the Preamble to the European Convention for Human Rights does not, unlike the American Convention, refer to the 'human personality'.

[211] Regarding peoples' rights and the relationship between peoples' rights and individual rights, see Rachel Murray, *The African Commission on Human and Peoples' Rights & International Law*, Oxford: Hart Publishing, 2000, pp. 103–110.

184 LEGAL AND EMPIRICAL SURVEY

The right to form and join trade unions is not expressly provided for. According to Umozurike, who is a member of the African Commission, the right is incorporated in the right to free association in Article 10.[212]

Literally, the right to free association is a purely individual right. Although several cases before the Commission have concerned the right to free association, the Commission's case-law does not provide much information on whether the right may include corporate elements.[213] A few cases concerning the right to free association touch briefly on the question of rights pertaining to NGOs as such.

In the case of *Civil Liberties Organization in Respect of the Nigerian Bar Association v. Nigeria*, a Nigerian NGO brought a communication alleging a violation of the right to freedom of association.[214] The communication was filed in protest against a decree which established a new governing body of the Nigerian Bar Association, namely the Body of Benchers. According to the decree the vast majority of members of the new governing body should be nominated by the government. One of the functions of the Body was to discipline legal practitioners. The complaining NGO claimed a violation of Nigerian lawyers' right to freedom of association. The Commission's opinion was somewhat contradictory: 'Freedom of association is enunciated as an individual right and is first and foremost a duty for the State to abstain from interfering with the free formation of association ... In regulating the use of this right, the competent authorities should not enact provisions which could limit the exercise of this freedom ... The Body of Benchers is dominated by representatives of the government and has wide discretionary powers. This interference with the free association of the Nigerian Bar Association is inconsistent with the preamble of the African Charter in conjunction with UN basic Principles on the Independence of the Judiciary and thereby constitutes a violation of Article 10 of the African Charter.'[215]

---

[212] U. Oji Umozurike, *The African Charter on Human and Peoples' Rights*, Dordrecht: Martinus Nijhoff, 1997, p. 36. See also Evelyn A. Ankumah, *The African Commission on Human and Peoples' Rights. Practices and Procedures*, Dordrecht: Martinus Nijhoff, 1996, p. 137.

[213] See, e.g., Communication No. 144/95, *William A. Courson v. Equatorial Guinea, Eleventh Annual Activity Report*, 1997–1998; No. 212/98, *Amnesty International v. Zambia, Twelfth Annual Activity Report*, 1998–1999; Nos. 147/95 and 149/96, *Sir Dawda K. Jawara v. The Gambia*; and No. 205/97 *Kazeem Aminu v. Nigeria, Thirteenth Annual Activity Report*, 1999–2000 and the communications described below.

[214] Communication No. 101/93, *Civil Liberties Organization in Respect of the Nigerian Bar Association v. Nigeria*, African Commission on Human and Peoples' Rights, *Eighth Annual Activity Report*, 1994–1995.

[215] Communication No. 101/93, *Civil Liberties Organization in Respect of the Nigerian Bar Association v. Nigeria*, paras. 14–16, African Commission on Human and Peoples' Rights, *Eighth Annual Activity Report*, 1994–1995.

RIGHTS AND OBLIGATIONS 185

While describing the right to free association as an individual right, the Commission stated that the interference with 'the free association of the Nigerian Bar Association' is a violation of the Charter. It also stated that the case concerned 'a violation of Nigerian lawyers' right to freedom of association', and thus an individual right. In other words, it cannot be concluded from this case alone that the right to free association under Article 10 protects NGOs as such.

The case of *International Pen, Constitutional Rights Project, Interights on behalf of Ken Saro-Wiwa, Jr. and Civil Liberties Organisation* v. *Nigeria* concerned individual victims but nevertheless briefly touched on the interests of an NGO.

The case was filed on behalf of, *inter alia*, the writer Ken Saro-Wiwa, who was also the president of the Movement for the Survival of the Ogoni People (MOSOP). The communication alleged that Article 10(1) was violated because the victims were tried and convicted by a special tribunal for their opinions, as expressed through their work in MOSOP. In its judgement, the Tribunal held that by their membership in MOSOP, the condemned persons were responsible for the murders of four Ogoni leaders. The Commission stated that the tribunal had demonstrated 'a clear prejudice against the organisation MOSOP, which the government has done nothing to defend or justify. Therefore the Commission finds a violation of Article 10.1.'[216]

The case of *Huri-Laws* v. *Nigera*, was submitted on behalf of the NGO Civil Liberties Organisation.

The applicant claimed that 'since the formation of Civil Liberties Organisation on 15th October 1987, it has experienced all forms of harassment and persecutions from the Nigerian Government. These harassment and persecutions have always been carried out in the form of arrests and detention of key members and staff of the Organisation and by way of raids and searches without warrants in the Organisation's offices by its Security Agency, the State Security Services (SSS).'[217] The applicant claimed violations of, *inter alia*, Article 9 on

[216] Communications Nos. 137/94, 139/94, 154/96, 161/97, *International Pen, Constitutional Rights Project, Interights, on behalf of Ken Saro-Wiwa, Jr. and Civil Liberties Organisation* v. *Nigeria*, para. 108, *Twelfth Annual Activity Report*, 1998–1999.
[217] Communication No. 225/98, *Huri-Laws* v. *Nigeria, Fourteenth Annual Activity Report*, 2000–2001, annex 5, p. 58. See also Inger Österdahl, *Implementing Human Rights in Africa: The African Commission on Human and Peoples' Rights and Individual Communications*, Uppsala: Iustus Förlag, 2002, p. 98.

186   LEGAL AND EMPIRICAL SURVEY

the right to freedom of expression and Article 10 on the right to free association. The Commission found violations of both rights without clarifying who was the victim of these violations.[218]

Another case which concerned the right to free association was *Kenya Human Rights Commission* v. *Kenya*.

Academic staff at four public universities in Kenya decided to form an 'umbrella' trade union to represent their interests in negotiation with their respective employers. An application for registration of the organisation was submitted to the registrar of trade unions. The registrar refused to register the union on the ground that 'the union is used for unlawful purposes and as such, peace, welfare, and good order in Kenya would otherwise be likely to suffer prejudice' ... The trade union officials were later arrested and harassed. The Commission declared the communication inadmissible because of failure to exhaust local remedies.[219]

The Commission's report on the case does not include any information on the articles under which the communication was brought. Neither does the Commission's own opinion discuss which rights came into question.

In sum, the Commission's case-law does not demonstrate a consistent practice as regards whether NGOs as such are protected under Article 10 of the Charter. It can be observed that other rights closely connected to the activities of NGOs, such as the right to freedom of information and expression under Article 9 and the right to freedom of assembly under Article 11 are, like the right to free association, bestowed upon 'every individual'. The right to freedom of religion and profession under Article 8 are impersonal, stating simply that the right is 'guaranteed'.

The communication procedure may be of some interest for the examination of the character of the rights under the Charter. According to Article 55, the Commission may receive communications 'other than those of state parties' about violations of the rights enunciated in the Charter. Although it is not clarified in the Charter or in the Commission's Amended Rules of Procedure who may submit such communications, it is clear from the Commission's practice that individuals, groups of individuals and NGOs are entitled to file

---

[218] *Ibid.*, pp. 64–65.
[219] Communication No. 135/94, *Kenya Human Rights Commission* v. *Kenya, Ninth Annual Activity Report*, in 4 IHRR (1997), pp. 86–88.

complaints.[220] There is no victim requirement for the author of a communication, and the Commission routinely registers communications submitted by NGOs on behalf of the victim. The complainant is not even required to be a citizen of a state member of the OAS, and a complaining NGO does not have to be registered in one of the member states. Several communications have been filed by international NGOs based outside Africa. It is in other words obvious that most complaints are not brought by NGOs in their capacity as right-holders but in their role of spokespersons of victims, with or without authorisation.

Because of the high number of communications submitted by NGOs to the African Commission, the Commission's practice is likely to provide an answer in the future to the question whether NGOs as such are protected under the African Charter on Human and Peoples' Rights.

4.3 International obligations

Introduction

While the individual has taken a step on the international plane as a rights-holder within the area of international human rights law, there are also clear international legal obligations for the individual to refrain from certain conduct. The Nuremberg International Military Tribunal stated in 1946 that 'international law imposes duties and liabilities upon individuals as well as upon States'.[221] These duties were elaborated and clarified during the 1990s through the development of international criminal law with the creation of International Criminal Tribunals for Yugoslavia (ICTY) and Rwanda (ICTR) and the adoption of the Statute of the International Criminal Court.

---

[220] See above and section 5.3. See also Umozurike, *The African Charter on Human and Peoples' Rights*, p. 75; Murray, *The African Commission on Human and Peoples' Rights & International Law*, pp. 67–68; and Ankumah, *The African Commission on Human and Peoples' Rights*, p. 24. Umozurike is a former member and Chairman of the Commission.

[221] See Judgement of the Nuremberg International Military Tribunal, 1 October 1946, in 41 AJIL (1947), p. 220. Another example of a treaty that imposes duties directly upon individuals is the 1969 International Convention on Civil Liability for Oil Pollution Damage. According to the Convention's Article III, the owner of a ship shall be liable for any pollution damage caused by oil which has escaped from the ship. 'Owner' is to be understood as the 'person or persons registered as the owner of the ship', and 'person' means 'any individual or partnership or any public or private body' (Article I). Corporate bodies such as commercial companies can accordingly be held directly liable under this provision of international treaty law.

188   LEGAL AND EMPIRICAL SURVEY

As the role and influence of other non-state actors in international law are increasing, the discussion regarding their responsibilities outside the fields of armed conflict and international crime is intensifying. Within the area of human rights, there is interest among some states about the subject of 'human responsibilities', of which other states are, however, highly critical. In 2000, the UN Commission on Human Rights, 'Recalling that human responsibilities were an integral part of the negotiating process leading to the Universal Declaration for Human Rights and are an important part of the Universal Declaration, but have since been ignored', requested the Sub-Commission to undertake a study on the topic.[222] The issue is controversial, and the resolution, which was introduced by Pakistan, was adopted by only 22 votes to 21, with 10 abstentions.[223] The study requested was prepared by the Special Rapporteur Miguel Alfonso Martínez and a pre-draft declaration on human social responsibilities is presented in his report.[224] In Article 1 of the pre-draft declaration, it is made clear that the terms 'responsibilities' and 'duties' are used interchangeably 'to indicate actions and attitudes that are judged on the extralegal social plane and not as mandatory obligations under the law'. Nevertheless, the declaration enumerates a considerable number of duties in different areas of societal and human life, and states that: 'The rights of the individual and his or her social responsibilities are indissolubly linked. They mutually reinforce each other and for that reason deserve express recognition of their equal value and importance

---

[222] E/CN.4/RES/2000/63, *Human Rights and Human Responsibilities*, 27 April 2000. According to the Universal Declaration of Human Rights, Article 29(1), 'everyone has duties to the community'. Another restriction is made in Article 30, according to which nothing in the Declaration 'may be interpreted as implying for any State, group or person any right to engage in any activity or to perform any act aimed at the destruction of any of the rights and freedoms set forth herein'. The duties of the individual are also mentioned in the Preambles of the ICCPR and the ICESCR (para. 5 states that 'Realising that the individual, having duties to other individuals and to the Community to which he belongs, is under a responsibility to strive for the promotion and observance of the rights recognised in the present Covenant') and in the African Charter on Human and Peoples' Rights, chapter 2. According to Clapham, individuals are obliged to respect the human rights contained in the ICCPR, see Andrew Clapham, *Human Rights in the Private Sphere*, Oxford: Clarendon Press, 1993, p. 97. See also Torkel Opsahl and Vojin Dimitrijevic, 'Articles 29 and 30', in Gudmundur Alfredsson and Asbjørn Eide (eds.), *The Universal Declaration of Human Rights: A Common Standard of Achievement*, The Hague: Martinus Nijhoff, 1999, pp. 637–642.

[223] E/CN.4/2000/SR.65, 4 May 2000, *Commission on Human Rights, Fifty-Sixth Session, Summary Record of the 65th Meeting*, paras. 80 and 99.

[224] E/CN.4/2003/105, *Promotion and Protection of Human Rights: Human Rights and Human Responsibilities*, 17 March 2003, annex I.

RIGHTS AND OBLIGATIONS   189

to life in society' (Article 5). At its 60th session in 2004, the Commission on Human Rights decided, by a slim majority, to accept a draft decision presented by China and thereby requested the Office of the High Commissioner for Human Rights to circulate to member states and relevant organisations the pre-draft declaration on human social responsibilities, requesting their views on it, to submit to the Commission at its next session a compilation of the essential aspects of the replies received, and to continue the consideration of the issue at its 61st session.[225] At the subsequent session of ECOSOC, the Netherlands presented a draft decision on behalf of a group of states attempting to revoke the decision of the Commission on Human Rights. In this draft, the group of states expressed concern that the content of the pre-draft declaration on human social responsibilities ran counter to fundamental human rights principles by seeking to make the enjoyment of human rights conditional, and proposed that the Office of the High Commissioner should be asked not to proceed with the issue.[226] However, the draft decision was rejected, again by a slim majority, by ECOSOC, which thus accepted the decision of the Commission on Human Rights to proceed with the processing of the pre-draft declaration on human social responsibilities.[227]

The international responsibilities of TNCs, as well as the international legal accountability of armed non-state actors, have been other major issues.[228] Agreements on standards of conduct have been concluded between non-state parties to conflicts and states, and between IGOs and non-state armed groups.[229] The threat from terrorist groups calls fundamental rules of international law, such as the right to self-defence, into question, and the sanctions issued by the UN Security Council on Al-Qaida and other non-state actors bridge traditional divides, such as public–private and international–national.[230]

---

[225] E/2004/23, *Commission on Human Rights: Report on the 60th Session*, Part I, p. 346, Decision 2004/117, *Human Rights and Human Responsibilities*. The draft decision was adopted with 26 votes for, 25 against and 2 abstentions.

[226] E/2004/L.21, *Commission on Human Rights Decision 2004/117 on Human Rights and Human Responsibilities*, 14 July 2004.

[227] A/59/3, *Report of the Economic and Social Council for 2004* (preliminary version), 6 August 2004, pp. 99–100. The draft decision was rejected by a vote of 25 to 24 with 5 abstentions.

[228] See, e.g., E/CN.4/2004/90, *Promotion and Protection of Human Rights: Fundamental Standards of Humanity. Report of the Secretary-General*, 25 February 2004. On standards of conduct for transnational corporations, see section 4.3.

[229] For examples, see E/CN.4/2001/91, paras. 40–45.

[230] See, for instance, S/RES/1373, 29 September 2001, S/RES/1526, 30 January 2004 and S/RES/1530, 11 March 2004.

190   LEGAL AND EMPIRICAL SURVEY

Although the concept of 'NGO' is understood in this study as exclusive of violent groups, these developments demonstrate that assumptions cannot be made *a priori* when issues relating to the behaviour of non-state actors are discussed.[231]

The international legal obligations of NGOs are still a rather undeveloped area in international law. The few international instruments that formulate some sort of responsibilities for NGOs will be examined below.[232] There has also been some progress in the area of self-regulation. NGOs that enter into formal relations with IGOs voluntarily undertake certain responsibilities. NGOs also seek to enhance their accountability by elaborating and adhering to codes of conduct, as will be discussed below. Obligations under international humanitarian law will be examined in the section which deals specifically with this area of law.[233]

Limitations of organisation rights

The above survey of human rights instruments treaties has demonstrated that some international and regional human rights, notably the right to freedom of association, protect not only individuals, but also NGOs. However, international law also requires that states restrict the right to freedom of association. Article 4 of the International Convention on the Elimination of all Forms of Racial Discrimination (1965) obliges state parties to:

condemn all propaganda and all organizations which are based on ideas or theories of superiority of one race or group of persons of one colour or ethnic origin, or which attempt to justify or promote racial hatred and discrimination in any form.

---

[231] See section 1.3.

[232] One document which will not be examined in this section is, however, the Council of Europe Fundamental Principles on the Status of Non-Governmental Organisations in Europe. The Principles can be regarded as guidelines to states for the formulation of appropriate national legislation on NGOs. The rather detailed Principles, however, also contain provisions which can be seen as recommendations to NGOs. For instance, it is stated that NGOs should employ lawful means in pursuing their objectives, that they should have statutes, that the bodies for management and decision-making of NGOs should be in accordance with their statutes and the law and that NGOs should observe all applicable employment standards and insurance obligations in the treatment of their staff. *Fundamental Principles on the Status of Non-Governmental Organisations in Europe and Explanatory Memorandum*, Council of Europe, May 2003. See also section 4.2.

[233] See section 4.4.

State parties undertake to adopt immediate and positive measures designed to eradicate all incitement to, or acts of, such discrimination and:

shall declare illegal and prohibit organizations, and also organized and all other propaganda activities, which promote and incite racial discrimination, and shall recognize participation in such organizations or activities as an offence punishable by law.[234]

The Committee on the Elimination of all Forms of Racial Discrimination has explained its views on this provision in two of its general recommendations. In General Recommendation No. 7, issued in 1985, the Committee recommended state parties whose legislation did not satisfy the provisions of Article 4 to 'take the necessary steps with a view to satisfying the mandatory requirements of that article'.[235] General Recommendation No. 15 is more elaborate. In this recommendation, the Committee explained that it held the opinion that the prohibition of dissemination of ideas based upon racial superiority or hatred was compatible with the right to freedom of opinion and expression. The Committee noted that some states had maintained that it was inappropriate in their legal orders to declare an organisation illegal before its members had promoted or incited racial discrimination, but emphasised that 'These organizations, as well as other organized and other propaganda activities, have to be declared illegal and prohibited'.[236]

Article 4 of CERD thus imposes a legal obligation which, although it is directed to contracting states, is of direct concern to NGOs as it in practice prohibits certain actions being undertaken by them. CERD Article 4 also circumscribes the right to freedom of association as conferred on NGOs by other treaties. In the survey of organisation rights above, it was found that, outside the area of labour law, the convention that most clearly confers rights on NGOs as organisations is the European Convention on Human Rights and Fundamental Freedoms.[237] This was due to the standing of NGOs as victims before the European Court of Human Rights provided by Article 34 of the Convention in the case

---

[234] International Convention on the Elimination of All Forms of Racial Discrimination (1965), Article 4(b).

[235] CERD General Recommendation No. 7, *Legislation to Eradicate Racial Discrimination (Art. 4)*, 25 August 1985, para. 1, in A/40/18, *Report of the Committee on the Elimination of Racial Discrimination*, 1985.

[236] CERD General Recommendation No. 15, *Organized Violence based on Ethnic Origin (Art. 4)*, 19 March 1993, para. 6, in A/48/18, *Report of the Committee on the Elimination of Racial Discrimination*, 1993.

[237] See section 4.2.

192   LEGAL AND EMPIRICAL SURVEY

of a violation of an organisation right. Most state parties to the European Convention on Human Rights are also parties to CERD. Thus, within these states, the rights to freedom of association, assembly and expression as conferred on NGOs by the European Convention are qualified by Article 4 of CERD, albeit the European Convention also entitles states to make restrictions of rights on other grounds.[238]

The ILO Conventions

A few ILO Conventions have been discussed above as examples of treaties which bestow rights on NGOs as such. At least one of the Fundamental ILO Conventions also imposes an international obligation on organisations of workers and employers. Article 8(1) of the Freedom of Association and Protection of the Right to Organise Convention (No. 87, 1948), provides that workers' and employers' organisations shall, like other persons or organised collectivities, respect the law of the land in exercising the rights provided for in the Convention.

The UN Declaration on Human Rights Defenders

The UN Declaration on Human Rights Defenders seems to be the only international instrument which formulates responsibilities for NGOs in general.[239] Article 18 states that:

1. Everyone has duties towards and within the community, in which alone the free and full development of his or her personality is possible.
2. Individuals, groups, institutions and non-governmental organizations have an important role to play and a responsibility in safeguarding democracy, promoting human rights and fundamental freedoms and contributing to the promotion and advancement of democratic societies, institutions and processes.
3. Individuals, groups, institutions and non-governmental organizations also have an important role and a responsibility in contributing, as appropriate, to the promotion of the right of everyone to a social and international order in which the rights and freedoms set forth in the Universal Declaration of Human Rights and other human rights instruments can be fully realized.

The wording of these provisions is vague. The expressions 'important role' and 'responsibility' are used instead of more legal terms, such as

---

[238] See Articles 10(2), 11(2), 16, 17.
[239] A/RES/53/144, *Declaration on the Right and Responsibility of Individuals, Groups and Organs of Society to Promote and Protect Universally Recognized Human Rights and Fundamental Freedoms*, 8 March 1999, annex.

'duties' or 'obligations'. There were different views on the notion of responsibilities of human rights defenders during the preparatory work on the Declaration. Some members of the working group of the Human Rights Commission argued that the text unnecessarily incorporated references to duties of human rights defenders: while individuals and groups had moral responsibilities in promoting human rights it was states that had the obligation.[240] The representatives of, *inter alia*, Turkey, Cuba and Malaysia were more in favour of the formulation of duties and responsibilities for human rights defenders than the representatives of, among others, Sweden, France, the Netherlands, as well as a group of NGOs.[241] Turkey stated that it could not give its consent to a text lacking a consolidated article enumerating the responsibilities of human rights defenders, and the representative of Cuba expressed a similar view. The Swedish representative argued that if a reference on duties and responsibilities had to be included in the declaration, it should be an exact replica of Article 29(1) of the Universal Declaration of Human Rights.[242] The representative of Malaysia suggested that by laying down loose guidelines on the responsibilities of human rights defenders, their credibility as a whole would hopefully be enhanced.[243]

The final result was, as demonstrated above, the inclusion in Article 18 of a rather vague reference to the duties of 'Everyone' and the 'important role ... and ... responsibility' of individuals, groups, institutions and NGOs. It should be noted that it is stressed in the Preamble of the Declaration that 'the prime responsibility and duty to promote and protect human rights and fundamental freedoms lie with the State'. The Declaration indicates that while states are under a primary legal obligation to comply with international human rights law, it cannot be excluded that human rights NGOs will be under a supplementary international obligation to do so in the future.

The obligations of NGOs in their co-operation with IGOs

Formal IGO–NGO co-operation

The different regional and international instruments that regulate the arrangements for co-operation between NGOs and IGOs include provisions on how NGOs should behave in relation to the IGO and

---

[240] E/CN.4/1998/98, 29 March 1998, para. 21.
[241] E/CN.4/1997/92, *Drafting of a Declaration on the Right and Responsibility of Individuals*, 25 March 1997, paras. 53–63 and E/CN.4/1998/98, 29 March 1998, para. 21.
[242] E/CN.4/1997/92, paras. 55 and 57.   [243] E/CN.4/1998/98, para. 41.

194   LEGAL AND EMPIRICAL SURVEY

otherwise once their application for a formalised relationship has been accepted. NGOs in formal relationship with an IGO thus voluntarily take on an obligation to refrain from certain conduct in order not to be excluded from further co-operation. The general aspects of consultative or similar arrangements for NGOs with different IGOs will be more thoroughly described in chapter 7.[244] In the present context, it is sufficient to examine what kind of conduct NGOs in consultative status are under an obligation to refrain from according to the different resolutions regulating such relations.

The most important and extensive provisions regarding consultative status for NGOs on the international plane are those contained in ECOSOC resolution 1996/31 regarding consultative relationship between the United Nations and NGOs. These arrangements have the purpose of enabling the ECOSOC and its subsidiary bodies to secure expert information or advice from NGOs with special competence and to enable NGOs that represent important elements of public opinion to express their views.[245] The resolution contains a particular chapter on suspension and withdrawal of consultative status, specifying which types of conduct NGOs in consultative status must refrain from if they wish to keep their status with ECOSOC. There is a general obligation for organisations which have been granted consultative status to 'conform at all times to the principles governing the establishment and nature of their consultative relations with the Council'.[246]

There are three main grounds for suspension or withdrawal of consultative status. First, consultative status shall be suspended for up to three years or withdrawn if an NGO clearly abuses its status by engaging in a pattern of acts contrary to the purposes and principles of the UN Charter, 'including unsubstantiated or politically motivated acts against Member States of the United Nations incompatible with those purposes and principles'.[247] Secondly, suspension or withdrawal shall take place if there is substantiated evidence of influence from proceeds resulting from internationally recognised criminal activities, such as illicit drugs or arms trade or money laundering. Finally, there is a positive obligation on NGOs in consultative status to make a positive or effective contribution to the work of the United Nations. If the NGO

---

[244] See section 7.2 and E/RES/1996/31, *Consultative Relationship between the United Nations and Non-Governmental Organizations*, 25 July 1996.
[245] E/RES/1996/31, para. 20.   [246] *Ibid.*, para. 55.   [247] *Ibid.*, para. 57(a).

has not complied with this provision within the preceding three years of its examination, its status shall be suspended or withdrawn.[248]

As will be described later in this book, the regular monitoring of consultative relations with NGOs is performed by the Council Committee of NGOs.[249] Its decisions thus demonstrate how the obligations formulated for NGOs in the resolution on consultative arrangements are interpreted in practice. Alleged acts which have been criticised by Committee members for being in breach of the provisions are, *inter alia*, the supporting and financing of subversive activities, the distribution of 'aggressive publications' and having links with separatist organisations or accrediting members of such organisations.[250] It should be noted, however, that there are often very different views among Committee members as well as among NGO representatives as to what has really happened.[251] Such discrepancies may cause insecurity as to what have been the real motives for some decisions, which in turn might blur the contours of the obligations bestowed on NGOs in consultative status with the Council. Moreover, the alleged acts that Committee members refer to as a basis for suspension or withdrawal of consultative status are wide-ranging and can sometimes not be regarded as clearly falling within a reasonable interpretation of the ECOSOC resolution 1996/31 on consultative arrangements. Actions which have been mentioned during these discussions, apart from those which were mentioned above, include the obtaining of interpretation service 'through unjust means' (i.e. to make a request at a late stage before a meeting with the intention to 'cause chaos'), and to 'rub shoulders with heretical cults'.[252] Criticism has also been raised against acts which fall within a 'grey zone' in relation to the provisions of the resolution, such as being 'not a non-governmental organization but a political organization', to divide the 'membership of the Council Committee on NGOs

---

[248] *Ibid.*, para. 57(b–c). As to the UN specialised agencies, the obligations of NGOs that maintain formal relations with the United Nations Educational, Scientific and Cultural Organization (UNESCO) are rather elaborate and mainly focused on the contribution of NGOs to UNESCO's work. 28 C/43, *Directives Concerning UNESCO's Relations with Non-Governmental Organizations*, 28 August 1995, para. 7. The FAO upholds similar requirements, see *FAO Policy Concerning Relations with International Non-Governmental Organizations, Basic Texts of the Food and Agriculture Organization of the United Nations*, 1998 edn., II, para. 22.

[249] Section 7.2.

[250] E/2000/88, *Report of the Committee on Non-Governmental Organizations*, 13 July 2000, paras. 70 ff.

[251] *Ibid.*   [252] *Ibid.*, para. 99.

196 LEGAL AND EMPIRICAL SURVEY

into "democratic" and "undemocratic" countries', or to promote 'the legalization of drugs by launching civil disobedience campaigns, distributing drugs and denouncing anti-drug legislation'.[253] In sum, it is not possible to say exactly what actions NGOs in consultative status with the ECOSOC are obliged to refrain from.

The obligations on NGOs in consultative status with regional organisations are of a similar nature. According to the resolution regulating participatory status for international NGOs with the Council of Europe, NGOs which have obtained such status shall undertake, in short, to:

- keep themselves regularly informed of CoE activities and developments in standards,
- furnish the different bodies of the CoE with information, documents or opinions,
- work to promote the respect of the CoE's standards, conventions and legal instruments in the member states, and assist in the implementation of these standards, and this in close contact with local, regional and national NGOs,
- give maximum publicity to the initiatives and achievements of the CoE in their own field(s) of competence,
- disseminate information on CoE standards, instruments and activities to their members, and
- submit every four years a report to the Secretary-General, containing certain specified information.[254]

Participatory status may be withdrawn, *inter alia*, if an NGO no longer meets the conditions for participatory status (for example, by failing to be particularly representative in its field of competence), if it has failed to comply with its obligations under the rules described above, or if it has 'taken any action which is not in keeping with its status as an INGO'.[255] The decision to remove an organisation from the list is taken by the Secretary-General, and submitted for tacit approval to the Committee of Ministers, the Parliamentary Assembly and the Congress of Local and Regional Authorities. The decisions of the

---

[253] *Ibid.*, paras. 105, 99, 101.
[254] Committee of Ministers, Resolution (2003)8, *Participatory Status for International Non-Governmental Organisations with the Council of Europe*, adopted on 19 November 2003, appendix, para. 9. Resolution (2003)9 on *Status of Partnership for National Non-Governmental Organisations with the Council of Europe* (19 November 2003) lays down similar responsibilities, however without expressly describing these as obligations or undertakings, see appendix, para. 4.
[255] Committee of Ministers, Resolution (2003)8, *Participatory Status for International Non-Governmental Organisations with the Council of Europe*, appendix, para. 16.

Secretary-General under the former resolution on consultative status, which had a similar wording as the present resolution on participatory status, demonstrate that the most common grounds for removing an NGO from the list of those NGOs enjoying consultative status is that they have ceased their activities or have failed to contribute to the work programme of the Council of Europe or to make known its activities to the European public.[256] During the period October 1997–January 2001, there did not seem to be any cases where the consultative status of an NGO was withdrawn on the ground that it had 'taken action which is not in keeping with its status as an international non-governmental organization'.

The formal relations of the OAS with NGOs are labelled 'participation of civil society organizations in OAS activities'.[257] By entering into such relations, NGOs and other civil society organisations undertake certain, rather limited, responsibilities, such as to answer inquiries from the organs, agencies and entities of the OAS and provide advisory services to them upon request, to disseminate information on OAS activities to its members and to present a yearly report on their participation in OAS activities to the OAS General Secretariat.[258] Other obligations are implied in the provision regarding suspension or cancellation of registration of civil society organisations. The Committee on Inter-American Summits Management and Civil Society Participation in OAS Activities may recommend to the Permanent Council that it suspend or cancel the registration if an organisation has:

- acted in a manner that is inconsistent with the essential aims and principles of the OAS,
- failed to make a positive or effective contribution to the work of the OAS,
- failed to submit reports for two consecutive years; or
- furnished manifestly false or inaccurate information.[259]

In other words, NGOs and other civil society organisations that register for participation in OAS activities undertake to refrain from such conduct. The documentation of the meetings of the Committee on

---

[256] Communications of the Secretary-General, Docs. No. 7950, 15 October 1997, paras. 7–8; No. 8027, 19 February 1998, para. 6; No. 8497, 6 September 1999, para. 4; No. 8550, 29 September 1999, para. 7; No. 8873, 16 October 2000, para. 8; No. 8933, 22 January 2001. See also Doc. SG/Inf(2003)32, 29 September 2003, para. 7.

[257] The arrangements are regulated by CP/RES. 759 (1217/99), *Guidelines for the Participation of Civil Society Organizations in OAS Activities*, 15 December 1999. For more detailed information on these arrangements, see section 7.8.

[258] CP/RES. 759 (1217/99), 15 December 1999, para. 11.   [259] *Ibid.*, para. 15.

198   LEGAL AND EMPIRICAL SURVEY

Inter-American Summits Management and Civil Society Participation does not include any recommendation for withdrawal or suspension of the registration of a civil society organisation during the period 2002–4. This may be due to the fact that the arrangements for consultation with civil society organisations were adopted fairly recently.[260]

NGOs enjoying observer status with the African Commission on Human and Peoples' Rights undertake to 'establish close relations of co-operation with the African Commission and to engage in regular consultations with it on all matters of common interest' and to present activity reports to the Commission every two years.[261]

Operational IGO–NGO co-operation

Just as with the formalised co-operation between IGOs and NGOs, operational co-operation may result in obligations on the part of NGOs. IGOs often conclude memoranda of understanding (MOU), framework agreements or contracts with NGOs, according to which NGOs undertake contractual obligations. Such agreements often lack provisions on applicable law, and sometimes even refer only to general principles of law. Disputes are often referred to arbitration. Some agreements on IGO–NGO co-operation provide that the NGO shall apply a specific code of conduct, which seems to increase the normative status of the otherwise voluntary codes (see below). The different kinds of agreements concluded between IGOs and NGOs will be examined in a later chapter.[262]

Codes of conduct

Codes of conduct are increasingly being used for voluntary regulation of different sectors of society. The OECD Guidelines for Multinational Enterprises, first adopted in 1976, for instance, are recommendations on responsible business conduct which governments make to MNEs operating in or from the adhering countries.[263] In contrast to the various codes of conduct that businesses develop for self-regulation, the OECD Guidelines are thus endorsed multilaterally by states.

---

[260] By the end of 1999. See section 7.6.
[261] *Resolution on the Criteria for Granting and Enjoying Observer Status to Non-Governmental Organisations Working in the Field of Human Rights with the African Commission on Human and Peoples' Rights*, adopted by the ACHPR at its 25th session, 26 April–5 May 1999, chapter III. See section 7.7.
[262] Chapter 9.   [263] *The OECD Guidelines for Multinational Enterprises*, Revision 2000, p. 5.

The ILO Tripartite Declaration of Principles concerning Multinational Enterprises and Social Policy was adopted in 1977, and has been amended several times since.[264] The effect given by governments and employers to the principles laid down in the Declaration is followed through quadrennial questionnaires, sent out by the ILO, through which member states and national employers' and workers' organisations provide information on the implementation of the Declaration. The responses received are examined by the ILO Governing Body. There is also a procedure for the examination of disputes concerning the Declaration, under which governments and organisations of workers and employers may request an interpretation from the ILO and the Officers of the Committee on Multinational Enterprises.[265]

The issue of codes of conduct is also being discussed within the United Nations. In 1999, the Sub-Commission on the Promotion and Protection of Human Rights decided to establish a sessional working group to examine the working methods and activities of TNCs.[266] In 2003, the Sub-Commission approved draft norms on the responsibilities of TNCs and other business enterprises with regard to human rights and transmitted them to the Commission on Human Rights. In the first paragraph of the draft norms, it is stated that

States have the primary responsibility to promote, secure the fulfillment of, respect, ensure respect of and protect human rights recognized in international as well as national law, including ensuring that transnational corporations and other business enterprises respect human rights. Within their respective spheres of activity and influence, transnational corporations and other business enterprises have the obligation to promote, secure the fulfillment of, respect, ensure respect of and protect human rights recognized in international as well as national law, including the rights and interests of indigenous peoples and other vulnerable groups.[267]

---

[264] Document OB vol. LXI, 1978, Series A, No. 1, *Tripartite Declaration of Principles concerning Multinational Enterprises and Social Policy*, adopted by the Governing Body of the International Labour Office at its 204th Session, Geneva, November 1977.

[265] *Procedure for the Examination of Disputes concerning the Application of the Tripartite Declaration of Principles Concerning Multinational Enterprises and Social Policy by Means of Interpretation of its Provisions*, adopted by the Governing Body of the ILO at its 232nd Session, Geneva, March 1986.

[266] E/CN.4/SUB.2/DEC/1999/101, *Establishment of a Sessional Working Group on the Working Methods and Activities of Transnational Corporations*, 3 August 1999.

[267] E/CN.4/Sub.2/2003/12/Rev.2, Economic, Social and Cultural Rights. Norms on the responsibilities of TNCs and other business enterprises with regard to human rights, 26 August 2003. See also the Commentary contained in E/CN.4/Sub.2/2003/38/Rev.2.

200 LEGAL AND EMPIRICAL SURVEY

The draft norms enumerate various human rights which should be respected and promoted by business enterprises, including the right to freedom of association and to collective bargaining. In line with the recommendation of the Commission on Human Rights, ECOSOC requested the Office of the UN High Commissioner on Human Rights to compile a report on the issue, and affirmed, *inter alia*, that the document had not been requested by the Commission and, as a draft proposal, had no legal standing.[268] In other words, the status of the draft norms is uncertain, although they indicate a growing acceptance of the theory that business has international legal obligations in the field of human rights.

In order to enhance their accountability and legitimacy, NGOs are increasingly creating joint standards for self-regulation. Particularly in the area of humanitarian response, it has been regarded as important to create greater NGO accountability. *The Code of Conduct for the International Red Cross and Red Crescent Movement and NGOs in Disaster Relief* was prepared jointly in the mid-1990s by the International Federation of Red Cross and Red Crescent Societies and the ICRC with the co-operation of Caritas Internationalis, Catholic Relief Services, International Save the Children Alliance, the Lutheran World Federation, Oxfam and The World Council of Churches.[269] The Code of Conduct was presented to and welcomed by the 26th International Conference of the Red Cross and Red Crescent in 1995.[270] By August 2004, it had 307 NGO signatories.[271]

The Code of Conduct for the International Red Cross and Red Crescent Movement and NGOs in Disaster Relief is a voluntary code which 'seeks to maintain the high standards of independence, effectiveness and impact to which disaster response NGOs and the International Red

---

[268] E/2004/23, *Commission on Human Rights: Report on the Sixtieth Session*, Part I, Decisions 2004/116, pp. 345–346.

[269] *The Code of Conduct for the International Red Cross and Red Crescent Movement and NGOs in Disaster Relief*, International Review of the Red Cross No. 310, pp. 55–130, annex VI, footnote 1.

[270] 26th International Conference of the Red Cross and Red Crescent, Geneva, 3–7 December 1995, Resolution No. 4, *Principles and Action in International Humanitarian Assistance and Protection*, para. E, in International Review of the Red Cross No. 310, 1996, pp. 55–130.

[271] *Code of Conduct for the International Red Cross and Red Crescent Movement and NGOs in Disaster Relief, List of Signatories*, 20 August 2004 (public record kept by the International Federation of Red Cross and Red Crescent Societies).

Cross and Red Crescent Movement aspires'.[272] The provisions of the code state, *inter alia*, that

- Aid is given regardless of the race, creed or nationality of the recipients and without adverse distinction of any kind. Aid is calculated on the basis of need alone.
- Aid will not be used to further a particular political or religious standpoint.
- We shall endeavour not to act as instruments of government foreign policy.
- We shall hold ourselves accountable to both those we seek to assist and those from whom we accept resources.[273]

The normative language varies from one provision to another; while the first and most basic provisions are expressed in the form of straight statements ('Aid is ...'), 'shall' or 'must' are used in other provisions. Although it is clear that the Code of Conduct is a voluntary means of self-regulation, it does at the same time have a certain degree of normative force among the over 300 NGOs that have adhered to it. This normativity is strengthened by the fact that several donors have made funding conditional on agencies adhering to the Code.[274] Moreover, as was stated above, agreements on IGO–NGO co-operation sometimes require that the NGO applies the Code.[275] On the other hand, the Code does not establish any procedures for implementation or monitoring. A possible future development could be the creation of such a procedure or of links between codes of conduct and consultative status or other types of formal relationship between NGOs and IGOs.

4.4 International humanitarian law and non-state actors

Introduction

Armed conflicts often create situations where organised non-state actors are involved, either as parties to the conflict or as independent

---

[272] *ICRC Annual Report 1999*, p. 39 and *The Code of Conduct for the International Red Cross and Red Crescent Movement and NGOs in Disaster Relief*, Purpose, in the International Review of the Red Cross No. 310, 1996, pp. 55–130.

[273] *Code of Conduct for the International Red Cross and Red Crescent Movement and NGOs in Disaster Relief*, paras. 2, 3, 4, 9.

[274] Toby Porter, 'The Partiality of Humanitarian Assistance – Kosovo in Comparative Perspective', *The Journal of Humanitarian Assistance*, June 2000, posted online at http://www.jha.ac/articles/a057.htm, accessed on 30 November 2000, endnote (ii).

[275] See section 9.3.

202 LEGAL AND EMPIRICAL SURVEY

actors offering humanitarian assistance. The definition of 'NGO' used in the present study excludes all armed groups and organisations.[276] Nonetheless, it is interesting to observe that humanitarian law creates international rights and duties for non-state groups which are parties to a conflict. In the nineteenth century there was already a way for states to create an international legal setting for a conflict not of an international character. By recognising insurgents fighting against it as belligerents, the insurgents could be subjects of rights and duties under the laws of war.[277] When the Geneva Conventions were adopted in 1949, basic humanitarian rules became applicable to non-state parties to armed conflicts not of an international character. Common Article 3 of the Conventions provides that 'each Party to the conflict shall be bound to apply, as a minimum the following principles', meaning that obligations are placed on states as well as non-state bodies parties to the conflict. It is automatically applicable to non-international armed conflicts, without any condition of reciprocity.[278] Non-state parties to armed conflict are also under a customary legal obligation to apply basic humanitarian standards.[279]

---

[276] See section 1.3.

[277] Hans Aufricht, 'Personality in International Law', XXXVII *The American Political Science Review* (1943), p. 221; Hersch Lauterpacht, 'The Subjects of the Law of Nations', 63 *The Law Quarterly Review* (1947), p. 444; Yves Sandoz et al. (eds.), *Commentary on the Additional Protocols of 8 June 1977 to the Geneva Conventions of 12 August 1949*, International Committee of the Red Cross, Geneva: Martinus Nijhoff, 1987, pp. 1320–1321 (hereafter, '*Commentary on the Additional Protocols*'); Edward Kwakwa, *The International Law of Armed Conflict: Personal and Material Fields of Application*, The Hague: Kluwer Academic Publishers, 1992, p. 48.

[278] Jean S. Pictet (ed.), *The Geneva Conventions of 12 August 1949: Commentary*, Geneva: International Committee of the Red Cross, *I Geneva Convention*, 1952, p. 48. The character of the non-state party is not further specified in the Convention, but during the Diplomatic Conference in Geneva in 1949 some criteria were discussed. Among those were (1) that the party in revolt against the *de jure* government possesses an organised military force, an authority responsible for its acts, acting within a determinate territory and having the means of respecting and ensuring respect for the Convention, (2) that the *de jure* government has recognised the insurgents as belligerents, or that it has claimed itself the rights of a belligerent, or that it has accorded the insurgents recognition as belligerents for the purposes of the Convention, (3) that the insurgents have an organisation purporting to have the characteristics of a state and a civil authority exercising *de facto* authority over persons within a determinate territory, (4) that the armed forces act under the direction of the organised civil authority and are prepared to observe the ordinary laws of war and (5) that the insurgent civil authority agrees to be bound by the provisions of the Conventions, Pictet (ed.), *The Geneva Conventions*, pp. 49–50.

[279] Lisbeth Zegveld, *The Accountability of Armed Opposition Groups in International Law*, Cambridge University Press, 2000, p. 10.

With the Additional Protocol I of 1977, more developed humanitarian rules were formulated for 'armed conflicts in which peoples are fighting against colonial domination and alien occupation and against racist régimes in the exercise of their right of self-determination'.[280] Liberation movements were now given the possibility to submit to international humanitarian law, beyond the requirements of Common Article 3 and customary international law, by declaring unilaterally to undertake to apply the Conventions and the Protocol.[281] The consequence of such a declaration is that the authority which makes this declaration assumes the same rights and obligations as a state party to the Conventions and the Protocol.[282] The requirements as regards the application of the Protocol to the non-state party are an authority representing the people engaged in the struggle and an organised structure of its armed forces, including a responsible command, in accordance with the requirements of Article 43.[283]

Protocol II relating to Protection of Victims of Non-International Armed Conflicts extended the rules of humanitarian law even further.[284] While Protocol II, like Common Article 3, is automatically applicable to non-international conflicts, its protection goes beyond the minimum standards of the latter. The intensity of the conflict, however, has to be greater to trigger applicability than what is required under Common Article 3.[285] The Protocol applies to armed conflicts which are not covered by Protocol I 'and which take place in the territory of a High Contracting Party between its armed forces and dissident armed forces or other organized groups which, under responsible command, exercise such control over a part of

---

[280] Protocol Additional to the Geneva Conventions of 12 August 1949, and relating to the Protection of Victims of International Armed Conflicts (Protocol I), 8 June 1977, Article 1(4).

[281] Protocol I, Article 96(3), *Commentary on the Additional Protocols*, pp. 1089–1090.

[282] *Commentary on the Additional Protocols*, p. 1090.

[283] *Ibid.*, p. 55. Article 43(1) reads: 'The armed forces of a Party to a conflict consist of all organized armed forces, groups and units which are under a command responsible to that Party for the conduct of its subordinates, even if that Party is represented by a government or an authority not recognized by an adverse Party. Such armed forces shall be subject to an internal disciplinary system which, *inter alia*, shall enforce compliance with the rules of international law applicable in armed conflict.' As to the definition of a national liberation movement, see Kwakwa, *The International Law of Armed Conflict*, pp. 50–52. As to the general scope *ratione personae* of the Conventions and the Additional Protocols, see pp. 85–127.

[284] Protocol Additional to the Geneva Conventions of 12 August 1949, and relating to the Protection of Victims of Non-International Armed Conflicts (Protocol II), 8 June 1977.

[285] *Commentary on the Additional Protocols*, p. 1350.

204   LEGAL AND EMPIRICAL SURVEY

its territory as to enable them to carry out sustained and concerted military operations and to implement this Protocol'.[286]

The provisions of Common Article 3 and the Additional Protocols impose duties on non-state parties in a seemingly unproblematic way. It might be questioned, however, how non-state groups can be bound by rules to which they are not formal parties. The explanation offered by the ICRC Commentary is that the commitment made by a state applies also to any established authorities and private individuals within its territory.[287] International obligations – as well as international rights – can therefore be imposed upon individuals and other non-state entities without their approval, according to the Commentary.[288] It has also been confirmed by the ICTY that not only states but also non-state actors such as terrorist groups or organisations can be responsible for acts of genocide and crimes against humanity.[289] Customary international law thus places non-state actors under an obligation not to commit such crimes. The adoption of the Statute of the International Criminal Court has taken the development of international humanitarian obligations for non-state entities even further.[290]

---

[286] Article 1(1). As to the definition of the non-state party to the conflict, see *Commentary on the Additional Protocols*, pp. 1351–1353, and Antonio Cassese, 'The Status of Rebels under the 1977 Geneva Protocol on Non-International Armed Conflicts', in Judith Gardam (ed.), *Humanitarian Law*, Dartmouth: Ashgate, 1999, pp. 241–264.

[287] *Commentary on the Additional Protocols*, p. 1345. For a thorough account of the problem of the origin of obligations of armed groups under interstate treaties, see Zegveld, *The Accountability of Armed Opposition Groups in International Law*, pp. 15 ff.

[288] The issue is, however, not unproblematic. The question of assent by the non-state party to rights and duties under Article 3 and the Additional Protocols is discussed by Cassese, 'The Status of Rebels', pp. 253–255. As regards individuals, see the *East German Border Guard* case, German Federal Constitutional Court, 24 October 1996, in 18 HRLJ (1997), pp. 65–78. As regards insurrectional movements which become a government, see Article 10 of the Draft Articles on State Responsibility, A/56/10, *Report of the International Law Commission*, 2001, p. 45. Van Boven suggests that the duties of non-state actors to comply with international law 'must be regarded as inherently linked with the claim that they qualify as acceptable parties in national and international civil society', Theo Van Boven, 'Non-State Actors; Introductory Comments', in Theo Van Boven et al. (eds.), *The Legitimacy of the United Nations: Towards an Enhanced Legal Status of Non-State Actors*, Netherlands Institute of Human Rights, SIM Special, 19, Utrecht, 1997, p. 8.

[289] ICTY, *Prosecutor v. Dusko Tadić a/k/a 'Dule'*, Judgement of 7 May 1997, paras. 654–655. The Tribunal referred to, *inter alia*, the ILC's *Draft Code of Crimes Against the Peace and Security of Mankind*, in A/51/10, *Report of the International Law Commission*, 1996, pp. 93–96.

[290] A/CONF.183, *Rome Statute of the International Criminal Court*, 17 July 1998. For instance, Article 7(2)(a) states that 'Attack directed against any civilian population' should be understood as 'a course of conduct involving the multiple commission of acts referred

RIGHTS AND OBLIGATIONS   205

International humanitarian law and humanitarian organisations

The presence of international humanitarian organisations in situations of armed conflict goes back a long way. The long history and special status of the Order of Malta, as well as the important role and status of the ICRC in international humanitarian law, have been described earlier. The Geneva Conventions and their Additional Protocols include a wide set of rules regulating the work and protection of humanitarian personnel and organisations.[291] While some of these rules apply specifically to different bodies of the Red Cross and Red Crescent Movement, others refer to humanitarian organisations in general.

It should first be observed that the ICRC does not consider itself to be an NGO, although it falls roughly into the definition of 'NGO' used here.[292] The International Red Cross and Red Crescent Movement also embraces the National Societies and the International Federation of Red Cross and Red Crescent Societies, which are likewise understood as NGOs for the purpose of the study.[293] Nevertheless, provisions of humanitarian law which refer to humanitarian organisations in general, rather than solely to the International Red Cross and Red Crescent Movement or its different components, are of primary interest to this study on the legal status of NGOs, and the focus will therefore be on those provisions.

There are a considerable number of provisions in the Geneva Conventions (GC) and their Additional Protocols (AP) which refer to humanitarian organisations.[294] The direct references include:

---

to in paragraph 1 against any civilian population, pursuant to or in furtherance of a State or *organizational* policy to commit such attack' (emphasis added).

[291] It can also be observed that NGO personnel deployed by a humanitarian NGO for a UN operation for the purpose of maintaining or restoring international peace and security is afforded protection by the Convention on the Safety of United Nations Personnel, adopted by A/RES/49/59, 9 December 1994.

[292] See section 2.4.

[293] For information on the character and status of the International Federation of the Red Cross and Red Crescent Societies and on the national societies, see Yves Beigbeder, *The Role and Status of International Humanitarian Volunteers and Organizations: The Right and Duty to Humanitarian Assistance*, Dordrecht: Martinus Nijhoff, 1991, pp. 61–78; Christophe Lanord, 'The Legal Status of National Red Cross and Red Crescent Societies', *International Review of the Red Cross*, No. 840 (2000), pp. 1053–1077; and Peter Nobel, 'The Red Cross–Red Crescent Movement: A Model for Non-State Participation?', in Van Boven, *The Legitimacy of the United Nations*, pp. 77–86.

[294] Convention (I) for the Amelioration of the Condition of the Wounded and Sick in Armed Forces in the Field, 1949, Convention (II) for the Amelioration of the Condition of Wounded, Sick and Shipwrecked Members of Armed Forces at Sea, 1949,

206   LEGAL AND EMPIRICAL SURVEY

Common Article 3 of the Conventions:

Article 9 of GC I, II and III and Article 10 of GC IV
Article 10 of GC I, II and III and Article 11 of GC IV
GC I, Articles 18, 26, 28, 34, 44, 53
GC II, Articles 14, 24, 25
GC III, Articles 33, 35, 72, 75, 123, 125
GC IV, Articles 15, 26, 30, 39, 53, 59, 61, 63, 96, 98, 140, 142
AP I, Articles 5, 8, 9, 17, 32, 60, 81
AP II, Articles 12, 18.

There is no need for a discussion of all these provisions here; the Geneva Conventions and Additional Protocols have been elaborately described elsewhere. Within the framework of a study on the international legal status of NGOs, the most interesting provisions and aspects are the following.

The different expression used in the Geneva Conventions and the Additional Protocols for referring to NGOs include 'the International Committee of the Red Cross', 'National Red Cross Societies', 'any other impartial humanitarian organization' or 'body', 'other Voluntary Aid Societies, 'an organization which offers all guarantees of impartiality and efficacy', 'international religious organizations', 'any other organiza- tion giving assistance to prisoners', 'relief societies' and 'social or coop- erative organizations'. It is interesting to note that such diverse categories of NGOs are afforded rights, protection and obligations under interna- tional humanitarian law. Because of the general recognition and support for the ICRC and the national societies of the Red Cross and Red Crescent, it is probable that the possibilities for other organisations to act under the provisions are seldom used in practice; that would be an interesting field for research in itself. Nevertheless, the possibilities are there and they do indeed confer legal status on any NGO which falls under the categories mentioned and which decides to act under the provisions.

According to Common Article 3, para. 2 of the Conventions, an 'impartial humanitarian body, such as the International Committee of the Red Cross, may offer its services to the parties of the conflict' in the case of a conflict not of an international character. This Article

Convention (III) relative to the Treatment of Prisoners of War, 1949, Convention (IV) relative to the Protection of Civilian Persons in Time of War. Geneva, 1949, Protocol Additional to the Geneva Conventions of 12 August 1949, and relating to the Protection of Victims of International Armed Conflicts (Protocol I), 1977, Protocol Additional to the Geneva Conventions of 12 August 1949, and relating to the Protection of Victims of Non-International Armed Conflicts (Protocol II), 1977.

represents what is often described as a convention 'in miniature' which prohibits protected persons from certain acts. It is of special import- ance, as it is automatically applicable without any condition of recipro- city, and since several states have still not ratified Additional Protocol II relating to non-international armed conflicts.[295] The Commentary to the provision notes that it 'is obvious' that any organisation can offer its services. The importance lies in the fact that the codification of this possibility means that it cannot be regarded as an unfriendly act to offer charitable services.[296] It is also obvious, according to the Commentary, that it is in the first place for the National Red Cross Society of each country to offer help. Sometimes, however, this may not be possible. The provision therefore leaves it open for any 'impartial body' to offer its services. For such offers to be legitimate and acceptable, they must come from an organisation which is 'both humanitarian and impartial', the Commentary explains. The ICRC is mentioned as an example of such a body.[297] The organisations which fall into that category are further specified in the Commentary on Article 9 of Geneva Convention I, which states that:

The provisions of the present Convention constitute no obstacle to the huma- nitarian activities which the International Committee of the Red Cross or any other impartial humanitarian organization may, subject to the consent of the Parties to the conflict concerned, undertake for the protection of wounded and sick, medical personnel and chaplains, and for their relief.

Article 9 of Geneva Convention I, II and III and Article 10 of Geneva Convention IV have a similar wording, adjusted only to the subject matter of the respective Conventions. As it is mainly on behalf of prison- ers of war and civilians that humanitarian organisations carry out humanitarian assistance, the practical scope of Article 9/10 is greater in Geneva Convention III and IV. The meaning of the provision is that none of the other provisions of the Conventions excludes humanitarian participation on the part of the ICRC or a similar organisation. Although the Article thus leaves the door open for humanitarian NGOs to provide humanitarian assistance in armed conflict, it at the same time clarifies that the consent of the state parties to the conflict is a general condition.

---

[295] Pictet (ed.), *The Geneva Conventions*, p. 48. (The four ICRC commentaries – I Geneva Convention, 1952, II Geneva Convention, 1960, III Geneva Convention, 1960, and IV Geneva Convention, 1958 – will hereafter be referred to as '*Commentary I*', '*Commentary II*', etc.)

[296] *Commentary I*, pp. 57–58.   [297] *Ibid.*, pp. 58–59.

208   LEGAL AND EMPIRICAL SURVEY

The Commentary observes that: 'A belligerent Power can obviously not be obliged to tolerate in its territory activities of any kind of foreign organization. That would be out of the question.'[298] The Conventions and the Protocols thus do not establish a ground for a right for humanitarian organisations to provide humanitarian assistance, even if the possibility of a development in this area has been discussed by, among others, the International Conference of the Red Cross and Red Crescent.[299] It should be observed that, to the extent that other provisions of the Conventions establish rights for humanitarian NGOs providing assistance or obligations of state parties in relation to these organisations, such rights and obligations are conditioned by the consent of the conflicting parties to the presence of humanitarian organisations in the first place.

As regards the organisation comprised by the Article, the draft provision presented at the Diplomatic Conference in 1949 referred only to the ICRC. As there was a general fear that such a wording could close the door to other organisations, the Article was adopted without opposition with the addition 'or any other impartial humanitarian organization'.[300] Just as in Article 3 para. 2, the ICRC is mentioned as an example of what is meant by an 'impartial humanitarian organization'. The Commentary states regarding the characteristics of approved organisations that:

It is necessary for the organization to be *humanitarian*; in other words it must be concerned with the condition of man, considered solely as a human being without regard to the value which he represents as a military, political, professional or other unit. And the organization must be *impartial*. Article 9 does not require it to be international. As the delegate representing the United States at the Conference remarked, it would have been regrettable if welfare organizations of a non-international character had been prevented from carrying out their activities in time of war.[301]

---

[298] *Ibid.*, p. 110.
[299] The 26th International Conference of the Red Cross and Red Crescent (Geneva, 3-7 December 1995) recognised 'the right of humanitarian agencies - abiding by the principles of humanity, neutrality, impartiality and independence - to have access to victims', Resolution No. 4 of the Conference, *Principles and Action in International Humanitarian Assistance and Protection*, Preamble, para. 7. The resolution was adopted by consensus by the Conference, in which 143 States Party to the Geneva Conventions participated. See also Christina Rottensteiner, 'The Denial of Humanitarian Assistance as a Crime under International Law', *International Review of the Red Cross*, No. 835 (1999), pp. 555-582 and David P. Forsythe, 'International Humanitarian Assistance: The Role of the Red Cross', 3 *Buffalo Journal of International Law* (1996), pp. 235-260.
[300] *Commentary I*, p. 197.
[301] *Ibid.*, p. 108 (emphasis in original).

The activities of the organisation are also subject to certain conditions – they must be purely humanitarian in character and must not be affected by any political or military considerations. It follows from the text of the Article that the organisation and its activities must be impartial. This means that choices that are made in the distribution of relief assistance must not be dictated by prejudice or by considerations regarding the person of those who are given or refused assistance.[302]

Article 10 is common to Geneva Conventions I, II and III. Article 11 of Geneva Convention IV has an identical wording. These provisions state that the contracting parties may agree to 'entrust to an organization which offers all guarantees of impartiality and efficacy the duties incumbent on the Protecting Powers by virtue of the present Convention'. Thus, under Article 10 of Geneva Convention I–III, and Article 11 of Geneva Convention IV, states have the option to choose an organisation to assume the responsibilities of a protecting power, i.e. to safeguard the interests of a party, according to its instructions, in relation to other states.[303] For example, a protecting power may visit prisoners of war or safeguard the interests of the civilian population in occupied territory. The provision is sometimes mentioned in relation to the ICRC as a demonstration of its special status under international humanitarian law. The ICRC is the only organisation explicitly mentioned, which does indeed give it a special status. Nonetheless, it is interesting to note that the role of a protecting power may be played by another impartial and efficient NGO.

The requirement of impartiality for an organisation to be appointed as substitute for a protecting power should be understood as in Common Article 3. As regards the requirement of efficacy, the Commentary explains that:

it is difficult to define here the conditions for 'efficacy', since they will depend on the nature, extent and degree of localization of the conflict. The guarantees of efficacy are to be sought mainly in the financial and material resources which the organization has at its command and, even more perhaps, in its resources in qualified staff. Its independence in relation to the Parties to the conflict, the authority it has in the international world, enabling its representatives to deal with the Powers on a footing of equality, and finally its accumulated experience – all these are factors calculated to weigh heavily in deciding the parties to agree to its appointment. Without such agreement the special organization to which

---

[302] *Ibid.*, p. 109.
[303] The role of a protecting power is described in Article 8 of Geneva Convention I–III and in Article 9 of Geneva Convention IV.

210   LEGAL AND EMPIRICAL SURVEY

paragraph I relates cannot be appointed; and in the absence of such agreement the duties for which the Convention provides fall automatically to the Protecting Powers.[304]

Obviously, there is no right for an organisation to be appointed to take on the responsibilities of a protecting power, but a possibility for each organisation that fulfils the criteria, and the necessary degree of recognition within the international community, to enjoy this status.

Under Article 18, para. 2: 'The military authorities shall permit the inhabitants and relief societies, even in invaded or occupied areas, spontaneously to collect and care for wounded or sick of whatever nationality.' Individual inhabitants and relief organisations in the conflict area thus have a right to undertake relief action under this provision. It may be observed that there are no special requirements for an organisation to qualify for this right.[305]

Article 24 of Geneva Convention I states that medical personnel exclusively engaged in searching and caring for the wounded or sick, as well as administrative staff and chaplains engaged in related activities, have the right to be 'respected and protected in all circumstances'. According to Article 26, the staff of national Red Cross societies and of other voluntary aid societies, duly recognised and authorised by their governments, who are employed on the same duties as the personnel named in Article 24, have the right to the same respect and protection. That an NGO is 'duly recognised and authorised' by its government means that, in order for the organisation to enjoy protection, the government of its home country has to have recognised it as auxiliary to its own medical service and authorised it to lend its assistance.[306] Personnel designated under Articles 24 and 26 also enjoy specific rights in case they fall into the hands of the adverse party (see Article 28).

Article 44 is interesting because it formulates an obligation for organisations and their staff employed in relief assistance not to use the emblem of the red cross on a white ground and the words 'Red Cross' or 'Geneva Cross' other than in accordance with the Conventions. The provision is complemented by Article 53, which obliges state parties to prohibit the use by individuals, societies, firms or companies, either public or private, of the emblem or designations in breach of the provisions of the Convention.

---

[304] *Commentary I*, pp. 122–123.   [305] *Ibid.*, p. 189.   [306] *Ibid.*, p. 226.

Geneva Convention III relative to the treatment of prisoners of war includes several provisions that refer to organisations. The most interesting of these for the purpose of the present study is Article 125, which provides that:

Subject to the measures which the Detaining Powers may consider essential to ensure their security or to meet any other reasonable need, the representatives of religious organizations, relief societies, or any other organization assisting prisoners of war, shall receive from the said Powers, for themselves and their duly accredited agents, all necessary facilities for visiting the prisoners, for distributing relief supplies and material, from any source, intended for religious, educational or recreative purposes, and for assisting them in organizing their leisure time within the camps. Such societies or organizations may be constituted in the territory of the Detaining Power or in any other country, or they may have an international character.

The Detaining Power may limit the number of societies and organizations whose delegates are allowed to carry out their activities in its territory and under its supervision, on condition, however, that such limitation shall not hinder the effective operation of adequate relief to all prisoners of war.

The special position of the International Committee of the Red Cross in this field shall be recognized and respected at all times.

It is striking that the scope as regards the organisations referred to is so broad – religious organisations, relief societies, or any other organisation assisting prisoners of war. This last expression was added to the provision in order for public or semi-public institutions to be included. It also covers NGOs whose primary purpose is other than to assist prisoners of war, and which are therefore not 'relief societies', but which assume this task temporarily. The provision includes no requirement that relief societies must be properly established according to the law of their country.[307] As to the attitude and obligations of the detaining powers, the Commentary explains that the Convention 'obliges the Detaining Power to treat the relief societies correctly and thus gives the most important humanitarian right to private societies, even foreign societies in most cases, to enter its territory'.[308] It thus seems that, although this provision like many others relating to organisations, refers to the organisations' representatives rather than to the organisations as such, it does confer international rights or status on the organisations as well. Paragraph 2 of the Article demonstrates that, although the consent of the conflicting parties is a general requirement

---

[307] *Commentary III*, p. 595–596.   [308] *Ibid.*, p. 596.

212   LEGAL AND EMPIRICAL SURVEY

for the presence of NGOs in a conflict area according to Article 9 of the Convention (see above), a detaining power may not always refuse consent.

Geneva Convention IV deals with the protection of civilians. It is therefore natural that it includes many provisions which relate to the work of NGOs. According to Article 26:

Each Party to the conflict shall facilitate enquiries made by members of families dispersed owing to the war, with the object of renewing contact with one another and of meeting, if possible. It shall encourage, in particular, the work of organizations engaged on this task provided they are acceptable to it and conform to its security regulations.

Any organisation which satisfies both the conditions mentioned in the Article (being acceptable to the parties of the conflict and conforming to security regulations) must, as a rule, be allowed to carry out its work in connection with the reuniting of families. Belligerents are not only required to tolerate such activities, but are under an obligation to support and actively further the efforts of organisations engaged in the task.[309]

Under Article 30 of Geneva Convention IV, the ICRC, the National Red Cross, Red Crescent or Red Lion and Sun Society, and any organisation that may assist them, shall be granted all facilities for receiving applications, communications, complaints, etc. from protected persons, within the bounds set by military or security considerations. Under Article 30, the detaining or occupying powers shall also facilitate, as much as possible, visits to protected persons by representatives of the ICRC and other organisations whose object is to give spiritual aid or material relief to such persons.[310] The Commentary on this Article states that:

The Diplomatic Conference deliberately refrained from making the assistance of such organizations subject to any condition, other than that of being capable of assisting those who ask for their help. Under circumstances where distress assumes such proportions that there can never be enough assistance, it is essential to call upon all possible sources of relief. These organizations, however, whether national or international, must likewise strictly avoid, in their humanitarian activities, any action hostile to the Power in whose territory they are working or to the Occupying Power. These principles, needless to repeat, govern all forms of relief organized in connection with the Geneva Convention.[311]

---

[309] *Commentary IV*, p. 198.   [310] *Ibid.*, p. 214.   [311] *Ibid.*, pp. 217–218.

The Convention obliges the parties to the conflict not merely authorise organisations to carry out their work, but to facilitate and promote it. The authorities are under the duty to take all necessary steps to allow approved organisations to take rapid and effective action wherever they are asked to give assistance.[312] Article 30 should be read in conjunction with Article 142, which deals with the general obligation of detaining powers to offer facilities for relief organisations which assist protected persons. While the two provisions in some respects duplicate each other, they are complementary, as Article 142 defines relief societies and describes their activities. According to Article 142, relief organisations may be constituted in the territory of the detaining power, in any other country, or may have an international character.[313]

Article 53 of Geneva Convention IV prohibits 'Any destruction by the Occupying Power of real or personal property belonging individually or collectively to private persons, or to the State, or to other public authorities, or to social or cooperative organizations ... except where such destruction is rendered absolutely necessary by military operations'. The provision thus provides protection for NGOs, as well as any other owner of property, within occupied territory from destruction of property.

Impartial humanitarian organisations, such as the ICRC, have the right under Article 59 of GC IV to undertake relief schemes in situations where the whole or part of the population of an occupied territory is inadequately supplied. All contracting parties to the Convention are obliged to permit the free passage of such consignments and to guarantee their protection.

Article 63 of Geneva Convention IV formulates the right for recognised national Red Cross (Red Crescent, Red Lion and Sun) societies in occupied territories to pursue their activities in accordance with Red Cross principles, as defined by the International Red Cross Conferences. Other relief societies have the right 'to continue their humanitarian activities under similar conditions'. This seems to mean, according to the Commentary, that activities of an essentially humanitarian character cannot be interfered with by the occupation authorities.[314]

Article 142 of Geneva Convention IV is a provision of a general character which is of interest to all organisations engaged in relief for civilian population. The provision is almost identical to Article 125 of Geneva Convention III, with the exception of the last paragraph of the

---

[312] *Ibid.*, p. 218.   [313] *Ibid.*, p. 558.   [314] *Ibid.*, p. 332.

214   LEGAL AND EMPIRICAL SURVEY

latter (omitted above).[315] It also repeats some parts of Article 30. As explained above, the two provisions to some extent repeat each other, but are complementary in that Article 142 defines relief societies and describes their activities.[316]

Article 5, para. 3, of Additional Protocol I relating to the protection of victims in liberation wars formulates the right of the ICRC or any other impartial humanitarian organisation to offer its good offices to the parties to the conflict with a view to the designation without delay of a protecting power. If no protecting power has been designated, the conflicting parties 'shall accept without delay an offer which may be made by the International Committee of the Red Cross or by any other organization which offers all guarantees of impartiality and efficacy ... to act as a substitute' (Article 5, para. 4). This paragraph thus corresponds to Article 10 of Geneva Convention I–III and Article 11 of Geneva Convention IV. There are also other provisions which repeat rights guaranteed for organisations in the Geneva Conventions – for example, the right of aid societies to collect and care for the wounded, sick and shipwrecked (Additional Protocol II, Article 17, para.1) and the right to be offered 'all facilities' by the conflicting parties for the carrying out of humanitarian functions (Additional Protocol II, Article 81). Article 32 is interesting in the sense that it formulates a general obligation for contracting parties, conflicting parties and humanitarian organisations alike to 'be prompted mainly by the right of families to know the fate of their relatives' in the implementation of Section III relating to missing and dead persons.

The provisions of Additional Protocol II relating to the protection of victims of non-international armed conflicts become increasingly important as civil wars become more frequent. However, it includes only one provision which explicitly refers to humanitarian NGOs. Article 18 regarding relief societies and relief actions is important because it permits and facilitates humanitarian activities in non-international armed conflicts, while Common Article 3 of the Conventions does not mention relief actions. According to the Article, 'Relief societies located in the territory of the High Contracting Party, such as Red Cross (Red Crescent, Red Lion and Sun) organizations may offer their services for the performance of their traditional functions in relation to the victims of the armed conflict', and 'The civilian population may,

---

[315] For commentary on Article 142, see *Commentary IV*, pp. 556–566.
[316] *Ibid.*, p. 558.

even on its own initiative, offer to collect and care for the wounded, sick and shipwrecked'. The Commentary explains that:

The whole of this provision is based on the principle that States are primarily responsible for organizing relief. Relief societies such as the Red Cross and Red Crescent organizations are called upon to play an auxiliary role by assisting the authorities in their task. The term 'relief society' should be understood in its traditional broad sense. The Red Cross Movement, while playing a role of prime importance, does not have a monopoly on humanitarian activities, and there are other organizations capable of providing effective assistance.[317]

The 'traditional broad' meaning of 'relief society' is based on the usage of this expression in the Conventions, for instance Articles 18 and 26 of Geneva Convention I.[318] According to Article 18, para. 2, relief actions 'which are of an exclusively humanitarian and impartial nature and which are conducted without any adverse distinction' shall be undertaken in situations where the civilian population is suffering undue hardship owing to a lack of the supplies essential for its survival, such as foodstuffs and medical supplies, provided that the state concerned gives its consent. However, the fact that consent is required does not mean that the decision is left to the discretion of the parties. If the survival of the population is threatened, and a humanitarian organisation fulfilling the required conditions of impartiality offers assistance which might remedy this situation, the authorities responsible cannot refuse relief without good grounds.[319] Such a refusal would be a violation of Article 14 of the Protocol, which prohibits the use of starvation as a method of combat.[320] There is thus no explicit right for humanitarian organisations to deliver assistance in such situations, but something that might be regarded as an implied right, provided that the situation is grave and the other conditions mentioned in the provision are met.

4.5 Conclusions

The individual human rights which are most closely connected with the activities of NGOs, such as the right to freedom of association and

---

[317] *Commentary on the Additional Protocols*, p. 1477.   [318] See above.
[319] *Commentary on the Additional Protocols*, p. 1479.
[320] *Ibid.*, and Peter Macalister-Smith, *International Humanitarian Assistance: Disaster Relief Actions in International Law and Organization*, Dordrecht: Martinus Nijhoff, 1985, p. 31. See also Article 54 of Protocol I and Rottensteiner, 'The Denial of Humanitarian Assistance', pp. 555–582.

216   LEGAL AND EMPIRICAL SURVEY

assembly and the right to freedom of expression, enjoy strong protection under international law. It is clear that NGOs benefit from the clear recognition of these rights. Further, NGOs as such are guaranteed basic rights, organisation rights, in international and regional treaty law. While a number of individual human rights are recognised under international customary law, evidence of corresponding organisation rights under customary law would, on the other hand, probably be difficult to find.

The rules relating to the rights of organisations form a rather complex pattern because of the large number of instruments, and the different material and geographical scope of these instruments. As a result, the legal status of NGOs of different categories, as well as in different geographical regions, varies. NGOs in the states parties to the European Convention on Human Rights have a strong position through their standing as victims before the Court and the clear recognition of organisation rights in case-law of the European Court of Human Rights. The fact that NGOs have instituted cases before the convention monitoring bodies alleging violations of a wide range of rights, including the right to freedom of association and assembly, the right to freedom of expression, the right to freedom of religion and the right to a fair trial, demonstrates that NGOs can be holders of all convention rights which are not of a clearly physical or otherwise individual character.

On the international plane, trade unions enjoy substantial protection because of the guarantee of the right to form and join trade unions and the rights of trade unions to act without interference and to bargain collectively under international labour conventions and regional human rights treaties. These rights are also monitored under several different mechanisms, such as the freedom of association procedures under the ILO, the state reporting and complaints mechanisms under the UN human rights system, the collective complaints mechanism within the Council of Europe and the regional systems of human rights protection.

In other areas, however, the protection of NGOs as such is not as strong. Within the Inter-American system, for example, the rights of juridical entities are not recognised, which means that NGOs are afforded protection only through the individual rights of their members. In other words, a European trade union has a considerably stronger position than, for instance, an American or Asian NGO active outside the field of labour.

Environmental NGOs within the territory of state parties to the Convention on Access to Information, Public Participation in Decision-Making and Access to Justice in Environmental Matters as part of 'the public' and 'the public concerned' have the rights of access to information, public participation in decision-making and access to justice in environmental matters. Such NGOs also have the right to appropriate recognition and support from state parties, which must see to it that their national legal systems are consistent with this obligation. International humanitarian law, for its part, provides impartial humanitarian NGOs with several international rights, provided that the conflicting parties consent to the assistance of the organisations.

The field of international obligations of NGOs has not developed much as yet. There are good reasons for not bestowing international legal obligations on non-state actors outside some clearly defined areas, such as humanitarian law. Nevertheless, some areas of present responsibilities and possible future development can be discerned. IGOs which establish formal co-operation with NGOs require them to abide by certain rules, and NGOs which enter into operational co-operation with IGOs undertake contractual obligations. In addition, there is the developing field of voluntary codes of conduct, in which NGOs agree to follow certain norms, mainly within the field of humanitarian assistance. The different fields that relate to the international responsibilities of NGOs interact in a way which strengthens the normative force of formally non-binding instruments, as contracts on IGO–NGO co-operation sometimes refer to codes of conduct. It is possible that this area will develop, as it is in the interest of many NGOs to adhere to codes that can increase their support and goodwill among both the public and the state community.

5 Standing before international judicial and quasi-judicial bodies

5.1 Introduction

In an article published in 1947, Sir Hersch Lauterpacht observed that: 'It would thus appear that there is nothing inherent in the structure of international law which prevents individuals and, generally, persons other than States from being parties to proceedings before international tribunals.'[1] He was right. States are increasingly institutionalising the participation of non-state actors in international proceedings. This is particularly true concerning regional human rights mechanisms.

This chapter contains a description of the extent to which NGOs enjoy such procedural capacity in international law. The survey has two main components. It describes the existence and content of rules which provide some sort of *locus standi* to NGOs, and it includes a survey of cases instituted by NGOs intended to give a rough outline of the activity of NGOs before international tribunals and quasi-judicial bodies and the types of cases brought by them.

As regards the case-law material, a couple of points need to be explained. First, it has been necessary to limit the number of mechanisms and cases studied, for practical reasons. Secondly, the group of actors which is allowed to institute proceedings under the designation 'non-governmental organisation' is differently defined within the different mechanisms, and these definitions do not always correspond to the one adopted in the present study.[2] It would be too time-consuming to investigate whether the particular organisations acting which have filed in the different cases are 'NGOs' in the meaning of the term as it

---

[1] Hersch Lauterpacht, 'The Subjects of the Law of Nations', 63 *The Law Quarterly Review* (1947), p. 453.
[2] See section 1.3.

218

has been defined here. It can be mentioned as an example that 'non-governmental organisation' as used in the European Convention for Human Rights includes commercial entities. I have tried to exclude such cases from the study by using the name of the case and the information given in the introductory part of the judgement, but it is not completely certain that all commercial entities have been excluded. It should therefore be borne in mind that the figures presented concerning NGO participation in international and regional proceedings are to be seen as an estimate rather than accurate statistics.

5.2 International bodies

The International Court of Justice

It is, of course, clear that private parties cannot institute cases before the ICJ. Article 34 of the Court's Statute provides that: 'Only states may be parties before the Court.' The scope of entities entitled to request the ICJ to give an advisory opinion in accordance with Articles 65 and 96 of its Statute is wider, but non-state actors are excluded from this possibility as well. Apart from states, only the UN General Assembly, the Security Council and other organs of the United Nations and specialised agencies may request the Court to give an advisory opinion. Access to the PCIJ was likewise restricted to states, both in contentious cases and for advisory opinions.[3]

Nevertheless, it can be observed that – in spite of the restrictive rules on *locus standi* before the ICJ – NGOs sometimes act behind the scenes. A famous example is the NGO campaign which led to the *ICJ Nuclear Weapons Advisory Opinion*.[4] The project was launched in 1992 by three NGOs, the International Physicians for the Prevention of Nuclear War, the International Peace Bureau and the International Association of Lawyers Against Nuclear Arms.[5] The World Court Project sought to

---

[3] Article 35 of the PCIJ Statute reads: 'The Court shall be open to the Members of the League and also to States mentioned in the Annex to the Covenant.'
[4] On the role of NGOs in bringing this issue before the Court, see, e.g., Judge Rosalyn Higgins, 'The Reformation in International Law', in Richard Rawlings (ed.), *Law, Society and Economy: Centenary Essays for the London School of Economics and Political Science 1895–1995*, Oxford: Clarendon Press, 1997, p. 215 and Philippe Sands, 'International Law, the Practitioner and Non-State Actors', in Chanaka Wickremasinghe (ed.), *The International Lawyer as Practitioner*, London: The British Institute of International and Comparative Law, 2000, p. 103.
[5] Ved P. Nanda and David Krieger, *Nuclear Weapons and the World Court*, New York: Transnational Publishers, 1998, p. 70.

220 LEGAL AND EMPIRICAL SURVEY

influence member states at the WHO and the UN General Assembly to sponsor a resolution requesting an advisory opinion on the legality of using or threatening to use nuclear weapons. Naturally, the idea was that the ICJ should declare the use of nuclear weapons wholly illegal. Although the World Court Project was not formed until 1992, the idea of seeking an advisory opinion on the legality of nuclear weapons had deep roots within groups of civil society. For instance, the Lawyers' Committee on Nuclear Policy, formed as early as 1982, saw the idea as an integral part of its work.[6]

In 1992, there was intensive lobbying by the World Court Project at the WHO. The result of this lobbying was that fourteen governments agreed to sponsor a resolution at the World Health Assembly, which in its turn led to the adoption by the Assembly the following year of a resolution requesting an advisory opinion from the ICJ on the legality of the use of nuclear weapons.[7] The resolution, however, met strong opposition within the organisation, and some states considered that the request addressed an issue beyond the WHO's competence.[8] As is well known, the Court found that it was not able to give the advisory opinion requested by the WHO, since the question asked was not considered to be one arising within the scope of the activities of the organisation.[9]

The World Court Project also began to lobby the UN General Assembly in 1992. In spite of strong opposition from nuclear weapon states as well as other countries, the Assembly adopted a resolution in December 1994 requesting the ICJ 'urgently to render its advisory opinion on the following question: "Is the threat or use of nuclear weapons in any circumstance permitted under international law?"'[10]

---

[6] *Ibid.*, p. 71. Another initiative with the same objective was a Nuclear Warfare Tribunal organised in London in 1985 by the UK Ecology Party and Lawyers for Nuclear Disarmament. The Tribunal, which included Richard Falk among its members, recommended the initiation of an effort to obtain an advisory opinion of the ICJ, Nanda and Krieger, *Nuclear Weapons*, p. 72. See also the description of the history of the campaign contained in *Written Statement of the Government of the United Kingdom*, International Court of Justice, Legality of the Threat or Use of Nuclear Weapons, June 1995, paras. 2.2–2.3.

[7] Nanda and Krieger, *Nuclear Weapons*, p. 81.

[8] Laurence Boisson de Chazournes and Philippe Sands, (eds.), *International Law, the International Court of Justice and Nuclear Weapons*, Cambridge University Press, 1999, p. 4.

[9] *Legality of the Use by a State of Nuclear Weapons in Armed Conflict*, Advisory Opinion of 8 July 1996, ICJ Reports, 1996, p. 84.

[10] Nanda and Krieger, *Nuclear Weapons and the World Court*, pp. 82–83 and A/RES/49/75 K, *Request for an Advisory Opinion*, 15 December 1994.

The World Court Project obtained the support of more than 700 groups of civil society. Through these groups, the Project gathered 'Declarations of Public Conscience', in which individuals declared their opposition towards nuclear weapons. In June 1994, around 170,000 such declarations were presented to the ICJ Registrar, who received them and indicated that he would draw the judges' attention to them. At the outset of the oral hearings at the ICJ in October 1995, more than 3.5 million Declarations of Public Conscience were presented to the Court.[11] The material was not regarded as formal submissions to the Court but nevertheless made some impact on the proceedings.

Interestingly, the issue of the strong involvement of civil society in the issue brought to the ICJ was regarded as a relevant issue by some states as well as by some of the judges. The United Kingdom, which was opposed to the Court delivering an advisory opinion on the matter, gave a rather thorough description of the NGO activity preceding the UN General Assembly resolution in its written statement to the ICJ.[12] This activity was not mentioned as a problem as such, but as it was described in the context of the controversies in the General Assembly and the opposition with which the resolution was met, the text nevertheless gives the impression that the UK government sought to stress the political (and thus 'non-legal') character of the issue put to the Court.[13] The government of France did not refer explicitly to the NGO campaign, but stated that '*cette question n'est pas de nature juridique*'.[14]

A couple of judges referred to the NGO campaign in their opinions. Judge Oda gave a thorough description of the NGO activity and its lobbying efforts in his Dissenting Opinion, and summarised: 'This gives the impression that the Request for an advisory opinion which was made by the General Assembly in 1994 originated in ideas developed by some NGOs.'[15] The description of the campaign was mentioned

---

[11] Nanda and Krieger, *Nuclear Weapons*, p. 80.

[12] *Written Statement of the Government of the United Kingdom*, International Court of Justice, Legality of the Threat or Use of Nuclear Weapons, June 1995, paras. 1.2, 2.2–2.3.

[13] See also Boisson de Chazournes and Sands, *International Law*, pp. 9–10.

[14] *Exposé écrit du Gouvernement de la République française*, June 1995, p. 12. Regarding the reactions from states on the involvement of NGOs, see also Roger S. Clark and Madeleine Sann (eds.), *The Case against the Bomb: Marshall Islands, Samoa, and Solomon Islands before the International Court of Justice in Advisory Proceedings on the Legality of the Threat or Use of Nuclear Weapons*, Rutgers University School of Law, 1996, p. 15.

[15] *Legality of the Use by a State of Nuclear Weapons in Armed Conflict*, Dissenting Opinion of Judge Oda, ICJ Reports, 1996, pp. 335–336. See also Judge Oda's Dissenting Opinion to

222 LEGAL AND EMPIRICAL SURVEY

as a factor pointing to 'The Inadequacy of the Question put by the General Assembly in the Resolution as the Request for Advisory Opinion'. Judge Guillaume also described the General Assembly resolution as originating in NGO activity in his Separate Opinion and stated that:

> I am sure that the pressure brought to bear in this way did not influence the Court's deliberations, but I wondered whether, in such circumstances, the request for opinions could still be regarded as coming from the Assemblies which had adopted them or whether, piercing the veil, the Court should not have dismissed them as inadmissible. However, I dare to hope that Governments and intergovernmental institutions still retain sufficient independence of decision to resist the powerful pressure groups which besiege them today with the support of mass media. I also note that none of the States which appeared before the Court raised such an objection. In the circumstances I did not believe that the Court should uphold it *proprio motu*.[16]

Judge Guillaume thus suggested that the Court could have regarded the resolutions as inadmissible because of the pressure from civil society. Clearly, his view is that the role of civil society should be limited to the national plane and that governments should resist public opinion which 'besiege[s]' them on the international plane.

Judge Weeramantry, on the other hand, argued for an opposite view. He began the substantive part of his Dissenting Opinion by describing the 'wave of global interest unparalleled in the annals of this Court' and observed that the signatures and other material sent to the Court evidenced a groundswell of global opinion which was 'not without legal relevance'.[17] In a section of his Opinion titled 'The Attitude of the International Community Towards Nuclear Weapons', Judge Weeramantry stated that the law of the United Nations proceeded from the law of the peoples of the United Nations. In addition to describing the views of states concerning nuclear weapons, he observed that 'there is also a vast preponderance of public opinion across the globe' and mentioned the many NGOs formed with the objective of

---

the ICJ's Advisory Opinion *Legality of the Use by a State of Nuclear Weapons in Armed Conflict* of 8 July 1996, ICJ Reports, 1996, pp. 92–96. The attitude towards NGOs is more clearly negative in this Opinion, where Judge Oda stated that it seemed clear that the WHO request 'was initiated by a few NGOs', *ibid.*, p. 96.

[16] *Legality of the Use by a State of Nuclear Weapons in Armed Conflict*, Separate Opinion of Judge Guillaume, ICJ Reports, 1996, pp. 287–288.

[17] *Ibid.*, Dissenting Opinion of Judge Weeramantry, ICJ Reports, 1996, p. 438.

protesting nuclear weapons, as well as the millions of signatures sent to the Court. Judge Weeramantry thus seems to have regarded public opinion on the matter in focus of the opinion as an argument in support of the illegality of nuclear weapons.[18]

The majority of the Court found that there were no compelling reasons for it not to deliver an opinion on the question posed by the General Assembly. In its Advisory Opinion, which was issued in July 1996, the ICJ did not comment on the campaign which had preceded the adoption of the General Assembly resolution or the signatures which had been received by the Court.[19] In other words, it did not regard these circumstances as legally relevant, either in relation to the question whether it should deliver the opinion, or in relation to the issue of the legality of nuclear weapons as such. As the threat or use of nuclear weapons was not declared as clearly illegal in all circumstances, it might have been seen as a disappointment for parts of the civil society campaign which had exerted pressure for the Court's examination of the issue. In light of the opposition from many states as regards the appropriateness of bringing the issue of nuclear weapons to the Court, the turn of events also raised questions about the accountability and legitimacy of NGOs.[20] Judge Rosalyn Higgins commented on the events in these words:

Clearly, to some, these radical phenomena represent the democratization of international law. To others, it is both a degradation of the technical work of international lawyers in the face of pressure groups and a side-stepping of existing international law requirements and procedures.[21]

---

[18] *Ibid.*, pp. 533–534. In the *Case Concerning Application of the Convention on the Prevention and Punishment of the Crime of Genocide* (Preliminary Objections), Judge *ad hoc* Kreca noted in his Dissenting Opinion that 'An unfavourable position regarding the principle of universal punishment emerges also from declarations and reservations concerning the Genocide Convention, Communication of Governments, and by non-governmental organizations that have a consultative status with the Economic and Social Council'. ICJ Reports, 1996, p. 767.

[19] *Legality of the Threat or Use of Nuclear Weapons*, Advisory Opinion of 8 July 1996, ICJ Reports, 1996, pp. 226–267.

[20] See statement by Philippe Sands, *Plenary Theme Panel: The Challenge of Non-State Actors*, in ASIL Proceedings of the 92nd Annual Meeting (1998), p. 31. The campaign has, however, also been described as an 'NGO success story', see Manfred Mohr, 'Advisory Opinion of the International Court of Justice on the Legality of the Use of Nuclear Weapons under International Law – A Few Thoughts on its Strengths and Weaknesses', *International Review of the Red Cross*, No. 316 (1997), pp. 92–102.

[21] Rosalyn Higgins, 'The Reformation in International Law', p. 215.

International criminal courts

The ICC has the power to exercise jurisdiction over persons for the most serious crimes of international concern.[22] The Court may exercise its jurisdiction if a situation, in which one or more crimes referred to in its Statute appear to have been committed, is referred to the Prosecutor by a state party to the Statute or by the UN Security Council, or if the Prosecutor has initiated an investigation *proprio motu*.[23] It is, in other words, clear that NGOs cannot refer such a situation to the Court. However, when the Prosecutor analyses the seriousness of information received, he or she may seek additional information from NGOs according to Article 15(2) of the Statute.

The Statute of the ICTY includes a similar provision.[24] According to Article 18 on the Investigation and preparation of indictment, the Prosecutor '*shall* initiate investigations ex-officio or on the basis of information obtained from any source, particularly from Governments, United Nations organs, intergovernmental and non-governmental organizations'.[25] An identical provision applies to the Prosecutor of the ICTR.[26] NGOs are thus officially mentioned as an important source of information for all three international criminal courts.

The UN Treaty Bodies

The Human Rights Committee

The UN Human Rights Committee is a body of eighteen experts, appointed in their personal capacity, which has the task of monitoring the contracting states' compliance with the ICCPR of 1966. The Committee may also receive communications of alleged breaches of the Covenant under the Optional Protocol.[27] A state which becomes party to the Protocol recognises the competence of the Human Rights Committee to receive and consider communications from individuals who claim that their human rights have been violated by that state.[28]

---

[22] A/CONF.183/9, *Rome Statute of the International Criminal Court*, as corrected by the procès-verbaux of 10 November 1998 and 12 July 1999, Article 1.

[23] *Ibid.*, Article 13.

[24] Statute of the International Criminal Tribunal for the Former Yugoslavia, 25 May 1993, as amended 30 November 2000.

[25] Emphasis added.

[26] Statute of the International Criminal Tribunal for Rwanda, 8 November 1994, Article 17(1).

[27] Optional Protocol to the International Covenant on Civil and Political Rights (1966).

[28] *Ibid.*, Article 1.

The Committee cannot issue binding judgements, only 'forward its views to the state party concerned and to the individual'.[29] As was mentioned in chapter 4 the opinions delivered by the Committee are, however, publicised and generally considered as authoritative.[30]

The Committee started its work under the Optional Protocol in 1977. According to Article 2 of the Protocol, 'individuals who claim that any of their rights enumerated in the Convention have been violated' may submit a written communication to the Committee. The original Dutch draft to Article 2 also permitted communications from groups of persons, and the admissibility of such communications was proposed in the Commission on Human Rights several times during the work with the drafting of the Convention.[31] A draft protocol presented by the United States permitted petitions from both individuals and from NGOs. It was argued during the negotiations that NGOs with consultative status with ECOSOC could better than individuals defend the interests of humanity as a whole, since they would have to act with caution through fear of criticism from the Council and from their members.[32] These discussions on the right to petition demonstrate that the restriction to individuals in the text finally adopted in 1966 by the General Assembly was intentional. It was likely motivated by the fear that groups of individuals or NGOs would use the right to petition for political or propaganda purposes.[33]

Subsequently, it has been confirmed by the Committee's jurisprudence that organisations as such may not submit communications. In *J. R. T. and the W. G. Party* v. *Canada*, the communication had been submitted by an unincorporated political party. The Committee declared the part of the communication which concerned the political party inadmissible with reference to the fact that it was an association, which could not as such submit a communication to the Committee.[34] A similar case is *A Group of Associations for the Defence of the Rights of Disabled*

---

[29] *Ibid.*, Article 5(4).

[30] Dominick McGoldrick, *The Human Rights Committee: The Role in the Development of the International Covenant on Civil and Political Rights*, Oxford: Clarendon Press, 1994, pp. 151–152 and Manfred Nowak, *UN Covenant on Civil and Political Rights: CCPR Commentary*, Kiel: N. P. Engel, 1993, p. xix. See also section 4.2.

[31] Nowak, *UN Covenant*, pp. 657–658.

[32] Dominic McGoldrick, *The Human Rights Committee: Its Role in the Development of the International Covenant on Civil and Political Rights*, Oxford: Clarendon Press, 1994, p. 123.

[33] *Ibid.*, pp. 122–123 and Nowak, *UN Covenant*, p. 658.

[34] Communication No. 104/1981, A/38/40, *Report of the Human Rights Committee*, 1983, p. 236.

226   LEGAL AND EMPIRICAL SURVEY

and Handicapped Persons in Italy, etc. v. *Italy.*[35] The authors of the communication were a group of associations together forming an NGO (*Coordinamento*) and the representatives of those organisations. They claimed that they were acting for the Coordinamento but also on their own behalf. The Committee declared that

> According to Article 1 of the Optional Protocol, only individuals have the right to submit a communication. To the extent, therefore, that the communication originated from the Coordinamento, it has to be declared inadmissable because of lack of personal legal standing.[36]

Even if Articles 1 and 2 of the Optional Protocol had provided standing for NGOs, their possibility of submitting communications would have been limited by the victim requirement as most of the rights set out in the Convention are individual rights. Article 1 of the Convention, however, formulates the collective right of self-determination. The question of admissibility of a communication submitted by an individual on behalf of a group allegedly subjected to a violation of the group right to self-determination was actualised in the *Mikmaq* case.[37] The communication was declared inadmissible because of lack of authorisation, which seemed to indicate that, had the complainant been able to provide sufficient evidence for his standing as a representative of the society, the communication would have been accepted. In the case of *Lubicon Lake Band* v. *Canada*, however, the Committee found that 'the author, as an individual, could not claim under the Optional Protocol to be a victim of a violation of the right to self-determination enshrined in Article I of the Covenant, as it dealt with rights conferred upon peoples as such'.[38] The Committee's practice means, on the one hand, that only individual victims can submit communications and, on the other, that only groups may be considered to be victims of violation of the group right to self-determination. The right to self-determination, containing no individual element, has thus been excluded from the procedure

---

[35] Communication No. 163/1984, A/39/40, *Report of the Human Rights Committee, 1984*, pp. 197–198.

[36] *Ibid.*, p. 198. See also Communication No. R.9.40, *Hartikainen* v. *Finland*, which was submitted by the Secretary-General of the Union of Free Thinkers of Finland on behalf of the organisation as well as on his own behalf. The application was declared inadmissible as far as the organisation was concerned. A/36/40, *Report of the Human Rights Committee*, 1981, p. 148.

[37] Communication No. 78/1980, *A.D.* v. *Canada*, submitted on behalf of the Mikmaq tribal society, in A/39/40, *Report of the Human Rights Committee*, 1984, pp. 200–203.

[38] Communication No. 167/1984, *Lubicon Lake Band* v. *Canada*, in 96 ILR (1994), p. 668.

under the Optional Protocol. The only solution for a group of persons which has suffered a violation of the ICCPR is to file individual complaints. The Committee added in the *Lubicon Lake Band* case that there is 'no objection to a group of individuals, who claim to be similarly affected, collectively to submit a communication about alleged breaches of their rights'.[39] Such communications may be considered, for instance, under Article 27 on the rights of persons belonging to minorities.

An NGO which suffers a violation of the right of assembly under Article 21 or the right of association under Article 22 of the Covenant can thus submit a communication only by putting forward one or more individuals, not only because NGOs lack *locus standi* under the Optional Protocol, but also because of the limitation to individual rights developed in the practice of the Human Rights Committee.[40] It can also be observed that an individual affected by a violation suffered by a juridical person does not have *locus standi* before the Committee. In *Lamagna* v. *Australia*, the Committee declared the communication inadmissible since the alleged violation was committed against the author's company, which had its own juridical personality.[41]

The Committee may, in accordance with Rule 90(b) of its Rules of Procedure, accept a communication submitted *on behalf of* an alleged victim when it appears that the individual is unable to submit the communication personally.[42] According to the practice of the Human Rights Committee, the condition for acceptance is that there is a strong link between the victim and the author of the communication, such as a close family connection.[43] The Committee has also developed a clear interpretation of the provision as regards communications submitted by others than family members in its case-law.

In *L.A. on behalf of U.R.* v. *Uruguay*, the victim was detained in a prison in Uruguay. The author of the communication was a member of the Swedish Section of Amnesty International and had been working on the alleged victim's case for two years. He claimed to have the authority to act on behalf of the victim because he believed 'that every prisoner treated unjustly would appreciate further investigation of his case by the Human Rights Committee'. The

---

[39] *Ibid.*, p. 702.   [40] See McGoldrick, *The Human Rights Committee*, p. 170.
[41] Communication No. 737/1997, *Lamagna* v. *Australia*, CCPR/C/65/D/737/1997, 30 April 1999, para. 6.2.
[42] HRI/GEN/3, *Compilation of Rules of Procedure Adopted by Human Rights Treaty Bodies*, p. 56.
[43] According to McGoldrick, the Committee has taken a fairly liberal approach to the question of family connection. McGoldrick, *The Human Rights Committee*, p. 170.

228 LEGAL AND EMPIRICAL SURVEY

Committee stated that a communication submitted by a third party on behalf of an alleged victim can be considered only if the author can justify his authority to submit the communication. As the Committee could not accept on the basis of the information before it that the author had the authority to act, the communication was declared inadmissible.[44]

In the case of *X. on behalf of S. G. F.* v. *Uruguay*, the communication was submitted by an NGO on behalf of a Uruguayan citizen living in Sweden. The organisation stated that the request of S. G. F. for it to act on her behalf was made through close friends living in France whose identity, however, the organisation felt unable to disclose. The Committee noted that 'No written evidence with regard to the authority of the organization ... to act on behalf of the alleged victim has been provided' and declared the communication inadmissible.[45] Another, similar, communication led to the same result.[46]

It is clear that NGOs are not regarded as having any general authority to act on behalf of alleged victims within their field of competence.[47] On the other hand, although all the above communications were declared inadmissible, the decisions demonstrate that an NGO can act on behalf of an individual victim provided that there is enough evidence regarding the NGO's authority to do so.[48]

This is also in line with the possibility of an NGO acting as the duly authorised representative of a victim who is not, in contrast to what was the case in the examples above, unable to submit the communication

---

[44] Communication No. 128/1982, in *Selected Decisions of the Human Rights Committee*, 2 (1990), pp. 40–41.

[45] Communication No. 136/1983, in *Selected Decisions of the Human Rights Committee*, 2 (1990), p. 43.

[46] Communication No. 137/1983, *X. on behalf of J. F.* v. *Uruguay*, *Selected Decisions of the Human Rights Committee*, 2 (1990), pp. 43–44. See also Communication No. 183/1984, *D. F. on behalf of D. F. et al.* v. *Sweden*, A/40/40, *Report of the Human Rights Committee*, 1985, pp. 228–229. The latter had similarities to an *actio popularis*, as the author submitted the communication both on his own behalf and on behalf of Arabs and Muslims who had allegedly been the constant target of discrimination and abuse in Sweden. A similar case was Communication No. 187/1985 (*J. H.* v. *Canada*) regarding alleged discrimination of persons of English mother tongue in Canada. The Committee stated that it was not its task to review *in abstracto* national legislation or practices and declared the communication inadmissible with reference to the victim requirement. A/40/40, pp. 230–231.

[47] Nowak holds that a provision allowing for communications to be submitted on behalf of someone who is unable to do so, 'poses a danger that organizations might misuse it for popular complaints'. The Rule was therefore the subject of long discussions within the Committee. Nowak, *UN Covenant*, p. 662.

[48] See also McGoldrick, *The Human Rights Committee*, p. 172.

personally. According to the above-mentioned Rule 90(b), a communication should normally be submitted 'by the individual personally or by that individual's representative'. Even though a lawyer with a written power of attorney was what the Committee primarily had in mind here, the representative does not have to be a lawyer.[49] The point is that the representative has to be specifically authorised by the victim to act on his or her behalf. The possibility of acting as the duly appointed representative of a victim is not insignificant from a law-influencing perspective since specialised NGOs can identify 'pilot cases'. However, the appointment of NGOs or their officials as representatives of authors of communications to the Human Rights Committee is not a common phenomenon. The majority of authors are represented by counsels from law firms, and many individuals lack legal representation.

Nevertheless, the London-based human rights organisation Interights has acted as the victim's representative in a number of cases examined by the Committee. The cases concerned issues related to death sentences and unfair trials.[50] In the second and third of these cases, Interights argued that a long period of time spent on death row *per se* amounted to cruel, inhuman and degrading treatment in violation of Article 7 of the Covenant and contrary to the right under Article 10(1) to be treated with humanity and respect for the inherent dignity of the

---

[49] Nowak, *UN Covenant*, p. 661; McGoldrick, *The Human Rights Committee*, p. 134. See also the cases referred to below.

[50] See communications 594/1992 (*Phillip* v. *Trinidad and Tobago*, CCPR/C/64/D/594/1992, 3 December 1998); 554/1993 (*LaVende* v. *Trinidad and Tobago*, CCPR/C/61/D/554/1993, 14 January 1998); 555/1993 (*Bickaroo* v. *Trinidad and Tobago*, CCPR/C/61/D/555/1993, 14 January 1998); 665/1995 (*Brown and Parish* v. *Jamaica*, CCPR,/C/66/D/665/1995, 5 August 1999); 668/1995 (*Smith and Stewart* v. *Jamaica*, CCPR/65/D/668/1995, 12 May 1999); 676/1996 (*Yasseen and Thomas* v. *Guyana*, CCPR/C/62/D/676/1996, 7 May 1998); 928/2000 (*Sooklal* v. *Trinidad and Tobago*, CCPR/C/73/D/928/2000, 8 November 2001). Interights also assisted the author of communication 950/2000 (*Sarma* v. *Sri Lanka*, CCPR/C/78/D/950/2000, 31 July 2003). Interights has further acted on the national level in cases regarding the death penalty in a number of countries, including Trinidad and Tobago and Guyana, Interights, *Annual Review 98–99*, pp. 21, 31. Two other human rights NGOs, Amnesty International and Human Rights Watch, have been frequently referred to by the authors of communications and their counsels. References to reports, investigations and press releases by Amnesty International have been made in a number of cases regarding prison conditions in Jamaica, e.g. 546/1993, 587/1994, 590/1994, 592/1994, 607/1994, 611/1995, 619/1995, 634/1995, 639/1995, 640/1995, 647/1995, 649/1995, 653/1995, 730/1996, 734/1997. Material produced by Amnesty International has also been mentioned in 328/1988 (Nicaragua), 706/1996 (Australia) and 458/1991 (Cameroon). Material produced by Human Rights Watch has been mentioned in some of these cases, and in at least one additional case (663/1995, Jamaica).

230   LEGAL AND EMPIRICAL SURVEY

person (the so-called 'death row phenomenon'). The Human Rights Committee has consistently rejected this argument, in spite of the cases brought by Interights, where two of the complainants had been on death row for up to eighteen years.[51] In some of the later cases, Interights focused on the conditions during detention and argued that bad conditions could amount to violations of Articles 7 and/or 10(1), which has been accepted by the Committee. The Committee has also ruled that the imposition of a sentence of death upon conclusion of a trial in which the fair trial guarantees in Article 14 of the Covenant have not been met constitutes, if no further appeal against the sentence is possible, a violation of the right to life in Article 6.[52]

A representative of another NGO, the Fundación de Ayuda Social de las Iglesias Cristianas, has acted as counsel in a couple of cases against Chile.[53]

The Draft Optional Protocol to the ICESCR

In 1996, a draft Optional Protocol for the submission of individual communications was adopted by the Committee on Economic, Social and Cultural Rights and submitted to the Commission on Human Rights, where the matter is still under consideration.[54] The proposed text for Article 2 of the Draft reads:

Any individual or group claiming to be a victim of a violation by the State party concerned of any of the economic, social or cultural rights recognized in the

---

[51] A/53/40, *Report of the Human Rights Committee*, 15 September 1998, para. 457; Natalia Schiffrin, 'Current Development: Jamaica Withdraws the Right of Individual Petition Under the International Covenant on Civil and Political Rights', 92 AJIL (1998), p. 564; McGoldrick, *The Human Rights Committee*, p. lxiii. Schiffrin is a senior legal adviser at Interights and has acted as counsel before the Human Rights Committee in several of the cases described above.

[52] See, *inter alia*, the cases of *Phillip* v. *Trinidad and Tobago* (Communication No. 594/1992) and *Yasseen and Thomas* v. *Guyana* (No. 676/1996), described above.

[53] The complainants argued that, with the application of its amnesty law in relation to a number of persons who were executed in 1973, Chile had accepted the impunity of those responsible for the acts and renounced its obligation to investigate international crimes, thereby violating Article 15(2) of the Covenant. Both applications were, however, declared inadmissible *ratione temporis* by the Committee as they concerned deaths which had occurred prior to the entry into force of the Covenant in 1976. Communication No. 717/1996, *Inostroza* v. *Chile*, CCPR/C/66/D/717/1996, 16 September 1999 and No. 746/1997, *Aceituno and Vasquez* v. *Chile*, CCPR/C/66/D/746/1997, 4 August 1997.

[54] As of August 2004.

Covenant, or any individual or group acting on behalf of such claimant(s), may submit a written communication to the Committee for examination.[55]

'Groups' are thus included both in the range of victims who may submit communications and in the scope of actors who may act on behalf of the victim. NGOs are not expressly mentioned, and the issue whether organisations as such can be considered to be victims of violations of the rights set out in the ICESCR is not discussed in the Committee's report on the Protocol.[56] The Committee did, however, discuss the issue of a victim requirement versus a broader rule on standing – for instance, one requiring 'sufficient interest' in the matter. It considered that the broader formulation, which would make it possible for a 'public interest group or some other type of non-governmental organization' to bring a complaint without having to act with or on behalf of the alleged victim would, on the one hand, increase the capacity of the procedure to address every possible issue of relevance but, on the other, do this at the price of a vast number of complaints. The solution decided upon by the Committee was to extend the capacity to submit a complaint to individuals or groups acting on behalf of alleged victims. The Committee noted, however, that 'this formulation should be interpreted only to embrace individuals and groups who, in the view of the Committee, are acting with the knowledge and agreement of the alleged victim(s)'.[57] It thus seems that the Protocol, if it is adopted, will include a wider possibility for NGOs to act than the Optional Protocol to the ICCPR.

The Committee on the Elimination of Racial Discrimination

Article 14 of the International Convention on the Elimination of All Forms of Racial Discrimination (1965) authorises the Committee on the Elimination of Racial Discrimination to receive and consider communications from individuals or groups of individuals claiming to be victims of a violation by a right set out in this Convention. It is, however, a condition that the state party in question has declared that it recognises the competence of the Committee to receive such communications. There is, in other words, no possibility for NGOs to submit communications in the capacity of victim of a violation. Nevertheless, communications submitted on behalf of the alleged victim can be accepted by the

---

[55] E/CN.4/1997/105, *Status of the International Covenants on Human Rights*, 18 December 1996, annex, para. 31.
[56] *Ibid.*, paras. 19–20.   [57] *Ibid.*, paras. 22–23.

232   LEGAL AND EMPIRICAL SURVEY

Committee in exceptional cases when the victim is unable to submit the communication personally and the author can justify his or her acting on the victim's behalf.[58] Another possibility for NGOs to act under the Convention is to act as the representative of the alleged victim.

As of August 2004, the Committee had issued its decision on inadmissibility or on the merits in twenty-eight cases. In two cases, NGOs have acted as petitioner, thereby giving the Committee the opportunity to formulate the scope of possibility for NGOs to act as petitioners before the Committee.

Communication No. 22/2002 was lodged by the Umbrella Organization for the Ethnic Minorities (POEM), a Danish organisation with the aim of promoting ethnic equality in all spheres of society, and the Association of Muslim Students (FASM), which is also a Danish organisation with the aim of raising awareness on Muslim issues. The petition concerned a statement made by a leader of a Danish political party which, according to the petitioners, was prejudicial and islamophobic. Another organisation, the Documentation and Advisory Centre on Racial Discrimination (DRC), reported the statement to the Danish police for being in violation of the Criminal Code. The petitioners claimed that when such statements are made in public, 'both the petitioners and their members, including the non-Muslims, are affected'.[59] They argued that the state party had violated several of its obligations under the Convention, such as the obligation under Article 6 to ensure effective protection and remedies for everyone within their jurisdiction. The Committee noted that none of the petitioners was a plaintiff in the domestic proceedings and that the report to the Copenhagen Police was submitted only by the DRC. It considered that it was a basic requirement under Article 14, para. 7(a) that domestic remedies have to be exhausted by the petitioners themselves and not by other organisations or individuals. The Committee therefore found that the communication was inadmissible under the said Article.[60]

In the case regarding communication No. 28/2003, the DRC acted as petitioner, represented by Ms Mohammad, who was the head of the board of trustees of the Centre.[61] The communication concerned a job advertisement which, according to the petitioner, amounted to discrimination on the ground of national or ethnic origin. The advertisement read: 'The construction company BAC SIA seeks Danish foreman.' The petitioner reported the advertisement to the police, alleging a violation of the prohibition against discrimination in respect of employment and occupation on the labour market. The petitioner claimed

---

[58] Rule 91(b) of the Committee's Rules of Procedure, HRI/GEN/3, *Compilation of Rules of Procedure Adopted by Human Rights Treaty Bodies*, 6 June 2001, p. 93.

[59] *POEM and FASM* v. *Denmark*, CERD/C/62/D/22/2002, 15 April 2003, para. 2.3.

[60] Ibid., paras. 6.2–6.3.   [61] *DRC* v. *Denmark*, CERD/C/63/D/28/2003, 26 August 2003.

that, as the head of the board of trustees, Ms Mohammad represented the DRC when complaints were filed in her name. Although neither Ms Mohammad nor any other person of non-Danish origin applied for the advertised job, she should be considered a victim of the discriminatory advertisement, since it would have been futile for her to apply for the post. Moreover, the petitioner itself should be recognised as having the status of victim under Article 14 of the Convention, since it represented a large group of persons of non-Danish origin discriminated against by the job advertisement in question. In support of this claim, the petitioner stated that both the police and the Regional Public Prosecutor had accepted it as a party to domestic proceedings. The petitioner argued that it followed from the *travaux préparatoires* to the Convention that the expression 'individuals or groups of individuals' in Article 14, para. 1, should be interpreted broadly so as to be able to include NGOs among those entitled to bring a complaint before the Committee. In its decision, the Committee stated that it did not exclude the possibility that a group of persons representing, for example, the interests of a racial or ethnic group, might submit an individual communication, provided that it was able to prove that it had been an alleged victim of a violation of the Convention or that one of its members had been a victim, and if it was able at the same time to provide due authorisation to this effect. It noted that, according to the petitioner, no member of the board of trustees applied for the job. Moreover, the petitioner had not argued that any of the members of the board, or any other identifiable person whom the petitioner would be authorised to represent, had a genuine interest in, or showed the necessary qualifications for, the vacancy. While the relevant provision of Danish law prohibited discrimination of all persons of non-Danish origin in job advertisements, it did not automatically follow that persons not directly and personally affected by such discrimination could claim to be victims of a violation of any of the rights guaranteed in the Convention. Any other conclusion would open the door for popular actions (*actio popularis*) against the relevant legislation of states parties. The Committee concluded that the petitioner had failed, for the purposes of Article 14(1), to substantiate its claim that it constituted or represented a group of individuals claiming to be the victim of a violation by Denmark of the Convention. The Committee therefore decided that the communication was inadmissible *ratione personae* under the Convention.[62]

It can be concluded from these two cases that an NGO may file petitions before CERD if (a) it has itself been the victim of a violation of the Convention and has itself exhausted domestic remedies in the matter, or (b) if it can demonstrate that it is authorised to represent persons who are identifiable victims of violations of the Convention.

---

[62] *Ibid.*, paras. 6.4–7(a).

234   LEGAL AND EMPIRICAL SURVEY

Interestingly, the Committee did not exclude the possibility for NGOs to act as petitioners on their own behalf. In the decision in case 28/2003, it used the expression 'group of persons', thereby avoiding 'organisation', while at the same time mentioning 'members', which can imply organisations as well as informal groups. The case nevertheless demonstrates that some of the rights pronounced by CERD may protect not only individuals and groups, but also organisations. On the other hand, it should also be observed that NGOs (and other legal or physical persons) do not have the right to file *actio popularis* for the common good without any connection to concrete victims.

According to the twenty-eight case reports, the victim was represented by an NGO acting as counsel in four cases.[63] Many reports, however, simply state that the victim was 'represented by counsel'. According to a former member of the Committee, the victim is represented by an NGO in about half of the cases examined by the Committee, and in some others it can be assumed that an NGO has probably referred the victim to the counsel or been involved in some other way.[64]

The Committee Against Torture

According to Article 22(1) of the Convention against Torture (CAT), the Committee Against Torture is restricted to receiving communications from individuals. The Article reads:

A State Party to this Convention may at any time declare under this article that it recognizes the competence of the Committee to receive and consider communications from *or on behalf of* individuals subject to its jurisdiction who claim to be victims of a violation by a State Party of the provisions of the Convention.[65]

Rule 107(b) of the Committee's Rules of Procedure makes it clear that the Committee may receive communications on behalf of an alleged victim when it appears that the victim is unable to submit the communication personally.[66]

---

[63] Communications No. 13/1998 (*Koptova* v. *Slovakia*, CERD/C/57/D/13/1998, 1 November 2000); 18/2000 (*F.A.* v. *Norway*, CERD/C/58/D/18/2000, 17 April 2001); 11/1998 (*Lacko* v. *Slovakia*, CERD/C/59/D/11/1998, 1 August 2001); 25/2002 (*Sadiv* v. *Denmark*, CERD/C/62/D/25/2002, 16 April 2003). In case 25/2002, it was the organisation DRC (which has also lodged petitions on its own behalf before the Committee) that acted as counsel. The same organisation acted on the national level (but seemingly not before the Committee) in case no. 27/2002.

[64] Interview with Peter Nobel, 29 September 2000.   [65] Emphasis added.

[66] HRI/GEN/3, *Compilation of Rules of Procedure Adopted by Human Rights Treaty Bodies*, 6 June 2001, p. 169.

STANDING BEFORE INTERNATIONAL BODIES   235

As of August 2004, there were 134 decisions taken by CAT on inadmissibility or on the merits posted in the database of the treaty bodies.[67] In two of these cases, the communication had been submitted by an NGO.[68] In another twelve cases, the victim was explicitly said to have been represented by an NGO as counsel.[69] As for the Committee on the Elimination of Racial Discrimination, it is likely that NGOs have been active as counsel or otherwise in many more cases than those where it is explicitly stated in the decision of the Committee. For instance, material from Interights demonstrates that a communication (not among those mentioned above) was submitted by an NGO, although this is not mentioned in the Committee's decision.[70]

The Committee on the Elimination of Discrimination Against Women

Under the Optional Protocol to the Convention on the Elimination of Discrimination against Women, which entered into force in December 2000, communications may be submitted by or on behalf of individuals or groups of individuals claiming to be victims of a violation of a right set forth in the Convention. Where a communication is submitted on behalf of the alleged victim, his or her consent is required, unless

---

[67] The database is accessible online on the website of the UN High Commissioner for Human Rights at http://www.ohchr.org/english, as of 5 November 2004.

[68] Communications No. 23/1995, *The Spanish Refugee Aid Commission on behalf of X v. Spain* (CAT/C/15/D/23/1995, 15 November 1995) and 113/1998 (*Ristic v. Yugoslavia*, CAT/C/26/D/113/1998, 11 May 2001). In the first case, the Committee accepted the explanation of the NGO that it represented the victim, although its mandate did not explicitly mention application to the Committee (para. 7.2). In the second case, the author of the communication had deceased when the application was transmitted to the Committee by the NGO on behalf of the victim (introduction and para. 1).

[69] Communications No. 32/1995, *N.D. v. France* (CAT/C/15/D/32/1995, 20 November 1995); 45/1996, *D. v. France* (CAT/C/19/D/45/1996, 10 November 1997); 62/1996, *E.H. v. Hungary* (CAT/C/22/D/62/1996, 11 June 1999); 65/1997, *I.A.O. v. Sweden* (CAT/C/20/D/65/1997, 6 May 1998); 127/1999, *Z.T. v. Norway* (CAT/C/23/D/127/1999, 18 April 2000); 143/1999, *S.C. v. Denmark* (CAT/C/24/D/143/1999, 3 September 2000); 146/1999, *E.T.B. v. Denmark* (CAT/C/28/D/146/1999, 24 May 2002); 161/2000, *Dzemajl et. al. v. Yugoslavia* (CAT/C/29/D/161/2000, 2 December 2002); 189/2002, *Ltaief v. Tunisia* (CAT/C/31/D/189/2002, 20 November 2003); 188/2002, *Abdelli v. Tunisia* (CAT/C/31/D/188/2002, 20 November 2003); 187/2002, *Thabti v. Tunisia* (CAT/C/31/D/187/2002, 20 November 2003; 199/2002, *El Khalek Attia v. Sweden* (CAT/C/31/D/199/2002, 24 November 2003).

[70] According to Interights' *Annual Review 98–99* (pp. 32–33), communication No. 120/1998, *Sadiq Shek Elmi v. Australia*, was submitted by an Australian NGO on behalf of the victim. Interights also assisted in the case. The Committee's decision makes no mention of the NGOs, see CAT/C/22/D/120/1998, 25 May 1999.

236   LEGAL AND EMPIRICAL SURVEY

the author can justify acting without such consent.[71] In cases where the author seeks to submit a communication without the consent of the victim, she or he shall provide written reasons justifying such action.[72] There is thus a clear possibility for NGOs to act before the Committee. Considering the wording of the Protocol, this possibility seems more extensive than the corresponding possibility before the Human Rights Committee (HRC) and the Committee Against Racial Discrimination.

As of January 2004, the Committee on the Elimination of Discrimination against Women had received three communications.[73] No case reports have, however, been publicised.

The 1503 Procedure

The so-called '1503 Procedure', which applies to all states members of the United Nations, was established by ECOSOC in 1970 through the adoption of Resolution 1503 (XLVIII).[74] The procedure does not deal with individual cases as such but with situations that affect a large number of people: 'situations which appear to reveal a consistent pattern of gross and reliably attested violations of human rights'.[75] The procedure for dealing with the communications was revised in 2000.[76]

Under the procedure, individuals and groups of individuals can submit communications alleging human rights violations to the Working Group on Communications of the Sub-Commission for the Promotion and Protection of Human Rights. If the Working Group identifies reasonable evidence of a consistent pattern of gross violations of human rights, the matter will be referred for examination by the Working Group on Situations. This Working Group can refer situations to the Commission on Human Rights, which takes a decision concerning each particular situation brought to its attention. The procedure is

---

[71] Optional Protocol to the Convention on the Elimination of Discrimination against Women (1999), Article 2. See also Rule 68 of the Committee's Rules of Procedure, HRI/GEN/3, Compilation of Rules of Procedure Adopted by Human Rights Treaty Bodies, 6 June 2001, p. 124.

[72] CEDAW/C/ROP, *Rules of Procedure of the Committee on the Elimination of Discrimination against Women*, 26 January 2001, Rule 68(3).

[73] Press Release WOM/1432, *Women's Anti-Discrimination Committee Concludes Current Session*, 30 January 2004, A/56/38, *Report of the Committee on the Elimination of Discrimination Against Women*, 20 April 2001.

[74] Economic and Social Council Resolution 1503 (XLVIII), *Procedure for Dealing with Communications Relating to Violations of Human Rights and Fundamental Freedoms*, 27 May 1970.

[75] *Ibid.*, para. 1.

[76] E/RES/2000/3, *Procedure for Dealing with Communications Concerning Human Rights*.

confidential. The Chairman of the Commission on Human Rights may, however, announce the names of countries which have been under examination.

Any individual, group or organisation with direct and reliable knowledge of human rights violations may submit a communication under the 1503 Procedure. It covers material from all types of sources, but NGOs are in practice the most important source of information.[77] According to a UN Fact Sheet, NGOs submitting communications 'must be acting in good faith and in accordance with recognized principles of human rights'. The organisation should also have 'reliable direct evidence of the situation it is describing'.[78] Amnesty International submits detailed reports on country situations under the procedure; during 2003 it made four submissions.[79]

The '1503 Procedure' can be useful for NGOs which want the United Nations to investigate the general human rights situation in a particular country. However, the confidentiality of the procedure makes it difficult for NGOs to play an active role or to use the procedure for publicity purposes. It also makes the estimation of NGO activity uncertain.

The ILO freedom of association procedures

The ILO has adopted more than 180 conventions covering a broad range of subjects within the area of labour law, among which are several conventions establishing organisation rights for workers' and employers' organisations.[80] The organisation's special procedures for supervision (i.e. those regarding specific allegations) include two different mechanisms to which organisations of workers and employers have access. The Article 24 Procedure, under which national or international workers' or employers' organisations may submit so-called representations to the ILO has been described earlier in this book.[81]

The other procedure which provides standing for NGOs of the relevant categories is the complaints mechanism handled by the Committee on Freedom of Association, which was established in 1951 as a tripartite

---

[77] Nigel Rodley, 'Human Rights NGOs: Rights and Obligations', in Theo Van Boven *et al.* (eds.), *The Legitimacy of the United Nations: Towards an Enhanced Legal Status of Non-State Actors*, Netherlands Institute of Human Rights, SIM Special, 19, Utrecht, 1997, p. 55.
[78] Fact Sheet No.7/Rev.1, Complaint Procedures.
[79] Cook, 'Amnesty International at the United Nations', p. 201 and *Amnesty International Report 2004* (section 'AI's Activities, International and Regional Organizations).
[80] See section 4.2.   [81] *Ibid.*

238   LEGAL AND EMPIRICAL SURVEY

body following a decision by the ILO Governing Body.[82] The Committee on Freedom of Association examines complaints containing allegations of violations of the ILO conventions on freedom of association.[83] The consent of the state concerned is not necessary for complaints to be receivable, as the legal basis for the procedure is the ILO Constitution and the Declaration of Philadelphia, according to which member states are bound to respect the fundamental principles laid down in the Constitution by virtue of their membership of the organisation.[84]

Organisations of workers or employers, or governments, may lodge complaints either directly to the Committee on Freedom of Association or through the United Nations. Allegations are receivable only if the complaint has been lodged by (a) a national organisation directly interested in the matter, (b) an international organisation of workers or employers having consultative status with the ILO, or (c) another international organisation of workers or employers where the allegations relate to matters directly affecting their affiliated organisations.[85] Organisations in general consultative status with the ILO – presently eight organisations of workers and employers – may thus lodge complaints without a connection to the matters which are the subject of the allegations.[86] The fact that an organisation has not been officially recognised or has been dissolved by the government does not make a complaint incapable of being received when it is clear from the complaints that the organisation has at least a *de facto* existence.[87]

The responsibility of the Committee on Freedom of Association is mainly to consider whether cases are worthy of examination by the Governing Body, and to make a recommendation in this respect. The Committee may also recommend the Governing Body to communicate the Committee's conclusions to the government concerned, drawing its

---

[82] *ILO Law on Freedom of Association: Standards and Procedures*, Geneva: International Labour Office, 1995, p. 128.

[83] The ILO Conventions on freedom of association include the Convention No. 87 on Freedom of Association and Protection of the Right to Organise (1948), No. 98 on the Right to Organise and Collective Bargaining (1949), No. 11 (Right of Association, 1921), No. 135 (Workers' Representatives Convention, 1971), No. 141 (Rural Workers' Organisations Convention, 1975), No. 151 (Labour Relations Convention) and No. 154 (Collective Bargaining Convention, 1981).

[84] Report of the Committee of Experts on the Application of Conventions and Recommendations, *Freedom of Association and Collective Bargaining*, International Labour Conference, 81st Session, Geneva, 1994, para. 19.

[85] *ILO Law on Freedom of Association*, p. 132.   [86] See section 7.3.

[87] *ILO Law on Freedom of Association*, p. 132.

attention to discrepancies between national law and practice and the conventions and inviting the government to take appropriate measures to remedy the situation. If the ILO conventions on freedom of association are ratified and legislative issues are raised, the Committee's conclusions receive follow-up from the Committee of Experts, which makes regular supervision of the observance by member states of their obligations under conventions and recommendations.[88] Since its establishment, the Committee on Freedom of Association has examined over 2,000 cases.[89]

The UNESCO procedure for individual communications

In 1978 the UNESCO Executive Board established a procedure for the examination of communications concerning alleged violations of human rights in its fields of competence – namely, education, science, culture and information.[90] Communications must in particular relate to violations of human rights within UNESCO's field of competence. Among these are, *inter alia*, the right to education, the right to information, including the freedom of opinion and expression, the right to freedom of thought, conscience and religion and the right to freedom of assembly and association for the purposes of activities connected with education, science, culture and information. The procedure is, in other words, not tied to any particular human rights instrument, although the Universal Declaration of Human Rights is used as a standard for describing UNESCO's competence in relation to different rights. It is also stated in the decision laying down the procedure that, in order to be admissible, 'the communication must be compatible with the principles of the Organization, the Charter of the United Nations, the Universal Declaration of Human Rights, the international covenants on human rights and other international instruments in the field of human rights'.[91]

---

[88] *Ibid.*, pp. 128, 149.

[89] ILO Governing Body, GB.280/9, *324th Report of the Committee on Freedom of Association*, March 2001, para. 2. The Committee examines around 200 cases per year, see Provisional Record, Ninety-Second Session, Geneva, 2004, p. 8. See also Lee Swepston, 'Human Rights Law and Freedom of Association: Development through ILO Supervision', *International Labour Review*, 1937 (1998), No. 2, p. 176.

[90] 104 EX/Decision 3.3, *Study of the Procedures which should be Followed in the Examination of Cases and Questions*, Executive Board 104th Session, 24 April–9 June 1978, para. 14 (a iii).

[91] *Ibid.*, para. 14(a iv).

240 LEGAL AND EMPIRICAL SURVEY

Communications may be submitted by individuals, groups of individuals and NGOs. The author of a communication can be the victim of a violation of the human rights protected or a person or organisation with reliable knowledge of such violations.[92] Communications should concern cases of individual and specific violations or situations of massive, systematic or flagrant violations of human rights.[93] Persons who UNESCO regards as particularly likely to suffer violations of the rights relevant to the organisations are teachers, students, researchers, artists, writers, journalists and others who by virtue of their position come within UNESCO's fields of competence.[94]

Communications regarding alleged violations are examined by the Committee on Conventions and Recommendations in an entirely confidential procedure.[95] The confidentiality of the procedure is in line with its general character of a political mechanism for negotiation, where the Committee tries to find a solution in a spirit of co-operation and understanding. It is explicitly recalled in the decision establishing the procedure that 'UNESCO should not play the role of an international judicial body'.[96] Because of its character, the procedure is not regarded as incompatible with the other complaints procedures within the UN system, but rather as a complementary mechanism. The Committee sees its sole role as being to establish dialogue with the governments concerned in order to consider what might be done on behalf of alleged victims for humanitarian reasons. Its aim is to promote rights within its field of competence by trying to reach a friendly solution through seeking information and facilitating conciliation.[97]

After having concluded its examination, the Committee adopts a report with recommendations. This report is also confidential, and the author receives only a letter with a summary of the government's position and the Committee's decision.[98] If a communication warrants further consideration, the Committee shall act 'with a view to helping

---

[92] *Ibid.*, para 14 (a ii) and 159 EX/CR/2, *Committee on Conventions and Recommendations, Information Document*, 14 March 2000, p. 21.
[93] 104 EX/Decision 3.3, para. 10(b).
[94] 159 EX/CR/2, *Committee on Conventions and Recommendations, Information Document*, 14 March 2000, p. 4.
[95] *Ibid.*, para. 14(c).   [96] *Ibid.*, para. 7.
[97] 159 EX/CR/2, *Committee on Conventions and Recommendations, Information Document*, 14 March 2000, p. 19.
[98] *Ibid.*, p. 6, and 104 EX/Decision 3.3, para. 15.

to bring about a friendly solution designed to advance the promotion of human rights falling within UNESCO's field of competence'.[99]

Confidentiality is regarded as essential, and if the author of a communication does not respect this principle, the Committee may decide to strike the communication from its list or declare it inadmissible.[100] This means that the weakness of the procedure cannot be compensated by a complaining NGO through mass media pressure.

Almost all of UNESCO's member states have recognised the Committee's competence to examine individual communications.[101] From 1978, when the procedure for individual communications was established, to 1998, the Committee on Conventions and Recommendations examined 482 communications. The communications came from individuals as well as NGOs, such as Amnesty International, the International Association of Democratic Lawyers, the International Human Rights Law Group and the Women's International Democratic Federation.[102]

The World Bank Inspection Panel

The World Bank Inspection Panel was created in 1993 in response to environmental and human rights campaigns as a forum for private citizens who believe that their rights or interests have been or could be directly harmed by a project financed by the Bank.[103] The Panel was established by the Executive Directors of the World Bank and the International Development Association (IDA).[104] It consists of three members of different nationalities from Bank member countries appointed by the Executive Directors.[105]

Affected people in the territory of the borrower may bring their concerns to the attention of the Panel by filing a request for inspection. Such requests may be brought only by affected parties who are not

---

[99] 104 EX/Decision 3.3, para. 14(k).
[100] 159 EX/CR/2, *Committee on Conventions and Recommendations, Information Document,* 14 March 2000, p. 24.
[101] *Ibid.,* p. 8.
[102] Symonides, 'UNESCO and the Universal Declaration of Human Rights', p. 97.
[103] According to Fox, 'all parties' agree that the Panel was created in direct response to such campaigns. Jonathan A. Fox, 'The World Bank Inspection Panel: Lessons from the First Five Years', 6 *Global Governance* (2000), p. 279.
[104] The Panel was established by IBRD Resolution No. 93-10, *The World Bank Inspection Panel,* and the identical IDA Resolution No. 93-6, both adopted by the Executive Directors of the respective institutions on 22 September 1993.
[105] *Ibid.,* para. 2.

242 LEGAL AND EMPIRICAL SURVEY

single individuals, but groups, communities, organisations, associations, etc., or by the local representative of such parties. This means that NGOs may bring requests before the Panel, and this has occurred in several cases. The affected party must demonstrate that its rights or interests have been or are likely to be directly affected by an action or omission of the Bank as a result of a failure of the Bank to follow its own operational policies and procedures during the design, appraisal and/or implementation of a bank-financed project. It is a condition that such failure has had, or threatens to have, a material adverse effect.[106]

The Panel's method of functioning is laid out in Operating Procedures developed by the Panel members.[107] The role of the Panel is to carry out independent investigations. After the receipt of a request, the Panel sends it to the Bank Management, which has twenty-one working days to respond to the allegations. The Panel then conducts a short assessment and makes a recommendation to the Board of Executive Directors whether or not the matters complained of should be investigated. If the Board so decides, the Panel carries out an investigation and provides its findings and conclusions to the Board, which considers the actions (if any) to be taken by the Bank.

The procedure was reviewed and clarified by the Board in 1996 and in 1999. During the 1996 review, NGOs proposed that the access to the Panel should be broadened to cover requests submitted by foreign NGOs and to cover local NGOs whose rights or interests had not been affected by the project, or generally to claims submitted in the public interest.[108] The Board however declined the proposal.[109] Accordingly, it is still a requirement both that the requester be affected and that the affected group of persons be in the territory of the borrower. NGOs may also act as a representative of the group or community concerned, but representatives shall in general be local. An NGO from another region or country may thus be chosen as representative only if appropriate

---

[106] *Ibid.*, para. 12.

[107] World Bank Inspection Panel, *Operating Procedures*, as adopted by the Panel on 19 August 1994.

[108] Ibrahim F. I. Shihata, *The World Bank Inspection Panel: In Practice*, 2nd edn., Oxford University Press, 2000, p. 168. According to the 1993 Resolution establishing the Panel, the Board of Directors was to review the experience of the inspection function after two years from the date of the appointment of the first members of the Panel. IBRD Resolution No. 93–10, IDA Resolution No. 93–6, 22 September 1993, para. 27.

[109] Shihata, *The World Bank Inspection Panel*, p. 168, and Review of the Resolution Establishing the Inspection Panel, Clarification of Certain Aspects of the Resolution, IBRD Resolution No. 96–204.

representation is not locally available.[110] As of August 2004, the Panel had registered twenty-nine requests for inspection. Twenty of these were filed by NGOs.[111]

In seven of the cases, the NGOs were acting on their own behalf or on behalf of themselves as well as on behalf of affected individuals.[112] In the other cases, the NGOs acted as representatives of the affected group. The Panel has, so far, recommended an investigation in about half of all the cases received. Since the April 1999 clarifications of the Rules, the Board has authorised all of the investigations recommended by the Panel.[113]

All NGOs which acted as representative were local or based in the same country as the affected group except for one case, where a US NGO filed a request on behalf of people living in the project area in Tibet.[114]

A couple of examples of cases where the request was filed by an NGO can illustrate the role of NGOs before the World Bank Inspection Panel.

The Jamuna Bridge Project was planned to connect the eastern and western parts of Bangladesh through the construction, operation and maintenance of a bridge over the Jamuna River.[115] There are thousands of mid-channel islands,

---

[110] IBRD Resolution No. 93–10, IDA Resolution No. 93–6, 22 September 1993, para. 12.

[111] The requests are Brazil/Rondônia Natural Resources Management Project; Bangladesh/Jamuna Bridge Project; Argentina–Paraguay/Yacyretá Hydroelectric Project; Brazil/Itaparica Resettlement and Irrigation Project; India/Ecodevelopment Project; Nigeria/Lagos Drainage and Sanitation Project; Brazil/Land Reform Poverty Alleviation Project; China/Western Poverty Reduction Project; Argentina/Special Structural Adjustment Loan; Brazil/Land Reform Poverty Alleviation Project, 2nd request; Kenya/Lake Victoria Environmental Management Project; Ecuador/Mining Development and Environmental Control Technical Assistance Project; India/Coal Sector Environmental and Social Mitigation Project and Coal Sector Rehabilitation Project; Uganda/Third Power Project and Fourth Power Project; Papua New Guinea/Governance Promotion Adjustment Loan; Cameroon/Petroleum Development and Pipeline Project and Petroleum Environment Capacity Enhancement (CAPECE) Project; Philippines/Manila Second Sewerage Project; Colombia/Cartagena Water Supply, Sewerage and Environmental Management Project; India/Mumbai Urban Transport Project; India/Mumbai Urban Transport Project – Gazi Nagar.

[112] The requests in Brazil/Rondônia Natural Resources Management Project; Nigeria/Lagos Drainage and Sanitation Project; Uganda/Third Power Project and Fourth Power Project; Philippines/Manila Second Sewerage Project; Colombia/Cartagena Water Supply, Sewerage and Environmental Management Project; India/Mumbai Urban Transport Project; and India/Mumbai Urban Transport Project – Gazi Nagar were filed by NGOs only or partly on their own behalf.

[113] Inspection Panel, Annual Report, August 1, 2001 to June 30, 2002, p. 3.

[114] Request No. 16.

[115] The World Bank Inspection Panel, *Report and Recommendation, Bangladesh: Jamuna Bridge Project* (Credit 2569-BD), 26 November 1996.

244 LEGAL AND EMPIRICAL SURVEY

known as *chars*, in the Jamuna river. *Choura*, or *char* people, live on or derive their income from the *chars*. Some seventy-five *chars* with over 70,000 inhabitants are said to be located in the project area. The request for inspection was filed by a local NGO, the Jamuna Char Integrated Development Project (JCIDP) representing *char* people in the project area. The JCIDP requested an investigation of the harmful effects of the project on the livelihood of *choura* on the *char* islands and alleged violations relating to IDA policies. The Panel was not satisfied that the policies and procedures on Resettlement and Environmental Assessment had been fully complied with in relation to the *chars* and the *choura* in the Jamuna River. The Panel concluded, however, that an investigation of the matters alleged in the Request was not warranted, since the borrower had undertaken corrective measures towards the affected people by the time the Panel took its decision.[116] The Panel therefore never decided on the question whether the Bank's operational policies had been complied with.

The Ecuador Mining Development and Environmental Control Technical Assistance Project, financed by the World Bank (IBRD), was created with the main objectives of attracting new private mining investment and arresting mining-related environmental degradation.[117] The request for inspection was filed by an Ecuadorian NGO acting for and on behalf of persons living in the project area, known as the Intag area, and four representatives of another NGO. The requesters claimed that the public release of maps with mineral data collected under the project would attract mining companies and produce multi-fold negative impacts on their society and the local environment. The development of mining activities in the area, for instance, would have a destructive impact on protected areas and their buffer zones and prevent local communities from continuing to work at their traditional farming, livestock and ecotourism activities. They further argued that the project would violate specific World Bank policies and procedures. More specifically, the Requesters alleged, *inter alia*, that the management had failed to consult and take into account the views of local communities and NGOs in preparing the Environmental Assessment. The Bank management was of the view that it had complied with all operational polices and procedures applicable to the matters raised by the Request. With regard to consultation, it replied that it had consulted with eleven NGOs during the preparation, appraisal and implementation of the Project. For purposes of determining the eligibility of the Request and Requesters, the Inspection Panel carried out a field visit to the project area and met with representatives of a large number of NGOs. The discussions confirmed that there was support for the Request and that the other criteria for eligibility had been met. The Panel

[116] See also Fox, 'The World Bank Inspection Panel', n. 43.
[117] The World Bank Inspection Panel, *Report and Recommendation, Ecuador: Mining Development and Environmental Control Technical Assistance Project* (Loan No. 3566-EC), 28 April 2000.

STANDING BEFORE INTERNATIONAL BODIES   245

recommended an investigation, and its recommendation was approved by the Board. In its Investigation Report, the Panel concluded that the management had complied with certain procedures, while it had been in apparent violation of certain other policies and procedures on Environmental Assessment, including those concerning consultation during preparation. According to Operational Directive 4.01, the views of affected groups and local NGOs should be taken fully into account in project design and implementation, and in particular in the preparation of Environmental Assessments. In one part of the project area, meetings with NGOs had not commenced until five years after the Environmental Assessment Report had been completed. The Panel also found it worth noticing that the management did not characterise these as meetings 'to consult' but rather as 'meetings to inform'.[118]

Although the Inspection Panel provides an interesting example of NGO influence on an important international institution, several of the parties involved in the procedure have been dissatisfied with the experience. The Panel itself was concerned with some of the management's practices, such as agreeing with borrowers before the Panel's submittal of its recommendations to the Board. Affected parties have complained about lack of consultation and failure to inform them about the outcome in their own language.[119] Concerns raised by NGOs have included that the Panel's mandate is too narrow, and that it has been frustrated by both the management and the Board.[120] One writer, evaluating the results of Panel inspections and other reforms of the World Bank, suggests that, on the one hand, the Bank appears to be funding fewer 'obviously disastrous new infrastructure megaprojects' while, on the other, many projects continue to fall short of the Bank's own policies.[121] A general observation is that the number of requests for inspection has been relatively few. The twenty-nine requests received as of August 2004 should be seen in relation to the fact that the Bank has hundreds of projects underway each year.

Perhaps the most important aspect of the establishment of the World Bank Inspection Panel from the perspective of NGOs and affected groups in general is that their interests in being consulted regarding

---

[118] The World Bank Inspection Panel, Report No. 21870, *Investigation Report on Ecuador Mining Development and Environmental Control Technical Assistance Project*, 23 February 2001, in particular paras. 92–107.

[119] Shihata, *The World Bank Inspection Panel*, p. 259.   [120] *Ibid.*, p. 260.

[121] Fox, 'The World Bank Inspection Panel', n. 58. See also Chi Carmody, 'Beyond the Proposals: Public Participation in International Economic Law', 15 *American University International Law Review* (2000), p. 1321.

246 LEGAL AND EMPIRICAL SURVEY

Bank projects have been recognised as legitimate. It should also be observed that similar mechanisms have been created within the Asian Development Bank (ADB) and the Inter-American Development Bank (IADB).

5.3 Regional bodies

The European Convention on Human Rights and its monitoring bodies

The procedure

Until a few years ago, NGOs had only a limited procedural capacity within the monitoring system of the European Commission of Human Rights (the Commission). The ECHR could receive petitions from individuals, groups of individuals or NGOs which claimed to be the victim of a violation of the rights of the Convention. This individual complaints procedure was facultative; complaints were declared admissible only if the respondent state had recognised the competence of the Commission to receive such petitions. According to Article 44 of the Convention, only the contracting states and the Commission had the right to bring cases before the Court. Private applicants were not considered to be parties before the Court if the Commission referred their case to it. Initially, individual petitioners could appear before the Court only for the sake of rendering 'assistance' to the delegates of the Commission, and it was not until 1982 that the Rules were amended so as to require that the applicant be invited to be individually represented.[122]

The 9th Additional Protocol, which was adopted in 1990, gave Article 44 of the Convention a new wording, entitling individuals and NGOs who had filed a case with the Commission to refer the case to the Court. This right was, however, conditional. First, the Commission had to adopt a report on the case. Second, according to Article 5(2) of the Protocol, a case referred to the Court by a person, an NGO or a group of individuals should first be submitted to a screening panel of three judges, including the judge elected in respect of the state against which the complaint had been submitted. If the case did not raise any serious question affecting the interpretation or application of the Convention, and did not for any other reason warrant further consideration, the panel should decide that the case would not be considered by the Court.

---

[122] P. van Dijk and G. J. H. van Hoof, *Theory and Practice of the European Convention on Human Rights*, 3rd edn., The Hague: Kluwer Law International, 1998, pp. 228–235.

With the coming into force of the 11th Additional Protocol in November 1998, a new monitoring system became operational. The former system where petitions were tried in the Commission and Court was replaced by the Single Court of Human Rights. The new Article 34 on the right to bring cases before the Court reads:

> The Court may receive applications from any person, non-governmental organisation or group of individuals claiming to be the victim of a violation by one of the High Contracting Parties of the rights set forth in the Convention or the protocols thereto. The High Contracting Parties undertake not to hinder in any way the effective exercise of this right.

In other words, NGOs, as well as individual applicants, now have *locus standi* as parties before the ECHR.

The concept of 'non-governmental organisation' and the victim requirement

The term 'non-governmental organisation', as used in the former Article 25 of the Convention and in Article 34 in the present wording of the text, includes a wide range of private legal persons.[123] The same word is to be found in the former Commission's Rules of Procedure and in the Rules of the new Court without any further explanation.[124] The Commission decided, however, during its first session that an NGO must be established in a regular way according to the law of one of the state parties to the Convention. If the organisation has not been established legally, the application must be signed by all the persons belonging to the group.[125] The Commission and the Court have examined several cases brought by associations with no or questionable juridical personality.

In the case of *Freedom and Democracy Party (ÖZDEP) v. Turkey*, the Turkish authorities applied to the Constitutional Court to have the party dissolved when the application of the Democracy Party had already been filed with the

---

[123] It should be observed that although the definition of 'NGO', which has been outlined in section 1.3 for the purpose of the study excludes political parties, these entities will be included in the discussion below, as some of the cases involving political parties provide information which is interesting in relation to all NGOs.

[124] According to Rule 32(1) of the former Commission's Rules of Procedure 'persons, non-governmental organisations, or groups of individuals' could present and conduct applications under Article 25 of the Convention, *Rules of Procedure of the European Commission of Human Rights*, as in force at 28 June 1993. See also, e.g., Rules 1, 36(1) and 45(2) of the *Rules of Court*, 4 November 1998.

[125] Van Dijk and van Hoof, *Theory and Practice of the European Convention*, p. 46.

248   LEGAL AND EMPIRICAL SURVEY

Commission. Shortly afterwards, a meeting of the founding members of ÖZDEP decided to dissolve the party voluntarily. Nevertheless, the proceedings before the Commission and the Court were continued with ÖZDEP as applicant. The government objected before the Court that ÖZDEP could not be regarded as a victim of the dissolution as it had been dissolved voluntarily well before the Constitutional Court had ordered its dissolution. The Court found that the members of ÖZDEP had resolved to dissolve their party in the hope of avoiding certain effects of dissolution by the Constitutional Court, in their case a ban on holding similar office in any other political body. The decision had therefore not been taken freely. Moreover, the Turkish law on the regulation of political parties provided that if a decision to dissolve a political party had been taken by the competent body of the party after an application for its dissolution had been lodged by the authorities, this should not prevent the proceedings before the Constitutional Court from continuing or deprive any dissolution order of its legal effects. As domestic law provided that a voluntarily dissolved political party remained in existence for the purposes of dissolution by the Constitutional Court, the Government could not contend before the ECHR that ÖZDEP was no longer in existence when the dissolution order was made. The government's preliminary objection was therefore dismissed. As to the merits of the case, the Court found a violation of Article 11 of the Convention. The judgement was issued in the name of the party.[126]

It should be observed that the Turkish government did not raise the objection that ÖZDEP was no longer a party to the proceedings because it did not exist legally, but only that it could not be considered a victim because of the decision to dissolve the organisation voluntarily. In the case of *Stankov and United Macedonian Organisation Ilinden* v. *Bulgaria* the question arose whether an organisation which had been refused registration could be accepted as an applicant before the Commission.

The Government argued that where an NGO lacks legal standing under domestic law and where it is not open to the Commission to examine the conformity with the Convention of the decision which has led to such legal situation, the NGO has no standing to submit a petition. The Commission recalled that in earlier case-law concerning NGOs which had been refused

---

[126] *Freedom and Democracy Party (ÖZDEP)* v. *Turkey*, 8 December 1999. The Court, however, ordered the compensation for non-pecuniary damage sustained by the founders and members of the applicant party to be paid to ÖZDEP's representative for the purposes of the proceedings before the Court, para. 57. Judgements and decisions of the Convention monitoring bodies which are accessible online in the Council of Europe HUDOC database (at http://cmiskp.echr.coe.int/tkp197/default.htm, as of 6 November 2004) are referred to with title and date only. If the cases are not included in the database, reference is made to a publication where they are included.

registration or had been dissolved and which had complained about these very facts, the Commission had not questioned the applicants' *locus standi*. It stated that any other solution would to a substantial degree restrict the right of NGOs to petition. The government's objection was, however, not rejected only on that ground. The Commission noted that there was nothing to suggest that a non-registered association such as the applicant had no right under Bulgarian law to function and to perform its activities. It again recalled earlier case-law, according to which the refusal of registration of an association did not amount to an interference with the association's right to freedom of assembly if the association was able to perform its activities without registration. It followed that if the authorities sought to suppress the activities of such an association following the refusal of registration there must be a possibility for it to submit a complaint under Article 11 of the Convention. The government had in any event impliedly accepted the applicant association's *locus standi* before its own authorities. The Commission concluded that the government's objection should be rejected.[127]

In the case of *Canea Catholic Church* v. *Greece*, the application was treated by the Commission and the Court as filed by the Church as such, in spite of the fact that the Greek government denied that the church had legal personality.

The application was brought by a bishop belonging to the church. The Commission found in its report that the applicant was acting only as the representative of the Catholic Church of the Virgin Mary in Canea. Accordingly, it considered that the application should be treated as having been submitted by the church itself. The church claimed that refusals on the part of the Canea Court of First Instance (CFI) and the Court of Cassation to recognise the church as a legal person with capacity to bring or defend legal proceedings violated, *inter alia*, Article 6 of the Convention. In short, it was argued that the applicant church, like all other churches existing in Greece before the Civil Code entered into force, had legal personality '*sui generis*'. The government argued that the church had not *ipso facto* acquired legal personality because it had not complied with relevant national legislation, which offered a sufficient number of possibilities for organising its activities through the setting up of separate, independent legal entities such as associations or religious foundations. The Court noted that the legal personality of the Greek Catholic Church and of parish churches had never before been called into question by administrative authorities or courts. The Court of Cassation's ruling that the applicant church had no capacity to take legal proceedings had imposed on it a real restriction preventing it then and for the future from having any dispute relating to its property rights determined by the

---

[127] *Stankov and United Macedonian Organisation Ilinden* v. *Bulgaria*, Admissibility decision, 29 June 1998.

250 LEGAL AND EMPIRICAL SURVEY

courts. The Court concluded that such a limitation impaired the very substance of the church's right to a court and therefore constituted a breach of Article 6(1) of the Convention.[128]

Yet another case brought by an unregistered organisation was *Apeh Üldözötteinek Szövetsége and Others* v. *Hungary*, in which the Court came to the conclusion that domestic proceedings regarding the applicant association's registration came within the scope of Article 6 of the Convention, as associations obtained their legal existence under Hungarian law only by virtue of their court registration.[129]

The Commission made it clear during its first session that NGOs were private organisations, as opposed to public entities.[130] This has also been confirmed in the Commission's case-law. In the case of *16 Austrian Communes and some of their Councillors* v. *Austria*, the Commission rejected the application filed by the Communes at the admissibility stage.

The Commission examined the question whether the communes concerned could, as submitted by the applicants, be considered as 'non-governmental' organisations within the meaning of this provision. It found that local government organisations such as communes, which exercise public functions on behalf of the State, were clearly 'governmental organisations'. The Commission next examined the question whether the communes concerned could nevertheless be regarded as 'persons' or 'groups of individuals' in the sense of the wording of the Convention. It found that such a construction would not be consistent with the Convention, and concluded that the communes concerned could not bring an application under Article 25.[131]

In another case, the Court determined the status of a legal person as a non-governmental body independently of a government's assertion of an organisation's status as a public law entity.

In the *Holy Monasteries* case of 1994, the Greek government argued that the monasteries were not NGOs within the meaning of Article 25 of the Convention because of their integration into the Greek Church, which was attributed with legal personality under public law. The government argued further that the church and its constituent parts played a direct and active role in public administration. The Court noted, like the Commission, that the monasteries did not

---

[128] *Canea Catholic Church* v. *Greece*, 16 December 1997.
[129] *Apeh Üldözötteinek Szövetsége and Others* v. *Hungary*, 5 October 2000.
[130] Van Dijk and van Hoof, *Theory and Practice of the European Convention*, p. 46.
[131] *16 Austrian Communes and some of their Councillors* v. *Austria*, Admissibility decision, 31 May 1974; *Ayuntamiento de X.* v. *Spain*, Admissibility decision, 7 January 1991; *Ayuntamiento de Mula* v. *Spain*, Admissibility decision, 1 February 2001. See also van Dijk and van Hoof, *Theory and Practice of the European Convention*, p. 46.

STANDING BEFORE INTERNATIONAL BODIES 251

exercise governmental powers and that their objectives were not such as to enable them to be classed with governmental organisations established for public administration purposes. From the classification as public law entities it could be inferred only that the legislature wished to afford them legal protection against third parties. The monasteries were not under the supervision of the state, of which they were completely independent. The Court concluded that the applicant monasteries were therefore to be regarded as NGOs within the meaning of Article 25 of the Convention.[132]

Among the private bodies which have applied under the former Article 25 are companies, trade unions, religious congregations, political parties, radio stations, newspapers and interest organisations.[133] No distinction is made between profit- and non-profit making organisations. Commercial entities are thus often applicants in cases before the Court.[134] Several cases have been instituted by newspapers.[135] As it is not necessary for the Court to decide whether an entity is for profit or not, these judgements do not always reveal whether the newspapers would fall into the category of NGOs as understood in the present study. In the case of *Open Door and Dublin Well Woman v. Ireland*, the applicants were companies incorporated under Irish law with the non-profit-making aim of providing counselling and health services to pregnant women.[136]

The Convention does not allow for an *actio popularis*. An application will not be accepted if the applicant has not suffered personally from a violation of the convention, or if the complaint is brought about legislation *in abstracto*. According to the practice of the monitoring bodies, however, it suffices for the so-called 'victim requirement' to be satisfied that the complainant runs the risk of being directly affected by the particular matter which is brought.[137]

---

[132] *Holy Monasteries v. Greece*, 9 December 1994. See also *Finska församlingen i Stockholm and Hautaniemi v. Sweden*, Admissibility decision, 11 April 1996.

[133] See below.

[134] A few examples of judgements are *Tinnelly & Sons Ltd and Others and McElduff and Others v. the United Kingdom*, 10 July 1998; *Immobiliare Saffi v. Italy*, 28 July 1999; *Agoudimos and Cefallonian Sky Shipping Co. v. Greece*, 28 June 2001.

[135] *The Sunday Times v. the United Kingdom*, 26 April 1979; *The Sunday Times v. the United Kingdom*, 31 July 1987; *Observer & Guardian v. the United Kingdom*, 27 January 1988; *Bladet Tromsø and Stensaas v. Norway*, 25 May 1999; *Özgür Gündem v. Turkey*, 16 March 2000; *Bergens Tidende and Others v. Norway*, 2 May 2000.

[136] *Open Door and Dublin Well Woman v. Ireland*, 29 October 1992.

[137] *Campbell and Cosans v. the United Kingdom*, 25 February 1982; *Marckx v. Belgium*, 13 June 1979. See also van Dijk and van Hoof, *Theory and Practice of the European Convention*, pp. 48–54.

252   LEGAL AND EMPIRICAL SURVEY

The victim requirement is, naturally, equally valid for NGOs. Accordingly, an NGO can claim to be a victim only in the case of a violation against the organisation itself, which means that the possibilities for NGOs to institute cases in order to develop the Court's case-law are limited.

The case of *Brüggemann and Sheuten* v. *the Federal Republic of Germany* concerned a criminal law on the termination of pregnancy. An application was brought jointly by an NGO – the *Weltschutzbund* – and by three of its members, two women and one man. The complainants asserted that the legislation interfered with the right to respect for their private life as guaranteed by Article 8 of the Convention. The Commission declared the application inadmissible insofar as it had been brought by the organisation and by the man.[138]

The case of *Purcell and Others* v. *Ireland* concerned alleged restrictions on the applicants' freedom of expression resulting from a ministerial order stating that broadcasts related to certain organisations were not allowed. The complaint had been filed by several individuals as well as two trade unions. The Commission stated that in order to satisfy the conditions of Article 25, an applicant must be able to demonstrate that he or she had been personally affected by the alleged breach of the Convention. The measure complained of in the case did not affect the rights of the applicant trade unions themselves, and the fact alone that the organisations considered themselves as guardians of the collective interests of their members did not suffice to make them victims within the meaning of Article 25. The application was declared inadmissible *ratione personae* insofar as it had been brought by the two trade unions.[139]

In *X. Union* v. *France*, the complaint had been filed by a professional union of teachers.[140] The union was an NGO which possessed legal personality under French law and which was entitled to take legal proceedings to defend the interests of the profession. In its application, the union challenged the obligation imposed upon secondary school teachers to reside in the town in which they worked. The Commission pointed out that the union fell into the category of applicants mentioned in Article 25, but that it did not itself claim to be the victim of a violation. The complaint was therefore rejected as incompatible *ratione personae* with the Convention.[141]

---

[138] The man had filed his application as the chairman of the organisation. It can therefore not be excluded that he would have been recognised as a victim had he filed the complaint in his capacity as a husband or a partner. *Brüggemann and Sheuten* v. *the Federal Republic of Germany*, 10 D&R (1978) p. 101.

[139] *Purcell and Others* v. *Ireland*, Admissibility decision, 16 April 1991.

[140] *X. Union* v. *France*, 32 D&R (1983), p. 261.

[141] See also *National Federation of Self-Employed* v. *the United Kingdom*, 15 D&R (1979), p. 198.

A related case was *X. and Church of Scientology* v. *Sweden*. The question arose whether the church itself was capable of possessing and exercising the right to freedom of religion contained in Article 9(1) of the Convention. The Commission found that the church did in fact possess this capability in its own capacity as a representative of its members.[142]

The case of *Modinos* v. *Cyprus* had similarities to an action brought for the common good, even though the applicant was an individual victim.[143] The applicant was the president of the Liberation Movement of Homosexuals in Cyprus. He complained that the prohibition on male homosexual activity constituted a continuing interference with his right to respect for private life in breach of Article 8 of the Convention. It might well have been the initiative of the organisation to file the complaint in order to influence the application of Article 8 in Cyprus. In the same case, the International Lesbian and Gay Association sought leave to submit written comments, but the President of the Court decided not to grant such leave.[144]

NGOs as parties before the Commission and the Court

From its establishment in July 1954 until 31 December 1997, the Commission received over 39,000 individual applications, of which more than 4,000 individual applications were declared admissible.[145] Since the Council of Europe does not provide any official statistics on the number of applications made by NGOs, and because of the vast number of individual applications, I have limited my investigation to NGO activity before the Court, with a few exceptions.

The ECHR delivered 1,009 judgements from 1959 until 1 November 1998 (when the Single Court system became operational).[146] The new Court delivered 3,307 judgements from 1999 until 2003.[147] All but three

---

[142] *X. and Church of Scientology* v. *Sweden*, 16 D&R (1979), p. 68. See also section 4.2. As regards the application of the victim requirement to individual members of an organisation, see *Gorraiz Lizarraga and Others* v. *Spain*, 27 April 2004. In this case, the individual applicants were not parties to the domestic proceedings but belonged to the applicant association which brought those proceedings in order to defend their interests.
The Court accepted the victim status of the applicants, having regard in particular to the fact that the applicant association had been set up for the specific purpose of defending its members' interests before the courts and that those members were directly affected by the issue at stake.
[143] *Modinos* v. *Cyprus*, 22 April 1993.   [144] *Ibid.*, para. 4.
[145] Information obtained in 5 May 1999 at the Council of Europe Human Rights website. The site has now been changed.
[146] Council of Europe, European Court of Human Rights, *Survey: Forty Years of Activity 1959–1998*, p. 25.
[147] European Court of Human Rights, *Survey of Activities*, 1999, 2000, 2001, 2002 and 2003.

254   LEGAL AND EMPIRICAL SURVEY

of the cases adjudged upon originated in an application from an individual or a private entity against a respondent state.[148] The number of judgements on the merits which originated in an application filed by an NGO can be estimated to (at least) twenty-nine, including those involving political parties.[149]

Sixteen cases originated in applications from different kinds of NGOs: *Plattform 'Ärzte für das Leben'* v. *Austria*, 21 June 1988; *Open Door & Dublin Well Woman* v. *Ireland*, 29 October 1992; *Informationsverein Lentia & Others* v. *Austria*, 24 November 1993; *Otto-Preminger Institut* v. *Austria*, 20 September 1994; *Vereinigung demokratischer Soldaten Österreichs & Gubi* v. *Austria*, 19 December 1994; *Vereniging Weekblad Bluf!* v. *The Netherlands*, 9 February 1995; *Procola* v. *Luxembourg*, 28 September 1995; *Radio ABC* v. *Austria*, 20 October 1997; *Clube de Futebol União de Coimbra* v. *Portugal*, 30 July 1998; *Apeh Üldözötteinek Szövetsége and Others* v. *Hungary*, 5 October 2000; *Stankov and the United Macedonian Organisation Ilinden* v. *Bulgaria*, 2 October 2001; *Verein Gegen Tierfabriken* v. *Switzerland*, 28 June 2001; *Ekin Association* v. *France*, 17 July 2001; *Unabhängige Initiative Informationsvielfalt* v. *Austria*, 26 February 2002; *Wynen and Centre hospitalier interrégional Edith-Cavell* v. *Belgium*, 5 November 2002; *Informationsverein Lentia* v. *Austria*, 28 November 2002.

Three cases originated in applications filed by trade unions: *National Union of Belgian Police* v. *Belgium*, 27 October 1975; *Swedish Engine Drivers' Union* v. *Sweden*, 6 February 1976; *Wilson, National Union of Journalists and Others* v. *the United Kingdom*, 2 July 2002.

Five cases originated in applications from political parties: *United Communist Party of Turkey and Others* v. *Turkey*, 30 January 1998; *Socialist Party and Others* v. *Turkey*, 25 May 1998; *Freedom and Democracy Party (ÖZDEP)* v. *Turkey*, 8 December 1999; *Refah Partisi (Prosperity Party) and Others* v. *Turkey*, 31 July 2001; *Yazar and Others* v. *Turkey*, 9 April 2002.

Six cases originated in applications from religious congregations or associations: *Holy Monasteries* v. *Greece*, 9 December 1994 and 1 September 1997; *Canea Catholic Church* v. *Greece*, 16 December 1997; *Cha'are Shalom ve Tsedek* v. *France*, 27 June 2000; *Institute of French Priests and Others* v. *Turkey*, 14 December 2000; *Grande Oriente d'Italia di Palazzo Giustiniani* v. *Italy*, 2 August 2001; *Metropolitan Church of Bessarabia and Others* v. *Moldova*, 13 December 2001.

It is obvious that the cases instituted by organisations are relatively few. During the period when non-state actors lacked standing before the Court

---

[148] The interstate cases were *Ireland* v. *the United Kingdom*, 16 December 1971; *Denmark* v. *Turkey*, 5 April 2000 (friendly settlement); *Cyprus* v. *Turkey*, 10 May 2001.

[149] The cases have primarily been identified through searches in the HUDOC database. The list of cases below includes only those where the application has been filed by an NGO, alone or together with other (physical or juridical) persons. Cases related to NGO activity (e.g. cases brought by individual members of an NGO, but not on behalf of the organisation) have not been included.

STANDING BEFORE INTERNATIONAL BODIES   255

it was natural that many cases brought by NGOs never reached the Court. With the present Single Court system in operation, the data will be more representative. This is also demonstrated by the fact that so many of the cases brought by NGOs have been adjudged during recent years.

Issues raised in cases brought by NGOs

Because of the victim requirement, cases instituted by NGOs concern alleged violations of the complaining organisation's rights under the Convention. Most cases concern alleged violations of the right to freedom of association and assembly and the right to freedom of expression. In spite of the victim requirement, the cases often have general political implications.

In addition to the cases concerning the right to freedom of association which have been described earlier, a few more can be mentioned.

The case of *United Communist Party of Turkey and Others* v. *Turkey* concerned a political party which was dissolved by the Turkish Constitutional Court. The applicants – the party itself together with two Turkish nationals – claimed that the decision was contrary to the right to freedom of association as protected by Article 11. The Court found that Article 11 also had to be considered in light of Article 10, as the party's activities formed part of a collective exercise of freedom of expression. It stressed that political parties had an essential role in ensuring pluralism and the proper functioning of democracy and that there could be no doubt that political parties came within the scope of Article 11. The Court concluded that Article 11 had been violated.[150]

In the *case of Socialist Party and Others* v. *Turkey*, the party had been dissolved by the Constitutional Court and claimed, *inter alia*, that the decision constituted a breach of Article 11. The Court found a violation of Article 11, referring to its argument in the case of *United Communist Party of Turkey and Others* v. *Turkey*.[151]

The three cases brought by trade unions, *National Union of Belgian Police* v. *Belgium*, *Swedish Engine Drivers' Union* v. *Sweden* and *Wilson, National Union of Journalists and Others* v. *the United Kingdom* likewise concerned the right to

---

[150] *United Communist Party of Turkey and Others* v. *Turkey*, 30 January 1998.
[151] *Socialist Party and Others* v. *Turkey*, 25 May 1998. See also *Refah Partisi (Prosperity Party) and Others* v. *Turkey*, 31 July 2001 and *Yazar, Karatas, Aksoy and the People's Labour Party (HEP)* v. *Turkey*, 9 April 2002, which both dealt with questions about the right to freedom of association and political parties.

256   LEGAL AND EMPIRICAL SURVEY

freedom of association, as did the case of *Grande Oriente d'Italia di Palazzo Giustiniani* v. *Italy*.[152]

The right to freedom of assembly has also been brought up by NGOs before the Court.

The case of *Plattform 'Ärzte für das Leben'* v. *Austria* originated in an application brought by an association of doctors campaigning against abortion. In 1980 and 1982 the organisation held two demonstrations which were disrupted by counter-demonstrators despite the presence of police. The organisation complained to the Commission that it had not had sufficient police protection during the demonstrations and submitted that there had been breaches of, *inter alia*, Articles 11 and Article 13. The complaint under Article 13 was declared admissible, and the Court examined the right to freedom of peaceful assembly in connection with Article 13. It stated that participants in a demonstration should not have to fear that they would be subjected to physical violence by their opponents, as such a fear would be liable to deter associations or other groups supporting common ideas or interests from openly expressing their opinions on highly controversial issues affecting the community. The Court did, however, not find a violation of the Convention.[153]

In the above-mentioned case of *Stankov and the United Macedonian Organisation Ilinden* v. *Bulgaria*, the applicants alleged a violation of Article 11 of the Convention in respect of the authorities' refusal to allow the holding of their commemorative meetings. The organisation applied for, but was refused, registration by the Bulgarian courts, which found that the association's aims were directed against the unity of the nation, that it advocated national and ethnic hatred and that it was dangerous for the territorial integrity of Bulgaria. The applicant association also applied on several occasions for authorisation to hold public meetings. Each application was refused as the applicant association was not duly registered by the courts. The Court considered that, while past findings of national courts which had screened an association were relevant in the consideration of the dangers that its gatherings might pose, an automatic reliance on the fact that an organisation had been considered anti-constitutional and been refused registration could not suffice to justify a practice of systematic bans on the holding of peaceful assemblies. As there had been no real foreseeable risk of violent action or of incitement to violence or any other form of rejection of democratic principles, the authorities' prevention of the dissemination of the applicants' views at demonstrations was not justified under

---

[152] *National Union of Belgian Police* v. *Belgium*, 27 October 1975; *Swedish Engine Drivers' Union* v. *Sweden*, 6 February 1976; *Wilson, National Union of Journalists and Others* v. *the United Kingdom*, 2 July 2002; *Grande Oriente d'Italia di Palazzo Giustiniani* v. *Italy*, 2 August 2001. Regarding the latter case, see also section 4.2 on the right to freedom of association.
[153] *Plattform 'Ärzte für das Leben'* v. *Austria*, 21 June 1988.

Article 11(2). The Court concluded that the authorities had overstepped their margin of appreciation and that the measures banning the applicants from holding commemorative meetings were not necessary in a democratic society within the meaning of Article 11 of the Convention, which had thus been violated.[154]

Many of the cases brought by NGOs before the Court actualised the right to freedom of expression. These cases are in their character rather similar to cases instituted for more general political reasons, as they involve the organisations' right freely to express the ideas they have been formed to promote. Five of the cases concerned TV, radio or film.[155] Four cases had to do with printed material.[156] In the case of *Open Door and Dublin Well Woman* v. *Ireland* the applicants were not-for-profit companies incorporated under Irish law with the aim of providing counselling and health services to pregnant women.[157]

The three cases which raised the right to fair trial have been described above.[158]

The European Social Charter collective complaints procedure

The European Social Charter underwent a process of revitalisation during the 1990s.[159] In 1991, the Committee on the European Social Charter (also known as the Revitalisation Committee) was appointed and given the task to draft proposals in order to remedy some of the Charter's weaknesses. In 1994, the Revised Social Charter was adopted, bringing together all the rights guaranteed in the Charter and the 1988 Additional Protocol, as well as introducing a number of new rights.[160] The Revised Charter entered into force in July 1999.

One of the problems which had been identified by the Revitalisation Committee was the absence of actual participation of the social partners

---

[154] *Stankov and the United Macedonian Organisation Ilinden* v. *Bulgaria*, 10 February 2001.

[155] *Informationsverein Lentia & Others* v. *Austria*, 24 November 1993; *Otto-Preminger Institut* v. *Austria*, 20 September 1994; *Radio ABC* v. *Austria*, 20 October 1997; *Vgt Verein gegen Tierfabriken* v. *Switzerland*, 28 June 2001; *Informationsverein Lentia* v. *Austria*, 28 November 2002 (friendly settlement). See also *Groppera Radio AG and Others* v. *Switzerland*, 23 March 1990, in which case the radio station was a limited company incorporated under Swiss law.

[156] *Vereinigung demokratischer Soldaten Österreichs and Gubi* v. *Austria*, 19 December 1994; *Vereniging Weekblad Bluf!* v. *the Netherlands*, 9 February 1995; *Ekin Association* v. *France*, 17 July 2001; *Unabhängige Initiative Informationsvielfalt* v. *Austria*, 26 February 2002.

[157] *Open Door and Dublin Well Woman* v. *Ireland*, 29 October 1992.

[158] See also *Wynen and Centre hospitalier interrégional Edith-Cavell* v. *Belgium*, 5 November 2002, and *Ekin Association* v. *France*, 17 July 2001.

[159] ETS No. 35.   [160] ETS No. 163.

258 LEGAL AND EMPIRICAL SURVEY

in the supervisory procedure.[161] The Committee's work led to the adoption of two additional protocols, including the 1995 Additional Protocol to the European Social Charter Providing for a System of Collective Complaints, which entered into force in July 1998.[162] According to the Explanatory Report to the Protocol, the new mechanism was:

> designed to increase the efficiency of supervisory machinery based solely on the submission of governmental reports. In particular, this system should increase participation by management and labour and non-governmental organisations ... The way in which the machinery as a whole functions can only be enhanced by the greater interest that these bodies may be expected to show in the Charter ... The system of collective complaints is to be seen as a complement to the examination of governmental reports, which naturally constitutes the basic mechanism for the supervision of the application of the Charter.[163]

The collective complaints system is optional and applies to states parties to the Protocol. However, states that are parties to the Revised Charter may also make a declaration under Article D(2) of the Revised Charter that they accept the supervision under the collective complaints system. As of August 2004, eleven states had ratified the Protocol and an additional two states had made a declaration under Article D(2) of the Revised Charter.

As a collective complaints system, the procedure is accessible only to organisations, not to individuals or states. Individual situations may not be submitted, but can be described as an illustration of a state's failure to comply with the Charter.[164] Complaints may relate to the obligations undertaken by a party in respect of any of the rights in the Charter, including those concerning full employment policy in Article 1(1).[165] When a collective complaint has been submitted, it is examined by the Committee of Independent Experts (also known as the European Committee of Social Rights) which must first decide on the question of admissibility. If the Committee decides that the complaint is admissible, it collects information from the complainant, from the state

---

[161] Nathalie Prouvez, 'The European Social Charter, an Instrument for the Protection of Human Rights in the 21st Century?', International Commission of Jurists, *The Review*, No. 58–59, Geneva, 1997, p. 31.

[162] ETS No. 158.

[163] Additional Protocol to the European Social Charter Providing for a System of Collective Complaints, *Explanatory Report*, para. 2.

[164] *Ibid.*, para. 31, Prouvez, 'The European Social Charter', p. 39.

[165] *Explanatory Report*, para. 31, Donna Gomien, David Harris and Leo Zwaak, *Law and Practice of the European Convention on Human Rights and the European Social Charter*, Strasbourg: Council of Europe Publishing, 1996, p. 426.

concerned, from the other state parties to the Charter and from both sides of industry. The Committee may also organise a hearing with the representatives of the parties (Article 7). When the case has been examined, the Committee draws up a report containing its conclusions as to whether the state concerned has ensured the satisfactory application of the provision of the Charter referred to in the complaint. The report is transmitted to the Committee of Ministers, to the organisation that lodged the complaint, to the contracting parties to the Charter and to the Parliamentary Assembly. The report is made public (Article 8).

On the basis of the report, the Committee of Ministers shall adopt a resolution by a majority of those voting, or – if the Committee finds that the Charter has not been applied in a satisfactory manner – it shall adopt a recommendation addressed to the Contracting Party concerned by a majority of two-thirds of those voting (Article 9). The state against which the complaint is brought is authorised to sit in the Committee of Ministers and to vote, a fact that has been criticised by NGOs. The general involvement of the Committee of Ministers, which is of course a political body, in the collective complaints procedure process has also been criticised.[166] The Committee of Ministers may not reverse the legal assessment made by the Committee of Independent Experts, but may base its decision on considerations of social and economic policy.[167] The recommendations issued by the Committee of Ministers are not legally binding.[168]

The categories of organisations which may submit complaints are set out in Article 1 of the protocol, which reads:

The Contracting Parties to this Protocol recognise the right of the following organisations to submit complaints alleging unsatisfactory application of the Charter:

(a) international organisations of employers and trade unions referred to in paragraph 2 of Article 27 of the Charter;

(b) other international non-governmental organisations which have consultative status with the Council of Europe and have been put on a list established for this purpose by the Governmental Committee;

(c) representative national organisations of employers and trade unions within the jurisdiction of the Contracting Party against which they have lodged a complaint.

---

[166] Prouvez, 'The European Social Charter', pp. 40–41. See also Gomien, Harris and Zwaak, *Law and Practice*, p. 429.

[167] *Explanatory Report*, para. 46.

[168] Gomien, Harris and Zwaak, *Law and Practice*, p. 428; Prouvez, 'The European Social Charter', p. 40.

260 LEGAL AND EMPIRICAL SURVEY

Para. 1(a) refers to employers' organisations and trade unions which have been invited to take part in the work of the sub-committee of the Governmental Social Committee in accordance with Article 27(2) of the Charter.[169] According to para. 1(b), international NGOs (INGOs) can file complaints provided that they have been included in a special list established by the Governmental Committee. The Explanatory Report to the Additional Protocol specifies which circumstances should be considered by the Governmental Committee in the drawing up of this list, namely:

1. that the INGO holds consultative status with the Council of Europe and is particularly competent in any of the matters governed by the Charter,
2. that its application is supported by detailed documentation showing that the organisation has access to authoritative sources of information and is able to carry out the necessary verifications, to obtain appropriate legal opinions etc. in order to draw up complaint files that meet basic requirements of reliability, and
3. that the application is accompanied by an opinion of the Secretary-General reflecting a sufficient degree of interest and participation shown by the INGO in its other dealings with the Council of Europe.[170]

An application by the Governmental Committee is considered accepted unless it is rejected by a simple majority of the votes cast. Inclusion on the list is valid for a period of four years.[171] All decisions on inclusion or exclusion should be published and the reasons for the decision presented.[172] As of August 2004, fifty-seven international NGOs with consultative status had been included in the special list in accordance with Article 1(b).[173]

The third category of organisations mentioned in Article 1(c) is 'representative national organisations of employers and trade unions within the jurisdiction of the Contracting Party against which they have lodged a complaint'. The criterion of representativity was introduced in view of the large number of trade unions in some states. It was left to the Committee of Experts to judge whether the applying organisations

---

[169] The sub-committee examines the reports of the Contracting States and the conclusions of the Committee of Experts.

[170] Additional Protocol to the European Social Charter Providing for a System of Collective Complaints, *Explanatory Report*, para. 20.

[171] *Ibid.*   [172] Prouvez, 'The European Social Charter', p. 38.

[173] The list is publicised at the Council of Europe Social Charter website, accessible online at http://www.coe.int/T/E/Human_Rights/Esc/5_Collective_complaints.

meet this requirement.[174] The Committee has now discussed the issue of representativity in a number of cases. The first case dealing with a complaint from a national trade union was *Syndicat National des Professions du Tourisme* v. *France*. In its decision on admissibility, the Committee stressed that 'the representativity of national trade unions is an autonomous concept, beyond the ambit of national considerations, as well [as] the domestic collective labour relations context'.[175] After 'an overall assessment of the documents in the file', and noting that the representative character of the complaining trade union had not been contested by the government, the Committee considered that the organisation was representative in the meaning of Article 1(c) of the Protocol.[176] In a later case, the French government challenged the representativity of the complaining trade union with reference to a judgement from an Administrative Court of Appeal, according to which the trade union did not fulfil the conditions of representativity as laid down by French law. The Committee again referred to the autonomy of the concept, which was 'not necessarily identical to the national notion of representativity'.[177] It noted that it appeared from the documents in the file that the union exercised activities in defence of the material and moral interests of personnel in the education sector, of which it represented a considerable number, and this in total independence from the employing authorities. The Committee thus concluded that the union was representative for the purposes of the collective complaints procedure.[178]

All states which have accepted supervision under the collective complaints system recognise the right of an organisation falling into one of the three categories described in Article 1 to bring a complaint. In addition, each contracting state may, in a declaration to the Secretary-General of the Council of Europe, authorise national NGOs to lodge

---

[174] Additional Protocol to the European Social Charter Providing for a System of Collective Complaints, *Explanatory Report*, paras. 22–23.

[175] Complaint No. 6/1999, *Syndicat National des Professions du Tourisme* v. *France*, Decision on admissibility, para. 6.

[176] *Ibid.*, paras. 7–8.

[177] Complaint No. 23/2003, *Syndicat occitan d'éducation* v. *France*, Decision on admissibility, para. 4.

[178] *Ibid.*, para. 5. See also the decisions on admissibility in complaints Nos. 9/2000, *Confédération Française de l'Encadrement – CGC* v. *France*; 10/2000, *Tehy r.y. and STTK r.y.* v. *Finland*; 12/2002, *Confederation of Swedish Enterprise* v. *Sweden*; and Robin R. Churchill and Urfan Khaliq, 'The Collective Complaints System of the European Social Charter: An Effective Mechanism for Ensuring Compliance with Economic and Social Rights?', 15 EJIL (2004), pp. 425–426.

complaints against it in accordance with Article 2 of the Protocol. The declaration may be made for a specific period. On the other hand, declarations may not be restricted to specific national NGOs or to particular provisions of the Charter.[179]

Article 2 requires that national NGOs should be representative and have 'particular competence in the matters governed by the Charter'. These are the same requirements that are laid down for international NGOs and national organisations of employers and trade unions. According to the Explanatory Report, the Committee of Independent Experts will judge whether these criteria are met when examining whether the complaint is admissible in the light of information submitted by both parties.[180] So far, only Finland has made a declaration that it accepts complaints from national NGOs, and in the absence of decisions from the Committee it is uncertain what the requirements of representativity and 'particular competence in the matters governed by the Charter' will mean in practice. As is observed by Churchill and Khaliq, the latter criterion may not be so difficult to assess, while the former is more complicated.[181] In particular, it may be complicated to measure the representativity of NGOs that promote general interests rather than the interests of a certain group, since it is unclear of which group such NGOs should be representative.

In general, there is no victim requirement under the collective complaints procedure, and the complaining organisations need not have any connection to the alleged violation. Article 1 makes it clear that it is sufficient that the complaint concerns alleged 'unsatisfactory application of the Charter'. However, organisations may submit complaints only in respect of those matters regarding which they have been recognised as having particular competence (Article 3). This question has also been left to the Committee to deal with in its practice. The competence of the complaining NGO has been challenged in a couple of cases. In complaint No. 17, the World Organisation against Torture (OMCT) stated that Greek law had not effectively prohibited corporal punishment of children, in breach of Article 17 of the Charter. The government alleged that OMCT was 'not particularly qualified in the field of degrading treatment of children'.[182] However, the Committee simply noted

---

[179] *Explanatory Report*, para. 28.   [180] *Ibid.*, para. 26.

[181] Churchill and Khaliq, 'The Collective Complaints System', p. 426.

[182] Complaint No. 17/2003, *World Organisation Against Torture (OMCT)* v. *Greece*, Decision on admissibility, para. 2.

that 'the OMCT is a non-governmental organization whose aim is to contribute to the struggle against torture ... regardless of the age of the persons against whom such treatments are directed' and considered that it was particularly qualified in the meaning of Article 3.[183] The Greek government also contested the competence of the Quakers (QCEA) in complaint No. 8/2000, which related to Article 1(2) on prohibition of forced labour.[184] The complainant alleged that the application in practice of the act authorising alternative forms of military service for conscientious objectors did not respect the prohibition of forced labour. The government stated that it was not clear from the complaint that the QCEA engaged in any activity that made it particularly qualified in the field of the protection of the right to work. Nevertheless, the Committee found that the aim of the QCEA was to bring to the attention of the European institutions the concerns of the members of this society, which relate to peace, human rights and economic justice, and therefore considered that the QCEA had introduced a complaint in a field in which it had particular competence.[185] It thus seems that the complainants do not need to demonstrate a very high degree of specialisation in order to meet the requirement of competence under Article 3.[186]

As of August 2004, twenty-seven complaints had been registered.[187] Twelve of these were lodged by INGOs.[188] All the others had been filed by (national and international) organisations of workers or employers. Only Finland has accepted communications from national NGOs (that are not organisations of workers or employers), but the only communication regarding Finland was lodged by a trade union. Nine complaints led to the adoption of a resolution or recommendation by the Committee of Ministers.[189]

---

[183] *Ibid.*, para. 6.
[184] Complaint No. 8/2000, *Quaker Council for European Affairs (QCEA)* v. *Greece*, Decision on admissibility, para. 4.
[185] *Ibid.*, paras. 8–9.
[186] See also Churchill and Khaliq, 'The Collective Complaints System', pp. 427–428.
[187] The list of complaints is published at the website of the Council of Europe, accessible online at www.coe.int/T/E/Human_Rights/Esc/5_Collective_complaints/List_of_collective_complaints.
[188] Nos. 1, 7, 8, 13, 14, 15, 17–21, 27. Several communications have been lodged by the same NGOs. For instance, the OMTC has filed five communications and the European Roma Rights Center has lodged two.
[189] RecChS(2001)1 on Collective complaint No. 6/1999, *Syndicat National des Professions du Tourisme* v. *France*, ResChS(2001)2 on No. 2/1999; *European Federation of Employees in Public Services* v. *France*, ResChS(2001)3 on No. 4/1999; *European Federation of Employees in Public*

264   LEGAL AND EMPIRICAL SURVEY

It is doubtful what effect the collective complaints procedure will have on state parties' compliance with the Charter.[190] It is nevertheless interesting that the participation by and interest of organisations of workers and employers, as well as of other NGOs, in the Charter machinery as a whole was seen as an important impetus for creating the collective complaints mechanism.

The European Court of Justice

The European Court of Justice (ECJ) is the judicial organ of all three European Communities. The Court has jurisdiction to hear cases to determine whether a member state has fulfilled its obligations under Community law, cases on annulment of Community legislation, on the legality of a failure to act by a Community institution and on action for damages, based on non-contractual liability of the Community for damage caused by its institutions or servants in the performance of their duties. The ECJ may also hear appeals on points of law against judgements given by the CFI, and has limited jurisdiction over certain EU third-pillar matters.

The CFI was set up in 1989 as a response to an increasing case-load and in order to enable the ECJ to concentrate on the uniform interpretation of Community law. It is not a fully independent court; its legal basis is to be found in Article 168a of the European Community (EC) Treaty, which provides that: 'A Court of First Instance shall be attached to the Court of Justice.' Instead of providing the CFI with its own statute, certain new articles were added the ECJ's Statute, and other articles were extended.

Private litigants cannot sue member states for alleged breaches of Community law. However, private parties have *locus standi* before the CFI as regards the actions of Community institutions.[191] Natural or legal persons may institute four categories of cases. First, the Court hears disputes between the Community and its servants under Article 236 of the Treaty Establishing the European Community (the EC Treaty).

Services v. *Italy*, ResChS(2001)4 on No. 5/1999; *European Federation of Employees in Public Services* v. *Portugal*, ResChs(2001)6 on No. 7/2000; *International Federation of Human Rights* v. *Greece*, ResChS(2002)2 on No. 10/2000; *STTK r.y. and Tehy r.y.* v. *Finland*, ResChs(2002)3 on No. 8/2000; *Quakers' Council for European Affairs* v. *Greece*, ResChS(2002)4 on No. 9/2000; *Confédération française de l'Encadrement CFE-CGC* v. *France*, ResChS(2002)5 on No. 11/2001; *European Council of Police Trade Unions* v. *Portugal*.

[190] For a discussion on this question, see Churchill and Khaliq, 'The Collective Complaints System', pp. 455–456.

[191] The investigation on NGO participation in proceedings before the CFI and the ECJ is limited to the European Economic Community (EEC).

Secondly, private parties may seek judicial review under Article 230 (para. 4), i.e. the annulment of a decision taken by a Community institution. Such actions may be brought by the addressee of the decision or by a party to whom the decision is of direct and individual concern. The meaning of the expression 'direct and individual concern' was clarified by the ECJ in the case of *Plaumann & Co.* v. *Commission*, and has been settled in subsequent case-law.[192] The Court concluded that a decision could be of individual concern to persons other than the addressee only if it affects third parties 'by reason of certain attributes which are peculiar to other persons and by virtue of these factors distinguishes them individually just as in the case of the person addressed'.[193]

Thirdly, natural or legal persons may complain that an institution of the Community has failed to act when such failure is contrary to Community law (Article 232, para. 3). This type of action is subject to a double restriction: the failure must concern an act of a binding character and the act must be addressed to the complaining person individually. Finally, natural and legal persons may bring claims for compensation as a consequence of the Community's non-contractual liability for damage caused by its institutions or servants in the performance of their duties (Articles 235, 288). The scope *ratione personae* of the first three types of cases is the same – 'any natural or legal person' – while the fourth category is open to anyone who has suffered damage caused by a Community institution.

About half of the cases brought before the CFI are staff cases. These will be left aside here as they are not particularly relevant to the central issues of the study. It can be mentioned, however, that trade unions often appear in support of the applicants in these cases, especially the *Union Syndicale*, which is the Community civil servants' union.[194] The majority of the other cases concern economic issues, mostly competition law. In view of the dominant subject matters of Community

---

[192] European Court of Justice, *Plaumann & Co.* v. *Commission of the European Economic Community*, Case 25/62, 15 July 1963. See also, e.g, *Spijker Kwasten BV* v. *Commission* (Case 231/82), 14 July 1983 and *Piraiki-Patraiki et al.* v. *Commission* (Case 11/82), 17 January 1985.

[193] European Court of Justice, *Plaumann & Co.* v. *Commission of the European Economic Community*, Case 25/62, 15 July 1963, Summary para. 4.

[194] Neville March Hunnings, *The European Courts*, London: Cartermill Publishing, 1996, p. 211.

266 LEGAL AND EMPIRICAL SURVEY

legislation and of the cases before the Courts, it is thus not surprising that there are few cases which have been instituted by NGOs. Nevertheless, there are a few cases worth mentioning.

An interesting case brought up the central question of *locus standi* under Article 230 (formerly Article 173) for NGOs formed for the protection of collective interests in cases concerning judicial review.[195]

The case, *Stichting Greenpeace Council (Greenpeace International) and others* v. *Commission*, was brought by Greenpeace International before the CFI and later to the ECJ. The background to the case was a decision adopted by the Commission in 1991 to grant Spain financial assistance for the building of two power stations in the Canary Islands by Unión Eléctrica de Canarias SA (Unelco). Two of the applicants in the case informed the Commission by letter in December 1991 that the works carried out on Gran Canaria were unlawful as Unelco had failed to undertake an environmental impact assessment study in accordance with a Council Directive, and asked the Commission to intervene to stop the works. Subsequently, several environmental NGOs and other applicants in the case contacted the Commission and instituted domestic proceedings against the project. In May 1993, Greenpeace asked the Commission for full disclosure of all information relating to measures it had taken with regard to the construction of the two power stations. The request was rejected.

The applicants brought an action before the CFI seeking annulment of the decision of the Commission to disburse funds to the Spanish government in reimbursement of expenses incurred in the construction of the power stations. The Commission raised an objection of inadmissibility in support of which it raised two pleas, one of which concerned the nature of the contested decision, and the other the applicants' lack of *locus standi*. The CFI upheld the Commission's objection and declared the action inadmissible. It recalled that it had consistently been held in the case-law that an association formed for the protection of the collective interests of a category of persons could not be considered to be directly and individually concerned for the purposes of (former) Article 173, para. 4 by a measure affecting the general interests of that category. An association was therefore not entitled to bring an action for annulment where its members could not do so individually. The CFI went on to

---

[195] The question of *locus standi* under Article 230 is a complicated subject, and I am not attempting to provide the full picture, merely to describe some of the issues which may arise for NGOs seeking to advance public interests on the basis of this Article. For more general information, see, e.g., Angela Ward, *Judicial Review and the Rights of Private Parties in EC Law*, Oxford University Press, 2000, pp. 239 ff.; Hunnings, *The European Courts*, pp. 211–213; Paul Craig, 'The Jurisdiction of the Community Courts Reconsidered', in Graínne de Búrca and J. H. H. Weiler, *The European Court of Justice*, Oxford University Press, 2001, pp. 177–214.

observe that special circumstances, such as the role played by an association in a procedure which led to the adoption of an act within the meaning of Article 173, might justify treating an action as admissible, even if it had been brought by an association whose members were not directly and individually concerned by the contested measure. The Court concluded, however, that the exchange of correspondence and the discussions which Greenpeace had with the Commission concerning the financing of the project for the construction of the power stations did not constitute special circumstances of that kind since the Commission had not initiated any procedure in which Greenpeace participated prior to the adoption of the contested decision.

The appellants argued in their appeal, *inter alia*, that the approach adopted by the CFI created a legal vacuum in ensuring compliance with Community environmental legislation, since in this area the interests were by their very nature common and shared. The rights relating to those interests were also liable to be held by a potentially large number of individuals so that there could never be a closed class of applicants satisfying the criteria adopted by the CFI. The appellants further argued that environmental protection was one of the Community's essential objectives in accordance with earlier judgements and submitted that Community environmental legislation could create rights and obligations for individuals. According to the appellants, environmental associations should be recognised as having *locus standi* where their objectives concerned chiefly environmental protection and one or more of their members was individually concerned in the contested Community decision, but also where their primary objective was environmental protection and they could demonstrate a specific interest in the question at issue.

The ECJ observed that the interpretation of Article 173(4) which the CFI had applied in concluding that the appellants did not have *locus standi* was in accordance with the settled case-law of the Court. As far as natural persons were concerned, it followed from this case-law that where the specific situation of the applicant was not taken into consideration in the adoption of an act, which concerned the applicant in a general and abstract fashion like any other person in the same situation, the applicant was not individually concerned in the act. The same applied to associations claiming to have *locus standi* on the basis of the fact that the persons whom they represented were individually concerned by the contested decision.[196]

It has been suggested that the reluctance on the part of the CFI to revise the criteria for *locus standi* under Article 230(4), as determined in the *Plaumann* and subsequent cases, was partly due to a fear of being

---

[196] European Court of Justice, Case C-321/95 P, *Stichting Greenpeace Council (Greenpeace International) and others v. Commission*, Judgement of 2 April 1998.

268 LEGAL AND EMPIRICAL SURVEY

flooded with appeals.[197] It thus seems clear that an expansion of *locus standi* cannot take place without a treaty amendment.[198]

Svenska Journalistförbundet v. *Council of the European Union* is another example of a case instituted by an NGO for reasons of public interest.

Svenska Journalistförbundet is the Swedish Journalists' Union. Following Sweden's accession to the European Union, the applicant decided to test the way in which Swedish authorities applied Swedish citizens' right of access to information in respect of documents relating to European Union activities. For that purpose, the organisation contacted forty-six Swedish authorities seeking access to Council documents relating to the setting up of Europol, and was granted access to eighteen of the twenty documents requested. The applicant also applied to the Council of the European Union requesting access to the same twenty documents under Council Decision 93/731/EC on public access to Council documents. The Council's General Secretariat allowed access to only two documents, while access to the other eighteen documents was refused on the ground that they were 'subject to the principle of confidentiality as laid down in Article 4(1) of Decision 93/731'. The applicant then submitted a confirmatory application to the Council in order to obtain re-examination of the decision refusing access. The Council replied that it agreed to grant access to two other documents but rejected the application for the remaining sixteen. It explained that, in its opinion, 'access to those documents cannot be granted because their release could be harmful to the public interest (public security) and because they relate to the Council's proceedings, including the positions taken by the members of the Council'. The documents were therefore covered by the duty of confidentiality.

The applicant instituted an action before the CFI applying for the annulment of the Council's decision of refusing access to the documents. Denmark, Netherlands and Sweden were granted leave to intervene in support of the applicant, while France and the United Kingdom intervened in support of the defendant. The Council requested the Court to, *inter alia*, declare the application inadmissible or reject it as unfounded. It held that, although it was conscious of the fact that the applicant was the addressee of the contested decision, it questioned whether the applicant was really affected by that decision within the meaning of Article 173 of the EC Treaty, as that article did not allow individual actions in the public interest but only permitted individuals to challenge acts which concerned them in a way in which they did not concern other individuals. The applicant's interest was of a general and political nature,

---

[197] Paul Joan George Kapteyn and Pieter VerLoren van Themaat, *Introduction to the Law of the European Communities*, 3rd edn., London: Kluwer International, 1998, pp. 487–488.

[198] For proposals of amendments of Article 230 that could create more effective judicial protection, see Ward, *Judicial Review and the Rights of Private Parties in EC Law*, pp. 256–260.

its intention being to ensure that the Council gave proper effect to its own Code of Conduct and Decision 93/731. The Council further contended that the release of the documents in question by the Swedish authorities to the applicant constituted a breach of Community law, since no decision had been taken to authorise such a disclosure.

The Court found that the applicant was the addressee of the contested decision and, as such, not obliged to prove that the decision was of direct and individual concern to it. It needed to prove only that it had an interest in the annulment of the decision. The objective of Decision 93/731 was to give effect to the principle of the largest possible access for citizens to information with a view to strengthening the democratic character of the institutions and the trust of the public in the administration. According to the Council's decisions, it was not required that members of the public put forward reasons for seeking access to requested documents. It therefore followed that a person who was refused access to a document or to part of a document had, by virtue of that very fact, established an interest in the annulment of the decision. The application was thus declared admissible. In its consideration of the merits of the case, the Court found that the contested decision should be annulled.[199]

Again, one of the central questions of the case was whether the NGO had a sufficiently strong interest in the contested decision – if the decision was of 'direct and individual concern' to the organisation, as provided in Article 230, para. 4. As the Journalists' Union had established such an interest already by the Council's decision to refuse access to the documents, the fact that the Union's reasons for the request were of a general and political nature became irrelevant. It is probable that there are other practices by Community institutions that could be challenged in a similar way by a private person or by an NGO.

An earlier case which actualised the question of *locus standi* in cases concerning judicial review was instituted by the ecologist party *Les Verts*, an NGO headquartered in Paris.

In the case of *Parti écologiste 'Les Verts'* v. *European Parliament* the party brought an action requesting the Court to declare void a decision of the Bureau of the European Parliament. The decision concerned the apportionment and use of funds destined to reimburse political groups for expenditures to be incurred in the 1984 European elections. The Court found that a political grouping which, unlike its rivals, was not represented in the European Parliament but which was able to put up candidates in the direct elections to the Parliament must, in

---

[199] Court of First Instance, Case T-174/95, *Svenska Journalistförbundet* v. *Council of the European Union*, 17 June 1998.

270   LEGAL AND EMPIRICAL SURVEY

order to avoid inequality in the protection afforded by the Court to groupings competing in the same elections, be regarded as being both directly and individually concerned by measures adopted by the Parliament for the purpose of allocating appropriations entered in its budget for the financing of the information campaign preceding those elections. The challenged decision was thus declared void by the Court.[200]

In addition to the cases described above, there are examples of cases brought by consumers' organisations, trade unions, industrial organisations and producers' associations.[201]

The requirements for *locus standi* formulated in Article 230 have been discussed by the ECJ as well as by scholars. The report of the Court of Justice on Certain Aspects of the Application of the Treaty on European Union discusses the Court's role in examining whether fundamental rights have been respected by the Community authorities and the member states. In this context the question is put whether the right for private parties to bring an action for annulment under Article 230 is sufficient to guarantee effective judicial protection against possible infringements of fundamental rights arising from the legislative activity of the Community institutions.[202] In another report on the Role and Function of the European Court of Justice, published in 1996 by Members of the EC Section of the Advisory Board of the British Institute of International and Comparative Law, it is suggested that the *locus standi* provision in Article 230 should be broadened.[203] It is observed that although the rule on direct and individual concern has been somewhat relaxed in the Court's case-law, the situation is still far from satisfactory, especially in relation to representative bodies. The writers

---

[200] Case 294/83, *Parti écologiste 'Les Verts'* v. *European Parliament*, 23 April 1986.

[201] Examples include Cases T-256/97, *Bureau Européen des Unions de Consummateurs (BEUC)* v. *Commission*, 27 January 2000; T-224/95, *Syndicat des Exploitants de Lieux de Loisirs (SELL)* v. *Commission*, 27 November 1997; T-82/96, *Associação dos Refinadores de Açúcar Portugueses (ARAP)* v. *Commission*, 17 June 1999; C-313/90, *Comité International de la Rayonne et des Fibres Synthétiques* v. *Commission*, 24 March 1993; T-135/96, *Union Européenne de l'artisanat et des petites et moyennes entreprises (UEAPME)* v. *Council*, 17 June 1998. See also *Forum des migrants de l'Union européenne* v. *Commission*, 9 April 2003, regarding the Commission's decision to terminate its financial support to an international NGO, and *Internationaler Hilfsfonds eV* v. *Commission*, 18 September 2003, on the Commission's decision to refuse applications for the co-financing of projects submitted by the applicant.

[202] *Report of the Court of Justice on Certain Aspects of the Application of the Treaty on European Union*, May 1995, para. 20. Reprinted in Hunnings, *The European Courts*, p. 172.

[203] *The Role and Function of the European Court of Justice*, A Report by Members of the EC Section of the British Institute's Advisory Board chaired by the Rt Hon. the Lord Slynn of Hadley, The British Institute of International and Comparative Law, 1996, pp. 93–94.

STANDING BEFORE INTERNATIONAL BODIES 271

suggest that the provision should be relaxed provided that the capacity of the CFI is expanded through an increase in the number of judges, the creation of specialised chambers and other measures.[204]

The Inter-American System for Human Rights

The procedure

The Inter-American Commission, established in 1960, examines individual communications regarding human rights violations within the territory of the OAS member states under two parallel procedures. First, the Commission was authorised through a re-formulation of its Statute in 1965 to examine individual complaints or petitions regarding specific cases of violations of human rights as expressed in the American Declaration of the Rights and Duties of Man of 1948.[205] Secondly, when the American Convention on Human Rights was adopted in 1969, the individual complaints procedure was included in the Convention and thereby became operational towards all the contracting parties.[206] The American Convention on Human Rights also completed the legal structure of the Inter-American human rights system with the establishment of the Inter-American Court of Human Rights.

The present Statute of the Commission was approved by the OAS General Assembly in 1979. The Statute distinguishes between the Commission's competence *vis-à-vis* state parties to the Convention and in relation to member states of the OAS not parties to the Convention.[207]

The right to file petitions with the Commission concerning violations of the human rights enumerated in the Convention is based on Article 44:

> Any nongovernmental entity legally recognized in one or more member states of the Organization, may lodge petitions with the Commission containing denunciations or complaints of violation of this Convention by a State Party.

As is clear from this provision, the possibilities for NGOs to act within the Inter-American system are in some respects more extensive than

---

[204] It can be noted that the Treaty of Nice allows for this, see Article 2(32) regarding new Article 225 a.

[205] American Declaration of the Rights and Duties of Man, adopted by the Ninth International Conference of American States, Bogotá, Colombia, 1948.

[206] OAS Treaty Series No. 36.

[207] Statute of the Inter-American Commission on Human Rights, October 1979, Articles 19, 20.

272   LEGAL AND EMPIRICAL SURVEY

within the European human rights system, although NGOs and individuals do not have *locus standi* before the Inter-American Court. It is no condition for a complaint to be accepted that the petitioner has been subjected to a violation of the Convention, and the petitioner does not need to be legally empowered to act on behalf of the victim. While the Convention does not recognise *actio popularis*, or communications lodged *in abstracto* without the naming of a victim, it suffices that the alleged victim is only potentially affected by, for instance, a legal provision.[208] The generous *locus standi* rules are an important advantage to human rights NGOs, which can lodge petitions that concern identified victims but which are also of general interest. The circle of actors entitled to lodge petitions is also wide; 'any nongovernmental entity' includes individuals and groups as well as commercial and non-commercial entities.[209] Furthermore, the complaining NGO does not have to be legally recognised in the respondent state. It suffices that it is recognised by one of the OAS member states. In fact, the alleged victim need not even approve of the complaint. Article 23 of the Commission's Rules of Procedure states that petitions may be submitted by persons and non-governmental entities 'on their own behalf or on behalf of third persons, concerning alleged violations', and according to Article 28(e) of the Rules, a petition shall contain the name of the victim 'if possible'.[210]

As regards the possibility of NGOs as victims of a violation enshrined by the American Convention, it should be noted that the Convention protects 'persons', who are defined as every human being (Article 1, paras. 1–2). The Convention thus does not protect NGOs or other legal persons as such.[211] Rights which can be associated with organisations or other legal entities, such as the right to freedom of

---

[208] American Convention on Human Rights, Article 44, *Rules of Procedure of the Inter-American Commission on Human Rights* (as Approved by the Commission at its 109th Special Session, December 4–8, 2000); Article 28, Case of *Metropolitan Nature Reserve*, Report No. 88/03 in OEA/Ser.L/V/II.118, *Annual Report of the Inter-American Commission 2003*, December 29, 2003, paras. 29–32; Thomas Buergenthal, 'The Inter-American Court of Human Rights', 76 AJIL (1982), p. 237.

[209] See Article 28(a) of the Commission's Rules of Procedure. Most juridical persons that lodge petitions are (non-commercial) NGOs. For an example of a case instituted by a (presumably) commercial actor, see Report No. 127 in OEA/Ser.L/V/II.114, *Annual Report of the Inter-American Commission 2001*, 16 April 2002, where a law firm acted as petitioner.

[210] *Rules of Procedure of the Inter-American Commission on Human Rights*, Approved by the Commission at its 109th Special Session, December 4–8, 2000, last amended on October 7–24, 2003.

[211] See section 4.2.

association under Article 16 of the Convention, are protected as individual rights.[212]

Twenty-five of the thirty-five member states of the OAS are parties to the Convention.[213] For OAS member states that are not parties to the Convention, the Commission continues to apply the American Declaration of the Rights and Duties of Man. It is clear from the Commission's Rules of Procedure that it employs the same rules on *locus standi* regarding violations of the Declaration as it does for violations of the Convention.[214] The Declaration was not legally binding at the time of its adoption. According to Scott Davidson, the Declaration has become an instrument which creates legally binding obligations for all OAS member states, although it is not possible to ascertain the precise nature of these obligations.[215]

If a friendly settlement cannot be reached between the parties, the Commission prepares a report which may include its conclusions and recommendations to the state concerned. This report is confidential.[216] If, after a period of three months, the matter has not been settled and

---

[212] In the case of *Statehood Solidarity Committee v. USA*, the petition was filed by an individual on behalf of the members of an NGO (as well as on behalf of all US citizens resident in the District of Columbia), whose rights under the American Declaration the state had allegedly violated, see Report (on the merits) No. 98, *Annual Report of the Inter-American Commission 2003*, OEA/Ser.L/V/II.118, 29 December 2003.

[213] As of 2003, OEA/Ser.L/V/II.118, *Annual Report of the Inter-American Commission on Human Rights 2003*, December 29, 2003, annex 2.

[214] Article 28(f) provides that petitions shall contain information regarding 'the State the petitioner considers responsible, by act or omission, for the violation of any of the human rights recognized in the American Convention on Human Rights and other applicable instruments'. In general, the Article does not distinguish between petitions concerning the Convention and petitions regarding the Declaration.

[215] Scott Davidson, *The Inter-American Human Rights System*, Aldershot: Dartmouth 1997, pp. 23–30. This evaluation of the Declaration is made by reference to, *inter alia*, the judgement of the Court in its Advisory Opinion OC-10/89 of 14 July 1989, *Interpretation of the American Declaration of the Rights and Duties of Man Within the Framework of Article 64 of the American Convention on Human Rights*, and the decision in 1981 of the Inter-American Commission in the *Baby Boy* case. According to Eriksson, the Declaration represents an authoritative interpretation of the OAS Charter, Maja Kirilova Eriksson, *Skydd av mänskliga rättigheter: Det Interamerikanska Systemet*, 2nd edn., Uppsala: Iustus Förlag (1994), p. 19.

[216] Article 50. As regards confidentiality, the Article states only that 'the report shall be transmitted to the states concerned, which shall not be at liberty to publish it'. The Court held in the *Certain Attributes* case that the presumption of equality between the parties implied that the Commission was not free to publish this report. Advisory Opinion OC-13/93, *Certain Attributes of the Inter-American Commission on Human Rights*, 16 July 1993, para. 48. See further Davidson, *The Inter-American Human Rights System*, pp. 183–185.

274 LEGAL AND EMPIRICAL SURVEY

the case has not been submitted by the state party or the Commission to the Court, the Commission may set out its opinions and conclusions in a second report under Article 51. The Commission has no power to offer compensation or other remedies. It may, however, make recommendations to the respondent state, prescribe the remedial measures that should be taken and the time period within which this should be done.[217] If the state concerned does not solve the situation, the Commission may decide to publish its report, as part of its Annual Report to the OAS General Assembly or in some other suitable manner.[218] Its decisions and recommendations are not legally binding.

Rather than preparing a second report for publication, the Commission may decide to take the case to the Inter-American Court. According to Article 62(3) of the Convention, the Court's adjudicatory or contentious jurisdiction comprises all substantive rights protected by the Convention, provided that the state parties to the case recognise or have recognised the jurisdiction of the Court. Only state parties and the Commission have *locus standi* before the Court. The alleged victims, their next of kin or their representatives may, however, submit requests, arguments and evidence, autonomously, throughout the proceedings under Rule 23(1) of the Court's Rules of Procedure.[219] The Court may also hear the petitioner, who is often someone else than the alleged victim (in many cases, an NGO), under Rule 44(1) as a 'witness, expert witness or in any other capacity'.[220] If the Court finds that there has been a violation of a right or freedom protected by the Convention, the Court shall rule that the injured party be ensured the enjoyment of the right. The Court can also rule that a fair compensation be paid to the injured party.

The Inter-American Commission

The annual reports of the Inter-American Commission contain all case reports on the merits that the Commission has decided to publish. Relatively few reports are published; as of 2003, the Commission had examined more than 13,000 complaints, resulting in the publication of

---

[217] American Convention on Human Rights, Article 51(1-2), and *Rules of Procedure of the Inter-American Commission on Human Rights*, December 2000, Article 45(1-2). See also Davidson, *The Inter-American Human Rights System*, pp. 118, 179.

[218] Article 51(3) of the Convention and *Rules of Procedure of the Inter-American Commission on Human Rights*, Article 45(3).

[219] *Rules of Procedure of the Inter-American Court of Human Rights*, as Approved by the Court at its Forty-Ninth Regular Session, November 16-25, 2000.

[220] See also Davidson, *The Inter-American Human Rights System*, pp. 138-139.

STANDING BEFORE INTERNATIONAL BODIES 275

some 600 case reports.[221] It should also be observed that the case reports often do not state who has filed the petition, which means that it is impossible to determine exactly how many cases have been lodged by NGOs on the basis of these reports.

The Commission's Annual Report for 2003 included six case reports on the merits and eleven friendly settlements.[222] Thirteen of these seventeen cases originated in petitions filed by NGOs.[223] The report for 2002 contained eleven reports on the merits and three friendly settlements. Of these fourteen cases, at least seven were cases lodged by NGOs.[224] For the year 2001, the Commission published four case reports on the merits and eight friendly settlements. Out of these twelve cases, nine originated in petitions filed by NGOs.[225] During the previous three-year period, the Annual Reports contained seventy-seven case reports on the merits and eighteen friendly settlements. Out of these ninety-five cases, at least forty-three were instituted by NGOs.[226] This means that out of a total of 138 case reports on the merits and on friendly settlements covering a period of six years, at least seventy-two cases had been instituted by NGOs, alone or together with other bodies or individuals. It can be assumed that NGOs have been involved in the preparation of many more petitions.[227]

The cases lodged before the Inter-American Commission are, generally speaking, different in their character as compared to, for

---

[221] OEA/Ser.L/V/II.118, *Annual Report of the Inter-American Commission on Human Rights 2003*, December 29, 2003, para. 5.

[222] According to the report, the Commission adopted 121 case reports during the two sessions covered by the report, OEA/Ser.L/V.II.118, paras. 11, 15.

[223] *Ibid.*, Reports No. 40, 63, 64, 66–69, 71, 91, 97, 98, 100. In No. 91, the NGO acted as co-petitioner together with an individual. The identity of the petitioner was withheld in one case (No. 70).

[224] OEA/Ser.L/V/II.117, *Annual Report of the Inter-American Commission on Human Rights 2002*, March 7, 2003, Reports No. 23, 32, 33, 52, 62, 78, 75. In one case (Report No. 57), the identity of the petitioners was withheld.

[225] OEA/Ser.L/V/II.114, *Annual Report of the Inter-American Commission on Human Rights 2001*, April 16, 2002, Reports No. 66, 100, 104–110. Eight of these petitions were filed by the same NGO, Comisión Ecuménica de Derechos Humanos (CEDHU).

[226] OEA/Ser.L/V/II.102, *Annual Report of the Inter-American Commission on Human Rights 1998*, April 16, 1999; OEA/Ser.L/V/II.106, *Annual Report of the Inter-American Commission on Human Rights 1999*, April 13, 2000; OEA/Ser.L/V/II.111, *Annual Report of the Inter-American Commission on Human Rights 2000*, April 16, 2001.

[227] For instance, NGOs sometimes act as the victim's formal representative, see, e.g., OEA/Ser.L/V/II.111, *Annual Report of the Inter-American Commission on Human Rights 2000*, April 16, 2001, Reports 93/00, 94/00, 98/00. In addition to such cases, it is reasonable to assume that NGOs sometimes act 'behind the scenes'.

276   LEGAL AND EMPIRICAL SURVEY

instance, cases before the (former) European Commission or Court. The situations examined are often violent, and many cases concern disappearances or killings. It is natural that human rights NGOs play an important role in bringing such cases to the attention of the Commission. It can even be assumed that the Commission depends on permissive *locus standi* rules, as the institution of a case may be associated with risks for the petitioner, and the extent and nature of many violations require resources and general knowledge for the establishment of facts, as well as legal expertise of how to meet the admissibility criteria.[228] Another factor which supports this supposition is that illiteracy rates in some countries in Latin America are high.

The violent character of the cases examined by the Commission also has the consequence that the reports publicised are focused more on determining the admissibility and facts of the case than on interpreting and analysing the different rights enshrined in the Convention.[229] The main strategy of NGOs acting before the Commission thus appears to be to bring cases to public attention rather than to promote a dynamic development of the case-law. One exception in this regard, however, is the organisation Interights, which has worked with issues related to the death penalty over a number of years. Interights has submitted a petition to the Inter-American Commission in such a case and has advised lawyers in other cases.[230] Another exception is the case of *María Eugenia Morales de Sierra* v. *Guatemala*, which was submitted by the Center for Justice and International Law (CEJIL) together with the alleged victim as a method for questioning the Guatemalan Civil Code *in abstracto*, as the Code was considered to create discriminatory distinctions between men and women.[231]

A few NGOs appear as petitioners in many cases. These include CEJIL, the Colombian Commission of Jurists, Asociación Pro Derechos

---

[228] Tragically, a number of persons who have reported on human rights violations or witnessed in cases before the Commission have been assassinated, disappeared or been driven into exile. David J. Padilla, 'The Inter-American Commission on Human Rights of the Organization of American States: A Case Study', 9 *American University Journal of International Law and Policy* (1993), p. 106. See also Davidson, *The Inter-American Human Rights System*, p. 140.

[229] See also Davidson, *The Inter-American Human Rights System*, p. 261.

[230] Interights, *Annual Review 98–99*, p. 48, and *Annual Review 99–2000*, p. 48.

[231] Case 11.625, included in OEA/Ser.L/V/II.111, *Annual Report of the Inter-American Commission on Human Rights* 2000, April 16, 2001. Interights and several other NGOs participated as *amici* at the admissibility stage of the case, see section 6.1.

Humanos (APRODEH), Americas Watch (now Human Rights Watch) and Comisión Ecuménica de Derechos Humanos (CEDHU).

According to an article by the Assistant Executive Secretary of the Commission, one of the explanations of the important role played by NGOs in the Inter-American human rights system is that they have created transnational networks.[232] Thanks to these networks, victims can present a complaint regarding a human rights violation to an NGO in the victim's home country and, once the complaint has been investigated, the case may be argued before the Commission and eventually the Court by an international team of lawyers. NGOs also carry out important functions at other stages of the proceedings, as well as in the work of the Commission in general. For instance, NGOs participate in the investigation of cases, assist in the conduct of on-site visits, request provisional measures in serious and urgent cases and monitor compliance with the recommendations of the Commission and the decisions of the Court.[233]

The Inter-American Court

The Court's mandate is described in Article 1 of its Statute as 'an autonomous judicial institution whose purpose is the application and interpretation of the American Convention on Human Rights'.[234] Although NGOs are unable to refer cases to the Court, it is an interesting question to what extent NGOs manage to influence the case-law of the Court through the cases lodged by them before the Commission and which are later referred to the Court. The advisory jurisdiction of the Court cannot be invoked by private parties.[235]

As of August 2004, the Inter-American Court had delivered judgements on the merits in forty-five contentious cases. At least fifteen of these originated in petitions filed by NGOs (alone or together with other

---

[232] Padilla, 'The Inter-American Commission on Human Rights', p. 98.

[233] *Ibid.* It is also demonstrated by several judgements of the Court that experts from NGOs have acted as the Commission's assistants before the Court – see, e.g., Series C: Decisions and Judgments, *Case of El Amparo* v. *Venezuela*, 18 January 1995, para. 6. In other judgements, it is not mentioned that the experts are NGO officers, but the persons appointed as assistants of the Commission are in fact NGO staff members. For instance, in judgement No. 69 in the case of *Cantoral Benavides* v. *Perú* of 18 August 2000, the Commission appointed José Miguel Vivanco and Viviana Krsticevic of the NGOs Human Rights Watch – Americas and CEJIL as assistants. The assistants also acted as representatives of the victim. CEJIL has further filed petitions before the Commission and submitted *amicus* briefs to the Court. See also section 6.4 on *amicus curiae* submissions.

[234] *Statute of the Inter-American Court of Human Rights*, October 1979.

[235] American Convention on Human Rights, Article 64.

278   LEGAL AND EMPIRICAL SURVEY

entities or individuals) before the Inter-American Commission.[236] One
additional case originated in an 'urgent action' appeal, which had probably been filed by an NGO.[237] It can be observed that during 2003 and
2004, nine out of ten judgements on the merits concerned cases which
originated in petitions filed with the Commission by NGOs.

A couple of cases can be briefly described as an illustration.

The *Blake* case was initiated by International Human Rights Law Group through a
petition lodged against Guatemala. The petition concerned the alleged abduction
and murder of a US citizen and journalist by agents of the Guatemalan state and
his disappearance, which lasted over seven years. The Court declared that the
state had violated the judicial guarantees set out in Article 8(1), the right to
humane treatment enshrined in Article 5 and that it was obliged to use all
means to investigate the acts denounced and punish those responsible. The
Court delivered separate judgements on the questions of preliminary objections, the merits, reparations, as well as on the interpretation of the judgement
on reparations.[238] The International Human Rights Law Group, which filed the
petition, also acted as representative of the injured party at the reparations
stage of the proceedings on a *pro bono* basis.

The case of *Baena Ricardo et al. v. Panama* originated in a petition filed with the
Commission by the Comité Panameño por los Derechos Humanos on behalf of
270 workers. The case concerned the adoption of a law which had the effect of
arbitrarily dismissing workers who had participated in a demonstration concerning labour-related issues. While the demonstration was held, a former head
of the National Police Force and other members of the armed forces who had
been detained, escaped from a prison and took the principal barracks of the
National Police Force. The state related this act to the march organised by
the trade union leaders and accused the workers who had participated in the

---

[236] The Inter-American Court of Human Rights, Series C: Decisions and Judgments, No. 36,
Blake v. Guatemala, 24 January 1998; No. 52, *Castillo Petruzzi et al.* v. *Perú*, 30 May 1999;
No. 63, *Villagrán Morales et al.* v. *Guatemala*, 19 November 1999; No. 72, *Baena Ricardo et al.* v.
Panamá, 3 February 2001; No. 73, *'The Last Temptation of Christ'* v. *Chile*, 5 February 2001;
No. 75, *Barrios Altos* v. *Perú*, 14 May 2001; No. 98, *Cinco Pensionistas* v. *Perú*, 28 February
2003; No. 99, *Juan Humberto Sánchez* v. *Honduras*, 7 June 2003; No. 100, *Bulacio* v.
Argentina, 18 September 2003; No. 101, *Myrna Mack Chang* v. *Guatemala*, 25 September
2003; No. 103, *Maritza Urrutia* v. *Guatemala*, 27 November 2003; No. 105, *Masacre Plan de
Sánchez* v. *Guatemala*, 29 April 2004; No. 106, *Molina Theissen* v. *Guatemala*, 4 May 2004;
No. 109, *19 Comerciantes* v. *Colombia*, 5 July 2004; and No. 110, *Los Hermanos Gómez
Paquiyauri* v. *Perú*, 8 July 2004. The identity of the petitioner is sometimes withheld,
so the petitioner might have been an NGO in some of the other cases as well.

[237] *Ibid.*, No. 22, *Caballero Delgado y Santana* v. Colombia, 8 December 1995.

[238] *Ibid.*, *Blake* v. *Guatemala*, No. 27 (Preliminary objections), 2 July 1996; No. 36 (Merits),
24 January 1998; No. 48 (Reparations), 22 January 1999; No. 57 (Interpretation of the
judgement on reparations), 1 October 1999.

demonstration of being accomplices of the military riot. As a consequence, the government sent a draft law to the legislative assembly and, without waiting for approval, dismissed the 270 workers. The Court declared that the state had violated the rights contained in Articles 8, 9, 15, 16 and 25 of the Convention, and recommended the state to, *inter alia*, re-employ the workers who had been dismissed.[239] The NGOs Centro de Asesoría Laboral del Perú, Centro de Derechos Económicos y Sociales, Centro de Estudios Legales y Sociales and the Colombian Commission of Jurists presented a joint *amicus curiae* brief.[240] The Court delivered a separate judgement on Preliminary Objections.[241]

As has been shown, a large part of cases decided upon by the Inter-American Court originated in a petition filed by an NGO. In general, the overall importance of NGOs in proceedings before the Commission and the Court must be regarded as considerable, as they act in many different capacities. As has been discussed above, NGOs submit a large part of the petitions before the Commission, act as the representative of the victim and co-operate with the Commission in several ways. NGOs also often file *amicus curiae* briefs in proceedings before the Commission and the Court, as will be further described in chapter 6.

The African Commission and Court for Human and Peoples' Rights

In June 1981, the Assembly of Heads of States and Governments of the Organization of African Unity (OAU) adopted a human rights treaty, the African Charter on Human and Peoples' Rights, also known as the Banjul Charter. The Charter entered into force in October 1986.

According to the Banjul Charter, the Member states shall recognise a number of human and peoples' rights, both civil and political rights (such as equality before the law, the right of association and assembly and the right to receive information) and economic, social and cultural rights (such as the right to education and the right to work). Group rights enshrined by the Charter include, *inter alia*, the right to existence and self-determination and the right of peoples to freely dispose over their wealth and natural resources.[242]

The African Commission

The African Commission on Human and Peoples' Rights is established under Article 30 of the Banjul Charter with the mandate to promote

---

[239] Ibid., No. 72, *Baena Ricardo et al. v. Panamá*, 3 February 2001.　[240] *Ibid.*, para. 46.
[241] Series C: Decisions and Judgments, No. 61, 18 November 1999.　[242] See section 4.2.

280   LEGAL AND EMPIRICAL SURVEY

human and peoples' rights and ensure their protection in Africa. The eleven commissioners are nominated by member states and appointed by the OAU Heads of States and governments but serve in their personal capacity.[243]

The jurisdiction of the Commission to review communications regarding human rights violations is compulsory, i.e. it is automatically accepted by the state upon ratification or accession to the Banjul Charter. State parties can submit a communication to the Commission if it has good reasons to believe that another state party has violated the provisions of the Charter.[244] According to Article 55, the Commission may also receive communications 'other than those of state parties'. The Commission's Rules of Procedure do not specify which type of non-state complaints can be received.[245] Article 114 of the old Rules gave this explanation:

(1)   Communications may be submitted to the Commission by:
   (a)   an alleged victim of a violation by a State party to the Charter of one of the rights enunciated in the Charter or, in his name, when it appears that he is unable to submit the communication himself;
   (b)   an individual or an organization alleging, with proofs in support, a serious or massive cases of violations of human and peoples' rights.
(2)   The Commission may accept such communications from any individual or organization irrespective of where they shall be.[246]

As will be shown below, it is clear from the Commission's practice that individuals, groups of individuals, NGOs and other non-state entities are entitled to bring communications also under the new Rules.[247]

---

[243]   Articles 31, 33. There have, however, been problems regarding the independence and credibility of the members of the commission. Two former members served as Attorney General and Minister of the Interior in their respective countries, and a couple of members have held ministerial positions under repressive governments. Evelyn A. Ankumah, *The African Commission on Human and Peoples' Rights. Practices and Procedures*, The Hague: Martinus Nijhoff, 1996, pp. 18–19.

[244]   Article 47.

[245]   *Rules of Procedure of the African Commission on Human and Peoples' Rights*, 6 October 1995.

[246]   *Rules of Procedure of the African Commission on Human and Peoples' Rights*, 13 February 1988.

[247]   U. Oji Umozurike, *The African Charter on Human and Peoples' Rights*, The Hague: Martinus Nijhoff, 1997, p. 75; Ankumah, *The African Commission*, p. 24. Umozurike is a former member and Chairman of the Commission. See, however, Rachel Murray, *The African Commission on Human and Peoples' Rights & International Law*, Oxford: Hart Publishing, 2000, pp. 67–68. For an example of a (presumably) commercial petitioner, see, e.g., 220/98, in which the communication was filed by the law firm Law Offices of Ghazi Suleiman 'on behalf of all students and university teachers in Sudan', *Fifteenth Annual Activity Report*, 2001–2002, p. 45.

There is no victim requirement for the author of a communication, and the Commission routinely registers communications submitted by NGOs on behalf of the victim, i.e. NGOs acting without formal authorisation from the alleged victim.[248] According to the Commission's Guidelines on the Submission of Communications:

Anybody, either on his or her own behalf or on behalf of someone else, can submit a communication to the Commission denouncing a violation of human rights. Ordinary citizens, a group of individuals, NGOs, and states Parties to the Charter can all put in claims. The complainant or author of the communication need not be related to the victim of the abuse in any way, but the victim must be mentioned.'[249]

Although it is stated in these Guidelines that the victim must be mentioned, the Commission does not require a concrete victim, but accepts *actio popul014ris* communications which concern hypothetical and collectively defined victims.[250] Further, the complainant is not required to be a citizen of a state member of the OAS, and a complaining NGO does not have to be registered in one of the member states. Several communications have been filed by international NGOs based outside Africa.

Article 55(2) of the Charter provides that communications 'other than those of state parties' shall be considered if a simple majority of the Commission so decides. Prior to any substantive consideration, all communications shall be brought to the knowledge of the state concerned. According to Article 56, communications shall be considered if they, among other things, indicate their authors even if anonymity is requested, are compatible with the OAU Charter and the Banjul Charter, are sent after exhausting local remedies, if any, unless it is obvious that this procedure is unduly prolonged and are not written in disparaging or insulting language directed against the state concerned.

---

[248] Naturally, NGOs can also act in the capacity of the victim's counsel, but in that case the victim is the petitioner, not the NGO. For a discussion on the distinction between formal representatives of the victim and petitioners acting on behalf of the victim under the individual communication procedure, see Inger Österdahl, *Implementing Human Rights in Africa: The African Commission on Human and Peoples' Rights and Individual Communications*, Uppsala: Iustus Förlag, 2002, pp. 95–96, 99.

[249] African Commission on Human and Peoples' Rights, *Information Sheet No. 2, Guidelines on the Submission of Communications*, p. 5.

[250] For example, the communication in case 220/98, *The Law Offices of Ghazi Suleiman v. Sudan*, was filed 'on behalf of all students and university teachers in Sudan', *Fifteenth Annual Activity Report*, 2001–2002, p. 45. See also Österdahl, *Implementing Human Rights in Africa*, pp. 101 ff.

282 LEGAL AND EMPIRICAL SURVEY

A communication lodged by an NGO in a case against Cameroon was declared inadmissible on this latter ground.

> Communication 65/92 in the case of *Ligue Camerounaise des Droits de l'Homme* v. *Cameroun* was declared inadmissible by the Commission during its 21st Ordinary Session. The Commission stated that 'the allegations submitted by the Ligue Camerounaise are of a series of serious and massive violations of the Charter. The Communication contains statements such as "Paul Biya [i.e. the President of Cameroon] must respond to crimes against humanity", "regime of torturers", and "government barbarisms". This is insulting language.'[251]

Because of its subjective character, there could be a risk that the provision regarding insulting language would be used as a means of dismissing communications alleging serious human rights violations. However, the Commission's six last Annual Activity Reports do not include any case where the provision has been used.[252]

The procedural steps that the Commission should take with respect to 'other' communications are specified in Chapter XVII of the Amended Rules of Procedure. If the Commission decides that a communication is admissible, its decision and the text of all relevant documents shall be submitted as soon as possible to the state party, which shall submit a written explanation or statement to the Commission within three months (Rule 119). After considering the communication in the light of all information that the individual and the state has submitted in writing, the observations of the Commission shall be communicated to the Assembly of Heads and State and Government and to the state party (Rule 120).

In 1994, the Commission initiated a practice of inviting the representatives of the parties to its ordinary sessions. At such sessions, the parties may submit additional information on the case, including oral arguments. Individuals have been allowed to be represented by NGOs.[253]

---

[251] Chidi Anselm Odinkalu and Camilla Christensen, 'The African Commission on Human and Peoples' Rights: The Development of its Non-State Communication Procedures', 20 HRQ (1998), p. 255.

[252] *Eleventh Annual Activity Report of the African Commission on Human and Peoples' Rights, 1997–1998, Twelfth Annual Activity Report, 1998–1999, Thirteenth Annual Activity Report, 1999–2000, Fourteenth Annual Activity Report 2000–2001, Fifteenth Annual Activity Report, 2001–2002, Sixteenth Annual Activity Report, 2002–2003.*

[253] Odinkalu and Christensen, *The African Commission on Human and Peoples' Rights*, p. 273. The fact that the parties are represented before the Commission is also clear from its reports: see, e.g., Communications No. 140/94, 141/94, 145/95, *Constitutional Rights Project, Civil Liberties Organisation and Media Rights Agenda v. Nigeria*, paras. 13–14, in *Thirteenth Annual Activity Report, 1999–2000*.

The Charter also outlines a procedure to be employed by the Commission with respect to non-state communications which 'apparently relate to special cases which reveal the existence of a series of serious or massive violations of human and peoples' rights' (Article 58). In such a situation, the Commission shall draw the case to the attention of the Assembly, which may request the Commission to undertake an in-depth study and make a factual report, accompanied by its finding and recommendations.

According to Article 59 of the Charter, all measures taken under the chapter on non-state communications remain confidential until the Assembly of Heads of State and Government decides otherwise, and the reports of the Commission are published upon the decision of the Assembly. Rule 106 states that the sessions of the Commission during which communications are considered shall be private. The principle of confidentiality was much discussed during previous years, as the expression 'all measures taken' in Article 59 was interpreted by the Commission as meaning that it could not disclose the names of states against which complaints had been filed or mention the status of cases pending before it.[254] However, this problem has been solved. A workshop organised by the International Commission of Jurists prior to the Commission's session in 1993 concluded that the provision of confidentiality did not prohibit making the proceedings and the jurisprudence of the Commission known. Sixty NGO representatives and six Commissioners participated in the meeting.[255] In the Commission's Seventh Activity Report from 1994, the cases considered were for the first time cited with a short summary of the facts and the recommendations of the Commission.[256] The Commission has continued its practice of publishing the reports, which are now elaborate and include information on both the admissibility and merits stages of the proceedings.

The Commission's Activity Reports from 1997 to 2003 contain forty-eight case reports. In twenty-eight of the cases, the communications had been filed by one or several NGOs.[257] It is thus obvious that NGOs play a

---

[254] Ankumah, *The African Commission*, pp. 38–39.

[255] International Commission of Jurists, *The Participation of Non-Governmental Organizations in the Work of the African Commission on Human and Peoples' Rights: A Compilation of Basic Documents*, October 1991–March 1996, p. 34.

[256] *Seventh Activity Report of the African Commission on Human and Peoples' Rights*, 1993–1994.

[257] *Eleventh Annual Activity Report of the African Commission on Human and Peoples' Rights*, 1997–1998, *Twelfth Annual Activity Report*, 1998–1999, *Thirteenth Annual Activity Report*,

284   LEGAL AND EMPIRICAL SURVEY

central role in the individual communications procedure. Some NGOs appear as petitioners in many cases. Examples of NGOs which have lodged several communications include the Nigerian organisations Constitutional Rights Project and Civil Liberties Organisation (CLO) and the British organisation Interights. Other non-African NGOs that have instituted cases before the African Commission include International Pen, Amnesty International, and Rights International. The *locus standi* of these NGOs was not questioned by the Commission.[258]

It appears that when filing a communication with the African Commission, there are both advantages and disadvantages for NGOs in comparison with other complainants. When authors of communications have neglected to communicate with or respond to the Commission, the Commission has sometimes treated this as evidence of withdrawal, depending on the facts of the case. This has been the case especially when the author has been an independent NGO. In its decision in the case of *Henry Kalenga* v. *Zambia*, the Commission stated that: 'Where the complainant is an individual, the Commission cannot automatically interpret silence as withdrawal of the communication, because individuals are highly vulnerable to circumstances that might prevent them from continuing to prosecute a communication.'[259] This is, of course, an understandable explanation to the differences in the Commission's practice.[260]

1999-2000, *Fourteenth Annual Activity Report* 2000-2001, *Fifteenth Annual Activity Report*, 2001-2002, *Sixteenth Annual Activity Report*, 2002-2003.

[258] See, e.g., *Twelfth Annual Activity Report of the African Commission on Human and Peoples' Rights*, 1998-1999, Communications Nos. 137/94, 139/94, 154/96, 161/97, *International Pen, Constitutional Rights Project and Interights on behalf of Ken Saro-Wiwa Jr and Civil Liberties Organisation* v. *Nigeria* and No. 212/98, *Amnesty International* v. *Zambia*.

[259] *Seventh Annual Activity Report of the African Commission on Human and Peoples' Rights*, 1993-1994, Communication No. 11/88, *Henry Kalenga* v. *Zambia* and Odinkalu and Christensen, *The African Commission*, pp. 247-248.

[260] On the other hand, Odinkalu and Christensen assert that NGOs which are well known to the Commission seem to have an advantage over political parties. In its decision on Communication 63/93, submitted by the *Congress for the Second Republic of Malawi* v. *Malawi*, the Commission declared the communication inadmissible on the grounds that it was of a general nature and did not as such disclose a *prima facie* violation of the Charter. During the same session, three other communications were declared admissible as they gave evidence of several serious or massive violations of human rights in Malawi. One of these communications was in the form of a report submitted by Amnesty International. The only apparent difference between the communications was that one of them was submitted by a political party and the other by a well-known international NGO. *Eighth Annual Activity Report of the African Commission on Human and Peoples' Rights*, 1994-1995, Communications No. 63/93, *Second Republic of Malawi* v. *Malawi*, Nos. 68/92 and 78/92, *Amnesty International* v. *Malawi* and Odinkalu and Christensen, *The African Commission*, pp. 253-254.

The nature of the cases examined by the Commission resemble those lodged within the Inter-American system. The facts alleged often concern serious human rights violations and the Commission appears to find violations of the Charter in the vast majority of the cases examined. This may be an explanation as to why NGOs play such a dominant role within the complaints system. As with the Inter-American Commission on Human Rights, which also employs generous *locus standi* rules, the system seems to depend on NGOs for its proper functioning.

The African Court

The idea of an African Court was raised during the initial discussions on the African Charter. An additional Protocol to the African Charter establishing an African Court on Human and Peoples' Rights was adopted by the OAU Council of Ministers in June 1998. The Protocol entered into force in January 2004, but the Court is not yet (as of November 2004) in operation.

According to Article 5(1) of the Protocol, only the Commission, state parties and 'African Intergovernmental Organizations' have direct access to the Court. Nevertheless, Article 5(3) provides that the Court may entitle 'relevant Non Governmental Organizations (NGOs) with observer status before the Commission, and individuals, to institute cases directly before it'. The possibility for individuals and NGOs to file petitions under this provision is conditional. According to Article 34(6), the Court may not receive a petition involving a state party which has not made a declaration accepting the competence of the Court to receive cases under Article 5(3). The state parties to the Protocol undertake, according to Article 30, to comply with the judgements of the Court.[261]

The Aarhus Convention procedure for individual communications

The Aarhus Convention on Access to Information, Public Participation in Decision-Making and Access to Justice in Environmental Matters has been described earlier in this book.[262] The Convention is open for states members of the Economic Commission for Europe and for states having consultative status with this organisation. As of August 2004, twenty-nine states were parties to the treaty.[263]

---

[261] For further information on the Court and NGO access to it, see Nsongurua J. Udombana, 'Toward the African Court on Human and Peoples' Rights: Better Late Than Never', 3 *Yale Human Rights & Development Law Journal* (2000), pp. 45–111.

[262] See section 4.2. [263] See http://www.unece.org/env/pp/ctreaty.htm.

286   LEGAL AND EMPIRICAL SURVEY

Article 15 of the Convention requires the Meeting of the Parties, which is the primary policy-making body of the Aarhus Convention, to establish arrangements for reviewing compliance with the Convention. In October 2002 the parties adopted a *Decision on Review of Compliance* and elected the first Compliance Committee, which has eight members elected in their personal capacity.[264] According to the decision, the Committee shall consider submissions by state parties, referrals by the secretariat and 'communications ... brought before the Committee by one or more members of the public concerning that Party's compliance with the Convention, unless that Party has notified the Depositary ... that it is unable to accept ... the consideration of such communications by the Committee'.[265] The Compliance Committee has made it clear that any natural or legal person may submit a communication to the Committee and that communications may be filed by NGOs, including environmental or human rights NGOs. The communicant is not required to be a citizen of or, in the case of an organisation, based in the state party concerned.[266] Communications may concern a person's rights under the Convention (such as the right to access to justice under Article 9). However, the Committee has stressed that the compliance procedure is designed to improve compliance with the Convention and is not a redress procedure for violations of individual rights.[267]

Communications should fulfil certain formal criteria. For instance, the Committee will not consider communications that are anonymous or manifestly unreasonable. Although there is not a strict requirement that all domestic remedies must be exhausted, the Committee may decide not to pursue the substance of a communication if it considers that the communicant has not sufficiently explored the possibilities for resolving the issue through national administrative or judicial review procedures.[268] Once the Committee has determined that a communication is admissible, it shall take into account all written information made available to it, and may hold hearings. In line with the overall

---

[264] ECE/MP.PP/2/Add.8, *Report of the First Meeting of the Parties, Addendum, Decision I/7, Review of Compliance*, 2 April 2004.

[265] *Ibid.*, para. 18.

[266] Aarhus Convention Compliance Committee, *Fact Sheet on Communications from Members of the Public*, Version 1.2, 26 January 2004, p. 3.

[267] *Ibid.* p. 1.

[268] ECE/MP.PP/2/Add.8, *Report of the First Meeting of the Parties, Addendum, Decision I/7, Review of Compliance*, 2 April 2004, paras. 20–21.

STANDING BEFORE INTERNATIONAL BODIES   287

purposes of the Convention, the decision on the Compliance Committee and procedures for the review of compliance expressly states that 'no information held by the Committee shall be kept confidential'.[269]

If the Committee determines that the state party concerned is or has been failing to comply with the Convention, it will consider what measures would be appropriate. The measures that the Committee can suggest to remedy a situation of non-compliance include, *inter alia*, to provide advice and facilitate assistance to the party concerned regarding its implementation of the Convention, make recommendations, issue declarations of non-compliance, issue cautions and/or suspend the special rights and privileges accorded to the party concerned under the Convention. The final conclusions are communicated to the party and the communicant. Information concerning the consideration of individual communications is also included in the reports on the meetings of the Compliance Committee.[270]

So far, five communications have been submitted to the Compliance Committee.[271] None of them has been considered on the merits, but all have been determined as admissible. All five communications were submitted by NGOs, or what seem to be NGOs. A couple of the submissions show that the Communication procedure under the Aarhus Convention may become an important way to attract international attention not only to particular procedures and decisions in environmental matters, but also more generally to the conditions for NGOs to exist and act in the Convention states.

Communication no. 1 was submitted by the NGO Green Salvation against Kazakhstan. The communicant alleged that its right to information was violated when a request for information to the National Atomic Company was not answered. It was also alleged that subsequent appeal procedures in several courts failed to meet the requirements of Article 9.1 on access to justice. According to the communication, the lawsuits were rejected, *inter alia*, on procedural grounds as the courts did not acknowledge the right of an NGO to file a suit in its own name rather than as an authorised representative of its members. The Committee determined that the communication was admissible.[272]

In Communication no. 5, *BIOTICA Ecological Society* v. *Turkmenistan*, the communicant alleged that by introducing a new regime for registration, operation and

---

[269] *Ibid.*, para. 26. See, however, also the exception in para. 27.   [270] *Ibid.*, paras. 35, 37.
[271] As of August 2004. The list is available at the Committee's website, accessible online at http://www.unece.org/env/pp/pubcom.htm.
[272] Communication ACCC/C/2004/01, Datasheet, last updated 19 May 2004.

288 LEGAL AND EMPIRICAL SURVEY

liquidation of NGOs through the adoption of the Law on Public Associations in November 2003, Turkmenistan was in breach of Article 3.4 of the Convention, which requires it to provide for appropriate recognition of and support to associations, organisations or groups promoting environmental protection and to ensure that its national legal system is consistent with this obligation. The communication was determined as admissible by the Committee.[273]

The findings of the Compliance Committee in these and other cases will surely provide important material for analysis of the international rights and status of NGOs. Even if the Convention concerns public participation and access to justice and information in environmental matters, it may indicate possible developments of the role of NGOs also in other areas of law.

One of the communicants under the Aarhus Convention procedure previously tried to file a submission with the Implementation Committee established under the Convention on Environmental Impact Assessment in a Transboundary Context (Espoo Convention, 1991). Although that Committee acknowledged receipt of the information, the majority agreed not to consider it on the grounds that unsolicited information from NGOs and the public relating to specific cases of non-compliance was not within the Committee's mandate. A minority disagreed, interpreting the Committee's mandate to mean that there were no restrictions on how the Committee became aware of a case of possible non-compliance, preferring to examine the information further.[274]

The citizen submission procedure under the North American Agreement on Environmental Cooperation

The North American Agreement on Environmental Cooperation (NAAEC) is one of two side agreements to the North American Free Trade Agreement (NAFTA). Developed to support the environmental provisions of NAFTA, it was signed by Canada, Mexico and the United States and came into force in 1994. According to Article 1, the objectives of the agreement are, *inter alia*, to promote sustainable development, enhance compliance with and enforcement of environmental laws and regulations and to promote transparency and public participation in the development

---

[273] *Ibid.*

[274] MP.EIA/WG.1/2004/4, Economic Commission for Europe, Meeting of the Parties to the Convention on Environmental Impact Assessment in a Transboundary Context, *Report of the Fifth Meeting of the Implementation Committee*, 8 April 2004, paras. 5–7. See also Communication No. 3 to the Aarhus Compliance Committee, ACCC/C/2004/03, Datasheet, last updated 19 May 2004.

of environmental laws, regulations and policies.[275] The Agreement does not specify any particular level of environmental protection, but requires only that the state parties shall enforce the legislation they have.[276]

The signing of NAFTA gave rise to a great deal of public criticism. One concern was that the United States and Canada would lower the level of their environmental enforcement standards in order to minimise production costs, protect employment levels and their economies in general, thereby creating a 'race to the bottom' of environmental standards.[277] This was an important reason for the adoption of NAAEC, which has been described as 'the price of passage of NAFTA through the US Congress ... intended to prevent the environment from bearing the costs of increased trade among the three signatory countries'.[278] The public controversy concerning NAFTA was probably also an important explanation of the creation under NAAEC of the so-called 'citizen submission procedure', which is a procedure for complaints from private parties.[279] The other NAFTA side agreement, the North American Agreement on Labor Cooperation, sets up another submission process, although of a weaker nature.[280]

---

[275] North American Agreement on Environmental Cooperation Between the Government of Canada, the Government of the United Mexican States and the Government of the United States of America, 1993, Articles 1(b), (g), (h).

[276] Article 3 of the NAAEC states: 'Recognizing the right of each Party to establish its own levels of domestic environmental protection and environmental development policies and priorities, and to adopt or modify accordingly its environmental laws and regulations, each Party shall ensure that its laws and regulations provide for high levels of environmental protection and shall strive to continue to improve those laws and regulations.'

[277] Beatriz Bugeda, 'Is NAFTA Up to its Green Expectations? Effective Law Enforcement under the North American Agreement on Environmental Cooperation', 32 *University of Richmond Law Review* (1999), p. 1592.

[278] David L. Markell, Director, Submissions on Enforcement Matters Unit, Commission for Environmental Cooperation, in 'The Commission for Environmental Cooperation's Citizen Submission Process', 12 *Georgetown International Environmental Law Review*, Spring (2000), p. 547.

[279] Raymond MacCallum, 'Evaluating the Citizen Submission Procedure under the North American Agreement on Environmental Cooperation', 8 *Colorado Journal of International Environmental Law and Policy* (1997), pp. 395–396. For a detailed description on the political background to NAAEC in the United States, see Jack I. Garvey, 'Trade Law and Quality of Life – Dispute Settlement under the NAFTA Side Accords on Labour and the Environment', 89 AJIL (1995) pp. 439–453.

[280] For more information on that procedure, see Garvey, 'Trade Law and Quality of Life', pp. 439–453 and A. L. C. De Mestral, 'The Significance of the NAFTA Side Agreements on Environmental and Labour Cooperation', 15 *Arizona Journal of International and Comparative Law* (1998), pp. 169–185.

290 LEGAL AND EMPIRICAL SURVEY

The Commission for Environmental Cooperation is established under NAAEC to oversee implementation of the agreement and monitor the abilities of the parties to meet the obligations.[281] The Commission is composed of three bodies: the Council, the Joint Public Advisory Committee (JPAC) and the Secretariat. The Council is the governing body of the Commission and is composed of the environment ministers, or the equivalent, of the state parties. It is authorised directly under the NAAEC to 'seek the advice of non-governmental organizations or persons, including independent experts'.[282] The JPAC is composed of fifteen members, five from each of the three member countries. The members are appointed by their respective governments, but act independently. The Committee labels itself a 'public, nongovernmental advisory group'.[283] The Committee's Rules of Procedure state that the Committee may provide advice to the Council on any matter within the scope of the Agreement.[284]

The Commission for Environmental Cooperation also has a quasi-judicial function. According to Article 14 of NAAEC, individuals or NGOs may make submissions on enforcement matters to the Secretariat of the Commission. Article 14(1) reads:

The Secretariat may consider a submission from any non-governmental organization or person asserting that a Party is failing to effectively enforce its environmental law, if the Secretariat finds that the submission:

(a) is in writing in a language designated by that Party in a notification to the Secretariat;

(b) clearly identifies the person or organization making the submission;

(c) provides sufficient information to allow the Secretariat to review the submission, including any documentary evidence on which the submission may be based;

(d) appears to be aimed at promoting enforcement rather than at harassing industry;

(e) indicates that the matter has been communicated in writing to the relevant authorities of the Party and indicates the Party's response, if any; and

(f) is filed by a person or organization residing or established in the territory of a Party.

---

[281] The role and structure of the Commission are clarified in Part Three of NAAEC.

[282] NAAEC, Article 9(5)b.

[283] North American Commission for Environmental Cooperation, Joint Public Advisory Committee, *Public Consultation Guidelines* (Preamble).

[284] Commission for Environmental Cooperation, Joint Public Advisory Committee, *Rules of Procedure*, Rule 5(1).

According to the first sentence of the Article, submissions may only be considered if they have been made by 'any nongovernmental organization or person'. Article 45(1) of NAAEC defines 'nongovernmental organization' as 'any scientific, professional, business, non-profit, or public interest organization or association which is neither affiliated with, nor under the direction of, a government'. In addition, Article 14(1) requires (i) that submissions concern environmental law(s), (ii) failure to effectively enforce such law(s) and (iii) that such omissions are of an ongoing nature.[285] The first requirement excludes some international instruments, such as the 1986 Agreement between the United States and Canada Concerning the Transboundary Movement of Hazardous Waste.[286] The requirement of 'enforcement' means that a submission which challenges a law as such or which concerns the adoption of new legislation that lowers the standards as compared with previous environmental law will be dismissed by the Secretariat.[287] Finally, the temporal requirement excludes submissions concerning failures relating to laws which are no longer in force.[288]

Seemingly, the Article 14 procedure (also called the 'citizen submission procedure') does not require any connection between the submitter and an actual damage suffered through lack of law enforcement. In that respect, it appears to resemble the collective complaints procedure established under the Additional Protocol to the European Social Charter, which establishes the right to submit complaints regarding

---

[285] NAAEC Article 45(2)a defines 'environmental law' as 'any statute or regulation of a Party, or provision thereof, the primary purpose of which is the protection of the environment, or the prevention of a danger to human life or health, through (i) the prevention, abatement or control of the release, discharge, or emission of pollutants or environmental contaminants'. See also Article 5 of the Guidelines for Submissions, in Council Resolution 99–06, *Adoption of the Revised Guidelines for Submissions on Enforcement Matters Under Articles 14 and 15 of the North American Agreement on Environmental Cooperation*, Banff, 28 June 1999.

[286] TIAS No. 11099.

[287] See also Article 3 of NAAEC. In the case of *Spotted Owl*, the Secretariat concluded: 'The enactment of legislation which specifically alters the operation of pre-existing environmental law in essence becomes a part of the greater body of environmental laws and statutes on the books. This is true even if pre-existing law is not amended or rescinded and the new legislation is limited in time. The Secretariat therefore cannot characterize the application of a new legal regime as a failure to enforce an old one.' Submission SEM-95–001, *Secretariat's Determination under Article 14(2)*, 21 September 1995, Section V.

[288] The Commission's practice as regards the different requirements is explained in Markell, 'The Commission for Environmental Cooperation's Citizen Submission Process', pp. 551 ff.

292   LEGAL AND EMPIRICAL SURVEY

'unsatisfactory application of the Charter'.[289] However, the Secretariat's determination of whether a submission merits a response from the state party in question is based on whether the submission alleges harm to the person or organisation making the submission, as well as on several other factors. Article 14(2) of NAAEC provides that the Secretariat shall be guided by whether:

- the submission alleges harm to the person or organisation making the submission;
- the submission, alone or in combination with other submissions, raises matters whose further study in this process would advance the goals of this Agreement,
- private remedies available under the Party's law have been pursued; and
- the submission is drawn exclusively from mass media reports.[290]

In order for the Secretariat to request a response from the state party concerned, the submission should fulfil the conditions in Article 14(2).[291] The criteria are, however, not absolute, but are to be weighed depending on the particular situation.[292]

The question of 'harm' to the person or organisation making the submission was discussed by the Secretariat with regard to the *Cozumel* Submission (see below). The submitters did not claim that any actual harm had occurred, and the government objected that the submitters

---

[289] Additional Protocol to the European Social Charter Providing for a System of Collective Complaints, 1995, Article 1. See also section 5.3.

[290] The Guidelines for submissions specify these factors. For instance, it is stated in the Guidelines that in determining whether a submission is aimed at promoting enforcement rather than harassing industry, the Secretariat will take into account whether or not 'the submission is focused on the acts or omissions of a Party rather than on compliance by a particular company or business; especially if the Submitter is a competitor that may stand to benefit economically from the submission' and 'the submission appears frivolous'. *Guidelines for Submission of Enforcement Matters*, attached to Council Resolution 99–06, 28 June 1999, Article 5.4.

[291] The procedure may also be terminated by the Secretariat at a later stage if the situation concerning one of the Article 14 factors has changed during the time of the procedure: see, e.g., the submission *Oldman River I*, SEM-96-003, *Determination pursuant to Articles 14 & 15 of the North American Agreement on Environmental Cooperation*, 2 April 1997.

[292] Regarding the submission *Great Lakes*, the Secretariat stated that: 'In deciding whether to request a response from a Party, the Secretariat is to be guided by the four factors listed in Article 14(2). Thus, during this phase of the process the Secretariat may assign weight to each factor as it deems appropriate in the context of a particular submission.' Secretariat of the Commission for Environmental Cooperation, SEM-98-003, Determination pursuant to Article 14(1) and (2) of the North American Agreement on Environmental Cooperation, 8 September 1999, Section III B.

had failed to establish the necessary relationship between damage and failure to enforce environmental legislation.[293] The Secretariat stated:

In considering harm, the Secretariat notes the importance and character of the resource in question – a portion of the magnificent Paradise coral reef located in the Caribbean waters of Quintana Roo. While the Secretariat recognizes that the submitters may not have alleged the particularized, individual harm required to acquire legal standing to bring suit in some civil proceedings in North America, the especially public nature of marine resources bring the submitters within the spirit and intent of Article 14 of the NAAEC.[294]

So far, the Secretariat has not discontinued the processing of any submission with reference to the 'harm' criterion.[295]

Proceedings may also be discontinued under Article 14(3), which provides that the state party concerned by a submission shall inform the Secretariat as to whether the matter is or has been the subject of pending national proceedings, and whether private remedies in relation to the matter are available to the submitter and whether they have been pursued.

If the Secretariat considers that the submission, in the light of any response provided by the state party, warrants further action, it shall inform the Council and provide its reasons. The Council decides by a two-thirds vote if the Secretariat shall prepare a so-called 'factual record', which is a report prepared on the basis of 'any relevant technical, scientific or other information'. The Secretariat submits a draft factual record to the Council, and state parties may provide comments on the accuracy of the draft within forty-five days. After incorporating such comments, as appropriate, in the final factual record, it is submitted to the Council. A final factual record contains a summary of the submission and of the response by the concerned party, as well as of any other relevant factual information. The factual record also includes the facts presented by the Secretariat with respect to the matters raised in the submission, but it does not contain any conclusions as to whether the state party has

---

[293] *Final Factual Record of the Cruise Ship Pier Project in Cozumel, Quintana Roo*, Prepared in Accordance with Article 15 of the North American Agreement on Environmental Cooperation, Commission for Environmental Cooperation 1997, pp. 3–7.

[294] SEM-96–001, *Recommendation of the Secretariat to Council for the Development of a Factual Record in accordance with Articles 14 & 15 of the North American Agreement on Environmental Cooperation*, 7 June 1996. See also Markell, 'The Commission for Environmental Cooperation's Citizen Submission Process', p. 560.

[295] The proceedings concerning three cases have been discontinued under Article 14(2): SEM-95–001; SEM-95–002; SEM-96–002 (as of August 2004).

294 LEGAL AND EMPIRICAL SURVEY

actually failed to enforce its environmental law.[296] The Council decides whether the final factual record should be made publicly available.[297]

Since the establishment of the procedure for submissions on enforcement matters until October 2001, the Secretariat of the Commission on Environmental Cooperation had received a total of forty-four submissions, but only nine final factual records had been prepared.[298] Several submissions have been dismissed under Article 14(1), often with reference to failure to meet the criterion of 'asserting that a Party is failing to effectively enforce its environmental law'.[299] In other cases, the Secretariat has not recommended, or the Council has decided not to request the preparation of a factual record.[300] It can be observed that no submission has been dismissed with reference to failure to meet the criterion 'from any non-governmental organization or person'.

Of the forty-four submissions which have been made so far, twenty-five were filed by (non-commercial) NGOs and three by business corporations.[301] The other submissions were made by private individuals or by a person or entity whose identity was withheld. Some NGOs have filed more than one submission.[302] Several submissions were submitted jointly by large groups of NGOs.[303]

A brief description of two cases which have led to the adoption of a final factual record might shed some light on the procedure and the issues involved.

The first final factual record to be prepared and made public concerned the construction of a cruise ship pier in the Mexican island of Cozumel in

---

[296] *Guidelines for Submission of Enforcement Matters*, Article 12.

[297] North American Agreement on Environmental Cooperation, Article 15.

[298] The Registry and Public File of Submission is accessible online at the Commission's website at www.cec.org, as of August 2004. All the final factual records have been made public.

[299] See, e.g., SEM-97-004; SEM-97-005; SEM-98-001; SEM-98-002; SEM-00-003; SEM-01-002.

[300] See, e.g., SEM-98-003; SEM-98-005; SEM-01-001; SEM-03-001.

[301] NGOs made the submissions SEM-95-001-002; SEM-96-001; SEM-96-003-004; SEM-97-001-007; SEM-98-001; SEM-98-003-007; SEM-99-002; SEM-00-003-004; SEM-01-001; SEM-01-003; SEM-03-001; SEM-03-002. The submissions SEM 99-001; SEM-00-002; SEM-01-003 were made by corporations.

[302] For instance, Academia Sonorense de Derechos Humanos AC submitted SEM-98-005 (*Cytrar*); SEM-00-005 (*Molymex II*) and SEM-01-001 (*Cytrar II*); Sierra Club of British Columbia SEM-98-004 (*BC Mining*) and SEM-00-004 (*BC Logging*); and Instituto de Derecho Ambiental and SEM-97-007 (*Lake Chapala*); SEM-98-001 (*Guadalajara*); SEM-99-002 (*Migratory Birds*).

[303] For example SEM-95-002 (*Logging Rider*); SEM-97-003 (*Quebec Hog Farms*, which was filed by a group of nineteen NGOs); SEM-99-002 (*Migratory Birds*).

the Caribbean sea.[304] The submission was presented in January 1996 by the NGOs the Committee for the Protection of Natural Resources, the International Group of One Hundred and the Mexican Center for Environmental Law. The NGOs alleged 'failure on the part of Mexican authorities to enforce their environmental law effectively with regard to the totality of the works of the "port terminal project in Playa Paraíso, Cozumel, Quintana Roo"'. The submitters argued, *inter alia*, that the project, as it was planned, failed to comply effectively with Mexican legislation, since the Consortium would not have to present a comprehensive Environmental Impact Statement regarding all works that made up the project.[305] The Mexican government responded with a number of arguments of procedural and material nature. As regards the submitters, the government argued that they had 'failed to provide reliable evidence demonstrating the character of the organizations they say they represent, since they did not supply any information regarding the incorporation particulars of the civil associations they purport to represent nor did they provide the by-laws of such associations'.[306] The government denied that it had failed to enforce its environmental legislation on the ground, *inter alia*, that since construction had not begun, the submitters demanded an Environmental Impact Report for works that had not yet been authorised.[307] The draft factual record was presented to the Council in April 1997. By July, the members of the Council had presented their comments on the draft. The Secretariat submitted the final factual record to the Council, which made the record public in October 1997.

Reading this first factual record is a rather disappointing experience. It is, as is clear already from its designation, a very thorough presentation of facts, as submitted by the NGOs and the government, together with relevant information gathered from other sources by the Secretariat itself. It does not include any conclusions whatsoever as to what the facts mean in terms of whether Mexico had failed to effectively enforce its environmental legislation or not. The arguments of the Mexican government as regarded the failure of the submitters to present evidence demonstrating the character of the organisation itself and whom it represented were not addressed by the Secretariat.[308] The conclusions

---

[304] *Final Factual Record of the Cruise Ship Pier Project in Cozumel, Quintana Roo*, Prepared in Accordance with Article 15 of the North American Agreement on Environmental Cooperation, Commission for Environmental Cooperation 1997.

[305] *Ibid.*, pp. 3–4.   [306] *Ibid.*, p. 7.   [307] *Ibid.*, pp. 8–12.

[308] The decision that the organisation met the criteria in Article 14, taken at a previous stage in the procedure, was discussed by the Secretariat in its *Recommendation of the Secretariat to Council for the Development of a Factual Record in accordance with Articles 14 & 15 of the North American Agreement on Environmental Cooperation*, SEM-96-001, 7 June 1996. The recommendation mentions the government's views on this point, but the Secretariat notes only that: 'The Secretariat concluded that the submitters complied with the requirements of Article 14(1).'

296   LEGAL AND EMPIRICAL SURVEY

are left entirely to the reader, and considering the vast amount of information presented, they are not easily reached. Beatriz Bugeda, former Head of the Mexico Liaison Office of the Commission for Environmental Cooperation, has commented as follows on the reaction to and effect of the *Cozumel* case:

When the submission was presented, and particularly when the Secretariat requested a response from the Mexican government, it captured the attention of the media in the three countries ... The submission was presented in January of 1996, and almost two years passed before the final Cozumel Factual Record was released to the public on October of 1997. By then, the initial interest of environmental groups and the media had all but vanished. Very few newspapers in North America covered the release of the report or the reaction by the parties involved. In Mexico, it practically went unnoticed ... The submitters held a press conference and distributed a document with their interpretation of the Cozumel Factual Record, alleging that 'it proved failure by the part of the Mexican environmental authorities to effectively enforce environmental law'. On the other hand, some Mexican officials have said off-the-record that they are 'pleased' with the Cozumel Factual Record because they believe that, even if it reaches no conclusions, it supports their position. Meanwhile, the JPAC has said nothing, and the Council remains silent to this day. For the CEC [Commission on Environmental Cooperation], with the release of the Cozumel Factual Record, the process is terminated ... The truth is that the procedure had very little impact on the environmental community, and none whatsoever on the tourist project in Cozumel that led to the submission. The fact that the record does not provide any judgement or evaluation regarding the allegations made by the submitters might have disappointed the public. Indeed, the efficiency of the procedure was compromised as the political momentum faded during the long process.[309]

The second final factual record to be prepared and made public concerned SEM-97–001, *BC Hydro*, filed by several NGOs against Canada.[310] The submitters alleged that the Canadian government was failing to enforce parts of its national legislation to ensure the protection of fish and fish habitat in British Columbia's rivers from ongoing and repeated environmental damage caused by hydro-electric dams. The record is less neutral in its character and also more comprehensible since it includes

---

[309] Bugeda, 'Is NAFTA Up to its Green Expectations?', pp. 1615–1616. See, however, Angela D. Da Silva, 'NAFTA and the Environmental Side Agreement: Dispute Resolution in the Cozumel Port Terminal Controversy', *Environs Environmental Law and Policy Journal*, 1998, p. 61.

[310] *Factual Record for Submission SEM-97–001 (BC Aboriginal Fisheries Commission et al.)*, made public on 11 June 2000.

a summary, as opposed to the Cozumel record. Some findings presented in the draft record are formulated in a way that could be regarded as recommendations.[311] This led to opposition from the state parties. According to NAAEC Article 15(5), any party may provide comments on the draft factual record within 45 days after it has been submitted by the Secretariat to the Council. Article 45(6) states that the Secretariat shall incorporate, as appropriate, any such comments in the final factual record and submit it to the Council. After the submission of the draft factual record on the *BC Hydro* dispute, all three state parties submitted comments that clearly demonstrated their view that the citizen's submission procedure is of a purely fact-finding procedure. For instance, the US government stated that:

In this process the Secretariat has been given the important role of serving as a neutral and independent fact-finder. Consequently, it is important that the Secretariat refrain from offering comments in a factual record that appear to provide the Secretariat's own views about whether or not there has been effective enforcement of the law with respect to the assertions in a particular submission. In this regard, the US government is concerned with three portions of the draft factual record. The portion of the draft factual record of most concern to us is the last bullet of section 233. In that bullet the secretariat discusses the tools Canada would need to use under particular circumstances in order to effectively enforce its law.[312]

It can be noted that the US government was sceptical even in the matter of the Secretariat's discussion over which measures could be needed in order for the law to be effectively enforced. The government recommended that some sections of the draft record should be modified in the final factual record. However, the Council instead instructed the Secretariat to make public the final factual record and to attach the comments sent by the Parties to the final factual record.[313] Criticism of the

---

[311] *Ibid.*, for example paras. 141, 217, 233.

[312] *Ibid.*, Comments from the Parties, *Letter to the Executive Director of the Secretariat from William A. Nitze*, US Alternate Representative to the Council, May 11, 2000. The Mexican government concluded in its comment that 'it is clear that the Secretariat put procedures into practice that have no basis', *Observations of Mexico on the Draft Factual Record*, 8 May 2000. Canada was less critical in its approach, noting that the record went beyond a compilation of facts, but also noting that the procedure was under review. *Letter to the Secretariat from Morine Smith*, Assistant Deputy Minister, May 11, 2000.

[313] Council Resolution 00–04, *Instruction to the Secretariat of the Commission for Environmental Cooperation to make public the Factual Record Regarding the Assertion that Canada is failing to effectively Enforce s. 35(1) of the Fisheries Act with Respect to Certain Hydro-Electric Installations in British Columbia, Canada*, Dallas, 11 June 2000.

298   LEGAL AND EMPIRICAL SURVEY

Secretariat has also been expressed in more recent cases. For instance, in the *BC Logging* case, the Canadian government observed that the Secretariat appeared to use language that reflected conclusions and provided commentary, and stated that this was 'beyond the mandate of the Secretariat which is to set out facts in an objective and impartial manner'.[314]

In the perspective of the international legal status of NGOs, it is interesting that NGOs have been granted the possibility to make submissions on enforcement matters under NAAEC. It has been demonstrated above that NGOs are the most active actors under this procedure. However, the facts that many submissions have been dismissed or their processing discontinued, and only nine have led to the preparation of a final factual record raise doubts as regards the effectiveness of the procedure. Moreover, since the final factual records do not contain any conclusions, they are not likely to have any real impact on the enforcement of environmental legislation. It is evident that, if the citizen's submission procedure has any importance, it lies on the political plane.

5.4 Conclusions

This chapter has dealt with the role of NGOs as parties before courts and quasi-judicial bodies, while chapter 6 will discuss their role as *amicus curiae*. In addition to these two roles, NGOs often act as the representative of private parties. The survey of international and regional procedures which provide NGOs with *locus standi* demonstrates that NGOs have an important role to play in many compliance mechanisms. The number of procedures open to NGOs as parties is increasing. An important development in this regard was, of course, the coming into force of the 9th Additional Protocol to the ECHR in 1990, which made it possible for NGOs to refer cases that had first been considered by the Commission to the European Court of Human Rights and, in 1998, the 11th Protocol, which gave direct access for NGOs and individuals to the Court. As of yet, the European Court of Human Rights and the ECJ are the only courts which are directly accessible to NGOs as parties (the latter providing only limited access). However, when the African Court of Justice comes into operation, NGOs will be able to institute cases there too.

---

[314] Factual Record, BC Logging Submission, SEM 00–004, p. 187 (Comment of Canada). The US government also stressed that a factual record should be limited to factual information, p. 205.

In addition to the quasi-judicial mechanisms within, for example, the Inter-American and African human rights systems, where NGOs have already played an important role as parties for some time, a number of new mechanisms have been established. These include the World Bank Inspection Panel, the Aarhus Convention procedure for individual communications and the citizen submission procedure concerning the NAAEC. Within the Council of Europe, the collective complaints procedure has been established, making it possible for NGOs to lodge complaints regarding alleged non-compliance with the European Social Charter. Some of these procedures are open exclusively to NGOs, i.e. the ILO freedom of association procedures and the European Collective Complaints procedure. Although other mechanisms are accessible to both individuals and groups and NGOs, it can be concluded that several of these procedures depend on NGOs acting as parties. This is particularly the case with the mechanisms with generous *locus standi* rules, notably the Inter-American and the African systems.

6 Non-party participation before judicial and quasi-judicial bodies

6.1 Introduction

The international legal system can be seen as a set of bilateral consensual relationships within which rights and obligations are formulated and values allocated between the parties. There is a correlation between rights and duties, as in Hohfeld's systematisation, although one and the same party may have the same claim or obligation towards several parties. Such bilateralism brings order to the appearance of the law, not only because it identifies who is the holder of a right, but also who may enforce it.[1] At the same time, international agreements and disputes often affect the interests of third states, nations or groups, or of the international community as a whole. Hermann Mosler suggests that:

> International law cannot be defined solely in terms of bilateral or multilateral relations between subjects which possess legal capacity. The collection of subjects participating in the international legal order constitutes a community living according to common rules of conduct.[2]

Interests which affect actors other than the parties might be of many different kinds – material interests in economic values or natural resources, or more political interests in legal developments in one direction or another, such as protection of the environment or respect of human rights standards.

The fact that the interests of many are affected by a bilateral and multilateral legal relationship raises issues about who may intervene or

---

[1] See Christine Chinkin, *Third Parties in International Law*, Oxford: Clarendon Press, 1993, pp. 1–2.

[2] Hermann Mosler, *International Legal Community*, in EPIL, 2, Amsterdam: North-Holland, 1995, p. 1252. See also Chinkin, *Third Parties in International Law*, p. 5.

otherwise make submissions during international judicial proceedings. A very strict view on the right to intervention may hinder or delay a development of the law in the direction of common interests, while a permissive practice may undermine the parties' control over the dispute or cause extra costs and work for the court. The need to strike a balance between different interests calls for a variety of forms of participation in legal proceedings, ranging from full participation as a party at one end of the scale to non-party contributions in the form of written or oral submissions at the other. The court as well as the parties and the public also has a common interest that the court should receive the fullest information possible on the matter before it.

Some basic distinctions between the different roles which NGOs may hold before tribunals and quasi-judicial bodies need to be upheld. The most basic distinction is the difference between parties, on the one hand, and 'non-parties' or 'third parties' on the other. Christine Chinkin, who prefers the latter term, stresses that there is no single definition which can be used for the identification of third parties, as such identification depends on the context of the claim. Nevertheless, she explains that: 'Third parties are those outside a bilateral relationship, whether formally created, for example by treaty or the commencement of proceedings, or occurring through events such as the outbreak of armed conflict.'[3] Chinkin's explanation is illustrative, although it should be observed that her study on third parties covers not only situations before a tribunal, but also treaty relationships or international legal relationships in general.[4] Since NGOs are explicitly excluded from being a party before many international courts and bodies, notably the ICJ, the expression 'non-party' will be used here for all cases of *amicus curiae* submissions. Moreover, some international judicial bodies distinguish between the intervention of third parties and other types of participation.[5]

---

[3] Chinkin, *Third Parties in International Law*, p. 7.

[4] See also D. J. Harris, M. O'Boyle and C. Warbrick, *Law of the European Convention on Human Rights*, London: Butterworths, 1995, pp. 668–671 and Donna Gomien, David Harris and Leo Zwaak, *Law and Practice of the European Convention on Human Rights and the European Social Charter*, Strasbourg: Council of Europe Publishing, 1996, pp. 80–81. These authors use the expression 'third-party intervention' for the submission of *amicus curiae* briefs in accordance with the Rules of the European Court of Human Rights, see section 6.5.

[5] In November 2000, the WTO Appellate Body adopted an additional procedure to deal with *amicus curiae* briefs. In the communication from the Appellate Body, it is stated that 'Any person, whether natural or legal, other than a party or a third party to this dispute'

302   LEGAL AND EMPIRICAL SURVEY

Although the distinction between the participation of parties and non-parties is made here, it is of interest to note that this distinction is not entirely clear within all fields of law, especially regional human rights law and environmental law. As was demonstrated in chapter 5 on the standing of NGOs before different human rights supervisory bodies, both the Inter-American Commission on Human Rights and the African Commission on Human and Peoples' Rights employ permissive *locus standi* rules in the sense that NGOs can file complaints concerning an alleged human rights violation without any direct connection with the victim. The existence of these types of procedures indicates that the respect for human rights standards is regarded as a public interest within these regional organisations, in line with Mosler's reasoning on the international legal community. It also means that NGOs have the possibility to choose between the role of a party and other avenues for advocating their interests before these regional bodies. The European Court of Human Rights, however, upholds the victim requirement.[6] Further, the rules on standing before the ECJ and CFI grant leave to institute proceedings for judicial review only for actors who have a direct interest in the matter. In the case of *Stichting Greenpeace Council* v. *the Commission* the rules on *locus standi* were given a restrictive interpretation, even though it concerned environmental interests, which might well be regarded as affecting a broad group of people.[7]

As has been described in chapter 5, NGOs often act as self-appointed advocates of both individual and common interests in the capacity of parties before international tribunals and quasi-judicial bodies. It will now be demonstrated that NGOs also intervene rather frequently in tribunal proceedings without having the standing of a party. There are three main platforms for such interventions. The first one, *amicus curiae* interventions, will be in the focus of this chapter as it is often (and seemingly to an increasing extent) used by NGOs. Secondly, NGOs may appear as expert witnesses before courts and quasi-judicial bodies. Finally, NGOs sometimes appear as counsel of a party. This latter possibility will be only briefly examined within the framework of this study, as it is difficult in practice to distinguish cases where a person employed by an NGO accepts to act as counsel in her or his personal

---

could file a written brief. WT/DS135/9, *European Communities – Measures Affecting Asbestos and Asbestos-Containing Products*, 8 November 2000.

[6] See section 5.3.

[7] European Court of Justice, *Stichting Greenpeace Council (Greenpeace International) and Others* v. *Commission*, Case C-321/95 P, Judgement of 2 April 1998. See also section 5.3.

capacity as lawyer or expert from cases where it is actually the organisation that is appointed as counsel.

An *amicus curiae* is a person or an organisation with an interest in or views on the subject matter of a case who, without being a party, petitions the court for permission to file a brief suggesting matters of fact and/or law in order to suggest a rationale consistent with its own views.[8] The interest of an *amicus* in the matter is often of a general nature, such as the desire to promote public interests.[9] *Amici curiae* are not bound by the decision and can therefore relitigate issues if the outcome is not favourable, and they are not limited to the issues presented by the parties. These circumstances make the *amicus* position favourable to NGOs which might wish to participate on the basis of a general interest or in order to support a private person, such as the victim of a human rights violation. On the other hand, *amici* cannot control the direction of the action, they cannot offer evidence or examine witnesses and they cannot be heard without special leave of the court.[10]

While an *amicus* intervenes on proper initiative or on the initiative of one of the parties, an *expert* is appointed by the court or by a party. The expert can make an oral or written statement on matters of which the court lacks sufficient knowledge.[11]

6.2 The World Court

The Statute of the ICJ admits non-party participation in the form of submission of information on matters relevant in a case. According to Article 34(2) of the Statute of the International Court of Justice, the Court may request and receive such information in contentious proceedings only from '*public* international organisations'.[12] Information from public international organisations shall also be received by the Court when it is presented on an organisation's own initiative. Article 69(4) of the Court's Rules of Procedure explains that the term 'public international organization' denotes an international organisation of states.[13]

In the *Asylum* case, the non-governmental International League for the Rights of Man (now the International League for Human Rights),

---

[8] *Black's Law Dictionary*, Abridged 6th edn., St Paul, MN: West Publishing Co., 1991, p. 54.
[9] Dinah Shelton, 'The Participation of Nongovernmental Organizations in International Judicial Proceedings', 88 AJIL (1994), p. 612.
[10] *Ibid.*, pp. 611–612.　　[11] *Black's Law Dictionary*, p. 401.　　[12] Emphasis added.
[13] International Court of Justice, *Rules of Court (1978), as Amended on 5 December 2000*.

304   LEGAL AND EMPIRICAL SURVEY

requested permission to submit written or oral statements.[14] A member of the League's Board of Directors wrote to the Court's Registrar and requested that the Court determine whether the League was a public international organisation within the meaning of Article 34 of the Statute.[15] The Court's Registrar rejected the League's participation in a telegram saying simply that the 'Court finds Article 34 not applicable since International League of Rights of Man cannot be characterized as public international organization as envisaged by Statute'.[16] It is thus clear that NGOs have no possibility to intervene in the ICJ's contentious proceedings as independent actors. There is, however, the possibility that a government may file an *amicus* brief as part of its own submissions. This occurred in the case concerning the *Gabcikovo-Nagymaros Dam Project* (1997), in which the Hungarian government submitted an *amicus* brief prepared by the National Heritage Institute and the International River Network.[17]

Article 66 regarding the Court's right to hear non-parties during its advisory proceedings is less restrictive, as regards both states and organisations. It can be assumed that it has been considered important that the Court receives as full information as possible if the advisory opinion is to be respected by the international community. Moreover, there is no need in advisory proceedings to pay respect to party autonomy as in contentious cases.[18] According to Article 66, the Court may decide to notify '*international* organisations' likely to be able to furnish relevant information that the Court will be prepared to receive written statements or to hear oral statements. The Rules of Procedure do

---

[14] *Asylum* case (*Colombia* v. *Perú*), 1949–1950, judgement on the merits delivered on 20 November 1950.

[15] Letter from Robert Delson, *Asylum* case, 1950 ICJ Pleadings, II, 1950, p. 227. See also Shelton, 'The Participation of Nongovernmental Organizations', p. 623 and Nigel Rodley, 'Human Rights NGOs: Rights and Obligations', in Theo Van Boven *et al.* (eds.), *The Legitimacy of the United Nations: Towards an Enhanced Legal Status of Non-State Actors*, Netherlands Institute of Human Rights, SIM Special, 19, Utrecht, 1997, p. 57.

[16] Telegram from the Registrar, *Asylum* case, 1950 ICJ Pleadings, II, p. 228.

[17] Daniel Schacht and Lori Pottinger, 'Devastating the Danube and Drave with Dams', *World Rivers Review*, January 1996 and 'NHI's Historic Involvement in Transboundary Water Issues', paper by the Natural Heritage Institute. The brief was filed by Hungary on 20 June 1995.

[18] See Chinkin, *Third Parties in International Law*, p. 229. An exception to this is, however, the situation where an instrument provides in advance that the ICJ's advisory opinion shall be binding, as is the case with the ILO Tribunal, see Article XII (2) of the Statute of the Administrative Tribunal of the International Labour Organization.

NON-PARTY PARTICIPATION 305

not include any explanation of the term 'international organisations' as used in Article 66 of the Statute.[19]

Seemingly, the Court has never notified an NGO of the request for an advisory opinion, but NGOs have on their own initiative asked for permission to submit information as *amici curiae*.[20] The International League for the Rights of Man is one example. When the President of the Court had set the date for the receipt of written statements from states in the proceedings leading to the 1950 *Advisory Opinion on the International Status of South-West Africa*, the same member of the League's board who had requested determination of the League's status wrote to the Registrar of the Court and asked permission for the League to participate by oral or written statement in the proceedings.[21] The Registrar responded in a letter to the League that the Court was prepared to receive a written statement of information which was likely to assist the Court in its examination of legal questions. The League was instructed not to include any statement of facts which the Court had not been asked to appreciate.[22] However, because of mistakes on the part of the League, notably the failure to submit its statement on time, the Court took no notice of the statement.[23]

The League later requested to intervene in the proceedings leading to the 1971 *Advisory Opinion on Namibia*, referring to the permission it had been granted in 1950 in the *South-West Africa* case.[24] This time the League was refused, although the decision did not include any challenge of the legitimacy of the request.[25] Several other organisations, such as the OAU and the NGO American Committee on Africa, also asked for leave to make submissions along with individual petitioners from Namibia, but all but the OAU were rejected.[26] The permission granted in 1950 to the League for the Rights of Man appears to be the only time

---

[19] See, however, the Court's Practice Directions, below.

[20] Chinkin, *Third Parties in International Law*, p. 230.

[21] *International Status of South-West Africa*, 1950 ICJ Pleadings, II, p. 324. See also Roger S. Clark, 'The International League for Human Rights and South West Africa 1947–1957: The Human Rights NGO as Catalyst in the International Legal Process', 3 HRQ (1981), pp. 116–120; Shelton, 'The Participation of Nongovernmental Organizations', p. 623; Rodley, 'Human Rights', p. 57.

[22] *International Status of South-West Africa*, 1950 ICJ Pleadings, II, p. 327.

[23] *Ibid.*, p. 346. See also Clark, 'The International League for Human Rights', p. 118–119.

[24] *Legal Consequences for States of the Continued Presence of South Africa in Namibia (South-West Africa) Notwithstanding Security Council Resolution 276 (1970)*, 1972 ICJ Pleadings, II, pp. 639–640, 678.

[25] *Ibid.*, pp. 672, 679. See also Clark, 'The International League for Human Rights', p. 119.

[26] 1970 ICJ Pleadings, II, pp. 649, 652, 672, 678.

306   LEGAL AND EMPIRICAL SURVEY

the ICJ has been prepared to receive a statement from an NGO independently.[27] Interestingly, the episode demonstrates that there is nothing
to prevent the Court from admitting an NGO to file a statement.

There have been requests from NGOs for permission to submit statements in other advisory proceedings before the ICJ. In the Advisory
Proceedings of *Legality of the Use by a State of Nuclear Weapons in Armed
Conflict*, requested by the WHO, the Physicians for the Prevention of
Nuclear War requested the ICJ for permission to submit information.
Although the Court noted the physicians' close working relationship
with the WHO and their contribution to a relevant publication, it
decided not to grant leave for the organisation to submit a written or
oral statement.[28]

Individuals have also sought leave to file statements with the Court.[29]
For example, during the *Legal Consequences for States of the Continued
Presence of South Africa in Namibia (South-West Africa)* proceedings,
Michael Reisman wrote to the Registrar asking about the 'possibilities
of submitting some form of *amicus curiae* brief' to the Court. Reisman
held that *amicus curiae* briefs had been an institution which had provided
useful information to courts and had, overall, 'served as a means for
integrating and buttressing the authority and conflict-resolving capacities of domestic tribunals'.[30] In his reply, the Registrar went into the
matter at some length, and referred to the expression 'international
organization' in Article 66(2) of the Statute and stating that the Article
was 'limitative and exclusive'. He asserted that the decision to grant the
International League for the Rights of Man permission to submit a statement could not be regarded as a precedent for the participation of

---

[27] Rodley, *'Human Rights'*, p. 57.
[28] *Legality of the Use by a State of Nuclear Weapons in Armed Conflict*, Letter from the Registrar to
Dr Barry D. Levy, 28 March 1994, in Shelton, 'The Participation of Nongovernmental
Organizations', p. 624.
[29] See, e.g., Letter from the Reverend Michael Scott to the Registrar, *Legal Consequences for
States of the Continued Presence of South Africa in Namibia (South-West Africa) Notwithstanding
Security Council Resolution 276 (1970)*, 1970 ICJ Pleadings, II, pp. 644–645 and the
Registrar's reply, p. 647. A rather interesting attempt by individuals to intervene in the
same proceedings was made by a group of indigenous inhabitants of the territory of
South-West Africa. The group, which called itself the South-West Africa National United
Front (SWANUF), submitted an application to be heard as 'petitioners' by the Court.
Since the request did not satisfy the conditions formulated in Article 66(2), it was
denied by the Registrar, see pp. 677–678.
[30] Letter from Professor Reisman to the Registrar, *Legal Consequences for States of the
Continued Presence of South Africa in Namibia (South-West Africa) Notwithstanding Security
Council Resolution 276 (1970)*, 1970 ICJ Pleadings, II, pp. 636–637.

individuals and concluded that 'the Court would be unwilling to open the floodgates to what might be a vast amount of proffered assistance'.[31]

The PCIJ permitted participation of NGOs in several advisory proceedings under Article 73 of its Rules.[32] This was a practice which evolved in cases concerning labour law involving the ILO. In its first advisory proceeding in 1922, concerning workers' delegates to the International Labour Conference, the PCIJ permitted participation by any organisation that wished to be heard. Numerous trade unions filed statements in the proceedings.[33] International trade unions often participated in the Court's advisory proceedings; in its *Third Annual Report* the PCIJ listed ten organisations permitted to submit information to the Court, of which almost all were NGOs.[34]

In conclusion, it can be observed that the ICJ seems to have applied Article 34 of its Statute regarding the submission of information in contentious cases and Article 66 regarding advisory proceedings in the same way, despite the fact that the former refers to 'public international organizations' and the latter to 'international organizations'. The only exception to this practice appears to have been the permission granted in 1950 to the International League for the Rights of Man. Christine Chinkin has expressed the following critical view of this practice:

The Court's attitude towards submissions from non-governmental sources is an excessively restrictive one which denies to itself a potential source of information, and to non-governmental organizations any legitimate interest in important questions of international law. No exception is made for those bodies with

---

[31] Letter from the Registrar to Professor Reisman, *Legal Consequences for States of the Continued Presence of South Africa in Namibia (South-West Africa) Notwithstanding Security Council Resolution 276 (1970)*, 1970 ICJ Pleadings, II, pp. 638–639.

[32] Article 73(1), para. 2 reads: 'The Registrar shall also, by means of special and direct communication, notify any ... international organization considered by the Court as likely to be able to furnish information on the question, that the Court will be prepared to receive ... written statements, or to hear, at a public sitting to be held for the purpose, oral statements related to the question.'

[33] Advisory Opinion No. 1, *Designation of the Workers' Delegate for the Netherlands at the Third Session of the International Labour Conference*, 1922 PCIJ Series C, No. 1, pp. 443, 446, 453, 454, 456. See also Shelton, 'The Participation of Nongovernmental Organizations', pp. 622–623.

[34] Third Annual Report of the PCIJ, 1927 PCIJ Series E, No. 3, p. 227. The organisations were the International Agricultural Commission, the IFTU, the ILO, the International Association for Legal Protection of Workers, the International Confederation of Agricultural Trades Unions, the International Federation of Landworkers, the International Institute of Agriculture, the International Federation of Christian Trades Unions of Landworkers, the International Organization of Industrial Employers and the International Confederation of Christian Trades Unions.

308 LEGAL AND EMPIRICAL SURVEY

observer status before organs of the United Nations such as ECOSOC, or which participate in human rights committees. Even in its advisory jurisdiction the Court distinguishes itself from the political organs of the United Nations in its extreme position with respect to non-governmental organizations.[35]

The most probable explanation to the ICJ's restrictive practice with respect to *amicus* briefs is the one which was given by the Registrar in his letter to Reisman, i.e. that 'the Court would be unwilling to open the floodgates to what might be a vast amount of proffered assistance'.[36] Another, possible, reason might be that the Court seeks to protect its integrity by avoiding every risk of bias. Considering that several other international and regional courts employ a more generous approach to *amicus curiae* participation, as will be demonstrated below, it might be held that the ICJ is unnecessarily cautious.[37]

However, the Court has recently recognised written statements submitted by NGOs in connection with advisory proceedings as a source of information. With the objective of increasing its productivity, the Court first adopted Practice Directions in 2001 for the use of states appearing before it. In July 2004, it amended the Practice Directions and adopted new Directions.[38] Part XII of the new Directions states:

1. Where an international non-governmental organization submits a written statement and/or document in an advisory opinion case on its own initiative, such statement and/or document is not to be considered as part of the case file.
2. Such statements and/or documents shall be treated as publications readily available and may accordingly be referred to by States and intergovernmental organizations presenting written and oral statements in the case in the same manner as publications in the public domain.
3. Written statements and/or documents submitted by international non-governmental organizations will be placed in a designated location in the Peace Palace. All States as well as intergovernmental organizations presenting written or oral statements under Article 66 of the Statute will be informed as to the location where statements and/or documents submitted by international non-governmental organizations may be consulted.[39]

---

[35] Chinkin, *Third Parties in International Law*, p. 232.
[36] Letter from the Registrar to Professor Reisman, *Legal Consequences for States of the Continued Presence of South Africa in Namibia (South-West Africa) Notwithstanding Security Council Resolution 276 (1970)*, 1970 ICJ Pleadings, II, pp. 638–639.
[37] See further section 6.9.   [38] International Court of Justice, *Press Release*, 30 July 2004.
[39] International Court of Justice, *Practice Directions*, as at 30 July 2004, Practice Direction XII.

It was already clear that the Court would receive material sent to it by NGOs on their own initiative. For instance, as was described in chapter 5, many 'Declarations of Public Conscience' were sent to the Court and received by the Registrar in connection with the advisory proceedings on *Legality of the Use by a State of Nuclear Weapons in Armed Conflict* in 1994 and 1995.[40] However, these were not regarded as formal submissions. It is not surprising that the new Practice Directions reflect the same view – that statements and other material sent by NGOs on their own initiative are not to be regarded as part of the case file. On the whole, Practice Directions XII reflect the restrictive approach earlier established by the Court towards NGO participation, and do not indicate any possibility for NGOs to seek permission to submit material to be regarded as formal submissions.[41] There are, however, two points worth observing. The Court explains that all states and IGOs presenting statements under Article 66 will be informed about where to find material from international NGOs, thus implicitly inviting INGOs to submit such material and recognising that such material will be taken care of. The Practice Directions also make clear that states and IGOs are free to refer to the NGO submissions in their own statements, although such submissions are explicitly put on the same level as any kind of material available to the public. It can also be observed that, in accordance with Article 66, the Practice Directions mention only international NGOs, thus excluding national NGOs.

Finally, the possibilities for NGOs to submit their views as experts before the ICJ should be mentioned. The Court may, according to Article 50 of its Statute, 'at any time, entrust any individual, body, bureau, commission, or other organization that it may select, with the task of carrying out an enquiry or giving an expert opinion'. NGOs are not excluded by this provision or by the Rules, and their possibilities therefore depend on the Court's need for additional information in the case at hand.[42] In the case of *Competence of the ILO to Regulate, Incidentally, the Personal Work of the Employer*, the PCIJ heard oral statements of experts from the baking industry selected by the International Federation of

---

[40] See section 5.2.
[41] On the other hand, the Practice Directions are addressed to states and may not be the right place for information intended for NGOs.
[42] International Court of Justice, *Rules of Court (1978) as Amended on 5 December 2000*, Rules 62(2), 67(1).

310   LEGAL AND EMPIRICAL SURVEY

Trade Unions (IFTU).[43] It has been suggested that an NGO could use Article 50 as a basis for a request that the ICJ appoints it to submit an expert opinion if the NGO has relevant information.[44] Apart from this possibility, NGOs can be heard as experts on the request of one of the parties according to Articles 57 and 63 of the Court's Rules of Procedure.

6.3 International criminal courts

The International Criminal Court

The Statute of the International Criminal Court does not include a provision on the participation of *amicus curiae* in Court proceedings. It should be observed, however, that Article 44(4) provides for a possibility for the Court to 'employ the expertise of gratis personnel offered by States Parties, intergovernmental organizations or non-governmental organizations to assist with the work of any of the organs of the Court'.[45]

The Rules of Procedure, on the other hand, do provide a legal basis for NGOs or other bodies or persons to act as *amici curiae*. Rule 103(1) states that:

At any stage of the proceedings, a Chamber may, if it considers it desirable for the proper determination of the case, invite or grant leave to a State, organization or person to submit, in writing or orally, any observation on any issue that the Chamber deems appropriate.[46]

According to Article 103(2), the Prosecutor and the defence shall have the opportunity to respond to such submissions. The Court is thus free to accept written or oral submissions from NGOs. It remains to be seen how the Rule will be applied in practice.

The International Criminal Tribunal for the former Yugoslavia

The ICTY and the ICTR both admit *amicus curiae* interventions by NGOs. Rule 74 of the Rules of Procedure of the ICTY states that:

---

[43] *Competence of the ILO to Regulate, Incidentally, the Personal Work of the Employer*, PCIJ Advisory Opinion No. 2 (1922), Serie A/B, p. 13. The PCIJ also heard statements from the International Agricultural Commission.

[44] Shelton, 'The Participation of Nongovernmental Organizations', p. 628.

[45] A/CONF.183/9, *Rome Statute of the International Criminal Court*, as corrected by the procès-verbaux of 10 November 1998 and 12 July 1999.

[46] PCNICC/2000/1/Add.1, *Report of the Preparatory Commission for the International Criminal Court*, 2 November 2000, p. 53.

A Chamber may, if it considers it desirable for the proper determination of the case, invite or grant leave to a State, organization or person to appear before it and make submissions on any issue specified by the Chamber.

Rule 74 of the Rules of Procedure of the ICTR is identical, and the Rules of the Special Court for Sierra Leone include a similar provision.[47]

So far, judgements have been issued by the ICTY in thirty-three cases.[48] NGOs have filed *amicus* briefs in at least four of these.[49] In at least one case, the Court has denied an NGO leave to file an *amicus* brief.[50] Briefs have also been filed by states, individuals and by academic institutions. A couple of cases will be described as an illustration.

The first *amicus curiae* briefs to be submitted to the ICTY were filed in the *Tadić* case.[51] In June 1995, a joint brief was submitted to the Trial Chamber by four persons on behalf of the Jacob Blaustein Institute for the Advancement of Human Rights of the American Jewish Committee, the Center for Constitutional Rights, the International Women's Human Rights Law Clinic of the City University of New York, the Women Refugees Project of the Harvard Immigration and Refugee Program and the Cambridge and Somerville Legal Services. Professor Christine Chinkin also filed an *amicus* brief. The joint NGO brief pointed to the failure of the Prosecutors to treat rape as an indictable offence in the motion for deferral of

---

[47] Article 74 of the Rules of Procedure of the Special Court for Sierra Leone reads: 'A Chamber may, if it considers it desirable for the proper determination of the case, invite or grant leave to any State, organization or person to make submissions on any issue specified by the Chamber.'

[48] As of September 2004. The list of judgements is accessible online on the ICTY website at www.un.org/icty/cases/jugemindex-e.htm.

[49] *The Prosecutor* v. *Tihomir Blaskić*, Order submitting the matter to Trial Chamber II and inviting *amicus curiae*, 14 March 1997; *Prosecutor* v. *Dusko Tadić*, Opinion and Judgement of Trial Chamber II, 7 May 1997, para. 11; *Prosecutor* v. *Anto Furundžija*, Order granting leave to appear as *amicus curiae*, 10 November 1998; and *Prosecutor* v. *Blagoje Simić et al.*, Order granting leave to appear as *amicus curiae* and Scheduling Order, 16 March 1999 (cited in Trial Chamber Decision on the Prosecution Motion under Rule 73 for a ruling concerning the testimony of a witness, 27 July 1999). It should be observed, however, that the number of cases in which NGOs have filed briefs might be higher. Decisions regarding *amicus curiae* participation are sometimes included in the judgement, sometimes in a court order or decision and sometimes in none of these, but in the *Annual Report.*

[50] *Prosecutor* v. *Stanislav Galić*, Judgement and Opinion of Trial Chamber I, 5 December 2003, para. 806. The Court simply stated in the judgement that 'the Trial Chamber did not find it necessary for the proper determination of the case to admit the brief and rejected the application for leave to submit it'. See also below on the *Erdemović* case.

[51] *Prosecutor* v. *Dusko Tadić*, Opinion and Judgement of Trial Chamber II, 7 May 1997, para. 11.

312   LEGAL AND EMPIRICAL SURVEY

the case from the German court to the ICTY.[52] The NGO Juristes sans Frontières later sought and was also granted leave to file a brief.[53] There were no references to the content of the *amicus* briefs in the judgement of the Trial Chamber or in the judgement of the Appeals Chamber. One individual was refused leave to appear as *amicus*.[54]

In the *Furundžija* case, eleven applicants who were scholars and/or NGO representatives sought and were granted leave to make an *amicus curiae* submission.[55] The applicants requested that the Tribunal should reconsider its decision on the right of witness A to 'equality, privacy, and security of the person, and to representation by counsel'.[56] Another *amicus* brief was filed by three applicants on behalf of the Center for Civil and Human Rights of the Notre Dame Law School in Indiana.[57] Both the briefs dealt with issues pertaining to the re-opening of the instant proceedings. The Chamber stated in the judgement that 'Timely assistance in this manner is generally appreciated', but noted that by the time the two briefs were received, the re-opening of the proceedings had already been decided upon and commenced. The Chamber also explained that it was not due to circumstances relating to witness A that the proceedings had been re-opened.[58] It can be observed that three of the persons filing *amicus* briefs had been members of an expert group following the 1995 UN Fourth World Conference on Women in Beijing together with one of the Prosecutors in the instant case before the ICTY.[59]

---

[52] To tie this question to the issue of deferral, the *amici* questioned whether the tribunal should accept the case from Germany since it was not clear that the Prosecutor would follow the precepts of universal justice. Rhonda Copelon, 'Gender Crimes as War Crimes: Integrating Crimes Against Women into International Criminal Law', 46 *McGill Law Journal* (2000), p. 229. Rhonda Copelon was one of the authors of the brief.

[53] *Prosecutor* v. *Dusko Tadić*, Opinion and Judgement of Trial Chamber II, 7 May 1997, para. 15.

[54] *Ibid.*, Order Denying Leave to Appear as *amicus curiae*, 25 November 1996.

[55] *Ibid.*, Judgement of the Trial Chamber, 10 December 1998, para. 35.

[56] *Prosecutor* v. *Anto Furundžija*, Order Granting Leave to Appear as *amicus curiae*, 10 November 1998.

[57] *Ibid.*, Judgement of the Trial Chamber, 10 December 1998, para. 35 and Order Granting Leave to Appear as *amicus curiae*, 11 November 1998.

[58] *Ibid.*, Judgement of the Trial Chamber, 10 December 1998, para. 107.

[59] *Ibid.*, Judgement of the Appeals Chamber, 21 July 2000, para. 167. Judge Mumba, the Presiding Judge in the Appellant's trial, had earlier been a member of the UN Commission on the Status of Women, which was responsible for the preparations of the Conference. The Appellant argued that Judge Mumba should have been disqualified because of her involvement in the Commission and her possible previous contacts with the Prosecutor and the authors of the *amicus* brief, who might also have been involved at some stage with the work of the Commission, see paras. 164–168. The Appeals Chamber found that there was no substance in the Appellant's allegations, para. 215.

In the *Blaskić* case, Judge Gabrielle Kirk McDonald invited requests for leave to submit *amicus* briefs on a number of legal issues.[60] Leave for the submission of *amicus* statements was sought by and granted to several individual experts on international law and organisations, including the Max Planck Institut for Comparative Public Law and International Law, Juristes sans Frontières, the Lawyers' Committee for Human Rights and the Coalition for International Justice.[61] The Trial Chamber invited representatives of all these organisations but the last-mentioned to attend a hearing in order to respond to questions from the Judges of the Trial Chamber and to provide any further assistance the Trial Chamber could require.[62] The *amicus* briefs were not mentioned in the judgement of the Trial Chamber.[63] The Appeals Chamber invited states, organisations and persons to submit requests for *amicus curiae* participation on the same legal issues as the Trial Chamber.[64] Nine briefs were filed, among which were one from Juristes sans Frontières and one from the Max Planck Institut.[65]

The *Erdemović* case is mentioned in the *Annual Report* of the Tribunal as an example of a case where persons and organisations have sought leave to appear as *amicus curiae*.[66] As there is no Court Order granting such leave, and no mention of *amicus* participation in the judgements, it may be assumed that leave was refused.

An NGO also appeared in the case of *Karadžić and Mladić*. In June 1996, the Court invited Human Rights Watch to appear during the proceedings pursuant to Rule 61. This Rule contains provisions on the procedure in case of failure to execute a warrant. In such proceedings, the Trial Chamber examines all evidence in order to determine whether there are reasonable grounds for believing that the accused has committed all or any of the charges in the indictment. Rule 61 B provides that the Prosecutor or the Trial Chamber may call any witness whose

---

[60] *The Prosecutor* v. *Tihomir Blaskić*, Order submitting the matter to Trial Chamber II and inviting *amicus curiae*, 14 March 1997.

[61] *Ibid.*, Orders Granting Leave to Appear as *amicus curiae*, 11 April 1997 (twelve different orders) and 14 April 1997 (one order) and A/52/375, *Report of the International Tribunal ...*, 18 September 1997, paras. 50–52 and n. 1. There is no order refusing leave for the submission of an *amicus* brief.

[62] *The Prosecutor* v. *Tihomir Blaskić*, Orders Granting Leave to Appear as *amicus curiae*, 11 April 1997.

[63] *Ibid.*, Judgement of the Trial Chamber, 3 March 2000.

[64] *Ibid.*, Appeals Chamber, Order Granting Extension of Time, 17 September 1997 and A/52/375, *Report of the International Tribunal ...*, 18 September 1997, para. 52.

[65] A/53/219, *Report of the International Tribunal ...*, 10 August 1998, para. 99 and n. 17.

[66] A/52/375, *Report of the International Tribunal ...*, 18 September 1997, para. 50.

314   LEGAL AND EMPIRICAL SURVEY

statement has been submitted to the confirming judge. Hearings were held with Human Rights Watch on 27 June to 5 July 1996.[67]

Although this is not a form of *amicus curiae* participation, it can be observed that Article 18 of the Statute of the Tribunal states that: 'The Prosecutor shall initiate investigations *ex officio* or on the basis of information obtained from any source, particularly from Governments, United Nations organs, intergovernmental and non-governmental organisations.'

The International Criminal Tribunal for Rwanda

The ICTR was set up by the UN Security Council in November 1994 to prosecute serious violations of human rights and humanitarian law committed in Rwanda in 1994. As of September 2004, nine cases had been completed and eleven were on appeal.[68] The Tribunal's reporting of *amicus curiae* participation of NGOs is scarce.[69] It is not possible to say for certain how many times non-governmental *amici* have participated in proceedings before the ICTR, as the Tribunal does not seem to report on all such submissions.[70] I have found information on non-governmental *amicus* participation in only four cases.

In the *Akayesu* case, the prosecutor had initially not charged for rape or other crimes of sexual violence, although rape is included in the Statute of the Tribunal as a crime against humanity and a war crime.[71] During the trial, witnesses who were called in relation to other crimes testified that rapes had occurred in Akayesu's commune. However, NGOs received the information that the prosecutor was not planning to amend the indictment. The NGOs the Working Groups on Engendering the Rwanda Tribunal and the Center for Constitutional Rights prepared and circulated an *amicus curiae* brief which was signed by almost thirty NGOs before it was submitted to the Tribunal. The brief called upon the Prosecutor to ensure the inclusion of rape in charges of genocide, as well as war crimes and crimes against humanity.[72] A couple of

---

[67] ICTY, Summary of Judicial Activities, accessible online at www.un.org/icty/summary/summar.htm, as of 3 September 2004.

[68] The list is accessible online on the tribunal's website at www.ictr.org/ENGLISH/cases/completed.htm, as of 6 September 2004.

[69] For the text of the relevant Article in the Tribunal's Rules of Procedure, see section 6.3.

[70] An *amicus* brief was filed in the case of the *Prosecutor* v. *Jean Paul Akayesu*, according to Rhonda Copelon, who was one of the authors. However, there is no court order granting leave for this submission, and the brief is not mentioned in the judgement. Copelon, 'Gender Crimes as War Crimes', pp. 225–226.

[71] ICTR, Chamber I, *The Prosecutor* v. *Jean-Paul Akayesu*, 2 September 1998.

[72] Copelon, 'Gender Crimes as War Crimes', p. 225 and Human Rights Watch Press Release, Montreal, 1 September 1998.

weeks later, the Prosecutor changed the indictment to include charges of rape, allegedly not as a result of the *amicus* brief, but because of the witnesses' testimonies. The *amicus* brief is not listed in the docket of the case, although the Chamber had acknowledged receipt of the brief in a fax message, and it is not mentioned in the judgement.[73] The *Akayesu* judgement was the first international conviction for the crime of genocide and the first to recognise rape and sexual violence as constitutive acts of genocide.

At the appeals stage of the *Akayesu* case, the International Criminal Defence Attorneys Association applied for leave to submit an *amicus curiae* brief.[74] In the petition for intervention, the NGO stated that it would submit that an accused who faces the most serious charges which can be brought against a human being must be entitled to choose, in a fully confident and informed manner, his defence counsel from the list maintained by the Tribunal's Registrar.[75] The background was, according to the association, that Akayesu had requested a Canadian defence counsel. This request was rejected by the Registrar, who gave several different explanations thereto, *inter alia*, that he could not assign French or Canadian counsels as they were over-represented on the Tribunal's list.[76] The brief was not mentioned in the judgement of the Appeals Chamber and there is no Court Order or Decision on the matter.[77] However, it is stated in the Annual Report of the petitioning NGO that the brief was indeed submitted in June 1999. On 27 July, the Appeals Chamber recognised the right to free choice of the counsel in the *Akayesu* case and directed the Registrar to assign to him the counsel of his choice.[78]

In the case of *Alfred Musema*, the NGO African Concern sought leave to appear as *amicus curiae* before the Trial Chamber. The *amicus* participation concerned the powers of the Tribunal to prosecute for serious violations of a number of instruments of international humanitarian law and to order restitution under the Statute and Rules of the Tribunal. The application is discussed at some length in the Trial Chamber's decision.[79] The Defence and the Prosecutor filed

---

[73] Copelon, 'Gender Crimes as War Crimes', pp. 225–226.
[74] A/54/315, *Report of the International Criminal Tribunal* ..., 7 September 1999, para. 116.
[75] International Criminal Defence Attorneys Association, *Petition for Intervention as amicus curiae*, April 1999.
[76] *Brief of the International Criminal Defence Attorneys Association*, June 1999.
[77] ICTR Appeals Chamber, *The Prosecutor v. Jean-Paul Akayesu*, 1 June 2001. In fact, it is not clear from the *Annual Report* of the Tribunal whether leave was granted for the brief to be filed. It is mentioned in the same report that another NGO sought leave to file a brief in the *Musema* case (see below), but it is not mentioned that it was refused. A/54/315, *Report of the International Criminal Tribunal* ..., 7 September 1999, para. 116.
[78] *ICDAA Annual Report*, 1998–1999 (Major Projects; Activities concerning the International Criminal Tribunal for Rwanda).
[79] *The Prosecutor v. Alfred Musema*, Decision on an Application by African Concern for Leave to Appear as *amicus curiae*, 17 March 1999.

316   LEGAL AND EMPIRICAL SURVEY

written responses to African Concern's application. The Prosecutor argued that, although she was not 'particularly against' any person filing an *amicus* brief, the main purpose of African Concern's application was to have a platform to promote its interests as regarded restitution in Rwanda. The Defence submitted that the Chamber should not grant leave as the case against the accused did not allege any pillage or unlawful taking of property by the accused, which meant that the brief would not be pertinent for the proper determination of the specific case.[80] The Chamber recalled that, according to Article 74 of the Rules of Procedure, the submissions of the *amicus curiae* must be relevant to the case and of assistance for the proper determination thereof. The Chamber considered that there appeared no specific legal or factual arguments in the application to support the applicant's two requests. The *amicus* brief was thus not considered desirable for the proper determination of the case and was rejected.[81]

African Concern also sought leave to file a brief in the case of *Théoneste Bagosora*.[82] It is not clear from the Tribunal's documentation whether the leave was granted or refused.

In the case of *Prosecutor* v. *Samuel Imanishimwe et al.*, Trial Chamber III, the Coalition For Women's Human Rights in Conflict Situations applied for leave to file an *amicus curiae* brief.[83] The Trial Chamber dismissed the application, and the Coalition filed a motion applying for reconsideration of this decision. In its motion, the Coalition expressed concern that the decision appeared to prohibit *amicus* intervention in relation to issues that were not already under consideration by the Trial Chamber and would thereby prevent an intervenor from bringing a new or unconsidered issue to the attention of the Trial Chamber. The Applicant suggested that the Chamber adopt the test applied by Chamber I in the *Akayesu* case, permitting *amicus* intervention where the third party may be of assistance for the proper determination of the case.[84] The Trial Chamber emphasised that the circumstances of the case were clearly distinguishable from the facts that precipitated the decision in *Prosecutor* v. *Akayesu*. The Chamber also observed that the Prosecutor had indicated that she would file a separate indictment with respect to the matter raised in the *amicus* brief. With regard to the possibility of review of the previous decision not to grant leave for the Coalition to

---

[80] *Ibid.*, paras. 4–6.

[81] *Ibid.*, paras. 8–14. See also *The Prosecutor* v. *Alfred Musema*, Judgement of the Trial Chamber, 27 January 2000, para. 26.

[82] A/54/315, *Report of the International Criminal Tribunal ...*, 7 September 1999, para. 116.

[83] Case No. ICTR 99-46-T, Trial Chamber III, *Decision on the Coalition for Women's Human Rights in Conflict Situations Motion for Reconsideration of the Decision on Application to File an amicus curiae Brief*, 24 September 2001.

[84] This decision granted leave to a representative of the UN Secretariat to make a statement on the lifting of the immunity of the witness Major-General Dallaire, who was the former Commander-in-Chief of UNAMIR, February 1998, *The Prosecutor* v. *Jean-Paul Akayesu*, Order granting leave for *amicus curiae* to appear, ICTR-96-4-T 12.

appear as *amicus curiae*, the Chamber stated that review, as regulated in Article 25 of the Court's Statute and Article 120 of its Rules, was an exceptional measure that could be invoked only where a new and potentially decisive fact had been discovered. In its request for review, the Applicant had not raised any new fact that could serve to trigger the exceptional jurisdiction of the Chamber to reconsider a previous decision. Therefore, the Chamber did not need to address whether review proceedings were available to non-parties or in relation to decisions other than judgements, and dismissed the motion.[85]

In the case of *Samuel Imanishimwe*, described above, it was alleged by one of the defence counsels that an *amicus* brief could not be filed without a previous invitation from the Court specifying a specific issue that should be addressed.[86] The Chamber did not address this issue in its decision. It can be assumed that the reason for this was that it was already sufficiently clear that such an invitation was not needed. Although the UN Secretariat was indeed invited in the *Akayesu* case to send a representative to appear as *amicus curiae* before the Court in order to make a statement on a specific matter, it is clear from the Court's case-law that it can accept *amicus* submissions without previous invitation.[87]

Finally, it can be noted that, as for the ICTY, the Statute of the ICTR provides that: 'The Prosecutor shall initiate investigations *ex officio* or on the basis of information obtained from any source, particularly from Governments, United Nations organs, intergovernmental and non-governmental organisations.'[88]

6.4 The WTO dispute settlement procedure

The legal basis for the dispute settlement procedure of the World Trade Organization (WTO) is the Dispute Settlement Understanding (DSU), which was one of the WTO agreements that came out of the Uruguay Round negotiations.[89] The dispute procedure applies only to the state

---

[85] Case No. ICTR 99-46-T, Trial Chamber III, *Decision on the Coalition for Women's Human Rights in Conflict Situation's Motion for Reconsideration of the Decision on Application to File an amicus curiae Brief*, 24 September 2001.

[86] *Ibid.*, para. 4.

[87] *The Prosecutor* v. *Jean-Paul Akayesu*, Order granting leave for *amicus curiae* to Appear, ICTR-96-4-T 12.

[88] Statute of the International Tribunal for Rwanda, Article 17.

[89] Agreement Establishing the World Trade Organization (1994), annex 2, Understanding on Rules and Procedures Governing the Settlement of Disputes (Dispute Settlement Understanding, DSU).

318   LEGAL AND EMPIRICAL SURVEY

members of the WTO.[90] If a dispute arises between WTO member states regarding their rights and obligations under the WTO agreements and the dispute cannot be settled through consultations, a panel of (normally) three persons is set up by the Dispute Settlement Body (DSB) to resolve the conflict, provided that the complaining party so requests.[91] Such a panel 'shall be composed of well-qualified governmental and/or non-governmental individuals'.[92] The Understanding provides, however, that panelists shall serve in their individual capacities and not as government representatives, nor as representatives of any organisation.[93] Appeals may be brought to a standing Appellate Body, composed of seven independent experts.[94]

The question of non-governmental participation in a governmental delegation in a dispute before a panel was discussed in the *Indonesia Auto* case.

The United States noted that Indonesia's delegation list included several private lawyers, and objected to the participation of these non-governmental employees in meetings of the Panel.[95] The Panel concluded that it was for the government of Indonesia to nominate the members of its delegation, and found no provision in the WTO Agreement or the DSU which prevented a WTO member from determining the composition of its delegation to WTO panel meetings. The Panel emphasised that all members of parties' delegations – whether or not they are government employees – are present as representatives of their governments.[96]

The issue of *amicus curiae* participation of NGOs was much discussed during the 1990s. It was made clear first in the case of *United States – Import Prohibition of Certain Shrimp and Shrimp Products* that panels and the Appellate Body may receive *amicus curiae* briefs submitted by NGOs. The dispute concerned a US law according to which nations catching wild shrimp and exporting them to the United States had to be certified as having adopted certain measures requiring shrimp trawls to be equipped with 'turtle-excluder' devices. In January 1997, India, Malaysia, Pakistan and Thailand requested the establishment of a Panel to examine their complaint, arguing that the law was an illegal

---

[90] DSU, Article 1.1.   [91] DSU, Articles 4.7, 6.1, 8.5.   [92] DSU, Articles 1.1, 8.1.
[93] DSU, Article 8.9.   [94] DSU, Article 17.
[95] WT/DS54/R, WT/DS55/R, WT/DS59/R, WT/DS64/R, *Indonesia – Certain Measures Affecting the Automobile Industry*, Report of the Panel, 2 July 1998, paras. 4.1–4.7.
[96] The Panel also noted that, unlike in the *Indonesia Auto* case, the working procedures of the Panel in the *Bananas III* case, which had been referred to by the United States in support of its view, contained a specific provision requiring the presence only of government officials. *Ibid.*, paras. 4.4, 14.1.

restriction on shrimp exports. In the course of proceedings before the Panel, two *amicus curiae* briefs were submitted by NGOs.[97] The Panel acknowledged receipt of the two briefs, which were also sent to the parties. The complaining parties requested the Panel not to consider the contents of the briefs in dealing with the dispute, while the United States urged the Panel to avail itself of any relevant information in the two briefs, as well as in any other similar communications.[98] The Panel rejected the two briefs, arguing that:

We had not requested such information as was contained in the above-mentioned documents. We note that, pursuant to Article 13 of the DSU, the initiative to seek information and to select the source of information rests with the Panel. In any other situations, only parties and third parties are allowed to submit information directly to the Panel. Accepting non-requested information from non-governmental sources would be, in our opinion, incompatible with the provisions of the DSU as currently applied. We therefore informed the parties that we did not intend to take these documents into consideration. We observed, moreover, that it was usual practice for parties to put forward whatever documents they considered relevant to support their case and that, if any party in the present dispute wanted to put forward these documents, or parts of them, as part of their own submissions to the Panel, they were free to do so. If this were the case, the other parties would have two weeks to respond to the additional material. We noted that the United States availed themselves of this opportunity by designating Section III of the document submitted by the Center for Marine Conservation and the Center for International Environmental Law as an annex to its second submission to the Panel.[99]

The Panel thus interpreted the DSU in a restrictive way, stating that accepting non-requested information from non-governmental sources would be 'incompatible with the provisions of the DSU as currently applied'. However, it still allowed the parties to the dispute to put forward 'whatever documents they considered relevant' as part of its own submissions to the Panel.

The United States appealed the decision of the Panel. On the question of *amicus* briefs, the Appellate Body noted that:

It may be well to stress at the outset that access to the dispute settlement process of the WTO is limited to Members of the WTO. This access is not available, under the *WTO Agreement* and the covered agreements as they currently exist, to individuals or international organizations, whether governmental or

---

[97] WT/DS58/R, *United States – Import Prohibition of Certain Shrimp and Shrimp Products*, Report of the Panel, 15 May 1998, p. 280.
[98] *Ibid.* [99] *Ibid.*, p. 281.

320 LEGAL AND EMPIRICAL SURVEY

non-governmental ... Thus, under the DSU, only Members who are parties to a dispute, or who have notified their interest in becoming third parties in such a dispute to the DSB, have a *legal right* to make submissions to, and have a *legal right* to have those submissions considered by, a panel. Correlatively, a panel is *obliged* in law to accept and give due consideration only to submissions made by the parties and the third parties in a panel proceeding.[100]

The Appellate Body believed, however, that the issue would be most appropriately addressed by examining what a panel was *authorised* to do under the DSU. It therefore went on to interpret Article 13 of the Dispute Settlement Understanding, which reads:

1. Each panel shall have the right to seek information and technical advice from any individual or body which it deems appropriate ...
2. Panels may seek information from any relevant source and may consult experts to obtain their opinion on certain aspects of the matter. With respect to a factual issue concerning a scientific or other technical matter raised by a party to a dispute, a panel may request an advisory report in writing from an expert review group.[101]

The Appellate Body found that, within the context of the broad authority vested in panels by the DSU, and given the object and purpose of the Panel's mandate, the word 'seek' should not be read too literally.[102] Authority to seek information was not properly equated with a prohibition on accepting information submitted without having been requested by a Panel. The Appellate Body stated that a Panel has the discretionary authority either to accept and consider, or to reject information and advice submitted to it – whether requested by a Panel or not.[103] It concluded:

We find, and so hold, that the Panel erred in its legal interpretation that accepting non-requested information from non-governmental sources is incompatible with the provisions of the DSU. At the same time, we consider that the Panel acted within the scope of its authority under Articles 12 and 13 of the DSU in allowing any party to the dispute to attach the briefs by non-governmental organizations, or any portion thereof, to its own submissions.[104]

The United States attached three exhibits to its appellant's submission, containing additional *amicus* briefs submitted by three different groups of NGOs. In addition, one NGO filed a revised version of the brief which

---

[100] WT/DS58/AB/R, *United States – Import Prohibition of Certain Shrimp and Shrimp Products*, Report of the Appellate Body, 12 October 1998, para. 101 (emphasis in original).
[101] *Ibid.*, para. 102.   [102] *Ibid.*, para. 107.   [103] *Ibid.*, para. 108.   [104] *Ibid.*, para. 110.

it had earlier submitted to the Panel.[105] The complaining states objected to the briefs and argued, *inter alia*, that these were not in conformity with Article 17(6) of the DSU, which states that an appeal shall be 'limited to issues of law covered in the panel report and legal interpretations developed by the panel'. They further argued that the submission of exhibits that presented the views of NGOs was not contemplated by, or authorised by the DSU or the Working Procedures, which vest the discretion to request additional submissions with the Appellate Body.[106] The Appellate Body issued a preliminary ruling stating that:

> We have decided to accept for consideration, insofar as they may be pertinent, the legal arguments made by the various non-governmental organizations in the three briefs attached as exhibits to the appellant's submission of the United States, as well as the revised version of the brief by the Center for International Environmental Law *et al.*, which was submitted to us on 3 August 1998.[107]

The Appellate Body considered that the attaching of a brief or other material to the submission of the appellant or appellee, no matter its origin, rendered that material at least *prima facie* an integral part of that participant's submission. In the appeal in question, the United States had made it clear that its views on the legal issues of the appeal were found in its main submission. The United States had also confirmed its agreement with the legal arguments of the NGOs, but only to the extent that those arguments concurred with the arguments set out in its main submission. Considering that the United States had itself accepted the briefs in a tentative and qualified manner only, the Appellate Body decided to focus on the legal arguments in the main appellant's submission.[108] The brief submitted separately by an NGO was accepted in the Preliminary Ruling by the Appellate Body, but does not seem to have been considered by it.[109]

One of the three groups of NGOs commented on the matter of an *amicus* brief in its submission.[110] It argued more or less in line with the Appellate Body that Article 13 of the DSU empowered panels to receive NGO briefs, but also stated that they had offered considerable expertise in the Panel's deliberations. Further, the acceptance of *amicus* briefs was

---

[105] *Ibid.*, para. 79.   [106] *Ibid.*, paras. 79–82.   [107] *Ibid.*, para. 83.

[108] *Ibid.*, paras. 89–91.   [109] *Ibid.*, para. 91, *e contrario*.

[110] *Amicus brief to the Appellate Body on United States – Import Prohibition of Certain Shrimp and Shrimp Products*, submitted by the Center for International Environmental Law (CIEL), the Center for Marine Conservation (CMC), the Environmental Foundation Ltd (EFL), Mangrove Action Project (MAP), Philippine Ecological Network (PEN), Red Nacional de Acción Ecológica (RENACE) and Sobrevivencia, printed by the CIEL, 1999, pp. 45–47.

322   LEGAL AND EMPIRICAL SURVEY

supported by the context, object and purpose of the WTO Agreements, in the view of the NGOs. First, the WTO Preamble – forming an important part of the DSU's interpretative context – endorsed the objective of sustainable development, for which public participation was central. Secondly, public participation was supported by the reference in the Preamble to 'international law relations between parties', as well as by developing norms of customary international law. The Rio Declaration and Agenda 21 recognised the necessity of adequate public participation in the decision making of international bodies and called for the inclusion of contributions from NGOs and broad access to dispute settlement mechanisms. Furthermore, the acceptance of *amicus* briefs was common practice in other multilateral judicial bodies.[111]

The dispute *United States – Imposition of Countervailing Duties on Certain Hot-Rolled Lead and Bismuth Carbon Steel Products Originating in the United Kingdom* was initiated by a complaint brought by the European Communities with respect to countervailing duties imposed by the United States on such products originating in the United Kingdom. In February 2000, the Appellate Body received two *amicus curiae* briefs submitted by the American Iron and Steel Institute and the Speciality Steel Industry of North America.[112] A week later, the EC filed a letter arguing that these *amicus curiae* briefs were inadmissible in appellate review proceedings, and stating that it did not intend to respond to the content of the briefs. The EC argued that the basis contained in Article 13 of the DSU for allowing *amicus* briefs in Panel proceedings did not apply to the Appellate Body and that, in any case, the provision was limited to factual information and technical advice and would not include legal arguments or legal interpretations received from those other than members. Furthermore, the EC stated that neither the DSU nor the Working Procedures allowed *amicus* briefs to be admitted in Appellate Body proceedings, as the DSU and the Working Procedures confined participation in an appeal to participants and third participants. Moreover, Article 17(10) of the DSU provided for the confidentiality of Appellate Body proceedings.

The third participants, Brazil and Mexico, agreed with the EC that the Appellate Body did not have the authority to accept *amicus curiae*

---

[111] *Ibid.*, pp. 46–47.

[112] *United States – Imposition of Countervailing Duties on Certain Hot-Rolled Lead and Bismuth Carbon Steel Products Originating in the United Kingdom*, Report of the Appellate Body, WT/DS138/AB/R, 10 May 2000, para. 36.

briefs. The United States, for its part, argued that the Appellate Body did indeed have this authority and urged it to accept the briefs submitted by the steel industry associations. The United States noted that, as was explained by the Appellate Body in the *United States – Shrimp* case, the DSU granted to a panel 'ample and extensive authority to undertake and to control the process by which it informs itself both of the relevant facts of the dispute and of the legal norms and principles applicable to such facts'.[113] The United States held that it was clear that the Appellate Body also had such authority, as the DSU authorised it to draw up its own working procedures and did not agree that acceptance of an unsolicited *amicus curiae* brief would compromise the confidentiality of the Appellate Body proceedings.[114]

The Appellate Body noted that the DSU made clear that it had broad authority to adopt procedural rules that did not conflict with any rules and procedures in the DSU or the covered agreements. While again emphasising that non-members of the WTO had no legal right to make submissions to nor to be heard by the Appellate Body, it was of the opinion that it had the legal authority under the DSU to accept and consider *amicus* briefs in an appeal in which it found it pertinent and useful to do so. In the appeal in question, however, the Appellate Body did not find it necessary to take the two *amicus* briefs filed into account in rendering its decision.[115]

The case of *European Communities – Measures Affecting Asbestos and Asbestos-Containing Products* gave rise to the next discussion on *amicus curiae* participation. The case was brought in May 1998 by Canada, which requested the DSB to establish a Panel to examine the French measure concerning the prohibition of asbestos and products containing asbestos. In 1999, the Panel received four *amicus* briefs from the NGOs Collegium Ramazzini, the Ban Asbestos Network, the Instituto Mexicano de Fibro-Industrias AC and the American Federation of Labor and Congress of Industrial Organizations.[116] Referring to the position taken in the case of *United States – Import Prohibition of Certain Shrimp and Shrimp Products*, the Panel

---

[113] WT/DS58/AB/R, 12 October 1998, para. 106.
[114] *United States – Imposition of Countervailing Duties on Certain Hot-Rolled Lead and Bismuth Carbon Steel Products Originating in the United Kingdom*, Report of the Appellate Body, WT/DS138/AB/R, 10 May 2000, para. 38.
[115] *Ibid.*, paras. 39–42.
[116] WT/DS135/R, *European Communities – Measures Affecting Asbestos and Asbestos-Containing Products*, Report of the Panel, 18 September 2000, para. 6.1.

324   LEGAL AND EMPIRICAL SURVEY

sent the briefs to the parties for their information. Canada notified the Panel that, bearing in mind the general nature of the opinions expressed by the NGOs in those submissions, they would not be useful to the Panel at this advanced stage of the proceedings. Canada thus urged the Panel to reject the four briefs. The EC incorporated the submission of the first- and last-mentioned organisations, while it proposed that the Panel should reject the submissions from the Ban Asbestos Network and the Instituto Mexicano de Fibro-Industrias AC, as their briefs contained no information of relevance to the dispute.[117]

The Panel informed the parties that it would consider the two briefs which had been incorporated into the EC's submission, and Canada was given the opportunity to reply to these documents. By contrast, the Panel decided not to take the submission from the Ban Asbestos Network and the Instituto Mexicano de Fibro-Industrias AC into account. In June 2000, the Panel received another *amicus* brief from an NGO, Only Nature Endures. The Panel decided not to accept the brief since it was submitted at a stage in the procedure when it could no longer be taken into account. It also decided that it would accept no more *amicus* briefs from that point until the end of the procedure.[118]

The Panel issued its report on 18 December 2000, in which it upheld the French ban on asbestos. Canada appealed the decision. The Appellate Body wrote to the Parties, recognising the possibility that it might receive submissions in the appeal from persons other than parties and third parties to the dispute. The Appellate Body was of the view that the fair and orderly conduct of this appeal could be facilitated by the adoption of appropriate procedures, pursuant to Rule 16(1) of the Working Procedures, to deal with any possible submissions received from such persons. After having received the different views of the parties and the third parties and consultation among the members of the Appellate Body, it did adopt such an additional procedure, for the purposes of the appeal only, to deal with written submissions received from persons other than the parties and third parties to the *Asbestos* dispute. The Additional Procedure provided, *inter alia*, that 'Any person, whether natural or legal, other than a party or a third party to this dispute, wishing to file a written brief with the Appellate Body, must apply for leave to file such a brief from the Appellate Body *by noon* on

---

[117] *Ibid.*, para. 6.2.   [118] *Ibid.*, paras. 6.3–6.4.

Thursday, 16 November 2000.'[119] According to the report of the Appellate Body, it received thirteen written submissions from NGOs that were not submitted in accordance with the Additional Procedure. Several of the submissions were received while the Body was still considering the possible adoption of an Additional Procedure. After the adoption of the Procedure, each of the submissions was returned to its sender, along with a letter informing it of the procedure. Only one of the NGOs subsequently submitted a request for leave in accordance with the Additional Procedure.[120] After the adoption of the Additional Procedure, the Appellate Body received another seventeen applications requesting leave to file *amicus* briefs. Six of these requests were received after the deadline. All these applicants were denied leave. Eleven requests were received within the time limits. Surprisingly, all these requests were also denied. In its report, the Appellate Body stated that:

> We carefully reviewed and considered each of these applications in accordance with the Additional Procedure and, in each case, decided to deny leave to file a written brief.[121]

Thus, all in all, thirty briefs and applications for leave to file an *amicus* brief were received, and all were denied. Many NGOs, having first welcomed the adoption for the first time of a formal framework for *amicus curiae* participation, expressed disappointment and criticism over this turn of events.[122] Some NGOs challenged the Appellate Body's rejection of their requests by submitting a joint *amicus* brief

---

[119] WT/DS135/AB/R, *European Communities – Measures Affecting Asbestos and Asbestos-Containing Products*, Report of the Appellate Body, 12 March 2001, paras. 50–51 (emphasis in original). Applicants for leave were also asked to adhere to a number of requirements, such as stating their legal status, their general objectives, the nature of their activities and their sources of financing, as well as specifying the nature of their interest in the appeal. *Ibid.* and WT/DS135/9, *Communication from the Appellate Body* with attachment AB-2000-11, *Additional Procedure Adopted Under Rule 16(1) of the Working Procedures for Appellate Review.*

[120] WT/DS135/AB/R, *European Communities – Measures Affecting Asbestos and Asbestos-Containing Products*, Report of the Appellate Body, 12 March 2001, para. 53.

[121] *Ibid.*, paras. 55–56.

[122] See, e.g., *A Court Without Friends? One Year After Seattle the WTO Slams the Door on NGOs*, Joint Press Release by Greenpeace International, IBAS, FIELD, WWF and CIEL, 22 November 2000; 'WTO General Council Slaps Appellate Body on Amicus Briefs', 45 *ICTSD BRIDGES Weekly Trade News Digest*, No. 45, 28 November 2000; and Alice Palmer and Jacob Werksman, 'World Trade Organization, European Communities – Measures Affecting Asbestos and Asbestos-Containing Products, Panel Report', 10 RECIEL (2001), pp. 129–130.

326   LEGAL AND EMPIRICAL SURVEY

under the Body's general authority to receive such submissions, but the Appellate Body did not accept it.[123]

The adoption of the Additional Procedure by the Appellate Body also gave rise to controversy among WTO members. Shortly after the adoption of the Procedure, the WTO General Council convened to discuss the matter of *amicus curiae* participation.[124] The majority of the delegates that spoke were of the opinion that it was unacceptable for the Appellate Body to receive and consider *amicus* submissions. Uruguay, for example, stated that the WTO dispute settlement system had been described as the 'jewel' of the Uruguay Round and that it should not be allowed to 'lose its brilliance or its value'. Uruguay noted with great concern the decision of the Appellate Body to adopt an Additional Procedure and emphasised that decisions on WTO relations with NGOs statutorily belonged to the General Council.[125] Although there was no consensus, the Chairman stated that he believed that, in light of the views expressed and in the absence of clear rules, the Appellate Body should exercise 'extreme caution' in future cases until members had considered what rules were needed. The Chairman was, however, instructed by the Council to initiate informal discussions with members to establish procedures on *amicus* briefs.[126]

So far, no rules have been elaborated, and the issue of *amicus curiae* participation is dealt with on an *ad hoc* basis by the Panel and the Appellate Body. Unsolicited *amicus* briefs have been submitted in several later disputes.[127] Most submissions have not been considered by the

---

[123] Palmer and Werksman, 'World Trade Organization', p. 130, and WT/DS135/AB/R, *European Communities – Measures Affecting Asbestos and Asbestos-Containing Products*, Report of the Appellate Body, 12 March 2001, para. 57.

[124] General Council, *Minutes of Meeting*, WT/GC/M/60, 23 January 2001.

[125] *Ibid.*, paras. 4-6.   [126] *Ibid.*, paras. 119-131.

[127] See WT/DS141/R, *European Communities – Anti-Dumping Duties on Imports of Cotton-Type Bed Linen from India*, 30 October 2000, para. 6.1 and n. 10; WT/DS122/AB/R, *Thailand – Anti-Dumping Duties on Angles, Shapes and Sections of Iron or Non-Alloy Steel and H-Beams from Poland*, 12 March 2001, paras. 62-78; WT/DS248/AB/R (joined with several other numbers); WT/DS212/AB/R, *United States – Countervailing Measures Concerning Certain Products from the European Communities*, 9 December 2002, paras. 9-10, 76; *United States – Definitive Safeguard Measures on Imports of Certain Steel Products*, 10 November 2003, paras. 9-10, 268; WT/DS257/AB/R, *United States – Final Countervailing Duty Determination with Respect to Certain Softwood Lumber from Canada*, 19 January 2004, para. 9; WT/DS277/R, *United States – Investigation of the International Trade Commission in Softwood Lumber From Canada*, 22 March 2004, n. 75 with Corrigendum WT/DS257/R/Corr.11, 29 August 2003; WT/DS231/AB/R, *European Communities – Trade Description of Sardines*, 26 September 2002 (at several places).

Panel or the Appellate Body.[128] The standard explanation is that submissions are not useful for the determination of the dispute or that arguments raised by *amici curiae* can be considered by the Panel or the Appellate Body only to the extent that those arguments are taken up in the written submissions and/or oral statements of a party or third party. Nevertheless, in *European Communities – Trade Description of Sardines*, the Appellate Body explicitly reiterated its view that it is indeed entitled to accept and consider *amicus* briefs.[129]

In conclusion, it can be observed that both the Panel and the Appellate Body have received a number of submissions from NGOs, also independently from the submissions of the parties. It was made clear by the Appellate Body in the *Shrimp* case that Panels and the Appellate Body itself both have a right, but not an obligation, to accept *amicus* briefs. In the *Asbestos* case, the Appellate Body even adopted an Additional Procedure to deal with such submissions. However, in spite of the great number of submissions made by NGOs, *amicus* briefs have very rarely been actually considered, and then only as part of the submissions of one of the parties. The issue of *amicus* briefs is clearly more controversial within the WTO context than in many other fields of international law, probably because of the considerable commercial interests at stake. It is interesting to note that during the discussions on *amicus* briefs in different WTO disputes, it has never been argued that such submissions lack importance.[130] Rather, the controversy seems to indicate that the WTO members believe that they may affect the outcome of a dispute.

---

[128] In *United States – Preliminary Determinations with Respect to Certain Softwood Lumber from Canada*, the Panel decided to consider an unsolicited *amicus curiae* brief from a Canadian NGO, the Interior Alliance. The brief was submitted to the Panel prior to its first substantive meeting with the parties and the parties and third parties were given an opportunity to comment on the brief. After that meeting, the Panel received three additional unsolicited *amicus curiae* briefs. The Panel stated that 'for reasons relating to the timing of these submissions, we decided not to accept any of these later briefs', WT/DS236/R, 27 September 2002, para. 7.2.

[129] WT/DS231/AB/R, *European Communities – Trade Description of Sardines*, 26 September 2002, para. 157. The main topic of this discussion was an *amicus curiae* submission from a WTO member that had not been a third party before the panel and, therefore, could not become a third participant in the appellate proceedings.

[130] On the probability that *amicus* submissions assert an influence on the outcome of WTO disputes as compared to other judicial proceedings, see Andrea Kupfer Schneider, 'Institutional Concerns of an Expanded Trade Regime: Where Should Global Social and Regulatory Policy be Made? Unfriendly Actions: The Amicus Brief Battle at the WTO', 7 *Widener Law Symposium Journal* 87 (2001), pp. 101–107.

328   LEGAL AND EMPIRICAL SURVEY

6.5 The European Commission and Court of Human Rights

The Commission

In line with the confidentiality of the Commission's procedure, its Rules included no provision for the submission of *amicus* briefs.[131] The applicant's lawyer could, however, incorporate NGO reports or opinions as part of the written submissions. A few examples of cases where this was done are *Gündem* v. *Turkey* (in which the applicant submitted a report by Human Rights Watch/Helsinki and extracts from a report by the Kurdish Human Rights Project), *Kılıc* v. *Turkey* (reports by Human Rights Watch/Helsinki and by Amnesty International), *Aydin* v. *Turkey* (report by Amnesty International), *Nsangu* v. *Austria* (report by Amnesty International), *Bahaddar* v. *the Netherlands* (letter and report by Amnesty International) and *Paez* v. *Sweden* (report by Human Rights Watch and report and letter by Amnesty International).[132] In its reports on these cases, the Commission has often described in detail the material produced by NGOs, and in some cases attributed evidential value to it.[133]

One example of a different type of NGO involvement in the proceedings before the Commission is the case of *Sutherland* v. *the United Kingdom*, where the applicant was represented by a representative of the NGO 'Stonewall', an organisation working for lesbian and gay equality.[134]

The Court

Bearing in mind that before 1998 private applicants were not considered full parties before the European Court of Human Rights, it is perhaps

---

[131] Rules of Procedure of the European Commission of Human Rights (as in force at 28 June 1993), Strasbourg, 1993.

[132] Reports of the Commission in the cases of *Gündem* v. *Turkey* (Application No. 22275/93), 3 September 1996, paras. 54, 147; *Kılıc* v. *Turkey* (No. 22492/93), 23 October 1998, para. 52; *Aydin* v. *Turkey* (No. 23178/94), 7 March 1996, paras. 59, 183; *Nsangu* v. *Austria* (No. 25661/94), 22 May 1995, para. 51; *Bahaddar* v. *the Netherlands* (No. 25894/92), 13 September 1996, paras. 37, 51–55, 58–63; *Paez* v. *Sweden* (No. 29482/95), 6 December 1996, paras. 26, 40–45. The case of *Aydin* v. *Turkey* was also examined by the Court, see below. See also Harris, O'Boyle and Warbrick, *Law of the European Convention on Human Rights*, p. 589.

[133] In the case of *Paez* v. *Sweden*, the NGO material was cited at length, see *Paez* v. *Sweden* (No. 29482/95), 6 December 1996, paras. 40–45. In the case of *Gündem* v. *Turkey*, at least some evidential value was attributed to the NGO material, see *Gündem* v. *Turkey* (No. 22275/93), 3 September 1996, para. 147.

[134] He was also represented by a solicitor and a barrister. *Sutherland* v. *The United Kingdom* (Application No. 25186/94), 1 July 1997, para. 2.

NON-PARTY PARTICIPATION   329

not surprising that there were limited possibilities for *amicus* submissions.[135] The first request from a non-party to submit information was made in 1978 in the case of *Tyrer v. the United Kingdom*.[136] The National Council for Civil Liberties, which had represented the applicant before the Commission, asked for leave to file a written memorandum and make oral submissions, but was refused by a chamber of the Court without explanation.[137] The first time a permission to intervene was granted was in 1979, when the United Kingdom was allowed to submit written information to be presented before the Court by delegates of the Commission in the case of *Winterwerp v. The Netherlands*.[138] This submission was made under Rule 38(1), which provided that the Chamber could decide to hear any person whose evidence or statements seemed likely to assist it, either at the request of a Party or the Commission, or *proprio motu*. In the case of *Young, James and Webster v. the United Kingdom* the Court for the first time accepted information submitted by an NGO, the Trades Union Congress (TUC), using the same procedure as for the UK intervention in the *Winterwerp* case.[139] A representative of the TUC was also allowed to make a presentation during the oral proceedings.[140]

In 1989, the Court amended its Rules of Procedure, incorporating a somewhat more permissive provision on non-party submissions:

The President may, in the interest of the proper administration of justice, invite or grant leave to any Contracting State which is not a party to the proceedings to submit written comments within a time-limit and on issues which he shall specify. He may extend such an invitation or grant such leave to any person concerned other than the applicant.[141]

This provision remained in force until the coming into force of the 11th Protocol in 1998. Under the old system, the scope of *amicus* interventions was in other words restricted to the submission of written comments on issues specified by the President of the Court. It was also

---

[135] On the other hand, the Inter-American Court of Human Rights has an extensive *amicus* practice, although only the Inter-American Commission or state parties can refer cases to the Court, see section 6.7.
[136] The European Court of Human Rights, *Tyrer v. the United Kingdom*, 24 April 1978.
[137] Shelton, 'The Participation of Nongovernmental Organizations', p. 630.
[138] *Winterwerp v. the Netherlands*, 24 October 1979, para. 7 and Shelton, 'The Participation of Nongovernmental Organizations', pp. 630–631.
[139] *Young, James and Webster v. The United Kingdom*, 13 August 1981, para. 8 and Shelton, 'The Participation of Nongovernmental Organizations', p. 631.
[140] *Young, James and Webster v. The United Kingdom*, 13 August 1981, paras. 8–9.
[141] European Court of Human Rights, *Rules of Court A* (as in force at 1 February 1994), Article 37(2).

330   LEGAL AND EMPIRICAL SURVEY

a requirement for leave to be granted that the intervenor could demonstrate a discernible interest in the case – that the person was 'concerned' by the case. In the case of *Malone* v. *the United Kingdom*, which dealt with alleged interference with telephone communications, the Post Office Engineering Union requested leave to submit written comments indicating its 'specific occupational interest' in the case and was granted leave to file a brief.[142] In the case of *Ashingdane* v. *the UK*, the National Association for Mental Health (MIND) was granted leave to submit comments in a case regarding the detention of a person in a psychiatric hospital. The President specified, however, that the comments should be strictly limited to certain matters which were closely connected with the case.[143]

The other requisite for leave to be granted was that the submission of an *amicus* brief was 'in the interest of the proper administration of justice'.[144] The rationale in this regard was that the Court should have as full information as possible before judging on the case. This seems to have been the ground for the leave granted to NGOs with special expertise related to the central issue of the case. One example is the intervention of Amnesty International in the case of *Soering* v. *the United Kingdom*, which concerned the decision to extradite the applicant from the United Kingdom to the United States where he suffered the risk of being sentenced to death.[145] The President did on many other occasions grant leave to NGOs with special expertise to intervene as *amicus curiae* with written comments on questions at issue in the case. From 1959 to the end of September 1998, the Court delivered 1,009 judgements. *Amicus curiae* briefs were filed by NGOs in at least thirty-six of these cases.[146]

---

[142] The President granted leave only 'in so far as such matters relate to the particular issues of alleged violation of the Convention which are before the Court for decision in the Malone case'. *Malone* v. *The United Kingdom*, 2 August 1984, para. 8.
[143] *Ashingdane* v. *The United Kingdom*, 28 May 1985, para. 6.
[144] Harris, O'Boyle and Warbrick, *Law of the European Convention on Human Rights*, p. 669.
[145] European Court of Human Rights, *Soering* v. *the United Kingdom*, 7 July 1989. See also below.
[146] These cases have been identified through searches in the Council of Europe HUDOC database. Since the references to *amicus* interventions are similar in the cases, the search terms are relatively easy to identify. It is, however, not possible to exclude the eventuality that leave may have been granted also in other cases and that the reference has been phrased differently in the judgement. Apart from the thirty-six cases where leave for written comments has been granted, NGO material, such as country reports from Amnesty International, has been used by the applicants in other cases. In *Weeks* v. *The United Kingdom*, 2 March 1987, an NGO legal officer (of Justice, the British section of the International Commission of Jurists) acted as the applicant's counsel. The thirty-six cases in which *amicus curiae* briefs were filed are: *Malone* v. *The United Kingdom*, August 1984; *Ashingdane* v. *The United Kingdom*, 28 May 1985; *Lingens* v. *Austria*, 8 July

NON-PARTY PARTICIPATION   331

Among the intervenors the five most active NGOs were Amnesty International (nine interventions), Article 19 (the International Centre against Censorship: nine), Interights (eight), Liberty (eight) and Rights International (eight). All these organisations are human rights NGOs based in the United Kingdom, except for Rights International, which is based in New York. Gomien, Harris and Zwaak observed regarding the Court's procedures during this period that – bearing in mind the import- ance of the case-law of the Court for the formulation of a common European human rights standard – it was surprising that third-party inter- ventions were so few.[147] It can be mentioned in this context that legal aid was not available for the purpose of *amicus curiae* briefs.[148]

The cases where an intervention was admitted demonstrate that the written comments submitted by NGOs had an impact on the Court in some, but far from all, cases. In twenty of the thirty-six cases in which *amicus* briefs had been filed, the Court did not refer to the contents of the *amicus* submissions at all. In sixteen cases, the contents of the *amicus* briefs were mentioned in the judgement, and six of these included a more extensive description.[149] Amnesty International was involved in all but one of the cases where a more elaborate description of the

1986; *Monnell and Morris* v. *The United Kingdom*, 2 March 1987; *Capuano* v. *Italy*, 25 June 1987; *Brogan and Others* v. *The United Kingdom*, 29 November 1988; *Soering* v. *The United Kingdom*, 7 July 1989; *The Observer and the Guardian* v. *The United Kingdom*, 26 November 1991; *Sunday Times* v. *The United Kingdom*, 26 November 1991; *Open Door and Dublin Well Woman* v. *Ireland*, 29 October 1992; *Brannigan and McBride* v. *The United Kingdom*, 26 May 1993; *Infomationsverein Lentia and Others* v. *Austria*, 24 November 1993; *Otto- Preminger-Institut* v. *Austria*, 20 September 1994; *Jersild* v. *Denmark*, 23 September 1994; *Prager and Oberschlick* v. *Austria*, 26 April 1995; *McCann and Others* v. *The United Kingdom*, 27 September 1995; *John Murray* v. *The United Kingdom*, 8 February 1996; *Goodwin* v. *The United Kingdom*, 27 March 1996; *Akdivar and Others* v. *Turkey*, 16 September 1996; *Chahal* v. *The United Kingdom*, 15 November 1996; *Wingrove* v. *The United Kingdom*, 25 November 1996; *Saunders* v. *The United Kingdom*, 17 November 1996; *Laskey, Jaggard and Brown* v. *The United Kingdom*, 19 February 1997; *Gregory* v. *The United Kingdom*, 25 February 1997; *Mantovanelli* v. *France*, 18 March 1997; *X, Y and Z* v. *The United Kingdom*, 22 April 1997; *H. L. R.* v. *France*, 29 April 1997; *Halford* v. *The United Kingdom*, 25 June 1997; *Aydin* v. *Turkey*, 25 September 1997; *Kurt* v. *Turkey*, 25 May 1998; *Incal* v. *Turkey*, 9 June 1998; *Teixera de Castro* v. *Portugal*, 9 September 1998; *McGinley and Egan* v. *The United* Kingdom, 9 June 1998; *Sheffield and Horsham* v. *The United Kingdom*, 30 July 1998; *Ahmed and Others* v. *The United Kingdom*, 2 September 1998; and *Assenov* v. *Bulgaria*, 28 October 1998.

[147] Gomien, Harris and Zwaak, *Law and Practice of the European Convention*, p. 81.
[148] Harris, O'Boyle and Warbrick, *Law of the European Convention on Human Rights*, p. 669.
[149] The six cases were *Brannigan and McBride* v. *The United Kingdom*, 26 May 1993; *John Murray* v. *The United Kingdom* 8 February 1996; *Chahal* v. *The United Kingdom*, 15 November 1996; *Aydin* v. *Turkey*, 25 September 1997; *Kurt* v. *Turkey*, 25 May 1998; *Sheffield and Horsham* v. *The United Kingdom*, 30 July 1998.

332   LEGAL AND EMPIRICAL SURVEY

brief was made in the judgement. Of the nine cases where Amnesty International made an intervention, its comments were at least briefly described in eight.[150]

The *amicus* briefs can be divided into two categories: statements regarding the facts and statements regarding relevant law. From the perspective of legal personality, it can be argued that statements on legal issues are more relevant as, to the extent that they are referred to by the Court, they indicate an influence on the interpretation and development of international law. However, statements regarding facts are not irrelevant. Even though an NGO might choose to intervene in a case of great interest with important information regarding facts – i.e. the treatment of prisoners in a certain country – its underlying interest might be that the Court clarifies or develops a certain area of the law.

It would be valuable therefore to take a closer look at a few examples of the cases where *amicus curiae* briefs have been filed by NGOs.

In the case of *Brannigan and McBride* v. *the United Kingdom* (1993) the applicants complained that they had not been brought promptly before a judge during detention in breach of Article 5(3). They also complained that they did not have an enforceable right to compensation in breach of Article 5(5), and that there was no effective remedy in respect to their complaints in breach of Article 13.[151]

The detentions occurred in Northern Ireland under the 1984 Act, which proscribed the Irish Republican Army (IRA) and conferred special powers of arrest and detention on the police in order to deal with terrorism. In 1988, the UK government had used the possibility under Article 15(1) of the Convention to derogate in times of emergency from the obligations imposed by Article 5(3) to the extent that the exercise of powers under the 1984 Act might be inconsistent with the Convention.

The President of the Court granted leave to Amnesty International and the Northern Ireland Standing Advisory Commission on Human Rights to submit *amicus* briefs. Interights, Liberty and the Committee on the Administration of Justice were also granted leave to submit a joint written statement.[152]

Amnesty International maintained in its submission that strict scrutiny was required by the Court when examining derogation from fundamental procedural guarantees which were essential for the protection of detainees at all times, and

---

[150] Out of the eight *amicus* briefs filed by Rights International, none was described or referred to in the judgement, while the contents of the briefs submitted by Interights were briefly discussed in one of the eight cases in which it filed a brief.

[151] *Brannigan and McBride* v. *The United Kingdom*, 26 May 1993.   [152] *Ibid.*, para. 5.

particularly in times of emergency. Liberty, Interights and the Committee on the Administration of Justice ('Liberty and Others') submitted that, if states were to be allowed a margin of appreciation at all, it should be narrower the more permanent an emergency becomes. The Court found that the contracting parties had a wide, but not unlimited, margin of appreciation in determining both the presence of an emergency and the nature and the scope of derogations necessary to avert it. In examining the question whether the state had gone beyond what was strictly required by the exigencies of the crisis, the nature of the rights affected by the derogation, the circumstances leading to and the duration of the emergency situation should be taken into account.[153]

Concerning the question of a public emergency, it was suggested by Liberty and Others in their written submissions that at the relevant time there was no longer any evidence of an exceptional situation of crisis. In the view of the Standing Advisory Commission on Human Rights, on the other hand, there was a public emergency in Northern Ireland at the relevant time of a sufficient magnitude to entitle the government to derogate. The Court considered there could be no doubt that such a public emergency existed at the relevant time.[154]

As regards safeguards against abuse of detention power, Liberty and Others and Amnesty International maintained that the safeguards were negligible and that during the period of detention the detainee was completely cut off from the outside world. Amnesty International stressed that international standards ruled out *incommunicado* detention by requiring access to lawyers and members of the family, and submitted that being brought promptly before a judicial authority in accordance with Article 5(4) was especially important since in Northern Ireland *habeas corpus* had been shown to be ineffective in practice. In the view of Amnesty International, Article 5(4) should be considered non-derogable in times of public emergency. The Court found that, although submissions had been made by the applicants and the NGOs concerning the absence of effective safeguards against abuse, such safeguards did in fact exist and provided an important measure of protection against arbitrary behaviour and *incommunicado* detention.[155]

It came to the conclusion that the government had not exceeded its margin of appreciation. The derogation was strictly required by the exigencies of the situation and satisfied the requirements of Article 15. The applicants could therefore not validly complain of a violation of Article 5(3). It followed that there was no obligation under Article 5(5) to provide the applicants with an enforceable right to compensation. The Court found no breach of Article 13.[156]

The fact that the Court described the arguments of the NGOs indicates that their viewpoints were considered. However, the majority was not

---

[153] *Ibid.*, paras. 42–43.   [154] *Ibid.*, paras. 45, 47.   [155] *Ibid.*, paras. 61–62.
[156] *Ibid.*, paras. 62–76.

334 LEGAL AND EMPIRICAL SURVEY

convinced by them. Two of the separate opinions gave considerable support to NGOs, however.

Judge Pettiti cited the Amnesty statement at length in his Dissenting Opinion. He concluded, in accordance with this statement, that international law prohibits *incommunicado* detention.[157] Judge Martens took the *amicus curiae* briefs into serious consideration in his concurring opinion. He stated, *inter alia*, that:

'I would add, however, that I have voted in this way only after considerable hesitations. I was impressed by Amnesty International's argument that under a derogation regular judicial review of extended detention is an essential guarantee to protect the detainee from unacceptable treatment – a risk which is all the greater where there is the possibility of *incommunicado* detention – even if the procedure to be followed does not meet fully the requirements implied in Article 5 para. 3 ... For my part, I found Amnesty International's arguments against so deciding persuasive, especially where Amnesty emphasised developments in international standards and practice in answer to world-wide human rights abuses under cover of derogation and underlined the importance of the present ruling in other parts of the world. Consequently, I regret that the Court's only refutation of those arguments is its reference to a precedent which is fifteen years old.'

Judge Martens wrote further: 'However that may be, the old formula was also criticised as unsatisfactory *per se* both by Amnesty International and Liberty, Interights and the Committee on the Administration of Justice, the latter referring to the 1990 Queensland Guidelines of the ILA (International Law Association). I agree with these criticisms.'[158]

The judgement in the case of *Chahal* v. *the United Kingdom* (1996) provides a good description of how an *amicus curiae* brief regarding facts and law can be used by the Court.[159]

The case concerned four applicants belonging to a Sikh family from the Punjab province in India. The first applicant, the father and an Indian citizen, complained, *inter alia*, that the UK authorities' decision to deport him to India would expose him to a real risk of torture or inhuman or degrading treatment in violation of Article 3 of the Convention. The background to the complaint was that the UK Home Secretary had decided that Mr Chahal should be deported, as his continued presence in the UK was unconducive to the public good for reasons of national security and other reasons of a political nature, namely

---

[157] *Ibid.*, Dissenting Opinion of Judge Pettiti.
[158] *Ibid.*, Dissenting Opinion of Judge Martens, paras. 1, 3, 4.
[159] *Chahal* v. *The United Kingdom*, 15 November 1996.

the international fight against terrorism. A couple of days later, Mr Chahal applied for asylum, in the United Kingdom. All the applicants also alleged breaches of Article 8 and that they had not been provided with effective remedies before the national courts in breach of Article 13 of the Convention. They maintained that the only remedy available to them in respect of their claims was judicial review and an advisory panel procedure, none of which was a 'remedy', nor 'effective'.[160]

Amicus briefs were filed in the case by Amnesty International, Justice and by Liberty jointly with the Centre for Advice on Individual Rights in Europe (the AIRE Centre) and the Joint Council for the Welfare of Immigrants (JCWI), all London-based human rights organisations.[161] Amnesty International also submitted two reports alleging that the Punjab police was known to have carried out abductions and executions of suspected Sikh militants in other Indian states outside their jurisdiction, and that high-profile individuals continued to 'disappear' in police custody.[162]

As regards the government's argument that Article 3 could be subject to implied limitations under exceptional circumstances, such as a threat to national security, Amnesty International held that such an argument was erroneous and dangerous, and that no derogation was allowed.[163] This view was shared by Liberty.[164] The Court came to the same conclusion after a brief reference to the *amicus* briefs.[165]

In its written submission, Amnesty also informed the Court that prominent Sikh separatists still faced a serious risk of disappearance, detention without charge or trial, torture and extra-judicial execution, frequently at the hands of the Punjab police.[166] The government urged the Court to proceed with caution in relation to the reports prepared by Amnesty International since it was not possible to verify the facts of the cases referred to and since the situation in Punjab had changed in recent years.[167] The Court, however, stated that it attached 'weight to some of the most striking allegations contained in those reports, particularly with regard to extra-judicial killings allegedly perpetrated by the Punjab police outside their home State'.[168] It also referred to a judgement by the UK Immigration Appeal Tribunal in another case and to materials from the US State Department and the National Human Rights Commission for

---

[160] *Ibid.*, paras. 12, 68.   [161] *Ibid.*, para. 6.

[162] *Punjab Police: Beyond the Bounds of the Law*, Amnesty International, May 1995 and *India: Determining the Fate of 'Disappeared' in Punjab*, Amnesty International, October 1995. *Chahal v. The United Kingdom*, 15 November 1996, paras. 55–56.

[163] Written comments submitted by Amnesty International, received at the Court's Registry on 15 January 1996, pp. 5–6.

[164] Written comments submitted by Liberty, received at the Court's Registry on 24 January 1996, pp. 7–11.

[165] *Chahal v. The United Kingdom*, 15 November 1996, paras. 78–81.

[166] *Ibid.*, paras. 89–90.   [167] *Ibid.*, para. 90.   [168] *Ibid.*, para. 99.

336   LEGAL AND EMPIRICAL SURVEY

assessing the situation in Punjab.[169] After a description of these different reports, the Court stated that it was 'persuaded by this evidence, which has been corroborated by material from a number of different objective sources'.[170] The Court found the allegations substantiated that there was a real risk of Mr Chahal being subjected to treatment contrary to Article 3 and that the order for Mr Chahal's deportation to India would, if executed, give rise to a violation of the Article.[171]

As regards the question of alleged violation of Article 13, all of the *amicus curiae* were of the view that judicial review did not constitute an effective remedy in cases involving national security. Article 13 required at least that some independent body should be appraised of all the facts and evidence and entitled to reach a decision which would be binding on the Secretary of State. Amnesty International, Liberty, the AIRE Centre and JCWI drew the Court's attention to the procedure applied in Canada, where a Federal Court judge holds an *in camera* hearing of all the evidence, at which the applicant is provided with a statement summarising the case and has the right to be represented and to call evidence.[172] The government pointed out that in previous cases the Court had held that Article 13 required only a remedy that was 'as effective as can be' in circumstances where national security considerations did not permit the divulging of certain sensitive information. The Court held, however, that the requirement of a remedy which is 'as effective as can be' was not appropriate in respect of a complaint that a person's deportation would expose him or her to a real risk of treatment in breach of Article 3, where the issues concerning national security were immaterial. In such cases the notion of an effective remedy required independent scrutiny of the claim that there existed substantial grounds for fearing a real risk of treatment contrary to Article 3. Such scrutiny need not be provided by a judicial authority. After a discussion on the powers and guarantees afforded by the judicial review and the advisory panel used in the United Kingdom, the Court reached the conclusion that the remedies taken together did not satisfy the requirements of Article 13.[173]

As in the case of *Brannigan and McBride*, the Court described the arguments of the *amicus curiae* in the judgement at some length. It seems clear that at least the statements of facts submitted by Amnesty International as regards the situation in Punjab had some influence on the Court's findings.

---

[169] *Ibid.*   [170] *Ibid.*, para. 100.   [171] *Ibid.*, para. 107.   [172] *Ibid.*, para. 144.

[173] *Ibid.*, paras. 150–155. See further Iain Cameron, *National Security and the European Convention on Human Rights*, The Hague and Uppsala: Kluwer Law International/Iustus Förlag, 2000, pp. 270–276.

In the case of *John Murray* v. *the United Kingdom* (1996), Amnesty International and Justice – the British Section of the International Commission of Jurists – were granted leave to submit written comments. Briefs were also submitted jointly by the Committee on the Administration of Justice, Liberty and British–Irish Rights Watch 'Liberty and Others'.[174]

The case concerned a British citizen, John Murray, who alleged that his rights under Article 6 of the Convention had been violated for two reasons. First, he had been deprived of the right to silence in the criminal proceedings against him. Secondly, his right of access to a solicitor during his detention had been violated. Moreover, he alleged that the fact that the practice concerning access to solicitors differed between Northern Ireland, England and Wales was in violation of Article 14 of the Convention.

Amnesty International submitted that permitting adverse inferences to be drawn from the silence of the accused was an effective means of compulsion which shifted the burden of proof from the prosecution to the accused and was inconsistent with the right not to be compelled to testify against oneself or to confess guilt. Amnesty pointed out that Article 14(3g) of the ICCPR explicitly provides that an accused shall 'not be compelled to testify against himself or to confess guilt', and also referred to other international legal instruments protecting the right to remain silent. Liberty and Others made a submission of similar content, while Justice stressed that such encroachments on the right to silence increased the risk of miscarriages of justice.[175]

The Court stated that there could be no doubt that the right to remain silent under police questioning and the privilege against self-incrimination were generally recognised international standards which lay at the heart of the notion of a fair procedure under Article 6. It held, however, that the question whether the right to silence was absolute must be answered in the negative. It could not be said therefore that a decision on the part of the accused to remain silent throughout criminal proceedings should necessarily have no implications when the trial court sought to evaluate the evidence against him. In conclusion, the Court did not consider that the criminal proceedings were unfair or that there had been an infringement of the presumption of innocence. Accordingly, there had been no violation of Articles 6(1) or 6(2).[176]

The applicant also submitted that he had been denied access to any legal advice for forty-eight hours, and had been interviewed on twelve occasions without a solicitor being present to represent his interests. Amnesty International and Liberty and Others stressed that access to a lawyer when in police custody is an integral part of well-established international standards

---

[174] *John Murray* v. *The United Kingdom*, 8 February 1996, para. 5.
[175] *Ibid.*, para. 42.   [176] *Ibid.*, paras. 44–58.

338 LEGAL AND EMPIRICAL SURVEY

concerning protection against the dangers of *incommunicado* detention. It was also a vital element in enabling access to the procedural guarantees of the courts in respect of illegal detention. Both submissions stressed, *inter alia*, that in the context of Northern Ireland where adverse inferences could be drawn from the applicant's failure to answer questions by the police it was particularly important to be assisted by a solicitor at an early stage. The Court observed that it had not been disputed by the government that Article 6 applied even at the stage of the preliminary investigation into an offence by the police. It found that the applicant had undoubtedly been directly affected by the denial of access and the ensuing interference with the right to defence and concluded that there had been a breach of Article 6(1) in conjunction with 6(3) as regards the applicant's denial of access to a lawyer during the first forty-eight hours of his police detention.[177]

The NGO submissions were described in detail in the judgement and the Court seems to have taken the arguments put forward into account. In the end, however, it reached a conclusion regarding the right to silence which differed from those of Amnesty as well as the other NGOs. As regards the argument on the issue of access to a lawyer, the *amicus* briefs focused on the right to access to lawyer in itself, without discussing the actual effects of the forty-eight hours of denial. Since the government had not questioned that the applicant had the right to access to a lawyer during the whole of the proceedings, the arguments put forward in the briefs were not relevant in the Court's discussion.

The case of *Aydin* v. *Turkey* (1997) originated in an application filed by a Turkish woman of Kurdish origin.[178]

Evidence proved beyond reasonable doubt that the applicant had been raped by a state official and that she had also been subjected to other forms of physical and mental suffering. Amnesty International intervened in the case with an *amicus* brief observing that the rape of a female detainee by an agent of the state for purposes such as the extraction of information or confessions or the humiliation, punishment or intimidation of the victim was considered as an act of torture under current interpretations of international human rights standards.[179] The Court did not refer to the *amicus* brief in its assessment. It found, however, that 'the accumulation of acts of violence inflicted on the applicant and the especially cruel act of rape to which she was subjected amounted to torture in breach of Article 3 of the Convention', and added that it would have reached that conclusion on either of those grounds taken separately.[180] It is

---

[177] *Ibid.*, paras. 59–70.   [178] *Aydin* v. *Turkey*, 25 September 1997.
[179] *Ibid.*, para. 51.   [180] *Ibid.*, para. 86.

impossible to conclude from the text of the judgement what impact Amnesty's brief had on the Court's reasoning.

The case of *Sheffield and Horsham* v. *the United Kingdom* (1998) concerned two transsexual persons who had changed sex.[181]

The applicants argued that refusal on the part of the United Kingdom to annotate or update information inscribed on the register of birth to take account of post-operative gender status constituted a breach of Article 8 of the Convention, since this refusal led to situations where the applicants had to disclose their previous names.[182] The applicants also argued violations of Articles 12, 14 and 13. The London-based NGO Liberty filed an *amicus* brief containing a comparative legal study on the legal recognition of transsexuals. Liberty suggested that there had been an unmistakably clear trend in the member states of the Council of Europe towards giving full recognition to gender reassignment. The organisation found that, out of thirty-seven countries analysed, only four (including the United Kingdom) did not permit a change to be made in a person's birth certificate to reflect the re-assigned sex of the person.[183]

The findings of the *amicus* brief were described in the judgement under the heading 'Other relevant materials'. The Court discussed Liberty's investigation, but was 'not fully satisfied that the legislative trends outlined by *amicus* suffice to establish the existence of any common European approach to the problems created by the recognition in law of post-operative gender status'. 'In particular', the Court stated, 'the survey does not indicate that there is yet any common approach as to how to address the repercussions which the legal recognition of sex may entail for other areas of law'.[184]

The Court did thus not seem to question the trustworthiness of the investigation, although it considered that its scope was too narrow. The Court held, by 11 votes to 9, that there had been no violation of Article 8. A joint partly dissenting opinion was filed by seven judges. This minority put considerable weight on the *amicus* brief:

Today, according to information submitted by Liberty in this case, twenty-three member States (out of thirty-seven surveyed) permit such birth-certificate entries in respect of post-operative transsexuals and only four countries ... expressly prohibit any change. The position in the remaining States is

---

[181] *Sheffield and Horsham* v. *The United Kingdom*, 30 July 1998.
[182] In the judgement, the terms 'sex' and 'gender' are used alternately; see, e.g., paras. 12–13.
[183] *Sheffield and Horsham* v. *The United Kingdom*, 30 July 1998, para. 35.
[184] *Ibid.*, para. 57.

340   LEGAL AND EMPIRICAL SURVEY

not clear. These figures in themselves – without needing to go into the varying details of such legislation – demonstrate convincingly that the problems of such transsexuals are being dealt with in a respectful and dignified manner by a large number of Convention countries.[185]

In the case of *Kurt* v. *Turkey* (1998), Amnesty International filed an *amicus* brief on forced disappearances.

The applicant of the case was the mother of a man who had disappeared after having been seen with Turkish security forces in a village in south-east Turkey.[186] The applicant held the Turkish government responsible for her son's disappearance and claimed breaches of, *inter alia*, Articles 2, 3 and 5. The brief by Amnesty International was described in detail under the heading 'Relevant international material'. Amnesty made a general analysis of the crime of disappearances and referred to case-law from the UN Human Rights Committee and the Inter-American Court of Human Rights.[187] The Court did not explicitly refer to the brief in its assessment of the legal issues of the case. Because of lack of evidence, the Court did not find that there had been breaches of Articles 2 or 3.[188] It concluded that there had been a particularly grave violation of Article 5, but did not mention Amnesty's brief on disappearances in this part of the judgement.[189]

One example of a case where the *amicus* briefs were only briefly described is *Soering* v. *the United Kingdom* (1989), in which Amnesty International obtained leave to submit written comments.[190] The case concerned the possible extradition from the United Kingdom of the applicant, who had committed homicide in the United States and who, in the event of an extradition, suffered the risk of being sentenced to death and thereby exposed to the 'death row phenomenon' (i.e. that the time spent on death row is so long that it in itself amounts to cruel, inhuman or degrading treatment). Amnesty International argued that the evolving standards in Western Europe regarding the existence and use of the death penalty required that it should be considered as an

---

[185] *Ibid.*, Joint Partly Dissenting Opinion of Judges Bernhardt, Thór Vilhjálmsson, Spielmann, Palm, Wildhaber, Makarczyk and Voicu.

[186] *Kurt* v. *Turkey*, 25 May 1998.   [187] *Ibid.*, paras. 68–71.   [188] *Ibid.*, paras. 106–117.

[189] *Ibid.*, paras. 118–129.

[190] *Soering* v. *The United Kingdom*, 7 July 1989. For another example of a judgement where the *amicus* submission is briefly described, see *McCann* v. *The United Kingdom*, 7 July 1989, 27 September 1995, paras. 5, 157. In this case, Amnesty International, Liberty, Inquest, the Committee on the Administration of Justice and the British–Irish Rights Watch were granted leave to submit written comments.

NON-PARTY PARTICIPATION 341

inhuman and degrading punishment within the meaning of Article 3 of the Convention.[191] The Court referred to and cited Amnesty's brief, and concluded that the exposure of the applicant to the 'death row phenomenon' would in itself constitute a breach of Article 3.[192]

McGinley and Egan v. *United Kingdom* (1998) provides an example of the many cases where the comments submitted by NGOs were not mentioned at all in the judgement.[193] The case concerned two persons who had been exposed to radiation from UK nuclear tests on Christmas Island in the Pacific Ocean druing 1957–8. Written comments were submitted by Liberty and The Campaign for Freedom of Information, while the New Zealand Nuclear Test Veterans' Association was refused leave to intervene.

The Court has refused leave for NGOs to submit *amicus curiae* briefs on several occasions. This happened in, *inter alia*, the case of *Modinos* v. *Cyprus* (1993), when the International Lesbian and Gay Association sought leave to submit written comments, but was refused.[194] In Harris, O'Boyle and Warbrick's guide to the Court's case-law, as well as in Gomien, Harris and Zwaak's book, it is presumed that the intervention was considered unnecessary because there was already settled case-law on the issue in focus of the case.[195] The Court has refused all applications from NGOs for leave to submit written statements in at least another five cases during the period before the Single Court system.[196]

In the case of *Young, James and Webster* v. *the United Kingdom* (1981) another kind of NGO intervention was made.[197] The Court decided *proprio motu*, in pursuance of Rule 38, para. 1, that during the oral proceedings it would hear, on certain questions of fact (including English law and practice) and for the purpose of information, a representative of the British TUC.[198] The case concerned a 'closed shop' agreement between British Rail and three trade unions, providing that membership of one of those unions was a condition for employment. The British TUC therefore had a close connection with the case. The organisation filed a memorial

---

[191] *Ibid.*, para. 101.   [192] *Ibid.*, paras. 102, 111.

[193] *McGinley and Egan* v. *The United Kingdom*, 9 June 1998.

[194] *Modinos* v. *Cyprus*, 22 April 1993, para. 4.

[195] Harris, O'Boyle and Warbrick, *Law of the European Convention on Human Rights*, p. 670; Gomien, Harris and Zwaak, *Law and Practice of the European Convention*, p. 81.

[196] These cases are: *Glasenapp* v. *Germany*, 28 August 1986; *Kosiek* v. *Germany*, 28 August 1986; *Y* v. *The United Kingdom*, 29 October 1992; *Ahmet Sadik* v. *Greece*, 15 November 1996; *Van Mechelen* v. *The Netherlands*, 23 April 1997.

[197] *Young, James and Webster* v. *The United Kingdom*, 13 August 1981.   [198] *Ibid.*, para. 8.

342   LEGAL AND EMPIRICAL SURVEY

with submissions on fact and law, and the Court decided that it would take the document into account as regarded factual information.[199]

When Protocol No. 11 entered into force in 1998, a new article on third-party intervention was incorporated into the Convention. According to Article 36(2):

The President of the Court may, in the interest of the proper administration of justice, invite any High Contracting Party which is not a party to the proceedings or any person concerned who is not the applicant to submit written comments or take part in hearings.

Thus, *amicus* participation which was earlier regulated only in the Rules has now become a permanent arrangement explicitly recognised by the parties to the Convention. Article 61(3) of the new Rules of Procedure, states that:

In accordance with Article 36(2) of the Convention, the President of the Chamber may, in the interests of the proper administration of justice, invite or grant leave to any Contracting State which is not a party to the proceedings, or any person concerned who is not the applicant, to submit written comments or, in exceptional cases, to take part in a hearing. Requests for leave for this purpose must be duly reasoned and submitted in one of the official languages, within a reasonable time after the fixing of the written procedure.[200]

As compared to the former rule on third-party intervention, which was found in Rule 37(2), the new Rules are more generous towards non-parties, as they explicitly provide for the possibility of taking part in a hearing. Apart from that, the content of the rule is the same in the old and new versions of the Rules, although the wordings are not identical.[201] Both Rules provide that an invitation or granting of leave to a third- or non-party shall be in the 'interest of the proper administration of justice', and both Rules state that a person should be 'concerned' in order to be invited or granted leave.

It can also be observed that there are possibilities for NGOs to participate in proceedings before the Court under Rule 42 on Measures for taking evidence. According to para. 1, a Chamber of the Court may, at the request of a party or a third party, or of its own motion, obtain any

---

[199] *Ibid.*, para. 10.
[200] European Court of Human Rights, *Rules of Court*, Strasbourg 1999 (As in force at 1 November 1998).
[201] European Court of Human Rights, *Rules of Court A*, Strasbourg 1990 (as in force at 1 February 1994), Rule 37(2).

NON-PARTY PARTICIPATION   343

evidence which it considers capable of providing clarification of the facts of the case. The Chamber may decide to hear as a witness or expert or in any other capacity any person whose evidence or statements seem likely to assist it in the carrying out of its tasks. Under Rule 42(3), it may also ask any person or institution of its choice to obtain information, express an opinion or make a report on any specific point.

Since the new Court became operational on 1 November 1998 until September 2004, NGOs have submitted *amicus* briefs in at least thirty-one cases.[202] In nine of these, the contents of the *amicus* submissions were not described in the judgement, while there was a short account of the NGOs' arguments in twelve cases. The remaining judgements included a more thorough description of the *amicus* submissions. It seems to have become a practice in recent years to include a special section with a rather detailed description of *amicus* submissions in the judgement, while these submissions are not explicitly referred to in the evaluating section.[203] As before 1998, some NGOs, such as the European Roma Human Rights Centre, Liberty and Interights, have acted as *amici* in several cases. Some NGOs also sometimes act as the victim's representative – for example, the Kurdish Human Rights Project, Lawyers for Human Rights, the AIRE Centre and Liberty.[204]

---

[202] The cases were *Beer and Regan v. Germany*, 18 February 1999; *T. v. The United Kingdom*, 16 December 1999; *Waite and Kennedy v. Germany*, 18 February 1999; *V v. The United Kingdom*, 16 December 1999; *Khan v. The United Kingdom*, 12 May 2000; *Cha'are Timurtas v. Turkey*, 13 June 2000; *Shalom Ve Tsedek v. France*, 27 June 2000; *Chapman v. The United Kingdom, Beard v. The United Kingdom, Coster v. The United Kingdom, Lee v. The United Kingdom* and *Jane Smith v. The United Kingdom*, all 18 January 2001; *T. P. and K. M. v. The United Kingdom*, 10 May 2001; *Z and Others v. The United Kingdom*, 10 May 2001; *Sadak and Others v. Turkey*, 17 July 2001; *Nikula v. Finland*, 21 March 2002; *Pretty v. The United Kingdom*, 29 April 2002; *Kingsley v. The United Kingdom*, 28 May 2002; *Sadak and Others v. Turkey (No. 2)*, 11 June 2002; *I v. The United Kingdom*, 11 July 2002; *Christine Goodwin v. The United Kingdom*, 11 July 2002; *Mamatkulov and Abdurasulovic v. Turkey*, 6 February 2003; *Sylvester v. Austria*, 24 April 2003; *Tahsin Acar v. Turkey*, 6 May 2003; *Pedersen and Baadsgaard v. Denmark*, 19 June 2003; *Hatton and Others v. The United Kingdom*, 8 July 2003; *Karner v. Austria*, 24 July 2003; *M. C. v. Bulgaria*, 4 December 2003; *Nachova and Others v. Bulgaria*, 26 February 2004; *von Hannover v. Germany*, 24 June 2004; *Vo v. France*, 8 July 2004.

[203] See, e.g., *Nikula v. Finland*, 21 May 2002; *Pretty v. The United Kingdom*, 29 April 2002; *I v. The United Kingdom* and *Christine Goodwin v. The United Kingdom*, 11 July 2002; *Sylvester v. Austria*, 24 April 2003; *Tahsin Acar v. Turkey*, 6 May 2003; *Pedersen and Baadsgaard v. Denmark*, 19 June 2003; *M. C. v. Bulgaria*, 4 December 2003; *Nachova and Others v. Bulgaria*, 26 February 2004; *Vo v. France*, 8 July 2004.

[204] *Binbay v. Turkey*, 21 October 2004; *Michael Edward Cooke v. Austria*, 18 February 2000; *T. P. and K. M. v. The United Kingdom*, 10 May 2001; *A v. The United Kingdom*, 17 December 2002; and *Prodan v. Moldova*, 18 May 2004.

344 LEGAL AND EMPIRICAL SURVEY

After having examined the different cases of *amicus curiae* participation of NGOs before the Court since the coming into force of the Single Court system, a couple of points can be raised concerning the Court's interpretation of the two requisites for such participation contained in Article 36(2) of the Convention. As described above, the President of the Court may grant such leave (i) when this is in the interest of the proper administration of justice, and (ii) when leave is sought by 'any High Contracting Party which is not a party to the proceedings or any person concerned who is not the applicant'. The idea behind the first condition is clear, and it seems to be rather easily met by NGOs that are specialised in a particular area. On the other hand, the requirement that an intervenor be 'concerned' is somewhat more surprising. In a couple of older cases from the time before the possibility of *amicus* participation was incorporated into the Convention, the condition of being 'concerned' (which was contained in the Rules of Procedure) was more strictly interpreted.[205] In more recent years, the Court does not seem to require more in this regard than a general interest in the issue of the case. The question of being 'concerned' is discussed in one of the more recent cases where three NGOs sought leave to intervene. In the case of *Karner* v. *Austria*, where leave was sought by ILGA-Europe (the European Region of the International Lesbian and Gay Association), Liberty and Stonewall, the Court stated that:

> The Court considers that the subject matter of the present application – the difference in treatment of homosexuals as regards succession to tenancies under Austrian law – involves an important question of general interest not only for Austria but also for other Member States of the Convention. In this respect the Court refers to the submissions made by ILGA-Europe, Liberty and Stonewall, whose intervention in the proceedings as third parties was authorised *as it highlights the general importance of the issue*. Thus, the continued examination of the present application would contribute to elucidate, safeguard and develop the standards of protection under the Convention.[206]

It thus seems that more persons and organisations are 'concerned' when the issue at stake is of general importance. In sum, it can be concluded from this case as well as the other cases with *amicus curiae* interventions that the condition of being 'concerned' has been given a generous interpretation which allows for NGOs with a general interest in the issue to intervene, provided that this is in the interest of the proper

---

[205] See, e.g., *Malone* v. *The United Kingdom*, 2 August 1984, para. 8 and *Ashingdane* v. *The United Kingdom*, 28 May 1985; para. 6.
[206] *Karner* v. *Austria*, 24 July 2003; para. 27 (emphasis added).

administration of justice – i.e. that they can demonstrate specific knowledge which can be of assistance to the Court in reaching its decision.

It can be concluded regarding the European Court of Human Rights that, considering the high number of judgements delivered by the Court, *amicus curiae* submissions are not particularly frequent. On the other hand, leave is seldom refused when requested, and the Court seems to take the *amicus* briefs into account when leave has been granted. This is demonstrated by the fact that most judgements, in particular since 2002, include descriptions of the contents of the *amicus* briefs and that the arguments put forward are sometimes (although not often) commented on in the Court's own reasoning. It should, however, also be noted that many briefs are very detailed, which means that the descriptions that are made in the judgements are only a minor portion of what has actually been submitted.[207] It is also worth observing that submissions from the large and well-established NGOs often seem to be more seriously considered by the Court than briefs submitted by less well-known organisations.

6.6 The European Court of Justice

The Statute of the European Court of Justice, its Rules of Procedure, and the Rules of the Court of First Instance all lack an explicit legal basis for *amicus curiae* submissions. The Advocates General have been given a similar task within the framework of the ECJ itself, as they deliver impartial and independent opinions on cases brought before the Court. It can therefore be argued that there is less need, from the Court's point of view, for *amicus* submissions. Nevertheless, Article 40 of the Statute provides a possibility for intervention by states and Community institutions, and by persons with an interest in the case:

Member States and institutions of the Community may intervene in cases before the Court.

The same right shall be open to any other person establishing an interest in the result of any case submitted to the Court, save in cases between Member

---

[207] This is at least the case with the following briefs: *Written comments submitted by Interights and Article 19 in the case of Wingrove v. The United Kingdom; Third Party Intervention of Liberty, Interights and the Committee on the Administration of Justice in the case of Brannigan and McBride v. The United Kingdom; Written comments submitted by Justice in the case of Chahal v. The United Kingdom; Written comments submitted by Amnesty International in the case of Chahal v. The United Kingdom;* and *Written comments submitted by Liberty in the case of Chahal v. The United Kingdom.*

346   LEGAL AND EMPIRICAL SURVEY

States, between institutions of the Community or between Member States and institutions of the Community ...

Submissions made in an application to intervene shall be limited to supporting the submissions of one of the parties.[208]

This provision applies also to the CFI.[209] Evidently, the purpose of the provision is to give persons and entities a possibility to intervene in order to protect a previously established interest in the result of the case. This requirement contrasts with the possibilities for *amicus* participation before other international tribunals, such as the European Court of Human Rights or the ICTY, where the President of the Court may invite anyone to submit a statement, if this is in the interest of the proper administration of justice. Even though the initiative for such an *amicus* submission well may come from the intervenor, the basis for the intervention is the Court's interest that the information in the case be as complete as possible. The intervening person or body in such cases is a friend of the court, an *amicus curiae*, while the intervenor under Article 40 of the ECJ Statute seeks to protect proper interests in the case. The two categories of intervention thus have different purposes. I will therefore not use the term '*amicus curiae*' for interventions made in cases before the ECJ and the CFI.

According to Article 93(1)(f) of the Rules of the European Court of Justice, the applications for leave submitted under this provision must contain a statement explaining the circumstances establishing a right to intervene.[210] The level of interest must be direct and concrete. The signification of this requirement is well illustrated by the case of *CAS Succhi di Frutta SpA* v. *Commission of the European Communities*, in which the CFI stated that:

For the purposes of granting leave to intervene, the Community judicature must ascertain, in the case of an action for annulment, whether the applicant for such leave is directly affected by the contested decision and whether his interest in the result of the case is established. Similarly, the prospective intervener must establish a direct, existing interest in the grant of the order as sought and not an

---

[208] *Protocol on the Statute of the Court of Justice annexed to the Treaty on European Union*, signed at Nice on 26 February 2001, as last amended on 19 April 2004. As with section 5.3 on NGOs as parties before the ECJ and CFI, this survey will be limited to cases lodged under the EC Treaty.

[209] According to Article 53 of the Statute, Title III on Procedure shall apply to the CFI, with certain possibilities for modifications.

[210] *Rules of Procedure of the Court of Justice of the European Communities*, 19 June 1991, last amended on 8 April 2003.

interest in relation to the pleas in law put forward. The interest necessary in this respect must not relate merely to abstract legal arguments but to the actual form of order sought by a party to the main action. More specifically, it is necessary to distinguish between prospective interveners establishing a direct interest in the ruling on the specific act whose annulment is sought and those who can establish only an indirect interest in the result of the case by means of similarities between their situation and that of one of the parties.[211]

For an organisation wishing to intervene, it is required that it represents members who have a direct and concrete interest in the case.

The case of *Ludwigshafener Walzmühle Erling KG* v. *European Economic Community* concerned an action which had the purpose of obtaining compensation for loss which the applicants claimed to have suffered as a result of the Community having fixed an inappropriate price for durum wheat.[212] A trade union applied for leave to intervene stating that, depending on the outcome of the case, many skilled workers employed by the applicant undertakings stood to lose their employment and, as a result of the fixing of excessive prices for imports of durum wheat from non-member countries, a number of jobs had already been directly affected in previous years. The Court found that:

In its capacity as an organization representing workers employed in the industrial sector in which the applicant undertakings are engaged, the applicant trade union has no specific interest in any payment of compensation to those undertakings. The purpose of the union's application to intervene is to support judicial proceedings which, if successful, could have a favourable impact on the economic well-being of the undertakings in question and, consequently, on the number of persons they employ. Such an interest, which is indirect and remote in its nature, is not sufficiently clearly defined to justify intervention in the proceedings.[213]

An older case regarding consumers, *Générale Sucrière* v. *The Commission*, is of a more permissive character.[214]

The Unione Nazionale Consumatori (the National Consumers' Union of Italy) sought leave to intervene in the case, which concerned application of

---

[211] *CAS Succhi di Frutta SpA* v. *Commission of the European Communities*, Case T-191/96, Order of the Court of First Instance, 20 March 1998.
[212] *Ludwigshafener Walzmühle Erling KG* v. *European Economic Community*, Joined cases 197-200/80, 243, 245, 247/80, European Court of Justice, Order of the Court, 8 April 1981.
[213] *Ibid.*, paras. 8–9.
[214] *Société anonyme Générale Sucrière and Others* v. *Commission of the European Communities*, Joined cases 41/73, 43–48/73, 50/73, 111/73, 113/73, 114/73, European Court of Justice, Order of the Court, 11 December 1973.

community provisions in the field of competition in the Italian market. According to its statute, the Union's objective was 'the representation and protection ... of all Italian consumers ... in judicial proceedings', where 'the interests of the whole category of consumers or of a considerable part of the latter are in issue'. Further, it was the Union's intention to 'contribute to the abolition of obstacles imposed by the market and by institutions upon the free competition of producers and traders and upon the free and conscious choice of consumers'. The Court stated that 'since it is the particular objective of the union to represent and protect consumers, it can show an interest in the correct application of community provisions in the field of competition, which not only ensure that the common market operates normally but which also tend to favour consumers ... Accordingly, the intervention must be permitted insofar as it supports the submissions of the commission with regard to its finding as to the protection of the Italian market'.[215]

Legal personality is not a condition for permission to intervene. The Court has held that an entity may intervene if it is sufficiently independent and responsible to function as a separate identity. In the case of *Générale Sucrière* v. *The Commission*, the Unione Nazionale Consumatori was admitted to intervene, although it was not a legal person. The Court held that 'bodies not having legal personality may be permitted to intervene if they display the characteristics which are at the foundation of such personality, in particular, the ability, however circumscribed, to undertake autonomous action and to assume liability'.[216]

Article 40 of the ECJ Statute provides a narrow scope for the intervenors' submissions: these 'shall be limited to supporting the submissions of one of the parties'. Moreover, interventions by private parties are allowed only in cases between another private party and a member state or Community institution. Nor can private parties intervene in actions for preliminary rulings, as these are not 'cases before the Court' within the meaning of Article 40, para. 1.[217] On the other hand, once an

---

[215] *Ibid.*, paras. 5, 7, 8. See also Richard Plender, 'Intervention', in Richard Plender (ed.), *European Courts: Practice and Precedents*, London: Sweet & Maxwell, 1997, p. 633.

[216] *Société anonyme Générale Sucrière and Others* v. *Commission of the European Communities*, Joined cases 41/73, 43–48/73, 50/73, 111/73, 113/73, 114/73, European Court of Justice, Order of the Court, 11 December 1973, para. 3. See also Chinkin, *Third Parties in International Law*, p. 221 and Shelton, 'The Participation of Nongovernmental Organizations', p. 629 (n. 117), and Plender, 'Intervention', p. 629.

[217] Chinkin, *Third Parties in International Law*, p. 220; Plender, 'Intervention', p. 615; Neville March Hunnings, *The European Courts*, London: Cartermill Publishing, 1996, p. 78.

intervention has been accepted, the intervenor is regarded as a party to the case. Documentation served on the parties is provided also to the intervening party, however with the possibility of omitting secret confidential documents.[218]

Because of the requirements for intervention in direct actions, it would be a matter of coincidence if an NGO had the possibility to intervene in a case of more general or political interest. Interventions have nonetheless been made by a great variety of associations and organisations. There are many examples of trade unions intervening, which is a category of cases which often involve issues of great interest to many employees.

For example, the Union Syndicale-Bruxelles, which represented officials of the European Communities, applied for leave to intervene in the case of *Mireille Meskens* v. *European Parliament*.[219] The Union alleged that its members had given it general authority to defend by all legal means their professional interests, both economic and non-material, where those interests were common. It considered that the pleas in law put forward by the applicant in support of her action raised questions of principle relating to the organisation of the European civil service. The defendant expressed reservations with regard to the intervention, stating that the Union had not established an interest in taking part in the proceedings. The CFI stated that:

The question as to what are the duties of a Community institution following the annulment of a decision rejecting the application of some of its staff to take part in a competition comes within the sphere of collective interests the defence of which is one of the objects of the Union Syndicale, as stated in its statutes. In those circumstances, the Union Syndicale's application to intervene must be granted.[220]

---

[218] Rules of Procedure, Article 93(3).

[219] *Mireille Meskens* v. *European Parliament*, Case T-84/91, Order of the Court of First Instance, 12 March 1992.

[220] *Ibid.*, para. 14. Other examples of cases where trade unions have sought leave to intervene are *Ludwigshafener Walzmühle Erling KG* v. *European Economic Community*, Joined cases 197–200/80, 243, 245, 247/80, European Court of Justice, Order of the Court, 8 April 1981 (application dismissed as ill-founded) and *G. R. Amylum NV and Others* v. *Council and Commission of the European Communities*, Joined cases 116, 124, 143/77, European Court of Justice, Order of the Court, 12 April 1978. The ECJ rejected the application with the following argument: 'Since the third paragraph of Article 37 of the above-mentioned statute limits the conclusions contained in an application to intervene in support of the conclusions of one of the parties in the main action, it follows that the interest in question must exist in relation to the said conclusions and not in relation to the submissions or arguments put forward. This is not the case in the present proceedings': *Ibid.*, paras. 7–8.

350   LEGAL AND EMPIRICAL SURVEY

Other bodies which have sought leave to intervene include organisations of small enterprises, transport associations and producers' organisations of different kinds.[221]

It can be concluded that the scope for NGOs to advocate public interests through intervention in cases before the ECJ and the CFI is limited. Nevertheless, the Court's conclusion in the case of *Générale Sucrière* v. *The Commission* shows that representative organisations do have a possibility of showing an established interest within the field of their objective.

6.7 The Inter-American Commission and Court of Human Rights

The Inter-American Commission

The Commission occasionally permits *amicus* interventions by NGOs and other private bodies, in spite of the fact that an explicit legal basis for such submissions is lacking in the American Convention on Human Rights, the Commission's Statute and its Rules of Procedure.[222] In 2002, the Commission addressed the question of *amici curiae* in its *Annual Report*. In the case of *Mary and Carrie Dann* v. *United States*, there were *amicus* submissions from a number of entities and persons, including several tribes. The Commission stated that:

After having reviewed the requests for intervention set forth above and the related *amici* briefs, the Commission considered that they essentially reiterated arguments already presented by the Petitioners and accordingly did not require further processing in these proceedings.[223]

Although the Commission decided not to consider the *amici* briefs, it clearly confirmed its capacity to receive such briefs and to consider

---

[221] See, e.g., *Union Européenne de l'Artisanat et des Petites et Moyennes Entreprises (UEAPME)* v. *Council of the European Union*, Case T-135/96, Order of the Court of First Instance, 18 March 1997, *Atlantic Container Line AB and Others* v. *Commission of the European Communities*, Case T-395/94 R, Order of the President of the Court of First Instance, 10 March 1995 and *Asociación Española de Empresas de la Carne* v. *Council of the European Union*, Case T-99/94, Order of the Court of First Instance, 20 October 1994.

[222] American Convention on Human Rights (1969), *Statute of the Inter-American Commission on Human Rights*, adopted in October 1979, *Rules of Procedure of the Inter-American Commission On Human Rights*, adopted in December 2000. This has also been confirmed by a staff attorney with the Commission (e-mail message of 27 September 2001, on file with the author).

[223] OEA/Ser.L/V/II.117, *Annual Report of the Inter-American Commission on Human Rights 2002*, March 7, 2003, Report No. 75/02, para. 34.

them, when it wishes to. Despite the fact that there are otherwise very few explicit references to *amicus curiae* interventions in the *Annual Reports* of the Commission, material prepared by NGOs has been submitted in other cases, by both the petitioner and by the NGOs themselves.

In the case of *Amparo Tordecilla Trujillo* v. *Colombia*, the Commission received 'reports and information on the facts of the case from non-governmental human rights organizations such as Justice et Paix and Amnesty International'. Also, the *Colectivo de Abogados 'José Alvear Restrepo'* joined the case as a co-petitioner. The Commission did not refer to the NGO reports in its analysis of the merits of the case.[224]

Ignacio Ellacuría, S.J. et al. v. *El Salvador* originated in an application filed by the NGO Americas Watch. The petitioners presented a report prepared by the organisation Christian Legal Aid 'Archbishop Oscar Romero'. Subsequently, the Lawyers' Committee for Human Rights replaced Americas Watch as the petitioner in the case, and presented additional information.[225]

In *Desmond McKenzie* v. *Jamaica* and four other cases described in the same *Annual Report*, the petitioners filed material from various governmental and non-governmental organisations concerning prison conditions in Jamaica. In the *Carl Baker* case, material produced by Americas Watch, the Jamaica Council for Human Rights and Amnesty International was submitted. The Commission commented on the contents of this material in its analysis of the cases, citing a part of an Americas Watch Report. It noted that the respondent state had criticised the reports as being out of date and indicated that there had been improvements in prison conditions since the reports were prepared. The Commission observed that the state had, however, not provided the Commission with any specific information with regard to such improvements.[226]

In the case of *Rafael Ferrer-Mazorra et al.* v. *the United States*, the petitioner submitted two reports of the Minnesota Lawyers International Human Rights Committee.[227] The Commission did not refer to the material in its analysis of the case.

---

[224] OEA/Ser.L/V/II.106, *Annual Report of the Inter-American Commission on Human Rights 1999*, April 13, 2000, Report No. 7/00, *Amparo Tordecilla Trujillo* v. *Colombia*, para. 4.

[225] *Ibid.*, Report No. 136/99, *Ignacio Ellacuría, S.J. et al.* v. *El Salvador*, paras. 7–8.

[226] *Ibid.*, Report No. 41/00, *Desmond McKenzie et al.* v. *Jamaica*, paras. 9, 81–82, 275–276.

[227] OEA/Ser.L/V/II.111, *Annual Report of the Inter-American Commission on Human Rights 2000*, April 16, 2001, Report 51/01, *Rafael Ferrer-Mazorra et al.* v. *the United States*, paras. 19(d) and (f).

352   LEGAL AND EMPIRICAL SURVEY

It should be noted that it was only in the first of these cases that the NGOs themselves had submitted material, while in the other cases the petitioner used reports prepared by NGOs to support their claim.

A case report on admissibility from 1997 demonstrates that NGO participation in the Commission's proceedings can also take the form of oral expert intervention.

The case of María Eugenia Morales de Sierra v. Guatemala was instituted by means of a petition in abstracto concerning various provisions of the Guatemalan Civil Code, which allegedly created discriminatory distinctions between men and women within marriage in breach of Articles 2, 17 and 24 of the Convention. The petitioners later modified their communication and named María Eugenia Morales de Sierra as an individual victim. During a hearing on the question of admissibility, the petitioners produced three experts who testified as amici curiae to support the standing of María Eugenia Morales de Sierra as a direct victim in the case. The amici were experts from Interights, the Center for Civil and Human Rights at Notre Dame Law School, and one person representing both the International Women's Human Rights Law Clinic and the Concertación de Mujeres Activistas Para los Derechos Humanos. The experts, citing case-law from the monitoring bodies of the ECHR, asserted that members of a class targeted by legislation which is discriminatory on its face were to be considered victims for the purpose of bringing petitions. Interights also submitted written statements which are not mentioned in the Commission's report.[228] The state, for its part, indicated that María Eugenia Morales had not in reality suffered any harm by the disputed legislation.

The Commission stated that, with respect to its jurisdiction ratione personae, its competence under the individual case process pertained to facts involving the rights of a specific individual or individuals. With regard to the standing of the petitioner in the case as a victim, the Commission held that international jurisprudence had established that a law may violate the right of an individual, even in the absence of any specific measure of subsequent implementation by the authorities, if the individual is directly affected or is at imminent risk of being directly affected by a legislative provision. In this context, the Commission cited the same cases from the European Convention monitoring bodies as the amicus curiae had mentioned. The Commission concluded that the direct effect of the challenged legislative provisions on the rights and daily life of the victim had been adequately demonstrated, and declared the case admissible.[229]

---

[228] Written Comments Submitted by Interights, the International Centre for the Legal Protection of Human Rights, in Case No. 11.625 between María Eugenia Morales de Sierra and Guatemala, provided by the organisation.

[229] Annual Report of the Inter-American Commission on Human Rights 1997, February 17, 1998, Report No. 28/98, María Eugenia Sierra v. Guatemala. For the amicus curiae intervention, see para. 16.

It thus seems that the oral intervention of the NGOs influenced the Commission's conclusion in the case. The Commission's report on *Desmond McKenzie* and the other cases against Jamaica mentioned above give the same impression. It can also be mentioned that the Commission in a couple of other cases referred to an *amicus curiae* brief which Amnesty International had submitted in a case before the Inter-American Court.[230]

The report on the case of *Juan Carlos Abella v. Argentina* describes an interesting discussion on the value of NGO material.

The case concerned an attack that was carried out by forty-two armed persons against military barracks at La Tablada in the province of Buenos Aires in 1989. The attack precipitated a thirty-hour combat between the attackers and Argentine military personnel, resulting in the deaths of twenty-nine of the attackers and several state agents. In their complaint, the petitioners alleged, *inter alia*, that after the fighting had ceased, state agents participated in summary executions, the disappearance of several persons and the torture of a number of attackers. Amnesty International undertook a detailed study of the events at La Tablada, the relevant parts of which were used in the Commission's case report. The NGO carried out interviews, analysed autopsies with the help of forensic experts and gathered medical information on injuries on the detainees.

The state questioned Amnesty's report and the probative value which the Commission assigned to it, in so far as 'it cannot be assumed that it was prepared as thoroughly as a report of the Inter-American Commission on Human Rights would be'. The Commission stated:

The Commission will refer, firstly, to the probative value which it attaches to the report of Amnesty International, which was apparently challenged by the State as one of the elements of proof to support several conclusions contained in report 22/97, particularly those relating to the inadequacy of the autopsies carried out on the corpses of the attackers, as well as the treatment which the attackers received in the days following the recapture of the RIM 3 barracks in La Tablada. The Inter-American Court has recognized the authority of an international organ to freely evaluate proof, stating that 'for an international tribunal, the criteria for evaluating proof are less formal than in internal legal systems'. Consequently, probative elements which are different from direct proof, such as circumstantial evidence, clues, presumptions, press articles and, where relevant, reports of non-governmental organizations may be used, provided that the conclusions drawn

---

[230] OEA/Ser.L/V/II.102, *Annual Report of the Inter-American Commission on Human Rights 1998*, April 16, 1999, Report No. 50/99, *Héctor Félix Miranda v. Mexico*, para. 27, and OEA/Ser.L/V/II.106, *Annual Report of the Inter-American Commission on Human Rights 1999*, April 13, 1999, Report No. 130/99, *Victor Manuel Oropeza v. Mexico*, n. 16. In both cases, the Commission referred to a memorial on impunity submitted by Amnesty International in the case of *Consuelo Benavides Cevallos v. Ecuador* before the Court.

354 LEGAL AND EMPIRICAL SURVEY

therefrom are consistent with the facts and corroborate the testimony or events alleged by the complainants. Assigning this power of discretion to an international organ is particularly relevant, 'in cases involving the violation of human rights in which the State cannot allege as its defence the complainant's inability to provide proof which, in many cases, cannot be obtained except with the State's cooperation'. Taking these principles into consideration and in the face of the near absolute silence of the State, the Commission based part of its considerations in the present case on the report of Amnesty International. That report, in addition to corroborating the substance of the petitioners' complaints, permitted conclusions to be drawn that were consistent with the facts, in so far as it was based on information gathered directly at the place where the events took place and immediately after their occurrence.[231]

It has thus been demonstrated that the Commission does accept *amicus* submissions from NGOs and that it seems to give weight to such material. However, the NGO interventions are relatively few. According to a staff attorney with the Commission, the Commission rarely receives *amicus* briefs. One explanation may be the lack of explicit legal basis in the Commission's Rules of Procedure, since it might lead potential *amici* to believe that briefs will be rejected. Another explanation may be that the proceedings before the Commission are usually confidential. Accordingly, NGOs may not be informed of the cases which are pending before it.[232]A third possible explanation is that NGOs often act as petitioners in cases before the Commission, which can be regarded as a stronger position than that of an *amicus*.[233]

Another possibility for NGOs is to join the petitioner as co-petitioner before the Commission. This occurred in the cases of *Monsignor Oscar Romero* v. *El Salvador* and *Leonel de Jesús Isaza Echeverry* v. *Colombia*, where the organisation CEJIL joined the original petitioners.[234]

The Inter-American Court of Human Rights

The Inter-American Court has an extensive *amicus curiae* practice. As this practice differs between its contentious jurisdiction and its advisory jurisdiction, I shall deal with these two categories separately.

---

[231] *Annual Report of the Inter-American Commission on Human Rights 1997*, February 17, 1998, Report No. 55/97, *Juan Carlos Abella* v. *Argentina*, paras. 403–408.

[232] E-mail message of 27 September 2001, on file with the author.

[233] On the standing of NGOs before the Commission, see section 5.3.

[234] OEA/Ser.L/V/II.106, *Annual Report of the Inter-American Commission on Human Rights 1999*, April 13, 1999, Report 37/00, para. 7, and OEA/Ser.L/V/II.111, *Annual Report of the Inter-American Commission on Human Rights 2000*, April 16, 2001, Report No. 64/01, para. 7.

Contentious cases

There is no explicit legal basis in the Convention or in the Statute of the Court for *amicus curiae* interventions in the Court's contentious proceedings.[235] Nor did the old Rules of Procedure, which were still in force when the Court examined the cases discussed below, include any such provision.[236] Article 34(1) of those Rules, however, gave a broad competence for the Court as regards evidence and information in contentious cases:

> The Court may, at the request of a party or the delegates of the Commission, or *proprio motu*, decide to hear as a witness, expert, or in any other capacity, any person whose testimony or statements seem likely to assist in carrying out its function.[237]

Thomas Buergenthal, who is an ex-President of the Court, has argued that since this provision authorised the Court *proprio motu* to hear persons whose statements might assist it in carrying out its function, it could also be regarded as permitting the receipt of *amicus* briefs.[238] According to Scott Davidson, the provision appeared to provide the Court with an appropriate constitutional basis for the Court to receive such submissions.[239]

In 1985, when Buergenthal wrote his article, the Court had been operational for only a few years, and no *amicus* briefs had yet been submitted in a contentious case.[240] Since then, the Court has clearly demonstrated its position on the issue of *amicus* submissions by accepting the filing of briefs in many cases and by formally noting its receipt of them in each case where such a submission has been made. In June 2001, new Rules of Procedure for the Court entered into force. Although there is no new rule on *amicus* submissions in contentious cases, the new rule on *Procedure for Taking Evidence* provides the Court with as broad competence as the old Rules did.[241]

---

[235] *Statute of the Inter-American Court of Human Rights*, October 1979.

[236] *Rules of Procedure of the Inter-American Court of Human Rights*, adopted on January 9–18, 1991, amended on January 25, 1993.

[237] *Ibid.*

[238] Thomas Buergenthal, 'The Advisory Practice of the Inter-American Human Rights Court', 79 AJIL (1985), p. 15.

[239] Scott Davidson, *The Inter-American Human Rights System*, Aldershot: Dartmouth, 1997, p. 147.

[240] Buergenthal, 'The Advisory Practice of the Inter-American Human Rights Court', p. 15.

[241] Article 45 of the new Rules is similar to the former Article 34. Rule 45(1) provides that 'The Court may, at any stage of the proceedings: Obtain, on its own motion, any evidence it considers helpful. In particular, it may hear as a witness, expert witness,

356 LEGAL AND EMPIRICAL SURVEY

Of the forty-four contentious cases in which judgements have been delivered on the merits (judgements on competence, preliminary objections, reparation, interpretation of previous judgements, etc. thus excluded), NGOs have submitted *amicus curiae* briefs in seventeen cases at the merits stage of the proceedings.[242] The cases in which NGOs intervened as *amici* include the following examples.

In *Loayza Tamayo* v. *Peru*, *amicus curiae* briefs were presented by a foundation, Fundación Ecuménica para el Desarrollo y la Paz (FEDEPAZ) and an individual concerning the principle of *non bis in idem*. Peru applied that the *amicus* briefs should be declared inadmissible. The President of the Court informed the state that 'documents of this type are added to the file without being formally incorporated into the record of the proceedings' and that the Court would evaluate those documents in due course.[243] No further discussions on the *amicus* briefs were included in the judgement.

In *Bámaca Velásquez* v. *Guatemala*, the International Commission of Jurists presented an *amicus curiae* brief on the right to truth for the next of kin to victims of forced disappearances.[244] The organisation argued, *inter alia*, that the right to truth was an established principle of international humanitarian law and implicit in international human rights law, as well as in the Convention in so much as Article 29(c) prohibited interpretations of the Convention which preclude 'rights

> or in any other capacity, any person whose evidence, statement or opinion it deems to be relevant.' According to Rule 44(3), the Court may: 'Request any entity, office, organ or authority of its choice to obtain information, express an opinion, or deliver a report or pronouncement on any given point.' *Rules of Procedure of the Inter-American Court of Human Rights*, Approved by the Court during its XLIX Ordinary Period of Sessions, held from November 16–25, 2000, and partially reformed by the Court during its LXI Ordinary Period of Sessions, held from November 20–December 4, 2003.

[242] Inter-American Court of Human Rights, Series C: Decisions and Judgments, No. 4, *Velásquez Rodríguez* v. *Honduras*, July 29, 1988, para. 38; No. 5, *Godínez Cruz* v. *Honduras*, January 20, 1989, para. 40; No. 6, *Fairén Garbi and Solís Corrales* v. *Honduras*, March 15, 1989, para. 47; No. 16, *Gangaram Panday* v. *Surinam*, January 21, 1994, para. 37; No. 30, *Genie Lacayo* v. *Nicaragua*, January 29, 1997, para. 41; No. 33, *Loayza Tamayo* v. *Perú*, September 17, 1997, para. 21; No. 35, *Suárez Rosero* v. *Ecuador*, November 12, 1997, para. 20, n. 2; No. 38, *Benavides Ceballos* v. *Ecuador*, June 19, 1998, paras. 24, 31; No. 56, *Cesti Hurtado* v. *Perú*, September 29, 1999, para. 34, n. 2; No. 63, *Villagrán Morales et al.* v. *Guatemala*, November 19, 1999, n. 1; No. 70, *Bámaca Velásquez* v. *Guatemala*, November 25, 2000, para. 64; No. 71, *Case of the Constitutional Court* v. *Perú*, January 31, 2001, para. 19; No. 72, *Baena Ricardo et al.* v. *Panamá*, February 2, 2001, para. 46; No. 74, *Ivcher Bronstein* v. *Perú*, February 6, 2001, paras. 27, 43; No. 79, *The Mayagna (Sumo) Awas Tingni Community* v. *Nicaragua*, August 31, 2001, paras. 38, 41, 42, 52, 61; No. 98, *Five Pensioners* v. *Perú*, February 28, 2003, para. 47; and No. 107, *Herrera-Ulloa* v. *Costa Rica*, July 2, 2004, paras. 39–41, 45, 47, 49, 52.

[243] Inter-American Court of Human Rights, Series C: Decisions and Judgments, No. 33, *Loayza Tamayo* v. *Perú*, September 17, 1997, paras. 21, 22.

[244] *Ibid.*, No. 70, *Bámaca Velásquez* v. *Guatemala*, November 25, 2000, para. 64.

NON-PARTY PARTICIPATION   357

or guarantees that are inherent in the human personality'. It was further stated that the right extended not only to the fate of the disappeared but to the reason for the disappearance, the totality of the circumstances surrounding the disappearance and the identity of all persons complicit in the act.[245] The Court briefly mentioned the subject of the brief in the judgement. While the Court found violations of several rights enshrined in the Convention, it did not find a violation of the right to truth. Judge Cançado Trindade supported a right to truth in his separate opinion.

In *Baena Ricardo et al.* v. *Panamá*, the NGOs Centro de Asesoría Laboral del Perú, Centro de Derechos Económicos y Sociales, Centro de Estudios Legales and the Colombian Commission of Jurists submitted a joint *amicus* brief.[246] There is no description of the contents of the brief in the judgement.

In the case of *The Mayagna (Sumo) Awas Tingni Community* v. *Nicaragua*, several different entities and one individual submitted written *amicus* briefs. These included the Organization of Indigenous Syndics of the Nicaraguan Caribbean (OSICAN), the Canadian organisation Assembly of First Nations (AFN), International Human Rights Law Group, the Mohawks Indigenous Community of Akwesasne and the National Congress of American Indians (NCAI).[247] There is, however, no mention of the contents of the briefs in the judgement.

The question might be put whether NGOs have sought leave to submit briefs on other occasions and been refused. This is, however, not the case. In the *Loayza Tamayo* case of 1997 the Court made it clear that its position is that *amicus* briefs should not be declared inadmissible since they do not belong to the formal record of the proceedings. Rather, the screening is carried out through the Court's estimation of the evidential or legal value of a particular brief.[248]

The question of oral interventions has been more dubious. Former Rule 34(1) did not distinguish between written and oral interventions, but in practice written interventions have been far more common. According to Buergenthal, the rule appeared to empower the Court to grant permission for an NGO to make an oral presentation, if this would

---

[245] *Memorial en Derecho Amicus Curiae Presentado por la Comisión Internacional de Juristas ante la Corte Interamericana de Derechos Humanos en el Caso Efraín Bámaca Velásquez c. Guatemala*, submitted on June 20, 2000.

[246] Inter-American Court of Human Rights, Series C: Decisions and Judgments, No. 72, *Baena Ricardo et al.* v. *Panamá*, February 2, 2001, para. 46.

[247] *Ibid.*, No. 79, *Mayagna (Sumo) Awas Tingni Community* v. *Nicaragua* paras. 38, 41, 42, 52, 61.

[248] It has been observed by Dinah Shelton that the Inter-American Court appears never to have refused a request for permission to submit an *amicus* brief, see Shelton, 'The Participation of Nongovernmental Organizations', p. 638.

358   LEGAL AND EMPIRICAL SURVEY

have assisted the court in carrying out its function.[249] Under the new Rules, the Court has the authority to request both oral and written submissions. From the text of the judgements of the Court, however, it seems that only written *amicus* interventions have so far been made in the contentious cases examined by the Court. It can also be observed that when such submissions are made, the judgements provide no description of the arguments presented, and the briefs are not referred to in the Court's reasoning.

Another point worth noticing is that NGOs sometimes serve as legal advisors to the Commission when a case is referred to the Court. In that role, NGOs have, *inter alia*, drafted memoranda to the Court, proposed and examined witnesses and experts and rendered oral arguments. Americas Watch has played an important role as advisor to the Commission.[250]

Advisory opinions

Any member state of the OAS may request an advisory opinion from the Court in accordance with Article 64(1) or 64(2) of the American Convention on Human Rights, whether or not it has become a party to the Convention. OAS organs listed in Chapter VIII of the OAS Charter can seek rulings within their sphere of competence. Private bodies cannot request advisory opinions from the Court.

According to Article 64 of the Court's Rules of Procedure, the Court may apply the rules governing contentious proceedings to its advisory proceedings. In other words, Article 45 on Procedure for Taking Evidence can be applied for advisory opinions. This was also the case under the old Rules.[251]

---

[249] Buergenthal, 'The Advisory Practice of the Inter-American Human Rights Court', p. 16.

[250] David J. Padilla, 'The Inter-American Commission on Human Rights of the Organization of American States: A Case Study', 9 *American University Journal of International Law and Policy* (1993), pp. 108–109. Padilla is the Assistant Executive Secretary of the Inter-American Commission. It is also clear from several judgements of the Inter-American Court of Human Rights that experts from NGOs have assisted the Commission before the Court – see, e.g., Series C: Decisions and Judgments, *El Amparo* v. *Venezuela*, January 18, 1995, para. 6. In other judgements, it is not mentioned that the experts are NGO officers, while the persons appointed as assistants of the Commission are in fact NGO staff members. For instance, in judgement No. 69 in the case of *Cantoral Benavides* v. *Perú* of 18 August 2000, the Commission appointed José Miguel Vivanco and Viviana Krsticevic of the NGOs Human Rights Watch – Americas and CEJIL as assistants. The assistants also acted as representatives of the victim. CEJIL has also filed petitions before the Commission and submitted *amicus* briefs to the Court.

[251] See Buergenthal, 'The Advisory Practice of the Inter-American Human Rights Court', p. 15.

NON-PARTY PARTICIPATION   359

The Court accepted *amicus* participation in the proceedings leading to its first advisory opinion. It has so far delivered eighteen advisory opinions. NGOs have intervened as *amicus curiae* in fifteen of these.[252] A few examples will now be mentioned.

Advisory Opinion No. 1 (1982): *'Other Treaties' Subject to the Advisory Jurisdiction of the Court*: The International Human Rights Law Group, the International League for Human Rights and the Lawyers' Committee for International Human Rights submitted *amicus curiae* briefs. Briefs were also presented by the academic institutions the Inter-American Institute of Human Rights and the Urban Morgan Institute for Human Rights of the University of Cincinnati College of Law.[253]

Advisory Opinion No. 5 (1985): *Compulsory Membership in an Association Prescribed by Law for the Practice of Journalism*: The following organisations acted as *amici curiae*: the American Newspaper Publishers' Association, the American Society of Newspaper Editors and the Associated Press, the Americas Watch Committee and the Committee to Protect Journalists, the Colegio de Periodistas of Costa Rica, the Federación Latinoamericana de Periodistas, the International Press Institute, the International League for Human Rights, the Inter-American Press Association, the Lawyers' Committee for Human Rights, the Newspaper Guild

---

[252] Inter-American Court of Human Rights, Series A: Judgements and Opinions, Advisory Opinions OC-1/82, *'Other Treaties' Subject to the Advisory Jurisdiction of the Court*, September 24, 1982, para. 5; OC-2/82, *The Effect of Reservations on the Entry into Force of the American Convention on Human Rights*, September 24, 1982, para. 5; OC-3/83, *Restrictions to the Death Penalty*, September 8, 1983, para. 5; OC-5/85, *Compulsory Membership in an Association Prescribed by Law for the Practice of Journalism*, November 13, 1985, paras. 5, 8; OC-7/86, *Enforceability of the Right to Reply or Correction*, August 29, 1986, para. 5; OC-8/87, *Habeas Corpus in Emergency Situations*, January 30, 1987, para. 5; OC-9/87, *Judicial Guarantees in States of Emergency*, October 6, 1987, para. 8; OC-10/90, *Interpretation of the American Declaration of the Rights and Duties of Man Within the Framework of Article 64 of the American Convention on Human Rights*, July 14, 1990, para. 7; OC-11/90, *Exceptions to the Exhaustion of Domestic Remedies*, August 10, 1990, para. 8; OC-13/93, *Certain Attributes of the Inter-American Commission On Human Rights*, July 16, 1993, paras. 9, 11–12; OC-14/94, *International Responsibility for the Promulgation and Enforcement of Laws in Violation of the Convention*, December 9, 1994, paras. 8, 10–11; OC-15/97, *Reports of the Inter-American Commission on Human Rights*, November 14, 1997, paras. 18, 21; OC-16/99, *The Right to Information on Consular Assistance in the Framework of the Guarantees of the Due Process of Law*, October 1, 1999, paras. 14, 22; OC-17/02, *Juridical Condition and Human Rights of the Child*, August 28, 2002, paras. 9–11, 15; OC-18/03, *Juridical Condition and Rights of the Undocumented Migrants*, September 17, 2003, e.g. paras. 18, 19, 23, 27–31, 37–39, 41.

[253] Inter-American Court of Human Rights, Series A: Judgements and Opinions, No. 1, Advisory Opinion OC-1/82, September 24, 1982, para. 5.

360   LEGAL AND EMPIRICAL SURVEY

and the International Association of Broadcasting, the World Press Freedom Committee. The Colegio de Periodistas of Costa Rica and the Inter-American Press Association were also heard at the hearing.[254]

Advisory Opinion No. 14 (1994): *International Responsibility for the Promulgation and Enforcement of Laws in violation of the Convention*: Briefs were submitted by the CEJIL jointly with Americas Watch and the Comisión Andina de Juristas (Andean Commission of Jurists). In addition, several professors made *amicus* interventions. The President authorised Americas Watch, CEJIL, the Comisión Andina de Juristas and the Red Latinoamericana de Abogados Católicos to participate in the hearing. CEJIL and Americas Watch were represented at the hearing.[255]

Advisory Opinion No. 16 (1999): *The Right to Information on Consular Assistance in the Framework of the Guarantees of the Due Process of Law*: *Amicus* briefs were filed by Amnesty International, la Comisión Mexicana para la Defensa y Promoción de Derechos Humanos (CMDPDH), Human Rights Watch/Americas, CEJIL, Death Penalty Focus of California and Minnesota Advocates for Human Rights. *Amicus* briefs were also filed by International Human Rights Law Institute of DePaul University College of Law, MacArthur Justice Center of the University of Chicago Law School and a number of individuals.[256] The Court commented briefly on the contents of some of the submissions.[257] All the NGOs were represented at the public hearing of the Court.[258]

During the proceedings on *Juridical Condition and Human Rights of the Child*, (Advisory Opinion No. 17, 2002) and *Juridical Condition and Rights of the Undocumented Migrants* (Advisory Opinion No. 18, 2003) a high number of NGOs, other entities and individuals submitted *amicus curiae* briefs. In both cases, the *amici* were invited to participate in the oral proceedings. Several NGOs made oral submissions at the hearings. Both opinions included detailed accounts of the written as well as the oral submissions of the *amici*.[259]

It is somewhat surprising that so many NGOs have made submissions in some cases. According to a former assistant executive secretary of the Inter-American Commission, over 100 *amicus* briefs (from both NGOs

---

[254] *Ibid.*, No. 5, Advisory Opinion OC-5/85, November 13, 1985, paras. 5, 8.
[255] *Ibid.*, No. 14, Advisory Opinion OC-14/94, December 9, 1994, paras. 8, 10–11.
[256] *Ibid.*, No. 16, Advisory Opinion OC-16/99, October 1, 1999, paras. 14, 22.
[257] *Ibid.*, paras. 46, 62.   [258] *Ibid.*, para. 16.
[259] OC-17/02, *Juridical Condition and Human Rights of the Child*, August 28, 2002, paras. 9–11, 15; OC-18/03, *Juridical Condition and Rights of the Undocumented Migrants*, September 17, 2003, e.g. paras. 18, 19, 23, 27–31, 37–39, 41.

and individuals) had been submitted to the Court as of 1993.[260] The advisory opinions give the impression that *amicus* participation has become even more frequent since then.

It is difficult to assess whether the *amicus* submissions have had any influence on the Court's reasoning. It can be observed, however, that before 2002, only one of the advisory opinions (No. 5 on *Compulsory Membership in an Association Prescribed by Law for the Practice of Journalism*) contained a description of the opinions submitted, while the two latest opinions (Nos. 17 and 18 from 2002 and 2003) include a quite detailed account of the submissions.[261] There also seems to be a trend towards a more permissive approach to NGO participation in the hearings of the Court as NGOs have been represented at the hearings in the cases resulting in the six most recent advisory opinion described above. While there is no indication in the earlier four of these opinions that the NGOs were allowed to make oral interventions, the two latest include summaries of such interventions.

6.8 The African Commission and Court of Human and Peoples' Rights

Under Article 46 of the African Charter on Human and Peoples' Rights, the Commission may 'resort to any appropriate method of investigation', including to 'hear from the Secretary General of the Organization of African Unity or any other person capable of enlightening it'.[262] Article 119 of the Commission's Rules of Procedure regarding the procedure for the consideration of non-state communications does not mention *amicus* participation, but refers solely to the submissions of the petitioner and the state party concerned.[263] This is not surprising considering the confidential nature of the Commission's proceedings.[264] Nevertheless, the author of a communication is informed of the Commission's decision on admissibility and

---

[260] Padilla, 'The Inter-American Commission', p. 111.
[261] See also Davidson, *The Inter-American Human Rights System*, p. 148.
[262] African Charter on Human and Peoples' Rights, adopted on 27 June 1981.
[263] *Amended Rules of Procedure of the African Commission on Human and Peoples' Rights*, adopted on 6 October 1995.
[264] Article 59 of the African Charter provides that: 'All measures taken within the provisions of the present Chapter shall remain confidential until such a time as the Assembly of Heads of State and Government shall otherwise decide.'

provided with the statements submitted by the state party and can therefore request assistance from an NGO which has previously not been involved in the case.[265] According to Odinkalu and Christensen, the Commission clearly has the power to receive *amicus* submissions, should it wish to do so.[266] It is also clear from the Activity Reports of the Commission that the Commission feels at liberty to receive a letter from an NGO which is not the complainant but has been requested to assist in the case at a later stage.[267] It thus seems that NGOs may act as *amici*, even if that particular designation is not used.

It should, however, be observed that the practical importance for NGOs of making *amicus curiae* submissions is less than before many other bodies, as any NGO can lodge communications on its own behalf or on behalf of a victim, individually or jointly.[268] The Commission has also in recent years allowed individual victims to be represented by NGOs acting as counsel or co-counsel. This was first done in October 1995, when Interights represented John Modise before the Commission.[269]

As mentioned in chapter 5, an additional Protocol to the African Charter establishing an African Court on Human and Peoples' Rights was adopted by the OAU Council of Ministers in June 1998. According to Article 34 of the Protocol on Establishment, the African Court shall draw up its rules and determine its own procedure. The Court had, as of November 2004, not yet become operational.

---

[265] Rules 118(1), 119(3).

[266] Chidi Anselm Odinkalu and Camilla Christensen, 'The African Commission on Human and Peoples' Rights: The Development of its Non-State Communication Procedures', 20 HRQ (1998), p. 279.

[267] An Annual Review of the NGO Interights demonstrates that the organisation received instructions from and worked with the complaining NGOs in the case of *Constitutional Rights Project and Civil Liberties Organisation* v. *Nigeria*. Interights, *Annual Review 98–99*, p. 7. According to the Commission's own Activity Report, the Secretariat of the Commission received a letter from Interights with regard to that case and thirteen others. The letter included objections and observations to a mission which had visited Nigeria in connection with a number of cases brought against the country. *Twelfth Annual Activity Report of the African Commission on Human and Peoples' Rights 1998–1999*, annex V, case 102/93, paras. 31–32.

[268] See section 5.3.

[269] Odinkalu and Christensen, 'The African Commission on Human and Peoples' Rights', p. 273 and Interights, *Annual Review 98–99*, p. 7.

6.9 Conclusions

It has been demonstrated that NGOs, as well as actors and individuals, have the possibility to act as *amici curiae* before several international and regional courts. Different courts, however, make different use of the rules on submissions from non-parties. The ICJ has the most restrictive practice of the courts surveyed, although its Statute provides a possibility for it to accept *amicus* briefs from NGOs in advisory proceedings. There may be several explanations for this hesitation. First, the ICJ is the only international court which has a jurisdiction comprising any matter of international law. The cases before it often concern politically sensitive issues, and states' acceptance of its jurisdiction implies a considerable sacrifice in terms of sovereignty. Further, all contentious cases are disputes between states, which are less likely to request or accept assistance from non-state actors than, for example, individual victims of human rights violations. Finally, the Court is often the focus of international attention, and would surely receive plenty of submissions if it started to invite NGOs to make submissions or grant formal leave for *amicus* participation. It is thus not surprising that the Court seeks to protect its integrity by being cautious about letting the interests of non-state actors enter the Court room. If it were not, there would probably be strong opposition from states.

Some cases involve public interests which are independent of national borders. This was particularly clear in the case of *Legality of the Use by a State of Nuclear Weapons in Armed Conflict*, which caused considerable public opinion.[270] It could be argued that the Court should be more permissive towards non-state submissions in such cases, especially considering that there is no need in advisory proceedings to protect the interests of the parties to remain in control of the case. Dinah Shelton has argued in an article on the participation of NGOs in international judicial proceedings that a role for NGOs as *amici curiae* seems particularly appropriate in cases which concern obligations *erga omnes*.[271] In my view, this is a reasonable point.

The restrictive approach of the WTO is in line with the above argument. While Dispute Settlement Panels and the Appellate Body have limited jurisdiction, the financial interests at stake are considerable. Accordingly, the reaction of member states was strongly sceptical when

---

[270] See section 5.2.
[271] Shelton, 'The Participation of Nongovernmental Organizations', p. 627.

364   LEGAL AND EMPIRICAL SURVEY

the Appellate Body adopted an Additional Procedure for the submission of *amicus* briefs in the *Asbestos* case, even though the DSU provides a legal basis for both Dispute Settlement Panels and the Appellate Body to accept briefs. The fact that states have accepted *amicus* briefs from NGOs as part of their own submissions is something different, as this practice permits the parties to a dispute to remain in control of the case.

The Rules of Procedure of the international criminal courts, as well as the practice of the ICTY and the ICTR, reflect a permissive attitude in relation to *amici*. This is somewhat surprising, as such submissions may be a disadvantage for the accused. In the *Akayesu* case before the ICTR, almost thirty NGOs filed a joint brief requesting that the Prosecutor amend the indictment to include crimes of sexual violence. The Prosecutor did indeed change the indictment, and although there were good grounds for doing this even without the NGO pressure, as witnesses had testified about sexual crimes, it is not impossible that the *amicus* brief had an influence on the decision. At the same time, cases within international criminal law often involve problems of clarifying the facts and providing evidence, and humanitarian NGOs may play an important role in providing such information.

Among the regional human rights courts, both the European Court of Human Rights and the Inter-American Court employ a generous *amicus* practice. While the latter accepts large numbers of briefs, especially in its advisory cases, it does not regard the submissions as part of the formal record of the case. This might provide for more freedom for the Court in its assessment of the briefs. It can also be observed that the Inter-American Court seldom mentions the content of briefs in its judgements, even though the two latest advisory opinions discussed have included summaries of *amicus* submissions. The European Court of Human Rights, for its part, has a considerable case-load. In relation to the total number of judgements delivered, the cases where *amicus* briefs have been accepted are few. On the other hand, the Court's judgements occasionally provide elaborate descriptions and discussions on the briefs which have been accepted.

The ECJ employs a restrictive practice towards *amici*, requiring that the intervenor has a direct interest in the case. This might be explained by the role of the Advocates General, which is similar to that of an *amicus*. The Court thus has no significant interest in additional information from NGOs.

From the perspective of the international legal status of NGOs, it is interesting to note that there seems to be a trend towards a more permissive approach in relation to the role of NGOs as non-parties in international tribunals and quasi-judicial bodies. The ICJ has, with its new Practice Directions, indicated that material submitted by international NGOs on their own initiative may be of interest to states and IGOs presenting written or oral statements under Article 66 of the Court's Statute. The material of international NGOs is explicitly placed on the same level as any 'publication in the public domain', and thus not regarded as formal submissions in a case, but is nevertheless mentioned, unlike material produced by individuals, research institutions or, for that part, national NGOs. Within the European human rights system, an explicit legal basis for third-party intervention was incorporated into the Convention with the coming into force of Protocol No. 11 in 1998. At the Inter-American Court, *amicus* participation has been extensive for a number of years, but still seems to be increasing. Moreover, with its last advisory opinions the Court appears to be establishing a practice to invite NGOs to make oral interventions during advisory proceedings and to incorporate descriptions of NGO submissions in advisory opinions. Within the WTO dispute settlement mechanism, the opposition to non-governmental *amicus* participation is strong. Nevertheless, with the acceptance of a number of briefs and the adoption of the additional procedure by the Appellate Body, *amicus* participation has become a possibility under discussion.

7 Co-operation with intergovernmental organisations

7.1 Introduction

IGOs are the main fora for international law- and policy-making. With very few exceptions, full membership in these fora is open exclusively to states, and non-members may not vote. NGOs and other non-state actors are therefore excluded from the actual decision-making within most IGOs. However, many IGOs grant some form of observer status to states that are not members, other IGOs, liberation movements, NGOs and other entities. Schermers and Blokker note that 'The word "observer" might give the impression that these entities with observer status have a passive role. However, the opposite is often true. Observers often participate actively, transmitting their ideas to international organisations.'[1]

The relations between IGOs and NGOs are of interest in a study on the international legal status of NGOs for two main reasons. First, consultative status or other forms of institutionalised co-operation implies some form of recognition of NGOs as partners in the international legal system. Secondly, the instruments and practices which regulate such co-operation constitute platforms which can be used by NGOs for influencing decision-making and the gradual development of international law which occurs within intergovernmental fora.

As will be shown below, NGOs engage in institutionalised co-operation with IGOs to an increasing extent, and appear to have some influence on their decision-making processes. In order to evaluate this co-operation and its meaning in legal terms, the formal relations between different IGOs and NGOs will be surveyed. Aspects of interest in this respect are,

---

[1] Henry G. Schermers and Niels M. Blokker, *International Institutional Law: Unity within Diversity*, 3rd rev. edn., Dordrecht: Martinus Nijhoff, 1999, p. 119.

366

inter alia, membership, observer status, consultative status and other forms of participation in decision-making bodies. The operational co-operation between IGOs and NGOs will be briefly examined in chapter 9 on international agreements.[2]

This book cannot provide space for an exhaustive survey of intergovernmental bodies. As the purpose of the study is to discuss the legal status of NGOs in international law, IGOs which are arenas for the drafting, adoption and monitoring of treaties are of primary interest. I have also chosen to focus on IGOs which have a more or less extensive co-operation with NGOs, rather than describing all organisations within a particular category of IGOs. This means that the IGOs presented here may not be typical or constitute a representative selection of all intergovernmental bodies, or of all such law-making bodies.[3]

7.2 The United Nations

Introduction

The United Nations has co-operated with NGOs from its very establishment. According to Article 71 of the UN Charter, the ECOSOC:

may make suitable arrangements for consultation with non-governmental organizations which are concerned with matters within its competence. Such arrangements may be made with international organizations and, where appropriate, with national organizations after consultation with the Member of the United Nations concerned.[4]

---

[2] See also section 4.3 on the obligations of NGOs in operational co-operation with IGOs.

[3] For instance, it should be noted that the WTO still has very limited formal contacts with NGOs. Article V:2 of the Marrakesh Agreement establishing the WTO provides that 'the General Council may make appropriate arrangements for consultation and cooperation with non-governmental organizations concerned with matters related to those of the WTO'. The General Council adopted Guidelines for Arrangements on Relations with Non-Governmental Organizations in 1996 under this provision, see WT/L/162, 23 July 1996. Article VI of these Guidelines states that: 'Members have pointed to the special character of the WTO, which is both a legally binding intergovernmental treaty of rights and obligations among its Members and a forum for negotiations. As a result of extensive discussions, there is currently a broadly held view that it would not be possible for NGOs to be directly involved in the work of the WTO or its meetings.' The Guidelines instead focus on making WTO documents publicly available and on informal contacts with NGOs, see Articles III–V. For information about WTO activities which are open to NGOs, see the *WTO Monthly Bulletin for NGOs*.

[4] For a description of the drafting process of this provision, and the role of NGOs in this discussion, see Bill Seary, 'The Early History: From the Congress of Vienna to the San Francisco Conference', in Peter Willets (ed.), '*The Conscience of the World': The Influence of Non-Governmental Organisations in the UN System*, Oxford: Hurst & Co., 1996, pp. 26–27.

368   LEGAL AND EMPIRICAL SURVEY

In his report on *Renewing the United Nations: A Programme for Reform* of 1997, the former Secretary-General explained some of the underlying reasons for the UN to co-operate with NGOs. He stated that the increasing influence of civil society was 'contributing to a process of enlargement of international cooperation and spurring the United Nations system and other intergovernmental structures towards greater transparency and accountability and closer linkages between national and international levels of decision-making and implementing'.[5] NGOs and other civil society actors were 'now perceived not only as disseminators of information or providers of services but also as shapers of policy, be it in peace and security matters, in development or in humanitarian affairs'.[6]

It is clear that some concrete aspects of NGO co-operation contribute to the work of the United Nations. One important form of co-operation is the information provided regarding factual situations and policies within particular countries, including violations of treaty obligations, from a 'third party', i.e. actors which are not members of the United Nations, nor contracting parties to treaties. This type of information is perhaps particularly important to the UN treaty bodies, as will be described below.[7] Independent actors such as NGOs can put pressure on states which violate international law without diplomatic considerations. Many NGOs also possess considerable expertise within their field of operation, which is useful to the United Nations and other IGOs.[8]

Naturally, co-operation also has problems, one of which is the fast-growing number and diversity of NGOs coupled with the financial and practical constraints within which the United Nations operates.[9] The United Nations also sees a risk that the illegitimate groups of 'uncivil society' may take advantage of the process of globalisation and increased IGO–NGO co-operation to advance their own agendas.[10]

---

[5] A/51/950, *Renewing the United Nations: A Programme for Reform, Report of the Secretary-General*, 14 July 1997, para. 212.

[6] *Ibid.*, para. 213.   [7] Section 7.2.

[8] The Secretary-General mentions this factor by stating that NGOs have themselves become primary sources and disseminators of information. A/53/170, *Arrangements and Practices*, 10 July 1998, para. 71.3. See also Schermers and Blokker, *International Institutional Law*, p. 128.

[9] A/53/170, *Arrangements and Practices*, 10 July 1998, para. 71.

[10] A/51/950, *Renewing the United Nations: A Programme for Reform, Report of the Secretary-General*, 14 July 1997, para. 209.

The forms for the United Nations' co-operation with civil society are now being considered within the organisation, with possible reforms in view. In 1998, Secretary-General Kofi Annan presented a report on the *Arrangements and Practices for the Interaction of NGOs in All Activities of the United Nations System*. In the report, which was compiled as a result of an initiative by ECOSOC, the Secretary-General noted that there had been 'striking changes' in United Nations–NGO relations since the 1980s, and referred to 'the universal movement towards greater citizen action, sometimes described as the "global associational revolution"'.[11] He observed that reform and restructuring of the United Nations coincided with the emergence of 'a new participatory international system responding to the forces of globalisation sweeping our world'.[12] In his report to the General Assembly in 2002, the Secretary-General highlighted the engagement of civil society as an aspect of the UN reform process and announced that he would 'assemble a group of eminent persons representing a variety of perspectives and experiences to review past and current practices and recommend improvements for the future in order to make the interaction between civil society and the United Nations more meaningful'.[13] The panel published its final report in July 2004. Its considerations and recommendations will be discussed below.

The General Assembly and the Security Council

Article 9(1) of the UN Charter provides that the General Assembly shall consist of all the members of the United Nations.[14] The Rules of Procedure do not contain any provisions regarding the participation of observers in the work of the Assembly.[15] Decisions on the admission of new observers are taken in the form of resolutions by the Assembly. Apart from the observers of non-member states, the UN specialised agencies and other IGOs, the General Assembly has accepted observers from a few liberation movements. In 1974, the General Assembly

---

[11] A/53/170, 10 July 1998, para. 2.
[12] *Ibid.*, para 3. In a later statement the Secretary-General has used the expression 'NGO revolution', UN Press Release SG/SM/7411 GA/9710, *Secretary-General, Addressing Participants at Millennium Forum, Calls for Intensified 'NGO revolution'*, 22 May 2000.
[13] A/57/387, *Strengthening the United Nations: An Agenda for Further Change*, 9 September 2002, para. 141.
[14] According to Article 4(1), membership is open only to states.
[15] A/520/Rev. 15, *Rules of Procedure of the General Assembly*, with amendments and additions adopted on 31 December 1984.

370 LEGAL AND EMPIRICAL SURVEY

decided to invite representatives of the national liberation movements recognised by the OAU to participate in the regular meetings of the Assembly main committees and subsidiary bodies, as well as in conferences, seminars and other meetings held under the auspices of the United Nations which related to their countries.[16] The same year, the General Assembly invited the Palestine Liberation Organization (PLO) to participate in the sessions and the work of the Assembly and all international conferences convened under its auspices in the capacity of observer.[17] The South-West Africa People's Organization (SWAPO) was granted observer status by the Assembly in 1976.[18] The General Assembly also decided in 1988 that the designation 'Palestine' should be used instead of 'Palestine Liberation Organization' within the UN system.[19]

NGOs do not have observer status with the UN General Assembly, with three exceptions. The ICRC was granted observer status in 1990 with reference to the mandates conferred upon it by the Geneva Conventions of 12 August 1949 and its 'special role . . . in international humanitarian relations'.[20] In 1994, the Assembly conferred observer status on the International Federation of Red Cross and Red Crescent, referring to 'the special functions of the member societies . . . which are recognised by their respective Governments as auxiliaries to the public authorities in the humanitarian field on the basis of the Geneva Conventions'.[21] It is thus clear that the special status conferred on these organisations by the Assembly is due to their special legal position

---

[16] A/RES/3280 (XXIX), *Co-Operation between the United Nations and the Organization of African Unity*, adopted on 10 December 1974.

[17] A/RES/3237 (XXIX), *Observer Status for the Palestine Liberation Organization*, adopted on 22 November 1974.

[18] A/RES/31/152, *Observer Status for the South-West Africa People's Organization*, adopted on 20 December 1976. In 1988, the General Assembly decided that the PLO and the SWAPO were entitled to have their communications relating to the sessions and work of the Assembly or to all its international conferences issued and circulated directly as official UN documents, A/43/160, *Observer Status of National Liberation Movements*, adopted on 9 December 1988.

[19] A/43/177, *Question of Palestine*. Additional rights and privileges, including the right to participate in the general debate of the Assembly, to speak under agenda items other than Palestinian and Middle East Issues at any meeting of the plenary, and to exercise the right to reply, were conferred upon Palestine in its capacity of observer ten years later, see A/RES/52/250, *Participation of Palestine in the Work of the United Nations*, 13 July 1998.

[20] A/RES/45/6, *Observer Status for the International Committee of the Red Cross*, 16 October 1990.

[21] A/RES/49/2, *Observer Status for the International Federation of Red Cross and Red Crescent Societies in the General Assembly*, 19 October 1994.

in international humanitarian law. The co-sponsors of the draft resolution, which was adopted by the Assembly without alterations, pointed
out that the granting of observer status to the ICRC should not be
considered as a precedent. In practical terms, the observer status
means that the organisations have access to the meetings of the
General Assembly and its committees, and that they can deliver statements on subjects within their competence.[22]

The third NGO with observer status in the UN General Assembly is the
Order of Malta, which was granted this status in 1994 because of its
'long-standing dedication ... in providing humanitarian assistance and
its special role in international humanitarian relations'.[23] In other
words, this resolution does not refer to treaties or special status under
international law, as in the case of the ICRC, but only to the Order's role
as regards humanitarian assistance and relations. As it is often held
that the Sovereign Military Order of Malta has a general kind of international legal personality, however, the Order's legal status is likely to
have been important for achieving a special position as an observer.[24]
Such considerations are reflected in the Explanatory Memorandum
annexed to the request for an additional item on the Assembly's agenda
that was put forward by the twenty-four states which raised the issue of
observer status for the Order of Malta. In the Memorandum, it is stated
that the Order has earned recognition by sixty-four member states of
the United Nations 'of its full sovereignty as an equal member of the
international community'.[25]

Considering the lack of Charter provisions and rules of procedure
regarding the granting and modalities of observer status, it is not
impossible that the General Assembly will adopt some form of arrangements for co-operation with NGOs. The Panel of Eminent Persons on
Civil Society and UN Relationships has proposed that the dialogue
should be strengthened, as will be discussed below. The possibility of
NGO participation in the General Assembly has been debated within

---

[22] Christian Koenig, 'Observer Status for the International Committee of the Red Cross at
the United Nations: A Legal Viewpoint', *International Review of the Red Cross*, No. 280, 1991,
pp. 37–48 and 'The ICRC is Granted Observer Status at the United Nations', *International
Review of the Red Cross*, No. 279, 1990, pp. 581–586.
[23] A/RES/48/265, *Observer Status for the Sovereign Military Order of Malta in the General Assembly*,
24 August 1994.
[24] See section 2.4.
[25] A/48/957, *Request for the Inclusion of an Additional Item in the Agenda of the 48th Session*, 29
June 1994, annex, para. 1.

372   LEGAL AND EMPIRICAL SURVEY

ECOSOC for several years. ECOSOC decided in 1993 to undertake a general review of the arrangements with NGOs with a view to updating the resolution on consultative arrangements. One of the most controversial issues from the beginning was whether the arrangements for consultation with NGOs should be extended to cover the General Assembly.[26] In the end it was decided that the main resolution should be applicable to ECOSOC only, and the new arrangements were launched in July 1996 with Resolution 1996/31.[27] ECOSOC, however, recommended the General Assembly to examine the 'question of the participation of non-governmental organizations in all areas of the work of the United Nations, in the light of experience gained through the arrangements for consultation between non-governmental organizations and the Economic and Social Council'.[28] The United States opposed the Resolution until the President of ECOSOC explained in the interpretative statement that it was the understanding of ECOSOC that the recommendation to the Assembly fell 'within the competence of the General Assembly as set forth in Article 10 of the United Nations Charter'.[29] As Article 10 on the functions and powers of the General Assembly to make recommendations to UN member states makes an exception for the competence of the Security Council, the point of the statement seems to have been to exclude the Council from the scope of the resolution.

The open-ended working group on UN reform set up a sub-group on NGO participation in 1997, but did not achieve any results.[30] However, in the same year the General Assembly itself marked a change by inviting NGOs to take part in the Special Session to Review and Appraise the Implementation of Agenda 21 ('Earth Summit + 5'). Some 1,000 NGOs were accredited to the session.[31] The plenary of the special session was, for the first time in UN history, addressed by 'representatives of major groups, including non-governmental organizations working on behalf of the environment, women, indigenous peoples, farmers, trade unions, the private sector and youth'.[32]

---

[26] Peter Willetts, 'From "Consultative Arrangements" to "Partnership": The Changing Status of NGOs in Diplomacy at the UN', 6 *Global Governance* (2000), p. 198.

[27] See section 7.2.

[28] E/1996/L.24, *Non-Governmental Organizations*, Draft decision of 16 July 1996 submitted by the President, adopted without amendment as ECOSOC Decision 1996/297, 25 July 1996.

[29] Willetts, 'From "Consultative Arrangements"', p. 198.   [30] *Ibid.*, p. 200.

[31] A/53/170, *Arrangements and Practices*, 10 July 1998, para. 10.

[32] UN Press Release, *Special Session of General Assembly on Implementation of Agenda 21 Concludes at Headquarters, 23–27 June*, GA/9276, ENV/DEV/442, 27 June 1997.

Although the President of the General Assembly stated in 1997 that the participation of NGOs in the Earth Summit + 5 would not create a precedent for other special sessions, NGOs have in fact been invited to several other special sessions since then.[33] At the twentieth special session of the General Assembly on the World Drug Problem, held in June 1998, accreditation was granted to all NGOs with a serious interest in the questions of drug abuse and illicit trafficking.[34] In the Special Session of the International Conference on Population and Development (ICPD + 5), held in July 1999, NGOs were also allowed to address the plenary.[35] In the Special Session on Children in 2000, 1,700 representatives of 700 NGOs participated. The participating NGOs included not only those accredited by ECOSOC, which is the ordinary practice for UN conferences, but also NGO partners of the United Nations Children's Fund (UNICEF). A limited number of NGO representatives were allowed to address the plenary.[36]

Permanent consultative arrangements for NGOs with the General Assembly still seem far away, however. A group of NGOs which is lobbying for such arrangements to come into existence has drafted a resolution for which it is attempting to gain support.[37] In the draft resolution, it is proposed that NGOs should be invited to participate in the work of the Assembly's main committees, special sessions and, as appropriate, subsidiary and *ad hoc* bodies, and that the ECOSOC consultative arrangements should apply to special sessions of the Assembly. It is further proposed that NGOs with consultative status with ECOSOC should be granted consultative status with the Assembly, and that the Assembly should establish procedures in relation to other NGOs without such status.[38]

Even though formal participation for NGOs in the meetings of the Security Council appears politically impossible, informal consultations do take place. These consultations are informally called the 'Arria consultations', or 'Arria formula meetings' after the former Venezuelan representative who initiated the practice in 1992 during the crisis in

---

[33] Willetts, 'From "Consultative Arrangements"', p. 201.
[34] A/53/170, *Arrangements and Practices*, 10 July 1998, para. 10.
[35] UN Press Release, *General Assembly Concludes Twenty-First Special Session on 1994 Cairo Population and Development Conference Outcome*, GA/9577, 2 July 1999.
[36] UN Special Session on Children, *Newsletter No. 5*, October 2002, p. 4.
[37] The group is called the International Task Group on Legal and Institutional Matters (INTGLIM), and is chaired by the World Federalist Movement. See also below on the discussions on reform of UN–civil society relationships.
[38] INTGLIM, *General Assembly NGO Resolution*, November 2000, on file with the author. Also accessible online at the World Federalist Movement's website at wfm.org/ACTION/pdf/2000_NGO_GA_Resolution.pdf.

374   LEGAL AND EMPIRICAL SURVEY

the former Yugoslavia.[39] There is in fact a legal basis for such consultations in the Council's provisional rules of procedure. Rule 39 provides that 'The Security Council may invite members of the Secretariat or other persons, whom it considers competent for the purpose, to supply it with information or to give other assistance in examining matters within its competence'.[40] According to an appendix to the rules, the Council may receive written statements 'from private individuals and non-governmental bodies'. A list of all such communications relating to matters of which the Security Council is seized shall be circulated to all representatives on the Security Council.[41] This procedure has been used by NGOs, for example in a letter-writing campaign directed towards the US government.[42] Arria consultations regularly take place; during the Norwegian chairmanship of the Council in March 2002, for example, four Arria consultations on different subjects were organised.[43] The NGO Global Policy Forum reports that Germany organised an Arria meeting in May 2004 at the suggestion of Médecins sans Frontières and Human Rights Watch. The topic of the discussions was the situation in Darfur. Médecins sans Frontières, Care International, Oxfam, International Crisis Group, Human Rights Watch and World Vision were invited to speak. The Arria formula has been discussed by the Panel of Eminent Persons on Civil Society and UN Relationships, as will be described below.

ECOSOC consultative arrangements

General

As stated above, Article 71 of the UN Charter entitles ECOSOC to make suitable arrangements for consultation with NGOs which are concerned with matters within its competence. According to this provision, such

---

[39] Ruth Wedgwood, 'Legal Personality and the Role of Non-Governmental Organizations and Non-State Political Entities in the United Nations System', in Rainer Hofmann, *Non-State Actors as New Subjects of International Law. International Law – From the Traditional State Order Towards the Law of the Global Community*, Proceedings of an International Symposium, Berlin: Duncker & Humblot, 1999, p. 27 and Willetts, 'From "Consultative Arrangements"', p. 200.

[40] S/96/Rev.7, *Provisional Rules of Procedure of the Security Council*, New York, 1983.

[41] Ibid., appendix, *Provisional Procedure for Dealing with Communications from Private Individuals and Non-Governmental Bodies*, Rule A.

[42] Willetts, 'From "Consultative Arrangements"', p. 199.

[43] S/2002/663, *Letter Dated 12 June 2002 from the Permanent Representative of Norway to the United Nations Addressed to the President of the Security Council*, 13 June 2002, pp. 7–8.

CO-OPERATION WITH INTERGOVERNMENTAL ORGANISATIONS   375

arrangements may be made with international NGOs and, where appropriate, with national organisations after consultation with the member state concerned.

The formulation of the first guidelines for consultative relationship between ECOSOC and NGOs was among the matters discussed during the first meetings of the UN General Assembly. In 1946, the Assembly adopted a resolution according to which ECOSOC should provide for consultative relationship with certain NGOs.[44] These first initiatives came mainly from the trade unions movement; it was the World Federation of Trade Unions, the American Federation of Labor, the International Co-Operative Alliance and 'other non-governmental organizations' that requested that their representatives should be allowed to take part in the work of ECOSOC. The same year, ECOSOC adopted a report, prepared by the Committee for consultations with non-governmental organisations, which provided for arrangements for consultation, including the establishment of a standing committee with the task to review applications from NGOs for consultative status and to make recommendations to the Council.[45] Among the conditions for an NGO to be granted consultative status was that it should be concerned with matters falling within the competence of ECOSOC with respect to international economic, social cultural, educational, health and related matters, that its aims and purposes were in conformity with the spirit, purposes and principles of the UN Charter, that it was of recognised standing and represented a substantial proportion of the organised persons within its interest field, that it was international in its structure and that its members could exercise voting rights in relation to policies or action of the organisation. Organisations which were proved to be 'discredited by past collaboration in fascist activities' were explicitly excluded from consultative status.[46]

---

[44] GA Resolution 4(I), *Representation of Non-Governmental Bodies on the Economic and Social Council*, 14 February 1946. The resolution reads 'the Economic and Social Council should, as soon as possible, adopt suitable arrangements enabling the World Federation of Free Trade Unions and the International Co-Operative Alliance as well as other international non-governmental organizations whose experience the Economic and Social Council will find necessary to use, to collaborate for purposes of consultation with the Economic and Social Council'. The WFTU had launched a persistent campaign at the beginning of 1946 in order to achieve representative status for itself in the ECOSOC, Chiang Pei-Heng, *Non-Governmental Organizations at the United Nations: Identity, Role and Function*, New York: Praeger, 1981, pp. 86–89.

[45] E/43/Rev. 2, *Arrangements for Consultation with Non-Governmental Organizations*, 21 June 1946.

[46] *Ibid.*, paras. 1–4, 7.

376   LEGAL AND EMPIRICAL SURVEY

The purpose in establishing consultative arrangements mentioned in the resolution was twofold: first, to secure expert information or advice from organisations with special competence and, secondly, to enable organisations representing important elements of public opinion to express their views.[47] The report also expressed the general view that the arrangements for consultation with NGOs were an important means for ensuring that the interests of the peoples of the United Nations in the UN's policies and operations be fulfilled.[48] As regards the principles governing the nature of the relationship, the report stated that:

> It is important to note that a clear distinction is drawn in the Charter between participation without vote in the deliberations in the Council, and the arrangements for consultations ... It is considered that this distinction, deliberately made in the Charter, is fundamental and that the arrangements for consultation should not be such as to accord to non-governmental organisations the same rights of participation accorded to States not members of the Council and to the specialized agencies brought into relationship with the United Nations.[49]

It was further emphasised as a basic principle that the arrangements should not be such as to overburden the Council or 'transform it into a general forum for discussion'.[50] Both these principles have been kept to this day in the provisions regulating ECOSOC consultative arrangements.[51] Among the NGOs which were granted consultative status during the first five years of consultations were the International Chamber of Commerce (ICC), Lions International, the International Union of Producers and Distributors of Electric Power, the International Student Service, the World Association of Girl Guides and Girl Scouts, Rotary International and the World Organization of the Teaching Profession.[52]

In 1950, the arrangements were reviewed and a new resolution was adopted by ECOSOC.[53] One of the new aspects of the relationship was that it explicitly required an input by NGOs – it is stated that 'the organizations shall undertake to support the work of the United

---

[47] *Ibid.*, part III, para. 3.   [48] *Ibid.*, part VI.   [49] *Ibid.*, part III, para. 1.
[50] *Ibid.*, part III, para. 2.
[51] See E/RES/96/31, *Consultative Relationship between the United Nations and Non-Governmental Organizations*, 25 July 1996, paras. 18–19.
[52] ECOSOC Resolution E/189/Rev. 2, *Arrangements for Consultation* ... , 1 October 1946 and ECOSOC Resolution 334 (XI), *Review of Non-Governmental Organizations in Consultative Status*, 20 July 1950.
[53] ECOSOC Resolution 288 (X), *Review of Consultative Relationship with Non-Governmental Organizations*, 27 February 1950.

Nations and to promote knowledge of its principles and activities'.[54] The following year, ECOSOC requested the General Assembly to examine the question of the attendance of NGOs at Assembly discussions or committees on problems which concerned NGOs.[55]

The modern basis for the consultative relationship was established by ECOSOC in 1968 with Resolution 1296, which governed the relationship until 1996, when it was superseded by ECOSOC Resolution 1996/31.[56] According to the former arrangements, national NGOs were granted consultative status only in special cases and after consultation with the member state concerned.[57] In the 1996 resolution, it is simply stated that relationships may be established with 'international, subregional and national organizations'.[58] The requisite of consultation with member states as regards national NGOs is, however, maintained in the 1996 arrangements. It is further stated that participation of NGOs from all regions, and particularly from developing countries, should be ensured.[59]

The resolution, 'acknowledging the breadth of non-governmental organizations' expertise and the capacity of non-governmental organizations to support the work of the United Nations' lays down the following principles to be applied in the establishment of consultative relations:

1. The organization shall be concerned with matters falling within the competence of the Economic and Social Council and its subsidiary bodies.
2. The aims and purposes of the organization shall be in conformity with the spirit, purposes and principles of the Charter of the United Nations.
3. The organization shall undertake to support the work of the United Nations and to promote knowledge of its principles and activities, in accordance with its own aims and purposes and the nature and scope of its competence and activities ...
9. The organization shall be of recognized standing within the particular field of its competence or of a representative character ...
10. The organization shall have an established headquarters, with an executive officer. It shall have a democratically adopted constitution, a copy of which shall be deposited with the Secretary-General of the

---

[54] *Ibid.*, part I, para. 4.
[55] ECOSOC Resolution 413 (XIII), *Non-Governmental Organizations*, 20 September 1951.
[56] E/RES/1296 (XLIV), *Arrangements for Consultation with Non-Governmental Organizations*, 3 May 1968 and 1996/31, *Consultative Relationship between the United Nations and Non-Governmental Organizations*, 25 July 1996.
[57] E/RES/1296 (XLIV), para. 9.   [58] E/RES/96/31, para. 5.   [59] *Ibid.*

378 LEGAL AND EMPIRICAL SURVEY

United Nations, and which shall provide for the determination of policy by a conference, congress or other representative body, and for an executive organ responsible to the policy-making body.

11. The organization shall have authority to speak for its members through its authorized representatives. Evidence of this authority shall be presented, if requested.

12. The organization shall have a representative structure and possess appropriate mechanisms of accountability to its members, who shall exercise effective control over its policies and actions through the exercise of voting rights or other appropriate democratic and transparent decision-making processes. Any such organization that is not established by a governmental entity or intergovernmental agreement shall be considered a non-governmental organization for the purpose of these arrangements, including organizations that accept members designated by governmental authorities, provided that such membership does not interfere with the free expression of views of the organization.

13. The basic resources of the organization shall be derived in the main part from contributions of the national affiliates or other components or from individual members ... Any financial contribution or other support, direct or indirect, from a Government to the organization shall be openly declared to the Committee through the Secretary-General and fully recorded in the financial and other records of the organization and shall be devoted to purposes in accordance with the aims of the United Nations.[60]

The conditions for NGOs to be granted consultative status are basically the same in the 1968 and the 1996 arrangements. As regards the standing of an organisation, the former version required a 'recognised *international standing*' (emphasis added) as opposed to the current version which, as mentioned above, is more permissive towards national NGOs. A former condition that organisations represented a 'substantial proportion ... of the population or of the organized persons within the particular field of its competence' was removed in the 1996 arrangements. As regards members designated by governmental authorities, both the old and the

---

[60] E/RES/96/31, part I. See also section 1.3 regarding the definition of 'NGO'. During its resumed 2000 session, the Committee on NGOs discussed the topic of NGOs whose defining characteristics 'were not in strict conformity with Council resolution 1996/31, namely commercial/industrial, professional, religious, research/educational or government-funded'. It was agreed that the topic should be reconsidered in the future. It seems that the Committee is considering a more restrictive interpretation of the resolution, as the categories of organisations mentioned have indeed been granted consultative status in the past. E/2000/8, *Report of the Committee on Non-Governmental Organizations* ..., 22 February 2001, para. 116.

new arrangements allow for this, provided that such membership does not interfere with the free expression of views of the organisation. The requirement that financial and other contributions direct or indirect from a government shall be openly declared is also the same.

A new section in the 1996 resolution as compared to the former arrangements includes provisions on the participation of NGOs in international conferences convened by the United Nations and their preparatory process.[61] These will be discussed in a subsequent chapter.[62]

The distinction between participation without a vote in ECOSOC and the consultative relationship that was laid down in 1946 is repeated with emphasis. NGOs shall not have the same rights of participation as non-member states and the specialised agencies.[63] An additional clause underlining state control over the relationship was included in the 1996 resolution:

The granting, suspension and withdrawal of consultative status as well as the interpretation of norms and decisions relating to this matter, are the prerogative of Member States exercised through the Economic and Social Council and its Committee on Non-Governmental Organizations.[64]

The purpose of the consultative arrangements are described as being twofold: on the one hand, the consultative relationship should enable the Council or one of its bodies to secure expert information or advice from organisations having special competence in the subjects for which consultative arrangements are made and, on the other, the arrangements should enable organisations that represent important elements of public opinion to express their views. The group of NGOs granted consultative status 'should, in sum, as far as possible reflect in a balanced way the major viewpoints or interests in these fields in all areas and regions of the world'.[65]

Part VIII of the resolution governs the suspension and withdrawal of consultative status.[66] The consultative status of NGOs with ECOSOC and

---

[61] *Ibid.*, part VII.   [62] Section 8.2.
[63] E/RES/96/31, paras. 18–19 reads: 'A clear distinction is drawn in the Charter of the United Nations between participation without vote in the deliberations of the Council and the arrangements for consultation ... This distinction, deliberately made in the Charter, is fundamental and the arrangements for consultation should not be such as to accord to non-governmental organizations the same rights of participation as are accorded to States not members of the Council and to the specialized agencies brought into relationship with the United Nations. The arrangements should not be such as to overburden the Council or transform it from a body for coordination of policy and action, as contemplated in the Charter, into a general forum for discussion.'
[64] *Ibid.*, para. 15.   [65] *Ibid.*, para. 20.   [66] *Ibid.*, paras. 55–59.

the listing of those on the Roster shall be suspended for up to three years or withdrawn in three cases: (1) if an organisation clearly abuses its status by engaging in a pattern of acts contrary to the purposes and principles of the UN Charter, (2) if there exists substantiated evidence of influence from proceeds resulting from internationally recognised criminal activities, or (3) if within the preceding three years an organisation did not make any positive or effective contribution to the work of the United Nations.[67] The last ground for suspension or withdrawal is interesting in that it underlines that NGOs in consultative status undertake an obligation to contribute to the work of ECOSOC and the United Nations.[68]

The consultative status is granted by a decision of ECOSOC on the recommendation of its standing Committee on Non-Governmental Organizations.[69] There are three categories of consultative relationship. *General consultative status* can be accorded to NGOs which are concerned with most of the activities of the Council and its subsidiary bodies and can demonstrate that they have a substantive and sustained contribution to make to the achievement of the objectives of the United Nations. These organisations should also be closely involved with the economic and social life of the peoples of the areas they represent and broadly representative in membership of major segments of society in a large number of countries in different regions of the world.[70] Organisations which have a special competence in, and are concerned specifically with, only a few of the fields of activity covered by the Council and its subsidiary bodies and that are known within the fields for which they have or seek consultative

---

[67] The second ground for suspension or withdrawal of consultative status is vaguely phrased. The corresponding provision in the previous resolution on consultative status, ECOSOC Resolution 1296 of 1968, stated that consultative status should be suspended or withdrawn if there was 'substantiated evidence of secret governmental financial influence to induce an organization to undertake acts contrary to the purposes and principles of the Charter of the United Nations'. It is interesting that today's threats are considered to be criminal activities such as drugs trade, while governments were regarded as a threat in the 1960s. The threats have, in other words, moved from being governmental to being non-governmental.

[68] See also section 4.3.   [69] E/RES/96/31, part IX.

[70] *Ibid.*, para. 22. Examples of organisations in general consultative status include Caritas Internationalis, Consumers International, Greenpeace International, the International Chamber of Commerce, Liberal International, Médecins sans Frontières International and the World Federation of Trade Unions. *List of NGOs in Consultative Status with the ECOSOC*, 8 August 2004.

status can acquire *special consultative status*.[71] Finally, NGOs which the Council or the UN Secretary-General consider can make occasional and useful contributions to the work of the Council or its subsidiary bodies or other UN bodies within their competence can be included in a list, the *Roster*.[72]

The different categories enjoy different privileges. The provisional agenda of the Council shall be communicated to all three groups, but only organisations with general consultative status may propose to the Committee on Non-Governmental Organizations that the Committee request the Secretary-General to place items of special interest to the organisations on the provisional agenda of the Council.[73] Organisations in general or special consultative status may designate representatives to sit as observers at public meetings of the Council and its subsidiary bodies. Those on the Roster may send representatives to meetings concerned with matters within their field of competence.[74] Only NGOs in general or special consultative status may submit written statements on subjects in which these organisations have a special competence. Such statements shall be circulated by the UN Secretary-General to the members of the Council.[75] Organisations in general consultative status may make oral presentations to the Council upon recommendation of the Committee on Non-Governmental Organizations, while those with special consultative status may only do so under certain circumstances and after recommendation by the Committee.[76]

In 1948, when the consultative arrangements had been operational for two years, forty-one NGOs had been granted consultative status.[77] At present, there are 2,534 NGOs in consultative status with ECOSOC, of

---

[71] *Ibid.*, para. 23. The list of NGOs in special consultative status includes Amnesty International, Anti-Slavery International, Baha'i International Community, the European Roma Rights Center, the European Women's Lobby, Freedom House, Handicap International, Human Rights Watch, the International Commission of Jurists and the Union of International Associations. *List of NGOs in Consultative Status with the ECOSOC*, 8 August 2004.

[72] *Ibid.*, para. 24. Organisations on the Roster include the American Foreign Insurance Association, the Cherokee Nation of New Jersey, the Hunger Project, the International Buddhist Foundation and the National Rifle Association of America Institute for Legislative Action. *List of NGOs in Consultative Status with the ECOSOC*, 8 August 2004.

[73] *Ibid.*, para. 28.   [74] *Ibid.*, para. 29.   [75] *Ibid.*, para. 30.   [76] *Ibid.*, para. 32.

[77] E/1998/43, *Work of the Non-Governmental Section of the Secretariat, Report of the Secretary-General*, 8 May 1998, para. 5. The report includes a table of the increasing number of NGOs in consultative status between the years 1948 and 1997.

which 134 organisations have general consultative status, 1,477 have special consultative status and 923 are on the Roster.[78]

ECOSOC Standing Committee on Non-Governmental Organizations

As is clear from the above description of the ECOSOC consultative arrangements with NGOs, the standing Committee on Non-Governmental Organizations plays a central role. The Committee, which was established in 1946, is an intergovernmental body composed of nineteen member states. Its main tasks are to consider applications for consultative status, to consider quadrennial reports submitted by NGOs and to monitor consultative relationships in general, including the withdrawal or suspension of status. The Committee makes recommendations to ECOSOC, which decides on the granting, suspension and withdrawal of consultative status and on the reclassification of organisations from one category to another. The Committee also makes recommendations regarding the participation of NGOs not in consultative status for participation in working groups and other bodies.[79]

Obviously, the intergovernmental nature of the Committee leaves the decision-making power regarding consultative status in the hands of member states. On the surface, the Committee's handling of applications on consultative status does not seem problematic. At its 2003 regular session, the Committee had 107 applications before it. Of those, the Committee recommended fifty-seven for consultative status and deferred forty-eight applications for consideration at a later date (two having withdrawn their applications).[80] During its 2002 regular session, the Committee decided to close its consideration of three applications, of which one had requested the Committee to do so. At the same session, the Committee granted consultative status to ninety-three NGOs.[81] However, it can be observed that the Committee's

---

[78] List of NGOs in Consultative Status with ECOSOC, 4 August 2004, accessible online at www.un.org/esa/coordination/ngo/pdf/INF_List.pdf.

[79] E/1998/72, Report of the Committee on Non-Governmental Organizations on the first part of its 1998 session, 19 June 1998, p. 6. See also, generally on the Committee, Jurij Daniel Aston, 'The United Nations Committee on Non-Governmental Organizations: Guarding the Entrance to a Politically Divided House', 12 EJIL (2001), pp. 943–962.

[80] E/2003/32 (Part I), Report of the Committee on Non-Governmental Organizations on its 2003 Regular Session, 16 June 2003, p. 1.

[81] E/2002/71 (Part I), Report of the Committee on Non-Governmental Organizations on its 2003 Regular Session, 3 July 2002, pp. 1, 7.

CO-OPERATION WITH INTERGOVERNMENTAL ORGANISATIONS   383

deferment of applications seems to be used in some cases as a means of delaying controversial candidatures.[82]

The Committee's documentation provides illustrative examples of the political implications of the granting of consultative status to some NGOs. Long statements delivered by state representatives in politically sensitive cases are common in the reports, and decisions are rather frequently adopted by vote.[83] The case of Human Rights in China (HRIC), which was discussed during the Committee's 1999 session, provides an example of a controversial candidature for consultative status.

HRIC is an international NGO which was founded in 1989 by Chinese scientists and scholars. It monitors the implementation of international human rights standards in the People's Republic of China and carries out human rights advocacy and education activities. At its 693rd meeting on 4 June 1999, the Committee on Non-Governmental Organizations had before it the application of HRIC for consultative status with ECOSOC. The representative of China advocated strongly that the Committee should not recommend consultative status to HRIC, stating, *inter alia*, that 'The overwhelming majority of the members of HRIC have never set foot on Chinese soil ... Because of their total ignorance of the realities in China, they are totally disqualified to make any comments on the human rights situation in my country ... Among members of the Board of Directors of that organization are criminals who have been duly punished by judicial organs, criminals who have fled the country but have remained on the wanted list of the Chinese Government, and prisoners who, because of their physical conditions, have been granted medical paroles. The so-called human rights activities they are engaged in have all been born out of their personal vendetta against the Chinese Government and have nothing whatsoever to do with the human rights of the Chinese people in general.'[84]

The representative of China requested a vote on the delegation's proposal not to recommend consultative status for HRIC. The proposal was adopted by a vote of 13 to 3 with 2 abstentions. Among the states which voted in favour of the proposals were, *inter alia*, Algeria, Cuba, Lebanon, Sudan and Turkey, while France, Ireland and the United States voted

---

[82] Aston, 'The United Nations Committee on Non-Governmental Organizations', p. 950.

[83] See, e.g., E/1999/109/Add.2 (Part II), *Report of the Committee on Non-Governmental Organizations on its resumed 1999 session*, 28 March 2000, para. 2 ff. regarding the applications from the Assyrian National Congress, Human Rights Guard, Universidad Latinoamericana de la Libertad Frederich Hayek, etc.

[84] E/1999/109, *Report of the Committee on Non-Governmental Organizations on its 1999 session*, 15 July 1999, para. 24.

384   LEGAL AND EMPIRICAL SURVEY

against.[85] HRIC has not been granted consultative status by ECOSOC; the organisation was also refused accreditation to the World Conference Against Racism in 2001 after opposition from China, in spite of the Conference Secretariat's favourable recommendation.[86]

As regards suspension of consultative status, a couple of examples may be described as an illustration.

In July 2000, the Committee on Non-Governmental Organizations recommended to ECOSOC that it should suspend the consultative status of the International Council of the Association for Peace in the Continents (ASOPAZCO). The discussion regarding ASOPAZCO was initiated by the Cuban delegation, which alleged that the organisation had violated the provisions of ECOSOC Resolution 1996/31 in several ways, for example by organising, supporting and financing subversive activities in Cuba and in other countries.[87] The Cuban delegation proposed that the consultative status of ASOPAZCO should be withdrawn. The organisation responded to, and denied, the allegations in a report which was submitted to the Committee. A direct dialogue between the Committee and the organisation could never take place during the Committee's meetings, as the session was lengthy and the representative of the organisation had to leave New York before the matter was taken up.[88] As the request from the representative of Cuba to take action on ASOPAZCO was formulated during the last days of the Committee's session, some delegations were of the opinion that the matter should be postponed. This motion was, however, rejected by the majority of Committee members, and the representative of ASOPAZCO was given forty-eight hours to appear before the Committee. In spite of protests

---

[85] After the adoption of the proposal, the US representative stated: 'June 4, 1999 – a sad date – the tenth anniversary of the events in Tiananmen Square, which remains unexplained, and also a date we shall recall as one on which the Committee chose to overlook not just the United Nations Charter, the Universal Declaration of Human Rights and the Vienna Declaration and Programme of Action, but also the significant piece of human rights legislation – the Defenders Declaration. Today, this Committee chose to deny accreditation to a non-governmental organization which embodies and advances these objectives, despite the fact that this non-governmental organization meets all the technical criteria which this Committee is mandated to examine'. E/1999/109, para. 27.

[86] Human Rights in China Press Release, *Human Rights in China Excluded from World Conference Against Racism*, 22 May 2001.

[87] E/2000/88 (Part II), *Report of the Committee on Non-Governmental Organizations*, 5 July 2000, paras. 71 ff.

[88] During the same session, the Committee took up as an inherent problem of the procedure for attendance of NGOs under discussion, that the Committee's programme of work could specify only a broad period during which an application or other matter would be considered. It was therefore decided that the NGO representatives with the longest distances to travel should be heard at the beginning of each session. E/2000/88 (Part II), *Report of the Committee on Non-Governmental Organizations*, 5 July 2000, para. 65.

CO-OPERATION WITH INTERGOVERNMENTAL ORGANISATIONS 385

from, among others, the representatives of the United States, France and Germany, the Committee decided to recommend to ECOSOC that the consultative status of ASOPAZCO should be suspended for three years.[89] ECOSOC decided to follow the recommendation, with 11 votes in favour to 5 against, with 2 abstentions.[90]

At the same session of the Committee on NGOs, the Committee recommended ECOSOC to suspend the status of the organisation Transnational Radical Party (TRP) as a result of a protest from the Russian delegation.

The Russian representative alleged that TRP had accredited a Chechen separatist and terrorist to the UN Commission on Human Rights. At the session of the Commission on Human Rights, the representative had identified himself as a representative of the President of Chechnya in Europe and to the United Nations. In its written response, the TRP acknowledged that it had accredited Mr Idigov from Chechnya to speak about gross and systematic violations of human rights, the right to self-determination and the need to end the Chechnya conflict through negotiations. Mr Idigov denied that he was a terrorist or had ever participated in such activities. The decision to recommend suspension of the consultative status of TRP was taken by consensus, but with reservations from some delegations, such as the German delegation, which stated that the measure was out of proportion and that the allegations about TRP had not been verified.[91] In the ECOSOC debate, several speakers questioned the procedure followed in the Committee on Non-Governmental Organizations when considering the case of the TRP, saying that the NGO had not been given a chance to respond to all the allegations made against it and that no conclusive evidence had been presented to confirm allegations of terrorism, drug trafficking and paedophilia. The Council rejected the Committee's draft decision to suspend the status of TRP by a vote of 20 in favour to 23 against, with 9 abstentions.[92]

---

[89] E/2000/88 (Part II), *Report of the Committee on Non-Governmental Organizations*, 5 July 2000, paras. 86 ff.

[90] ECOSOC Decision 2000/307, in E/2000/INF/2/Add.3, *Resolution and Decisions Adopted by the Economic and Social Council*, 1 December 2000, p. 12, UN Press Release 367, *Non-Governmental Organization Committee Recommends Status Suspension*, 23 June 2000. On the Commission's decisions regarding suspension and withdrawal of consultative status, see Aston, 'The United Nations Committee on Non-Governmental Organizations', pp. 952–957.

[91] E/2000/88 (Part II), *Report of the Committee on Non-Governmental Organizations*, 5 July 2000, paras. 101–117.

[92] UN Press Release 5934, *Economic and Social Council Establishes New UN Forum on Forests*, 18 October 2000. For an example of withdrawal of consultative status see, for instance, the example of Christian Solidarity International in E/1999/109, *Report of the Committee on Non-Governmental Organizations on its 1999 session*, 15 July 1999, paras. 69–81, with the ECOSOC discussions that followed in ECOSOC in E/1999/SR.46, *Substantive Session of 1999*,

386   LEGAL AND EMPIRICAL SURVEY

The two-step procedure, with the Committee of Non-Governmental Organizations as a preparatory body and ECOSOC as the decision-making body, compensates for some of the risk that the Committee may adopt a politicised decision or a decision contrary to Resolution 1996/31. It should be noted, however, that in the case of the NGO Christian Solidarity International, the organisation's privileges were temporarily suspended although the Committee had not applied its procedure correctly and was asked to re-examine the case.[93] This means that it is possible for states to prevent an NGO in consultative status from attending a particular session of, for instance, the Sub-Commission on the Promotion and Protection of Human Rights, which meets in July and August.

Observers from NGOs in consultative status with ECOSOC may attend open meetings of the Committee on Non-Governmental Organizations, as well as meetings of all the subsidiary bodies of the Council.[94] In accordance with ECOSOC consultative arrangements, the Committee shall also hold, before each of its sessions and at other times as necessary, consultations with organisations in consultative status to discuss questions of interest to the Committee or to the organisations relating to the relationship between the NGOs and the United Nations.[95]

The ECOSOC standing Committee on Non-Governmental Organizations is served by the Non-Governmental Section of the Secretariat, which prepares documentation for the Committee and provides accreditation for NGOs in consultative status with ECOSOC. It also maintains contact with the Conference of NGOs in Consultative Relationship with the United Nations (CONGO).[96]

Provisional Summary Record of the 46th Meeting, p. 13; ECOSOC Decision 1999/268, in E/1999/INF/2/Add.2, *Resolutions and Decisions Adopted by the Economic and Social Council*, 30 August 1999, pp. 186–187, E/1999/SR.46, p. 15; ECOSOC Decision 1999/292, in E/1999/INF/2/Add.3, *Resolutions and Decisions Adopted by the Economic and Social Council*, p. 9. See also *Statement to ECOSOC on Case of CSI*, By Danielle Bridel, First Vice-President, Conference of CONGO, Geneva, 28 July 1999. Accessible online at www.globalpolicy.org/ngos/docs99/bridel99.htm, as of 20 September 2004.

[93] See n. 92 above.   [94] E/RES/1996/31, para. 35.   [95] *Ibid.*, para. 61(a).

[96] E/1998/43, *Work of the Non-Governmental Section of the Secretariat*, Report of the Secretary-General, 8 May 1998. In 1948, NGOs in consultative status with ECOSOC established CONGO, which is an independent membership association of NGOs that aims at facilitating the participation of NGOs in UN debates and decisions. CONGO convenes meetings on NGO access to the United Nations and issues statements on that subject, and organises discussions with the members of the ECOSOC Committee on NGOs. It does not take positions on substantive matters.

ECOSOC subsidiary bodies and extra-conventional mechanisms

The UN functional commissions have both political and law-making tasks. International conventions and other instruments are drafted here, and the commissions also have functions as regards monitoring compliance with the conventions. NGOs are involved in the work of the functional commissions in accordance with ECOSOC consultative arrangements, which also apply to the subsidiary bodies of ECOSOC. The functional commissions of ECOSOC have common rules of procedure, which include regulations for their relations with NGOs.[97] The Rules, which refer to the ECOSOC consultative arrangements as specified in resolution 1996/31, provide, *inter alia*, that:

- the provisional agenda of the commissions shall include all items which have been proposed by an NGO in general consultative status in accordance with the procedure prescribed by the rules, provided that a two-thirds majority of the members of the commission support this (Rule 5.2(h) and 5.4),
- the agenda and the basic documents related to each item shall be communicated to all NGOs in consultative status (Rule 6),
- NGOs in general or special consultative status may designate authorised representatives to sit as observers at public meetings of the commissions and their subsidiary organs, while NGOs on the Roster may do so when matters within their field of competence are being discussed (Rule 75),
- the functional commissions may consult with NGOs in general or special consultative status, and, on the recommendation of the Secretary-General and at the request of the commission, with organisations on the Roster, either directly or through a committee established for the purpose (Rule 76).

The *Commission on Human Rights* consists of fifty-three state representatives. It prepares studies, makes recommendations and drafts international human rights conventions and declarations. Among the instruments drafted within the Commission are the Universal Declaration of Human Rights, the two human rights Covenants of 1966, and the issue-oriented human rights conventions, such as the CAT and the Convention on the Rights of the Child (CRC). As described

---

[97] E/5975/Rev.1, *Rules of Procedure of the Functional Commissions of the Economic and Social Council*, 3 June 1994.

388   LEGAL AND EMPIRICAL SURVEY

in chapter 5, the Commission also investigates allegations of human rights violations and handles communications relating to them under the 1503 Procedure.[98]

Almost 250 NGOs were represented at the 2003 session of the Commission on Human Rights.[99] NGOs may submit written and oral statements as provided for in resolution 1996/31 on consultative arrangements. Because of the large number of NGOs that participate in the sessions of the Commission, the number and length of their oral statements is limited.[100] Written statements by NGOs in general or special consultative status are issued as official UN documents, and are made available in the three working languages of the Commission if submitted in sufficient time before the session.[101] NGOs are, however, not allowed to distribute any of their own material in the conference room.[102] Apart from direct participation, parallel meetings focused on items dealt with by the Commission or its preparatory committee may be organised by NGOs in the UN conference rooms.[103]

NGOs have been involved in the Commission's consideration and drafting of many human rights instruments. A few examples are the draft optional protocol to the ICESCR,[104] the Optional Protocol to the CAT[105] and the identification of Fundamental Standards of Humanity.[106] The Commission also drafted the Optional Protocol to

---

[98] Section 5.2.

[99] E/2003/23/E/CN.4/135/*Commission on Human Rights, Report on The Fifty-Ninth Session*, 30 September 2003, annex II.

[100] See, e.g., E/CN.4/2001/167, *Commission on Human Rights*, 20 July 2001, Part II, paras. 14–15.

[101] *Ibid.*, para. 29. See also, e.g., E/CN.4/2001/NGO/1,16 January 2001, and E/CN.4/2001/NGO/102, 6 February 2001.

[102] E/CN.4/2001/167, *Commission on Human Rights*, 20 July 2001, Part II, para. 34.

[103] Information note for NGOs, issued on 4 February 2000 in relation to the 56th Session of the Commission on Human Rights, Office of the United Nations High Commissioner for Human Rights.

[104] E/CN.4/2000/49, *Draft Optional Protocol to the International Covenant on Economic, Social and Cultural Rights, Report of the High Commissioner for Human Rights*, 14 January 2000. See para. 4 regarding NGO statements.

[105] E/CN.4/2000/58, *Report of the Working Group on the Draft Optional Protocol to the Convention against Torture*, 2 December 1999. For attendance and statements by NGOs, see paras. 8, 73.

[106] E/CN.4/2000/94, *Fundamental Standards of Humanity, Report of the Secretary-General Submitted Pursuant to Commission Resolution 1999/65*, 27 December 1999. Comments and views from states and NGOs are integrated throughout the document. The matter was considered in consultation with the ICRC, see E/CN.4/2001/91, *Promotion and Protection of Human Rights*, 12 January 2001, para. 1.

the Convention on the Rights of the Child on the involvement of children in armed conflicts and the Optional Protocol to the Convention on the Rights of the Child on the sale of children, child prostitution and child pornography.[107] NGOs have sent observers to the meetings of standard-setting working groups – such as the (former) Working Group on a Draft Optional Protocol to the Convention against Torture and the (former) Working Group on a Draft Optional Protocol to the Convention on the Rights of the Child on the sale of children, child prostitution and child pornography – and have presented their views on the drafts under discussion.[108]

The *Open-Ended Working Group on a Draft Declaration on the Rights of Indigenous Peoples* (to be distinguished from the Working Group on Indigenous Populations of the Sub-Commission, discussed below) involves NGOs in its work to a large extent. As with all the subsidiary bodies of ECOSOC, NGOs may participate in the proceedings. In addition to the ECOSOC arrangements for consultation with NGOs, the Commission on Human Rights has set up a procedure for the participation of 'organisations of indigenous people' without consultative status with ECOSOC in the meetings of the Working Group.[109] The meetings are attended by a high number of representatives from indigenous organisations and other NGOs. As an illustration, it can be mentioned that the Working Group held nineteen meetings during the period 15–26 September 2003, during which forty-four governments and eighty-two indigenous and non-governmental organizations were represented.[110] The Working Group's debates on the draft declaration include statements and text proposals of participating states as well as of indigenous and other NGOs.[111]

---

[107] Adopted by A/RES/54/263, 25 May 2000. See also E/CN.4/2000/WG.13/3, *Report of the Chairperson of the WG on a Draft Protocol on Children in Armed Conflicts*, 6 December 1999, which describes broad informal consultations with, *inter alia*, governments, UN bodies and specialised agencies, IGOs and NGOs.

[108] See, e.g., Working Group reports E/CN.4/2000/58, 2 December 1999, paras. 8, 73; E/CN.4/1999/59, 26 March 1999, paras. 8, 59, 90; E/CN.4/1999/74, 25 March 1999, para. 15; E/CN.4/1998/103, 24 March 1998, paras. 13–15.

[109] E/CN.4/RES/1995/32, *Establishment of a Working Group*, para. 7 and annex.

[110] E/CN.4/2004/81, *Indigenous issues*, 7 January 2004, para. 2.

[111] *Ibid.*, paras. 21 ff. See also E/CN.4/2000/84, 6 December 1999, on the meetings in November and December 1999. The high degree of non-governmental representation at this meeting was regarded as a problem by some of the state representatives. During the meeting it was proposed that possibilities should be provided for informal consultations between governments during the session of the Working Group. The indigenous caucus opposed the suggested 'formalisation of informal meetings'

390   LEGAL AND EMPIRICAL SURVEY

Another of the Commission on Human Rights' working groups, of special interest from a civil society point of view, is the *ad hoc Open-Ended Working Group on a Permanent Forum for Indigenous People in the United Nations System*, which was established by the Commission in 1998. The working group organised its work in a rather untraditional way, with both state representatives and representatives of indigenous peoples participating in the Working Group's discussions and acting as facilitators for its meetings.[112] In July 2000, ECOSOC decided to establish the *Permanent Forum on Indigenous Issues* as an advisory body to the Council. It consists of sixteen members, eight members to be nominated by governments and elected by the Council, and eight members to be appointed by the President of the Council. Indigenous organisations shall be consulted before the appointment of the latter eight members. All members serve in their personal capacity as independent experts on indigenous issues for a period of three years. NGOs in consultative status with ECOSOC may participate in the Forum as observers, as may organisations of indigenous people in accordance with the procedures which have been applied in the Working Group on Indigenous Populations of the Sub-Commission on the Promotion and Protection of Human Rights.[113] The findings of the Council are, *inter alia*, addressed to ECOSOC, the United Nations and its member states in the form of recommendations.[114]

The *Sub-Commission on the Promotion and Protection of Human Rights* (formerly the Sub-Commission on Prevention of Discrimination and Protection of Minorities) is the main subsidiary body of the Commission on Human Rights. The twenty-six members of the Sub-Commission are nominated by states but act in an independent capacity

> excluding the participation of indigenous peoples. A representative of one of the indigenous organisations stated that to legitimise informal governmental meetings during the Working Group session would violate the principle established in Commission on Human Rights resolution 1995/32, which provided for the participation of indigenous representatives. The United States and Canada – both states with indigenous peoples within their territories – endorsed the proposal for informal consultations while New Zealand agreed to striking informal governmental meetings from the work plan. The Working Group adopted a revised work programme which allowed for the plenary to be suspended if requested by the participants. The indigenous representatives were allowed to be present at the informal consultations in order to allow for transparency, but could not take an active role, see paras. 18–25.

[112] E/CN.4/2000/86, *Report of the Open-Ended Inter-Sessional*, 28 March 2000.

[113] E/RES/2000/22, *Establishment of a Permanent Forum on Indigenous Issues*, 28 July 2000, paras. 1–2.

[114] See, e.g., the recommendations of the Forum's third session, E/2004/43, *Permanent Forum on Indigenous Issues, Report on the Third Session*, 10–21 May 2004, paras. 2 ff.

as experts. The functions of the Sub-Commission include the preparations of studies, the review of specific country situations and human rights standard-setting, although the last function has been given less emphasis in favour of promotion and implementation during recent years.[115] The Sub-Commission has adopted guidelines for its application of the Rules of Procedure of the Functional Commissions. These guidelines establish rules for consultation with and representation of NGOs that are identical with the rules of the functional commissions.[116]

The meetings of the Sub-Commission are regularly attended by a large number of NGO observers; NGOs by far outnumber states, as both organisations and as individual representatives.[117] Written statements submitted by NGOs to the Sub-Commission are published as official UN documents.[118] David Weissbrodt, who is a former member of the Sub-Commission, emphasises the role of NGOs in the work of the Sub-Commission, in particular as regards country situations. During the sessions of the Sub-Commission, NGOs submit reports and make written and oral statements which, together with other information, provide a basis for the Sub-Commission's decisions as to which country situations to review and address in resolutions. In general, the Sub-Commission attempts to maintain an open dialogue between its members and representatives of NGOs, IGOs and governments.[119]

The Sub-Commission has established several working groups. The annual *Working Group on Indigenous Populations*, established by ECOSOC in 1982, is probably one of the UN bodies with the highest level of NGO attendance.[120] The Working Group consists of independent experts and members of the Sub-Commission and is open to *all* representatives of indigenous peoples and their communities and organisations, as well as to representatives of governments, NGOs and UN agencies. As an

---

[115] David Weissbrodt, 'An Analysis of the Fifty-First Session of the United Nations Sub-Commission on the Promotion and Protection of Human Rights', 22 HRQ (2000), p. 790.

[116] *Guidelines for the Application by the Sub-Commission on the Promotion and Protection of Human Rights of the Rules of Procedure of the Functional Commissions of the Economic and Social Council and other Decisions and Practices Relating Thereto*, in E/CN.4/2000/2, 11 November 1999, Decision 1999/114.

[117] See, e.g., E/CN.4/Sub.2/AC.4/1999/INF.2, *Final List of Attendance*, 30 July 1999.

[118] See, e.g., E/CN.4/Sub.2/2000/NGO/10, *Written Statement Submitted by North–South XXI*, 12 July 2000.

[119] Weissbrodt, 'An Analysis of the Fifty-First Session', pp. 791–792.

[120] E/RES/1982/34, *Study of the Problem of Discrimination*, 7 May 1982.

392   LEGAL AND EMPIRICAL SURVEY

example, over 1,000 persons participated in the 2000 session of the Working Group, including representatives of forty-five member states and 248 indigenous and (other) NGOs.[121] Information received by the Working Group from NGOs on different issues is published and distributed as UN documents. Indigenous and other NGO representatives also deliver oral statements in the meetings of the Working Group, as reflected in its reports.[122]

The Working Group has considered and delivered studies on different themes, such as indigenous peoples and their relationship to land.[123] Its most important achievement in terms of standard-setting has been the elaboration of the Draft UN Declaration on the Rights of Indigenous Peoples, which was completed in 1993 after nearly ten years of work with the participation of many hundreds of indigenous organisations. After the draft was adopted by the Sub-Commission and submitted to the Commission on Human Rights, the Commission set up the Open-Ended Working Group on a Draft Declaration on the Rights of Indigenous Peoples noted above, which has not yet completed its work. When or if the declaration is finally adopted, the participation of indigenous groups and NGOs in the Working Group is likely to increase the possibility that the instrument is perceived as legitimate by the groups whose rights it is intended to protect.

The Working Group also reviews developments related to the situation of indigenous groups in different parts of the world. The Working Group provides an important forum in this respect, as the indigenous communities themselves may participate in the meetings and discuss their situation with state representatives.[124]

Following the UN Conference on Environment and Development in 1992, the General Assembly requested ECOSOC to set up a *Commission on Sustainable Development* (CSD) in order to ensure effective follow-up to the Conference, to enhance international co-operation for the integration of environment and development issues and to examine progress in the implementation of Agenda 21.[125] ECOSOC established the Commission in 1993 with several functions enumerated by the Assembly, among

---

[121] E/CN.4/Sub.2/2000/24, *Human Rights of Indigenous Peoples*, 17 August 2000, para. 6.

[122] *Ibid.*, paras. 19–23.

[123] E/CN.4/Sub.2/1997/17, *Preliminary Working Paper*, 20 June 1997 and Corr.1 and E/CN.4/Sub.2/1999/19, *Report of the Working Group*, 12 August 1999.

[124] For more details regarding the work of the Working Group, see Weissbrodt, 'An Analysis of the Fifty-First Session', pp. 825–829.

[125] A/RES/47/191, *Institutional Arrangements*, 29 January 1993, paras. 2–3.

them to monitor progress in the implementation of Agenda 21, to consider information provided by governments, to review and analyse relevant input from competent NGOs, including those in the scientific and the private sector, in the context of the implementation of Agenda 21, and to enhance dialogue with NGOs and the independent sector.[126] The CSD does not draft international environmental instruments, but is of interest because two of its functions are specifically related to NGOs. This was a natural consequence of the large involvement of NGOs in the Rio Conference and the recognition of the role of NGOs and 'major groups' expressed in Agenda 21.[127] The Commission has drawn up its own Roster for relations with NGOs, in addition to NGOs which participate on the basis of their consultative status with ECOSOC.[128] This means that NGOs in consultative status with ECOSOC, as well as NGOs included on the CSD's Roster, may participate in the sessions of the Commission; 145 NGOs were represented as observers at the Commission's eleventh session in 2003.[129] The modalities for co-operation are regulated by ECOSOC consultative arrangements.

The *extra-conventional mechanisms* include the country and thematic rapporteurs, the special representatives and a range of working groups created by the General Assembly and the functional commissions. Although the thematic mechanisms have no formal complaints procedure, some of them do receive communications regarding human rights violations. These are submitted from different sources, such as the victims or their relatives, or NGOs.

The Working Group on Enforced or Involuntary Disappearances assists the relatives of disappeared persons in ascertaining their fate and whereabouts and acts as a channel of communication between the families and the governments concerned. In 2003, 41,934 cases were under active consideration by the Working Group, as they had not yet been clarified or discontinued.[130] During the same year, the Working Group clarified 837 cases of enforced disappearance.[131] The Working Group has also established an urgent action procedure under which its

---

[126] E/1993/207, *Establishment of the Commission on Sustainable Development*, 12 February 1993.

[127] See section 8.3.

[128] E/1998/29, *Commission on Sustainable Development, Report on the Sixth Session*, pp. 90–91.

[129] E/2003/29, *Commission on Sustainable Development, Report on the Eleventh Session*, para. 10 and annex II.

[130] E/CN.4/2004/58, *Civil and Political Rights, Including the Questions of Disappearances and Summary Executions*, 21 January 2004, p. 2.

[131] *Ibid.*, para. 5.

394   LEGAL AND EMPIRICAL SURVEY

chairperson is authorised to process cases immediately. In 2003, the Working Group sent urgent action appeals to governments concerning forty-three cases.[132] Information on disappearances is submitted to the Working Group by representatives of human rights NGOs, associations of relatives of missing persons and by relatives of disappeared persons.[133] It also meets with representatives of NGOs to discuss its methods of work.[134]

Similar methods are used by the Working Group on Arbitrary Detention, which is entrusted with the investigation of instances of alleged arbitrary deprivation of liberty. During the reporting period January–December 2001, the Working Group submitted 167 individual cases to governments. Of these, sixty-three were based on information communicated by local or regional NGOs, seventy-eight on information provided by international NGOs in consultative status with ECOSOC, and twenty-six by private sources.[135] Obviously, NGOs constitute the most important source of information on individual cases of arbitrary detention investigated by the Working Group.

Generally speaking, NGOs are an important source of information for many of the country and thematic rapporteurs. Sir Nigel Rodley, who held the position of Special Rapporteur of the Commission on Human Rights on the question of torture from 1993 until 2001, considered that he could not have carried out his work adequately without the information submitted by NGOs, which provided around 90 per cent of all information received by him.[136] The working methods of the rapporteur include the sending of urgent appeals, the transmittal of information alleging violations to governments and the carrying out of missions to UN member states.[137]Apart from receiving reports and other types of information from NGOs, the rapporteur meets with NGOs on his country visits.[138]

---

[132] *Ibid.*
[133] E/CN.4/2001/68, *Civil and Political Rights, Including the Questions of Disappearances and Summary Executions*, 18 December 2000, para. 19.
[134] *Ibid.*, paras. 21–23.
[135] E/CN.4/2002/77, *Civil and Political Rights, Including the Questions of Torture and Detention*, 19 December 2001, para. 13.
[136] *Interview with Sir Nigel Rodley*, 16 November 2000. In an article, Rodley observes that the non-treaty-based mechanisms 'would simply not be able to function effectively without NGOs', see 'Human Rights NGOs: Rights and Obligations', in Theo Van Boven *et al.* (eds.), *The Legitimacy of the United Nations: Towards an Enhanced Legal Status of Non-State Actors*, Netherlands Institute of Human Rights, SIM Special, 19, Utrecht, 1997, p. 55.
[137] Regarding the Special Representative of the Secretary-General on the situation of human rights defenders, see section 4.2.
[138] See also, e.g., E/CN.4/2000/9/Add.4, *Civil and Political Rights*, 9 March 2000, para. 4.

The UN treaty bodies

Introduction

The status of NGOs as petitioners or counsel to petitioners before the treaty bodies has been described earlier.[139] This section focuses on other forms of relations between the treaty bodies and NGOs.

Seven committees have been established to monitor the implementation of the principal international human rights treaties: the Human Rights Committee (which monitors the implementation of the ICCPR), the Committee on Economic, Social and Cultural Rights (which monitors the ICESCR), the Committee against Torture (which monitors CAT), the Committee on the Elimination of Racial Discrimination (which monitors CERD), the Committee on the Elimination of Discrimination against Women (which monitors CEDAW), the Committee on the Rights of the Child (which monitors the CRC) and the Committee on the Protection of the Rights of All Migrant Workers and Members of their Families (which monitors the Convention on the Protection of the Rights of All Migrant Workers and Members of Their Families).

In general, it can be observed that NGOs play an increasingly important role in the work of human rights treaty bodies. At a joint meeting in 1996 on the effective implementation of human rights instruments, the chairpersons of the treaty bodies affirmed 'once again that non-governmental organizations play a vital role in supplying the treaty bodies with documentation and other information on human rights developments that is extremely useful for their monitoring activities and that each treaty body should consider how best to monitor and facilitate this role'. The chairpersons encouraged NGOs to continue to take an active role in critically examining the work of the treaty bodies.[140] Sir Nigel Rodley holds that NGOs play a most important role in submitting information to members of the respective bodies, thereby ensuring that they are in a position to question the version presented in official state reports.[141] With the exception of the Committee on Economic, Social and Cultural Rights, the treaty bodies are not subsidiary bodies of ECOSOC, and the ECOSOC consultative arrangements are therefore not applicable to NGO–treaty body relations.

---

[139] Section 5.2.
[140] A/51/482, *Human Rights Questions*, 11 October 1996, paras. 35–36. See also A/52/507, 21 October 1997, para. 61.
[141] Rodley, 'Human Rights NGOs', p. 52.

396   LEGAL AND EMPIRICAL SURVEY

The Human Rights Committee

Neither the ICCPR nor the Human Rights Committee's Rules of Procedure contain any provisions on co-operation with or information from NGOs. However, under Rule 62 of its Rules of Procedure, the Committee establishes working groups which meet before each session to prepare lists of issues concerning the state party reports to be considered by the Committee during that particular session, and it is an established practice of the working group to hold discussions with representatives of NGOs.[142] This practice is reflected in the Committee's annual reports to the General Assembly.[143] The purpose of these discussions is to obtain advance information on the state party reports to be considered during the session.[144] The information submitted by NGOs to the different treaty bodies is often presented in the form of parallel (or 'shadow') reports to state party reports.[145]

In its reports, the Committee has welcomed the presence of NGOs at open meetings for the consideration of state party reports, although these organisations may not take part in the dialogue between state parties and the committee.[146] Meetings for the consideration of individual or state communications regarding violations of the Convention are closed.[147] In its consideration of the report prepared by Nigeria in 1996, the Committee emphasised that NGOs are entitled to take part in the meetings at which state reports are under consideration and that state parties should not prevent this:

> The Committee wishes to emphasize that the consideration of reports submitted under article 40 of the Covenant takes place in public meetings and in the presence of representatives of the State party concerned. Representatives of non-governmental organizations, whether internationally or locally based, are entitled to attend the meetings at which reports are being considered and to

---

[142] CCPR/C/3/Rev.7, *Rules of Procedure of the Human Rights Committee*, 4 August 2004.

[143] See, e.g., the *Reports of the Human Rights Committee (Vol. I)*, A/54/40, 21 October 1999, para. 18; A/55/40, 10 October 2000, para. 17; A/57/40, 30 October 2002, para. 17. Amnesty International, Human Rights Watch and the Lawyers Committee for Human Rights were among the NGOs heard on these three occasions.

[144] A/57/40, *Report of the Human Rights Committee*, 30 October 2002, para. 17.

[145] See also regarding meetings between Committee members and NGOs prior to the sessions, Andrew Clapham, 'UN Human Rights Reporting: An NGO Perspective', in Philip Alston and James Crawford (eds.), *The Future of UN Human Rights Treaty Monitoring*, Cambridge University Press, 2000, pp. 176–181.

[146] See, e.g., A/54/40, 21 October 1999, para. 144 and A/52/40, 21 September 1997, para. 80.

[147] Rules 75 and 96.

provide information to members of the Committee on an informal basis. The Government of Nigeria should ensure that individuals (including members of non-governmental organizations) are not prevented from leaving Nigeria to attend the Committee's sessions, should conduct immediate investigations into the allegations mentioned in paragraph 290 above, and should inform the Committee of the result of these investigations.[148]

The background to this statement was allegations by a Nigerian NGO that two of its officials had been prevented by the State Security Service from attending the session of the Committee and had had their passports impounded.

The Committee sometimes refers to written information submitted by NGOs in its concluding observations on state party reports when the state's information has been incomplete or contradictory of other sources, or even expresses its regret that no NGO submitted information.[149] A formulation often used by the Committee is that: 'The information submitted by a wide range of non-governmental organizations also assisted the Committee in its understanding of the human rights situation in the State party.'[150] State co-operation with NGOs on the national plane in activities related to the implementation of the Covenant is seen as a positive factor by the Committee.[151]

The Committee on Economic, Social and Cultural Rights

The functions of the Committee on Economic, Social and Cultural Rights are similar to those of the treaty bodies, although it was not established under a treaty but by means of an ECOSOC resolution.[152] The Committee is thus a subsidiary body of ECOSOC, and the latter's arrangements for consultation with NGOs are applicable to it. Because of the treaty monitoring function of the Committee, however, it has established its own procedures for relations with NGOs in addition to those of ECOSOC in general. The Committee adopted a procedure

---

[148] A/51/40, 24 July 1996, paras. 290, 304.
[149] See, e.g., A/54/40, 21 October 1999, para. 141, A/53/40; 15 September 1998, para. 139; A/52/40, 21 September 1997, paras. 266, 418.
[150] A/52/40, 21 September 1997, para. 266 (regarding Colombia). See also A/53/40, 15 September 1998, para. 139 (regarding Belarus).
[151] See, e.g., A/54/40, 21 October 1999, paras. 102, 222; A/53/40, 15 September 1998, paras. 56, 123, 208.
[152] E/RES/1985/17, *Review of the Composition, Organization*, 28 May 1985.

concerning the participation of NGOs in its activities in 1993, which was supplemented in 2000 by detailed guidelines.[153]

The main activities that are open to NGO participation are consideration of state party reports, days of general discussion and drafting of general comments. As regards the consideration of state party reports, NGOs can participate at several stages of the procedure.[154] National NGOs working within the field of economic, social and cultural rights are encouraged to contact the Committee Secretariat when a party has ratified the Covenant. Once a state party has submitted a report, the Secretariat of the Committee establishes a list of national NGOs and contacts them in writing to solicit information regarding the implementation of the Covenant. NGOs can submit any type of information they consider relevant to the Secretariat or to the pre-sessional working groups which are set up to prepare for the consideration of state reports during the next session. During the Committee's session, information can be submitted in the form of a parallel report and/or oral statements within the framework of the Committee's NGO hearings which are arranged on the first day of each reporting session. The Committee is also interested in information as a follow-up to its concluding observations regarding a country. The information thus collected is included in the Committee's country file.

NGOs in general or special consultative status with ECOSOC may submit written statements to the Committee at its reporting sessions. NGOs without such status may submit written statements if they are supported by an NGO with consultative status. Statements thus submitted are translated into the working languages of the Committee and issued as UN documents if they have been submitted three months prior to the session.

NGO information regarding non-reporting states is considered as 'especially valuable'. NGO reports structured as an official state report, i.e. discussing article by article the implementation of the Covenant, are especially appreciated. According to the guidelines, it is also 'highly recommended' as regards non-reporting states that NGOs participate in the Committee's NGO hearings and submit oral information regarding the country in question.[155]

---

[153] E/1994/23, *Report of the Committee on Economic, Social and Cultural Rights*, 1993, para. 354; E/C.12/1993/WP.14, *Non-Governmental Organizations Participation in Activities of the Committee on Economic, Social and Cultural Rights*, 12 May 1993; E/C.12/2000/6, *Substantive Issues*, 7 July 2000.
[154] *Ibid.*, paras. 4–29.   [155] *Ibid.*, paras. 28–29.

As mentioned above, NGOs are entitled to participate in the Committee's days of general discussions on particular rights or aspects of the Covenant. Specialised NGOs may submit background information to the Committee, as well as send their experts to participate in the meetings.[156]

Finally, the Committee receives information from NGOs for the purpose of drafting its General Comments on the Articles of the Covenant. During the stages and drafting of such Comments, specialised NGOs may address the Committee in writing. NGOs may also make short oral interventions during the discussion of a Comment.[157]

The Committee Against Torture

As part of its examination of state party reports on the implementation of the Convention, the CAT regularly receives information from NGOs.[158] The legal basis of this practice is contained in Rule 62(1) of the Committee's rules of procedure, which states that 'the Committee may invite ... non-governmental organizations in consultative status with the Economic and Social Council to submit to it information, documentation and written statements, as appropriate, relevant to the Committee's activities under the Convention'.[159] The participation of NGOs in national activities undertaken to contribute to the implementation of the Convention is also regarded by the Committee as a positive factor.[160]

Article 20(1) of the Convention states that if the Committee receives reliable information which appears to contain well-founded indications that torture is being systematically practised in the territory of a state party, the Committee shall invite that state to co-operate in the examination of the information. On the basis of the initial information, the Committee may decide to request additional information, from the representatives of the state concerned, from IGOs, NGOs or individuals.[161] It can be presumed that NGOs are an important source of information for the procedure under Article 20, even if information

---

[156] *Ibid.*, paras. 30–31.   [157] *Ibid.*, paras. 32–33.

[158] See e.g. A/53/44,16 September 1998, para. 111; A/54/44, *Report of the Committee against Torture*, 24 June 1999, para. 160; A/57/44, 1 November 2002, paras. 125, 130, 134.

[159] CAT/C/3/Rev. 4, *Rules of Procedure*, 9 August 2002.

[160] See, e.g., A/54/44, *Report of the Committee against Torture*, 24 June 1999, paras. 134 and 143; A/53/44, 16 September 1998, para. 247.

[161] CAT/C/3/Rev. 4, *Rules of Procedure*, 9 August 2002, Rules 75(1), 76(4).

400 LEGAL AND EMPIRICAL SURVEY

on such cases is published only if the Committee decides so after the inquiry has been concluded. During the 1990s, information on Article 20 inquiries was published in only two cases; Amnesty International was an important source of information in both investigations.

In an inquiry on Egypt which was begun in 1996, the initial information was submitted by Amnesty International.[162] The Committee decided to invite Amnesty International to submit additional relevant information substantiating the facts of the situation, including statistics. Information was also submitted by other NGOs.[163] In its conclusions, the Committee noted that the information on allegations of torture in Egypt had been provided mainly by the Special Rapporteur of the Commission on Human Rights on questions relating to torture, Amnesty International, the Egyptian Organization for Human Rights, and the World Organization against Torture. Other non-governmental sources had occasionally provided information during the inquiry. The NGOs claimed that torture had been regularly practised by the Egyptian police forces, especially by the State Security Intelligence, while the government stated that it remained committed to applying the articles of the Convention and that violations of the laws prohibiting torture constituted exceptional individual cases. The Committee found that there was a clear contradiction between the allegations made by non-governmental sources and the information provided by the government with regard to the role of the Egyptian security forces and the methods they used. As the government did not accept a visit by the Committee, it had to draw its conclusions on the basis of the information available to it. The Committee stated that: 'On the basis of this information, the Committee is forced to conclude that torture is systematically practised by the security forces in Egypt, in particular by State Security Intelligence, since in spite of the denials of the Government, the allegations of torture submitted by reliable non-governmental organizations consistently indicate that reported cases of torture are seen to be habitual, widespread and deliberate in at least a considerable part of the country.'[164]

It is interesting to note that the Committee preferred to trust the non-governmental information rather than that of the government in this case. One factor which was explicitly mentioned by the Committee as a ground for relying on the information provided by NGOs was that a great number of coinciding allegations had come from different sources.[165] The other case on which the Committee decided to publish information concerned Turkey, concerning which an account was included in its *Sixth Annual Report* of 1993.[166] In this case, the

---

[162] A/51/44, 3 May 1996, para. 181.   [163] *Ibid.*, paras. 182–183.   [164] *Ibid.*, paras. 201–220.
[165] *Ibid.*, para. 219.   [166] A/48/44/Add.1, 15 November 1993.

Committee received numerous allegations of torture in Turkey originating mainly from five international and five Turkish human rights NGOs.[167] In 2001 and 2002, the Committee also published information on the situations in Peru and Sri Lanka. In these two cases, the initial information also came from NGOs.[168]

As has been discussed in chapter 5, the Committee also receives individual communications regarding violations of the Convention.

The Committee on the Elimination of Discrimination against Women

Apart from the complaints mechanism described in chapter 5, the Committee co-operates with NGOs in several ways. The Committee's Rules of Procedure include a general provision regarding co-operation with NGOs:

Representatives of non-governmental organizations may be invited by the Committee to make oral or written statements and to provide information or documentation on areas relevant to the Committee's activities under the Convention to meetings of the Committee or to the pre-session working group.[169]

Since 1997, the Committee has invited representatives of national and international NGOs to a meeting of the pre-session Working Group.[170] During the meeting, NGOs are invited to offer country-specific information on the state parties that are to be reviewed by the Committee. One form of providing such information consists of reports prepared by NGOs and disseminated to the Committee members parallel to state party reports. The Committee recommends that state parties consult national NGOs in the preparation of their reports as required

---

[167] *Ibid.*, para. 36.

[168] A/56/44, *Report of the Committee Against Torture*, 26 October 2001, para. 146; A/57/44, 1 November 2002, para. 125.

[169] *Rules of Procedure of the Committee on the Elimination of Discrimination Against Women*, Article 47, in HRI/GEN/3, *Compilation of Rules of Procedure Adopted by Human Rights Treaty Bodies*, 6 June 2001.

[170] See *Report of the Committee on the Elimination of Discrimination against Women* A/52/38/Rev.1, 12 August 1997, Decision 16/II; A/53/38/Rev.1, 14 May 1998, Decision 18/I; A/54/38, 4 May 1999, Decision 20/1. See also CEDAW/C/1997/5, *Ways and Means of Expediting the Work of the Committee*, 6 December 1996, paras. 28–48 and Mara R. Bustelo, 'The Committee on the Elimination of Discrimination Against Women at the Crossroads', in Philip Alston and James Crawford (eds.), *The Future of UN Human Rights Treaty Monitoring*, Cambridge University Press, 2000, pp. 104–108.

402 LEGAL AND EMPIRICAL SURVEY

by Article 18 of the Convention.[171] NGO comments are occasionally included in the official state party reports.[172]

NGOs are sometimes asked to pressurise their governments on different issues. In the report on its twentieth session, the Committee noted that a number of NGOs had been requested by the Committee's Chairperson to encourage ratification of the Convention. The Committee further noted that, as a result of those efforts, several states had accepted the Convention.[173] In general, co-operation between state parties and NGOs on the national plane in activities related to the implementation of the Covenant is seen as a positive factor by the Committee, and is encouraged.[174]

The Committee also collaborates with NGOs in its preparation of General Recommendations on particular Articles or aspects of the Convention.[175]

The Committee on the Elimination of Racial Discrimination

Like the other treaty bodies, the Committee on the Elimination of Racial Discrimination (CERD) examines state party reports. Originally, the Committee did not deal with information submitted by NGOs, as there is no explicit support for this in the Convention.[176] In 1991, however, the Committee decided that 'in examining the reports of State parties, members of the Committee must have access, as independent experts,

---

[171] A/52/38/Rev.1, 12 August 1997, Decision 16/II, *Non-Governmental Organizations*. In this decision, the Committee 'recommended that States parties consult national non-governmental organizations in the preparation of their reports required by article 18 of the Convention. It recommended that international non-governmental organizations and United Nations agencies, funds and programmes be encouraged to facilitate attendance at Committee sessions by representatives of national non-governmental organizations. It also recommended that specialized agencies and other United Nations entities with field representation work with non-governmental organizations to disseminate information on the Convention and on the work of the Committee and to call upon past and present experts of the Committee to participate in those efforts.' As regards the participation of NGOs in the preparation of State Party reports, see also, e.g., A/54/38, 4 May 1999, paras. 140, 334.

[172] A/52/38/Rev.1, 12 August 1997, para. 256.

[173] A/54/38, *Report of the Committee on the Elimination of Discrimination Against Women*, 4 May 1999, para. 33.

[174] *Ibid.*, paras. 59, 86, 224; A/53/38/Rev. 1, 14 May 1998, paras. 189 and 385; A/57/38 (Part I), 7 May 2002, paras. 84, 118, 135, 184.

[175] A/54/38, *Report of the Committee on the Elimination of Discrimination Against Women*, 4 May 1999, General Recommendation 24, para. 3; A/57/38 (Part I), 7 May 2002, para. 416.

[176] Interview with Peter Nobel, former member of the Committee, 29 September 2000.

CO-OPERATION WITH INTERGOVERNMENTAL ORGANISATIONS   403

to all other available sources of information, governmental and non-governmental'.[177] The Committee now regularly receives information from NGOs. According to Peter Nobel, who is a former member of the Committee, it would be difficult for it to carry out its work effectively without the information submitted by NGOs, as the information contained in state party reports tends to be one-sided and focused on legislation and statistics, rather than on actual realities.[178] The type of information from NGOs that is most useful for the Committee is shadow reports structured in the same way as the official state reports.[179] In general, information submitted by several NGOs jointly is regarded as more reliable than information filed by an individual organisation. There is no requirement that NGOs which submit information should be in consultative status with ECOSOC. In its concluding observations on state party reports, the Committee occasionally refers to information submitted by NGOs when the information provided by the state is incomplete or contradicts other sources.[180] The Committee welcomes the participation of NGOs in the preparation of state party reports.[181] It also regards co-operation between state parties and NGOs in activities aimed at promoting the implementation of the Convention on the national plane as something positive. One example of this approach is the recommendation of the Committee that 'the State party take measures aimed at establishing a genuine dialogue between the Government and non governmental organizations in the fight against racial and ethnic discrimination'.[182]

---

[177] Decision 1 (XL) of 13 August 1991; A/46/18, *Report of the Committee on the Elimination of Racial Discrimination*, 1992, p. 104.

[178] Interview with Peter Nobel, former member of the Committee, 29 September 2000.

[179] Some NGOs specialise in collecting and structuring information from other NGOs and submitting it to the country Rapporteur of the Committee prior to each session. As the Committee's Secretariat has limited capacity, this service is much appreciated by the Committee. One NGO, the Anti Racism Information Service (ARIS) has an important role in this respect and is sometimes referred to in the Committee as 'our nineteenth member'. *Ibid.*

[180] See, e.g., *Report of the Committee on the Elimination of Racial Discrimination*, A/53/18, 10 September 1998, paras. 102, 124; A/57/18, 1 November 2002, paras. 261, 498. See also the comments of Australia in A/55/18 (Annex X, p. 168), where the government stated that it was 'very disappointed that the Committee ... gave undue weight to NGO submissions, and strayed from its legitimate mandate'.

[181] See, e.g., A/54/18, 29 September 1999, paras. 421, 442, 483.

[182] A/54/18, 29 September 1999, para. 163. See also, e.g., A/57/18, 1 November 2002, paras. 151, 304.

404   LEGAL AND EMPIRICAL SURVEY

As a result of recommendations contained in the Report of the seventh meeting of persons chairing human rights treaty bodies, the Chairman of the Committee on the Elimination of Racial Discrimination began a practice at its fiftieth session in 1995 of holding a separate informal hearing with NGOs towards the end of each session.[183] NGOs are, however, not permitted to deliver oral statements during the Committee's formal sessions.[184]

Apart from the examination of state party reports, the Committee on the Elimination of Racial Discrimination has developed practices for dealing with early warnings and urgent cases. These activities depend on information from all types of sources, including NGOs. The Committee also hold thematic discussions, which sometimes include informal hearings with NGOs.[185]

The Committee receives complaints from individuals claiming to be the victims of a violation of the Convention. The participation of NGOs in this procedure has been discussed in chapter 5.

The Committee on the Rights of the Child

In spite of the fact that there is no complaints mechanism connected to the International Convention on the Rights of the Child (ICRC), the Committee on the Rights of the Child has extensive collaboration with NGOs. In contrast to the treaty bodies described above, the Committee on the Rights of the Child has a legal basis for co-operating with NGOs in the Convention. Article 45 of the Convention provides that:

In order to foster the effective implementation of the Convention and to encourage international co-operation in the field covered by the Convention:

   a. ... The Committee may invite the specialized agencies, the United Nations Children's Fund and other competent bodies as it may consider appropriate to provide expert advice on the implementation of the Convention in areas falling within the scope of their respective mandates.
   b. The Committee shall transmit, as it may consider appropriate, to the specialized agencies, the United Nations Children's Fund and other competent bodies, any reports from States Parties that contain a

---

[183] A/52/18, 26 September 1997, para. 654 (c). The recommendation of the chairpersons of the treaty bodies is contained in document A/51/482, *Human Rights Questions: Implementation of Human Rights Instruments*, 11 October 1996, paras. 35–36 (see also citation at the beginning of this chapter).

[184] Interview with Peter Nobel, former member of the Committee, 29 September 2000.

[185] *Ibid.*

CO-OPERATION WITH INTERGOVERNMENTAL ORGANISATIONS 405

request, or indicate a need, for technical advice or assistance, along with the Committee's observations and suggestions, if any, on these requests or indications.

The expression 'other competent bodies' was specifically intended to include NGOs. NGOs in general are thereby given a kind of mandate actively to participate in the implementation of the CRC.[186] The role of NGOs in this work is evidenced by the annual reports of the Committee on the Rights of the Child, which include information on the Committee's co-operation with the United Nations and 'other competent bodies'.[187] It can also be noted that the NGOs which co-operate with the Committee on the Rights of the Child are co-ordinated among themselves within the framework of the NGO Group, which had an important role in the drafting of the Convention.[188]

Article 45(c) of the Convention empowers the Committee to request that the Secretary-General undertake studies on matters of general interest to all state parties. The Committee on the Rights of the Child has in practice not only requested the Secretary-General to undertake such studies, but has also turned to NGOs, which have carried out a number of research projects.[189]

In order to facilitate the Committee's work with state party reports, as well as under Article 45 of the Convention, pre-session working groups are held, to which NGOs are regularly invited.[190] During these meetings, state party reports are reviewed and the main questions which

---

[186] Cynthia Price Cohen, 'The United Nations Convention on the Rights of the Child', in Theo C. Van Boven *et al.* (eds.), *The Legitimacy of the United Nations: Towards an Enhanced Legal Status of Non-State Actors*, Netherlands Institute of Human Rights, SIM Special, 19, Utrecht, 1997, p. 180 and 'The Role of NGOs in the Drafting of the Convention on the Rights of the Child', 12 HRQ (1990), p. 146.

[187] See, e.g., CRC/C/87, *Committee on the Rights of the Child, Report on the Twenty-First Session*, 30 July 1999, paras. 256–259. See also Claire Breen, 'The Role of NGOs in the Formulation of and Compliance with the Optional Protocol to the Convention on the Rights of the Child on Involvement of Children in Armed Conflict', 25 HRQ (2003), pp. 458–459.

[188] Price Cohen, 'The United Nations Convention on the Rights of the Child', pp. 173–184.

[189] *Ibid.*, p. 180.

[190] In the Working Group arranged prior to the thirty-fifth session, the NGO Group for the Convention on the Rights of the Child and several other NGOs were represented, CRC/C/137, *Report on the Thirty-Fifth Session*, 11 May 2004, para. 10. Most members of the Committee participated, as did representatives of ILO, OHCHR, UNESCO, UNHCR, UNICEF and WHO.

406   LEGAL AND EMPIRICAL SURVEY

need to be discussed with state representatives are identified. The
Committee also receives written information submitted by NGOs.[191]

Committee on the Protection of the Rights of All Migrant Workers and Members of Their Families

Just as in the case of the Committee on the Rights of the Child, there is a
basis in the Convention for co-operation between NGOs and the
Committee on the Protection of the Rights of All Migrant Workers and
Members of Their Families. Article 74(4) states that:

> The Committee may invite the specialized agencies and organs of the United
> Nations, as well as intergovernmental organizations and other concerned
> bodies to submit, for consideration by the Committee, written information on
> such matters dealt with in the present Convention as fall within the scope of
> their activities.[192]

The Committee's provisional Rules of Procedure made it clear that the
expression 'other concerned bodies' covers NGOs. According to Rule 28,
the expression refers to 'national human rights institutions, non-
governmental organizations, and other bodies'.[193] The Committee
held its first session in March 2004 and has so far not initiated its
considerations of state party reports. It remains to be seen what practice
it develops in relation to NGOs.

Discussions on reform of UN–civil society relationships

It has been mentioned earlier that, in his report to the Fifty-Seventh
General Assembly, the Secretary-General highlighted the engagement
of civil society as an aspect of the UN reform process and announced
that he would 'assemble a group of eminent persons representing a
variety of perspectives and experiences to review past and current
practices and recommend improvements for the future in order to
make the interaction between civil society and the United Nations
more meaningful'. According to the Panel's Terms of Reference, it
should, *inter alia*, (1) review existing guidelines, decisions and practices

---

[191] For more information on the reporting process under the ICESCR and the role of NGOs
in this regard, see Gerison Lansdown, 'The Reporting Process under the Convention on
the Rights of the Child', in Philip Alston and James Crawford (eds.), *The Future of UN
Human Rights Treaty Monitoring*, Cambridge University Press, 2000, pp. 113–127.

[192] International Convention on the Protection of the Rights of All Migrant Workers and
Members of Their Families (1990).

[193] CMW/C/L.1, *Provisional Rules of Procedure*, 13 February 2004.

regarding civil society organisations' access to and participation in UN deliberations and processes, (2) identify best practices in the UN and in other IGOs with a view to identifying new and better ways of interaction with NGOs and other civil society organisations and (3) examine the ways in which participation of civil society actors from developing countries could be facilitated. In February 2003 the Secretary-General appointed a group of eleven persons to form the Panel.[194] The Panel held three meetings and a large number of consultation meetings with NGOs. It published its final report under the title 'We the Peoples: Civil Society, The United Nations and Global Governance' in June 2004.[195]

In reaching its recommendations, the Panel built on four main principles, namely that the UN should (i) become an outward-looking organisation, (ii) embrace a plurality of constituencies, (iii) connect the local with the global, as the deliberative and operational spheres of the United Nations are separated by a wide gulf and (iv) help strengthen democracy for the twenty-first century. The discussions are detailed and provide a great deal of interesting thought and material on the issues of global governance, civil society, the role of the United Nations and the challenges it is facing. It is impossible to give justice to it within the context of this study. Some of the Panel's more general considerations have been mentioned in chapter 1; here, I shall mention only some of the more concrete reform proposals made by the Panel that have direct connections to the UN–NGO relationships described above.

Several of the proposals have the aim of improving and deepening the modalities for co-operation with NGOs. In general, it is considered that UN–civil society engagements should be strengthened. The main reason for this is that it would make the United Nations more effective. An enhanced engagement, it is stated, 'could help the United Nations do a better job, further its global goals, become more attuned and responsive to citizens' concerns and enlist greater public support'.[196]

In the description of UN–NGO relationships above, it was mentioned that there are presently no arrangements for consultation between the General Assembly and NGOs, although NGOs have been advocating for the establishment of such arrangements. The Panel proposes that the General Assembly 'should permit the carefully planned participation of actors besides central Governments in its processes'.[197] Civil society

---

[194] For Terms of Reference and composition of the Panel, see A/58/817, 11 June 2004, annex I.
[195] A/58/817, 11 June 2004.   [196] *Ibid.*, p. 8.   [197] *Ibid.*, p. 16.

408   LEGAL AND EMPIRICAL SURVEY

organisations should be included more regularly in the affairs of the
Assembly, since it no longer makes sense to restrict their involvement
in the intergovernmental process to ECOSOC. In particular, the
Assembly should regularly invite contributions to its committees and
special sessions from those offering high-quality independent
input.[198]

The 'Arria consultations' between NGOs and the Security Council
have also been described below. According to the Panel, today's conflicts
appear to be more complex than ever, and to address them adequately
demands on-the-ground knowledge, new tools, new skills in social and
cultural analysis, the active involvement of communities and their
leaders, links to vulnerable groups and bridges to mainstream development processes. Civil society organisations often have unique capacities
in all those areas, it is claimed. More concretely, Security Council
members should further strengthen their dialogue with civil society,
for instance by (i) improving the planning and effectiveness of the Arria
formula meetings by lengthening lead times and covering travel costs to
increase the participation of actors from the field, and (ii) ensuring that
Council field missions meet regularly with, *inter alia*, appropriate local
civil society leaders and international humanitarian NGOs.[199]

It has been mentioned already that the numbers of NGOs participating in UN meetings are very high. It has also been shown how the
process for considering applications for consultative status with
ECOSOC can in some cases get politicised. The Panel of Eminent
Persons states that it appreciates concerns raised by member states
over the number of civil society organisations seeking to take part in
UN meetings and that some NGO interventions are offensive. But, the
Panel states, 'using the accreditation process to restrict access of civil
society organizations either wholesale, by slowing the application process, or selectively, by arbitrary political judgements, is not a good way

---

[198] *Ibid.*, p. 9. 'Civil society organisations' are understood as associations of citizens
entered into voluntarily to advance their interests, ideas and ideologies. They are
non-profit and do not belong to the public sector. The term seems to be overlapping,
and both wider and narrower than 'non-governmental organisation' as used by the
Panel, as the latter is understood to include associations of businesses, parliamentar-
ians and local authorities. 'Civil society organisations', on the other hand, include
mass organisations (such as organisations of peasants, women or retired people), trade
unions, professional associations, social movements, indigenous people's
organisations, religious and spiritual organisations, academe and public benefit NGOs,
see A/58/817, p. 13.
[199] *Ibid.*, pp. 45–46.

to address such concerns'.[200] The Panel believes it is essential to depoliticise the accreditation process. It is also concerned about the growing phenomenon of accrediting NGOs that are sponsored and controlled by governments. The United Nations should realign accreditation with its original purpose – namely, it should be an agreement between civil society actors and member states based on the applicants' expertise, competence and skills. To achieve this, and to widen the access of civil society organisations beyond ECOSOC Council fora, member states should agree to merge the current procedures at UN Headquarters for the Council, the Department of Public Information and conferences and their follow-up into a single UN accreditation process. An Accreditation Unit should be established within the General Assembly Secretariat, and a designated General Assembly committee would decide on accreditation based on that guidance. The work of the General Assembly committee and the Accreditation Unit would be conducted as transparently as possible, and records of the governmental debate would be posted on the UN website.[201]

The Panel points to problems in the representation of civil society. It argues that civil society speakers come largely from the North, that speakers are largely male, that most civil society organisations have unclear accountability to the grass roots and that the voices of vulnerable groups are underrepresented. It is recommended that the Secretary-General makes redressing North–South imbalances a priority in enhancing UN–civil society relations, and that the UN establish a fund to enhance the capacity of civil society in developing countries to engage in UN processes and partnerships.[202]

Finally, it is worth observing that the Panel also takes a wider view on the importance of a strong civil society for the development of the United Nations. The Panel states that many of its proposals will be fully realisable only if civil society everywhere is given the chance to flourish and is respected by domestic governments as interlocutors and partners. The Panel claims that this would give practical meaning to the freedom of expression, association and assembly that is at the heart of the human rights framework. The priorities identified by the Panel in this area include discussing civil society freedoms in UN fora and at the highest-level meetings between the Secretariat and governments, including those issues in all programmes of good governance and legal reform

---

[200] *Ibid.*, p. 53. [201] *Ibid.*, pp. 54–55. [202] *Ibid.*, pp. 65–66.

410   LEGAL AND EMPIRICAL SURVEY

and promoting consultations with non-state actors in any governmental deliberative process in which the United Nations is party.[203]

For the purposes of the present study, it is indeed interesting to note that the Panel so strongly emphasises the importance of UN–civil society relations. It recommends that these contacts be extended to include new areas of the United Nations, such as the General Assembly and the Security Council, deepened to reach the country and local levels and that selection processes be streamlined and depoliticised. At the heart lie the fundamental freedoms of expression, association and assembly, which the United Nations should promote and protect through its organs and activities. The Chairman of the Panel states that the rise of civil society is one of the landmark events of our times, and that the growing participation and influence of non-state actors is enhancing democracy and reshaping multilateralism: given this reality, 'constructively engaging with civil society is a necessity for the United Nations, not an option'. At the same time, it should be observed that it is not proposed to alter the UN's basic intergovernmental character. Instead, opening up the United Nations to a plurality of constituencies and actors is to be regarded as 'a powerful way to reinvigorate the intergovernmental process itself'.[204]

7.3 The International Labour Organization

The tripartite structure

The ILO, created in 1919 as part of the Treaty of Versailles, was recognised as a specialised agency within the area of labour issues in 1946.[205] The ILO is unique among international organisations in its model, which brings together representatives of governments, employers and workers in the different bodies of the organisation. This model is usually referred to as 'tripartism'.[206] From the perspective of this study, the ILO is in particular interesting as a special model of institutionalised state–non-state co-operation. This tripartite organisation is

---

[203] *Ibid.*, p. 69.   [204] *Ibid.*, p. 3.

[205] *Freedom of Association and Collective Bargaining*, Report of the International Labour Conference, Geneva: International Labour Office, 1994, p. 5.

[206] Virginia Leary, 'The ILO: A Model for Non-State Participation?', in Theo C. Van Boven et al. (eds.), *The Legitimacy of the United Nations: Towards an Enhanced Legal Status of Non-State Actors*, Netherlands Institute of Human Rights, SIM Special, 19, Utrecht, 1997, p. 61 and Arend Lijphart, *Patterns of Democracy: Government Forms and Performance in Thirty-Six Countries*, New Haven: Yale University Press, 1999, p. 16.

also an active producer of international law in the form of treaties, mainly within the area of labour law, as has been discussed earlier in this book.[207]

It was the focus on labour legislation rather than general considerations about the participation of civil society which opened the doors of the ILO to NGOs from the field of labour. Employers' and workers' organisations were already often involved in drafting labour legislation on the national plane when the ILO was established as an organisation. Protests against non-state actors as international legislators were mollified when it was made clear that the instruments elaborated by the ILO would not be binding immediately after adoption by the General Conference, but only after ratification by the state in question.[208]

As provided by Article 1(1) of the ILO Constitution, only states can be members of the ILO. The permanent organisation consists of a General Conference of representatives of the Members, a Governing Body and an International Labour Office controlled by the Governing Body (Article 2). The Conference, which meets annually, elaborates and adopts international labour standards in the form of conventions and recommendations, and is a general forum for social and labour questions of international importance. The Conference also adopts the budget and elects the Governing Body.

According to Article 3 of the Constitution, the meetings of the International Labour Conference (or the General Conference) 'shall be composed of four representatives of each of the Members, of whom two shall be Government delegates and the two others shall be delegates representing respectively the employers and the workpeople of each of the Members'. Non-governmental delegates are nominated by the member states in agreement with the industrial organisations which are most representative of employers or workpeople in their respective countries.[209] The primacy of member states in nominating the non-governmental delegates is somewhat restricted by Article 3(9), which provides that the Conference 'may, by two-thirds of the votes cast by the delegates present, refuse to admit any delegate or adviser whom it deems not to have been nominated in accordance with this article'. The delegates vote individually on all matters taken into consideration by the Conference.[210]

---

[207] See sections 4.2, 5.2.
[208] Leary, 'The ILO: A Model for Non-State Participation?', pp. 62–63.
[209] ILO Constitution, Article 3(5).   [210] *Ibid.*, Article 4(1).

412   LEGAL AND EMPIRICAL SURVEY

The Governing Body is the executive council of the ILO. It takes decisions, *inter alia*, on the policy of the ILO and establishes the programme and the budget for adoption by the Conference. Article 7 provides that the Governing Body shall consist of fifty-six persons: twenty-eight representing governments, fourteen representing the employers, and fourteen representing the workers. The employer and worker representatives in the Conference organise themselves into an Employers' Group and a Workers' Group and (every three years) into Employers' and Workers' Electoral Colleges, which are responsible for electing the employer and worker members of the ILO Governing Body.[211] The Employers' and Workers' Groups of the Governing Body nominate the employers' and workers' representatives on the ILO's various consultative bodies.

For the purpose of this study, however, it is not only relevant to study the institutionalised co-operation between IGOs or governments and NGOs, but also what this co-operation means in terms of NGO input in the development and implementation of international law. One of the objectives of the ILO is to promote 'the recognition of the principle of freedom of association', through the development and promotion of a global system of international labour standards. As mentioned in chapter 4, the organisation has adopted more than 180 conventions covering a broad range of subjects.

The drafting procedure for conventions demonstrates that the ILO tripartite structure is crucial throughout the drafting process. Topics which might result in an international instrument are usually put on the agenda of the International Labour Conference by the Governing Body.[212] When the Conference meets, it normally appoints a tripartite committee to examine proposals for new standards. An important part of the work on international standards is carried out by these tripartite *drafting Committees*, which are set up under Article 6 of the Conference Standing Orders, and which consist of at least three persons. The drafting Committees are in general responsible for expressing in the form of conventions and recommendations the decisions adopted by the Conference and for ensuring agreement between the English and French versions of the texts of all formal instruments submitted to the Conference for adoption.[213] After having discussed

---

[211] *Ibid.*, Article 7(4) and (5) and Articles 49–50, Standing Orders of the International Labour Conference, February 1998.
[212] ILO Constitution, Article 14.
[213] Article 6, Standing Orders of the International Labour Conference, February 1998.

all the aspects of the subject, the tripartite committee adopts its report and proposed conclusions. The proposed text is then submitted to the full Conference. If the Conference adopts the report and conclusions of the committee, it also decides (if the single-discussion procedure is not used) to place the question on the agenda of the next session of the Conference for the second discussion. At the next session of the Conference, the provisional text of the proposed Convention and/or Recommendation is examined again by a tripartite Conference committee. The agreed text is then submitted to the full Conference for approval.

One example of a drafting Committee is the Committee on Child Labour, which originally consisted of 181 members. The Committee presented its first report, including conclusions with a view to a Convention, at the Conference in 1998.[214] The report with the conclusions was adopted by the Conference. The Committee on Child Labour reported a second time to the Conference at its session in 1999 and proposed that a Convention be adopted by the Conference.[215] At the same session, the Conference adopted the Convention concerning the Prohibition and Immediate Action for the Elimination of the Worst Forms of Child Labour (No. 182), which entered into force in November 2000.

The Conference Committee on Application of Standards, set up under Article 7 of the Standing Orders, is important for determining the scope and precise content of the international obligations which are undertaken by state parties to ILO conventions. Like the other ILO committees and bodies, it is tripartite, consisting of a minimum of three persons, of whom the chairperson represents a member state and the other two employers' and workers' organisations, respectively.[216] According to its Terms of Reference, the Committee has to consider, *inter alia*, the measures taken by members to give effect to the Conventions to which they are parties and the information and reports concerning Conventions and Recommendations communicated by

---

[214] International Labour Conference, *Report of the Committee on Child Labour*, 86th Session, Geneva, June 1998, para. 1 and Proposed Conclusions.

[215] International Labour Conference, *Report of the Committee on Child Labour (Corr.)*, 87th Session, Geneva, June 1999.

[216] *Handbook of Procedures Relating to International Labour Conventions and Recommendations*, Geneva: International Labour Office, Rev.2/1998, para. 56; Héctor G. Bartolomei de la Cruz *et al.*, *The International Labour Organization: The International Standards System and Basic Human Rights*, Boulder, Co: Westview Press, 1996, p. 81.

414   LEGAL AND EMPIRICAL SURVEY

Members in accordance with Article 19 of the Constitution.[217] As part of this work, the Committee studies individual cases of apparent failure on the part of states to comply with the conventions ratified by it in a procedure where the state party in question is asked to submit oral and written information to the Committee.[218] The initiative to study a specific case can originate in observations made by the Committee of Experts or in cases examined by the Committee on Freedom of Association.[219] In its annual report to the Conference, the Committee includes information on its discussions as to various states' compliance with specific obligations, failure to comply with reporting obligations, instances of progress, etc. The Committee points out the most serious cases of failure to apply ratified Conventions to the Conference and calls its attention to them. The Committee's reports are usually adopted by the Conference.[220]

Virginia Leary has studied the work of ILO, and in particular the work of the Conference Committee on Application of Standards. According to Leary, the most outstanding contribution to its work is made by the workers who, on the basis of material including official documents as well as NGO reports, consistently point out serious violations of the Conventions. The workers' members in the Committee, however, find that it is too weak a sanction to comment on a state party's violation of a convention in a paragraph in the Committee report, but their advocacy of more forceful sanctions has so far been in vain.[221]

As has been mentioned in chapters 4 and 5, the *Committee on Freedom of Association* examines complaints from governments, workers' and employers' organisations that member states of the ILO are not respecting basic principles of freedom of association.[222] The responsibility of the Committee is essentially to consider, with a view to making a recommendation to the Governing Body, whether cases are worthy of examination. Like the other Committees, the Committee on Freedom of Association is a tripartite body, although its members participate in their personal capacity.

---

[217] *Handbook of Procedures Relating to International Labour Conventions and Recommendations*, para. 57.

[218] *Ibid.*, para. 58(c).

[219] Cases which have not been dealt with at all by the Committee of Experts may not be discussed by the Conference Committee on the Application of Standards, Bartolomei de la Cruz *et al.*, *The International Labour Organization*, p. 82.

[220] *Handbook of Procedures Relating to International Labour Conventions and Recommendations*, para. 58; Bartolomei de la Cruz *et al.*, *The International Labour Organization*, pp. 82–83.

[221] Leary, 'The ILO: A Model for Non-State Participation?', pp. 67–69.

[222] Sections 4.2, 5.2.

Consultative status

In addition to the tripartism that characterises the ILO itself, the organisation also has a structure for consultative relationships with NGOs. Article 12 of the ILO Constitution provides that the organisation 'may make suitable arrangements for such consultation as it may think desirable with recognized non-governmental international organizations, including international organizations of employers, workers, agriculturists and co-operators'. This provision has resulted in the establishment of consultative status for three different categories of international NGOs. The first category includes *International NGOs with an Important Interest in a Wide Range of the ILO's Activities* that are granted either general or regional consultative status. Presently, eight NGOs are in general consultative status and eighteen organisations in regional consultative status with the ILO.[223] The second category, the *Special List of Non-Governmental International Organizations*, has been set up by the ILO Governing Body with a view to establishing working relations with international NGOs other than employers' and workers' organisations which share the principles and objectives of the ILO Constitution and Declaration of Philadelphia. There are presently about 150 NGOs in this category specialised in different fields, such as human rights, poverty alleviation, social security, gender issues, etc.[224] Thirdly, the ILO Governing Body extends *invitations to international NGOs* which meet certain established criteria to attend ILO meetings in which they have demonstrated a particular interest. Representatives of NGOs with general and regional consultative status are permitted at the sittings of the Conference. International NGOs which have been invited by the Governing Body are also allowed to be represented at the Conference.[225] NGOs may also, with the permission of the President, circulate statements for the information of the Conference on questions which are being considered, with the exceptions of administrative and financial questions.[226] NGOs in general or regional consultative status and organisations which have been

---

[223] ILO website at www.ilo.org/public/english/comp/civil/ngo/ngogen.htm and www.ilo.org/public/english/comp/civil/ngo/ngoreg.htm, 23 August 2004.

[224] ILO website at www.ilo.org/public/english/bureau/exrel/civil/ngo/index.htm, 23 August 2004.

[225] Standing Orders of the International Labour Conference, February 1998, Article 2, para. 3(j).

[226] *Ibid.*, Article 14, para. 10.

416   LEGAL AND EMPIRICAL SURVEY

invited by the Governing Body or by the Conference, may also be present at the meetings of the Conference Committees.[227]

7.4 The Council of Europe

The CoE first adopted a resolution on relations with NGOs in 1951. This resolution simply stated that: 'The Committee of Ministers may, on behalf of the Council of Europe, make suitable arrangements for consultation with international non-governmental organisations which deal with matters that are within the competence of the Council of Europe.'[228] The relations with NGOs were elaborated through new rules on consultative status in 1976.[229] A further basis for the arrangements came in 1993 with Resolution (93)38 of the Committee of Ministers and its appended Revised Rules for Consultative Status.[230] Under these arrangements, there was no possibility for national NGOs to enter into formal consultation with the CoE.

In October 2001, following an exchange of views with the Chairman of the Liaison Committee of NGOs Enjoying Consultative Status with the Council of Europe,[231] the Ministers' Deputies invited their Rapporteur on Relations with NGOs to examine the possibilities of adapting Resolution (93)38 in order that the Council might take greater advantage of its relations with NGOs in the pursuit of its aims.[232] A mixed working group composed of representatives of the NGOs enjoying consultative status and members of the Secretariat was set up with the mandate to prepare a draft legal framework updating Resolution (93)38 and permitting the reinforcement of co-operation between the Council of Europe and INGOs.[233] Since the 1993 update of the arrangements, relations between the CoE and INGOs had steadily evolved into an active

---

[227] *Ibid.*, Article 56, para. 9.

[228] Resolution (51) 30 F, *Relations with International Organisations, both Intergovernmental and Non-Governmental*, 3 May 1951, para. 4.

[229] *Relations between the Council of Europe and International Non-Governmental Organisations (Consultative Status)*, May 1976.

[230] Committee of Ministers, *Resolution (93)38 on Relations between the Council of Europe and International Non-Governmental Organisations*, 18 October 1993.

[231] The Liaison Committee of NGOs enjoying participatory (formerly consultative) status was formed in 1976. It is a committee under the responsibility of the NGOs themselves.

[232] RAP-ONG(2003)6, *Report by Mrs Gogoberidze, Rapporteur on Relations between the Council of Europe and Non-Governmental Organisations, to the 837th Meeting of the Ministers' Deputies*, 3 April 2003, para. 2.

[233] *Ibid.*, para. 7.

CO-OPERATION WITH INTERGOVERNMENTAL ORGANISATIONS 417

participation of INGOs in relevant CoE bodies and activities. The objective was thus to transform the consultative status into a participatory one, recognising the practice established in the 1990s. The working group produced a draft resolution on co-operation between the CoE and NGOs. This was transformed by the Secretariat, after several consultations and meetings, into two draft resolutions, one on participatory status for INGOs and one on partnership for national NGOs.[234] In November 2003, the Ministers' Deputies adopted Resolution (2003)8 on participatory status for INGOs with the CoE and Resolution (2003)9 on the status of partnership between the CoE and national NGOs.[235] Interestingly, INGOs were for the first time formerly consulted in the process of adoption of a Committee of Ministers resolution in relation to Resolutions (2003)8 and (2003)9. The Plenary Conference of INGOs enjoying consultative status with the CoE adopted official opinions on the draft resolutions in June 2003 in which it expressed its satisfaction in being consulted and its views on the drafts.[236]

With Resolution (2003)8 the Committee of Ministers wished 'to reflect the active and constructive role of NGOs, and to clarify, facilitate and intensify the co-operation between the Council of Europe and the INGOs, in particular underlining its participatory character'. In the Resolution, it is also stated that it is indispensable that the rules governing the relations between the CoE and NGOs evolve to reflect the active participation of INGOs in the organisation's policy and work programme, and to facilitate INGO participation and access to such bodies as the steering committees and governmental expert committees, and other subsidiary bodies of the Committee of Ministers.[237] It is also worth observing that the new resolution recognises 'the important role to be played by the Liaison Committee as the democratically elected representative body of all of the INGOs enjoying participatory status with the Council of Europe, and by the INGO thematic groupings as their collective voice and, thus, of millions of European citizens, working in each of

---

[234] *Ibid.*, paras. 8–16.
[235] Committee of Ministers, Resolution Res(2003)8, *Participatory Status for International Non-Governmental Organisations with the Council of Europe* and Resolution Res(2003)9, *Status of Partnership between the Council of Europe and National Non-Governmental Organisations with the Council of Europe*, both adopted on 19 November 2003.
[236] The opinions are accessible online at the CoE website at www.coe.int/T/E/NGO/Public/ NGO_PC_Opinion_2003_01.asp#TopOfPage and www.coe.int/T/E/NGO/Public/ NGO_PC_Opinion_2003_02.asp#TopOfPage, as of 27 September 2004.
[237] Committee of Ministers, Resolution Res(2003)8, *Participatory Status for International Non-Governmental Organisations with the Council of Europe*, 19 November 2003.

418   LEGAL AND EMPIRICAL SURVEY

the fields represented by them'.[238] These collective and representative NGO structures within the Council of Europe are considered to increase the efficiency of the co-operation of NGOs within the Council of Europe.[239]

The rules for participatory status of INGOs at the Council of Europe are specified in an appendix to Resolution (2003)8. In order to be granted participatory status, INGOs must meet certain conditions. These are that the INGO should:

- be particularly representative in the field(s) of their competence, which should correspond to the Council of Europe's fields of action,
- be represented at the European level, i.e. have members in a significant number of countries throughout greater Europe,
- be able, through their work, to support the achievement of the closer unity mentioned in Article 1 of the Council of Europe's Statute,[240]
- be capable of contributing to and participating actively in Council of Europe deliberations and activities, and
- be able to make known the work of the Council of Europe among European citizens.[241]

The requirements are basically the same as under the 1993 arrangements, but spelled out a little more elaborately. For example, the condition of being representative on the European level has been specified in the new Resolution as meaning to 'have members in a significant number of countries throughout greater Europe'. Resolution (93)38 simply stated that NGOs should be particularly representative at the European level without any further explanation. Clearly, the CoE did not see any need for conditions regarding established headquarters, a democratically adopted constitution, etc., as is required under the UN ECOSOC arrangements for consultative status.[242] Rather surprisingly,

---

[238] *Ibid.* See also the appendix, paras. 3–5, 7 and 13, 14, 18, which also demonstrates the important role of the Liaison Committee and the INGO thematic groupings.

[239] RAP-ONG(2003)8, *Draft Resolution on Participatory Status for International Non-Governmental Organisations (INGOs) with the Council of Europe and Draft Resolution on the Partnership between the Council of Europe and National Non-Governmental Organisations (NGOs)*, 14 October 2003, para. 4.

[240] Article 1 (a) of the Statute of the Council of Europe establishes that the aim of the CoE is to achieve a greater unity between its members for the purpose of safeguarding and realising the ideals and principles which are their common heritage and facilitating their economic and social progress.

[241] Committee of Ministers, Resolution Res(2003)8, *Participatory Status for International Non-Governmental Organisations with the Council of Europe*, 19 November 2003, appendix, para. 2.

[242] Section 7.2.

the conditions enumerated for participatory status do not even provide explicitly that the aims and purposes of organisations with consultative status shall be in conformity with the purposes and principles of the CoE. On the other hand, NGOs applying for participatory status must submit to the Secretary-General a declaration to the effect that it accepts the principles set out in the statute and other basic texts of the CoE, together with the application and other documents, such as its statute. Such a requirement might also be seen as implicitly included in the condition of being capable of supporting the achievement of a closer unity between the members of the Council. When considering the draft resolution on participatory status, the Parliamentary Assembly stated that it 'would like to draw the attention of the Committee of Ministers to the importance of requiring that the NGOs have a democratic structure, decision-making mechanism, as well as a truly non-governmental source of funding ... Furthermore, the Assembly is confident that the Council of Europe will not grant participatory status or conclude partnership agreements with those NGOs whose activities are incompatible with the principles of the Council of Europe, in such areas as the fight against racism and xenophobia.'[243] The Rapporteur on relations between the Council of Europe and NGOs later replied to the Assembly's comment by stating that 'it is obvious that only those INGOs and NGOs which support the ideals and objectives of the Organisation can obtain participatory status or conclude partnership agreements'.[244]

The decision on granting participatory status is taken by the Secretary-General based on the criteria mentioned in the resolution. In addition, the Secretary-General may take into consideration the main priorities of the CoE's programme of activities and the possible proliferation of an INGO in a given sector of activity.[245] From the explanations given by the Secretary-General over applications for consultative status under the 1993 arrangements, it seems that the main reasons for

---

[243] Parliamentary Assembly, Doc 9909, *Relations between the Council of Europe and Non-Governmental Organisations*, 15 September 2003, para. 17.

[244] RAP-ONG(2003)8, *Draft Resolution on Participatory Status for International Non-Governmental Organisations (INGOs) with the Council of Europe and Draft Resolution on the Partnership between the Council of Europe and National Non-Governmental Organisations (NGOs)*, 14 October 2003, para. 4.

[245] Committee of Ministers, Resolution Res(2003)8, *Participatory Status for International Non-Governmental Organisations with the Council of Europe*, 19 November 2003, appendix, para. 12.

420 LEGAL AND EMPIRICAL SURVEY

granting consultative status to a certain NGO during that period were that the NGO was 'useful' to the CoE in the sense that its programmes were in keeping with the Council, that it could provide expertise on specific issues relevant for the CoE and that it could contribute in general to its work.[246]

The Secretary-General communicates the list of INGOs suggested for participatory status to the INGO Liaison Committee for its opinion. After two months, the list is submitted for tacit approval to the Committee of Ministers, the Parliamentary Assembly and the Congress of Local and Regional Authorities. If no objection has been raised from these bodies within three months, the INGOs are added to the list of those enjoying participatory status.[247] Thus, as is the case with ECOSOC arrangements for consultation with NGOs, it is ultimately the member states that decide whether or not a particular NGO should be granted consultative status. There are presently 391 INGOs enjoying participatory status with the CoE.[248] All INGOs that enjoyed consultative status in accordance with Resolution (93)38 were automatically granted participatory status when the new Resolution was adopted.

Once an INGO has been granted participatory status, it may be involved in the steering committees, committees of governmental experts and other bodies of the Committee of Ministers in the definition of CoE policies, programmes and actions. More concretely, participatory status means that INGOs may, *inter alia*, address memoranda to the Secretary-General for submission to the different committees as well as to the Commissioner for Human Rights, may be invited to provide expert advice on CoE policies, programmes and actions, shall receive the agenda and public documents of the Parliamentary Assembly, shall be invited to public sittings of the Congress of Local and Regional Authorities of Europe and shall be invited to attend seminars, conferences and colloquies of interest to their work according to the applicable CoE rules. The committees of the Parliamentary Assembly and of

[246] See, e.g., Doc. 8550, Communication of the Secretary General, *Implementation of Committee of Ministers Resolution (93)38*, 29 September 1999.
[247] Committee of Ministers, Resolution Res(2003)8, *Participatory Status for International Non-Governmental Organisations with the Council of Europe*, 19 November 2003, appendix, paras. 13–14. For information on the procedure in cases where an objection is raised, see para. 15.
[248] The list is accessible online at the CoE website at www.coe.int/T/E/NGO/public/ Participatory_status/List_of_NGOs/liste_des_OING_2004_ internet. asp#TopOfPage, as of 27 September 2004.

the Congress of Local and Regional Authorities of Europe, as well as the Commissioner for Human Rights are encouraged to maintain or intensify their co-operation with NGOs.[249] In considering the draft resolution, the Assembly noted that:

at present the Assembly committees invite the NGOs to those meetings which they consider useful and put their documentation at the disposal of their members when appropriate. Several Assembly activities rely on information and advice provided by NGOs when organising hearings and seminars, preparing fact-finding visits, election observation and in the preparation of reports. As in the past, the Assembly and its committees should remain free to determine the methods used for co-operation with NGOs, while bearing in mind the Rules of Procedure and any pertinent text adopted on the matter by the Committee of Ministers. In this connection, it is recalled that according to Rule 44.5 of the Assembly's Rules of Procedure 'each committee may develop relations with non-governmental organisations which carry out activities within the committee's terms of reference'.[250]

In order for an INGO to assert influence on the drafting of new treaties, access to the Steering Committees of the Committee of Ministers is important. A right to participation in these Committees does not follow from the rules for participating status, but is granted on an *ad hoc* basis by the various committees in relation to subjects in which NGOs – with or without participating status – have special competence. According to the resolution on participatory status, the steering committees, committees of governmental experts and other bodies of the Committee of Ministers, 'may' involve the INGOs enjoying participatory status in their activities, 'in particular by granting observer status to the Liaison Committee and to the INGO thematic groupings'.[251] This possibility is based on Resolution 76(3) on Committee Structures, Terms of Reference and Working Methods, which states that any steering committee may, by a unanimous decision, admit observers from INGOs.[252] According to the Rules of Procedure for CoE committees which are appended to the Resolution, an observer does not have a right to vote, but may make oral or written statements on the subjects under discussion with the permission of the chairperson.

---

[249] *Ibid.*, paras. 5–6.
[250] Parliamentary Assembly, Doc 9909, *Relations between the Council of Europe and Non-Governmental Organisations*, 15 September 2003, para. 14.
[251] *Ibid.*, para. 4.
[252] Committee of Ministers, *Resolution (76)3 on Committee Structures, Terms of Reference and Working Methods*, 18 February 1976, para. 5.

422   LEGAL AND EMPIRICAL SURVEY

Proposals made by observers may be put to the vote if sponsored by a committee member. Committee meetings are held in private.[253]

Several of the Committees have granted observer status to a number of NGOs. For example, the Steering Committee for Human Rights has granted observer status to Amnesty International, the International Commission of Jurists, the International Federation of Human Rights (FIDH) and the European Co-Ordinating Group of National Institutions for the Promotion and Protection of Human Rights.[254] A former member of the Steering Committee of Human Rights cannot recall a meeting which has been closed to observers, who are generally respected for their expertise. At the meetings of the Committee, the observers distribute their own documents and draft provisions (which are sometimes 'adopted' by a member state) and make oral statements practically on an equal footing with governments.[255]

INGOs which are granted participatory status also have certain obligations. These include, *inter alia*, that INGOs should:

- furnish, either spontaneously or at the request of the CoE's different bodies, information, documents or opinions relating to their own field(s) of competence on matters which are under consideration or which could be addressed by the CoE,
- work to promote the respect of the CoE standards, conventions and legal instruments in the member states, and assist in the implementation of these standards, and this in close contact with local, regional and national NGOs;
- give maximum publicity to the initiatives and achievements of the CoE in their own field(s) of competence and disseminate information on CoE standards, instruments and activities, and
- submit every four years a report to the Secretary-General specifying, among other things, their participation in the work of the various CoE bodies, their attendance at events organised by the Secretariat General, and any action they have undertaken with a view to ensuring respect of CoE standards and to publicising its work.[256]

---

[253] *Ibid.*, appendix 2, *Rules of Procedure for Council of Europe Committees*, Articles 9, 5.

[254] I.A.00 CDDH e, *Specific Terms of Reference – Steering Committee for Human Rights (CDDH)*, 18 December 2002, para. 5 (e). See also, e.g., the list of observers of the European Committee on Migration in CM/Del/Dec(2004)877/6.2a/appendix8E, *Revised Specific Terms of Reference – European Committee on Migration*, 26 March 2004, para 5i.

[255] Interview on 14 February 2001 with Carl Henrik Ehrenkrona, at the time Director for Legal Affairs of the Swedish Ministry for Foreign Affairs and representative of Sweden to the Steering Committee on Human Rights.

[256] Committee of Ministers, Resolution Res(2003)8, *Participatory Status for International Non-Governmental Organisations with the Council of Europe*, 19 November 2003, appendix, para. 9.

CO-OPERATION WITH INTERGOVERNMENTAL ORGANISATIONS 423

In other words, INGOs enjoying participatory status with the CoE enter into a partnership, in which both sides have obligations to the other. In fact, the INGOs' obligations seem more extensive than the obligations of the CoE. While organisations enjoying participatory status 'shall' furnish the CoE with information, documents, reports, etc. INGOs 'may' be invited to provide expert advice. INGOs 'shall' be invited to certain seminars and conferences, but these are mostly meetings which are either public or specifically organised for NGOs. On the other hand, several of the obligations undertaken by NGOs are in their own interests, such as furnishing the CoE with information, documents and opinions. The obligation to submit a report every fourth year to the Secretary-General is a relaxation in relation to the former arrangements, under which the interval for reports was only two years.

Participatory status can be withdrawn. The Secretary-General may decide to remove an INGO from the list of organisations enjoying such status if it, in his or her opinion, has failed to comply with its obligations under the resolution, is represented twice through, for example, an affiliate organisation, no longer has activities included in the CoE's work programme, or 'has taken any action which is not in keeping with its status as an INGO'. A review of the list of INGOs with participatory status is undertaken periodically. The review is based on the report submitted by the INGOs every four years.[257] The INGO Liaison Committee shall be consulted by the Secretary-General before the list of INGOs which are proposed to be removed is submitted to the Committee of Ministers, the Parliamentary Assembly and the Congress of Local and Regional Authorities for tacit approval.[258] An INGO whose application has been refused or which has been removed from the list may not submit a new application until two years after the decision.[259]

At the time of the adoption of the new arrangements for participatory status, the Committee of Ministers also adopted Resolution (2003)9 on status of partnership between the CoE and national NGOs, as was mentioned above.[260] Partnership status has the aim of recognising existing co-operation between national NGOs and the CoE in the implementation of concrete activities through the conclusion of partnership

---

[257] *Ibid.*, paras. 16–17.   [258] *Ibid.*, paras. 18–19.   [259] *Ibid.*, para. 22.

[260] Committee of Ministers, Resolution Res(2003)9, *Status of Partnership between the Council of Europe and National Non-Governmental Organisations with the Council of Europe*, 19 November 2003.

424   LEGAL AND EMPIRICAL SURVEY

agreements. The conditions for the conclusion of such an agreement with a national NGO are that the NGO is (a) particularly representative in the field(s) of its competence, field(s) of action shared by the CoE, (b) able, through its work, to support the achievement of the closer unity mentioned in Article 1 of the Statute of the Council of Europe and (c) able to make known the work of the CoE in its country. National NGOs should also be able to contribute, through specific projects, programmes, events or manifestations, to the implementation of CoE programmes and public awareness-raising, to 'strengthening of the European idea', or capable of providing, through their specific activity or experience, expert advice on the definition of CoE policies, programmes and actions.[261] The conditions to be met by national NGOs seeking partnership with the CoE are thus rather elaborate.

The modalities for co-operation are more limited as compared to those for participatory status. Two privileges are enjoyed by national NGOs in partnership with the CoE: first, they have the possibility to attend the public sittings of the Parliamentary Assembly and the Congress of Local and Regional Authorities of Europe and, secondly, they have the possibility to attend seminars, conferences and hearings of interest to their work according to the relevant CoE rules. The obligations undertaken by national NGOs include the regular dissemination of information to their members on the standards, activities and achievements of the CoE in their own field(s) of competence, and the furnishing, either spontaneously or at the request of the CoE's different bodies, of information, documents or opinions relating to their own field(s) of competence.[262] The Secretary-General keeps the list of NGOs with which the CoE has concluded partnership agreements. The list shall be updated every two years.[263]

As was mentioned earlier, there was no possibility for national NGOs to obtain consultative status with the Council of Europe under the previous arrangements for co-operation. The Resolution on partnership for national NGOs with the CoE provides that the new rules shall remain in force for an initial period of five years, after which the implementation of the resolution shall be evaluated.[264] There is no corresponding provision in the Resolution on participatory status.

---

[261] *Ibid.*, appendix, paras. 2–3.   [262] *Ibid.*, para. 4.

[263] Committee of Ministers, Resolution Res(2003)9, *Status of Partnership between the Council of Europe and National Non-Governmental Organisations with the Council of Europe*, 19 November 2003, appendix, para. 5.

[264] *Ibid.*, para. 6.

CO-OPERATION WITH INTERGOVERNMENTAL ORGANISATIONS   425

There are several aspects of the establishment of the new arrangements for co-operation between the CoE and NGOs that are worthy of attention. First, arrangements for *consultative* status have been substituted for *participatory* status, a fact which clearly reflects a stronger position for INGOs, although the forms of co-operation may not be so different in practice. Secondly, a means of establishing formal co-operation with national NGOs has been introduced. Thirdly, NGOs have been involved in the drafting process of both resolutions and also for the first time formally consulted on draft resolutions by the Committee of Ministers. Finally, it is worth observing that the elaboration of the new arrangements has been paralleled by the drafting and adoption of the Fundamental Principles on the Status of Non-Governmental Organisations in Europe, discussed in chapter 4. The CoE has thus in several ways since the 1990s recognised the importance of NGOs on the national as well as the international plane.

7.5 The European Union

In spite of the intense lobbying efforts of NGOs within the European Union, the Union has no system-wide regulations for formalised co-operation with NGOs. There are, however, two institutionalised advisory bodies – the Economic and Social Committee (ESC) and the Committee of the Regions (CoR) – which have the function of assisting the Council, the Parliament and the Commission and of serving as channels for external contacts. While the CoR serves as a contact point with regional and local authorities, the ESC represents organised civil society. According to the Nice Treaty, which established the ESC, the Committee has advisory status and shall consist of 'representatives of the various economic and social components of organised civil society, and in particular representatives of producers, farmers, carriers, workers, dealers, craftsmen, professional occupations, consumers and the general interest'.[265] In 2001, the Commission concluded protocols on co-operation with the ESC and the CoR, respectively, in order to reinforce their function as intermediaries between EU institutions

---

[265] With the Treaty of Nice, Article 257 in the Treaty establishing the European Community was replaced by the cited text. Treaty of Nice Amending the Treaty on European Union, the Treaties Establishing the European Communities and Certain Related Acts (2001), Article 2, para. 39.

426   LEGAL AND EMPIRICAL SURVEY

and organised civil society and the regional and local authorities, respectively.[266]

The European Council maintains no direct relations with NGOs. The European Parliament (EP) is open for lobbying, although this possibility is not limited to NGOs. According to Rule 9(2) of the EP's Rules of Procedure with annexed *Provisions Governing the Application of Rule 9(2) – Lobbying in Parliament*, passes may be issued to persons who wish to enter Parliament's premises frequently with a view to supplying information to members within the framework of their parliamentary mandate.[267] In return, such persons shall be asked to respect the code of conduct on Lobbying in the Parliament, which is included in the provisions annexed to Rule 9(2). The code of conduct provides, *inter alia*, that persons who have been given passes for lobbying in the Parliament shall 'not claim any formal relationship with Parliament in any dealings with third parties' (Article 3.1.d).

According to Article 9 of the Protocol on the application of the principles of subsidiarity and proportionality, annexed to the treaty of Amsterdam, 'the Commission should ... consult widely before proposing legislation and, wherever appropriate, publish consultation documents'.[268] Although until recently there was no Commission-wide approach on how to undertake consultation with civil society, each of the Commission's departments had its own mechanisms and methods for consulting its respective sectoral interest groups.[269] Contacts included regular and *ad hoc* meetings, as well as more formalised arrangements. Within some areas of the Commission's work there is a formal or political commitment to consult an NGO or grouping of NGOs on a particular issue during the decision-making process. One such area covers the agricultural advisory committees, which have existed for some forty years as a formal mechanism for regular and systematic consultation with NGOs and socio-professional

---

[266] COM(2002) 704, Communication from the Commission, *Towards a Reinforced Culture of Consultation and Dialogue – General Principles and Minimum Standards for Consultation of Interested Parties by the Commission*, 11 December 2002, p. 8.

[267] *Rules of Procedure of the European Parliament*,16th edn., July 2004 and annex IX, *Provisions governing the application of Rule 9(2) – Lobbying in Parliament*.

[268] Treaty of Amsterdam Amending the Treaty on European Union, the Treaties Establishing the European Communities and Related Acts (1997), Protocol on the application of the principles of subsidiarity and proportionality.

[269] COM(2002) 704 final, Communication from the Commission, *Towards a Reinforced Culture of Consultation and Dialogue – General Principles and Minimum Standards for Consultation of Interested Parties by the Commission*, 11 December 2002, p. 4.

organisations.[270] NGOs have also participated in Community delegations to international conferences. While this was first done on an *ad hoc* basis, it has developed into a practice for the most important conferences. NGOs are allowed formal expert status within these delegations.[271]

In January 2000, a discussion paper was presented by the President and Vice President of the Commission with the aim of suggesting possible ways of developing the relationship between the Commission and NGOs.[272] In 2001, the Commission launched a White Paper on European governance and a consultation process which ran until Spring 2002.[273] The proposals for change included the establishment of minimum standards for consultations on EU policy, the establishment of partnership arrangements in selected areas, the publication of guidelines on collection and use of expert advice and improved dialogue with non-governmental actors of third countries for the purpose of developing policy proposals with an international dimension. Civil society organisations were mentioned in the White Paper as important in giving voice to the concerns of citizens.[274]

After the publication of the White Paper, many organisations expressed a desire to submit comments on the basis of an actual draft consultation framework. In June 2002 the Commission therefore published the consultation document 'Proposal for general principles and minimum standards for consultation of interested parties by the Commission' and invited all interested parties to submit their comments.[275] During the consultation process, the Commission received eighty-eight comments from governments, NGOs, regional and local authorities, individuals, etc. In December the same year, the

---

[270] *The Commission and Non-Governmental Organisations*, Discussion paper presented by President Prodi and Vice-President Kinnock to the Commission, adopted on 18 January 2000, para. 2.1.

[271] See further Peter Bombay, 'The Role of Environmental NGOs in International Environmental Conferences and Agreements: Some Important Features', 10 *European Environmental Law Review* (2001), p. 230–231. As regards operational co-operation between the Commission and NGOs for the purpose of humanitarian activities, see chapter 9.

[272] *The Commission and Non-Governmental Organisations*, Discussion paper presented by President Prodi and Vice-President Kinnock to the Commission, adopted on 18 January 2000.

[273] COM(2001), *European Governance: A White Paper*, 27 July 2001.   [274] *Ibid.*, p. 14.

[275] COM (2002) 277, *Towards a Reinforced Culture of Consultation and Dialogue – Proposal for General Principles and Minimum Standards for Consultation of Interested Parties by the Commission*, 5 June 2002.

428 LEGAL AND EMPIRICAL SURVEY

Commission adopted the final Communication *'Towards a reinforced culture of consultation and dialogue – General principles and minimum standards for consultation of interested parties by the Commission'*, which applied from 1 January 2003.[276] As a means of strengthening consultation processes, the Commission has also set up the CONECCS (Consultation, the European Commission and Civil Society) database, with the objective of providing information on formal consultative committees and other Commission frameworks through which the civil society organisations may be consulted in a formal or structured way.[277]

Before discussing the contents of the communication, it should be noted that the document is a policy document, which is not legally binding. This means that a Commission proposal cannot be challenged before the ECJ on the ground of alleged lack of consultation of interested parties. The Commission argues in the communication that such an approach would be 'over-legalistic' and 'incompatible with the need for timely delivery of policy, and with the expectations of the citizens that the European Institutions should deliver on substance rather than concentrating on procedures'.[278]

The communication sets up a coherent framework for consultation of different stake-holders, including NGOs, which is to be applied without prejudice to more advanced practices for consultation employed by Commission departments. The Commission's guiding principle for consultation is described as 'to give interested parties a voice, but not a vote'. It is emphasised that it is one of the Commission's duties to consult, while at the same time it is made clear that 'first and foremost, the decision-making process in the EU is legitimised by the elected representatives of the European peoples'.[279] The specific role of civil society organisations is regarded as being a facilitator of a broad policy dialogue. It is also placed in the context of the fundamental right of citizens to form associations in order to pursue a common purpose, as mentioned in Article 12 of the European Charter of Fundamental Rights.[280] The term 'civil society organisation' is described as an inclusive shorthand to refer to a range of organisations, including trade unions and employers' federations, organisations representing social and economic players (such as consumer organisations), NGOs

---

[276] COM(2002) 704, Communication from the Commission, 11 December 2002.
[277] The database is accessible online at http://europa.eu.int/comm/civil_society/coneccs/index.htm.
[278] COM(2002) 704, p. 10.   [279] *Ibid.*, pp. 5–6.   [280] *Ibid.*, p. 5.

(described as organisations which bring people together in a common cause, such as environmental organisations, human rights organisations, charitable organisations, etc.), CBOs (community-based organisations – i.e. organisations set up within society at grassroots level which pursue member-oriented objectives) and religious communities.[281]

The consultation between the Commission and interested parties should, according to the communication, be underpinned by certain general principles, which were identified in the Commission's White Paper on European governance. The principles are participation, openness, accountability, effectiveness and coherence. As regards participation, the Commission notes that it is 'committed to an inclusive approach when developing and implementing EU policies, which means consulting as widely as possible on major policy initiatives. This applies, in particular, in the context of legislative proposals.'[282] The general principles are said to be applicable to both sides of the consultation process. In relation to the principle of openness, this means that organisations seeking to contribute in consultation processes are expected to make it apparent which interests they represent and how inclusive that representation is.[283]

Although the general principles are rather elaborately explained, it is the minimum standards that provide the concrete information on how consultation is to be carried out. The minimum standards require the following:

(a) Clear content of the consultation process: certain information should be provided in publicity and consultation documents, including a summary of the context, scope and objectives of consultation, details of any hearings, meetings or conferences, where relevant, and reference to related documentation when these are not included.

(b) Consultation target groups: these should include, *inter alia*, those affected by the policy, those who will be involved in the implementation of the policy and bodies that have stated objectives giving them a direct interest in the policy, but can also be determined on the basis of 'specific experience, expertise or technical knowledge, where applicable', as well as other factors.

(c) Publication: the Commission should ensure adequate awareness-raising publicity and adapt its communication channels to meet the needs of all target audiences.

(d) Time limits for participation: the Commission should provide sufficient time for planning and responses to invitations and written contributions; the Commission should strive to allow at least eight

---

[281] *Ibid.*, p. 6.   [282] *Ibid.*, pp. 14 ff. (cited sentence on p. 16).   [283] *Ibid.*, p. 17.

430   LEGAL AND EMPIRICAL SURVEY

weeks for reception of responses to written public consultations and twenty working days notice for meetings.

(e) Acknowledgement and feedback: receipt of contributions should be acknowledged, such as through individual or collective response, and contributions should be analysed carefully to see whether, and to what extent, the views expressed can be accommodated in the policy proposals.[284]

It is interesting that these arrangements for consultation are so different from those applied within other intergovernmental organisations, such as the CoE. The differences should be seen against the background of the Union's unique character. On the one hand, the Union has extensive legislative and regulatory authority, directly affecting citizens in the member countries. This extensive authority can be regarded as an argument for extensive and institutionalised consultation with civil society. On the other hand, the channels between populations in the member countries and politically elected representatives within the Union institutions, notably the EP, is – at least in theory – more direct than in the case of IGOs such as the United Nations or the CoE. It could therefore be concluded that different views and concerns of population groups should be taken care of by their elected representatives, rather than by civil society organisations.

Bearing the special character of the European Union in mind, a few points can be mentioned about the Commission's guidelines and minimum standards for consultation. A first, obvious, point is that it is surprising that the guidelines for consultation were issued only in 2002, while many other IGOs have had formal arrangements for consultation with civil society for decades. Another point is that these first Commission arrangements for consultation are issued only as non-binding policy guidelines, thus providing no guarantee that consultation will actually be carried out in accordance with the document. Yet another point is that the category of the group to be consulted is wider than in most other IGOs, where the group to be consulted is often defined as NGOs or CSOs meeting certain formal conditions. On the other hand, a basic criterion for consultation is that the group, organisation, church, etc. is affected in one way or the other by the proposed policy initiative, or that it has specific experience or expertise, which is not required by many other IGOs. Consequently, the group to be consulted is determined on an *ad hoc* basis, rather than in accordance with

---

[284] *Ibid.*, pp. 19–22.

certain pre-determined criteria. Finally, it can be observed that the Commission consultations have the form of separate activities performed in order to consult those affected, while, for example, participatory status within the CoE means more streamlined access to the ordinary meetings and procedures of the organisation's different organs. With the system for consultation introduced by the Commission, it is up to the Commission itself to decide which parties are interested and affected, when in the case of, for example, ECOSOC or the CoE, organisations with consultative or participatory status determine which meetings and processes are of interest to them.

7.6 The Organization of American States

General

The Charter of the Organization of American States of 1948 includes several provisions which concern NGOs.[285] For example, Article 45 (g) provides that the member states recognise the importance of the contribution of organisations such as labour unions, co-operatives and cultural, professional, business, neighbourhood and community associations to the life of the society and to the development process. According to Article 91(d), the Permanent Council shall draft agreements to promote and facilitate co-operation between the OAS and other 'American agencies of recognized international standing'. These draft agreements shall be submitted to the General Assembly for approval.[286]

In 1949, the Permanent Council approved the first 'Standards for the Conclusion of Agreements or Special Arrangements between the Council and its Organs and Nongovernmental Organizations'.[287] These Standards were revised several times until the adoption in 1971 of the Standards on Cooperative Relations by the General Assembly.[288] The latter concerned not only the relations of OAS with NGOs, but also OAS

---

[285] Charter of the Organization of American States, signed in Bogotá in 1948, latest amended by the Protocol of Managua in 1993.
[286] Another provision which concerns NGOs is Article 112(h), which states that: 'the General Secretariat shall establish relations of co-operation, in accordance with decisions reached by the General Assembly or the Councils, with the Specialized Organizations as well as other national and international organizations.'
[287] OEA/Ser.G, CP/CSC-3/99, *Background Information on Civil Society Participation in OAS Activities*, 26 August 1999.
[288] General Assembly, AG/RES. 57 (I-0/71), *Standards on Cooperative Relations between the Organization of American States and the United Nations, Its Specialized Agencies, and other National and International Organizations*, April 23, 1971.

432 LEGAL AND EMPIRICAL SURVEY

relations with the United Nations, its specialised agencies and other international and national organisations.

In 1994, the Committee on Juridical and Political Affairs established the Working Group to Study the Possibility of Granting Status to Nongovernmental Organizations in the OAS, in response to a request by the Permanent Mission of Canada. In its note to the Permanent Council, the Canadian Mission stated, *inter alia*, that it believed that granting status to NGOs at the OAS would assist the organisation in the promotion and consolidation of representative democracy in the hemisphere.[289] The Working Group found that NGOs already had a status by the 1971 Resolution on standards on Cooperative Relations, and that these need not be amended.[290] Nevertheless, it concluded that practical guidelines based on the Standards would be useful in order to ensure consistent practices and enhance OAS–NGO relations, including selection criteria with regard to NGO participation in programmes, projects, and other activities. It also recommended the establishment of a register of NGOs which had relations with the OAS.[291]

In June 1999, the General Assembly adopted a resolution establishing the Committee on Civil Society Participation in OAS Activities within the Permanent Council, and instructed the Permanent Council and its Committee to prepare guidelines for civil society participation.[292] The guidelines were adopted by the Permanent Council the same year.[293] In the guidelines, the term 'civil society organizations' (CSOs) is used rather than 'NGOs', which had been used before the work on establishing the guidelines was initiated. The resolution defines a CSO as 'any national or

---

[289] OEA/Ser.G, CP/doc.2486/94, *Note from the Permanent Mission of Canada on the 'Study of the Possible Granting of Status to Non-Governmental Organizations, (NGOs) at the OAS'*, 2 May 1994.

[290] AG/RES. 57 (I-0/71), *Standards on Cooperative Relations Between the Organization of American States and the United Nations, Its Specialized Agencies, and Other National and International Organizations*, April 23, 1971.

[291] See further CP/CSC-3/99, *Background Information on Civil Society Participation in OAS Activities*, 26 August 1999 and OEA/Ser.G, CP/Doc.2946/97, *Report by the Committee on Juridical and Political Affairs on the Status of Non-Governmental Organizations (NGOs) in the OAS*, 11 July 1997.

[292] XXIX Regular Session of the General Assembly, OEA/Ser.P, AG/RES. 1661 (XXIX-O/99), *The Organization of American States and Civil Society*, 7 June 1999. The General Assembly also adopted another resolution urging member states to establish, or to continue to strengthen, means of co-operation between governments and civil society organisations at the state, provincial, and municipal levels, see XXIX Regular Session of the General Assembly. OEA/Ser.P, AG/RES. 1668 (XXIX-O/99), *Strengthening Cooperation between Governments and Civil Society*, 7 June 1999.

[293] CP/RES.759 (1217/99), *Guidelines for the Participation of Civil Society Organizations in OAS Activities*, 15 December 1999.

international institution, organization, or entity made up of natural or juridical persons of a nongovernmental nature'.[294] Evidently, 'CSO' is understood as a wider term that includes NGOs but also organisations which are not always regarded as belonging to this category, such as institutes and business and professional associations. The term CSO will be used here in order to avoid confusion in relation to the OAS terminology, although 'NGO' is understood in the present study as inclusive of private institutes, as well as business and professional organisations.[295]

Paragraph 4 of the guidelines clarifies the principles governing the relations. It is established, *inter alia*, that the matters with which NGOs are concerned 'must fall within the competence of the OAS, and the aims and purposes they pursue must be consistent with the spirit, aims, and principles established in the Charter of the OAS'. The purpose of CSO participation in OAS activities is to enable the organs, agencies, or entities of the OAS to benefit from expert advice or specialised information provided to them by the organisations. It is explicitly stated that participation by NGOs in OAS activities 'shall not be interpreted as a concession of negotiating functions – which are the exclusive preserve of the States – and shall not alter the intergovernmental nature of the organs, agencies, and entities of the OAS'.

Applications from CSOs are examined by the Committee on Inter-American Summits Management and Civil Society Participation in OAS Activities, which is a subsidiary body of the Permanent Council. The Committee makes a recommendation to the Permanent Council, after taking several conditions of eligibility into account. The most important of these conditions are the following:

- The organisation shall be of recognised standing within its particular field of competence and shall be of a representative nature.
- The organisation shall have an institutional structure that includes appropriate mechanisms for holding its officers accountable and subject to its members.
- The organisation shall obtain its resources primarily from its affiliates or individual members, and shall have provided a listing of its sources of financing and any donations received, including, in particular, those originating from government sources.
- The institutional and financial structure of the organisation is transparent and affords it a degree of independence.[296]

---

[294] *Ibid.*, appendix, para. 2.   [295] See section 1.3.
[296] CP/RES. 759 (1217/99), appendix, para. 8.

434   LEGAL AND EMPIRICAL SURVEY

In addition, the Committee takes the geographic origin of the organisation into account in order to ensure a balanced representation of different regions.[297] It follows from Article 91(d) of the OAS Charter that CSOs which co-operate with the OAS shall be 'American'.[298]

During the period of the Committee's examination of applications from CSOs to participate in OAS activities, the member states may submit comments and request information from the organisation in question. The final decision is taken by the Permanent Council, which comprises one representative for each member state. The Permanent Council is under the direct authority of the General Assembly.[299] CSOs which are approved by the Permanent Council for participation in OAS activities are included in a register which is kept by the General Secretariat. By September 2004, ninety CSOs had been accredited for participation in OAS activities.[300]

The privileges of the organisations that have been accepted for participation include the right to participation in OAS conferences and to attend, as observers, meetings of the Permanent Council and the Inter-American Council for Integral Development (CIDI), and their subsidiary bodies. The rules for participation in the work of the two Councils are described below. As regards participation in OAS conferences, the guidelines prescribe that registered CSOs may attend conferences after notifying the Secretariat.[301] CSOs which are not registered may apply to the Secretariat for accreditation. The forms and extent of participation by registered or accepted CSOs in the proceedings of the conferences are governed by the rules of the conference.

By registering for participation with the OAS, CSOs undertake, *inter alia*, to answer inquiries from the organs, agencies and entities of the OAS and provide them with advisory services upon request, to disseminate information on OAS activities to its members, and to present each year to the General Secretariat a report on their participation in OAS

---

[297] *Ibid.*, para. 9.

[298] See also the introduction to the *Guidelines for the Participation of Civil Society Organizations in OAS Activities*, CP/RES.759 (1217/99), 15 December 1999.

[299] Articles 70 and 80 of the Charter of the Organization of American States.

[300] Registry of Civil Society Organizations within the Organization of American States, accessible online at www.civil-society.oas.org.

[301] The guidelines for CSO participation in OAS conferences are contained in para. 12 of the *Guidelines for the Participation of Civil Society Organizations in OAS Activities*, CP/RES.759 (1217/99), appendix, 15 December 1999.

activities during that year, their financial situation and sources of funding, and the activities planned for the coming year.[302]

The registration of an organisation may be suspended or cancelled by the Permanent Council after recommendation of the Committee on Civil Society Participation. This may occur if an organisation has acted in a manner that is inconsistent with the essential aims and principles of the OAS, has failed to make a positive or effective contribution to the work of the OAS, has failed to submit reports for two consecutive years, or has furnished manifestly false or inaccurate information.[303]

In March 2003, the Permanent Council of the OAS approved a Resolution on *Strategies for Increasing and Strengthening Participation by Civil Society Organizations in OAS Activities*, thereby recognising that the participation of civil society in the activities of the OAS should be further developed within the different political and institutional organs of the organisation.[304] The resolution, which was endorsed by the General Assembly, called for a more active promotion of the registration process and participation of civil society organisations. It also strengthened the position of CSOs in relation to the General Assembly, as will be described below.[305]

The General Assembly and the General Secretariat

The Guidelines for the Participation of Civil Society in OAS Activities generally apply to all 'organs, agencies and entities' of the OAS. The Guidelines are, however, complementary to and do not modify the Rules of Procedure of the General Assembly.[306] According to these Rules, CSOs may participate in the annual General Assembly as 'special guests'.[307] The General Secretariat must provide all official documents

---

[302] *Ibid.*, para. 11.   [303] *Ibid.*, para. 15.

[304] CP/RES. 840 (1361/03), *Strategies for Increasing and Strengthening Participation by Civil Society Organizations in OAS Activities*, March 26 2003.

[305] AG/RES. 1915 (XXXIII-O/03), *Increasing and Strengthening Civil Society Participation in OAS Activities*, adopted on 10 June 2003. The Permanent Council resolution also asked the Secretariat to review, in a single document, 'all current provisions of the rules and procedures of the General Assembly, the Permanent Council, the Inter-American Council for Integral Development, the specialized conferences, and other organs and agencies that permit participation by CSOs'. This review is contained in document CP/CISC-106/04, *Review of the Rules of Procedure for Civil Society Participation with the Organization of American States*, 31 March 2004.

[306] CP/RES.759 (1217/99), *Guidelines for the Participation of Civil Society Organizations in OAS Activities*, appendix, 15 December 1999, paras. 1, 5 b.

[307] AG/RES. 1737, *Amendments to the Rules of Procedure of the General Assembly*, 5 June 2000, appendix, Article 10.

436   LEGAL AND EMPIRICAL SURVEY

of the General Assembly to the special guests.[308] In addition, the Resolution on Strategies for Increasing and Strengthening Participation by Civil Society Organizations in OAS Activities has led to a number of privileges for CSOs in relation to the General Assembly and the General Secretariat. First, the General Secretariat should hold regular informal dialogue between heads of delegation, the Secretary-General and civil society representatives. Second, the General Secretariat shall transmit electronically, in consultation with the chairs or presidents of the OAS' political organs, to the registered CSOs that so request, the draft resolutions presented for consideration by the General Assembly, thereby giving the CSOs the opportunity to comment and make suggestions on the drafts.[309] The General Secretariat should also transmit the resolutions adopted at each session of the General Assembly to CSOs.[310] Third, member states should invite registered civil society organisations to attend as guests and contribute to the agenda and preparation of the General Assembly.[311]

The OAS Councils

The Councils of the OAS – the Permanent Council and CIDI – may both present drafts of international instruments to the General Assembly and to the OAS Specialised Conferences. The Councils may also present studies and proposals, for example on the convening of specialised conferences or on the creation, modification, or elimination of specialised organisations and other inter-American agencies, as well as on the co-ordination of their activities.[312] Both councils are composed of one representative of each member state.[313] The functions of the Councils imply that access to their meetings and other participation in their work are important for CSOs seeking to influence the development of Inter-American treaties or other instruments.

As was mentioned above, CSOs that have been accepted for participation have the right to participate as observers in the public meetings of the two councils and their subsidiary bodies. CSOs may also attend closed meetings upon decision by the chair of the meeting in consultation with the participating member state delegations. The calendar of public meetings and the order of business shall be provided to CSOs by the Secretariat

---

[308] *Ibid.*, Article 17.
[309] CP/RES. 840 (1361/03), *Strategies for Increasing and Strengthening Participation by Civil Society Organizations in OAS Activities*, 26 March 2003, Article 1(1)d.
[310] *Ibid.*, Article 1(1)b.   [311] *Ibid.*, 1(3)a.   [312] OAS Charter, Article 73.
[313] *Ibid.*, Articles 71, 80, 93.

'in a timely manner'. Registered CSOs may give oral presentations at the beginning of the meetings of committees of the Permanent Council or CIDI, with prior approval from the committee in question. Written documents may be presented on questions that fall within the sphere of competence of the CSO and appear on the agenda of the meeting. The document shall be distributed by the General Secretariat to the member states. As regards the Committees of the Permanent Council and CIDI, registered CSOs may distribute documents in advance on the same conditions and may give oral presentations at the meetings with prior approval by the Committee. Furthermore, registered CSOs and other civil society organisations with special competence in the issue to be discussed may give oral statements to the meetings of expert groups and working groups of the Permanent Council or of CIDI.[314]

The Inter-American Commission on Human Rights

The Guidelines for the Participation of Civil Society in OAS Activities are complementary to the Commission's own Rules, which govern, *inter alia*, the procedure for the examination of individual complaints regarding violations of the American Convention on Human Rights.[315] As has already been described, NGOs often act as petitioners in these cases and sometimes also act as advisers to the Commission if a case is referred to the Inter-American Court of Human Rights.[316]

NGOs and other CSOs also provide the Commission with information for its work on monitoring the human rights situation in the OAS member states, both on their own initiative and at request of the Commission. In the planning of its on-site visits to the countries, the Inter-American Court of Human Rights takes into account, in addition to its own data, information provided by the state, the principal CSOs and individual members of civil society, in accordance with its priorities and observation plan. During its on-site investigations the Commission normally visits or holds hearings with a number of CSOs.[317] For

---

[314] CP/RES. 759 (1217/99), appendix, para. 13.

[315] *Ibid.*, paras. 1, 5b. The Commission's competence and procedures for the examination of such complaints are of course also governed by the American Convention on Human Rights.

[316] Section 5.3. See also OEA/Ser.G, CP/CSC-3/99, *Background Information on Civil Society Participation in OAS Activities*, 26 August 1999, Chapter VI.

[317] Committee on Civil Society Participation in OAS Activities, OEA/Ser.G, CP/CSC-3/99, *Background Information on Civil Society Participation in OAS Activities*, 26 August 1999, Chapter VI.

438   LEGAL AND EMPIRICAL SURVEY

example, the Commission carried out an on-site investigation to the Dominican Republic in 1997, during which it interviewed a considerable number of NGOs, women's groups and trade unions representatives, as evidenced by its report.[318]

The Commission has appointed Special Rapporteurs for different areas, including the Special Rapporteur on Freedom of Expression and the Rapporteur on the Rights of the Child. These rapporteurs receive information from NGOs during country visits and otherwise.[319]

7.7 The African Union

General

The OAU was established in 1963 with the purposes, *inter alia*, of promoting the unity and solidarity of the African states, to co-ordinate and intensify co-operation between the member states, and to defend their sovereigns, their territorial integrity and independence.[320] With the entering into force of the Constitutive Act of the African Union in 2002, the OAU and the African Economic Community were transformed into the African Union (AU).[321]

The OAU Charter did not include any explicit legal basis for relations with NGOs. Although the OAU did grant observer status to a few NGOs, NGO co-operation with the principal organs of the OAU seem to have been limited.[322] Neither does the Constitutive Act on the African Union contain any provisions that explicitly mention NGOs or civil society. According to Article 22, however, an Economic, Social and Cultural Council (ECOSOCC) is established as an advisory organ composed of different social and professional groups of the member states.

At its Third Ordinary session in July 2004, the AU General Assembly approved the Statutes of the ECOSOCC.[323] According to Article 2 of the Statutes, the objectives of the Commission include, *inter alia*, 'to forge

[318] OEA/Ser.L/V/II.104, Doc. 49 rev. 1, *Report on the Situation of Human Rights in the Dominican Republic*, 7 October 1999, paras. 13–15.
[319] See, e.g., *Report of the Office of the Special Rapporteur for the Freedom of Expression*, Chapters I.B.3 and I.C.2. and *Report of the Rapporteur on the Rights of the Child*, both included in the *Annual Report of the Inter-American Commission on Human Rights* 1998.
[320] OAU Charter, Article II(1).
[321] Constitutive Act of the African Union, 11 July 2000.
[322] Martin A. Olz, 'Non-Governmental Organizations in Regional Human Rights Systems', 28 *Columbia Human Rights Law Review* (1997), pp. 360–361.
[323] Assembly/AU/Dec 48 III, *Decision on the Economic, Social and Cultural Council (ECOSOCC)*, 6–8 July 2004.

strong partnerships between governments and all segments of the civil society, in particular women, the youth, children, the Diaspora, organized labour, the private sector and professional groups', to 'promote the participation of African civil society in the implementation of the policies and programmes of the Union' and to 'Promote and strengthen the institutional, human and operational capacities of the African civil society'.[324] Articles 3 and 4 on composition and membership state that ECOSOCC shall be composed of 150 CSOs in member states of the Union and the African Diaspora, including social groups (such as those representing women, children, the elderly and those with disabilities and special needs), professional groups, NGOs, CBOs, voluntary organisations and cultural organisations. Certain requirements must be met by organisations in order to be eligible for membership in ECOSOCC. The organisations should, for example:

- be national, regional, continental or of African Diaspora,
- have objectives and principles that are consistent with the principles and objectives of the Union,
- show proof that the ownership and management of the CSO is made up of not less than fifty per cent of Africans or of African Diaspora,
- have basic resources which are at least fifty per cent derived from contributions of its members, and any financial or other support or contribution from a government shall be declared, and
- not discriminate on the basis of religion, gender, tribe, ethnic, racial or political basis.[325]

The functions of ECOSOCC are rather vaguely formulated. They include, *inter alia*, to 'Contribute, through advise, to the effective translation of the objectives, principles and policies of the Union into concrete programmes, carry out studies, and to contribute to the promotion of popularisation, popular participation, and to the realisation of the vision and objectives of the Union.'[326]

The AU has thus established an advisory organ with broad civil society representation. Its mandate is wide but at the same time vague, and since ECOSOCC is an advisory body it is impossible to foresee what its actual position in the AU will be.

---

[324] Experts/PRC/ECOSOCC Statutes/Rev.5, *Statutes of the Economic, Social and Cultural Council of the African Union.*
[325] *Ibid.*, Article 6.   [326] *Ibid.*, Article 7.

440   LEGAL AND EMPIRICAL SURVEY

The African Commission on Human and Peoples' Rights

It is often pointed out that the African Commission has a close relationship with NGOs.[327] Some components of this relationship have been described earlier in this book.[328] There are, however, also several articles in the African Charter on Human and Peoples' Rights and the Commission's Rules of Procedure which concern the status of NGOs within the OAU bodies.

Article 45(1a) of the Banjul Charter declares that one of the functions of the Commission is to encourage national and local institutions concerned with human and peoples' rights. Article 45(1c) provides that the Commission should co-operate with other African and international institutions concerned with human rights. Chapter XIII of the Commission's Rules of Procedure deals with relations of the African Commission with NGOs and the representation of these organisations.[329] The formal relationship between the Commission and NGOs has the form of observer status, which can be granted to NGOs after application to the Commission under Rule 75. At its 25th ordinary session in 1999, the Commission adopted new criteria for the granting and enjoying of observer status.[330] The Resolution formulates three criteria for observer status:

- that the organisation's objectives and activities are in consonance with the fundamental principles and objectives enunciated in the OAU Charter and in the African Charter on Human and Peoples' Rights,
- that the organisation works within the field of human rights, and
- that the organisation declares its financial resources.[331]

---

[327] Rachel Murray, *The African Commission on Human and Peoples' Rights & International Law*, Oxford: Hart Publishing, 2000, p. 88; Evelyn A. Ankumah, *The African Commission on Human and Peoples' Rights: Practices and Procedures*, The Hague: Martinus Nijhoff, 1996, p. 47; Claude Welch, *Protecting Human Rights in Africa: Strategies and Roles of Non-Governmental Organizations*, Philadelphia: University of Pennsylvania Press, 1995, pp. 163–169; Chidi Anselm Odinkalu and Camilla Christensen, 'The African Commission on Human and Peoples' Rights: The Development of its Non-State Communication Procedures', 20 HRQ (1998), p. 236; U. Oji Umozurike, *The African Charter on Human and Peoples' Rights*, The Hague: Martinus Nijhoff, 1997, p. 71.

[328] Sections 5.3, 6.8.

[329] *Rules of Procedure of the African Commission on Human and Peoples' Rights*, Adopted on 6 October 1995.

[330] *Resolution on the Criteria for Granting and Enjoying Observer Status to Non-Governmental Organisations Working in the Field of Human Rights with the African Commission on Human and Peoples' Rights*, adopted at the 25th Ordinary Session, held on 26 April–5 May 1999.

[331] *Ibid., Annex – Criteria for the Granting of and Maintaining Observer Status with the African Commission on Human and Peoples' Rights*, Chapter I, para. 2.

To apply for observer status, an NGO needs to provide its statutes, proof of its legal existence, a list of its members, documentation on its constituent organs and its sources of funding, its last financial statement and a statement on its activities.[332] It can be observed that there is no requirement that the NGO should be based in a member state of the OAU. As of May 2003, there were 300 African and international organisations in observer status with the Commission.[333]

The privileges of NGO observers include access to the opening and closing meetings of all sessions of the Commission and access to all non-confidential documents which are of relevance to their interests. Observers may also be invited to closed sessions dealing with issues of particular interest to them. As regards oral statements, observers may be authorised to speak on issues of concern to them, provided that the text of the statement has been provided beforehand to the Chairman. Observers may also be given the floor to respond to questions from the commissioners. NGO observers may request that issues of particular interest to them be included in the provisional agenda. There is no provision governing the distribution of written statements.[334]

There are two obligations upon NGOs with observer status in the Commission. First, NGO observers shall 'undertake to establish close relations of co-operation with the African Commission and to engage in all regular consultations with it on all matters of common interest'. Secondly, they shall present their activity reports to the Commission every two years. Observers who do not comply with their obligations may be denied some of their privileges or have their observers status suspended or withdrawn.[335]

The participation of NGO observers as regulated in the criteria for observer status reflects only the most recent part of a long history of extensive co-operation between the Commission and NGOs. In fact, the Geneva-based NGO the International Commission of Jurists had an important role in the drafting and adoption of the Banjul Charter. The

---

[332] *Ibid.*, Chapter I, para. 3(b).

[333] *Sixteenth Annual Activity Report of the African Commission on Human and Peoples' Rights 2002–2003*, p. 16. The Directory of NGOs with observer status is accessible online at the Commission's website at www.achpr.org/english/_info/directory_ngo_en.html, as of 30 September 2004.

[334] *Resolution on the Criteria for Granting and Enjoying Observer Status to Non-Governmental Organisations Working in the Field of Human Rights with the African Commission on Human and Peoples' Rights*, adopted at the 25th Ordinary Session, held on 26 April–5 May 1999, annex, Chapter II, paras. 1–6.

[335] *Ibid.*, Chapter III, paras. 1–2, Chapter IV, paras. 2–3.

442   LEGAL AND EMPIRICAL SURVEY

International Commission of Jurists started its work towards the elaboration of the African Charter on Human and People's Rights in 1961, when it organised the Lagos Conference, which assembled 194 participants from different African countries and expressed a call to African governments to study the possibilities of adopting an African convention of human rights and of creating an African court.[336] In 1977, the International Commission of Jurists convened a colloquium in Dakar. The reports from these meeting were widely distributed and used by the United Nations in its later meetings in Cairo and Monrovia devoted to discussing a draft African human rights treaty. In what the International Commission of Jurists called the 'decisive step', it convened a new meeting with lawyers in Dakar in 1978. Four of the participants in these meetings lobbied ten heads of state to support an African human rights treaty.[337] Judge Kéba Mbaye from Senegal, at the time the President of the International Commission of Jurists and concurrently chairman of the UN Commission on Human Rights, persuaded the Senegalese President to introduce a resolution to the OAU calling upon the organisation to convene African experts to draft a human rights treaty. In 1981, the experts had finished a draft strongly influenced by Mbaye, who served as the Rapporteur of the drafting committee.[338]

The African Charter was adopted at the OAU Summit in 1981. The International Commission of Jurists then embarked on a continent-wide campaign for its ratification in collaboration with African NGOs, such as the Council for the Development of Economic and Social Research in Africa (CODESRIA), the Union of African Lawyers and the African Bar Association.[339] The first part of the campaign, which included a seminar in Dakar in 1983, was targeted at persons and institutions that could influence decision-makers in the different governments. A second seminar was arranged in 1985 with the aim of

---

[336] Shadrack B. O. Gutto, *ICJ Workshops on NGO Participation in the African Commission on Human and Peoples' Rights 1991 to 1996: A Critical Evaluation*, Geneva: International Commission of Jurists, pp. 7, 21–24. See also Howard B. Tolley, Jr., who describes the International Commission of Jurists as the 'midwife' of the African Charter, *The International Commission of Jurists*, Philadelphia: University of Pennsylvania Press, 1994, pp. 178–181.

[337] Welch, *Protecting Human Rights in Africa*, p. 165; Ankumah, *The African Commission on Human and Peoples' Rights*, p. 4; *ICJ Report on Activities 1986–1988*, Geneva, 1989, p. 3.

[338] Welch, *Protecting Human Rights in Africa*, p. 165; Tolley, *The International Commission of Jurists*, p. 179.

[339] Gutto, *ICJ Workshops on NGO Participation in the African Commission on Human and Peoples' Rights 1991 to 1996*, pp. 26–27.

CO-OPERATION WITH INTERGOVERNMENTAL ORGANISATIONS   443

securing the additional eleven ratifications needed for the Charter to enter into force. This seminar brought together leading jurists from countries which had not yet ratified the African Charter. During the annual summit of the OAU heads of State in 1984, fourteen states ratified the Charter, which meant that the required number of ratifications for the Charter to enter into force had been met.[340]

The ICJ also assembled eleven jurists in June 1987 to work on the procedures to implement the Charter. Six of these jurists were subsequently elected to the African Commission. All but two of the recommendations made by the International Commission of Jurists were adopted as the Commission's rules of procedure.[341]

After the establishment of the African Commission on Human and Peoples' Rights in 1987, the International Commission of Jurists turned its attention to the implementation of the Charter's provisions. One of the models used for contributing to the strengthening of the African human rights mechanism was the NGO workshops organised by the International Commission of Jurists in collaboration with other NGOs prior to the Commission's ordinary sessions from the early 1990s. These workshops often adopted resolutions and recommendations which were presented to the Commission during its session. The Commission has adopted without major alterations a number of such resolutions submitted to it by NGOs.[342] Examples of such resolutions include:

- *Resolution on the Military*: The 7th NGO Workshop in October 1994 adopted a resolution on the military, which recognised that military take-overs contravene Articles 13 and 20 of the African Charter and called upon incumbent military governments to return political power to freely elected governments immediately.[343] During its subsequent 16th Ordinary Session, the African Commission adopted a Resolution on the Military with the same content.[344]
- *Contemporary Forms of Slavery*: The same NGO Workshop in October 1994 adopted a resolution on contemporary forms of slavery in Africa. The Workshop recommended the African Commission to contact all

---

[340] Welch, *Protecting Human Rights in Africa*, p. 166 and Gutto, *ICJ Workshops on NGO Participation in the African Commission on Human and Peoples' Rights 1991 to 1996*, pp. 26–27.

[341] Welch, *Protecting Human Rights in Africa*, p. 166.

[342] Ankumah, *The African Commission on Human and Peoples' Rights*, p. 26.

[343] *Seventh Workshop*, 23–24 October 1994, in *The Participation of Non-Governmental Organizations in the Work of the African Commission on Human and Peoples' Rights: A Compilation of Basic Documents, October 1991–March 1996*, p. 52.

[344] *Resolution on the Military*, adopted at the 16th Ordinary Session of the African Commission (1994).

444   LEGAL AND EMPIRICAL SURVEY

member states of the OAU and urge them to ratify and implement all existing international instruments relating to slavery.[345] During its subsequent Ordinary Session, the Commission adopted a similar Resolution on Contemporary Forms of Slavery.[346]

- *Resolutions on specific countries*: The same NGO Workshop in October 1994 adopted resolutions regarding the situation in Algeria, the Gambia, Nigeria and Rwanda.[347] The Commission adopted resolutions on these countries during its session.[348] The content of the resolutions of the African Commission and the resolutions adopted by the NGO Workshops are in large parts the same.[349]

The Commission's *Annual Activity Reports* often contain descriptions of extensive co-operation with different governmental and non-governmental organisations.[350]

7.8 Conclusions

This chapter has described some examples of arrangements for formal co-operation between IGOs and NGOs. Other IGOs that undertake formalised co-operation with NGOs are, for example, the United Nations Environment Programme (UNEP), FAO and UNESCO. It is, of course, also interesting to identify IGOs that have no system for formal consultation with NGOs. In this group we find, for instance, the IMF and the WTO. Several organisations have no system for formal consultation with NGOs integrated into their own decision-making structures, but maintain dialogue with civil society through special civil society meetings or advisory groups – e.g. the World Bank and the United Nations Development Programme (UNDP). Still others, such as UNHCR and the

---

[345] Seventh Workshop, 23–24 October 1994, in *The Participation of Non-Governmental Organizations in the Work of the African Commission on Human and Peoples' Rights: A Compilation of Basic Documents*, p. 51.

[346] *Resolution on Contemporary Forms of Slavery*, adopted at the 16th Ordinary Session of the ACHPR (1994).

[347] Seventh Workshop, 23–24 October 1994, in *The Participation of Non-Governmental Organizations in the Work of the African Commission on Human and Peoples' Rights: A Compilation of Basic Documents*, p. 50.

[348] 16th Ordinary Session of the African Commission on Human and Peoples' Rights, 25 October–3 November 1994, *Final Communiqué*, para. 46.

[349] *Resolution on Algeria, Resolution on the Gambia, Resolution on Nigeria and Resolution on Rwanda*, adopted at the 16th Ordinary Session of the African Commission (1994).

[350] See, e.g., *Thirteenth Annual Activity Report of the African Commission on Human and Peoples' Rights 1999–2000*, paras. 45–48, 56–69 and *Sixteenth Annual Activity Report of the African Commission on Human and Peoples' Rights 2002–2003*, pp. 10–11, 13, 34.

Organization for Security and Co-operation in Europe (OSCE) have extensive co-operation with NGOs on the operational level but little or none within central decision-making structures.[351]

Some general points can be made regarding the arrangements studied above. One interesting fact is that, since the late 1990s, there has been a clear trend towards enhanced co-operation between IGOs and NGOs, or civil society in general. Indications of this include the adoption of the first guidelines for consultation with civil society by the European Commission in 2003 (although these guidelines have the form of a non-binding policy document), the adoption of the first coherent arrangements for co-operation with NGOs within the OAS in 1999 and the transformation within the CoE in 2003 from a system for consultation with INGOs to a system for participation of INGOs and for partnership with national NGOs. It can also be noted that the AU has established ECOSOCC, an advisory body consisting of representatives of civil society organisations.

Another interesting indication of a development towards a stronger position for NGOs within IGOs is that the use of the term 'participation' seems to becoming more frequent, at the expense of 'consultation'. The former concept has been introduced within the CoE and the OAS while, for example, ECOSOC and the ILO still use 'consultation'. It can also be observed that some IGOs have gone from describing their civil society partners as 'NGOs' to calling them 'CSOs', the latter term being understood as broader and inclusive of NGOs as well as, for example, academic institutes, religious organisations and indigenous organisations.

Finally, the Report of the Panel of Eminent Persons on Civil Society and UN Relationships should be recalled. Although the Report has not yet led to any actual reforms within the United Nations, it is noteworthy that the Panel recommends a stronger relationship between the United Nations and civil society and enhanced co-operation between NGOs and central UN fora, such as the General Assembly and the Security Council.

---

[351] For examples of co-operation between IGOs and NGOs, see section 9.3.

8 Participation in international conferences

8.1 Introduction

One of the most obvious examples of increasing contacts between NGOs and IGOs during the 1990s was the participation of NGOs in international conferences. The rules which provide NGOs with the possibility to participate in such meetings probably provide the most important formal platform for NGOs which seek to influence international law-making. While rules which give NGOs standing as victims, complainants or *amici curiae* before international courts and quasi-judicial bodies are essential avenues for influencing the interpretation and development of already existing law, many international conferences create new law. The participation of NGOs in the conferences which adopted the Landmines Convention, the Statute of the International Court and, to some extent, environmental treaties such as the Framework Convention for Climate Change, therefore in a sense provide more direct examples of how NGOs influence law-making.[1]

---

[1] The influence of NGOs on the Convention on the Prohibition of the Use, Stockpiling, Production and Transfer of Antipersonnel Mines and on their Destruction has been described in detail elsewhere, see Maxwell A. Cameron *et al.* (eds.), *To Walk Without Fear: The Global Movement to Ban Landmines*, Oxford University Press, 1998; Louis Maresca and Stuart Maslen (eds.), *The Banning of Anti-Personnel Landmines: The Legal Contribution of the International Committee of the Red Cross 1955–1999*, Cambridge University Press, 2000; and Kenneth Anderson, 'The Ottawa Convention Banning Landmines, the Role of International Non-Governmental Organizations and the Idea of International Civil Society', 11 EJIL (2000), pp. 91–120. The influence of NGOs on environmental treaties is analysed in Bas Arts, *The Political Influence of Global NGOs: Case Studies on the Biodiversity Conventions*, Utrecht: International Books, 1998. Regrading the role of NGOs in the negotiations of the UN Convention on the Law of the Sea, the Ottawa Convention and the Multilateral Agreement on Investment, see John King Gamble and Charlotte Ku, 'International Law – New Actors and New Technologies: Center Stage for NGOs?', 31 *Law*

446

This chapter includes a description of the rules for and actual participation of NGOs in a few selected UN conferences. The limitation to UN conferences is mainly due to the universal character of these conferences, but also to the practical aspect of availability of documents and to the need for limitations. Among many possible UN conferences, I have decided to focus on the United Nations Rio Conference on Environment and Development UNCED, (1992), the World Conference on Human Rights (1993), the Third Session of the Conference of the Parties to the Framework Convention on Climate Change (FCCC, which adopted the Kyoto Protocol) (1997) and the Rome Conference for an International Criminal Court (1998). This selection includes both directly law-making conferences and conferences which have been important for the development of international law, although they did not adopt new treaties, and it covers different fields, such as environmental law, human rights law and humanitarian law. The conferences also represent different legal frameworks for the participation of NGOs, as the Rio Conference and the Conference on Human Rights both took place before the adoption in 1996 by ECOSOC of general rules for NGO participation in UN conferences, while the Rome Conference for an International Criminal Court occurred after the adoption of these rules. The Third Session of the Conference of the Parties to the FCCC took place after the adoption of the ECOSOC Resolution but followed its own rules for NGO participation on the basis of provisions in the Convention itself.

One of the examples – the Rome Conference for an International Criminal Court – includes not only a description of the rules and actual participation of NGOs in the proceedings, but also an evaluation of the influence which NGOs asserted on the negotiations in the view of five persons who were in key positions during the conference. This investigation is also an attempt to examine the practical significance of different rules formulating modalities for NGO participation. It should be observed that it is a difficult task to assess the influence of different actors and other factors on the outcome of international negotiations, and it is indeed not a task for which lawyers are trained, but rather something for sociologists or scholars of international relations.[2] The study of the Rome negotiations is therefore more of a qualitative than quantitative nature; it focuses on the developments as they were

---

and *Policy in International Business* (2000), pp. 246–258. The influence of NGOs on the adoption of the Statute of the ICC is analysed in section 8.6.

[2] This is demonstrated by the complexity and thoroughness of Arts' study of the influence of NGOs on the climate change negotiations, see Arts, *The Political Influence of Global NGOs*.

448   LEGAL AND EMPIRICAL SURVEY

experienced by a few people involved in the negotiations and should not be understood as an assertion of objective facts.

The fact that all the events described are examples of strong NGO participation in international conferences does not mean that NGOs always participate. As descriptions of the increasing participation of NGOs on the international scene often focus on a few examples, there is a risk that a false impression may be created. Even though NGOs have had an impact on the negotiations during some important law-making conferences, it can be assumed that the more concrete or politically sensitive the issue, the less likely it will be that NGOs are granted any real access to the negotiations, at least if the conference in question is not convened by the United Nations.[3] The Conference on Disarmament provides an illustration of this. The Rules of Procedure of the Conference includes rules for participation of non-member states as observers and for UN organs to provide information to the Conference, but do not provide a basis for participation of IGO or NGO observers. The only rule on NGOs states that all communications from NGOs shall be retained by the Secretariat and made available to delegations upon request, and that a list of all communications shall be circulated to the Conference.[4]

8.2 Rules for NGO participation in UN conferences

Before 1996, the rules for NGO participation in conferences hosted by the United Nations were determined on a case-by-case basis by the organ convening the conference.[5] With the adoption in 1996 of the ECOSOC Resolution on revised arrangements for consultative relationships between the United Nations and NGOs, a set of generally applicable provisions for the participation of NGOs in UN conferences became operational.[6] The first of these provisions states that if an NGO has

---

[3] In 1996, the United Nations adopted general rules for NGO participation in conferences convened by it, see section 8.2.

[4] CD/8/Rev.9, 19 December 2003, *Rules of Procedure of the Conference on Disarmament*, Rules IX, XI, XII. Earlier reports of the Conference demonstrated that NGOs were not invited, with the exception of a few special occasions. See, however, the decision on NGO participation taken by the Conference in 2004, CD/1744, 7 September 2004, paras. 18–20.

[5] E/AC.70/1994/5, *General Review of Arrangements for Consultations with Non-Governmental Organizations*, 26 May 1994, para. 100.

[6] E/RES/1996/31, *Consultative Relationship between the United Nations and Non-Governmental Organizations*, 25 July 1996, Part VII, Participation of non-governmental organizations in international conferences convened by the United Nations and their preparatory process.

PARTICIPATION IN INTERNATIONAL CONFERENCES 449

been invited to participate in a conference convened by the United Nations, it is the prerogative of member states to decide on its accreditation through the respective preparatory committee. Accreditation shall, according to the provision, be preceded by an appropriate process to determine the eligibility of the NGO.[7]

NGOs in general consultative status, special consultative status and on the Roster that so wish shall as a rule be accredited.[8] Other NGOs may apply to the Secretariat for accreditation. Such an application should be accompanied by detailed information, including:

- the competence of the organisation and the relevance of its activities to the work of the conference and its preparatory process
- the purpose of the NGO, its programmes and activities which are relevant to the conference and its preparatory process and the country or countries in which they are carried out
- copies of the annual or other reports with financial statements, and a list of financial sources and contributions, including governmental contributions
- a list of members of the governing body of the NGO and their countries of nationality
- a description of the membership of the organisation, indicating the total number of members, the names of organisations that are members and their geographical distribution
- a copy of the constitution and/or by-laws of the organisation.[9]

The applying NGOs shall also be asked to confirm their interest in the goals and objectives of the conference.[10] In the evaluation of applications, determination shall be made on the basis of the background and involvement of the NGO in the subject areas of the conference. Member states may submit comments on any of the applications. If the Secretariat finds that the applying NGO has demonstrated its competence and the relevance of its activities to the work of the preparatory committee, it recommends accreditation to the committee, which decides on the matter. An organisation which has been accredited to attend a session of the preparatory committee and related preparatory meetings of regional commissions may attend all its future sessions, as well as the conference itself.[11]

The status of NGOs which have been accredited to an international conference is of an observatory character. It is made clear in the

---

[7] *Ibid.*, para. 41. [8] *Ibid.*, para. 42. [9] *Ibid.*, paras. 42–44. [10] *Ibid.*, para. 44(b).
[11] *Ibid.*, paras. 45–47, 49.

450 LEGAL AND EMPIRICAL SURVEY

resolution that the nature of conferences convened by the United Nations and the preparatory processes for such conferences is intergovernmental, and that active participation of NGOs is welcome but does not entail a negotiating role.[12] Privileges of accredited organisations include that they may be given the opportunity to address the preparatory committee and the conference in plenary meetings and their subsidiary bodies, at the discretion of the chairperson and with the consent of the body concerned, and the right to make written presentations during the preparatory process.[13] Accreditation may be suspended or withdrawn on the same conditions as consultative status.[14]

8.3 The United Nations Conference on Environment and Development

The participation of NGOs in UNCED (or the Rio Conference) in Rio de Janeiro in 1992 and its preparatory process was, in the words of the UN Secretary-General, 'unprecedented'.[15] At the same time, it has been asserted that the rules for accreditation of NGOs to UNCED became adopted only after a 'fierce political battle'.[16] The final outcome, however, with some 2,400 accredited representatives of around 650 NGOs attending the conference, seems to have been an important factor in the process towards the adoption of new consultative arrangements in 1996, including general rules for participation of NGOs with or without consultative status in UN conferences.[17] Interestingly, it was another environmental conference – the UN Conference on the Human Environment in 1972 – which had marked the first step in a development towards increased NGO participation in UN conferences; the number of around 250 registered NGOs was at that time the highest at

---

[12] *Ibid.*, para. 50.   [13] *Ibid.*, paras. 51–52.   [14] *Ibid.*, paras. 55–59. See also sections 4.3, 7.2.

[15] E/AC.70/1994/5, *General Review of Arrangements for Consultations with Non-Governmental Organizations, Report of the Secretary-General*, 26 May 1994, para. 101.

[16] UN Briefing Papers, *The World Conferences: Developing Priorities for the 21st Century*, The United Nations, 1997, p. 20; Peter Willetts, 'From Stockholm to Rio and Beyond: The Impact of the Environmental Movement on the United Nations Consultative Arrangements for NGOs', 22 *Review of International Studies* (1996), p. 57.

[17] The United Nations, 1997, p. 20; Willetts, 'From Stockholm to Rio', p. 57. The 'hybrid NGO', the International Union for the Conservation of Nature (IUCN), which comprises states, government agencies and NGOs, also played a very important role in the Rio process, see Sally Morphet, 'NGOs and the Environment', in Peter Willetts (ed.), *'The Conscience of the World': The Influence of Non-Governmental Organisations in the UN System*, London: Hurst & Co., 1996, pp. 134–140.

any conference in the history of the United Nations and it probably continued to be the record until the Rio Conference.[18]

In terms of international instruments, UNCED produced the Rio Declaration on Environment and Development, the Authoritative Statement on Forest Principles and Agenda 21, which is an action plan on sustainable development. The Conference also established the UN Commission on Sustainable Development to monitor the implementation of Agenda 21. No legally binding instruments were adopted by the Conference, but many participating states signed the FCCC, which was opened for signature in Rio.[19]

In the resolution by which the General Assembly decided to convene the Conference, the Assembly requested 'relevant' NGOs in consultative status with ECOSOC 'to contribute to the Conference, as appropriate'.[20] There were thus initially no plans for NGOs which were not in consultative status to be invited to apply for accreditation, and among NGOs with consultative status only those 'relevant' were to be admitted. As regards the Preparatory Committee (PrepCom), the General Assembly decided that it was to be open to the 'participation of observers in accordance with the established practice of the General Assembly'.[21] The lack of reference to NGOs seemed to indicate that these organisations were not to be allowed to participate in the preparatory process at all. Nevertheless, eleven international NGOs attended the organisational session of the PrepCom three months later.[22] At the first substantive session, the PrepCom adopted rules for NGO participation which were then extended for the following meetings. These rules could be adopted only after a long debate, during which some delegates held that the rules would have to be referred back to the General Assembly for approval if they allowed for accreditation of NGOs without consultative status.[23]

---

[18] Willetts, 'From Stockholm to Rio', pp. 69–70; Morphet, 'NGOs and the Environment', p. 124.

[19] A/CONF.151/26 (vol. I), *Report of the United Nations Conference on Environment and Development*, 12 August 1992, Chapter 1, Resolution 1 (Adoption of texts).

[20] A/RES/44/228, *United Nations Conference on Environment and Development*, 22 December 1989, Part II, para. 12.

[21] *Ibid.*, Part II, para. 1.

[22] A/44/48, *Report of the Preparatory Committee*, 14 January 1991, para. 11. The Committee did not agree on rules for the participation of NGOs in the preparatory process at this session, but decided that the Secretariat should submit a proposal to the Committee at its first substantive session; *ibid.*, Decision IV, pp. 13–14.

[23] Willetts, 'From Stockholm to Rio', pp. 73–74. It is interesting to note that both NGOs with and without consultative status with ECOSOC were accredited to the Stockholm

452 LEGAL AND EMPIRICAL SURVEY

Nevertheless, the decision finally taken by the PrepCom allowed for participation of NGOs in consultative status with ECOSOC, as well as of other NGOs 'desiring to be accredited'. Applications for accreditation of NGOs lacking consultative status had to be accompanied by information on the NGOs' competence and relevance to the work of the PrepCom. All NGOs which had been granted accreditation to one of the sessions of the PrepCom could also attend its future sessions.[24]

The actual participation of NGOs in the preparatory process was strong; over 160 NGOs were represented at the second session of the PrepCom (PrepCom II) and 350 NGOs participated in PrepCom III.[25] Some NGOs participated in national preparatory committees and made contributions to the preparation of national reports to the conference. The NGOs also arranged a preparatory conference in Paris 1991 with over 800 participating NGO representatives.[26]

All NGOs which were accredited to participate in the work of the PrepCom by the conclusion of its fourth session were accredited to the Rio Conference;[27] 172 governments were represented at the conference and some 2,400 representatives of around 650 accredited NGOs attended it.[28] It has been asserted that during the whole preparatory

---

Conference in 1972 and that the rules of procedure allowed NGOs to speak at open plenary and committee sessions, Morphet, 'NGOs and the Environment', p. 124.

[24] PrepCom decision 2/1 on Procedure for determining non-governmental organizations' competence and relevance to the work of the Preparatory Committee, included in A/46/48, *Report of the Preparatory Committee for the United Nations Conference on Environment and Development*, p. 21. See also Decision 1/1 of the Preparatory Committee of the United Nations Conference on Environment and Development, *Role of Non-Governmental Organizations in the Preparatory Process*, reprinted in Willetts, *'The Conscience of the World'*, pp. 302–303. According to Willetts, Decision 1/1 was 'one of the most restrictive texts on NGOs ever adopted by the UN', mostly due to the phrase 'Non-governmental organizations shall not have any negotiating role in the work of the Preparatory Committee', see 'From Stockholm to Rio', pp. 74–75. The same phrase is used in the section on NGO participation in UN conferences (para. 50) of the ECOSOC resolution 1996/31 on consultative arrangements.

[25] A/46/48, *Report of the Preparatory Committee for the United Nations Conference on Environment and Development*, 1991, paras. 9–10, and Bertil Hägerhäll, 'The Evolving Role of NGOs', in Gunnar Sjöstedt et al. (eds.), *International Environmental Negotiations: Process, Issues and Contexts*, Swedish Council for Planning and Coordination of Research and the Swedish Institute of International Affairs, Report 93:1, p. 71.

[26] Hägerhäll, 'The Evolving Role of NGOs', p. 71.

[27] A/RES/46/168, *United Nations Conference on Environment and Development*, 19 December 1991, para. 9(f).

[28] The United Nations, 1997, p. 20 and Willetts, 'From Stockholm to Rio', p. 70. According to E/1993/12, *Rules of Procedure of the Commission on Sustainable Development*, 29 January 1993, para. 15, 1,400 NGOs were accredited to the conference. It thus seems that less than half of those who were accredited actually participated.

process and the conference, only four out of 1,420 NGOs were refused accreditation by the UNCED Secretariat.[29]

As for the modalities for participation, NGOs were allowed to make oral statements in the plenary and in the subsidiary bodies upon the invitation of the chairperson.[30] During the plenary meetings of the conference, only a few NGO statements were allowed.[31] Written statements could be distributed, but not as official documents and at the expense of the NGOs.[32] It was explicitly stated, in the rules for both NGO participation in the preparatory process and in the conference itself, that NGOs should not have a negotiating role in the conference or its preparatory process.[33] This rule, although seemingly obvious, had never been formulated as such before.[34] NGOs took part in fifteen national delegations, but were to a large extent excluded from the intergovernmental negotiations on the documents which were to be presented at UNCED, as these negotiations were held in informal meetings to which NGOs were not admitted.[35]

The parallel NGO Forum in Rio, which gathered together around 17,000 people, drafted and negotiated more than thirty alternative treaties.[36] Not only were environmental NGOs active in Rio and during the preparatory process, but also many other types of NGOs – such as industrial and business organisations, indigenous peoples' organisations, youth groups, scientific organisations, women's organisations and trade unions.[37]

---

[29] Pratap Chatterje and Matthias Finger, *The Earth Brokers: Power, Politics and World Development*, London: Routledge, 1994, p. 84.

[30] A/48/37, *Report of the Preparatory Commission for the United Nations Conference on Human Settlements (Habitat II)*, 9 March 1993, annex, *Rules of Procedure for the Participation of Non-Governmental Organizations* (analogous to the rules for the Rio Conference), para. 10, and A/CONF.165/5, *Accreditation of Non-Governmental Organizations*, 13 February 1996, para. 2.

[31] At most plenary session, only one NGO was allowed to deliver a statement. During two sessions, two or three NGO statements were delivered. A/CONF.151/26/Rev.1, vol. II (Proceedings of the Conference), pp. 9–12.

[32] A/48/37, annex, *Rules of Procedure for the Participation of Non-Governmental Organizations*, para 11.

[33] Decision 1/1 of the Preparatory Committee of the United Nations Conference on Environment and Development, *Role of Non-Governmental Organizations in the Preparatory Process*, para. 4(a), in Willetts, 'The Conscience of the World', p. 302, A/48/37, annex, *Rules of Procedure for the Participation of Non-Governmental Organizations*, para. 9.

[34] Arts, *The Political Influence of Global NGOs*, p. 29.

[35] Peter M. Haas and Marc A. Levy, 'Appraising the Earth Summit: How Should We Judge UNCED's Success?', 34 *Environment* (1992), p. 6, at n. 26 and Hägerhäll, 'The Evolving Role of NGOs', p. 71.

[36] Hägerhäll, 'The Evolving Role of NGOs', p. 73.

[37] Chatterje and Finger, *The Earth Brokers*, pp. 86–91; Hägerhäll, 'The Evolving Role of NGOs', p. 69.

454   LEGAL AND EMPIRICAL SURVEY

There are different views as to what extent NGOs influenced the text of Agenda 21 and other texts adopted by the conference.[38] Nevertheless, Agenda 21 in several ways expresses recognition of the role of NGOs and 'major groups', notably in a specific chapter titled 'Strengthening the Role of Non-Governmental Organizations: Partners For Sustainable Development'.[39] The chapter, being wide in scope but vague as to its character, includes a section on more access for NGOs to the UN system by reviewing 'formal procedures and mechanisms for the involvement of these organizations at all levels from policy-making and decision-making to implementation'.[40] However, Agenda 21 did not only recognise NGOs as important actors, but regarded 'the commitment and genuine involvement of *all* social groups' as critical to the effective implementation of the Agenda, and stated that a need for new forms of participation had emerged in the context of environment and development.[41] It was therefore concluded that any policies, definitions or rules affecting access to and participation by NGOs in the work of the UN institutions or agencies associated with the implementation of Agenda 21 should 'apply equally to all major groups'.[42] Agenda 21 also included an outline of how the follow-up to the Agenda was to be carried out within and outside the UN system. In general, it was said that the UN system should, in consultation with NGOs, take measures to 'design open and effective means to achieve the participation of non-governmental organizations, including those related to major groups, in the process established to review and evaluate the implementation of Agenda 21 at all levels and promote their contribution to it' and that 'Procedures should be established for an expanded role for non-governmental organizations, including those related to major groups, with accreditation based on the procedures used in the Conference'.[43]

Among the concrete recommendations included in Agenda 21 were, *inter alia*, to establish a Commission on Sustainable Development in accordance with Article 68 of the UN Charter with participation of

---

[38] Arts, *The Political Influence of Global NGOs*, p. 28.
[39] Agenda 21, Chapter 27, adopted by the plenary of the Rio Conference on 14 June, 1992, in A/CONF.151/26/Rev. 1, annex II, Volume I. As to the background of the expression 'major groups', see Willetts, 'From Stockholm to Rio', p. 75.
[40] *Ibid.*, Chapter 27.6.   [41] *Ibid.*, Chapters 23.1–23.2 (emphasis added).
[42] *Ibid.*, Chapter 23.3. In section III of Agenda 21, the following 'major groups' were identified: women, children and youth, indigenous people, NGOs, local authorities, workers and trade unions, business and industry, scientific and technological communities and farmers.
[43] *Ibid.*, Chapters 38.43, 38.44.

NGOs, including industry and the scientific community.[44] As a consequence, the UN Commission on Sustainable Development was set up by ECOSOC in 1993, following a request by the General Assembly.[45] The Commission is composed of representatives of UN member states, and NGOs participate in the Commission in a role as observers. Before the adoption of the present rules for consultative status in 1996, the Commission on Sustainable Development accredited a large number of NGOs without consultative status with ECOSOC for participation in its work.[46] Any NGO which was accredited to participate in the work of the PrepCom for UNCED by the conclusion of its fourth session could apply for and was to be granted Roster status with the Commission.[47] Even after the adoption of the new ECOSOC arrangements for consultation, the Commission keeps a Roster listing a large number of NGOs which participate in its work without being in consultative status with the ECOSOC.[48]

8.4 The World Conference on Human Rights

The World Conference on Human Rights of 1993 constituted the next landmark as regards NGO participation in UN conferences. The General Assembly expressed a clearly generous approach towards NGO participation from the outset. In the resolution whereby the Assembly decided to convene the conference, it requested:

non-governmental organizations concerned with human rights to assist the Preparatory Committee and to undertake reviews and submit recommendations concerning the Conference and the preparations therefor to the Preparatory Committee through the Secretary-General and to participate actively in the Conference.[49]

---

[44] Agenda 21, Chapters 38.11–38.13.

[45] E/1993/207, *Establishment of the Commission on Sustainable Development*, 12 February 1993 and A/RES/47/191, 29 January 1993. See also section 7.2.

[46] E/AC.70/1994/5, *General Review of Arrangements for Consultations with Non-Governmental Organizations*, para. 101.

[47] ECOSOC Decision 1993/215, *Procedural Arrangements for the Commission on Sustainable Development*, para. 2(c), in E/1993/INF/2, 4 March 1993. For a detailed description on the developments as regards co-operation between the Commission and NGOs, see Willetts, 'From Stockholm to Rio', pp. 76–79.

[48] See, e.g., E/CN.17/1998/20, *Commission on Sustainable Development. Report on the Sixth Session*, annex I (Attendance).

[49] A/RES/45/155, *World Conference on Human Rights*, adopted on 18 December 1990.

456 LEGAL AND EMPIRICAL SURVEY

This can be compared to the resolution by which the Assembly decided to convene the Rio Conference, in which it was stated that 'relevant' NGOs in consultative status with ECOSOC were requested to 'contribute to the Conference, as appropriate'.[50] In the PrepCom meetings, NGOs in consultative status with ECOSOC, as well as those which lacked such status but were active in the field of human rights and/or development, were allowed to participate.[51] A large number of NGOs were accredited to and participated in the meetings of the PrepCom.[52] In addition, many NGOs participated in the regional meetings that were held prior to the conference in Asia, Africa and Latin America.[53] To these regional meetings, the PrepCom decided to invite, first, NGOs in consultative status with ECOSOC active in the field of human rights and, secondly, other NGOs which were active in the field of human rights and/or development and had their headquarters in the region concerned. Concerning the latter category, however, the states in the region were to be consulted first.[54] A group of well-known NGOs (among them Amnesty International, QCEA (the Quakers), the International Commission of Jurists, the International Federation for Human Rights and Minority Rights Group) proposed to the PrepCom that a considerably wider range of organisations should be allowed to participate in the regional meetings. According to the proposal, NGOs with status similar to consultative status at the specialised agencies or at regional human rights IGOs, and indigenous peoples should be invited.[55]

The rules for accreditation to the conference were elaborated by the PrepCom and adopted by the conference itself as part of the Rules of Procedure. The rules had been the subject of fierce debate between states and NGOs during the preparatory process; Asian states in particular had tried to minimise NGO participation in the conference. It was not until PrepCom III that agreement could be reached on generous

---

[50] A/RES/44/228, *United Nations Conference on Environment and Development*, 22 December 1989, Part II, para. 12.

[51] E/AC.70/1994/5/Add.1, *General Review of Current Arrangements*, 7 June 1994, para. 8.

[52] For instance, almost 100 NGOs participated in PrepCom III and around 140 in PrepCom IV, A/CONF.157/PC/INF.1, 23 September 1992 and A/CONF.157/PC/INF.1, 26 May 1993.

[53] 166 NGOs participated in the regional meeting for Africa, 169 in the meeting for Latin America and 151 in the meeting for Asia, E/AC.70/1994/5/Add.1, *General Review of Current Arrangements*, 7 June 1994, para. 10.

[54] A/CONF.157/PC/54, *Report of the Preparatory Committee for the World Conference of Human Rights*, 8 October 1992, annex II, Decision PC.3/2.

[55] A/CONF.157/PC/50/Rev.1, *Recommendations Concerning the Participation*, 17 September 1992.

rules after firm lobbying from NGOs.[56] According to the rules, NGOs in consultative status with ECOSOC and with competence in the field of human rights, as well as other NGOs which had participated in the PrepCom meetings, could designate representatives to participate as observers in the conference, its committees and working groups, on questions within the scope of their activities.[57] This was an important development in terms of NGO participation in UN conferences, as many local and regional organisations without consultative status were able to participate. The total number of participants in the conference amounted to around 7,000.[58] Of these, 3,691 persons were NGO representatives from 841 organisations; 593 NGOs were not in consultative status with ECOSOC.[59] In other words, more NGOs and NGO representatives participated in the Vienna Conference than in the Earth Summit in Rio. Almost 600 organisations of the accredited NGOs were national;[60] it was also seen as an important achievement that many NGOs from the South took part in the conference, many of them for the first time in an international meeting of this kind.[61]

A pre-Conference NGO Forum was also held, which among other objectives aimed at submitting common recommendations to the UN conference.[62] Some 2,700 NGOs participated.[63] The final document of the NGO Forum included recommendations on, *inter alia*, the recognition of the right to self-determination of indigenous peoples and a holistic approach to the right to development.[64]

---

[56] For a detailed account of this debate, see William Korey, *NGOs and the Universal Declaration of Human Rights: A Curious Grapevine*, New York: Palgrave Macmillan, 1998, pp. 278–280.

[57] A/CONF.157/8, *Rules of Procedure of the World Conference on Human Rights*, 14 June 1993, Rule 66.

[58] The United Nations, 1997, p. 31.

[59] 47 *Yearbook of the United Nations*, Dordrecht: Martinus Nijhoff, 1993, p. 908; Korey, *NGOs and the Universal Declaration of Human Rights*, p. 288.

[60] E/AC.70/1994/5/Add.1, *General Review of Current Arrangements*, 7 June 1994, para. 13.

[61] The Joint Liaison Project, launched by the International Service for Human Rights in Geneva and the Ludwig Bolzmann Institute of Vienna had an important role in this respect. It was created with the purpose of achieving the 'fullest possible contribution and participation of NGOs particularly from the South', and kept NGOs throughout the world informed about the preparatory meetings, the NGO Forum and the World Conference itself. Korey, *NGOs and the Universal Declaration of Human Rights*, p. 280.

[62] Manfred Nowak (ed.), *World Conference on Human Rights, Vienna, June 1993: The Contribution of NGOs, Reports and Documents*, Vienna: Manz, 1994, p. 4.

[63] Korey, *NGOs and the Universal Declaration of Human Rights*, p. 288.   [64] *Ibid.*, p. 5.

458   LEGAL AND EMPIRICAL SURVEY

As mentioned above, the Rules of Procedure allowed for NGOs to designate representatives to participate in the meetings of the conference, its main committees and, 'as appropriate', any other committee or working group on questions within the scope of their activities.[65] However, the different bodies of the conference could require that a meeting be held in private.[66] NGOs were excluded from the main drafting committee and were physically separated from the government delegates.[67] Written statements by NGOs were issued as official documents, which is otherwise generally not the case.[68] For the sake of comparison, it can be noted that the 1996 ECOSOC arrangements for consultation with NGOs, which include rules on the participation of NGOs in UN conferences, provide that written statements by NGOs shall not be issued as official documents.[69] Eventually, permission was also granted for oral statements from NGOs at the conference, although under clear restrictions.[70]

As has become customary for this type of document, the Vienna Declaration and Programme of Action which was adopted by the 171 states participating in the conference repeatedly mentions NGOs.[71] The most important passage as regards NGOs is as follows:

The World Conference on Human Rights recognizes the important role of non-governmental organizations in the promotion of all human rights and in humanitarian activities at national, regional and international levels ... While recognizing that the primary responsibility for standard-setting lies with States, the Conference also appreciates the contribution of non-governmental organizations to this process. In this respect, the World Conference on Human Rights

---

[65] A/CONF.157/8, *Adoption of the Rules of Procedure: Rules of Procedure of the World Conference on Human Rights*, 14 June 1993, Rule 66.

[66] *Ibid.*, Rule 56.

[67] Michael H. Posner, 'ASIL Report: Reflections on the Vienna Conference', *ASIL Newsletter*, September 1993; Korey, *NGOs and the Universal Declaration of Human Rights*, pp. 292–293.

[68] Rule 67 on written statements of procedure by NGOs, as opposed to the rules of some other conferences, did not provide that statements would not be issued as official documents. NGOs at the Rio Conference could not issue statements as official documents: Decision 1/1 of the Preparatory Committee of UNCED, in Willetts, 'The Conscience of the World', p. 302. See also NGO statements, such as A/CONF.157/PC/79, 20 April 1993, presented by the American Society of International Law to the Preparatory Committee.

[69] E/RES/1996/31, para. 52.

[70] Korey, *NGOs and the Universal Declaration of Human Rights*, p. 292.

[71] The United Nations, 1997, p. 30. For mentions of NGOs in the Vienna Declaration and Programme of Action, see, e.g., paras. 13, 18, 38, 73.

emphasizes the importance of continued dialogue and cooperation between Governments and non-governmental organizations. Non-governmental organizations and their members genuinely involved in the field of human rights should enjoy the rights and freedoms recognized in the Universal Declaration of Human Rights, and the protection of the national law. These rights and freedoms may not be exercised contrary to the purposes and principles of the United Nations. Non-governmental organizations should be free to carry out their human rights activities, without interference, within the framework of national law and the Universal Declaration of Human Rights.[72]

From a general point of view, it was of importance for human rights NGOs that the Vienna Declaration and Programme of Action underlined that the promotion and protection of human rights was a legitimate concern of the international community and NGOs and a priority objective of the United Nations.[73] More specifically, the UN Centre for Human Rights (now the Office of the High Commissioner for Human Rights) was set up as part of the follow-up to the Conference with the High Commissioner for Human Rights as its head. Amnesty International and other NGOs had strongly advocated the creation of such an institution at the conference, as they had done several times before.[74] According to one writer, the decision of the conference to call the United Nations to establish a High Commissioner for Human Rights was 'a consequence of an unprecedented and unparalleled outburst of lobbying by nongovernmental organizations'.[75] It should be observed, however, that the recommendation of the conference on this matter was considerably weaker than that which had been advocated by the NGOs.[76] Some other demands put forward by NGOs, such as strengthening measures to protect the human rights of women, an unequivocal denunciation of racism, xenophobia and

[72] A/CONF.157/23, World Conference on Human Rights, *Vienna Declaration and Programme of Action*, 12 July 1993, para. 38.

[73] See also the *Vienna Declaration and Programme of Action*, para. 4.

[74] NGOs had previously supported the proposals of governments to create a UN High Commissioner for Human Rights in 1950, 1965 and in the late 1970s. Philip Alston, 'The United Nations High Commissioner for Human Rights', *ASIL Newsletter*, September 1995 and Posner, 'ASIL Report: Reflections on the Vienna Conference'; Nowak, *World Conference on Human Rights*, p. 9; Korey, *NGOs and the Universal Declaration of Human Rights*, p. 282.

[75] Korey, *NGOs and the Universal Declaration of Human Rights*, p. 273.

[76] Nowak, *World Conference on Human Rights*, p. 8. The High Commissioner has established regular contacts and co-operation with NGOs in different ways, including the programming of human rights activities, country visits and meetings of the UN human rights organs, see A/53/372, *Follow-Up to the World Conference on Human Rights*, 11 September 1998, para. 24 and E/CN.4/1998/122, *Report of the United Nations High Commissioner for Human Rights*, 23 February 1998, paras. 123–124.

460 LEGAL AND EMPIRICAL SURVEY

other forms of intolerance, and recognition of the right to asylum, found their way into the final document of the conference.[77]

8.5 Third Session of the Conference of the Parties to the Framework Convention on Climate Change

The UN FCCC was adopted in May 1992 and opened for signature at the Rio Conference the same year. The Convention establishes its own institutional arrangement, the yearly Conference of the Parties (COP), with the purpose of developing the normative content of the agreement and supervising the state parties' implementation of and compliance with the Convention. The Third Session of the COP met in Kyoto in December 1997. On its final day it adopted the Kyoto Protocol, which is a legally binding instrument for the reduction of greenhouse gas emissions.

The Convention also establishes an autonomous framework for co-operation between NGOs and the parties to the Convention.[78] Article 4, para. 1(i) provides that the state parties to the Convention shall promote and encourage wide participation, including that of NGOs, in education, training and public awareness related to climate change. Article 7, para. 2(l), regarding the supervision by the COP of the implementation of the Convention, states that the conference shall 'seek and utilize, where appropriate, the services and cooperation of, and information provided by, competent ... non-governmental bodies'.

Article 7(6) provides the legal basis for NGO participation in proceedings of the Conference of the parties by stating that:

Any body or agency, whether national or international, governmental or non-governmental, which is qualified in matters covered by the Convention, and which has informed the secretariat of its wish to be represented at a session of the Conference of the Parties as an observer, may be so admitted unless at least one-third of the Parties present object. The admission and participation of observers shall be subject to the rules of procedure adopted by the Conference of the Parties.

The understanding of the expression 'non-governmental body or agency' included in this Article of the Convention is, like the institutional framework, autonomous. In ECOSOC resolution 1996/31 on arrangements

[77] Nowak, *World Conference on Human Rights*, p. 10.
[78] On the participation and influence of NGOs on the climate change negotiations generally, see Asher Alkoby, 'Non-State Actors and the Legitimacy of International Environmental Law', 3 *Non-State Actors and International Law* (2003), pp. 36–41.

for consultations with NGOs, as well as within most corresponding arrangements within other IGOs, the term 'NGO' is specified in a more or less detailed manner.[79] The understanding of the term in the FCCC is broader. The expression 'non-governmental body or agency' is wider than the usual 'non-governmental organisation', probably chosen in order to embrace research institutes and (public) academic bodies. The same expression is used in the Rules of Procedure, as was mentioned above. There is, however, a practice of requiring non-governmental bodies to 'furnish proof of their non-profit (tax-exempt) status in a State member of the United Nations or of a specialized agency or of the International Atomic Energy Agency'.[80] In other words, profit-making bodies are not admitted as observers to the conference.

At its first session, the COP agreed that the Secretariat should invite to all future sessions of the conference and its subsidiary bodies all organisations which had been admitted before, unless an objection was raised by the state parties. Accordingly, all organisations which had been admitted to the first and second sessions of the COP were admitted to the third session. In addition, a number of new organisations which had requested admission were invited. No objections were raised to any of the organisations on the Secretariat's list by the COP Bureau before the third session or by the COP itself during the session.[81]

The lists of participants in the sessions of the COP present a varied group of non-governmental bodies. Many attending organisations and bodies were environmental NGOs, trade unions or research institutes. At least half of the non-governmental participants at the third session seem to have been industrial organisations – i.e. organisations formed by the industry to represent their interests, such as the Australian Coal Association and the Canadian Vehicle Manufacturers' Association.[82] The

---

[79] See chapter 7 and section 8.2.

[80] FCCC/CP/1997/4, *Organizational Matters: Admission of Organizations as Observers*, 12 November 1997, para. 3.

[81] *Ibid.*, paras. 2–3, 5 and FCCC/CP/1997/7, *Report of the Conference of the Parties on its Third Session*, 18 March 1998, para. 28.

[82] FCCC/CP/1997/4, *Organizational Matters: Admission of Organizations as Observers*, 12 November 1997, annex and Chiara Giorgetti, 'From Rio to Kyoto: A Study of the Involvement of Non-Governmental Organizations in the Negotiations on Climate Change', 7 *New York University School of Law Environmental Law Journal* (1999), pp. 220–222. However, it is very hard to tell whether organisations promote industrial and business interests or have other concerns without a detailed examination of each organisation, and the names of the organisations do not provide much guidance. For instance, coal and oil companies have formed an organisation called the Climate Council and the chemical sector is represented by the International Climate Change Partnership, *ibid.*

462 LEGAL AND EMPIRICAL SURVEY

total number of participants in the third session of the COP amounted to almost 10,000 people, of which 2,200 were official delegates and the rest observers from different kinds of organisations and representatives of the press.[83] The number of (all kinds of) NGOs represented at the session was 243.[84]

Provisions on the modalities for NGO participation in international conferences are normally provided by the rules of procedure. According to Article 7(3) of the FCCC, the COP should, at its first session, adopt its own rules of procedure. At Kyoto, however, the rules had still not been adopted, as the first and second as well as the third sessions of the COP were unable to agree on them. The President of the Conference thus decided that the draft rules of procedure should continue to be applied during the third session.[85] These Rules reiterated the wording of Article 7(6) of the Convention on the representation of IGOs and NGOs at the sessions of the COP and specified the modalities for such participation:

Such observers may, upon invitation of the President, participate without the right to vote in the proceedings of any session in matters of direct concern to the body or agency they represent, unless at least one third of the Parties present at the session object.[86]

According to draft Rule 30, meetings of the COP should be held in public, unless the conference decided otherwise. The daily programmes from the third session demonstrate that, while the plenaries and the meetings of the Committee of the Whole were public and accordingly open to NGOs, the meetings of negotiating groups, as well as several other meetings, were closed.[87] NGOs were allowed to deliver oral statements at the plenaries, but were given the floor on only twelve occasions during these meetings (as compared to around 130 statements delivered by state representatives and twenty-one by IGOs).[88]

---

[83] United Nations Press Release, *Industrialized Countries to Cut Greenhouse Gas Emissions by 5.2%*, Kyoto, 11 December 1997.

[84] FCCC/CP/1997/7, *Report of the Conference of the Parties on its Third Session*, 18 March 1998, annex II.

[85] FCCC/CP/1997/5, *Organizational Matters: Adoption of the Rules of Procedure*, 19 November 1997, paras. 3–4.

[86] FCCC/CP/1996/2, *Organizational Matters: Adoption of the Rules of Procedure*, 22 May 1996, Draft Rules of Procedure, Rule 7(2).

[87] Conference of the Parties, Third Session, 1–10 December 1997, *Daily Programme*, Nos. 1–3 and 9 (1–3 December and 10 December).

[88] FCCC/CP/1997/7, *Report of the Conference of the Parties on its Third Session*, 18 March 1998, annex I.

Written statements by NGOs were not issued as official conference documents.[89]

A study of the techniques used by different types of NGOs to influence the climate change negotiations at the three first COP sessions demonstrates that industrial organisations mainly used direct contacts with state representatives, the presentation of draft texts to governmental delegations and contacts with the mass media as their methods, while environmental NGOs used these techniques as well as other methods more directed at the public, such as publications (for instance the daily newspaper 'ECO'), and visible protests inside and outside the conference centre.[90] Perhaps surprisingly, environmental NGOs and industrial organisations also co-operated with each other on some issues, and some members of environmental NGOs participating in the sessions of the COP sat on the board of directors of companies of, for instance, renewable energies corporations.[91]

8.6 The Rome Conference for an International Criminal Court

Introduction

The Rome Conference held in 1998 for the establishment of an international court is of special interest to the present study, for several reasons. The adoption of the Statute of the Court on 17 July 1998 constituted a significant development of international law. In spite of – or because of – the importance of the instrument, the draft Statute which was before the conference was far from a finalised text, containing around 1,700 square brackets representing points of disagreement and different alternatives for the wording of provisions.[92] This fact, taken together with the Rules of Procedure and the actual proceedings of the Conference which admitted a considerable degree of NGO participation, created a very special opportunity for NGOs to influence an important step in international legal

---

[89] FCCC/CP/1996/2, *Organizational Matters: Adoption of the Rules of Procedure*, 22 May 1996, Draft Rules of Procedure, Rules 7, 36 *e contrario*.

[90] Giorgetti, 'From Rio to Kyoto', pp. 239–241 and 'Report of the Third Conference of the Parties to the United Nations Framework Convention on Climate Change', 12 *Earth Negotiations Bulletin*, No. 76, p. 15.

[91] *Ibid.*, pp. 234–235.

[92] Philippe Kirsch, 'The Development of the Rome Statute', in Roy S. Lee (ed.), *The International Criminal Court: The Making of the Rome Statute*, The Hague: Kluwer Law International, 1999, p. 452.

464   LEGAL AND EMPIRICAL SURVEY

development. With over 200 NGOs accredited to the conference, the level of civil society participation was unusually high for a law-making conference.[93] After the adoption of the Statute, it was generally recognised that NGOs had played an important role in the process.[94]

The study of the role of NGOs at the Rome Conference is more detailed than the descriptions of other conferences above and includes an examination of NGO influence on the negotiations as experienced by state and NGO representatives. More concretely, the influence of NGOs on the negotiation of the Rome Statute was investigated through interviews with persons who were in key positions during the Rome Conference itself and the preparatory process, as well as through an examination of the conference documents which provided the framework for NGO participation.

The discussions on establishing an international criminal court began only a few years after the founding of the United Nations when in 1948 the General Assembly assigned the project to the ILC. The International Commission of Jurists advocated a creation of such a court at the World Conference on Human Rights in 1993.[95] However, it was not until 1994, after several unsuccessful attempts by the ILC and other bodies, that the work on a draft Statute for the court could actually be completed and presented to the General Assembly.[96] The work on the draft Statute was then continued within an *ad hoc* Committee established by the General Assembly, and later within the Preparatory Committee on the Establishment of an International Criminal Court (the PrepCom).[97]

---

[93] A/53/1, *Annual Report of the Secretary-General on the Work of the Organization*, 27 August 1998, para. 180. Actually, according to the Secretary-General, it was 'unprecedented' for a law-making conference. However, it has already been mentioned that 234 NGOs (industrial organisations included) were accredited to the Third Session of the Parties to the UN FCCC, which adopted the Kyoto Protocol.

[94] *Ibid.*, para. 183 (speaking about 'civil society'), UN Press Release L/ROM/22, *UN Diplomatic Conference Concludes in Rome . . .*, 17 July 1998; CICC Press Release, *Momentum Builds*, 28 June 2001; and Adriaan Bos, 'The International Criminal Court: A Perspective', in Roy S. Lee (ed.), *The International Criminal Court: The Making of the Rome Statute*, The Hague: Kluwer Law International, 1999, p. 470.

[95] Nowak, *World Conference on Human Rights*, p. 10; Korey, *NGOs and the Universal Declaration of Human Rights*, p. 282.

[96] A/49/10, Supp. 10, *Report of the International Law Commission*, para. 91 and Roy S. Lee, 'The Rome Conference and its Contributions to International Law', in Roy S. Lee (ed.) *The International Criminal Court: The Making of the Rome Statute*, The Hague: Kluwer Law International, 1999, pp. 2–3.

[97] The *ad hoc* Committee was established by the General Assembly on 9 December 1994 by means of resolution A/RES/49/53, *Establishment of an International Criminal Court*, 17 February 1995, and the PrepCom on 11 December 1995 by means of Resolution A/RES/50/46, 18 December 1995.

The PrepCom held six sessions between 1996 and 1998 and presented a consolidated text for a Statute in its final report, together with draft Rules of Procedure and a draft Final Act for the conference.[98]

In December 1997, the UN General Assembly decided that a diplomatic conference of plenipotentiaries, open to all member states of the United States or its specialised agencies, would be held in Rome from 15 June to 17 July 1998 with a view to adopting a convention on the establishment of an international criminal court.[99]

Qualitative research interviewing

The decision to interview participants in the Rome Conference raised questions about how to select the interviewees, how to perform the interviews and how to treat the material arising from them. These problems are reflected in the sociological debate between quantitative and qualitative theories on how empirical data should be sought and interpreted. Quantitative research is here understood as a positivist approach to empirical material, where data are obtained through standardised means.[100] Interviews carried out with such a method would, typically, be carried out with questionnaires or a pre-determined set of questions – maybe also with a given set of alternative answers to choose from – put to a large number of people. The analysis of the material found could result in figures, tables and graphs.

By contrast, researchers who use a qualitative method generally have a different conception of empirical knowledge, emphasising experience, description and interpretation and the use of the subjects' perspective as a starting point.[101] Accordingly, the techniques for identifying the respondents, for structuring the interview and formulating the questions and for analysing the results are different. The qualitative interview is sometimes called 'non-standardised', and its purpose is to

---

[98] A/CONF.183/2, *Report of the Preparatory Committee on the Establishment of an International Criminal Court*, 14 April 1998, paras. 2–15.

[99] A/RES/52/160, *Establishment of an International Criminal Court*, 28 January 1998 (adopted at the 72nd plenary meeting on 15 December 1997).

[100] Mats Alvesson and Kaj Sköldberg, *Reflexive Methodology: New Vistas for Qualitative Research*, London: Sage, 2000, p. 3; David Silverman, *Interpreting Qualitative Data: Methods for Analysing Talk, Text and Interaction*, London: Sage, 1993, pp. 10, 21–22; Russell H. Bernard, *Social Research Methods: Qualitative and Quantitative Approaches*, London: Sage, 2000, pp. 418–419.

[101] Steinar Kvale, *InterViews: An Introduction to Qualitative Research Interviewing*, London: Sage, 1996, p. 38; Alvesson and Sköldberg, *Reflexive Methodology*, pp. 3–4; Silverman, *Interpreting Qualitative Data*, pp. 23 ff.

466   LEGAL AND EMPIRICAL SURVEY

obtain descriptions of the lived world of the subjects and their relation to it.[102] Underlying this choice of method is a sceptical attitude towards the possibility of obtaining 'objective' data about complex social issues and an emphasis on the subjective experiences of the interviewee as one of many possible stories.[103]

It is often held that the choice of method depends on what kind of information is sought. For instance, Silverman is critical of the placing of quantitative and qualitative methods as polar opposites, suggesting that 'It all depends upon what you are trying to do'.[104] The basic question I would like to answer, or at least discuss, in the light of information obtained from the interviews is whether, in the view of the informants, NGOs asserted an influence on the negotiation of the Statute of the ICC. If that question can preliminarily be answered in the affirmative, other issues that should be discussed are *how* NGOs managed to influence the negotiations – i.e. which methods were used – and in what respects the final text of the Statute was influenced. The different questions asked are clearly of a kind that cannot be answered in a clear-cut way. Rather, it can be assumed that the interview subjects will have rather complex and diverging views on what happened during the Rome Conference and the preparatory process. This means that data regarding the influence of NGOs on the negotiation of the Rome Statute can hardly be quantified in any meaningful way. The factors involved in a situation of political pressure, as well as in the interpretation of such a situation, are subjective. Although the process studied here led to a result that is in some sense objective, namely the treaty text as it was adopted by the conference, this does not offer much guidance. Even if the treaty text is a purely intergovernmental product on the surface, the questions asked must reach beneath this and before its adoption in time. It is on these grounds that I have chosen a method which borrows more from qualitative than from quantitative research.

A rather limited number of persons – three state representatives and two representatives of NGOs – who were in central positions during the Rome Conference and the preparatory process have been identified for the interviews. The interviews were semi-structured, i.e. carried out with a limited number of rather open questions that were put to all the interviewees.[105] In order not to circumscribe the

---

[102] Kvale, *InterViews*, pp. 13, 29.   [103] *Ibid.*, pp. 35, 41–44.

[104] Silverman, *Interpreting Qualitative Data*, p. 22. See also Alvesson and Sköldberg, *Reflexive Methodology*, p. 4.

[105] On informal, unstructured, semi-structured and structured interviewing, see Bernard, *Social Research Methods*, pp. 190–192.

possibility of describing what was really said, especially with regard to state representatives whose answers might otherwise appear as official statements, the information obtained through the interviews – both factual information and personal experiences and opinions – has been compiled into one coherent text without direct citations. Direct references are made only when information has been obtained through other sources, such as papers and articles on the conference. It should be observed that, although all interviewed persons were identified through their official positions during the conference, their answers reflect personal experiences which do not necessarily correspond to the standpoints of their respective governments or organisations.[106]

The legal framework for NGO participation

When the report of the ILC with the draft Statute for the international criminal court was debated in the UN General Assembly in 1995, a small group of NGOs monitored the session.[107] There are no arrangements for consultations between the Assembly and NGOs, and debates in the Assembly can be monitored only by accredited NGOs from the balcony in the General Assembly Hall. Accordingly, NGOs do not have any right to actual participation in the form of delivering oral or written statements or even walking around among the delegates in the meeting room. As the PrepCom was a body established by the Assembly it followed the Assembly's rules of procedure, so NGOs could listen to the plenary sessions only during the first PrepComs. The ICRC, however, was an exception in this regard, as it has had observer status with

---

[106] The persons interviewed and their official positions during the Conference were as follows: *Sir Franklin Berman*, legal adviser to the British Foreign and Commonwealth Office and Head of the UK delegation; *Christopher Hall*, Legal adviser at Amnesty International's International Secretariat; Ambassador *Philippe Kirsch*, Legal advisor to the Canadian Department of Foreign Affairs, Head of the Canadian delegation and Chairman of the Committee of the Whole; *William Pace*, Convenor of the NGO Coalition for an International Criminal Court and Executive Director of the World Federalist Movement; *Per Saland*, Director of Division, Swedish Ministry for Foreign Affairs, Vice Head of the Swedish delegation and Chairman of the Working Group on General Principles and the Working Group on Applicable Law. In addition, one member of a delegation from a Western European country gave some informal information. This concentration on persons from Northern, industrialised countries is unfortunate, but was necessary for practical reasons.

[107] William Pace and Mark Thieroff, 'Participation of Non-Governmental Organizations', in Roy S. Lee (ed.), *The International Criminal Court: The Making of the Rome Statute*, The Hague: Kluwer Law International, 1999, p. 391.

468   LEGAL AND EMPIRICAL SURVEY

the General Assembly since 1990.[108] NGOs did, nevertheless, attend the meetings of the PrepCom to an increasing extent during the preparatory process. Twenty representatives of the NGO Coalition for the Establishment of an International Criminal Court (hereafter the CICC or the NGO Coalition) attended the second session of the PrepCom, approximately fifty NGOs were represented at the fourth session, around 150 representatives of approximately eighty NGOs attended the fifth session, and over sixty NGOs were represented at the sixth session.[109] At the later PrepCom meetings, NGOs were allowed to attend not only the plenary sessions but also the working group meetings, while the informal drafting group meetings continued to be closed to NGO observers.[110]

There were also intersessional meetings during the preparatory period. Most of these took place at the International Institute of Higher Studies in Criminal Sciences in Syracuse. At these meetings, NGOs could participate almost on an equal footing with state representatives, i.e. attend the meetings and move freely among state representatives, distribute their materials and also participate in the discussion. Only the largest and best-known NGOs were, however, able to prepare for and attend these meetings.

In December 1997, the General Assembly decided to convene the Rome Conference. In the same resolution, it outlined the modalities for participation of NGOs by requesting the Secretary-General to invite NGOs accredited by the Preparatory Committee, with due regard to the provisions of part VII of ECOSOC resolution 1996/31 (which deals with the participation of NGOs in UN conferences) and in particular to the relevance of NGO activities to the work of the conference, to participate in the conference along the lines followed in the PrepCom.[111] The General Assembly also stated that NGOs were invited to the conference on the basis of the understanding that participation meant:

- attending meetings of its plenary and, unless otherwise decided by the conference in specific situations, formal meetings of its subsidiary bodies except the drafting group,

---

[108] A/RES/45/6, *Observer Status for the International Committee of the Red Cross*, 16 October 1990. The ICRC did in fact participate in the work of the PrepCom, see, e.g., A/AC.249/INF/2, *List of Delegations*, 29 August 1996.

[109] *ICC Monitor On-line*, No. 2, 1998, article by Mark Thieroff, 'CICC Report from Working Group 3 of PrepCom 4', 'Initial Summary report by William Pace on PrepCom 5', and 'Report on the March–April 1998 Session'.

[110] CICC, *Reports from Working Group 3 of PrepCom 4* and *PrepCom 6*.

[111] A/RES/52/160, *Establishment of an International Criminal Court*, 28 January 1998, para. 9.

PARTICIPATION IN INTERNATIONAL CONFERENCES 469

- receiving copies of the official documents,
- making available their materials to delegates, and
- addressing, through a limited number of their representatives, its opening and/or closing sessions, as appropriate, in accordance with the rules of procedure to be adopted by the conference.[112]

Interestingly, the work of identifying likely NGOs for accreditation to the conference by the PrepCom was carried out by the UN Secretariat in collaboration with the CICC.[113] This was a rather controversial solution, but since it was taken at a late stage when there was a shortage of time, there were no attempts to suggest other solutions. The rules for accreditation were also generous, and the role of the NGO Coalition was mainly to identify the organisations which had been active during the preparatory process. There was, however, a screening mechanism which made it possible for states to raise objections to the participation of particular NGOs. Such objections were made by China and Sri Lanka, for example, in the latter case in relation to an NGO which allegedly maintained contacts with a Tamil organisation.

On the basis of the lists of NGOs compiled by the Secretariat and the CICC, the PrepCom decided to invite around 236 NGOs, represented by around 450 accredited individuals, to the conference;[114] 160 governmental delegations participated, together with representatives of IGOs and the media.[115]

The Rules of Procedure for the conference included provisions for NGO participation which were almost identical to those outlined by the General Assembly in its Resolution. According to Rule 63, NGOs invited to the conference were allowed to participate through their designated representatives:

- by attending plenary meetings of the conference and, unless otherwise decided by the conference in specific situations, formal meetings of the committee of the Whole and of subsidiary bodies established by it,
- by receiving copies of official documents,

---

[112] *Ibid.*

[113] A/CONF.183/INF/3, *Non-Governmental Organizations Accredited to Participate in the Conference*, para. 2 and Pace, 'Participation of Non-Governmental Organizations', in Roy S. Lee (ed.), *The International Criminal Court: The Making of the Rome Statute*, The Hague, Kluwer Law International, 1999, p. 393.

[114] Pace and Thieroff, 'Participation of Non-Governmental Organizations', p. 392.

[115] UN Press Release, L/ROM/22, *UN Diplomatic Conference Concludes in Rome with Decision to Establish Permanent International Criminal Court*, 17 July 1998.

470 LEGAL AND EMPIRICAL SURVEY

- by making, through a limited number of their representatives, oral statements to the opening and closing sessions of the conference, upon the invitation of the President and subject to the approval of the conference.[116]

In addition, the Rules of Procedure provided that written statements by designated NGO representatives should be distributed by the Secretariat to delegations in the quantities and languages made available to it at the site of the conference, provided that the statement was related to the work of the conference and dealt with a subject on which the organisation had special competence. Written NGO statements were not produced at the expense of the United Nations and were not issued as official UN documents.[117]

As provided by the Rules of Procedure, the conference established two Committees – the Committee of the Whole, in which all participating states were represented, and the Drafting Committee.[118] The Committee of the Whole established a number of Working Groups, such as the Working Group on Applicable Law, the Working Group on Enforcement and the Working Group on General Principles. As far as I have been informed, NGOs were allowed to attend all formal meetings but one.

The majority of the NGOs which attended the Rome Conference were part of the CICC, which was formed in 1995 with the purpose of advocating a fair, effective and independent ICC. The Coalition has not acquired any legal personality, and the secretariat is hosted by the World Federalist Movement. The initiative to form the Coalition was taken by a small group of NGOs – among others, Amnesty International, Human Rights Watch, Lawyers for Human Rights and the World Federalist Movement.[119] As of August 2004, the Coalition brought together over 1,000 NGOs, international law experts and groups.[120]

Influence on the negotiations

General

There was general agreement among the informants that NGOs played a very important role in the negotiation of the Rome Statute, both before and during the conference. The views on what factors contributed to this influence and in what respects it made an impact differed between

---

[116] A/CONF183/6, *Rules of Procedure*, 23 June 1998.   [117] Rule 64.   [118] Rules 48, 49.
[119] Pace and Thieroff, 'Participation of Non-Governmental Organizations', p. 391.
[120] Website at www.iccuow.org.

state and NGO representatives, as will be described below. Several persons pointed out that the negotiation of the Rome Statute was a process with special characteristics because of its complexity and partly legal–technical nature, which created a special opportunity for NGOs to provide specialised knowledge and information, in particular in relation to smaller delegations. One state representative made the comparison with the Ottawa Land Mine Conference in 1997, which dealt with a 'simple' issue – i.e. whether or not to ban land mines – and which was not very controversial, as almost everyone could agree that land mines should be banned. That negotiation was therefore not a particularly interesting example of NGO pressure as compared to the Rome Conference, in the view of the state representative.

Another point of general agreement, among both state and NGO representatives, was that the forming of the CICC was central to NGOs' success. One NGO representative pointed to the fact that through the formation of the Coalition the NGOs together had by far the largest delegation, amounting to over 200 people and involving some 95 per cent of all NGO members participating in the conference.

The modalities for NGO participation

As is clear from the Rules of Procedure, NGOs could attend plenary meetings and formal meetings of the Committee of the Whole, as well as of subsidiary bodies established by it, unless otherwise decided in specific situations. This meant in practice that they could walk around in the meeting rooms among the governmental delegates during almost all the formal meetings, even if the seating was sometimes limited. Only the Working Group on General Principles, on one occasion, closed its doors to NGOs. When the definition of the term 'gender' was to be discussed, several delegations demanded that the NGOs should leave the Working Group. Some NGO representatives tried to stay in the room after the decision to close the doors had been taken, which produced a very tense atmosphere. One of the state representatives interviewed underlined that this kind of behaviour on the part of NGOs was very badly received by the governmental delegations and might even have been counterproductive in relation to NGO access to future meetings. Another state representative said that the more NGOs observed the kind of role that governments expected from them, the more they were welcome. If they overstepped it, there was a risk they would suddenly find they were not welcome, so it was in the NGOs' own interest to keep to their role.

472 LEGAL AND EMPIRICAL SURVEY

Apart from the formal meetings, there were, of course, informal meetings and consultations. One of the NGO representatives described the variety of meetings as the informal, the formal–informal, the formal and the negotiation meetings in halls and restaurants. The state representatives were all of the view that if NGOs are granted wide access to meetings, the 'real' negotiations tend to move elsewhere. On the other hand, one of the state representatives interviewed pointed out that NGOs often know within a few minutes after the conclusion of such a meeting what has happened. The same person thought that, generally speaking, almost all of the actual drafting during this kind of event takes place in meetings where NGOs are not present, but that these meetings concern matters of detail rather than of principles. He further stressed the importance of maintaining a space for informal meetings open to governmental delegates only. The issues discussed during negotiations are often politically sensitive, and considerable experience is required in order to find solutions where governments can adjust or alter their positions without losing face. Another state representative, on the other hand, was of the view that NGOs should have wide access even to informal meetings if possible, as closed doors tend to feed a lack of understanding.

Strategies and working methods of NGOs

The NGOs used a variety of techniques and strategies for asserting influence on the negotiations. Among the concrete methods were the distribution of written material through the Secretariat or privately, either generally (e.g. by placing them beside entrances to meeting rooms) or to a selected group of people or delegations. These materials included position papers, reports, text proposals and information about the NGOs themselves. Some of the larger NGOs sent material to governmental delegations before the conference started. In general, it was mentioned by both NGO and state representatives that the emphasis in the work performed by NGOs during the conference was not on advocacy but on information, education and service. The detailed and analytical material produced by in particular the larger and more well-known NGOs was widely used and appreciated. Through their specialisation, NGOs were able to produce wide-ranging analyses of many different issues. Since the Rome Statute was a very complex matter involving a wide range of issues, the smaller delegations especially (but not only) were assisted by the NGO material.

The CICC also produced two daily 'newspapers', *Terra Viva* and the *CICC Monitor*, as well as the electronic newsletter *On the Record*. According to one of the state representatives 'no one' paid attention to *Terra Viva* at first since it was an NGO product. Later, however, people started to notice that it commented on daily events in great detail, including what different delegates had said, sometimes with critical remarks, so that after a while people became very curious to find out who 'was the victim of the day'. The representative thought that this could in itself have had a certain influence on the negotiations, since no one wanted to be attacked personally.

The CICC did not produce draft provisions, but worked only with a few basic principles and by reacting to the drafts put forward by governments. According to one of the NGO representatives, governmental delegations in general often reacted negatively to draft provisions put forward by NGOs. This was to some extent confirmed by the state representatives. Individual NGOs, including those which belonged to the Coalition, did, however, produce and present drafts during the Rome negotiations. One of the state representatives interviewed said that it was not unusual for governments to adopt whole sections of drafts from NGOs – mostly the smaller delegations but also delegations which included NGO representatives.

A special kind of material produced by the CICC was the lists or compilations of state positions. According to one of the state representatives, NGOs used these lists in order to demonstrate when there was a sufficient majority for a certain position for a 'safe vote' on different parts of the draft Statute. However, voting took place only three times during the Conference.

The Rules entitled NGOs to deliver oral statements to the opening and closing sessions of the conference, but not in working groups. These statements seem to have been of little importance in terms of influence on the negotiations. Two factors were mentioned by the state representatives in this regard. First, it was considered important that the number of NGO statements during a meeting was limited. The UN Commission on Human Rights was mentioned as an example of a body where NGO statements were far too many. Second, it was held that when particular NGOs delivered very critical statements during or after the completion of difficult negotiations, this produced a bad atmosphere and a negative reaction towards NGOs among governmental delegations.

During the preparatory process and the conference itself, a complex web of personal contacts between state and NGO representatives was woven during meetings and seminars, lunches, receptions and so on. Lobbying started long before the conference; NGOs even contacted state

474   LEGAL AND EMPIRICAL SURVEY

representatives well in advance in order to try to make them take on certain functions during the conference. Meetings took place during the conference between NGOs and individual governments, with the 'Group of like-minded' or other governments (see below), and at the initiative of both states and NGOs. There were also meetings of different kinds between the sessions of the PrepCom. It was not unusual, for instance, for state representatives to meet one of the larger NGOs on their way to an official encounter in order to be briefed on recent developments. An NGO representative explained that when you are involved in a process like the Statute of the International Criminal Court for a period of several years, you get to know each other and become friends. This was to some extent confirmed by the state representatives, who on several occasions mentioned their appreciation of the central NGO figures who were regarded as highly knowledgeable and responsible.

The 'Group of like-minded', a bloc of developed and developing states which became the leading force for an effective and independent ICC, held special meetings with representatives of the CICC. In one state representative's view, these meetings were not particularly important, as the objectives of the state and the NGO side were to a great extent shared. It was more important, in his view, that the CICC arranged meetings with the heads of different delegations, and maybe even more so when the largest and best-known NGOs arranged such meetings on their own. These organisations 'have a name', the state representative pointed out, which they can use for creating publicity if a government alters or adjusts its position.

One issue on which the informants' opinions differed clearly was to what extent governmental positions could be, or were, adjusted at the stage of a diplomatic conference. One state representative claimed that if the governmental system was 'developed', most of the decisions were taken at home and the instructions to the governmental delegation were very detailed, which left little room for adjusting the position under NGO pressure at a conference. In general, the state representatives emphasised the importance of thorough consultation processes with domestic NGOs prior to meetings such as the Rome Conference. Another state representative, however, explained that some delegations hardly received any instructions at all, and that even delegations from Western democracies came to the Rome Conference with only a few pages of instructions. Moreover, the Rome Statute was a highly complicated and detailed text which left room for negotiation and adjustment of practically all governmental positions. One of the NGO representatives agreed that instructions were sometimes detailed, but still emphasised that there was always room for adjusting positions. More importantly, the NGO representative thought, was that the role of NGOs in these cases was more to prevent delegations from backing off from 'good' positions than to make them formulate particular positions. Most European governments had positions which were shared by the CICC, but there was a danger that these positions would be 'sold out' during the negotiations with governments which were not so keen on a strong ICC. If a government backed off from the official position under the pretext that the position had to be given up due to the 'hard' positions of other governments, NGOs could try to prevent this or at least make it known to the public what had happened.[121]

A related issue is the 'complex mutual using', as one of the interviewees described it, between governmental delegations and NGOs during the conference. People within the CICC, according to this description, would sometimes be told by a state representative that a certain delegation was secretly compromising its position. Since it could be sensitive at times for one governmental delegation to criticise another, the CICC could be used to do this job. The Coalition could then either use the media to provoke public criticism (at one point, some of the members of the Coalition published an article in the UK newspaper the *Guardian*) or phone the government in question in order to inform the minister what was happening. According to this NGO representative, there were sometimes significant variations in opinion between officials from foreign offices and responsible ministers so that publicly stated positions could be undermined by the actual negotiators. Another aspect of the 'mutual using' described by this interviewee was that strong NGO pressure on a government would sometimes leave more 'political space' for other delegations to publicly criticise its position. There were, however, also situations when NGOs were misled by one delegation into believing that another was 'selling out' when in fact it was the first that was doing so.

One of the state representatives made a general remark that to some extent contradicted this, however. He suggested that NGOs loved to 'tip off' people and think that they are 'pulling the strings', when in reality they were not. In the view of this representative, NGOs were generally not very good negotiators – at least they were far from having the skills

---

[121] The lists with estimations of majorities for or against different positions which were compiled by the Coalition might have been helpful to them in this regard.

of the more experienced diplomats. At the same time, however, he admitted that NGOs had more opportunity to walk around among the delegates during the negotiations and spread the information that a certain delegation was planning to back out, and that they did contact governments 'back home' when a delegation was making compromises. He also described the CICC's use of the 'shame factor' as an effective instrument for putting pressure on states to ratify the Statute.

A matter that was mentioned by state representatives was that the tendency of NGOs to go for the 'maximum position', or formulate 'wish lists' sometimes caused irritation among governmental delegations, especially when they were subjected to heavy criticism for making compromises. In their view, compromises were necessary, and NGOs did not always understand this. Such differences between government and NGO agendas and strategies were hardly surprising, as governments had to balance different interests, while many NGOs were promoting a single issue. Moreover, governmental delegations had to co-operate and make compromises with other delegations at future negotiations. One state representative said that he was happy to listen to the NGOs and to take their views into account, but if he would later 'get blasted' for achieving 80 per cent rather than 100 per cent, he would prefer not to bother. Another state representative pointed out that very critical attitudes by NGOs could sometimes ruin negotiation packages, which also caused irritation. On the other hand, one of the NGO representatives mentioned that it was not a question of understanding or not understanding negotiations: it was simply the role of NGOs to advocate the 'maximum solution'.

A somewhat special phenomenon which seems to be spreading is the contracting of NGO experts to perform negotiations on behalf of, especially smaller, states. This also occurred during the Rome Conference, as was confirmed by both state and NGO representatives. Examples of states represented by experts from NGOs or academia included Bosnia, Samoa, Sierra Leone and the Solomon Islands. One of the NGO representatives, however, emphasised that it was an unfortunate error by NGOs to suggest that states contracted NGOs to represent them: it was only a question of governments appointing individual experts, who might come from NGOs, academia or elsewhere. Another NGO representative pointed out that it was often harder for the NGO delegates to co-operate with state representatives who were on such contracts, as they were less experienced and therefore more anxious not to give away too much information as compared to more experienced diplomats. He also mentioned that it could sometimes create confusion when a person who had formerly attended negotiations in the capacity of an NGO representative turned up at the next conference as a state representative.

Many governments invited individual NGO experts to take part in their delegation as one of many members, in contrast to the situation described above where the whole delegation was on contract. The state representatives seemed to agree that the NGO members in these situations functioned as representatives only of the state. At the same time, at least a couple of the state representatives were of the opinion that they continued to promote the NGO's objectives even in this situation, and even if there were limits to what they could do. The normal procedure for appointing these persons seemed to be that the Foreign Office identified them personally; in other words it was not for the NGO to select from among its representatives. It was pointed out by one of the NGO representatives interviewed that it was incorrect to say that such an individual 'represented' the NGO in any sense at all. Many NGOs decided never to 'loan' their staff to governments like this, as it might compromise the independence of their organisation. On the other hand, some states never co-opted NGO experts on their delegations.

The internal strategy of the CICC

The CICC agreed on a number of basic points in order to maintain unity within the organisation. First, almost any NGO supporting the basic idea of an ICC could join the CICC. Secondly, the CICC did not submit draft provisions or even specific statements, but worked only with the promotion of a few principles forming a clear mandate, such as the principle of an independent prosecutor. On the other hand, NGOs which joined the CICC were free to issue statements and speak on their own behalf.

Another important characteristic of the CICC was that it was very large and thus able to form specialised groupings on different issues (such as the Victims' Working Group and the Women's Caucus), as well as for different geographical regions. In other words, the CICC formed one enormous delegation which included specialised groups on a wide range of issues. It created twelve teams to cover negotiations on different parts of the Statute, and reports from these teams were made generally available.[122]

---

[122] Pace and Thieroff, 'Participation of Non-Governmental Organizations', p. 394.

The role of different organisations

In the view of all the state representatives interviewed, the most important factors helping an NGO to build a good reputation among governmental delegations were knowledge and expertise. One of the state representatives made the observation that when organisations such as the ICRC, Human Rights Watch, Amnesty International or Lawyers for Human Rights produced material, it was not necessary to double-check the information provided. These organisations played an important role through the distribution of their materials, which were generally regarded as analytical and helpful. It was also mentioned by all the state representatives that the CICC was very well run and respected. At the same time one of them thought that the larger NGOs were probably more important for issues of substance in the Statute, while the main importance of the CICC was in pressurising for a Statute to be adopted at all.

As was described earlier the state representatives said that it created a negative attitude towards NGOs when they were unrealistic and 'too critical' of governmental positions and compromises. The deliberate breaking up of compromises was mentioned by a couple of state representatives and one described how leaders of the major NGOs at one point disassociated themselves from such behaviour by informing governments that their organisations had not supported it. In the view of at least two of the state representatives interviewed, dramatic demonstrations or manifestations, as well as accusations of 'treason', decreased the possibilities for NGOs to co-operate with governmental delegations. One of the NGO representatives also pointed to this kind of behaviour as counter-productive.

One state representative regarded it as positive that a wide range of NGOs were involved from an early stage of the preparatory process. In his view, it was partly due to the active role played by professional organisations, not belonging to the 'normal sort of pressure group people', for example, that there was such a strong and complex influence on the process from the non-governmental groupings. This influence was 'much, much wider' than anything this state representative had previously seen.

In what respect were the negotiations influenced?

Many different aspects of the ICC and the Statute were mentioned as examples of NGO influence on the negotiations. Most interviewees mentioned the role and independence of the prosecutor as a clear example of NGO influence. In one state representative's view, there was a 'tremendous opposition' on the part of many states on this point. Several interviewees also mentioned the scope of the Court's jurisdiction as another example of NGO influence.

Other examples that were mentioned were the question of whether the Statute should be extended to cover internal armed conflicts on more or less the same footing as international conflicts, the position of victims in proceedings before the Court and the turning down of the '*à la carte*' model of the Statute proposed by the ILC. The ICRC was send to have played a very important role as regards the formulation of war crimes.

A couple of state representatives shared the view that one of the most important roles of NGOs was to pressurise for the creation of the Court in general and to create an atmosphere which was favourable to this, especially during the preparatory process. It was also said that the CICC played, and continues to play, an important role in promoting state ratification of the Statute.[123]

8.7 Conclusions

There are several significant questions relating to the participation of NGOs in UN world conferences. One is the rules for accreditation and whether these have changed towards a more open or more restrictive approach as regards NGO participation. Another is how many NGOs, or how many NGO representatives, have actually been accredited and participated. A third question concerns the forms of participation, i.e. whether NGOs have been allowed to speak, to distribute written material, etc. The most difficult question is whether NGOs have actually had an influence on the proceedings. That issue needs to be examined from the perspective of those who have actually participated in the negotiations and, most of all, from that of those state representatives who decided what positions to take and what texts to endorse or reject. The number of conferences described above is too limited for any definite conclusions to be drawn. Nevertheless, a brief examination of differences and possible trends may be of interest.

---

[123] It should be observed that the respondents were not specifically asked about the role of NGOs on the developments in relation to the ICC *after* the conclusion of the Rome Conference. That this aspect is not mentioned should not therefore be understood as NGOs being insignificant in that regard.

480   LEGAL AND EMPIRICAL SURVEY

As described above, the rules for accreditation of NGOs to UN conferences were standardised in 1996 with the adoption of the new arrangements for consultative status. Before that, the rules for accreditation were
decided upon individually for each conference. Until the 1990s, accreditation was in most cases available only to NGOs which were in consultative
status with ECOSOC and which had specific competence in the subject
matter of the conference.[124] However, some of the conferences which
were held before 1996 did represent a new and more generous attitude
on the part of states as regards NGO participation. This was particularly the
case with the Rio Conference and the World Conference on Human Rights.
The Rio Conference had rules for accreditation of NGOs which were not in
consultative status but 'desired to participate'.[125] The Conference on
Human Rights allowed for accreditation of NGOs which were not in consultative status but were active in the field of human rights and/or development.[126] With the present arrangements for NGO participation in UN
conferences, organisations in consultative status shall as a rule be accredited for participation in international conferences convened by the
United Nations.[127] In addition, NGOs without consultative status can
apply for accreditation in all UN conferences in which they have a special
interest or competence. The decision whether to grant accreditation or not
is based on the background and competence of the particular NGO in the
subject areas of the conference.[128] The rules for accreditation of NGOs to
UN conferences in the 1990s thus demonstrated a trend towards wider
access for NGOs, and the adoption in 1996 of the general ECOSOC rules
for consultative arrangements and NGO participation in conferences transformed this practice into a permanent arrangement.

The Rio Conference, the World Conference on Human Rights and the
Women's Conference probably set the record as regards the number of
NGO representatives participating in conferences convened by the UN in
the 1990s; 2,400 NGO representatives attended the Rio Conference, over

---

[124] See table on criteria for NGO participation 1976–1996 in E/AC.70/1994/5/Add.1, *General
Review of Current Arrangements*, 7 June 1994, pp. 31–35.
[125] These were the rules for accreditation to PrepCom meetings. Later, it was decided that
all NGOs which had participated in these meetings should be accredited to the
conference. E/EC.70/1994/5, *General Review of Arrangements for Consultation*, 26 May 1994,
p. 33.
[126] A/CONF.157/8, *Adoption of the Rules of Procedure*, 14 June 1993, Rule 66 and Preparatory
Committee decision PC.3/2, *Participation of Representatives of Non-Governmental
Organizations at Regional Meetings*, in A/CONF.157/PC/54, *Report of the Preparatory
Committee for the World Conference on Human Rights*, 8 October 1992, p. 19.
[127] E/RES/1996/31, para. 42.   [128] *Ibid.*, para. 45.

3,600 participated in the World Conference on Human Rights and around 5,000 attended the Women's Conference. All three conferences were also combined with large NGO fora, the largest being the Forum at Beijing with between 25,000 and 30,000 participants, while the Forum arranged in Rio gathered 17,000 and the NGO Forum in Vienna around 2,700.[129]

The NGO Forums illustrate an increased mobilisation among NGOs in relation to state and IGO policies formulated at international meetings, but cannot provide much evidence as regards actual influence, since the NGO Forums are completely separated from the actual negotiations. It may even be the case that these events create a misleading image of UN conferences as being more NGO-friendly than they actually are. Some of the events have been criticised for their distance from the official meetings, the location of the NGO Forum in Beijing was even regarded by many as a deliberate attempt to keep NGOs out of the official meetings.[130] On the other hand, the numbers of NGOs participating in the meetings, and the co-ordination of their attempts to influence the negotiations, would possibly have been more limited had there been no NGO Forum at all.

It is clear that NGOs are, formally speaking, nothing more than observers at UN conferences. It is stated explicitly in the 1996 ECOSOC arrangements for consultation, as well as in the Rules of Procedure for the participation of NGOs in some conferences, that participation of NGOs does not entail a negotiating role.[131] The two formal avenues open for NGOs trying to influence intergovernmental negotiations are thus to deliver oral interventions during meetings and to distribute written statements. However, NGOs also use other methods of asserting an influence, and it seems that the most important methods are informal. The most effective of those is probably direct lobbying with state representatives by presenting views and proposals to them. It is crucial for this kind of lobbying to take place at conferences that NGOs are

---

[129] The United Nations, 1997, pp. 20, 56 and Korey, *NGOs and the Universal Declaration of Human Rights*, p. 288.

[130] An NGO report from the conference states that the unilateral decision of the China Organising Committee to relocate the NGO Forum to Huairou 'was seen widely by NGOs and a number of governments as a political decision by the Chinese government, indicative of a desire to isolate NGO participants both from the official proceedings and from contact with Chinese citizens', *Beyond Beijing: NGO Participation at the UN Fourth World Conference on Women*, report by Amnesty International et. al., October 1996, Chapter III. See also Marie Mansson, *NGOs*, 'Women and Beijing', The Swedish Institute of International Affairs, *Occasional Papers*, Stockholm, 1996, pp. 9, 15, 33.

[131] E/RES/1996/31, para. 50 and A/48/37, *Report of the Preparatory Commission for the United Nations Conference on Human Settlements*, 9 March 1993, annex, para. 9.

482   LEGAL AND EMPIRICAL SURVEY

allowed to sit among and walk around governmental delegates during the negotiations (as opposed to being seated on a balcony or the like or not being allowed in the room at all), even if NGOs also often manage to keep themselves informed of what is happening at closed meetings. Personal contacts are, of course, very important, and it is clear that some of the staff of the large and well-known NGOs maintain close contacts with state representatives both during and in between meetings. Other important techniques used by NGOs to spread their message to governmental delegations as well as the media and the public are the publication of materials, such as reports and analyses, and the issuing of daily newsletters. Some governmental delegations are small, and all state representatives are busy during a conference, so governmental delegates often appreciate the analyses which specialised NGOs are able to produce. Visual protests, such as demonstrations outside meetings or the carrying out of manifestations of different kinds at the Conference Centre may be important for attracting media attention and creating public opinion, but seem unpopular among state representatives. Some parts of the NGO sector, such as industrial organisations, in fact seldom or never seem to arrange these types of protest activity.[132]

A special feature of NGO participation in IGO conferences is that some states appoint NGO experts to take part in or even form the governmental delegation. This occurred during the Rome Conference, as was described earlier, and is also not uncommon at environmental meetings. The Foundation for International Environmental Law and Development (FIELD), for example, has built up a relationship with small island states, which have been represented by experts from the organisation at different meetings. This can be regarded as a normal lawyer–client relationship, and from a traditional perspective on international law the NGO experts become state representatives when they accept such an assignment. At the same time, however, NGOs may choose to represent only states which have interests generally consistent with those of the NGO. Considering that the work performed by an NGO which represents a state may be on a *pro bono* basis or on the basis of external financial support, the role of one particular NGO may be very important for a state.[133] By actually taking part in intergovernmental negotiations, the NGO has the possibility to exert a direct influence on the development of international law.

---

[132] Giorgetti, 'From Rio to Kyoto', p. 240.
[133] *Interview with Philippe Sands* (founder of FIELD), 13 December 2000.

The question may be raised whether the rules for NGO participation have changed as regards the form of such participation. Generally speaking, this has not been the case. The rules of procedure regarding NGO participation in UN conferences were basically the same before 1996, when the rules on NGOs were adopted separately for each conference, and after the new ECOSOC arrangements. NGOs may designate observers to public meetings of the conference and its preparatory process. As regards access to meetings, NGO observers may sit in the plenaries and the main committees, but in working Group meetings only on the condition that the particular working Group admits it. NGOs may make oral statements upon the invitation of the presiding officer on matters in which they have special competence. Usually, NGOs are allowed to deliver statements only in the plenary sessions, but the rules do not hinder such statements being delivered in the subsidiary bodies as well.[134] Written statements are distributed by the conference secretariats to all delegations in the languages in which they were written, but are usually not issued at the expense of the United States and not as official documents.[135] The World Conference on Human Rights was an exception in this respect, as statements from accredited NGOs were issued as UN documents.[136]

Naturally, the rules of procedure can be differently applied, particularly as regards oral statements, since these may be delivered only upon the invitation of the chairperson. At the Rio Conference, only a few NGO statements were allowed at plenary meetings, normally only one statement per session.[137] The negotiations on the final documents were to a large extent carried out in informal meetings to which NGOs were

---

[134] E/RES/1996/31, para. 51 states that: 'The non-governmental organizations accredited to the international conference may be given, in accordance with established United Nations practice and at the discretion of the chairperson and the consent of the body concerned, an opportunity to briefly address the preparatory committee and the conference in plenary meetings and their subsidiary bodies.'

[135] E/RES/1996/31, para. 52, includes a rule on written NGO statements during the preparatory process, but does not mention the conferences as such.

[136] The Rules of Procedure, as opposed to the other conferences, did not include the information that statements would not be issued as official documents, see A/CONF.157/8, *Adoption of the Rules of Procedure*, 14 June 1993, Rule 66. See also NGO statements, e.g. A/CONF.157/PC/79, 20 April 1993, presented by the American Society of International Law to the Preparatory Committee.

[137] At most plenary sessions, only one NGO was allowed to deliver a statement. During two sessions, two or three NGO statements were delivered. A/CONF.151/26/Rev.1, vol. II (Proceedings of the Conference), pp. 9–12.

484   LEGAL AND EMPIRICAL SURVEY

not admitted.[138] This was also the case with the Rome Conference, where NGOs were allowed to sit in all formal meetings but one. In Kyoto, many meetings were closed.

The final documents of major IGO conferences are normally drafted before the conference, albeit subjected to many changes during the conference itself. It is therefore important for NGOs to participate in the preparatory meetings which seek to influence the final documents. It is probably even better – if possible – for NGOs to take part in meetings on the national plane before the governments' positions have been fixed. The participation of NGOs in preparatory processes at UN conferences has been fairly strong, although not as extensive as in the conferences themselves.[139] A high number of NGOs participated in the four meetings of the UN PrepCom for the Rio Conference: over 160 NGOs were represented at PrepCom II, and 350 NGOs participated in PrepCom III.[140] At the regional meetings that preceded the Human Rights Conference in Vienna, NGOs significantly outnumbered states. The regional meeting for Latin America, for instance, was attended by delegations from twenty-three Latin American and a similar number of observer states, while the number of NGOs represented was over 160.[141] At the regional meetings for Asia and Africa, the situation was similar.[142] During all these meetings, NGOs made a large number of oral statements.[143] Written NGO statements were delivered as official UN documents and were on the table of the meetings under the respective agenda item.[144] The number of NGOs participating in the preparatory meetings for the Rome Conference was lower, probably because of the more specialised topic. As already mentioned, some fifty NGOs

[138] The above figures and information are presented in Hägerhäll, 'The Evolving Role of NGOs', pp. 69–71.
[139] Over 700 NGOs participated in the 39th session of the Commission on the Status of Women, which acted as a preparatory body for the Women's Conference, E/CN.6/1995/14, p. 69 and annex II–III.
[140] A/46/48, Report of the Preparatory Committee for the United Nations Conference on Environment and Development, 1991, paras. 9–10 and Hägerhäll, 'The Evolving Role of NGOs', p. 71.
[141] A/CONF157/LACRM/15, A/CONF157/PC/58, *Report of the Regional Meeting for Latin America and the Caribbean of the World Conference on Human Rights*, 11 February 1993, para. 6.
[142] A/CONF.157/AFRM/14, A/CONF157/PC/57, *Report of the Regional Meeting for Africa*, 24 November 1992, para. 4 and A/CONF.157/ASRM/8, A/CONF.157/PC/59, *Report of the Regional Meeting for Asia*, 7 April 1993, para. 6.
[143] See, e.g., the report on the Latin American meeting, paras. 25–26.
[144] See, e.g., written statement by Amnesty International, A/CONF157/AFRM/8, mentioned in the report on the African meeting, para. 37.

were represented at PrepCom IV, about eighty at PrepCom V and around sixty at PrepCom VI.

An important observation concerning the NGO participation in the major UN world conferences of the 1990s is that it functioned as an engine for greater NGO participation in the regular work of ECOSOC subsidiary bodies. Following several of the conferences, ECOSOC adopted *ad hoc* measures to facilitate NGO participation in the follow-up processes, while encouraging the organisations to apply for consultative status. By a decision in 1997, for instance, ECOSOC invited those NGOs which were accredited to the Women's Conference, the Social Summit or the Conference on Population and Development to attend the sessions of the relevant functional commissions of ECOSOC, provided that they had begun the process of applying for consultative status.[145] The Rio Conference led to another expansion of NGO participation in ECOSOC bodies through the establishment of the Commission on Sustainable Development as a follow-up to the Conference. All NGOs which were accredited to participate in the work of PrepCom IV for the Rio Conference could apply for and should be granted Roster status with the Commission.[146]

The number of conferences discussed above is too limited to provide a basis for any well-founded conclusions regarding differences in states' attitudes towards NGOs at intergovernmental conferences. Nevertheless, it is probable that states would be unwilling to provide access for NGOs to conferences which concerned important financial interests or politically highly sensitive issues. There is some support for this hypothesis in the study of conferences presented here. As was noted in the introduction to this chapter, before 2004 NGO observers were not generally allowed at the Conference on Disarmament, a negotiating process involving both considerable financial interests and politically sensitive issues. Environmental agreements may also put commercial interests at stake. The FCCC, however, includes surprisingly generous rules for participation of NGOs in the Conference of the Parties. Many meetings in Kyoto, on the other hand, were closed to NGOs. The Rio Conference demonstrated an early example of impressive NGO involvement, but was not convened with the aim of adopting a legally binding

---

[145] ECOSOC Decision 1997/298. See also E/1998/43, *Work of the Non-Governmental Organizations Section of the Secretariat*, 8 May 1998, para. 6.

[146] ECOSOC Decision 1993/215, *Procedural Arrangements for the Commission on Sustainable Development*, para. 2(c), in E/1993/INF/2, 4 March 1993.

environmental instrument. The Vienna Conference, for its part, involved issues which were more political than financial and did not have the objective of adopting a treaty and the attitude towards NGO participation was permissive from the outset, as demonstrated by the resolution by which the General Assembly decided to convene it.

9 Agreements with states and intergovernmental organisations

9.1 International agreements and non-state actors

It has become a common phenomenon that IGOs contract NGOs for humanitarian operations.[1] As will be described, the ICRC has also concluded headquarters agreements with several states. How should such agreements be categorised, and what law governs them? Is it possible for non-state entities to conclude agreements with states or IGOs under international law?[2] These questions will be briefly discussed in order to provide a basis for an examination of some more concrete examples of agreements.

The Vienna Convention on the Law of Treaties of 1969 (VCLT 1969) defines 'treaty' for the purposes of the Convention as:

an international agreement concluded between States in written form and governed by international law, whether embodied in a single instrument or in two or more related instruments and whatever its particular designation.[3]

At first sight, the Convention, which is generally regarded as reflective of customary international law in most parts, seems to exclude the possibility that entities other than states can conclude treaties.[4] However, it is made clear in Article 3 of the Convention that:

---

[1] Section 9.3.

[2] In order to avoid confusion, I will use the neutral term 'agreement' when one or more of the parties is a non-state entity.

[3] Article 2(1) a.

[4] *Restatement of the Law Third: The Foreign Relations Law of the United States*, The American Law Institute, 1987, vol. I, p. 145 (hereafter 'Restatement (Third)'); Sir Robert Jennings and Sir Arthur Watts (eds.), *Oppenheim's International Law*, I, 9th edn., London: Longman, 1996, p. 1199; Anthony Aust, *Modern Treaty Law and Practice*, Cambridge University Press, 2000, p. 14; Iain Brownlie, *Principles of Public International Law*, 5th edn., Oxford University Press, 1998, p. 608. Klabbers states that 'it would appear that at least the definition of treaty has

488   LEGAL AND EMPIRICAL SURVEY

The fact that the present Convention does not apply to international agreements concluded between States and other subjects of international law or between such other subjects of international law, or to international agreements not in written form, shall not affect:

a. the legal force of such agreements;
b. the application to them of any of the rules set forth in the present Convention to which they would be subject under international law independently of the Convention.

In its commentary on the Convention, the ILC explained that the primary purpose of the narrow scope of the Convention was to make it clear that all the following articles were formulated with particular reference to treaties concluded between states. It stated that the narrow definition of 'treaty':

although expressly limited to the purposes of the present articles, might by itself give the impression that international agreements between a State and an international organization or other subjects of international law, or between two international organizations, or between any other two non-Statal subjects of international law, are outside the purview of the law of treaties. As such international agreements are now frequent ... the Commission considered it desirable to make an express reservation in the present article regarding their legal force and the possible relevance to them of certain of the rules expressed in the present articles.[5]

Both the Convention and the ILC commentary thus admitted the possibility that subjects of international law other than states could enter into treaties. The question that arises is what kind of entities belong to this category. With the adoption of the Vienna Convention on the Law of Treaties between States and International Organizations or between International Organizations (VCLT 1986) it was confirmed that IGOs have the capacity to enter into treaties in accordance with the provisions of their constituent instruments.[6] The Convention, the legal

---

started to lead an existence of its own', Jan Klabbers, *The Concept of Treaty in International Law*, The Hague: Kluwer Law International, 1996, p. 41. In the case of *Qatar* v. *Bahrain* (Judgement of 1 July 1994, Jurisdiction and Admissibility, para. 23), the ICJ referred to VCLT 1969 in its discussion of whether the agreement between the parties, who had not ratified the Vienna Convention, was to be considered a 'treaty'. See also *Dissenting Opinion of Judge Oda*, para. 13 and Klabbers' comment on this, *The Concept of Treaty in International Law*, p. 41.

[5] YILC 1966, II, p. 190.

[6] The text of the treaty is reproduced in *International Legal Materials*, 25 (1986), pp. 543–592. 'International organization' is understood in the treaty as an IGO.

regime of which is in large parts a replication of VCLT 1969, has not yet (as of November 2004) entered into force.[7]

As with VCLT 1969, the VCLT 1986 includes a provision stating that the fact that the Convention does not apply to other agreements than the ones defined by it shall not affect the legal force of such agreements.[8] The drafting of this provision gave the ILC an opportunity to discuss the issue of the possibility that entities other than states and IGOs might enter into agreements under international law:

> It is pretty well beyond dispute that the situation under international law of certain international agreements not within the scope of the present articles needs to be safeguarded by a provision on the lines of article 3 of the Vienna Convention [of 1969]. Suffice it to point out that it is not unusual for an international agreement to be concluded between an international organization and an entity other than a State or than an international organization. Reference may be made here ... to agreements concluded between the Holy See and international organizations. Similarly, there can be little doubt that agreements concluded between the International Committee of the Red Cross and an international organization ... are indeed governed by international law. The development of world humanitarian law and its extension for the benefit of entities which have not yet been constituted as States will provide further examples of this kind, and there will even be agreements concluded between one or more international organizations, one or more States and one or more entities which are neither States nor international organizations.[9]

The ILC thus stopped referring to 'subjects of international law' for a more open attitude to possible developments inclusive of non-state actors. The Commission also pointed to the actual existence of agreements concluded by entities other than states under international law, although the concept of 'treaty' was not used to refer to such instruments. In the discussion below on agreements concluded by non-state entities the same language will be used, as 'treaty' is normally understood as an instrument regulating the relations between states and/or IGOs.

In spite of the position held by the ILC, it is sometimes asserted that entities other than the recognised subjects cannot enter into agreements under international law. For instance, it is stated in *Oppenheim's*

---

[7] United Nations Treaty Collection database accessible online at http://untreaty.un.org, as of 8 November 2004. For commentaries on the Convention, see Giorgio Gaja, 'A "New" Vienna Convention on Treaties Between States and International Organizations or Between International Organizations: A Critical Commentary, 58 BYIL (1987), pp. 253–269.

[8] Article 3 in both Conventions.   [9] YILC 1981, I, Part 2, p. 125.

490   LEGAL AND EMPIRICAL SURVEY

International Law that 'where the agreement is concluded between parties who have no international legal personality it will not be governed by international law'.[10] Anthony Aust adopts a similar view in his book *Modern Treaty Law and Practice*, as does Peter Malanczuk in an article on agreements concluded between MNEs and states.[11] The question of non-state actors as parties to agreements under international law has perhaps been discussed mainly in relation to such 'internationalised contracts' as are sometimes used when a state allows a private company to explore and exploit natural resources on its territory. In order to safeguard the interest of the company to place the contract outside the reach of the contracting state's national law, these agreements refer to international law in their 'applicable law clause', and disputes are often subjected to arbitration.[12] The doctrinal views on internationalised contracts are varied. One view is that such agreements are indeed concluded under and governed by international law. The Restatement accepts the validity of clauses referring to international law, but does not regard the contracts as international agreements.[13] Malanczuk holds that – although this does not solve the problem from the viewpoint of the company – one could at most argue that international law might be applied by way of analogy, on the basis of the will of the parties, while the contract remains subject to the national law of the host state.[14] On the basis of his review of the decisions in the *Libyan Oil*

---

[10] *Oppenheim's International Law*, I, p. 1200.

[11] Aust states: 'A treaty can be concluded between a state and another subject of international law, in particular an international organisation, or between international organisations, but this is outside the scope of the Convention, and of this book.' Aust, *Modern Treaty Law and Practice*, p. 15. Malanczuk's position is that: 'it is also clear that bilateral or multilateral treaties under public international law can only be concluded among the subjects of international law, such as States, international organizations or other recognized subjects of international law.' '[S]o-called State contracts or "internationalised contracts" are not treaties in the sense of international law and cannot elevate them [i.e. multinational enterprises] to "partial subjects of international law".' Peter Malanczuk, 'Multinational Enterprises and Treaty-Making – A Contribution to the Discussion on Non-State Actors and the "Subjects" of International Law', in Vera Gowlland-Debbas (ed.), *Multilateral Treaty-Making*, The Hague. Kluwer Law International, 2000, pp. 57, 71.

[12] In the case of *Anglo-Iranian Oil Company*, the ICJ found that it lacked jurisdiction in the dispute concerning a contract concluded between Iran and a company incorporated in the United Kingdom, the Anglo-Iranian Oil Company. (At the time, the parties were the Imperial Government of Persia and the Anglo-Persian Oil Company Ltd.) *ICJ Reports* 1952, p. 93. See also Klabbers, *The Concept of Treaty in International Law*, p. 49.

[13] This position is described in the Restatement as an intermediate view. Restatement (Third), II, p. 214.

[14] Malanczuk, 'Multinational Enterprises and Treaty-Making', p. 60.

Arbitrations, Christopher Greenwoood concluded, *inter alia*, that a contract between a state and a foreign company might be delocalised and that the legal system by which the contract is to be governed might be public international law.[15] The three concessions which were the subject of these cases all included an applicable law clause stating that they should be governed by and interpreted in accordance with principles of national law 'common to the principles of international law and in the absence of such common principles then by and in accordance with the general principles of law'.[16]

A relatively new area where contracts can be concluded by private actors under international law is the law of the sea. According to Article 21 of annex III to the UN Convention on the Law of the Sea (UNCLOS), contracts between the International Seabed Authority and corporations that regulate the conditions of prospecting, exploration and exploitation of the international seabed area beyond the limits of national jurisdiction 'shall be governed by the terms of the contract, the rules, regulations and procedures of the Authority, *Part XI and other rules of international law not incompatible with this Convention*'.[17] Such contracts may be concluded by 'natural or juridical persons which possess the nationality of States Parties', as provided by UNCLOS Article 153, para. 2(b). Disputes concerning the interpretation or application of a contract are settled by the Seabed Disputes Chamber, or – at the request of any party to the dispute – through binding commercial arbitration.[18]

The employment contracts which are concluded between IGOs and their personnel may be interesting for comparison with agreements concluded between IGOs and NGOs. Such contracts, which often lack an applicable law clause, are generally regarded as governed by the organisation's own regulations supplemented by general principles of law, rather than by domestic law, and disputes are often settled in international administrative tribunals. According to Van Hecke, it is generally accepted regarding all contracts concluded by IGOs that they may be subject to international rather than national law. The main arguments for this theory are that an IGO is a subject of international

---

[15] Christopher Greenwood, 'The Libyan Oil Arbitrations', 53 BYIL (1983), p. 79. The same conclusion is reached by Kaj Hobér, *Extinctive Prescription and Applicable Law in Interstate Arbitration*, Uppsala: Iustus Förlag, 2001, pp. 93, 113 (see also below).

[16] Greenwood, 'The Libyan Oil Arbitrations', p. 28.

[17] United Nations Convention on the Law of the Sea (1982), annex III, Basic Conditions of Prospecting, Exploration and Exploitation (emphasis added).

[18] Articles 187(c)(i), 188(2)(a).

492   LEGAL AND EMPIRICAL SURVEY

law as well as of its internal law, and that it is desirable to safeguard the independent and international character of IGOs' activity.[19]

In sum, there is some disagreement as to whether agreements, one party to which is a non-state entity, can be placed directly under international law. Some, such as the ILC, point to the actual existence of such agreements, while others argue that although there may be agreements that refer to international law, such instruments cannot in reality be governed by the international legal system – or, at most, by way of analogy (which leaves disputes on the actual contract to be determined under a national legal system). In my view, it should first be observed that the concepts of 'subjects of international law' and 'international legal personality' cannot provide much guidance for the determination of which actors can conclude agreements under international law. As has been demonstrated earlier, these concepts are rather ambiguous in their character and are sometimes defined in a circular manner.[20] It has also been stated earlier as a basic standpoint for a study on the legal status of NGOs that states are assumed to be able to confer upon non-state entities the rights and capacities they deem useful.[21] The inductive method used in the present study thus suggests, quite simply, that if agreements with non-state entities are purposely placed under international law by states or IGOs, these agreements are, at least in principle, actually governed by international law. It is therefore the intention of the parties, as expressed in actual agreements, which should be at the centre of the investigation.[22]

---

[19] Henry G. Schermers and Niels M. Blokker, *International Institutional Law. Unity within Diversity*, 3rd rev. edn., Dordrecht: Martinus Nijhoff, 1999, pp. 362, 434–439; Georges Van Hecke, *Contracts between International Organizations and Private Law Persons*, EPIL, 1, Amsterdam: North-Holland, 1992, p. 813. Sands and Klein observe that the problem with subjecting contracts between IGOs and private actors to national legislation 'is less significant than for contract between two states, where one party to the contract may have a direct interest in unilaterally modifying its terms by way of a unilateral act. States are less likely to engage in such acts to benefit the private persons who are normally the parties to private contracts with organisations.' Philippe Sands and Pierre Klein, *Bowett's Law of International Institutions*, 5th edn., London: Sweet & Maxwell, 2001, p. 463.

[20] Brownlie points to the circularity of this line of argument when he observes that the common *indicia* referred to for a subject of international law depend on the existence of a legal person, *Principles of Public International Law*, pp. 57, 609. See also section 2.3, 3.2.

[21] Or, as expressed in the Restatement 'private juridical entities can have any status, capacity, rights, or duties given them by international law or agreement', Restatement (Third), 1987, I, p. 70. See also section 3.2.

[22] In the *Case of Serbian Loans*, the PCIJ stated, however, that 'Any contract which is not a contract between States in their capacity as subjects of international law is based on the

The ILC has also emphasised the importance of the intention of the parties to create an agreement under international law in relation to the determination of a treaty:

The two main elements in the present definition are (i) 'intended to be governed by international law' ... As to the first element, the Commission felt ... that the element of subjection to international law is so essential a part of an international agreement that it should be expressly mentioned in the definition ... At any rate, the Commission was clear that it ought to confine the notion of an 'international agreement' for the purposes of the law of treaties to one the whole formation and execution of which (as well as the *obligation* to execute) is governed by international law.[23]

This emphasis on intent as the decisive factor also seems to be established in the customary international law of treaties.[24] Moreover, the question of the intention of the parties seems to explain the meaning of the reference to 'subjects of international law' in the Vienna Conventions and the ILC reports. In its draft articles to VCLT 1986, the ILC discussed the question whether some agreements concluded by IGOs could be of an 'internal' nature, i.e. governed by rules peculiar to the organisation in question. It stated that:

If an agreement is concluded by organizations with recognized capacity to enter into agreements under international law and if it is not by virtue of its purpose and terms of implementation placed under a specific legal system (that of a state or given organization), it *may be assumed that the parties to the agreement intended it to be governed by international law.*[25]

Thus, the fact that the contracting parties are recognised international legal subjects seems to mean that there is a presumption that they intended the agreement to be 'governed by international law'. The agreement itself or circumstances surrounding its conclusion may overcome this presumption. It is suggested in *Oppenheim's International Law* that, when the parties are subjects of international law, the intention to create international legal rights and obligations between them 'will

---

municipal law of some country.' PCIJ Series A, No. 20, p. 41. This statement has been criticised by many writers, see Greenwood, 'The Libyan Oil Arbitrations', p. 42.

[23] YILC 1962, II, p. 32 (emphasis in original).

[24] Restatement (Third), I, p. 145 (*e contrario*); Aust, *Modern Treaty Law and Practice*, pp. 10–11. Klabbers observes that the element of intent is useful in a twofold manner – on the one hand, for distinguishing binding agreements from non-binding instruments and on the other for the distinction between 'those agreements properly governed by international law, and those governed by the domestic laws of one or another state', with the exception of some cases. Klabbers, *The Concept of Treaty in International Law*, pp. 63–64.

[25] YILC 1981, I, Part 2, p. 122 (emphasis added).

494   LEGAL AND EMPIRICAL SURVEY

need to be determined in the light of all the circumstances of each case', such as the registration of an agreement with the UN or the statements made by governments before the adoption of the instrument.[26]

The hypothesis that it is the intention of the parties that determines which law is to govern an agreement is supported by the principle of party autonomy. Christopher Greenwood concluded after his examination of the *Libyan Oil Arbitrations*, mentioned earlier, that a contract between a state and a foreign company may be delocalised and that the legal system by which the contract is to be governed may be public international law.[27] The same conclusion is reached by Kaj Hobér, who observes that the doctrine of party autonomy allows the parties to choose any set of rules – whether they be characterised as law or something else – to serve as the basis for solving disputes. Hobér points out that:

> Not only do the parties have the discretion to choose any law, or rules, they wish, but they may also *exclude* the application of any national law by referring, for example, to the general principles of law ... It follows from the foregoing, that the parties are the masters over the law, or rules to be applied and also over the public policy of the law they may have chosen.[28]

It seems that the principle of party autonomy provides contracting parties with practically unlimited freedom in choosing the applicable law of the contract, including general principles of law.[29]

In order to determine the intention of the parties, it is necessary to examine concrete agreements. When one of the parties is not a recognised subject of international law, there is no presumption that international law is the applicable law, so the terms of the agreement are even more important. A few examples of agreements entered into by NGOs with states and IGOs will now be described.

9.2 Agreements between states and NGOs

As has been described in chapter 2, the ICRC is generally regarded as having a unique status in international law for an organisation

---

[26] *Oppenheim's International Law*, I, p. 1202.
[27] Greenwood, 'The Libyan Oil Arbitrations', p. 79.
[28] Kaj Hobér, *Extinctive Prescription and Applicable Law in Interstate Arbitration*, Uppsala: Iustus Förlag, 2001, pp. 93, 113 (emphasis in original).
[29] See also P. M. North and J. J. Fawcett, *Private International Law*, 12th edn., London: Butterworths, 1992, pp. 476–486 and J. G. Collier, *Conflict of Laws*, 2nd edn., Cambridge University Press, 1994, pp. 185–196.

AGREEMENTS WITH STATES AND INTERGOVERNMENTAL ORGANISATIONS 495

established under national law and by private initiative. The ICRC cannot therefore serve as a basis for general conclusions about all NGOs. It should also be observed that the ICRC, as has been mentioned, does not consider itself to be an NGO in the ordinary sense of the term.[30] The ICRC is, however, interesting as an illustration of a status that can, at least potentially, be acquired by other NGOs.

Because of the ICRC's special role in international humanitarian law and its development, one might assume that it would itself be a party to the Geneva Conventions of 1949 and its Additional Protocols. This is, however, not the case, although the ICRC does enter into agreements with states. One agreement of main interest here is the Agreement concluded in 1993 between the Swiss Federal Council and the ICRC to determine its legal status in Switzerland.[31] In Article 1 of the Agreement, the Swiss Federal Council recognises the international juridical personality of the ICRC. In Article 2, the Federal Council 'guarantees the ICRC independence and freedom of action'. Articles 3 and 4 grant the ICRC inviolability of premises and archives, while Article 5 guarantees the ICRC immunity from legal process and execution, with certain exceptions. The staff of the ICRC is also granted privileges and immunities under the Agreement.[32] The Committee has a favourable fiscal position in Switzerland according to Article 5, which exempts the ICRC from direct federal, cantonal and communal taxation. In other respects, such as customs and communications, the ICRC is granted the same status as IGOs.[33] The Agreement refers to the International Telecommunication Convention of 1982 in the latter respect.

The 'non-responsibility' of Switzerland is regulated in a special section of the Agreement. Article 20 states that 'Switzerland shall not incur, by reason of the activity of the ICRC on its territory any international responsibility for acts or omissions of the ICRC or its staff'.

As for settlement of disputes, the Agreement provides that any divergence of opinion concerning its application or interpretation may be submitted by either party to an arbitral tribunal consisting of three members, of which each party appoints one and the two appointed

---

[30] See section 2.4.
[31] *Agreement between the International Committee of the Red Cross and the Swiss Federal Council to Determine the Legal Status of the Committee in Switzerland*, 19 March 1993, reprinted in the *International Review of the Red Cross*, No. 293, pp. 152–160.
[32] Articles 11–17.   [33] Articles 7, 9.

496   LEGAL AND EMPIRICAL SURVEY

select the chairperson.[34] The arbitration award is binding on the parties.[35] The Agreement does not include any provision on applicable law.

According to the ICRC's *Annual Report*, the organisation has also concluded headquarters agreements with seventy-four states.[36] The ICRC considers its headquarters agreements to be international treaties.[37] The Agreement between the ICRC and the Federal Republic of Yugoslavia, for example, presents some differences in relation to the agreement concluded with Switzerland.[38] For instance, the Agreement does not recognise the international legal personality of the ICRC, but only its 'juridical personality'. On the other hand, it is stated that 'The ICRC shall be recognized the status given to intergovernmental organizations', and the ICRC is granted immunity, inviolability of premises and exemption from taxes and customs duties. Disputes arising from the Agreement shall be settled by negotiations, or – if negotiations fail – by a court of arbitration, whose decision shall be final. The headquarters agreement does not have an applicable law clause.

9.3 Agreements between IGOs and NGOs

Introduction

The collaboration between NGOs and UN agencies active in humanitarian emergencies, such as the WFP and the UNHCR, has increased dramatically.[39] This collaboration between IGOs and NGOs needs to be regulated in agreements of varying normative status, such as MOUs, letters of understanding, partnership agreements, etc.[40] The different kinds of agreements which have been concluded between IGOs and

---

[34] Articles 22(1–3).   [35] Article 22(7).

[36] *ICRC Annual Report 2003*, p. 21.

[37] Letter from the ICRC legal division, 22 June 2001, on file with the author.

[38] *Agreement between the International Committee of the Red Cross and the Federal Republic of Yugoslavia*, 14 June 1994, on file with the author.

[39] Leon Gordenker and Thomas G. Weiss, 'Devolving Responsibilities: A Framework for Analysing NGOs and Services', in Thomas G. Weiss (ed.), *Beyond UN Subcontracting: Task-Sharing with Regional Security Arrangements and Service-Providing NGOs*, New York: Macmillan/St Martin's Press, 1998, p. 31 and Andrew S. Natsios, 'NGOs and the UN System in Complex Humanitarian Emergencies: Conflict or Cooperation?', in Thomas G. Weiss and Leon Gordenker (eds.), *NGOs, the UN, and Global Governance*, London: Lynne Rienner, 1996, p. 74.

[40] During 1999, the UN Office for Projects Services began facilitating 'partnerships' among, *inter alia*, UN bodies and NGOs and new contracting mechanisms for the procurement of goods and services through co-operation with NGOs were created, A/55/1, *Report of the Secretary-General on the Work of the Organization*, 2000, para. 334.

AGREEMENTS WITH STATES AND INTERGOVERNMENTAL ORGANISATIONS   497

NGOs will be examined below after a general examination of IGO–NGO co-operation. It should be observed that the agreements examined were provided in 2001. Some of them might later have been replaced by other contracts. This would not, however, deprive them of their relevance as examples of agreements which are, or have been, in actual use.

The increase in IGO–NGO operational collaboration is confirmed in documentation from WFP, where it is also stated that NGOs are vital as implementing partners of WFP in relief situations for reasons of scope, scale and effectiveness.[41] In some cases, WFP needs to turn to NGOs for collaboration because of the weaknesses of government authorities – e.g. in situations of major disasters.[42] About 80 per cent of WFP relief operations involve NGOs as implementing partners, and about 16 per cent of the operations are carried out by NGOs alone.[43]

Since 1995, WFP has used 'global MOUs' for outlining partnerships with major international NGOs. These MOUs, which are of a standing character, are concluded with NGOs at headquarters level to set a general framework for collaboration at the global level.[44] The WFP has MOUs with some fifteen NGOs, including Catholic Relief Services, the Lutheran World Federation, the Danish Refugee Council and Save the Children (US).[45] The content of such MOUs will be examined below.[46] In addition to global MOUs, WFP signs local agreements with NGOs specifying arrangements for a specific operation;[47] in 2001, WFP had local agreements with over 1,100 NGOs.[48]

---

[41] Document WFP/EB.1/99/3-A, *Partnership with NGOs*, 21 December 1998, para. 1 and WFP/EB.A/2001/4-B, *WFP Working with NGOs: A Framework for Partnership*, 17 April 2001, para. 9.

[42] WFP/EB.A/2001/4-B, *WFP Working with NGOs: A Framework for Partnership*, 17 April 2001, para 2. For example, in the 1997 *Country Strategy Outline for Honduras*, it is stated that 'The participation of experienced NGOs often compensated for weak implementation by the public sector, and increased the coverage and efficiency of activities, and care for infant populations', WFP/EB.2R/97/3/Add. 4, *Country Strategy Outline for Honduras*, para. 52.

[43] WFP/EB.A/2001/4-B, *WFP Working with NGOs: A Framework for Partnership*, 17 April 2001, para. 3.

[44] WFP/EB.1/2000/5/2, *Thematic Evaluation of WFP–NGO Partnerships*, 20 December 1999, para. 13.

[45] WFP/EB.A/2000/3-A, *Annual Report of the Executive Director: 1999*, 26 April 2000, para. 57, WFP/EB.3/99/INF/8, *List of Memoranda of Understanding and Agreements signed by WFP and Other Organizations/Entities*, 1 October 1999 and the WFP website accessible online at www.wfp.org, as of 30 October 2004 (section 'WFP's Partners').

[46] Section 9.3.

[47] WFP/EB.1/2000/5/2, *Thematic Evaluation of WFP–NGO Partnerships*, 20 December 1999, para. 13.

[48] WFP/EB.A/2002/4, *Annual Report of the Executive Director: 2001* (Executive Board version), para. 96.

498   LEGAL AND EMPIRICAL SURVEY

UNHCR has worked closely with NGOs since its foundation in 1951. During 2003, the UNHCR funded 538 national and international NGO implementing partners through project agreements totalling approximately 19 per cent of its annual budget.[49] UNHCR has also adopted a Framework Agreement for Operational Partnership, which is a global agreement to be concluded by international NGOs at the headquarters level.[50]

NGOs are also of increased importance to the World Bank. The Bank, however, seldom funds NGOs directly. The most common way for an NGO to receive project funds is instead by working as a contractor to the borrowing government. NGOs are sometimes contracted directly by the World Bank – for example, to assist in project design or implementation.[51] Of all the projects approved by the World Bank in 1999, involvement of NGOs and other civil society organisations had increased to 52 per cent, up from 20 per cent in 1989.[52] NGOs are mostly involved at the planning, implementation and operation, and maintenance stages of projects.[53]

Memoranda of understanding and framework agreements

A 'memorandum' is, according to *Black's Law Dictionary*: 'An informal record, note or instrument embodying something that the parties desire to fix in memory by the aid of written evidence, or that is to serve as the basis of a future formal contract or deed.'[54] Thus, in general legal terms, a 'memorandum' refers to a non-binding instrument.

Aust analyses the difference between treaties and MOUs concluded between states in some detail and his analysis can help to elucidate the character of agreements concluded between IGOs and NGOs. In Aust's view, as a general rule, MOUs are non-binding instruments.[55] As the

---

[49] UNHCR, *Global Report 2003*, p. 103.

[50] Letter from the UNHCR NGO Coordinator, 12 January 2001, on file with the author.

[51] *Working Together: The World Bank's Partnership with Civil Society*, Washington, DC: World Bank, 2000, p. 30.

[52] *World Bank–Civil Society Relations, Fiscal 1999 Progress Report*, August 2000, p. 2. The expression 'civil society organisations' (CSOs) include, for the purposes of the report, 'NGOs, community-level and women's groups, churches, and labour unions, among others'. *Ibid*, p. 1.

[53] *Ibid.*, p. 3. In almost 30 per cent of World Bank projects which involve co-operation with NGOs, these organisations have also participated in the identification of the project.

[54] *Black's Law Dictionary*, Abridged 6th edn., St Paul, MN: West Publishing Co., 1991, p. 680.

[55] Aust, *Modern Treaty Law and Practice*, pp. 17–18, 26. See, however, Klabbers, who suggests that when an agreement is referred to as a 'memorandum of understanding', this provides little evidence to suggest that the negotiators actually contemplated whether the agreement was to be legally binding or not. Klabbers, *The Concept of Treaty in*

designation of an instrument may be misleading, Aust recommends that the instrument is classified by means of an analysis of the circumstances under which it was concluded, whether it has been registered with the United Nations, as well as an examination of its provisions on a number of points.[56] In Aust's opinion, the registration of an instrument with the United Nations pursuant to Article 102 of the UN Charter provides evidence that the instrument is a treaty.[57] As regards the content of the instruments, Aust observes that a dispute settlement clause according to which disputes are to be referred to compulsory international judicial process is hardly consistent with an intention to conclude a non-legally binding instrument. Typically, MOUs provide that disputes are to be settled by negotiation between the parties and not referred to any third party.[58]

Another point which may be of interest in the context of MOUs concluded between IGOs and NGOs is the terminology of the agreement. Aust points out that an intention to conclude a legally binding instrument is often indicated by the employment of imperative terms, such as 'shall', 'agree', 'undertake', 'rights', 'obligations' and 'enter into force'. The text of instruments which are not intended to be legally binding, by contrast, often includes terms such as 'will' and 'come into effect'.

As was noted above, WFP concludes MOUs with NGOs on both the global and local level. In its own words, the standard global MOU used by WFP 'sets the framework for achieving the overall goal of WFP and NGO cooperation', and is intended to improve the emergency response and the implementation capacity of both WFP and the partner NGO. It applies to different kinds of operational work, such as emergency operations and development programmes.[59] The MOU establishes 'basic principles of collaboration', but does not mention national or international law, or refer to treaties or other legal rules. As regards the division of responsibilities, the MOU states that WFP is

---

International Law, p. 68. For a general analysis on legal and non-legal agreements, see Christer Ahlström, *The Status of Multilateral Export Control Regimes – An Examination of Legal and Non-Legal Agreements in International Co-Operation*, Uppsala: Iustus Förlag, 1999.

[56] Aust, *Modern Treaty Law and Practice*, pp. 27–29. See also Klabbers, *The Concept of Treaty in International Law*, pp. 68 ff.

[57] Article 102(1) provides that: 'Every treaty and every international agreement entered into by any Member of the United Nations after the present Charter comes into force shall as soon as possible be registered with the Secretariat and published by it.'

[58] Aust, *Modern Treaty Law and Practice*, p. 38.

[59] Standard MOU provided by WFP in February 2001, para. 1, on file with the author.

500   LEGAL AND EMPIRICAL SURVEY

primarily responsible for resource mobilisation, for transport and delivery of food commodities and accountability for their proper use, while co-operating NGOs are primarily responsible for the final distribution and monitoring of all food commodities delivered to it by WFP.[60]

WFP's standard MOU includes fairly detailed provisions on a wide range of issues, such as target groups for operations, resource mobilisation, distribution of food commodities, financial reporting, co-ordination mechanisms (consultations, meetings, etc.) and public information activities. As for the settlement of disputes, the MOU states that conflicts which remain unresolved at the local level will be brought quickly to the attention of the respective headquarters, and officials of the two parties will immediately enter into discussions to reach a solution. The MOU may be amended with the mutual agreement of WFP and the partner NGO and remains 'in effect until terminated by written notice'. According to a WFP official, the global MOUs are not intended to be legally binding.[61]

An MOU concluded between WFP and a Danish NGO demonstrates that, while the subject matters regulated by it are basically the same as in the standard MOU, the individual clauses are considerably different. This is in spite of the fact that the MOU concluded with the Danish NGOs is of a standing character and does not refer to a specific operation.[62] Some provisions are clearly of importance from a legal point of view, such as the question of 'employer responsibility' for staff provided by the NGO, the selection of individuals to be deployed on each assignment and the period of deployment.[63] The provision on dispute settlement states that, if a dispute cannot be settled by mutual agreement between the parties, either party shall have the right to request arbitration by the ICC. The parties agree to be bound by such an arbitration award. Amendments may be made by mutual consent and in writing.[64] The agreement does not, however, refer to any national legal system or to international law. Nor does it state the period of validity. The clause on duration includes 'legal' expressions, such as that the MOU 'shall enter into force upon signature for a period of two years renewable subject to mutual consent'.[65]

---

[60] *Ibid.*, paras. 2–3.   [61] E-mail message of 27 June 2001, on file with the author.
[62] MOU concluded between WFP and the Danish Refugee Council, 30 March 1999, on file with the author.
[63] *Ibid.*, paras. 3, 4, 12.   [64] *Ibid.*, para. 22.   [65] *Ibid.*, para. 23.

One interesting aspect of the standard MOU used by WFP is that it includes the following requirement:

All NGO implementing partners of WFP in emergency operations must carry out their activities in compliance with the Code of Conduct for the International Red Cross and Red Crescent Movement and NGOs in Disaster Relief.[66]

As has been mentioned earlier, this type of connection between codes of conduct and agreements between NGOs and donor or partner IGOs seems to increase the importance and normative force of the codes, which have been adopted and adhered to voluntarily by NGOs and which lack formal sanction mechanisms.[67] A similar clause is included in the standard agreement used by UNHCR, as will be shown below, which refers to the same code of conduct – i.e. the Code of Conduct for the International Red Cross and Red Crescent Movement and NGOs in Disaster Relief.

UNHCR's *Framework Agreement for Operational Partnership* is a result of a long process involving both the organisation itself and NGOs.[68] The content and language of the agreement is of a general nature, setting a framework for co-operation, consultation, planning, etc. and stating, for example, that 'Contact at the Headquarters level is important' and that 'Partners will work together to determine the mechanisms required to enable agreement on specific guidelines and standards as required for a particular refugee operation.'[69] The responsibilities of the respective partners are discussed in general terms, such as 'The Partners recognise the primary protection role and responsibility of UNHCR in any refugee situation.'[70]

---

[66] *Ibid.*, para. 4. The clause is preceded by a general requirement that: 'All NGOs involved in the distribution of WFP-supplied commodities must be willing to work with all beneficiaries in complete impartiality, regardless of race, religion, nationality, political opinion or gender, without linking it, either directly or indirectly, to any religious or political persuasion.'

[67] Section 4.3.

[68] The Agreement is a follow-up to and an integral part of the Partnership in Action process and its 1994 Oslo Declaration and Plan of Action. Para. 2 of the *Framework Agreement for Operational Partnership between the United Nations High Commissioner for Refugees and NGOs*, provided by the UNHCR NGO Unit in January 2001, on file with the author.

[69] *Framework Agreement for Operational Partnership between the United Nations High Commissioner for Refugees and NGOs*, paras. 9, 11.

[70] *Ibid.*, para. 5.

502   LEGAL AND EMPIRICAL SURVEY

The Framework Agreement does not include any provision on entering into force or termination, but provides that its text is to be monitored regularly by a joint UNHCR/NGO working group. Nor does the Agreement refer to legal rules or to binding dispute settlement. It states that:

Problems arising from the implementation of this Agreement will be dealt with initially between the senior staff member of each partner at the field level. In the absence of a satisfactory conclusion, the matter can be referred by UNHCR offices to the NGO Coordinator and by [XNGO] staff to a designated staff member in [XNGO] for review.[71]

The UNHCR Framework Agreement is thus clearly less specific than the MOUs used by WFP and has a mechanism for dispute resolution which does not involve a third party or lead to binding decisions, such as the MOU concluded between a Danish NGO and WFP. An official of the UNHCR NGO Unit describes the Framework Agreement as a non-legal document, and points out that it has not been presented to the Executive Committee for endorsement as a fact supporting this.[72]

As with the WFP standard MOU, the UNHCR Framework Agreement refers to the Code of Conduct of the International Red Cross and Red Crescent Movement and NGOs in Disaster Relief. However, while the WFP standard MOU requires that 'All NGO implementing partners of WFP in emergency operations must carry out their activities in compliance with' the Code, the UNHCR Framework Agreement states that 'The Partners will be guided by the principles set down in' the Code.[73] In this respect, the UNHCR Framework Agreement thus also employs a less 'legal' language than the standard MOU used by WFP.

The WHO Department of Emergency and Humanitarian Action has concluded some broad framework agreements with NGOs. These agreements provide that a particular NGO shall maintain a roster of candidates who shall be ready for rapid mobilisation and deployment in support of the WHO's emergency relief operations.[74] The agreements are very specific and employ language which indicates an intention to create legally binding obligations. A legal officer at the WHO has

---

[71] *Ibid.*, para. 29.

[72] Letter from the UNHCR NGO Unit, 12 April 2001, on file with the author.

[73] Standard MOU provided by WFP in February 2001, para. 4 and *Framework Agreement for Operational Partnership between the United Nations High Commissioner for Refugees and NGOs*, para. 6. Both agreements on file with the author.

[74] *Agreement between the World Health Organization (WHO) and ... [XNGO]*, provided in 2001 by the WHO as example of the organisation's broad framework agreements, on file with the author.

confirmed that this is indeed the WHO's intention.[75] As an illustration, a few examples of provisions may be described:

A request by WHO to [XNGO,] for candidates available for deployment shall include details concerning the location of the emergency relief work, the nature of the work, the probable duration of the assignment ...

WHO and the [XNGO] may agree to share the budgeted costs, in which case WHO shall reimburse its agreed-upon portion of the budgeted costs to [XNGO] upon completion of the assignment, subject to any reduction should the budgeted costs be greater than the actual costs ...

The obligations of WHO are strictly limited to the express terms and conditions of this Agreement. WHO shall not provide any payments to the Officer unless expressly authorized by an amendment to this Agreement.[76]

The agreement includes detailed provisions on duration, termination and amendment, while there is no clause on choice of law.[77] Disputes which cannot be solved amicably or through conciliation shall be finally settled by arbitration. Arbitration is to be carried out in accordance with the arbitration rules of the United Nations Commission on International Trade Law (UNCITRAL) if the parties cannot agree on the modalities.[78]

Project agreements

WFP's global MOUs are complemented by local agreements concluded with each NGO for the particular operation. As of June 2001, WFP had not yet adopted a standard document for these agreements. A draft standard agreement has, however, been formulated.[79] This draft agreement, which has a content indicating an intent to create legally binding agreements, specifies the partner NGO as a 'non-governmental, non-profit, non-political organisation registered with the Government of ... '.[80] It contains detailed definitions and provisions on each partner's obligations, on assessment and evaluation of operations, damages and payments from WFP to the implementing partner. For instance, it states that: 'The Implementing Partner will be paid monthly by WFP on the basis of invoices submitted and approved, and according to the

---

[75] E-mail message of 28 September 2001, on file with the author.
[76] *Agreement between the World Health Organization (WHO) and ... [XNGO]*, paras. 2.1, 3.2, 7.3.
[77] *Ibid.*, paras. 9.3, 9.4.   [78] *Ibid.*, para. 9.6.
[79] *Draft Agreement Between the World Food Programme and ... [NGO's name] Regarding the Distribution of WFP-supplied Commodities*, provided by WFP in April 2001, on file with the author.
[80] *Ibid.*, Preamble, para. 3.

504   LEGAL AND EMPIRICAL SURVEY

agreed budget.'[81] It specifies the commencement, duration and termination of the agreement in precise terms.[82]

Disputes may be referred, upon agreement by the parties, to a single arbitrator – or, if agreement cannot be reached, to two arbitrators – to be appointed in accordance with the arbitration rules of UNCITRAL. The arbitration decision shall be binding upon the parties.[83] There is no reference as to which legal system is to govern the agreement. As opposed to the global or framework MOU, the draft for a standard local MOU also contains a clause on *force majeure*, which provides further support for the assumption that it is of a binding character.[84] WFP has confirmed that it is its intention to create legally binding agreements on the basis of the draft, while the global MOUs are not intended to be binding.[85]

It was mentioned above that the Framework Agreement used by UNHCR was general in its content and language and lacked reference to binding dispute settlement by a third party. By contrast, an example of a local operational agreement concluded between UNHCR and an international NGO as an annex to the Framework Agreement is more detailed and has to a greater extent the characteristics of a binding agreement.[86] The Agreement is, in its own words, concluded as an annex to the Framework Agreement for Operational Partnership in order to 'reflect the actual agreement on our joint efforts in delivery of humanitarian assistance to Refugees and Internally Displaced Persons in the Federal republic of Yugoslavia', but does not refer to a specific operation in that region.[87] According to the Agreement, both parties agree that they 'shall' carry out a number of activities. For instance, the partner NGO shall respond to UNHCR requests for assistance to beneficiaries, it shall attend co-ordination meetings and provide UNHCR with information.[88] UNHCR shall, for its part, provide the partner NGO with relief items for distribution to beneficiaries, with support in obtaining customs clearance, and with diesel fuel at cost price when available.[89] It is also stated that if the partner NGO uses benefits provided for purposes not related to the humanitarian activities described in the Framework Agreement, the UNHCR reserves the right to withdraw immediately the benefits extended in the Agreement.[90] There is no applicable law clause or reference to dispute settling mechanisms.

---

[81] *Ibid.*, para. 9.1.   [82] *Ibid.*, para. 3.1.   [83] *Ibid.*, para. 11.   [84] *Ibid.*, para. 10.

[85] E-mail message from a WFP official, 27 June 2001, on file with the author.

[86] *Local Operational Partnership Agreement between X [international NGO] and the United Nations High Commissioner for Refugees*, 21 March 2001.

[87] *Ibid.*, Preamble.   [88] *Ibid.*, para. 1.   [89] *Ibid.*, para. 2.   [90] *Ibid.*, para. 3.

As to the termination of the agreement, it states that 'it is valid' to a certain date but may be terminated earlier by written notification of UNHCR.[91] It can be amended on the basis of mutual consent.[92]

The WHO Department of Emergency and Humanitarian Action concludes two types of agreements with NGOs on the operational level.[93] The first category, project agreements, sets out that a particular NGO shall implement a specific project.[94] The provisions regulate the project's duration and financing, for instance that:

WHO shall reimburse the costs incurred by the Agency [i.e. the NGO] in the implementation of the Project in accordance with this agreement, up to a maximum amount of US$ ..., subject to the restrictions set forth below.[95]

The agreement also includes highly detailed provisions on the operational work and the reporting of the NGO to WHO.[96] Disputes which cannot be solved amicably or through conciliation shall be settled by a final arbitral award. If the parties cannot agree on the modalities of arbitration, it shall be carried out in accordance with the rules of the ICC.[97] In sum, it is clearly an agreement of a binding character. It does, however, not include any provision on choice of law.

The second type of agreement used by the WHO Department of Emergency and Humanitarian Action is called Agreements for the Performance of Work (APWs). It regulates details of payments and reporting. Disputes are to be settled in the same manner as in the case of the project agreements described above.[98]

The FAO uses the same standard Letter of Agreement for their co-operation with governmental, intergovernmental and non-governmental organisations. The common requirement regarding the 'recipient organisation' is that it is not-for-profit.[99] Each Letter of Agreement (LOA) consists of a standard letter and an annex, which outlines the terms

---

[91] *Ibid.*, para. 4. [92] *Ibid.*, Preamble.

[93] *Letter from the WHO Department of Emergency and Humanitarian Action*, 28 June 2001.

[94] *World Health Organization Project Agreement*, provided by the WHO Department of Emergency and Humanitarian Action, on file with the author.

[95] *Ibid.*, para. III(a). [96] *Ibid.*, paras. III(c)–(g), IV. [97] *Ibid.*, para. IV(l)a.

[98] *World Health Organization Agreement for the Performance of Work*, on file with the author.

[99] *Letter of Agreement*, provided by FAO, on file with the author, in *FAO Manual*, Section V 507, as updated on 9 October 1997, para 507.1(12). The LOA defines the recipient organisation as a 'governmental, regional, inter-governmental, parastatal or other *non profit institution*' (emphasis in original). According to an FAO official, the same standard LOA is used for co-operation with NGOs (telephone conversation, 6 September 2001).

506 LEGAL AND EMPIRICAL SURVEY

and conditions and clearly describes the services and/or work products to be provided under the agreement, and which constitutes an integral part of the LOA. The agreement is clearly of a legally binding nature, and the FAO Manual provides detailed instructions for its negotiation, on the responsibility for each agreement concluded, on control measures, etc.

Each LOA states an amount which is to be made available to the recipient organisation, and specifies the activities for which the funds provided are to be used. Further details about each project are given in the annex.[100] The General Conditions include provisions on, *inter alia*, division of responsibilities, the use of the FAO emblem, on intellectual property rights (IPRs) and on the status of project staff. This part of the agreement also includes an applicable law clause, in contrast to all the agreements examined above. Interestingly, the FAO LOAs 'shall be governed by general principles of law, to the exclusion of any single national system of law'.[101] Disputes shall be settled by arbitration in accordance with the UNCITRAL Arbitration Rules, if the parties are unable to reach a settlement by mutual agreement. The arbitral award is binding on the parties 'as the final adjudication of any such dispute'.[102] In addition, the LOA includes provisions on the reporting to be carried out by the recipient organisations, terms of payment, amendments and entry into force.[103]

9.4 Conclusions

The central issue which has been examined in this chapter is whether NGOs can and/or do conclude agreements under international law. In the discussion on this question, the term 'treaty' was not used, as it tends to be associated only with states and IGOs, although the VCLT 69 and VCLT 86 with accompanying ILC commentaries do not exclude the possibility that other entities may conclude treaties. Instead, the more neutral term 'agreement' was used.

---

[100] Standard Letter of Agreement, Introduction and Purpose.
[101] *Ibid.*, General Conditions, para. 6. The Humanitarian Office of the European Commission (ECHO) uses a Framework Partnership Agreement which is specified by means of General Conditions. According to Article 33 of the General Conditions, the Framework Partnership Agreement and operation contracts concluded with humanitarian NGOs are to be governed by Belgian law. These contracts were therefore not examined above.
[102] *Ibid.*, Settlement of Disputes.
[103] *Ibid.*, Reporting, Terms of Payment, Amendment, Entry into Force.

As is the case with most of the questions relating to legal status discussed in this book, the concepts of 'international legal personality' or 'subject of international law' as such do not provide much guidance. Discussions which take these concepts as their starting-point tend to be circular, since they often suggest that only subjects of international law have the capacity to conclude international agreements, while on the other hand those entities which do so are considered to be subjects of international law. In line with the inductive method outlined earlier in this study, it was considered that an examination of the issue should consider the existence and nature of agreements which have actually been concluded between NGOs and states or IGOs.

The status and headquarters agreements concluded by the ICRC are interesting in this respect. These agreements do indeed seem to be concluded under international law, notably through the subject matters regulated by them. The ICRC itself regards these agreements as 'international treaties'.[104] The existence of these agreements demonstrates the ability of the international legal system to confer legal status on NGOs and other private entities when this is necessary or practicable. Because of the ICRC's special status, it is however not particularly likely that agreements similar to those of the ICRC will be concluded by other NGOs within the near future.[105]

As regards the agreements concluded between IGOs and NGOs it can be concluded that their juridical character demonstrates a scale where some are clearly intended to be binding, while others are not intended to be binding or are difficult to characterise. Only one of the agreements examined includes an applicable law clause, the FAO LOA which, interestingly, subjects the agreement to 'general principles of law, to the exclusion of any single system of law'. According to the principle of party autonomy, contracting parties have almost unlimited freedom in choosing the applicable law of the contract, including general principles of law.[106] The ILC has also emphasised the importance of the intention of the parties in determining whether or not an agreement

---

[104] E-mail message from the ICRC legal division, 22 June 2001, on file with the author.

[105] With the exception of the Order of Malta, which maintains diplomatic relations with many states and is therefore likely to have concluded headquarters agreements under international law.

[106] See chapter 9 and P. M. North and J. J. Fawcett, *Private International Law*, 12th edn., London: Butterworths, 1992, pp. 476–486; Collier, *Conflict of Laws* pp. 185–196; Hobér, *Extinctive Prescription*, pp. 94, 113. As regards agreements between states and companies, see Greenwood, 'The Libyan Oil Arbitrations', pp. 79–80.

508 LEGAL AND EMPIRICAL SURVEY

is concluded under international law.[107] According to Van Hecke, it is also generally accepted that contracts concluded by IGOs may be subject to international rather than national law.[108] It thus seems that the FAO LOAs are indeed governed by international law.

The methods outlined in the different instruments examined for settling disputes vary in accordance with the binding or non-binding character of the document. Arbitration is the common method for the former category, and the decisions of such bodies are binding on the parties to the agreement. It seems rare that disputes concerning contracts between IGOs and NGO are actually referred to arbitration.[109] That is not surprising, as both parties have an interest in respecting the contract or solving disputes amicably. IGOs depend on NGOs to co-operate with them for the purpose of humanitarian operations, and there may not always be several NGOs available with the same type of expertise and capacity. NGOs, for their part, depend on the financial and other resources of IGOs. Nevertheless, if an IGO–NGO contract without an applicable law clause were to be subjected to arbitration, the arbitrator would in most cases be free to choose conflict of law rules, or to make a direct choice of substantive law. It is more and more common that arbitrators rely on general principles of law in the substantive part of the proceedings without having been expressly or tacitly authorised to do so by the parties.[110]

It may be asked whether the categorisation of an agreement as being concluded under international law renders it an 'international agreement', or indeed, a treaty. In the case of agreements concluded between IGOs and NGOs, however, this question does not seem to be of much practical significance. It is clear that such an agreement is not subject to

---

[107] YILC 1962, II, p. 32.

[108] Van Hecke, *Contracts between International Organizations and Private Law Persons*, p. 813. For a discussion on the situation where state parties to an agreement have not provided the arbitrator with any instructions as to choice of law, see Hobér, *Extinctive Prescription*, pp. 209 ff.

[109] According to a WFP official, no disputes concerning an agreement between WFP and an NGO seem to have been referred to arbitration, e-mail message of 11 April 2001, on file with the author. A WHO official believes that arbitration proceedings are few, possibly because of the relatively small amounts involved in individual agreements and the desire of the parties to resolve disputes amicably, e-mail message from the WHO Department of Emergency and Humanitarian Action, 25 July 2001, on file with the author.

[110] Ole Lando, 'The Law Applicable to the Merits of the Dispute', in Julian D. M. Lew (ed.), *Contemporary Problems in International Arbitration*, Dordrecht: Martinus Nijhoff, 1987, pp. 107–110.

the law of treaties, at least not as it is expressed in VCLT 1969 and VCLT 1986, which are designed for the relations among states and IGOs. Nor does the categorisation of an agreement as a treaty place it under the jurisdiction of the ICJ.[111] Instead, such disputes are solved in the manner stipulated by the agreement, in general through negotiation or arbitration. As regards agreements concluded by states or IGOs with entities with special status, such as the ICRC, the answer may be different. The ICRC considers its headquarters agreements to be international treaties and it can be observed that these agreements concern issues, such as immunity, which are otherwise regulated in treaties.[112] It seems possible that a conflict regarding, for instance, the interpretation of one of the ICRC's headquarters agreements could be solved by means of the law of treaties, at least by means of analogy. Although this type of agreement is not likely to be concluded by many, or any, other NGOs in the near future, the status and headquarters agreements of the ICRC demonstrate that there is at least a potential for such a development in international law.

If co-operation between IGOs and NGOs continues to increase, more contracting organisations may find it useful to refer explicitly to general principles of international law in order to determine a neutral legal ground for their agreements. Increasing responsibilities of NGOs for humanitarian and other operations could also create a need for provisions requiring compliance with international humanitarian law and human rights. As of today, some agreements state that contracted NGOs should carry out their activities in compliance with the Code of Conduct for the International Red Cross and Red Crescent Movement and NGOs in Disaster Relief.

---

[111] As regards agreements between IGOs and NGOs it should, however, be borne in mind that most specialised agencies of the United Nations may request an advisory opinion on legal questions arising within the scope of their activities. Article 65 of the Statute of the International Court of Justice, *Report of the International Court of Justice 1 August 1999–31 July 2000*, para. 49; Sands and Klein, *Bowett's Law of International Institutions*, p. 364.

[112] Letter from the ICRC legal division, 22 June 2001, on file with the author.

PART III • CONCLUSION

10 Summary and concluding remarks

10.1 The legal status of NGOs in international law

In the first part of this study it was demonstrated that the theories on international law look very differently on the legal role and position of non-state actors.[1] It was argued that it would be more constructive if an examination of the legal status of NGOs could be based on the common elements of such theories, a few basic assumptions that most international lawyers could accept, than if one particular theory was adhered to. The common assumptions that were identified as a platform for the purpose of the study on NGOs were, first, that states are the dominant actors of current international law; second, that they are able to confer legal status on non-state entities; third, that the increasing international role of non-state actors is a fact that international law needs to deal with; and, fourth, that treaties, case-law and resolutions dealing with the procedure of IGOs provide relevant information on the international legal status of NGOs.[2]

Further, an inductive method, or approach to international law, was outlined on the basis of the fundamental assumptions mentioned above. This inductive approach can be summarised as the standpoint that the rules, relations and practices that actually exist 'on the ground' are law itself and that, at least sometimes, general rules can be induced from many separate rules. It was asserted that the classical concepts relating to the actors of international law – such as international legal personality and subjects of international law – are rather ambiguous in their content, and cannot therefore help to clarify the situation. In spite of the unclear meaning of these concepts, they are sometimes

---

[1] Section 3.2.   [2] Section 3.2.

514   CONCLUSION

understood to reflect *a priori* notions of the 'real' nature of international law and its actors. If this understanding were accepted as the basis for an examination of the status of NGOs, it would seem to determine by means of deduction which material would be relevant and which would not. It was therefore suggested that the term 'legal status', considered as both wider and more neutral in relation to which fields of law should be examined, was a better concept. An investigation on the legal status of NGOs can, and should, deal with international legal material from all parts of international law that expressly relate to NGOs or can be used by these organisations for activities within the international legal system.[3]

In line with what has been said above, the material thus assembled and examined will not be measured against the notions of 'subject of international law' or 'international legal personality'. The answer to the question about the legal status of NGOs is the legal survey conducted in part II of the volume. In other words, the international legal status of NGOs is the sum of all the rules and practices laid down by states and IGOs for their interaction on the international plane with NGOs, and any more general norms which can possibly be induced from this material. It is the choice of the reader to decide if this material can be categorised in terms of international legal personality and, in that case, whether the answer is 'yes', 'no' or 'partial'.

The legal and empirical survey of part II was extensive, and the results need to be summarised. In the survey on rights and obligations, it was found that NGOs as organisations possess some international legal rights in their capacity as organisations, organisation rights, which are related to their existence and functioning.[4] Because of differences in the geographical and material scope of treaties which formulate such organisation rights, the rights of NGOs in different geographical regions and of different categories vary. As regards universal protection for all categories of NGOs, it can be argued that the ICCPR bestows organisation rights on all NGOs, notably the rights to freedom of association and assembly. However, the evidence that these rights include corporate elements is not strong, and the complaints system established under the Optional Protocol is open only to individuals. As compared to the general protection of NGOs on the universal level, international labour law gives a strong position to organisations of workers and employers. The ILO Conventions on freedom of association guarantee, *inter alia*, the

---

[3] Section 3.2.   [4] Chapter 4.

right to freedom of association for workers' and employers' organisations and the right to collective bargaining for the former. ICESCR also includes organisation rights for trade unions. The UN Declaration on Human Rights Defenders formulates some protection for human rights NGOs through the recognition of rights exercised by individuals in association with others, albeit the Declaration is not a binding instrument.

On the regional plane, instruments that create organisation rights for all types of NGOs include the ECHR, which provides strong protection for the rights of organisations. This is demonstrated by the fact that organisations have *locus standi* before the Court to institute cases concerning violations of the right to freedom of association, assembly, expression, religion and all other Convention rights which are not inherently linked to the physical person. International NGOs based within the territory of state parties to the European Convention on the Recognition of the Legal Personality of International Non-Governmental Organisations also have the right to be recognised as legal persons within the territories of other state parties to the Convention. In addition, the CoE Fundamental Principles on the Status of Non-Governmental Organisations in Europe formulate, if not legally binding rights, at least guidelines on the protection that should be afforded NGOs under national legislation, and express a general recognition of the importance and legitimate expectations of NGOs within European society.

Environmental NGOs within the territory of state parties to the Convention on Access to Information, Public Participation in Decision-Making and Access to Justice in Environmental Matters (the Aarhus Convention), which is a convention adopted within the UN Economic Commission for Europe, have clear rights in their capacity as organisations. As part of 'the public' and 'the public concerned', environmental NGOs have the right of access to information, public participation in decision-making and access to justice in environmental matters. Such NGOs also have the right to appropriate recognition and support from state parties, which shall see to it that their national legal systems are consistent with this obligation. The organisations' rights guaranteed under the Aarhus Convention are supported by the compliance mechanism which has been established and which is accessible to NGOs.

Organisation rights within the field of European regional labour law are laid down by the ECHR and the European Social Charter, which are also both connected to monitoring mechanisms accessible to NGOs. The American Convention on Human Rights, for its part, is expressly limited

516   CONCLUSION

to the protection of individual rights, while the character of rights formulated by the African Charter for Human and Peoples' Rights is ambiguous in this respect.

On the side of obligations, the position of NGOs is still vague, probably because of general concerns regarding the formulation of international legal duties for non-state actors outside clearly defined fields, such as international criminal and humanitarian law.[5] The discussions held within the UN Commission on Human Rights and ECOSOC regarding the pre-draft declaration on human social responsibilities illustrate the controversial character of this debate. Nevertheless, some 'grey zones' of normativity – fields of quasi-legal responsibilities – seem to exist within human rights law, where non-state actors have the responsibility, *inter alia*, not to 'engage in any activity or to perform any act aimed at the destruction of any of the rights' of others, as stated in Article 30 of the Universal Declaration of Human Rights. Moreover, state parties to the International Convention for the Elimination of all Forms of Racial Discrimination are obliged to prohibit racist organisations and their activities. This Convention thus lays down limits to the rights of organisations. NGOs which enter into formal relations with IGOs also undertake certain obligations formulated by the resolutions which form the basis for such co-operation. Finally, many NGOs voluntarily adhere to codes of conduct. Compliance with these codes is sometimes laid down as a requirement by IGOs in their agreements with NGOs, which increases the normative character of the formally voluntary codes.

International humanitarian law is an area of particular character, more accustomed to dealing with non-state actors. As for the status of NGOs within this field of law, there are numerous provisions in the Geneva Conventions and Additional Protocols which oblige state parties to respect and protect the work of humanitarian organisations, once their assistance has been accepted. The most interesting rule within this field of law from the perspective of the international legal status of NGOs is the provision of the Geneva Conventions that states that the contracting parties may agree to entrust to an organisation which offers all guarantees of impartiality and efficacy the duties of a protecting power. Although this is a possibility usually associated with the ICRC, it is not explicitly reserved for that organisation.[6]

[5] Section 4.3.   [6] Section 4.4.

An extensive part of the legal survey dealt with the standing of NGOs before international and regional tribunals and quasi-judicial bodies.[7] When the whole complex of such procedures is examined, it is striking to find that NGOs have acquired standing within so many fields and regions of law. It is also clear that the number of procedures accessible to NGOs is increasing. On the international level, however, NGOs still have access only to quasi-judicial procedures, which include the World Bank Inspection Panel, the ILO freedom of association procedures, the '1503 procedure' of the UN Commission on Human Rights and the UNESCO procedure for individual communications. In addition, NGOs are often active in individual cases examined by the UN treaty bodies, but lack standing of their own. The most important international court – the ICJ – is closed to non-state actors. This does, however, not mean that NGOs have not attempted to make use of this Court. It is generally recognised that it was a coalition of NGOs, the World Court Project, which managed to convince first the WHO and then the UN General Assembly to request the advisory opinion on the *Legality of the Use by a State of Nuclear Weapons in Armed Conflict*.[8]

The regional human rights systems all provide NGOs with *locus standi*. The Inter-American and African Commissions employ generous rules on standing, the latter allowing for *actio popularis*, and the European system provides NGOs which have suffered a violation of a Convention right with direct access to the Court. The EC field of law, for its part, provides only limited possibilities for NGOs to act directly before the Court, even though some NGOs have made use of the rules on judicial review. Other regional compliance mechanisms that provide NGOs with *locus standi* include the Aarhus Convention procedure for individual communications, the citizen submission procedure connected with NAAEC, and the Collective Complaints procedure established for the monitoring of the European Social Charter. The European Court of Human Rights and the ECJ are currently the only courts which are directly accessible to NGOs as parties, and the latter in particular pro-vides limited access. However, when the African Court of Justice comes into operation, NGOs will be able to institute cases before that court as well.

Rules on *amicus curiae* participation in international proceedings give NGOs a possibility to intervene in proceedings before some bodies from which they are otherwise excluded, such as the international criminal

---

[7] Chapter 5.   [8] Section 5.2.

518   CONCLUSION

tribunals and the WTO dispute settlement procedure, although within the latter *amicus curiae* briefs have very rarely been actually considered, and then only as part of the submissions of one of the parties.[9] The ICJ has the possibility under its Statute to notify 'international organisations' likely to be able to furnish relevant information that the Court will be prepared to receive written statements or to hear oral statements, but seems to have issued such a notification to an NGO only once. With its more recent Practice Directions, the ICJ has, however, recognised that material may be submitted by international NGOs and that such material will be taken care of by the Court and made available to states and IGOs, albeit not regarded as formal submissions. It is also made clear that states and IGOs presenting written and oral statements in an advisory case are free to refer to material submitted by INGOs. Furthermore, there is also a possibility for state parties to file *amicus* briefs from NGOs as part of their own submissions.

NGOs also have a possibility to act as *amici* within several procedures under which they also have standing of their own. The European Court of Human Rights provides the clearest examples of judgements which explicitly describe and discuss the information submitted by NGOs in their capacity of *amici*. The Inter-American Court of Human Rights has a generous *amicus* practice, in particular in its advisory cases, but has until the issuing of recent opinions not had the practice of describing or referring to *amicus* submissions in its judgements. The African Commission has the possibility to receive submissions from NGOs, although it does not seem to use the designation of *amicus curiae*. The ECJ employs a restrictive practice towards *amici*, requiring that the intervenor has a direct interest in the case.

In addition to making written or oral submissions in the capacity of *amicus*, NGO staff sometimes act before international and regional human rights bodies as the victim's counsel.

The co-operation of NGOs with IGOs in the form of consultative relationship or similar arrangements and submission of information to different bodies, such as the UN treaty bodies and the extra-conventional mechanisms, appears to be a relationship of mutual dependence.[10] The formal arrangements for co-operation between IGOs and NGOs, or civil society in general, have demonstrated an increasing trend since the late 1990s. In 1999, the first coherent arrangements for co-operation with civil society organisations were established

---

[9] Chapter 6.   [10] Chapter 7.

within the OAS. The European Commission issued its first guidelines for consultation with civil society in 2003, if only in the form of a non-binding policy document. In the same year, the CoE transformed its system for consultation with international NGOs to a system for participation of INGOs and partnership with national NGOs. It can further be observed that the recently formed AU has established an advisory body, ECOSOCC, consisting of representatives of civil society organisations.

Another interesting indication of a development towards a stronger position for NGOs within IGOs is that the use of the term 'participation' seems to be becoming more frequent at the expense of 'consultation'. The former concept has been introduced within the CoE and the OAS, while, for example, ECOSOC and the ILO still use 'consultation'. It can also be observed that the term 'civil society organisations', or 'CSOs' seems gradually to be replacing 'NGOs'.

Finally, the Report of the Panel of Eminent Persons on Civil Society and UN Relationships should be remembered. This report has not yet led to any actual reforms within the United Nations, but is interesting because of the Panel's recommendations for a stronger relationship between the United Nations and civil society in general and an enhanced co-operation between NGOs and central UN fora such as the General Assembly and the Security Council.[11] One interesting example of a close relationship between states and NGOs, which is not new but may nevertheless illustrate possible future developments within some fields of international law, is the ILO which, with its tripartite structure, incorporates representatives of states, employers' organisations and workers' organisations at all levels.[12]

NGO participation has also become a common characteristic of many international conferences. The study of UN Conferences demonstrated an increasing acceptance of NGOs as partners of dialogue at such fora, at both law-making and other meetings, on the part of states.[13] In fact, the number of NGO representatives often exceeds the number of state representatives. The negotiation of the Statute for an International Criminal Court during the Rome Conference was given special attention, and on the basis of interviews with state and NGO representatives it was concluded that NGOs had considerable influence on the negotiations, perhaps in particular in pressurising for the Court to be created at all, but also on the formulation of different parts of the Statute, such as the role and independence of the prosecutor.[14] This type of influence

[11] Section 7.2.　[12] Section 7.3.　[13] Chapter 8.　[14] Section 8.6.

can hardly in itself be considered as relevant for determining an actor's international legal status. After all, it is states that take the decisions, and a decision-maker may be influenced by many different persons and phenomena, inside and outside of meeting rooms. However, the influence that NGOs seem to have in some international fora demonstrates that the rules that allow for their presence and for their submissions are not just a façade, but evidence of an acceptance of the participation of NGOs in international legal discourse. Another interesting feature of intergovernmental negotiations is that states are sometimes represented by NGOs (or NGO staff) – for example, at environmental meetings. On the other hand, there are also conferences and bodies which have limited contacts with NGOs, such as the IMF.

Finally it was demonstrated that while only rather unique non-state entities such as the ICRC conclude agreements under international law with states, many NGOs enter into agreements on operational co-operation with IGOs.[15] Some of these instruments are not of a binding character, which can be explained by the fact that IGOs and NGOs often have a mutual interest in settling their conflicts amicably, and that disputes are rare. However, there are also examples of agreements between IGOs and NGOs which are intended to be legally binding and which refer explicitly to general principles of international law in their applicable law clause. Although there is some disagreement as to whether an agreement involving a non-state party can be located outside national legislation concerning both the law of the contract and the material rules, it seems that the principle of party autonomy generally allows the parties freely to choose any legal system, including international law, to govern the agreement. It therefore appears that NGOs have legal status to enter into agreements under international law when IGOs deem this useful. If states also accepted the possibility of concluding agreements under international law with NGOs other than the ICRC, there does not seem to be anything to prevent them doing so. The state community has accepted a strong international legal status for different *sui generis* entities, such as the Order of Malta, which is also a non-state actor, even if in historic times it controlled territory.[16]

This diverse picture of the international legal status of NGOs leads to the question whether there are any elements of this status which are common to all categories of NGOs throughout the world. As regards rights, this is uncertain. It is possible that the ICCPR enunciates

---

[15] Chapter 9. [16] See section 2.4.

organisation rights, but as was mentioned above, there is little evidence to support such a suggestion. As far as procedural capacity is concerned, there are three complaints systems which provide *locus standi* for NGOs both generally and universally. These include the '1503 Procedure' of the UN Commission on Human Rights and the UNESCO procedure for individual communications. In addition, the African Commission for Human and Peoples' Rights receives complaints from all categories of NGOs from all parts of the world regarding violations of the African Charter on Human and Peoples' Rights. It can also be observed that rules for *amicus curiae* submissions do not include any restrictions as to type or region of the NGO which seeks leave to make a submission. Consultative status with international organisations is another aspect of legal status which is potentially open for all NGOs. There is, however, generally a requirement that the NGO should be wholly or partly concerned with the issues of concern to the IGO with which consultative status is sought. NGOs may also participate in international conferences convened by the United Nations if they can demonstrate that their activities are of relevance to the conference and its preparatory process. Finally, many NGOs are potential partners in operational co-operation with intergovernmental bodies, and are therefore also potential parties to agreements concluded under international law. In sum, most elements of the international legal status of NGOs vary depending on which category of NGOs a particular organisation belongs to and in which region it is based.

10.2 Possible developments of the legal status of NGOs through standard-setting

Apart from gradual developments of the international legal status of NGOs through diverse rules in treaty-law, resolutions adopted within IGOs and customary law, states might in the future see advantages in clarifying and generalising the legal position of NGOs through international instruments. One way of doing this has already been explored on the regional plane. The European Convention on the Recognition of the Legal Personality of International Non-Governmental Organisations provides that the legal personality and capacity of international NGOs within the territory of the state party where they have their statutory offices shall also be recognised within other contracting states.[17]

---

[17] Section 4.2.

A similar instrument on the international plane would be likely to facilitate the work of some international NGOs. However, bearing in mind the weak support which the Convention has obtained in terms of the number of state parties, it is not probable that a corresponding treaty on the international plane would be successful. This is particularly true considering the threat of terrorism, which creates a strong demand among states for control of any foreign group that wishes to acquire property or perform other legal acts within a country. One possible solution would be to formulate very strict requirements for the acquisition of legal personality under such a global convention so that only well-established and scrutinised NGOs would come into question.

However, while the European Convention on the Recognition of the Legal Personality of INGOs provides a legal platform for NGOs which seek to extend their activities into new states, the main interest of many NGOs is to participate on the international plane. One way of attributing NGOs with a more general legal status on the international plane would be to create a common system among a selected group of IGOs for NGO participation. Today, there is a host of different mechanisms in operation within different intergovernmental bodies. INGOs often co-operate with several IGOs and report to different bodies on their own activities in accordance with the requirements of various resolutions on consultative status and similar mechanisms. At the same time, secretariats and NGO co-ordination units within different IGOs review applications and reports from the same NGOs. A shared system would thus mean that available resources could be used more rationally. Moreover, the systems for reviewing applications from NGOs that seek to participate could be made more based on expertise, and thus become less politicised. The bodies for granting consultative status and accreditation are usually composed of state representatives, and whether organisations are granted or denied access sometimes depends more on where they are based and which states are represented in the organ deciding on their application, than on to what extent they meet the formal requirements. A more general status that would provide access to a combination of international institutions after review of the organisation could also have the function of creating public confidence for the NGOs accepted, which could perhaps even lead to a more generally accepted understanding of the concept of 'NGO'. Furthermore, it could also create clearer accountability on the part of NGOs by requiring compliance with international legal rules or codes of conduct, in particular within the framework of operational collaboration. Finally, better methods for securing fair geographical and social representation could be established in relation to such arrangements for co-operation.

Shared or centralised arrangements for partnership with NGOs ought to be of particular interest within the UN system. The status thus acquired could provide access to selected organs of the United Nations and specialised agencies. This type of system already exists on a smaller scale under ECOSOC, and the Panel of Eminent Persons on Civil Society and UN Relationships has suggested that the system for consultative status should be extended outside ECOSOC. Depoliticisation of the process for revising applications has also been regarded as essential by the Panel.[18]

The thought of creating a possibility for a more generalised form of participatory status for NGOs might, however, mainly be the reflection of frustration over the diversity and complexity of today's system, or rather absence of a system. It is not clear that a general system for IGO–NGO co-operation would be better. Any reforms in these areas can be decided upon only after an open and participatory process of careful consideration in which the views of NGOs are, naturally, central. It is very probable that such deliberations would produce a strong negative reaction from NGOs, who have reasons to remain sceptical about centralisation which may entail risks that access will in reality be restricted or controlled in political, discriminatory or otherwise inappropriate ways. It is also possible that today's plurality of systems is needed in order to retain flexibility and the possibility of adapting mechanisms for co-operation to different situations and circumstances.

10.3 NGOs and the legitimacy of international law

Chapter 1 of the study placed the investigation of the international legal status of NGOs in a wider political and legal setting. A concept of legal legitimacy was chosen according to which law must ultimately be based on individual consent.[19] In consequence of this conceptualisation, the legitimacy of international law was considered to be flawed as long as its rules on the recognition of states and governments did not, in practice, require democratic government.[20] It was also suggested that even if all states were internally democratic and international law required governments to have been elected in order to be entitled to

---

[18] See section 7.2.   [19] Section 1.2.   [20] See section 1.2.

524   CONCLUSION

represent a state internationally, there would still be problems relating to the legitimacy of international law. The process of globalisation, with its diffusion of state power, can cause democratic deficits which weaken the legitimacy of international law in relation to people all over the world. In the report of the Panel of Eminent Persons on Civil Society and UN Relationships, it is observed that the weak influence of traditional democracy in matters of global governance is one reason why citizens in different parts of the world are urging greater democratic accountability from international organisations.[21] The legitimacy of international decision-making is also problematic in relation to nationally unrepresented or underrepresented groups, such as cultural, religious and linguistic minorities.

However, an international legal system based on states was accepted as a fact which is unlikely to be replaced by other systems, such as cosmopolitan democracy, at any time in the nearer future. Therefore, ways to strengthen the legitimacy of the state-centric system needed to be considered. Habermas has suggested that, although conventional democratic procedures for decision-making and political representation can never be entirely replaced, a discourse-theoretical understanding of democracy means that factors such as a functioning public sphere, the quality of discussion, accessibility and the discursive character of opinion and will formation can contribute to strengthening the legitimacy of international decision-making. In other words, the legitimacy of international law can be strengthened if international fora are rendered more transparent and more open for participation by a wide range of groupings and interests from different sectors and segments of society – such as indigenous peoples, minorities with cultural, linguistic or religious characteristics, academia, trade unions, religious associations, NGOs, etc. In accordance with the discourse principle, decisions should be based on rational discourse which provides access for all persons possibly affected. The reforms for greater access and transparency which have been taking place within some fields of international law and some international institutions ought therefore to be extended.[22]

It needs to be repeated that it was not suggested that NGOs should have a general right to vote or negotiate alongside governments in international bodies. The role of NGOs which has been in focus of this study is one of *participation*. It was argued that the regulated participation of NGOs as informants and partners of dialogue in intergovernmental

---

[21] See sections 1.2, 7.2.   [22] Section 1.2.

meeting rooms was a phenomenon that was healthy for the overall functioning of international law and that it contributed to strengthening its legitimacy, even if the participation of NGOs could not make international law 'democratic'. From a more pragmatic point of view, co-operation with NGOs can also help to bring information and expertise into intergovernmental fora and back again to the public. The role of NGOs in monitoring national implementation of international law and documenting breaches is important: in fact, some intergovernmental bodies seem to depend on co-operation with NGOs in order to function properly at all.

What has been stated above may give the impression that it has been assumed here that NGOs are 'good'. This is not the case. It is recognised that NGOs are self-appointed, single-issue-oriented and often not accountable to the people on whose behalf they claim to speak. The NGO sector is also dominated by the North in several respects, such as power and resources. In the first part of the study a definition of 'non-governmental organisation' was outlined on the basis of definitions which are contained in international instruments. This definition was fairly basic in its character and did in principle not distinguish between organisations on the basis of their objectives.[23] In line with this 'empty' definition, it should be observed that the focus of this study is more on non-governmental organisation as a form or a method of participation than on the character or role of particular NGOs. Although this distinction might seem artificial, it is important to make it for the purpose of a discussion on legitimacy. It is thus suggested that the question of whether international law should provide and protect a form of political participation through non-governmental organisation is on another and more fundamental level than the issue of which particular organisations should be entitled to participate in which particular situations, and what should then be required in terms of structure, objective, accountability, etc. in these different contexts.

It should also be observed that the points made here as regards the international participation of NGOs are not intended to be exclusive of other actors. The fact that it is suggested that the role of NGOs is important in some contexts does not thus mean that other actors are considered less important. The focus on NGOs in the discussion has been caused by the need for delimitation only. At the same time, it is argued that non-governmental organisation as a form or an instrument

---

[23] Section 1.3.

526   CONCLUSION

of participation is important, because it is neutral to different interests, sectors of society and objectives. It provides a common platform for a diversity which is also its strength.

The elements of the international legal status of NGOs which have been summarised earlier in this chapter are many and diverse. The international legal status of NGOs, as composed of these different factors, is considerable and this status is increasing. New complaints procedures which provide standing for NGOs were put in place during the 1990s and the *amicus* practice of some courts has become more permissive towards NGOs. New arrangements for consultation with NGOs have been established by IGOs, and some of the older mechanisms for consultation with NGOs have been replaced by arrangements for participation. The participation of NGOs in international conferences has also been incremental, and the influence of these organisations on international law-making more generally recognised. In 2001, the Convention on Access to Information, Public Participation in Decision-Making and Access to Justice in Environmental Matters (the Aarhus Convention) entered into force.[24] Interestingly, this Convention focuses specifically on the right to public participation, albeit only within the field of environmental law, and affords NGOs with several rights of a participatory nature.

In view of what has been said above about the role of NGOs in relation to the legitimacy of international law and the position that has actually been provided for NGOs in international law, the question can be raised if the international legal system will reach a point when NGOs have a general right to participate in international legal discourse. I suggest that, as of today, they have at least a legitimate expectation.

[24] Section 4.2.

Bibliography

Abbott, Kenneth W., 'International Relations Theory, International Law, and the Regime Governing Atrocities in Internal Conflicts', 93 AJIL (1999), pp. 361–379

Ahlström, Christer, *The Status of Multilateral Export Control Regimes – An Examination of Legal and Non-Legal Agreements in International Co-Operation*, Uppsala: Iustus Förlag, 1999

Åkermark, Athanasia Spiliopoulou, *Justifications of Minority Protection in International Law*, The Hague and Uppsala: Kluwer Law International/Iustus Förlag, 1997

Alkema, Evert, 'Freedom of Associations and Civil Society', 34 *A Yearbook of the European Convention on Human Rights* (1994), Freedom of Association, pp. 52–83

Alkoby, Asher, 'Non-State Actors and the Legitimacy of International Environmental Law', 3 *Non-State Actors and International Law* (2003), pp. 23–98

Alston, Philip, 'The United Nations High Commissioner for Human Rights', *ASIL Newsletter*, September 1995

Alston, Philip and Crawford, James (eds.), *The Future of UN Human Rights Treaty Monitoring*, Cambridge University Press, 2000

Alvesson, Mats and Sköldberg, Kaj, *Reflexive Methodology: New Vistas for Qualitative Research*, London: Sage, 2000

Amnesty International Report 2004, accessible online at http://www.amnesty.org/ailib/aireport/index.html

Anderson, Kenneth, 'The Ottawa Convention Banning Landmines, the Role of International Non-Governmental Organizations and the Idea of International Civil Society', 11 EJIL (2000), pp. 91–120

Ankumah, Evelyn A., *The African Commission on Human and Peoples' Rights. Practices and Procedures*, Dordrecht: Martinus Nijhoff, 1996

Archer, Clive, *International Organizations*, 2nd edn., London: Routledge, 1992

Archibugi, Daniele and Held, David, *Cosmopolitan Democracy: An Agenda for a New World Order*, Cambridge: Polity Press, 1995

Arend, Anthony Clark, *Legal Rules and International Society*, Oxford University Press, 1999

BIBLIOGRAPHY

Arts, Bas, *The Political Influence of Global NGOs: Case Studies on the Biodiversity Conventions*, Utrecht: International Books, 1998

Arzt, Donna E., and Lukashuk, Igor I., 'Participants in International Legal Relations', in Charlotte Ku and Paul F. Diehl (eds.), *International Law: Classical and Contemporary Readings*, Boulder, CO: Lynne Rienner, 1998, pp. 155–176

Aston, Jurij Daniel, 'The United Nations Committee on Non-Governmental Organizations: Guarding the Entrance to a Politically Divided House', 12 EJIL (2001), pp. 943–962

Aufricht, Hans, 'Personality in International Law', XXXVII *The American Political Science Review* (1943), pp. 217–243

Aust, Anthony, *Modern Treaty Law and Practice*, Cambridge University Press, 2000

Bartolomei de la Cruz, Héctor G., Potobsky, Geraldo von and Swepston, Lee, The *International Labour Organization: The International Standards System and Basic Human Rights*, Boulder, CO: Westview Press, 1996

Beck, Robert J., Arend, Anthony Clark and Lugt, Robert D. Vander (eds.), *International Rules: Approaches from International Law and International Relations*, Oxford University Press, 1996

Beck, Ulrich, *What is Globalization?*, Cambridge: Polity Press, 2000

Bederman, David J., 'The Souls of International Organizations: Legal Personality and the Lighthouse at Cape Spartel', 36 *Virginia Journal of International Law* (1996), pp. 275–377

Beigbeder, Yves, *Le rôle international des organisations non gouvernementales*, Brussels: Bruylant, 1992

  The Role and Status of International Humanitarian Volunteers and Organizations: The Right and Duty to Humanitarian Assistance, Dordrecht: Martinus Nijhoff, 1991

Bekker, Peter H. F., *The Legal Position of Intergovernmental Organizations*, Dordrecht: Martinus Nijhoff, 1994

Benvenuti, Paolo, 'The Nature and Features of International Non-Governmental Organizations', 4 *Italian Yearbook of International Law* (1978–1979), pp. 84–102

Berger, Jean-François, *The Humanitarian Diplomacy of the ICRC and the Conflict in Croatia (1991–1992)*, Geneva: International Committee of the Red Cross, 1995

Berger, Klaus Peter, *The Creeping Codification of Lex Mercatoria*, The Hague: Kluwer Law International, 1999

Bettati, Mario and Dupuy, Pierre-Marie (eds.), *Les O N G et le Droit International*, Paris: Economica, 1986

Beyond Beijing, *NGO Participation at the UN Fourth World Conference on Women: Report on Access, with Recommendations for Change*, Amnesty International *et al.*, October 1996

Black's Law Dictionary, Abridged 6th edn., St Paul, MW: West Publishing Co., 1991

Bodansky, Daniel, 'The Legitimacy of International Governance: A Coming Challenge for International Environmental Law?', 93 AJIL (1999), pp. 596–624

Boisson de Chazournes, Laurence and Sands, Philippe (eds.), *International Law, the International Court of Justice and Nuclear Weapons*, Cambridge University Press, 1999

Boli, John and Thomas, George M. (eds.), *Constructing World Culture: International Nongovernmental Organizations since 1875*, Stanford University Press, 1999

Bombay, Peter, 'The Role of Environmental NGOs in International Environmental Conferences and Agreements: Some Important Features', 10 *European Environmental Law Review* (2001), pp. 228–231

Breen, Claire, 'The Role of NGOs in the Formulation of and Compliance with the Optional Protocol to the Convention on the Rights of the Child on Involvement of Children in Armed Conflict', 25 HRQ (2003), pp. 453–481

Brett, Rachel, 'Non-Governmental Actors and Human Rights', in Raija Hansk and Markku Suksi (eds.), *An Introduction to the International Protection of Human Rights: A Textbook*, 2nd rev. edn., Turku and Åbo: Institute for Human Rights, Åbo Akademi University, 1999, pp. 399–413

'The Contribution of NGOs to the Monitoring and Protection of Human Rights in Europe: An Analysis of the Role and Access of NGOs to the Intergovernmental Organisations', in Arie Bloed *et al.* (eds.), *Monitoring Human Rights in Europe: Comparing International Procedures and Mechanisms*, Dordrecht: Martinus Nijhoff, 1993, pp. 121–144

Broms, Bengt, '*Subjects*: Entitlement in the International Legal System', in R. St J. MacDonald and Douglas M. Johnston (eds.), *The Structure and Process of International Law*, The Hague: Martinus Nijhoff, 1986, pp. 383–423

Brownlie, Ian, *Principles of Public International Law*, 5th edn., Oxford University Press, 1998

Treaties and Indigenous Peoples, Oxford: Clarendon Press, 1992

Buchanan, Allen, *Justice, Legitimacy, and Self-Determination: Moral Foundations for International Law*, Oxford University Press, 2004

Buergenthal, Thomas, 'Self-Executing and Non-Self-Executing Treaties in National and International Law', 235 *Recueil de Cours* 1992 IV, pp. 305–400

'The Advisory Practice of the Inter-American Human Rights Court', 79 AJIL (1985), pp. 1–27

'The Inter-American Court of Human Rights', 76 AJIL (1982), pp. 231–245

Bugeda, Beatriz, 'Is NAFTA Up to its Green Expectations? Effective Law Enforcement under the North American Agreement on Environmental Cooperation', 32 *University of Richmond Law Review* (1999), pp. 1591–1617

Butt, Philip Alan and Gray, Oliver (eds.), *Directory of Pressure Groups in the EU*, 2nd edn., London: Cartermill Publishing, 1996

Byers, Michael, *Custom, Power and the Power of Rules: International Relations and Customary International Law*, Cambridge University Press, 1999

Cameron, Iain, *An Introduction to the European Convention on Human Rights*, 3rd edn., Uppsala: Iustus Förlag, 1998

National Security and the European Convention on Human Rights, The Hague and Uppsala: Kluwer Law International/Iustus Förlag, 2000

Cameron, Maxwell A. *et al.* (eds.), *To Walk Without Fear: The Global Movement to Ban Landmines*, Oxford University Press, 1998

Carbonneau, Thomas E. (ed.), *Lex Mercatoria and Arbitration: A Discussion of the New Law Merchant*, rev. edn., The Hague: Kluwer Law International, 1998

530 BIBLIOGRAPHY

Carey, Henry F. and Richmond, Oliver P. (eds.), *Mitigating Conflict: The Role of NGOs*, London: Frank Cass, 2003

Carmody, Chi, 'Beyond the Proposals: Public Participation in International Economic Law', 15 *American University International Law Review* (2000), p. 1321

Cassese, Antonio, *Self-Determination of Peoples: A Legal Reappraisal*, Cambridge University Press, 1995

'The Status of Rebels under the 1977 Geneva Protocol on Non-International Armed Conflicts', in Judith Gardam (ed.), *Humanitarian Law*, Dartmouth: Ashgate, 1999, pp. 241–264

Castells, Manuel, *The Information Age: Economy, Society and Culture, II, The Power of Identity*, Oxford: Blackwell, 1997 and *III, End of Millennium*, 2nd edn., Oxford: Blackwell, 2000

Cavaglieri, A., 'I soggetti del diritto internazionale', IV *Rivista di Diritto Internazionale* (1925), pp. 18–32, 169–187

Charlesworth, Hilary, 'Feminist Methods in International Law', 93 AJIL (1999), pp. 379–394

Charlesworth, Hilary, Chinkin, Christine and Wright, Shelley, 'Feminist Approaches to International Law', 85 AJIL (1991), pp. 613–645

Chen, Lung-chu, *An Introduction to Contemporary International Law: A Policy-Oriented Perspective*, New Haven: Yale University Press, 1989

Chinkin, Christine, 'The Role of NGOs in Standard Setting, Monitoring and Implementation of Human Rights', in Joseph P. Norton *et al.* (eds.), *The Changing World of International Law in the Twenty-First Century: A Tribute to the Late Kenneth R. Simmonds*, The Hague: Kluwer Law International, 1998, pp. 45–66

Third Parties in International Law, Oxford: Clarendon Press, 1993

Churchill Robin R. and Khaliq, Urfan, 'The Collective Complaints System of the European Social Charter: An Effective Mechanism for Ensuring Compliance with Economic and Social Rights?', 15 EJIL (2004), pp. 417–456

Clapham, Andrew, *Human Rights in the Private Sphere*, Oxford: Clarendon Press, 1993

Clark, Roger S., 'The International League for Human Rights and South West Africa 1947–1957: The Human Rights NGO as Catalyst in the International Legal Process', 3 HRQ (1981), pp. 101–136

Clark, Roger S. and Sann, Madeleine (eds.), *The Case against the Bomb: Marshall Islands, Samoa, and Solomon Islands before the International Court of Justice in Advisory Proceedings on the Legality of the Threat or Use of Nuclear Weapons*, Camden: Rutgers University School of Law, 1996

Collier, J. G., *Conflict of Laws*, 2nd edn., Cambridge University Press, 1994

Conforti, Benedetto and Francioni, Francesco (eds.), *Enforcing International Human Rights in Domestic Courts*, The Hague: Martinus Nijhoff, 1997

Copelon, Rhonda, 'Gender Crimes as War Crimes: Integrating Crimes Against Women into International Criminal Law', 46 *McGill Law Journal* (2000), pp. 217–240

Craven, Matthew C. R., *The International Covenant on Economic, Social and Cultural Rights: A Perspective on its Development*, Oxford: Clarendon Press, 1995

Crawford, James, *The Creation of States in International Law*, Oxford: Clarendon Press, 1979

'The ILC's Articles on Responsibility of States for Internationally Wrongful Acts: A Retrospect', 96 AJIL (2002), pp. 874–890

(ed.), *The Rights of Peoples*, Oxford: Clarendon Press, 1988

Dahl, Robert A., *On Democracy*, New Haven: Yale University Press, 1998

Dahlén, Olle, 'The Relationship between the UN and the NGOs', 6–7 *International Association* (1976), pp. 326–331

Da Silva, Angela D., 'NAFTA and the Environmental Side Agreement: Dispute Resolution in the Cozumel Port Terminal Controversy', *Environs Environmental Law and Policy Journal*, 1998, pp. 43–62

Davidson, Scott, *The Inter-American Human Rights System*, Aldershot: Dartmouth, 1997

De Mestral, A. L. C., 'The Significance of the NAFTA Side Agreements on Environmental and Labour Cooperation', 15 *Arizona Journal of International and Comparative Law* (1998), pp. 169–185

Dinstein, Yoram, 'Collective Human Rights of Peoples and Minorities', 25 ICLQ (1976), pp. 102–120

Dunant, Henri, *Un souvenir de Solferino*, Geneva

Ebbesson, Jonas, 'The Notion of Public Participation in International Environmental Law', 8 *Yearbook of International Environmental Law* (1997), pp. 51–97

Economic Commission for Europe, *The Aarhus Convention: An Implementation Guide*, ECE/CEP/72, United Nations Sales Publication, New York and Geneva, 2000

Edwards, Michael and Hulme, David (eds.), *Non-Governmental Organisations – Performance and Accountability Beyond the Magic Bullet*, London: Earthscan Publications and Save the Children, 1995

Eriksson, Maja Kirilova, *Skydd av mänskliga rättigheter: Det Interamerikanska Systemet*, 2nd edn., Uppsala: Iustus Förlag, 1994

Falk, Richard A., 'International Legal Order: Alwyn V. Freeman v. Myres McDougal', 59 AJIL (1965), pp. 66–71

Law in an Emerging Global Village: A Post-Westphalian Perspective, New York: Transnational Publishers, 1998

'Nuclear Weapons, International Law and the World Court: A Historic Encounter', 91 AJIL 1997, pp. 64–75

'On the Quasi-Legislative Competence of the General Assembly', 60 AJIL (1966), pp. 782–791

Fine, Robert and Rai, Shirin (eds.), *Civil Society: Democratic Perspectives*, London: Frank Cass, 1997

Forsythe, David P., 'International Humanitarian Assistance: The Role of the Red Cross', 3 *Buffalo Journal of International Law* (1996), pp. 235–260

Fox, Gregory and Roth, Brad R. (eds.), *Democratic Governance and International Law*, Cambridge University Press, 2000

Fox, Jonathan A., 'The World Bank Inspection Panel: Lessons from the First Five Years', 6 *Global Governance* (2000), p. 279

BIBLIOGRAPHY

Franck, Thomas M., 'Community Based on Autonomy', in Jonathan I. Charney
et al. (eds.), *Politics, Values and Functions: Essays in Honour of Professor Louis Henkin*,
The Hague: Kluwer Law International, 1997, pp. 43–64
'The Democratic Entitlement', 29 *University of Richmond Law Review* (1994),
pp. 1–39
'The Emerging Right to Democratic Governance', 86 AJIL (1992), pp. 46–91
The Empowered Self: Law and Society in the Age of Individualism, Oxford University
Press, 1999
The Power of Legitimacy Among Nations, Oxford University Press, 1990
The Principle of Fairness in International Law and Institutions, Oxford University
Press, 1995
Freedom of Association and Collective Bargaining, Report of the International Labour
Conference, Geneva: International Labour Office, 1994
Gaja, Giorgio, 'A "New" Vienna Convention on Treaties Between States and
International Organizations or Between International Organizations:
A Critical Commentary', 58 BYIL (1987), pp. 253–269
Galenkamp, Marlies, 'Collective Rights: Much Ado About Nothing? A Review
Essay', 19 *Netherlands Quarterly of Human Rights* (1991), No. 3, pp. 291–307
Gamble, John King and Ku, Charlotte, 'International Law – New Actors and New
Technologies: Center Stage for NGOs?', 31 *Law and Policy in International
Business* (2000), pp. 221–262
Garvey, Jack I., 'Trade Law and Quality of Life – Dispute Settlement under the
NAFTA Side Accords on Labour and the Environment', 89 AJIL (1995)
pp. 439–453
Ghandi, P. R., 'The Human Rights Committee and the Right of Individual
Communication', 57 BYIL (1986), pp. 201–251
Giorgetti, Chiara, 'From Rio to Kyoto: A Study of the Involvement of Non-
Governmental Organizations in the Negotiations on Climate Change', 7
New York University School of Law Environmental Law Journal (1999), pp. 201–245
Gomien, Donna, Harris, David and Zwaak, Leo, *Law and Practice of the European
Convention on Human Rights and the European Social Charter*, Strasbourg: Council
of Europe Publishing, 1996
Gordenker, Leon, 'NGOs and Democratic Process in International
Organisations', in Monique Castermans-Holleman et al. (eds.), *The Role of the
Nation-State in the 21st Century: Essays in Honour of Peter Baehr*, The Hague:
Kluwer International, 1999, pp. 277–289
Gordenker, Leon and Weiss, Thomas G., 'NGO Participation in the International
Policy Process', 16 *Third World Quarterly* (1995), pp. 543–555
Greenwood, Christopher, 'The Libyan Oil Arbitrations', 53 BYIL (1983), pp. 27–81
Grugel, Jean (ed.), *Democracy without Borders: Transnationalization and Conditionality
in New Democracies*, London: Routledge, 1999
Guillet, Sara, '"Nous, Peuples des Nations Unies . . .": L'Action des Organisations
Non Gouvernamentales dans le Système International de Protection des
Droits de L'Homme', Centre de Droit International de Paris I, *Perspectives
internationales*, No. 10, Montchrestien, 1995

BIBLIOGRAPHY 533

Gutto, Shadrack B. O., *ICJ Workshops on NGO Participation in the African Commission on Human and Peoples' Rights 1991 to 1996: A Critical Evaluation*, Geneva: The International Commission of Jurists, 1996

Haas, Peter M. and Levy, Marc A., 'Appraising the Earth Summit: How Should We Judge UNCED's Success?', 34 *Environment* (1992), pp. 6–20

Habermas, Jürgen, *Between Facts and Norms: Contributions to a Discourse Theory of Law and Democracy*, Cambridge: Polity Press, 1996

'Postscript to Faktizität und Geltung', 20 *Philosophy and Social Criticism* (1994), pp. 135–150

The Inclusion of the Other: Studies in Political Theory, Cambridge: Polity Press, 1998

The Postnational Constellation. Political Essays, Cambridge: Polity Press, 2001

Harris, David J., *Cases and Materials on International Law*, 5th edn., London: Sweet & Maxwell, 1998

Harris, David J., O'Boyle, M. and Warbrick, C., *Law of the European Convention on Human Rights*, London: Butterworths, 1995

Harris, David D. J. and Livingstone, Stephen (eds.), *The Inter-American System of Human Rights*, Oxford: Clarendon Press, 1998

Hart, H. L. A., *The Concept of Law*, Oxford University Press, 1961

Hasenclever, Andreas, Mayer, Peter and Rittberger, Volker, *Theories of International Regimes*, Cambridge University Press, 1997

Held, David, *Democracy and the Global Order: From the Modern State to Cosmopolitan Governance*, Cambridge: Polity Press, 1995

Held, David and Koenig-Archibugi, Mathias (eds.), *Taming Globalization: Frontiers of Governance*, Cambridge: Polity Press, 2003

Henkin, Louis, *The Age of Rights*, New York: Columbia University Press, 1990

Herzfeld Olsson, Petra, *Facklig föreningsfrihet som mänsklig rättighet (The Workers' Freedom of Association as a Human Right)*, Uppsala: Iustus Förlag, 2003

Higgins, Alexander Pearce, *Studies in International Law and Relations*, Cambridge University Press, 1928

Higgins, Rosalyn, 'Policy Considerations and the International Judicial Process', 17 ICLQ (1968), pp. 58–84

Problems and Process: International Law and How We Use it, Oxford: Clarendon Press, 1994

'The Reformation in International Law', in Richard Rawlings (ed.), *Law, Society and Economy: Centenary Essays for the London School of Economics and Political Science 1895–1995*, Oxford: Clarendon Press, 1997, pp. 207–224

Hiroshi, Morita, 'International Human Rights and in Particular Reference to the Role of Non-Governmental Organizations', Dissertation, University of Alberta, Faculty of Law, 1993

Hobér, Kaj, *Extinctive Prescription and Applicable Law in Interstate Arbitration*, Uppsala: Iustus Förlag, 2001

Hofmann, Rainer (ed.), *Non-State Actors as New Subjects of International Law: International Law – From the Traditional State Order Towards the Law of the Global Community*, Proceedings of an International Symposium, Berlin: Duncker and Humblot, 1999

534 BIBLIOGRAPHY

Hohfeld, Wesley Newcomb, *Fundamental Legal Conceptions as Applied in Legal Reasoning*, New Haven: Yale University Press, 1919

Hollis, Martin and Smith, Steve, *Explaining and Understanding International Relations*, Oxford: Clarendon Press, 1990

Hudock, Ann C., *NGOs and Civil Society. Democracy by Proxy?*, Cambridge: Polity Press, 1999

Hunnings, Neville March, *The European Courts*, London: Cartermill Publishing, 1996

Hurd, Ian, 'Legitimacy and Authority in International Politics', 53 *International Organization* (1999), pp. 379–408

Hägerhäll, Bertil, 'The Evolving Role of NGOs', in Gunnar Sjöstedt *et al.* (eds.), *International Environmental Negotiations: Process, Issues and Contexts*, Swedish Council for Planning and Coordination of Research and the Swedish Institute of International Affairs, Report 93:1, pp. 50–76

ICC Monitor On-line, No. 2, 1998 (online version of the newspaper 'ICC Monitor' of the CICC)

ICRC Annual Report 2003, Geneva: International Committee of the Red Cross, 2004

ILO Law on Freedom of Association: Standards and Procedures, Geneva: International Labour Office, 1995

Interights 98–99 Annual Review

Interights 99–2000 Annual Review

International Commission of Jurists Report on Activities 1986–1988, Geneva, 1989

Irish, Leon E., Kushen, Robert and Simon, Karla W., *Guidelines for Laws Affecting Civic Organizations*, New York: Open Society Institute, 2004

Jessup, Philip C., *A Modern Law of Nations*, New York: Macmillan, 1948
Transnational Law, New Haven: Yale University Press, 1956

Johnsson, Christina, *Nation States and Minority Rights: A Constitutional Law Analysis*, Uppsala University, 2002

Jones, Peter, 'Human Rights, Group Rights, and People's Rights', 21 HRQ (1999), pp. 80–107

Joseph, Sarah, Schultz, Jenny and Castan, Melissa, *The International Covenant on Civil and Political Rights: Cases, Materials, and Commentary*, Oxford University Press, 2000

Kalyadin, A. N., 'The Role of Non-Governmental Organizations in UN Activities for Peace and Disarmament', 18 *Bulletin of Peace Proposals* (1987), pp. 393–398

Kapteyn, Paul Joan George and VerLoren van Themaat, Pieter, *Introduction to the Law of the European Communities*, 3rd edn., London: Kluwer Law International, 1998

Keane, John, *Global Civil Society?*, Cambridge University Press, 2003

Keck, Margaret E. and Sikkink, Kathryn, *Activists Beyond Borders: Advocacy Networks in International Politics*, Ithaca: Cornell University Press, 1998

Kelsen, Hans, *Principles of International Law*, 2nd edn., New York: Holt, Rinehart & Winston, 1966

Kempees, P., *A Systematic Guide to the Case-Law of the European Courts of Human Rights 1960–1994*, Dordrecht: Martinus Nijhoff, 1996

Keohane, Robert A., 'Global Governance and Democratic Accountability', in David Held and Mathias Koenig-Archibugi (eds.), *Taming Globalization: Frontiers of Governance*, Cambridge: Polity Press, 2003, pp. 130–159

Keohane, Robert A. and Nye, Joseph S. (eds), *Transnational Relations and World Politics*, Cambridge, MA: Harvard University Press, 1972

Kirsch, Philippe, 'The Development of the Rome Statute', in Roy S. Lee (ed.), *The International Criminal Court: The Making of the Rome Statute*, The Hague: Kluwer Law International, 1999, pp. 451–461

Kiss, Alexandre and Shelton, Dinah, *International Environmental Law*, 2nd edn., New York: Transnational Publishers, 2000

Kjaerum, Morten, 'The Contributions of Voluntary Organsations to the Development of Democratic Governance', in Ann McKinstry Micou and Birgit Lindsnaes (eds.), *The Role of Voluntary Organisations in Emerging Democracies: Experiences and Strategies in Eastern and Central Europe and South Africa*, The Danish Centre for Human Rights and the Institute of International Education, 1993

Klabbers, Jan, *An Introduction to International Institutional Law*, Cambridge University Press, 2002

The Concept of Treaty in International Law, The Hague: Kluwer Law International, 1996

Koenig, Christian, 'Observer Status for the International Committee of the Red Cross at the United Nations: A Legal Viewpoint', *International Review of the Red Cross*, No. 280, 1991, pp. 37–48

Koh, Harald Hongju, 'Transnational Legal Process', The 1994 Roscoe Pound Lecture, 75 *Nebraska Law Review* (1996), pp. 181–207

Korey, William, *NGOs and the Universal Declaration of Human Rights. A Curious Grapevine*, New York: Palgrave Macmillan, 1998

Koskenniemi, Martti, *From Apology to Utopia: The Structure of International Legal Argument*, Helsinki: Finnish Lawyers' Publishing Co., 1989

'Letter to the Editors of the Symposium', 93 AJIL (1999), pp. 352–361

Ku, Charlotte, 'The Developing Role of NGOs in Global Policy and Law Making', *Proceedings of the International Law Association, First Asian–Pacific Conference*, 1995, pp. 408–423

Kvale, S., *InterViews: An Introduction to Qualitative Research Interviewing*, London: Sage, 1996

Kwakwa, Edward, *The International Law of Armed Conflict: Personal and Material Fields of Application*, Dordrecht: Kluwer Academic Publishers, 1992

Lador-Lederer, J. J., *International Non-Governmental Organizations and Economic Entities: A Study in Autonomous Organization and Ius Gentium*, Leyden: A. W. Sythoff-Leyden, 1963

'Status Problems of International Non-Governmental Organizations', 37 *Nordisk tidsskrift for international ret* (1967), pp. 149–170

Lando, Ole, 'The Law Applicable to the Merits of the Dispute', in Julian D. M. Lew (ed.), *Contemporary Problems in International Arbitration*, Dordrecht: Martinus Nijhoff, 1987, pp. 101–112

BIBLIOGRAPHY

Lanord, Christophe, 'The Legal Status of National Red Cross and Red Crescent Societies', *International Review of the Red Cross*, No. 840 (2000), pp. 1053–1077

Lauterpacht, Elihu (ed.), *International Law: Being the Collected Papers of Hersch Lauterpacht*, 2, *The Law of Peace*, Cambridge University Press, 1975

Lauterpacht, Hersch, *International Law (Collected Papers), I: The General Works*, Cambridge University Press, 1970

'The Subjects of the Law of Nations', *The Law Quarterly Review*, 63 (1947), pp. 438–460 and 64 (1948), pp. 97–119

Lavoyer, J.-P., 'Refugees and Internally Displaced Persons: International Humanitarian Law and the Role of the ICRC', *International Review of the Red Cross*, No. 305, March–April 1995, pp. 162–191

Leary, Virginia, 'A New Role for Non-Governmental Organizations in Human Rights: A Case Study of NGO Participation in the Development of International Norms on Torture', in Antonio Cassese (ed.), UN Law/ Fundamental Rights, Alpen aan den Rijn: Sijthoff & Noordhoff, 1979, pp. 197–209

Lerner, Natan, *Group Rights and Discrimination in International Law*, Dordrecht: Martinus Nijhoff, 1991

Linklater, Andrew, *The Transformation of Political Community*, Cambridge: Polity Press, 1998

Macalister-Smith, Peter, 'Humanitarian Action by NGOs: National and International Law Perspectives', 18 *Bulletin of Peace Proposals* (1987), pp. 119–131

International Humanitarian Assistance: Disaster Relief Actions in International Law and Organization, Dordrecht: Martinus Nijhoff, 1985

MacCallum, Raymond, 'Evaluating the Citizen Submission Procedure under the North American Agreement on Environmental Cooperation', 8 *Colorado Journal of International Environmental Law and Policy* (1997), pp. 395–422

MacCormick, Neil, *Legal Right and Social Democracy*, Oxford: Clarendon Press, 1982

MacDermot, Niall, 'The Role of NGOs in Human Rights Standard-Setting', *UN Bulletin of Human Rights*, No 90/1, pp. 42–49

MacDougal, Myres S. and Reisman, Michael W., 'International Law In Policy-Oriented Perspective', in R. St J. MacDonald and Douglas M. Johnston (eds.), *The Structure and Process of International Law*, The Hague: Martinus Nijhoff, 1986

Mair, Peter, *Party System Change: Approaches and Interpretations*, Oxford: Clarendon Press, 1997

Malanczuk, Peter, *Akehurst's Modern Introduction to International Law, 7th edn.* London: Routledge, 1997

'Multinational Enterprises and Treaty-Making – A Contribution to the Discussion on Non-State Actors and the "Subjects" of International Law', in Vera Gowlland-Debbas (ed.), *Multilateral Treaty-Making*, The Hague: Kluwer Law International, 2000, pp. 45–72

Mansbach, Richard W., *The Global Puzzle: Issues and Actors in World Politics*, Boston: Houghton-Mifflin, 1994

Maresca, Louis and Maslen, Stuart (eds.), *The Banning of Anti-Personnel Landmines: The Legal Contribution of the International Committee of the Red Cross 1955–1999*, Cambridge University Press, 2000

Markell, David L., 'The Commission for Environmental Cooperation's Citizen Submission Process', 12 *Georgetown International Environmental Law Review* Spring, (2000), pp. 545–574

Marks, Susan, *The Riddle of All Constitutions: International Law, Democracy, and the Critique of Ideology*, Oxford University Press, 2000

Martin, Hans-Peter and Schumann, Harald, *The Global Trap: The Assault on Prosperity and Democracy*, London: Zed, 1997

McCoubrey, Hilaire, *International Humanitarian Law*, 2nd edn., Aldershot: Dartmouth, 1998

McGoldrick, Dominic, *The Human Rights Committee: Its Role in the Development of the International Covenant on Civil and Political Rights*, Oxford: Clarendon Press, 1994

Médicins sans Frontières, *Life Death and Aid*, London: Routledge, 1993

Meijers, H., 'New International Persons in the Caribbean', XXIV *Netherlands International Law Review: Essays in Honour of A. J. P. Tammes*, Special Issue 1/2 (1977), pp. 160–188

Meron, Theodor, *Human Rights and Humanitarian Norms as Customary Law*, Oxford: Clarendon Press, 1989

Morris, Virginia and Scharf, Michael P., *The International Criminal Tribunal for Rwanda*, New York: Transnational Publishers, 1998

Mosler, Hermann, 'Die Erweiterung des Kreises der Völkerrechtssubjekte', 22 *Zeitschrift für ausländisches öffentliches Recht und Völkerrecht* (1962), pp. 1–48

The International Society as a Legal Community, Alphen aan den Rijn: Sijthoff & Noordhoff, 1980

'Subjects of International Law', in *Encyclopedia of Public International Law*, 4, Amsterdam: North-Holland, 2000, pp. 710–727

Mosse, Gail M. L., 'US Constitutional Freedom of Association: Its Potential for Human Rights NGOs at Home and Abroad', HRQ 1997, pp. 738–812

Murray, Rachel, *The African Commission on Human and Peoples' Rights & International Law*, Oxford: Hart Publishing, 2000

Musgrave, Thomas D., *Self-Determination and National Minorities*, Oxford University Press, 1997

Månsson, Marie, *NGOs, Women and Beijing: A Study of NGOs at the NGO Forum on Women '95* in connection with the Fourth World Conference on Women in Beijing 1995, Stockholm: The Swedish Institute of International Affairs, 1996

Naldi, Gino J., *The Organization of African Unity: An Analysis of its Role*, 2nd edn., London: Mansell Publishing, 1999

Nanda, Ved P. and Krieger, David, *Nuclear Weapons and the World Court*, New York: Transnational Publishers, 1998

Newell, Peter and Grant, Wyn, 'Environmental NGOs and EU Environmental Law', 1 *Yearbook of European Environmental Law* (2000), pp. 225–252

Nino, Carlos Santiago, *The Ethics of Human Rights*, Oxford: Clarendon Press, 1991

North, P. M. and Fawcett, J. J., *Private International Law*, 12th edn., London: Butterworths, 1992

Nowak, Manfred, 'Survey of Decisions Given up till July 1986', 7 HRLJ (1986), pp. 287–306

UN Covenant on Civil and Political Rights: CCPR Commentary, Kiel: N. P. Engel, 1993

(ed.), *World Conference on Human Rights, Vienna, June 1993: The Contribution of NGOs, Reports and Documents*, Vienna: Manz, 1994

Nowrot, Karsten, 'Legal Consequences of Globalization: The Status of Non-Governmental Organizations Under International Law', 6 *Indiana Journal of Global Legal Studies* (1999), pp. 579–645

O'Connell, D. P., *International Law*, 2nd edn., London: Stevens & Sons, 1970

'La personnalité en droit international', *LXVII Revue Générale de Droit International Public* (1963), pp. 5–43

O'Connell, Mary Ellen, 'New International Legal Process', 93 AJIL (1999), pp. 334–351

Odinkalu, Chidi Anselm and Christensen, Camilla, 'The African Commission on Human and Peoples' Rights: The Development of its Non-State Communication Procedures', 20 HRQ (1998), pp. 235–280

OECD, *Understanding the Digital Divide*, Paris: OECD Publications, 2001

Oestreich, Joel E., 'Liberal Theory and Minority Group Rights', 21 HRQ (1999), pp. 108–132

Okeke, Chris N., *Controversial Subjects of Contemporary International Law: An Examination of the New Entities of International Law and their Treaty-Making Capacity*, Rotterdam University Press, 1974

Olz, Martin A., 'Non-Governmental Organizations in Regional Human Rights Systems', 28 *Columbia Human Rights Law Review* (1997), pp. 307–374

Oppenheim, Lassa, *International Law: A Treatise*, I, 4th edn., London: Longmans, Green & Co., 1928

International Law: A Treatise, I, 7th edn., London: Longmans, Green & Co., 1948

International Law: A Treatise, I, H. Lauterpacht, (ed.), 8th edn., London: Longmans, Green & Co., 1955

Oppenheim's International Law, I, Sir Robert Jennings and Sir Arthur Watts (eds.), 9th edn., London: Longman, 1996

Opsahl, Torkel and Domitrijevic, Vojin, 'Articles 29 and 30', in Gudmundur Alfredsson and Asbjørn Eide, (eds.), *The Universal Declaration of Human Rights: A Common Standard of Achievement*, The Hague: Martinus Nijhoff, 1999, pp. 633–652

Österdahl, Inger, *Implementing Human Rights in Africa: The African Commission on Human and Peoples' Rights and Individual Communications*, Uppsala: Iustus Förlag, 2002

Otto, Diane, 'Nongovernmental Organizations in the United Nations System: The Emerging Role of International Civil Society', 18 HRQ (1996), pp. 107–141

Pace, William and Thieroff, Mark, 'Participation of Non-Governmental Organizations', in Roy S. Lee (ed.), *The International Criminal Court: The Making of the Rome Statute*, The Hague: Kluwer Law International, 1999, pp. 391–398

Padilla, David J., 'The Inter-American Commission on Human Rights of the Organization of American States: A Case Study', 9 *American University Journal of International Law & Policy* (1993), pp. 95–115

Palmer, Alice and Werksman, Jacob, 'World Trade Organization, European Communities – Measures Affecting Asbestos and Asbestos-Containing Products, Panel Report', 10 RECIEL (2001), pp. 125–130

Parry, Clive, *The Sources and Evidences of International Law*, Manchester University Press, 1965

Pei-heng, Chiang, *Non-Governmental Organizations at the United Nations: Identity, Role and Function*, New York: Praeger, 1981

Pictet, Jean S. (ed.), *The Geneva Conventions of 12 August 1949 : Commentary, I Geneva Convention, 1952; II Geneva Convention, 1960; III Geneva Convention, 1960; IV Geneva Convention, 1958;* Geneva: International Committee of the Red Cross

Pilloud, Claude *et al.*, *Commentary on the Additional Protocols of 8 June 1977 to the Geneva Conventions of 12 August 1949, International Committee of the Red Cross*, Geneva/Dordrecht: Martinus Nijhoff, 1987

Plattner, Denise, 'ICRC Neutrality and Neutrality in Humanitarian Assistance', *International Review of the Red Cross*, No. 311, 1996, pp. 161–179

Plender, Richard, 'Intervention', in Richard Plender (ed.), *European Courts: Practice and Precedents*, London: Sweet & Maxwell, 1997, pp. 613–656

Poggi, Gianfranco, *The State: Its Nature, Development and Prospects*, Cambridge: Polity Press, 1990

Porter, Toby, 'The Partiality of Humanitarian Assistance – Kosovo in Comparative Perspective', *The Journal of Humanitarian Assistance*, June 2000, accessible online at http://www.jha.ac/articles/a057.htm

Posner, Michael H., 'ASIL Report: Reflections on the Vienna Conference', *ASIL Newsletter*, September 1993

Price Cohen, Cynthia, 'The Role of Nongovernmental Organizations in the Drafting of the Convention on the Rights of the Child', 12 HRQ (1990), pp. 137–147

Proceedings of the 92nd Annual Meeting: The Challenge of Non-State Actors, American Society of International Law, Washington DC, April 1–4, 1998

Prouvez, Nathalie, 'The European Social Charter, an Instrument for the Protection of Human Rights in the 21st Century?', International Commission of Jurists, *The Review*, No. 58–59, Geneva, 1997, pp. 30–44

Putnam, Robert D., *Making Democracy Work: Civic Traditions in Modern Italy*, Princeton University Press, 1993

Rama-Montaldo, Manuel, 'International Legal Personality and Implied Powers of International Organizations', 44 *British Yearbook of International Law* (1970), pp. 111–155

Raz, Joseph, 'Legal Rights', 4 *Oxford Journal of Legal Studies* (1984), pp. 1–21
The Morality of Freedom, Oxford University Press, 1986

Rechenberg, Hermann H.-K., 'Non-Governmental Organizations', in *Encyclopedia of Public International Law*, 3, Amsterdam: North-Holland, 1997, pp. 612–618

540   BIBLIOGRAPHY

Redgwell, Catherine J., 'Decisions by the African Commission on Individual Communications under the African Charter on Human and Peoples' Rights', 46 *International and Comparative Law Quarterly* (1997), pp. 412–434

Restatement of the Law Third: The Foreign Relations Law of the United States, The American Law Institute, St Paul, MN: American Law Institute Publishers, 1987

Rich, Roland, 'Recognition of States: The Collapse of Yugoslavia and the Soviet Union', 4 EJIL (1993), pp. 36–65

Risse-Kappen, Thomas (ed.), *Bringing Transnational Relations Back In: Non-State Actors, Domestic Structures and International Institutions*, Cambridge University Press, 1995

The Role and Function of the European Court of Justice, A Report by Members of the EC Section of the British Institute's Advisory Board chaired by the Rt Hon. the Lord Slynn of Hadley, The British Institute of International and Comparative Law, 1996

Rosas, Allan, 'So-Called Rights of the Third Generation', in Asbjørn Eide *et al.* (eds.), *Economic, Social and Cultural Rights: A Textbook*, Dordrecht: Martinus Nijhoff, 1995, pp. 243–245

'The Right to Self-Determination', Asbjørn Eide *et al.* (eds.), *Economic, Social and Cultural Rights: A Textbook*, Dordrecht: Martinus Nijhoff, 1995, pp. 79–86

Rottensteiner, Christina, 'The Denial of Humanitarian Assistance as a Crime under International Law', *International Review of the Red Cross*, No. 835 (1999), pp. 555–582

Russell, Bernard H., *Social Research Methods: Qualitative and Quantitative Approaches*, London: Sage, 2000

Sandoz, Yves, '"Droit" or "devoir d'ingérence" and the Right to Assistance: The Issues Involved', *International Review of the Red Cross*, No. 288 (1992), pp. 215–227

The International Committee of the Red Cross as Guardian of International Humanitarian Law, Geneva: ICRC, 1998

Sands, Philippe, 'International Law, the Practitioner and Non-State Actors', in Chanaka Wickremasinghe (ed.), *The International Lawyer as Practitioner*, London: The British Institute of International and Comparative Law, 2000

'The Role of Environmental NGOs in International Environmental Law', *Development* 1992:2, pp. 28–31

Sands, Philippe and Klein, Pierre, *Bowett's Law of International Institutions*, 5th edn., London: Sweet & Maxwell, 2001

Sands, Philippe and Werksman, Jakob, 'Procedural Aspects of International Law in the Field of Sustainable Development: Citizens' Rights', in Konrad Ginther *et al.* (eds), *Sustainable Development and Good Governance*, Dordrecht: Martinus Nijhoff, 1998, pp. 178–204

Schachter, Oscar, 'The Decline of the Nation-State and its Implications for International Law', in Jonathan I. Charney *et al.* (eds.), *Politics, Values and Functions, Essays in Honour of Professor Louis Henkin*, The Hague: Martinus Nijhoff, 1997, pp. 13–28

Schermers, Henry G. and Blokker, Niels M., *International Institutional Law: Unity within Diversity*, 3rd rev. edn., The Hague: Martinus Nijhoff, 1999

Schiffrin, Natalia, 'Current Development: Jamaica Withdraws the Right of Individual Petition Under the International Covenant on Civil and Political Rights', 92 AJIL (1998), pp. 563–568

Schneider, Andrea Kupfer, 'Institutional Concerns of an Expanded Trade Regime: Where Should Global Social and Regulatory Policy be Made? Unfriendly Actions: The Amicus Brief Battle at the WTO', 7 *Widener Law Symposium Journal* 87 (2001), pp. 87–107

Schreuer, Christoph, 'The Waning of the Sovereign State: Towards A New Paradigm for International Law?', 4 EJIL (1993), pp. 447–471

Seyersted, Finn, 'International Personality of Intergovernmental Organizations: Do their Capacities Really Depend upon the Conventions Establishing Them?', 34 *Nordisk Tidsskrift for International Ret og Jus Gentium* (1964), pp. 1–112

Shaw, Malcolm N., *International Law*, 4th edn., Cambridge University Press, 1997

Shearer, I. A., *Starke's International Law*, 11th edn., London: Butterworths, 1994

Shelton, Dinah, 'The Participation of Nongovernmental Organizations in International Judicial Proceedings', 88 AJIL (1994), pp. 611–642

Shihata, Ibrahim F. I., *The World Bank Inspection Panel: In Practice*, 2nd edn., Oxford University Press, 2000

Silverman, David, *Interpreting Qualitative Data*, London: Sage, 1993

Simma, Bruno and Paulus, Andreas L., 'The Responsibility of Individuals for Human Rights Abuses in Internal Conflicts: A Positivist View', 93 AJIL (1999), pp. 302–316

Siotto-Pintor, Manfredi, 'Les sujets du droit international autres que les etats', 41 *Recueil des Cours* (1932), pp. 245–361

Sire, H. J. A., *The Knights of Malta*, New Haven: Yale University Press, 1994

Slaughter, Anne-Marie, 'Building Global Democracy', 1 *Chicago Journal of International Law* (2000), pp. 223–229

'International Law and International Relations Theory: A Dual Agenda', 87 AJIL (1993), pp. 205–239

'International Law in a World of Liberal States', 6 EJIL (1995), pp. 503–538

Slaughter, Anne-Marie, Tulumello, Andrew S. and Wood, Stepan, 'International Law and International Relations: A New Generation of Interdisciplinary Scholarship', 92 AJIL (1998), pp. 367–397

Sloss, David, 'The Domestication of International Human Rights: Non-Self Executing Declarations and Human Rights Treaties', *Yale Law Journal* 24(1), 1999, pp. 129–221

Smith, Jackie *et al.*, 'Globalizing Human Rights: The Work of Transnational Human Rights NGOs in the 1990s', 20 HRQ (1998), pp. 379–412

Spiro, Peter J., 'Globalization, International Law, and the Academy', 32 *New York University Journal of International Law and Politics* (2000), pp. 567–590

542   BIBLIOGRAPHY

'NGOs versus the State', 18 *The Washington Quarterly* (1995), pp. 45–56

Stavenhagen, Rodolfo, 'Cultural Rights and Universal Human Rights', in Asbjørn Eide *et al.* (eds.), *Economic, Social and Cultural Rights: A Textbook*, Dordrecht: Martinus Nijhoff, 1995, pp. 63–77

Steinberger, Helmut, 'Sovereignty', in *Encyclopedia of Public International Law*, 4, Amsterdam: North-Holland, 2000, pp. 500–521

Steiner, Henry J., 'Diverse Partners. Non-Governmental Organizations in the Human Rights Movement: The Report of a Retreat of Human Rights Activists', Harvard Law School Human Rights Program, 1991

Swepston, Lee, 'Human Rights Law and Freedom of Association: Development through ILO Supervision', *1937 International Labour Review* (1998), pp. 169–194

Symonides, Janusz, 'UNESCO and the Universal Declaration of Human Rights', in Glen Johnson and Janusz Symonides, *The Universal Declaration of Human Rights: A History of its Creation and Implementation 1948–1998*, Paris: UNESCO Publishing, 1998

Taylor, Charles, 'The Dynamics of Democratic Exclusion', *9.4 Journal of Democracy* (1998), pp. 143–156

Taylor, Phillip, *Nonstate Actors in International Politics: From Transnational to Substate Organizations*, Boulder, CO: Westview Press, 1984

Teubner, Gunther (ed.), *Global Law Without a State*, Aldershot: Dartmouth, 1997

The Participation of Non-Governmental Organizations in the Work of the African Commission on Human and People's Rights: A Compilation of Basic Documents, International Commission of Jurists, October 1991–March 1996

The UN System and NGOs: A New Relationship for a New Era?, Report of the Twenty-Fifth United Nations Issues Conference, February 18–20, 1994

Thoolen, Hans and Verstappen, Berth, *Human Rights Missions: A Study of the Fact-Finding Practice of Non-Governmental Organizations*, Dordrecht and Aldershot: Martinus Nijhoff, 1986

Thornberry, Patrick, *International Law and the Rights of Minorities*, Oxford: Clarendon Press, 1991

Tolley, Howard B., Jr, *The International Commission of Jurists: Global Advocates for Human Rights*, Philadelphia: University of Pennsylvania Press, 1994

Udombana, Nsongurua J., 'Toward the African Court on Human and Peoples' Rights: Better Late Than Never', 3 *Yale Human Rights & Development Law Journal* (2000), pp. 45–111

Umozurike, U. Oji, *The African Charter on Human and Peoples' Rights*, The Hague: Martinus Nijhoff, 1997

UNDP, *Human Development Report 2001*, Oxford University Press, 2001

UNHCR, *Global Report 2003*, Geneva, 2004

Urquhart, Brian, 'Between Sovereignty and Globalisation: Where Does the United Nations Fit In?', The Second Dag Hammarskjöld Lecture, Dag Hammarskjöld Foundation, Uppsala, 2000

Valticos, Nicolas and von Potobsky, Geraldo W., *International Labour Law*, 2nd edn., The Hague: Kluwer Law and Taxation Publishers, 1995

Van Boven, Theo C. et al. (eds.), *The Legitimacy of the United Nations: Towards an Enhanced Legal Status of Non-State Actors*, Netherlands Institute of Human Rights, SIM Special, 19, Utrecht, 1997

Van Dijk, P. and van Hoof, Godefridus J. H., *Theory and Practice of the European Convention on Human Rights*, 3rd edn., The Hague: Kluwer Law International, 1998

Van Hecke, Georges, 'Contracts between International Organizations and Private Law Persons', in *Encyclopedia of Public International Law*, 1, Amsterdam: North-Holland, 1992, pp. 812–814

Van Hoof, Godefridus J. H., *Rethinking the Sources of International Law*, The Hague: Kluwer, 1983

Van Kleffens, E. N., 'Sovereignty in International Law', 82 *Recueil des Cours* (1953), pp. 1–130

Van Rooy, Alison, *The Global Legitimacy Game: Civil Society, Globalization and Protest*, New York: Palgrave Macmillan, 2004

Vázquez, Carlos Manuel, 'The Four Doctrines of Self-Executing Treaties', 89 AJIL, 1995, pp. 695–723

Von Weiss, Andreas, 'Die Non-Governmental Organizations und die Vereinten Nationen', 27 *Zeitschrift für Politik*, (1980), pp. 387–406

Waltz, Kenneth N., *Theory of International Politics*, New York: McGraw-Hill, 1979

Walzer, Michael, *Toward a Global Civil Society*, Providence and Oxford: Berghahn Books, 1995

Ward, Angela, *Judicial Review and the Rights of Private Parties in EC Law*, Oxford University Press, 2000

Warkentin, Craig, *Reshaping World Politics: NGOs, the Internet and Global Civil Society*, Oxford: Rowman & Littlefield, 2001

Weil, Prosper, 'Towards Relative Normativity in International Law?', 77 AJIL (1983), pp. 413–442

Weiss, Thomas G. (ed.), *Beyond UN Subcontracting: Task-Sharing with Regional Security Arrangements and Service-Providing NGOs*, New York: St Martin's Press, 1998

Weiss, Thomas G., and Gordenker, Leon (eds.), *NGOs, the UN, and Global Governance*, London: Lynne Rienner, 1996

Weissbrodt, David, 'An Analysis of the Fifty-First Session of the United Nations Sub-Commission on the Promotion and Protection of Human Rights', 22 HRQ (2000), pp. 788–837

'Non-State Entities and Human Rights Within the Context of the Nation-State in the 21st Century', in Monique Castermans-Holleman *et al.* (eds.), *The Role of the Nation-State in the 21st Century: Essays in Honour of Peter Baehr*, The Hague: Kluwer International, 1999, pp. 175–195

Welch, Claude E., Jr, *Protecting Human Rights in Africa: Strategies and Roles of Non-Governmental Organizations*, Philadelphia: University of Pennsylvania Press, 1995

(ed.), *NGOs and Human Rights: Promise and Performance*, Philadelphia: University of Pennsylvania Press, 2001

Wheatly, Steven, 'Deliberative Democracy and Minorities', 14 EJIL (2003), pp. 507–527

544 BIBLIOGRAPHY

White, Lyman Cromwell, *International Non-Governmental Organizations: Their Purposes, Methods and Accomplishments*, New Brunswick: Rutgers University Press, 1951

Wiessner, Siegfried and Willard, Andrew R., 'Policy-Oriented Jurisprudence and Human Rights Abuses in International Conflict: Toward a World Public Order of Human Dignity', 93 AJIL (1999), pp. 316–334

Willemin, Georges and Heacock, Roger, *The International Committee of the Red Cross*, Boston: Martinus Nijhoff, 1984

Willetts, Peter, 'From "Consultative Arrangements" to "Partnership": The Changing Status of NGOs in Diplomacy at the UN', 6 *Global Governance* (2000), pp. 191–212

'From Stockholm to Rio and Beyond: The Impact of the Environmental Movement on the United Nations Consultative Arrangements for NGOs', 22 *Review of International Studies* (1996), pp. 57–80

(ed.), *'The Conscience of the World': The Influence of Non-Governmental Organisations in the UN System*, London: Hurst & Co., 1996

Wolfke, Karol, *Custom in Present International Law*, 2nd rev. edn., Dordrecht: Martinus Nijhoff, 1993

WWF Annual Report 2002, Washington, DC: World Wide Fund for Nature, December 2002

Yearbook of International Organizations, 36, 1B, 1999/2000

Yearbook of the United Nations, 47, Dordrecht: Martinus Nijhoff, 1993

Young, Iris Marion, *Inclusion and Democracy*, Oxford University Press, 2000

Zegveld, Lisbeth, *The Accountability of Armed Opposition Groups in International Law*, Cambridge University Press, 2002

Interviews

Note: The titles specified are those held by the persons interviewed when the events relevant for the interview occurred.

Sir Franklin Berman, Legal Adviser to the British Foreign and Commonwealth Office and Head of the UK delegation to the Rome Conference for an International Criminal Court

Carl-Henrik Ehrenkrona, Director for Legal Affairs of the Swedish Ministry for Foreign Affairs

Cristopher Hall, Legal Adviser, Amnesty International

Peter Nobel, member of the United Nations Committee Against Racial Discrimination

Philippe Kirsch, Ambassador, Legal Advisor to the Canadian Department of Foreign Affairs, Head of the Canadian delegation and Chairman of the Committee of the Whole at the Rome Conference for an International Criminal Court

William Pace, Convenor of the NGO Coalition for an International Criminal Court and Executive Director of the World Federalist Movement

Emma Playfair, Executive Director, The International Centre for the Legal Protection of Human Rights (Interights)

Sir Nigel Rodley, Special Rapporteur of the United Nations Commission on Human Rights on the Question of Torture

Per Saland, Director, Swedish Ministry for Foreign Affairs, Vice Head of the Swedish delegation and Chairman of the Working Group on General

Principles and the Working Group on Applicable Law at the Rome Conference for an International Criminal Court

Philippe Sands, Professor, University of London, and Project Director of the Project on International Courts and Tribunals

Index

1503 Procedure 236–7, 521
16 Austrian Communes and some of their Councillors v. *Austria* case 250
Aarhus Convention on Access to Information, Public Participation in Decision-Making and Access to Justice in Environmental Matters 160–4, 515, 526
procedure for individual communications 285–8, 517
access to legal advice 337–8
actio popularis 302, 517
actors of international law 82–117
increasing role of non-state actors 111–12
new actors entering legal system 87–91, 96–9, 107–9
states as dominant actors of international law 111
who are the actors of international law 84–7, 91–6, 103–7
Advisory Opinion on Namibia 305
Advisory Opinion on the International Status of South-West Africa 305
African Charter on Human and Peoples' Rights 183–7, 440, 442, 515
African Commission on Human and Peoples' Rights 279–85, 440–4, 517, 518, 521
African Court 285, 517
NGOs and 198
non-party participation in legal process 361–2, 518
standing before 186–7, 279–85, 517, 521
African Concern 315–16
African Union, NGOs and 438–44, 445, 519
Agenda 21 451, 454–5
agreements *see* international agreements
aid programmes 7, 21
humanitarian aid *see* humanitarian aid
aims/objectives of NGOs 16, 47, 52

Akayesu case 314–15, 317, 364
Alfred Musema case 315–16
American Committee on Africa 305
American Convention on Human Rights 181–3, 515
Inter-American Commission on Human Rights 274–7, 350–4, 437–8, 517
Inter-American Court of Human Rights 277–9, 354–61, 364–5
non-party participation in legal process 350–61, 518
standing before 181–2, 271–9, 517: procedure 271–4
American Declaration of the Rights and Duties of Man (1948) 271
American Federation of Labor 375
Americas Watch 358
amicus curiae see non-party (third party) participation
Amnesty International 20, 21, 330, 331, 332, 333, 334, 335, 337, 340–1, 353, 400, 459
Amparo Tordecilla Trujillo v. *Colombia* case 351
Apeh Üldözötteinek Szövetsége and others v. *Hungary* case 173–4, 250
Arend, Anthony Clark 84, 106–9, 112
asbestos 323–6, 327
Ashingdane v. *UK* case 330
assembly rights 139, 142, 169–72, 183
issues raised in cases before ECHR 256
Association for Peace in the Continents (ASOPAZCO) 384–5
association rights
African Charter on Human and Peoples' Rights 183–6
American Convention on Human Rights 182
European Convention on Human Rights 169–72
European Social Charter 178
ICCPR 140–4, 147

548   INDEX

association rights (cont.)
  ILO freedom of association procedures
    237–9, 514
  issues raised in cases before ECHR 255–6
  limitations 190–2
  Universal Declaration of Human Rights
    139
Asylum case 303
Aust, Anthony 490, 498–9
autonomy 26, 27, 494
  NGOs and 7, 46–7, 52
Aydin v. *Turkey* case 328, 338–9

Bacchelli v. *Commune di Bologna* case 76
Baena Ricardo et al. v. *Panama* case 278–9, 357
Bahaddar v. *the Netherlands* case 328
Bámaca Velásquez v. *Guatemala* case 356–7
Bangladesh, Jamuna Bridge Project 243–4
Banjul Charter *see* African Charter on
  Human and Peoples' Rights
Bekker, Peter 61–2
belligerent groups 64
BIOTICA Ecological Society v. *Turkmenistan* case
  287
Blake case 278
Blaskić case 313
Blokker, Niels M. 61, 85, 366
Brannigan and McBride v. *The United Kingdom*
  case 332–4
Brownlie, Ian 89–90
Brüggemann and Sheuten v. *Federal Republic of*
  Germany case 252
Buchanan, Allen 25–6
budgets of NGOs 20
Buergenthal, Thomas 129, 355
Byers, Michael 77, 104–6, 107, 109

Canea Catholic Church v. *Greece* case 249–50
capacity *see* legal capacity
capital punishment 229–30, 276, 340–1
Carl Baker case 351
CAS Succhi di Frutta SpA v. *Commission of the*
  EU case 346
Castells, Manuel 13–14
Center for Justice and International Law
  (CEJIL) 276
Central American Court of Justice 55
Cha'are Shalom Ve Tsedek v. *France* case 175
Chahal v. *UK* case 334–6
Chen, Lung-chu 92
Chinkin, Christine 307–8
Christensen, Camilla 362
Christian Solidarity International 386
civil conflict 203, 206, 213, 214
Civil Liberties Organization in respect of the
  Nigerian Bar Association v. *Nigeria* case
  184–5

civil service, trade unions in 141
civil society 15–17, 31, 35, 104
  ICJ nuclear weapons opinion and 221,
    222
  UN and 406–10
closed shop 341
Coalition for Women's Human Rights in
  Conflict Situations 316–17
codes of conduct 198–201
Codex alimentarius 22
colonial system, wars of liberation 203, 214
communicative democracy 35
communitarianism 17
companies *see* corporations
Competence of the ILO to Regulate, Incidentally,
  the Personal Work of the Employer case
  309
conferences *see* international conferences
conflict/war
  care of wounded 210
  civil conflict 203, 206, 213, 214
  colonial wars of liberation 203, 214
  Geneva Conventions (1949) 70, 202–4,
    205, 495, 516: humanitarian
    organisations and 205–15
  humanitarian law and 202–4
  prisoners of war 211–12
  protection of civilians 212, 213, 214
  protection of property 213
  relief schemes 213
consent, state 25–6
constitution of NGOs 16, 50–1, 52
constructivism 102
consultation procedure
  European Social Charter 179
  ILO Conventions 157
  United Nations Economic and Social
    Council (ECOSOC) 374–86
contracts
  employment contracts 491
  law of the sea and 491
Convention Against Torture 234–5
Convention on the Elimination of All
  Forms of Discrimination against
  Women 139
Convention on Environmental Impact
  Assessment in a Transboundary
  Context 288
Convention on the Law of the Sea 491
Convention on the Prohibition of the Use,
  Stockpiling, Production and Transfer
  of Anti-Personnel Mines and on their
  Destruction (1997) 70
corporal punishment 262
corporations
  rights of 136, 143–4
    see also organisation rights

transnational *see* transnational
corporations
cosmopolitan democracy 26, 30, 31, 524
Council of Europe
Fundamental Principles on the Status
of NGOs 23-5, 140, 166-8,
170, 515
NGOs and 196-7: co-operation with
416-25, 445, 519; definitions 40-3
counsel, NGOs as 302
Court of First Instance (CFI) 264, 302, 346
Cox, Robert 101
Craven, Matthew 148
Crawford, James 9
criminal groups 45, 49, 52
criminal law, international 187
critical approach 80
customary law 113
legal personality and 77-8
recognition in 89

Dahl, Robert 14
Danzig Railway Officials case 55-6, 112, 123,
124, 127-8
Davidson, Scott 355
death penalty 229-30, 276, 340-1
decision-making, Aarhus Convention on
public participation in 160-4,
515, 526
procedure for individual
communications 285-8, 517
democracy
civil society and 15-17
communicative 35
cosmopolitan 26, 30, 31, 524
fairness and 24
globalisation and 14-15, 31, 524
international law and 6-12, 23, 29
nature of 10, 11
self-determination and 26
Desmond McKenzie v. *Jamaica* case 351, 353
digital divide 17
diplomatic protection 107, 124, 131
direct applicability
ILO Conventions 159-60
treaties 129
disappeared people 340
disarmament, Conference on
Disarmament 448, 485, 520
disaster relief, code of conduct for 200-1
discourse theory 27, 28-36, 524
discrimination, racial *see* racial
discrimination
drugs issues 373
Dunant, Henry 69
duties/obligations 187-201, 300
under Aarhus Convention 162, 163

under ECHR 135, 170-1
under European Convention on the
Recognition of the Legal Personality
of International Non-Governmental
Organisations 166
under European Social Charter 177, 178
under ICCPR 144-6
under ICESCR 150-2
under ILO Conventions 154, 157-8, 160,
192
NGOs 190, 192-3, 217, 516: co-operation
with IGOs 193-8
rights and 121, 122-3, 125
social responsibilities 188, 189, 516
UN Declaration on Human Rights
Defenders 192-3

Earth Summit 373
Ecuador, Mining Development and
Environmental Control Technical
Assistance Project 244-5
elections, process of 7, 8
employment contracts 491
enforcement of rights 124, 133
environmental issues
Aarhus Convention on public
participation in decision-making
160-4, 515, 526: procedure for
individual communications 285-8,
517
Conference on Environment and
Development (Rio 1992) 447,
450-5, 480, 483, 484, 485
Conference on the Human Environment
(1972) 450
Convention on Environmental Impact
Assessment in a Transboundary
Context 288
Framework Convention on Climate
Change 451, 460, 485: Conference of
the Parties to the Framework
Convention on Climate Change
(Kyoto) 447, 460-3, 484, 485
international law 29
Erdemović case 313
Espoo Convention on Environmental
Impact Assessment in a
Transboundary Context 288
*European Communities – Measures Affecting
Asbestos and Asbestos-Containing Products*
case 323-6, 327
*European Communities – Trade Description of
Sardines* 327
European Convention on Human Rights
48, 168-77, 191, 216, 219, 515
assembly and association rights
169-72

550 INDEX

European Convention on Human Rights (cont.)
fair hearing right 173-4
freedom of religion 174-5
legal nature of rights under 177
non-party participation in Court of Human Rights 328-45, 364, 365, 518
peaceful enjoyment of possessions right 176-7
respect for private life right 176
standing *(locus standi)* 171, 177, 216, 246-57, 298, 302, 515: concept of NGO and victim requirement 247-53; NGOs as parties before Commission and Court 253-5; procedure 246-7
European Convention on the Recognition of the Legal Personality of International Non-Governmental Organisations (1986) 40-1, 49, 164-6, 515, 521-2
European Court of Justice (ECJ) 264-71, 302
non-party participation 345-50, 364, 518
standing before 264-71
European Framework Convention for the Protection of National Minorities 139
European Social Charter 177-80, 515
collective complaint procedure 257-64, 517
European Union (EU) 13, 14, 85
co-operation with NGOs 425-31, 445
Court of First Instance (CFI) 264, 302, 346
EU Commission 425: NGOs and 426-31; non-party participation 328
EU Council 426
European Court of Justice 264-71, 302: non-party participation 345-50, 364
existence rights 134, 135-6
expert witnesses, NGOs as 302, 309-10
expression right *see* free expression right

fairness 24-5
fair hearing right 142, 173-4
Falk, Richard 104
FIELD 482
financial markets 13
Food and Agricultural Organization (FAO) 505-6, 507
forced labour 263
framework agreements 501-3
Framework Convention on Climate Change 451, 460, 485
Conference of the Parties to the Framework Convention on Climate Change (Kyoto) 447, 460-3, 484, 485
Franck, Thomas 7-8, 11, 17, 23-5, 28, 29, 104

free expression right 7, 172-3, 182
issues raised in cases before ECHR 257
Freedom and Democracy Party (ÖZDEP) v. Turkey case 247-8
freedom of religion 142, 174-5
Fundación de Ayuda Social de las Iglesias Cristianas 230
Furundzija case 312

Gabcikovo-Nagymaros Dam Project case 304
gender
transsexuality 339-40
see also women
Générale Sucrière v. Commission of the EU case 347-8, 350
Geneva Convention for the Amelioration of the Condition of the Wounded in Armies in the Field (1864) 70
Geneva Conventions (1949) 70, 202-4, 205, 495, 516
humanitarian organisations and 205-15
globalisation 12
civil society and 16
democracy and 14-15, 31, 524
diffusion of state power and 12-15, 524
inclusion and 32
legal pluralism and 95
protest campaigns against 18-19
government and the state
agreements with NGOs 494-6
conferral of international legal status and 112-13
consent by 25-6
as dominant actors of international law 111
globalisation and diffusion of power of 12-15, 524
government-organised NGOs 45
individuals' rights and 126-7
legitimacy 6, 22-8, 524
liberalism and 101
obligations: under Aarhus Convention 162, 163; under ECHR 135, 170-1; under European Convention on the Recognition of the Legal Personality of International Non-Governmental Organisations 166; under European Social Charter 177, 178; under ICCPR 144-6; under ICESCR 150-2; under ILO Conventions 154, 157-8, 160
realist/neo-realist view of 100, 102
recognition of 6-7, 9, 11
sovereignty 23
undemocratic regimes 9, 12
Grande Oriente d'Italia di Palazzo Giustiniani v. Italy case 256
Green Salvation 287

INDEX 551

Greenpeace 19, 266-7, 302
Greenwood, Christopher 491, 494
Group of Associations for the Defence of the Rights of Disabled and Handicapped Persons in Italy v. Italy case 225
group rights 134-6, 170-1
Gündem v. Turkey case 328

Habermas, Jürgen 26, 27-8, 30-2, 34, 524
Harris, David J. 85, 124, 125, 127, 131, 169
health and safety at work, European Social Charter and 177, 178
Held, David 11, 26-7, 30, 31
Henkin, Louis 123, 125
Henry Kalenga v. Zambia case 284
Higgins, Rosalyn 91, 93-4, 96-7, 111, 112
Hobér, Kaj 494
Hohfeld, Wesley 121-2, 125, 130, 131, 300
Holy Monasteries case 250-1
Holy See 64
human rights *see* rights
Human Rights in China (HRIC) 383-4
humanitarian aid 201-15, 217, 516
care of wounded 210
civil conflict 203, 206, 213, 214
code of conduct for 200-1
humanitarian organisations and 205-15
prisoners of war 211-12
protection of civilians in conflicts 212, 213, 214
Huri-Laws v. Nigeria case 185-6
hybrid NGOs 46

Ignacio Ellacuría SJ et al. v. El Salvador case 351
indigenous peoples, UN and 389, 390, 391-2
individuals
legitimacy and 28
NGOs as representatives of 228-30, 232
rights under international law 124, 125, 126-7, 131-2: group rights and 134, 135-6; organisation rights and 137-8; participation in organisations 139
as subjects of international law 55, 56, 96-7
see also standing *(locus standi)*
Indonesia Auto case 318
inductive method 115-17
informal bodies 43
Institut de Droit International 43
institutionalism 101
insurgent groups 64
intention of parties, rights and 127-8
Inter-American Commission on Human Rights 437-8

non-party participation in legal process 350-4
standing before 274-7, 517
Inter-American Court of Human Rights 277-9
non-party participation 354-61, 364, 518: advisory opinions 358-61; contentious cases 355-8
intergovernmental organisations
agreements with NGOs 496-506, 507-9
co-operation with NGOs 193-8, 366-7, 444-5, 518-19, 526: African Union 438-44, 445, 519; Council of Europe 416-25, 445, 519; European Union 425-31, 445; formal 193-8; ILO 410-16, 519; operational 198, 521; Organization of American States (OAS) 431-8, 445, 519; United Nations 367-410, 445, 519
customary law and 78
employment contracts and 491
powers 75
resolutions 113-14
as subjects of international law 58-63, 87
Interights 229-30, 276
international agreements 487-94, 506-9
between IGOs and NGOs 496-506, 507-9
between states and NGOs 494-6
framework agreements 501-3
memoranda of understanding (MOUs) 497, 498-501
project agreements 503-6 *see also* individual agreements
International Association of Lawyers Against Nuclear Arms 219
International Campaign to Ban Landmines (ICBL) 18
International Centre for Not-for-Profit Law 16
International Commission of Jurists 442, 464
International Conference on Population and Development (ICPD) 373
international conferences 446-8, 479-86, 519-20, 526
Conference of the Parties to the Framework Convention on Climate Change (Kyoto) 447, 460-3, 484, 485
Conference on Disarmament 448, 485, 520
Conference on Environment and Development (Rio 1992) 447, 450-5, 480, 483, 484, 485

552 INDEX

international conferences (cont.)
  Conference on the Human Environment (1972) 450
  Rome Conference for an International Criminal Court (1998) 447, 463–79, 482, 484: influence of NGOs on negotiations 468, 470–9, 519; legal framework for NGO participation 467–70; research interviewing 464, 465–7
  rules for NGO participation in 448–50, 480
  Women's Conference 480
  World Conference on Human Rights (1993) 447, 464, 480, 483, 484, 486
International Convention on the Elimination of all forms of Racial Discrimination 190–2, 516
  Committee on the Elimination of Racial Discrimination 231–4, 395, 402–4
International Co-Operative Alliance 375
International Court of Justice (ICJ) 115, 517
  non-party participation in 303–10, 363, 365, 518
  nuclear weapons opinion 219–23, 306, 307, 309, 363, 517
  standing before 219–23
International Covenant on Civil and Political Rights (ICCPR) 8, 51, 128, 132, 139, 140–7, 514, 520
  association rights under 140–4, 147
  obligations of states under 144–6
  reporting system 146
  supervision mechanism 145–6, 224–30
International Covenant on Economic, Social and Cultural Rights (ICESCR) 129, 137, 139, 147–52
  Draft Optional Protocol 230–1
  implementation in national law 151–2
  obligations of states under 150–2
  supervisory mechanism 152
  trade union rights under 148–50
International Criminal Court
  non-party participation 310
  Rome Conference for an International Criminal Court (1998) 447, 463–79, 482, 484
    influence of NGOs on negotiations 468, 470–9, 519
    legal framework for NGO participation 467–70
    research interviewing 464, 465–7
  standing before 224
  Statute 115
International Criminal Tribunal for Rwanda (ICTR), non-party participation 310, 314–17, 364

International Criminal Tribunal for the former Yugoslavia (ICTY)
  non-party participation 310–14
  standing before 224
International Federation of Trade Unions (IFTU) 309
International Human Rights Law Group 278
International Labour Organisation (ILO) 33, 307
  Committee on Child Labour 413
  Committee on Freedom of Association 237–9, 414
  Conference Committee on Application of Standards 413–14
  Conventions 154–60, 412–13, 514
    consultation procedure 157: direct applicability 159–60; obligations under 154, 157–8, 160, 192; right to organise under 155–7, 172; supervision of compliance 158–9, 237
  co-operation with NGOs 410–16
    consultative procedure 415–16, 521
    tripartite structure 410–16
  freedom of association procedures 237–9, 514
  General Conference 410–14
  Governing Body 412
  transnational corporations and 199
international law 6–36
  democracy and 6–12, 23, 29
  discourse theory and 27, 28–36, 524
  environmental 29
  humanitarian law 201–15, 516
  legal process see international legal process
  legitimacy and 6, 22–30, 523–6
  organisation rights in 139–40
  recognition of governments and 6–7
  sources of law 113–15
  subjects see legal personality/subjects of law
  theoretical issues in see theoretical issues in international law
International Law Commission 60, 464, 465–7, 488, 489, 492, 493, 507
International League for the Rights of Man 303, 305–6, 307, 309
international legal process 91, 94, 300–3
  new international legal process 91, 94, 98–9, 111
  transnational legal process 91, 94, 98–9
International Monetary Fund (IMF) 18, 520
International Organisation for Standardisation 22
International Peace Bureau 219

International Pen, Constitutional Rights Project and Interights v. *Nigeria* case 185
international relations theories 81, 82, 83, 100–9, 110, 111
  new actors entering legal system 107–9
  who are the actors of international law 103–7
International Union for the Conservation of Nature (IUCN) 47
ISKCON et al. v. *The United Kingdom* case 174

J. R. T. and the W. G. Party v. *Canada* case 225
Jamuna Bridge Project 243–4
Jessup, Philip 57
Jones, Peter 136–7
Juan Carlos Abella v. *Argentina* case 353–4

Karadžić and Mladić case 313
Karner v. *Austria* case 344
Kenya Human Rights Commission v. *Kenya* case 186
Keohane, Robert A. 33, 34
Kilić v. *Turkey* case 328
Koh, Harald Hongju 94, 95, 98
Koskenniemi, Martti 79, 109
Kurt v. *Turkey* case 340
Kyoto Protocol 460

L. A. on behalf of U. R. v. *Uruguay* case 227
LaGrand case 123
Lamagna v. *Australia* case 143, 227
landmines
  Convention on the Prohibition of the Use, Stockpiling, Production and Transfer of Anti-Personnel Mines and on their Destruction (1997) 70
  International Campaign to Ban Landmines (ICBL) 18
  Ottawa Land Mine Conference (1997) 471
Lauterpacht, Hersch 56–7, 97, 130, 131, 218
Lawyer's Committee on Nuclear Policy 220
League of Nations 54, 58, 63, 134
Leary, Virginia 414
legal advice, access to 337–8
legal capacity 75
  rule-oriented approaches 86, 88
Legal Consequences for States of the Continued Presence of South Africa in Namibia case 306
legal personality/subjects of law 51, 52, 54–7, 116, 514
  classical concepts relating to 74–7
  customary international law 77–8
  individuals 55, 56, 96–7: new actors entering legal system 107–9

intergovernmental organisations 58–63, 87
international law–international relations approach 103–7
process-oriented approach 91–6: new actors entering legal system 96–9
rule-based approaches 84–7: new actors entering legal system 87–91, 99
states as dominant actors of international law 111
'*sui generis*' subjects 63–74, 520:
  International Committee of the Red Cross (ICRC) 63, 68–74, 112; Order of Malta 63, 64–8, 112, 520
  see also legal status of NGOs
legal pluralism 95
legal process, international *see* international legal process
legal status of NGOs 81, 116, 168, 513–21, 526
  under European Convention on the Recognition of the Legal Personality of International Non-Governmental Organisations 165–6
  standard-setting and 521–3
  states and conferral of international legal status 112–13
legitimacy
  individual and 28
  international law and 6, 22–30, 523–6
  meaning of 23
  states 6, 22–8, 524
Leonel de Jesús Isaza Echeverry v. *Colombia* case 354
lex mercatoria 22, 95
liberalism 101, 103–4, 111
liberation movements 203, 214
Libyan Oil Arbitration case 490, 494
Ligue Camerounaise des Droits de l'Homme v. *Cameroun* case 282
Linklater, Andrew 32
Loaza Tamayo v. *Peru* case 356, 357
local government 47
locus standi see standing
Lubicon Lake Band v. *Canada* case 226, 227
Ludwigshafener Walzmühle Erling KG v. *EEC* case 347

MacCormick, Neil 122
McGinley and Egan v. *The United Kingdom* case 341
Malanczuk, Peter 75, 123–4, 125, 127, 130, 131, 490
Malone v. *The United Kingdom* case 330
manufacturing sector, globalisation and 13

554 INDEX

María Eugenia Morales de Sierra v. *Guatemala* case 276, 352
Marks, Susan 10, 27, 33
Martínez, Miguel Alfonso 188
Mary and Carrie Dann v. *US* case 350
The Mayagna (Sumo) Awas Tingni Community v. *Nicaragua* case 357
Mbaye, Kéba 442
Médecins Sans Frontières 18
media, globalisation and 13
membership of NGOs 20
memoranda of understanding (MOUs) 497, 498–501
methodological issues 79–82
inductive method 115–17
MEVOPAL SA v. *Argentina* case 181–2
Mikmaq case 226
military coups 443
mines *see* landmines
minorities 49
indigenous peoples 389, 390, 391–2
rights of 7, 12, 134, 136, 137, 139
Mireille Meskens v. *European Parliament* case 349
Modinos v. *Cyprus* case 253, 341
monitoring mechanisms 131–2
morality, legitimacy and 25–6
Morgenthau, Hans 102
Mosler, Hermann 88–9, 90, 99, 300, 302
multinational corporations *see* transnational corporations (TNCs)
Murphy, Sean D. 8
Murray v. *The United Kingdom* case 337–8

National Union of Belgian Police case 179, 255
National Union of Journalists and Others v. *The United Kingdom* case 255
neo-realism 100
New Haven school 91, 92, 108, 112
new international legal process 91, 94, 98–9, 111
NGO Coalition for the Establishment of an International Criminal Court (CICC) 468, 470–9
Nobel Peace Prize 18
non-governmental organisations (NGOs) 3, 4–5, 33–6
definitions 525: international instruments and doctrine 36–46; this study 46–52
increasing role of 16, 17–22
numbers 19
see also individual topics and organisations
non-party (third party) participation 301, 302, 363–5, 517–18, 521

African Commission and Court of Human Rights 361–2, 518
European Commission 328
European Court of Human Rights 328–45, 364, 365, 518
European Court of Justice 345–50, 364, 518
Inter-American Commission 350–4
Inter-American Court of Human Rights 354–61, 364, 518: advisory opinions 358–61; contentious cases 355–8
International Court of Justice (ICJ) 303–10, 363, 365, 518
International Criminal Court (ICC) 310
International Criminal Tribunal for Rwanda (ICTR) 310, 314–17, 364
International Criminal Tribunal for the former Yugoslavia (ICTY) 310–14
World Trade Organization (WTO) dispute settlement procedure 317–27, 363–364, 365
non-profit organisations 38, 39, 41, 42, 47–8
North American Agreement on Environmental Cooperation (NAAEC), citizen submission procedure 288–98, 517
North American Free Trade Agreement (NAFTA) 288, 289
Norway, aid programmes 21
Nowak, Manfred 140, 142, 144
nuclear weapons
ICJ opinion on 219–23, 306, 307, 309, 363, 517
testing 341
Nuremberg International Military Tribunal 187

O'Connell, Mary Ellen 98, 112
Odinkalu, Chidi Anselm 362
Open Door and Dublin Well Woman v. *Ireland* case 251, 257
Oppenheim, Lassa 54–5, 74, 131
Order of Malta 60, 205
as '*sui generis*' subject of international law 63, 64–8, 112, 520
United Nations and 371
Order of Santa Maria Gloriosa 76
Organization for African Unity (OAU) 305, 370, 438
see also African Union
Organization for Economic Co-operation and Development (OECD), Guidelines for Multinational Enterprises 198
Organization of American States (OAS) Councils 436–7

General Assembly 432, 435–6
General Secretariat 435–6
Inter-American Commission on Human
    Rights 437–8
NGOs and 43, 197–8, 431–8, 445, 519
organisation rights 134–87, 216–17, 514,
    520
  individual rights and 137–8
  instability threat from 137, 138
  in international law 139–40
  limitations 190–2
organisations, right to participate in 139
Oscar Romero v. *El Salvador* case 354
Ottawa Land Mine Conference (1997) 471

Paez v. *Sweden* case 328
Palestine Liberation Organisation (PLO)
    370
Parti écologiste 'Les Verts' v. *European
    Parliament* case 269
participation 524
  Aarhus Convention on public
    participation in decision-making
    160–4, 515, 526: procedure for
    individual communications 285–8,
    517
  non-parties in legal system *see* non-party
    (third party) participation
  process-orientation and 95
  right to participate in organisations 139
Paulus, Andreas 84, 112
Permanent Court of International Justice
    (PCIJ) 307
Physicians for the Prevention of Nuclear
    War 219, 306
Plattform 'Ärzte für das Leben' v. *Austria* case
    169, 256
Plaumann & Co v. *Commission* case 265
pluralism 95
policy orientation 91–3, 97–8, 111
political parties 18, 41, 42, 45, 48–9
population issues, International
    Conference on Population and
    Development (ICPD) 373
positivism 83, 108
power 104–6
prisoners of war 211–12
private contacts, transnational 19
private life, right to respect for 176
process-oriented theories 80, 82, 83, 91–9,
    111, 113
  new actors entering legal system 96–9
  who are the actors of international law
    91–6
professional associations 170
profit-making organisations 42
project agreements 503–6

property
  protection in conflicts 213
  right to peaceful enjoyment of
    possessions 176–7
Prosecutor v. *Samuel Imanishimwe et al.* case
    316–17
protest campaigns 18–19, 29
Purcell and Others v. *Ireland* case 252
Putnam, Robert 16

Quaker Council for European Affairs
    (QCEA) 263

racial discrimination 190–2
  Committee on the Elimination of
    Racial Discrimination 231–4, 395,
    402–4
  International Convention on the
    Elimination of all forms of
    Racial Discrimination 190–2,
    516
racist groups 138
Rafael Ferrer-Mazorra et al v. *US* case 351
Raz, Joseph 122, 134, 136
realism 100, 102
recognition
  customary law 89
  government/state 6–7, 9, 11
  international legal personality and
    76–7
Red Cross and Red Crescent Movement 20,
    21, 205, 516
  code of conduct 200–1
  Geneva Conventions (1949) and 206, 207,
    208, 209, 213
  international agreements 487, 494–6,
    507, 509
  International Committee (ICRC) as *'sui
    generis'* subject of international law
    63, 68–74, 112
  United Nations and 370–1
regime theory 101
regulation 22, 45
religion, freedom of 142, 174–5
religious congregations 42
remedies, rights and 130–3
*Reparation for Injuries Suffered in the Service of
    the United Nations* case 58–60, 87, 90,
    112
representatives, NGOs as 228–30, 232,
    302–3
rights 117, 121–3, 215, 520
  enforcement 124, 133
  group rights 134–6, 170–1
  intention of parties 127–8
  monitoring mechanisms 131–2
  non-state rights 123–33

556 INDEX

rights (cont.)
  organisation rights 134–87, 216–17, 514,
    520: individual rights and 137,
    137–8; instability threat from 137,
    138; in international law 139–40
  remedies and 130–3
  terms of treaties and 128–30
  theoretical issues 121–34
  transnational corporations and 199–200
  see also individual rights
Rio Conference on Environment and
  Development (1992) 447, 450–5, 480,
  483, 484, 485
Rodley, Nigel 394, 395
Rome Conference for an International
  Criminal Court (1998) 447, 463–79,
  482, 484
  influence of NGOs on negotiations 468,
    470–9, 519: examples of influence
    478–9; internal strategy of NGO
    Coalition 477; modalities for NGO
    participation 471–2; role of different
    organisations 478; strategies and
    working methods of NGOs 472–7
  legal framework for NGO participation
    467–70
  research interviewing 464, 465–7
rule-oriented theories 80, 81, 82, 83, 84–91,
  111, 112, 113, 115
  new actors entering legal system 87–91,
    99
  who are the actors of international law
    84–7
Rwanda, International Criminal Tribunal
  310, 314–17, 364

Schermers, Henry G. 61, 85, 366
sea, law of 491
self-determination right 7, 26, 134, 136, 147
Seyersted, Finn 61
Shaw, Malcolm N. 76
Sheffield and Horsham v. *UK* case 339–40
Shelton, Dinah 363
silence, right to 337
Silverman, David 466
Simma, Bruno 84, 112
Slaughter, Anne-Marie 10, 103–4, 109
slavery 443
social responsibilities, draft declaration on
  188, 189, 516
social security systems, globalisation and 13
Socialist Party and Others v. *Turkey* case 255
Soering v. *The United Kingdom* case 330, 340–1
sources of law 113–15
South West Africa case 84
South West Africa People's Organization
  (SWAPO) 370

sovereignty 23
standardisation 22, 95
standard-setting, legal status of NGOs and
  521–3
standing *(locus standi)* 218–19, 298–9, 517, 521
1503 Procedure 236–7, 521
  Aarhus Convention procedure for
    individual communications 285–8,
    517
  African Charter on Human and Peoples'
    Rights 186–7, 279–85: African
    Commission 279–85, 517, 521;
    African Court 285, 517
  American Convention on Human Rights
    181–2, 271–9: Inter-American
    Commission 274–7, 517;
    Inter-American Court 277–9;
    procedure 271–4
  Committee Against Torture 234–5
  Committee on Elimination of
    Discrimination Against Women
    235–6
  Committee on the Elimination of Racial
    Discrimination 231–4
  European Convention on Human Rights
    171, 177, 216, 246–57, 298, 302, 515:
    concept of NGO and victim
    requirement 247–53; procedure
    246–7
  European Court of Justice 264–71, 302
  European Social Charter collective
    complaint procedure 257–64, 517
  International Court of Justice (ICJ) 219–23
  International Criminal Court (ICC) 224
  International Criminal Tribunal for the
    former Yugoslavia (ICTY) 224
  International Labour Organization (ILO),
    freedom of association procedures
    237–9
  North American Agreement on
    Environmental Cooperation
    (NAAEC) 288–98, 517
  UN Human Rights Committee 224–31
  UNESCO procedure for individual
    communications 239–41, 521
  World Bank Inspection Panel 241–6
  see also non-party (third party)
    participation
*Stankov and United Macedonian Organisation
  Ilinden* v. *Bulgaria* case 248–9, 256–7
state *see* government and the state
*Stichting Greenpeace Council (Greenpeace
  International) and others* v. *Commission*
  case 266–7, 302
strike, right to 148, 149, 179
subjects of law *see* legal personality/
  subjects of law

INDEX   557

'*sui generis*' subjects of international law 63–74, 520
 International Committee of the Red Cross (ICRC) 63, 68–74, 112
 Order of Malta 63, 64–8, 112, 520
supervision mechanisms
 Aarhus Convention 163
 European Social Charter 178, 180
 ICCPR 145–6, 224–30
 ICESCR 152
 ILO Conventions 158–9, 237
Sutherland v. *UK* case 328
Svenska Journalistförbundet v. *Council of the EU* case 268–9
Sweden, aid programmes 21
Swedish Engine Drivers' Union v. *Sweden* case 255
Switzerland
 aid programmes 21
 Red Cross and 495
Syndicat National des Professions du Tourisme v. *France* case 261

Tadić case 311
terrorist groups 49, 52, 138, 204, 332–4, 522
Teubner, Gunther 95, 96
Théoneste Bagosora case 316
theoretical issues in international law 79–82, 109–11
 actors of international law and 82–117: increasing role of non-state actors 111–12; new actors entering legal system 87–91, 96–9, 107–9; states as dominant actors of international law 111; who are the actors of international law 84–7, 91–6, 103–7
 critical approach 80
 inductive method 115–17
 international law–international relations approach 81, 82, 83, 100–9, 110, 111: new actors entering legal system 107–9; who are the actors of international law 103–7
 process-oriented approach 80, 82, 83, 91–9, 111, 113: new actors entering legal system 96–9; who are the actors of international law 91–6
 rights 121–34
 rule-oriented approach 80, 81, 82, 83, 84–91, 111, 112, 113, 115: new actors entering legal system 87–91, 99; who are the actors of international law 84–7
 sources of law 113–15
 states and conferral of international legal status 112–13

states as dominant actors of international law 111
third parties *see* non-party (third party) participation
torture 338–9
 Convention Against Torture 234–5
 United Nations Committee Against Torture 234–5, 395, 399–401
 World Organisation against Torture 262
trade unions 41, 42, 307
 African Charter on Human and Peoples' Rights and 184
 civil service 141
 closed shop 341
 ECHR and 134, 170, 171–2
 European Social Charter and 179–80
 ICESCR and 137, 148–50
 ILO Conventions and 155–7, 172
 as non-party participants in court 347, 349
 rights to join 140, 216
transnational corporations (TNCs) 106
 human rights issues and 199–200
 ILO and 199
 international obligations 189
 OECD Guidelines for 198
 United Nations and 199–200
transnational legal process 91, 94, 98–9
transnational private contacts 19
Transnational Radical Party (TRP) 385
transnationalism 102
transsexuality 339–40
treaties 7, 52, 113
 directly applicable 129
 monitoring mechanisms 131–2
 non-state rights-holders on the international plane and 128–30
 self-executing 129
 Vienna Conventions 487–8, 488–9, 493, 506, 509
tripartism 410–16
Tyrer v. *The United Kingdom* case 329

undemocratic regimes 9, 12, 138
Union of Arab Banks 50
United Communist Party of Turkey and Others v. *Turkey* case 255
United Nations 117
 1503 Procedure 236–7, 521
 Charter 37, 38, 39, 47, 59
 civil society and 406–10
 codes of practice and 199–200
 Commission on Sustainable Development (CSD) 392–3, 451, 455, 485
 Committee Against Torture 234–5, 395, 399–401

558 INDEX

United Nations (cont.)
Committee on Conventions and
Recommendations 240-1
Committee on Economic, Social and
Cultural Rights 395, 397-9
Committee on the Elimination of
Discrimination Against Women
235-6, 395, 401-2
Committee on the Elimination of Racial
Discrimination 231-4, 395, 402-4
Committee on the Protection of the
Rights of All Migrant Workers and
Member of their Families 395, 406
Committee on the Rights of the Child
395, 404-6
Declaration on Human Rights Defenders
140, 152-4, 192-3, 515
draft declaration on social
responsibilities 188, 189, 516
Economic and Social Council (ECOSOC)
371, 519, 523: consultative
arrangements 374-86; standing
committee on NGOs 382-6;
subsidiary bodies and extra-
conventional mechanisms 387-94
Food and Agricultural Organization
(FAO) 505-6, 507
General Assembly 220, 221: co-operation
with NGOs 369-73
High Commissioner for Human Rights
459
High Commissioner for Refugees 498,
499-502, 504-5
Human Rights Commission 9, 387-9,
473, 516
Human Rights Committee 395, 396-7:
standing before 224-31, 224-30
International Committee of the Red
Cross and 74
international conferences 446-8,
479-86: Conference of the Parties to
the Framework Convention on
Climate Change (Kyoto) 447, 460-3,
484, 485; Conference on
Disarmament 448, 485, 520;
Conference on Environment and
Development (Rio 1992) 447, 450-5,
480, 483, 484, 485; Conference on
the Human Environment (1972)
450; Rome Conference for an
International Criminal Court
(1998) 447, 463-79, 482, 484, 519;
rules for NGO participation in
448-50, 480; Women's Conference
480; World Conference on Human
Rights (1993) 447, 464, 480, 483,
484, 486

legal personality 58-60, 87
NGOs and 19, 194-6, 523: co-operation
with 367-410, 445, 519; Council
Committee of NGOs 195-6;
definitions 37-40; reform proposals
406-10
Order of Malta and 67-8
Permanent Forum on Indigenous Issues
390
reform proposals 33, 406-10
Security Council 13: co-operation with
NGOs 373-4, 408
Sub-Commission on the Promotion and
Protection of Human Rights 390-1
UNESCO procedure for individual
communications 239-41, 521
Working Groups: on Arbitrary Detention
394; on draft declaration on the
rights of indigenous peoples 389,
392; on Enforced or Involuntary
Disappearances 393; on Indigenous
Populations 391-2; on permanent
forum for indigenous peoples in the
UN system 390
World Health Organization (WHO) 115,
220, 502-3, 505
*United States – Import Prohibition of Certain
Shrimp and Shrimp Products* case
318-22
*United States – Imposition of Countervailing
Duties on Certain Hot-Rolled Lead and
Bismuth Carbon Steel Products Originating
in the UK* case 322-3
Universal Declaration of Human Rights
139, 239, 516

Van Dijk, P. 170
Van Hecke, Georges 491, 508
Van Hoof, Godefridus 78, 170
Van Rooy, Alison 34
Vatican 64
*Verein 'Kontakt-Information-Therapie' and Jagen
v. Austria* case 175
Vienna Convention on the Law of Treaties
(1969) 487-8, 506, 509
Vienna Convention on the Law of Treaties
between States and International
Organizations or between
International Organizations (1986)
488-9, 493, 506, 509
Vienna Declaration and Programme of
Action 458-9

Waltz, Kenneth 100
war *see* conflict/war
Weil, Prosper 84
Weissbrodt, David 391

welfare systems, globalisation and 13
Westphalia, Peace Treaty of 54
Wiessner, Siegfried 96, 97
Willard, Andrew R. 96, 97
Williams, Jody 18
Winterwerp v. *Netherlands* case 329
women
  Convention on the Elimination of All
    Forms of Discrimination against
    Women 139
  rights of 139
  United Nations Committee on the
    Elimination of Discrimination
    Against Women 235-6, 395, 401-2
Women's Conference 480
World Bank 16, 18, 50, 498
  Draft Handbook on Good Practices
    Relating to Non-Governmental
    Organizations 45
  Inspection Panel 241-6
World Conference Against Racism 384
World Conference on Human Rights (1993)
  447, 464, 480, 483, 484, 486
World Court *see* International Court of
  Justice

World Court Project 219-21, 517
World Federation of Trade Unions 375
World Food Programme (WFP) 21, 497,
  499-502, 503-4
World Health Organization (WHO) 115,
  220, 502-3, 505
World Organisation against Torture 262
World Trade Organization (WTO) 18
  dispute settlement procedure 317-27,
    363-364, 365
World Wide Fund for Nature (WWF) 20
wounded, care of 210

X. and Church of Scientology v. *Sweden* case
  174, 253
X. on behalf of S. G. F. v. *Uruguay* case
  228
X. Union v. *France* case 252

Young, Iris Marion 35
Young, James and Webster v. *The United
  Kingdom* case 329, 341
Yugoslav war trials *see* International
  Criminal Tribunal for the former
  Yugoslavia

CAMBRIDGE STUDIES IN INTERNATIONAL AND COMPARATIVE LAW

Books in the series

Non-Governmental Organisations in International Law
Anna-Karin Lindblom

Democracy, Minorities and International Law
Steven Wheatley

Prosecuting International Crimes
Selectivity and the International Criminal Law Regime
Robert Cryer

Compensation for Personal Injury in English, German and Italian Law
A Comparative Outline
Basil Markesinis, Michael Coester, Guido Alpa,
Augustus Ullstein

Dispute Settlement in the UN Convention on the Law of the Sea
Natalie Klein

The International Protection of Internally Displaced Persons
Catherine Phuong

Imperialism, Sovereignty and the Making of International Law
Antony Anghie

Necessity, Proportionality and the Use of Force by States
Judith Gardam

International Legal Argument in the Permanent Court of International Justice
The Rise of the International Judiciary
Ole Spiermann

Great Powers and Outlaw States
Unequal Sovereigns in the International Legal Order
Gerry Simpson

Local Remedies in International Law
C. F. Amerasinghe

Reading Humanitarian Intervention
Human Rights and the Use of Force in the International Law
Anne Orford

Conflict of Norms in Public International Law
How WTO Law Relates to Other Rules of Law
Joost Pauwelyn

Transboundary Damage in International Law
Hanqin Xue

European Criminal Procedures
Edited by Mireille Delmas-Marty and John Spencer

The Accountability of Armed Opposition Groups in International Law
Liesbeth Zegveld

Sharing Transboundary Resources
International Law and Optimal Resource Use
Eyal Benvenisti

International Human Rights and Humanitarian Law
René Provost

Remedies Against International Organisations Basic Issues
Karel Wellens

Diversity and Self-Determination in International Law
Karen Knop

The Law of Internal Armed Conflict
Lindsay Moir

International Commercial Arbitration and African States
Practice, Participation and Institutional Development
Amazu A. Asouzu

The Enforceability of Promises in European Contract Law
James Gordley

International Law in Antiquity
David J. Bederman

Money-Laundering
A New International Law Enforcement Model
Guy Stessens

Good Faith in European Contract Law
Reinhard Zimmermann and Simon Whittaker

On Civil Procedure
J. A. Jolowicz

Trusts
A Comparative Study
Maurizio Lupoi

The Right to Property in Commonwealth Constitutions
Tom Allen

International Organizations Before National Courts
August Reinisch

The Changing International Law of High Seas Fisheries
Francisco Orrego Vicuña

Trade and the Environment
A Comparative Study of EC and US Law
Damien Geradin

Unjust Enrichment
A Study of Private Law and Public Values
Hanoch Dagon

Religious Liberty and International Law in Europe
Malcolm D. Evans

Ethics and Authority in International Law
Alfred P. Rubin

Sovereignty Over Natural Resources
Balancing Rights and Duties
Nico Schrijver

The Polar Regions and the Development of International Law
Donald R. Rothwell

Fragmentation and the International Relations of Micro-States
Self-determination and Statehood
Jorri Duursma

Principles of the Institutional Law of International Organizations
C. F. Amerasinghe

For EU product safety concerns, contact us at Calle de José Abascal, 56–1°,
28003 Madrid, Spain or eugpsr@cambridge.org.

www.ingramcontent.com/pod-product-compliance
Ingram Content Group UK Ltd.
Pitfield, Milton Keynes, MK11 3LW, UK
UKHW040413060825
461487UK00006B/483